D1619449

Space in America

Architecture Technology Culture 1

Editors

Klaus Benesch
(University of Bayreuth, Germany)
David E. Nye
(Warwick University, UK)
Miles Orvell
(Temple University, Philadelphia, USA)
Joseph Tabbi
(University of Illinois, Chicago, USA)

Editorial Address:
Prof. Dr. Klaus Benesch
Department of English/American Studies
University of Bayreuth
D-95447 Bayreuth
Germany

Space in America
Theory History Culture

Edited by
Klaus Benesch and Kerstin Schmidt

Rodopi

Amsterdam - New York, NY 2005

Cover illustration: Arakawa and Madeline Gins, *Biocleave House* –
Section showing slope of rammed-earth floor, Computer-generated model,
1999 – ongoing

Cover design: Pier Post

The paper on which this book is printed meets the requirements of "ISO
9706: 1994, Information and documentation - Paper for documents -
Requirements for permanence".

ISBN: 90-420-1876-3
Editions Rodopi B.V., Amsterdam - New York, NY 2005
Printed in The Netherlands

To
Madeline Gins + Arakawa

Pioneers of procedural architecture and relentless thinkers and re-thinkers of space in America and elsewhere

Contents

Concepts of Space in American Culture: An Introduction
KLAUS BENESCH   11

Theory

Imaginary Space; Or, Space as Aesthetic Object
WINFRIED FLUCK   25

Where Are We? Some Methodological Reflections on Space, Place, and Postmodern Reality
LOTHAR HÖNNIGHAUSEN   41

The Subject-Object Paradigm: Conflict and Convergence in Theories of Landscape, Consciousness, and Technoscape since Emerson and Thoreau
JOCHEN ACHILLES   53

Multiplicity: Foldings in Architectural and Literary Landscapes
HANJO BERRESSEM   91

Between, Beyond, Elsewhere: Mapping the Zones and Borderlands of Critical Discourse
SABINE SIELKE   107

Landscape / Nature

Foundational Space, Technological Narrative
DAVID E. NYE   119

Waste and Race: An Introduction to Sustainability and Equity
ROBIN MORRIS COLLIN and ROBERT W. COLLIN   139

The Cultural Spaces of Southern California: From Colonial Conquest to Postborder Region
HELLMUT FRÖHLICH   153

Simulated Safaris: Reading African Landscapes in the U.S.
KIRK A. HOPPE   179

Water and "the land's disease": Poetics and Politics of Muriel Rukeyser's "The Book of the Dead"
GERD HURM   193

Technoscape / Architecture / Urban Utopia

A Brief Introduction to *Architectural Body* by Madeline Gins and Arakawa
KLAUS BENESCH   211

The Architectural Body—Landing Sites
MADELINE GINS and ARAKAWA   215

Urban Exodus? The Future of the City
FLORIAN RÖTZER   253

Envisioning Progress at Chicago's White City
ASTRID BÖGER   265

Where Every Woman May Be a Queen: Gender, Politics, and Visual Space at the Chicago World's Fair, 1893
TRACEY JEAN BOISSEAU   285

Literature

Charles Sealsfield's and Ferdinand Kürnberger's Spatial Constructions of America
JOSEPH C. SCHÖPP   313

"Man Is Not Himself Only": Senses of Place in American Nature Writing
HEIKE SCHÄFER   327

Interior and Exterior Spaces: Versions of the Self in the American Novel around 1900
ULFRIED REICHARDT   341

Moving Earth: On Earthquakes and American Culture in Arthur C. Clarke's SF-Novel *Richter 10*
FLORIAN DOMBOIS   357

'Just driving': Contemporary Road Novels and the Triviality of the Outlaw Existence
RUTH MAYER   369

Sites of Community, Sites of Contest: The Formation of Urban Space in the American West
BRIGITTE GEORGI-FINDLAY   385

Borders and Catastrophes: T.C. Boyle's Californian Ecology
ELISABETH SCHÄFER-WÜNSCHE   401

Performance / Film / Visual Arts

Theatrical Space and Mediatized Culture: John Jesurun's "Pieces in Spaces"
KERSTIN SCHMIDT   421

Dancing the Digital: American and European Visions of Digital Bodies in Digital Spaces
MARTINA LEEKER   451

Slow Spaces. Remarks on the Music of John Cage
JULIA KURSELL and ARMIN SCHÄFER   469

African-American Contestations of Public and Ceremonial
Space during the Civil War: Freedom Jubilees, 1861-1865
GENEVIÈVE FABRE   489

The Ring and the Stage: African Americans in Parisian
Public and Imaginary Space before World War I
MICHEL FABRE   521

Belizaire the Cajun and the Post-CODOFIL Renaissance
of Cajun Cultural Capital and Space
BERNDT OSTENDORF   529

Brooklyn Bridge: Sign and Symbol in the Works of Hart
Crane and Joseph Stella
PAUL NEUBAUER   541

Contested Space: *Washington Crossing the Delaware* as a
Site of American Cultural Memory
KARSTEN FITZ   557

Contributors   581

Illustrations   589

Concepts of Space in American Culture: An Introduction

Klaus Benesch

> I take SPACE to be the central fact to man born in America, from Folsom cave to now. I spell it large because it comes large here. Large, and without mercy.
>
> Charles Olson, *Call Me Ishmael*
>
> Spatium est ordo coexistendi.
>
> G. W. Leibniz, *Initia rerum metaphysica*

What can be more suitable for a collection of essays dedicated to the contentious issue of space in American culture at the turn from the second to the third millennium than to begin with a text bluntly titled *Architecture 2000: Predictions and Methods*? Its author, Charles Jencks, is well known as an influential voice in postmodern debates and an astute critic of twentieth century architectural history. A former student of architect and historian Sigfried Giedion, Jencks published in 1977 a groundbreaking study of the language of postmodern architecture in which he argued that unlike the monumental design of high modernism, postmodern architecture addresses and communicates with a "spatial" reading public by way of complex semiotic strategies. Rather than privileging an overarching abstract idea (like their modernist predecessors), postmodern architects tend to engage the human in an interactive dialog with her/his urban surrounds, a dialog in which architecture becomes an aesthetic object accessible primarily by way of semiotic analysis. If *Language of Post-Modern Architecture* turns on the important idea, as Fredric Jameson keenly observed, that architecture "reinforces a [spatial] ideology of communication" (n2, 420), Jencks's earlier, lesser known study of architecture's immediate future, *Architecture 2000* (1971), appears to be even more relevant with regard to spatial considerations and ideologies in American culture.

While the title clearly refers to the realm of architecture and therefore, by way of implication, to the problem of space, its heuristic value for a "spatial" analysis of culture has more to do with the fact that Jencks sets out to define space as a fundamental category of human life, a site where different trends and traditions meet and where projections of the future blur with both memories of the past and the contested conventions of the present. Reviewing major trends in the history of modern and postmodern architecture, Jencks posits a general inclination towards a technology-driven evolutionary progress, a belief in technology's power to increase both "*efficiency* and the independence of, or *control* over, the environment" (13). Yet if computerized planning, new high-tech material, and the artificial environments of amusement parks, shopping malls or fake recreational worlds (such as Tokyo's gigantic "Summerland") corroborate this powerful "myth of the machine," there is also evidence that technological innovation has "both controlled, positive consequences and uncontrolled negative ones" (16), depending on whether one looks at biological and cultural systems as *open* or *closed*.[1] Though far from being a Luddite or technophobe, Jencks questions the ideology of technological progress by showing that the future remains vastly unpredictably and that the alleged negentropic effects of technological encroachment of natural spaces on a lower level are usually thwarted by a loss of control on a higher level.[2] Since open systems such as society and culture have an innate tendency towards continual self-transcendence, the number of possible consequences of any form of progress within those systems is by necessity infinite and, thus, incalculable.

Jencks's *Architecture 2000* delineates a decisive shift from landscape to technoscape in industrial societies, a merging of nature, culture, and the machine that renders effete any attempt to distinguish between acts of nature and those unleashed by human agency. It also registers a loss of boundary between country and city (a boundary Raymond Williams, two years later, found equally obsolete yet quite persistent as cultural mythology), a merging of outdoors and indoors environments, of day and night, summer and winter, north and south.

---

1   Criticism and critical studies of this modern belief in technology abound. See, among many others, the canonical texts by Carlyle, Arnold, Marcuse, and Mumford.
2   Jencks mentions the invention of the railroad or automobile that "did represent an increase in control, speed and energy over horse-drawn vehicles [but] also brought with it a decrease in control over pollution, noise and traffic jams" (*Architecture 2000* 15).

Regardless of whether one fully agrees with Jencks's contention of a widespread waning of the nature-culture paradigm, his other argument, namely, that within this context of dissolution and lack of (spatial) orientation "the arts induce [a] state of organization in us more effectively than the sciences because the artist is capable of presenting and reconciling a wide range of impulses whereas the scientist or statesman can concentrate at best on a few" (118), appears to be largely indisputable.[3] Yet how do artists organize or articulate these fundamental spatial concerns and why is it that by engaging aesthetic artifacts we often learn more about the status of space in a particular culture than by merely moving around in the actual geo-physical spaces of that culture? To answer these crucial questions about the perennial relation between space and the arts in America a brief excursion seems in order here.

Modern Aesthetics of Space

In an influential essay, Joseph Frank famously argued that modern literature followed the plastic arts by shifting from a preoccupation with time to the preoccupation with space. Modern art, according to Frank, sought to escape the tyranny of time by replacing historical depth with a temporal continuum "in which distinctions between past and present are wiped out. [...] past and present are apprehended *spatially*, locked in a timeless unity that [...] eliminates any feeling of sequence by the very act of juxtaposition" (59). The shift from an aesthetics of time to an aesthetics of space was caused, Frank believed, by the "insecurity, instability, the feeling of loss of control over the meaning and purpose of life amidst the continuing triumphs of science and technics" (55) in the modern world. By making space rather than time the realm in which literary works unfold, modern authors tried to escape and, ultimately, transcend the "wasteland" of technological society.

Though quite a contested construct in itself, space in modern literature thus often functions as a site of aesthetic relief and regeneration. Kafka's unfinished debut novel *Amerika* (originally titled "Der

---

3   Albert Einstein, in a revealing foreword (in German) to Max Jammer's magisterial study *Concepts of Space* (1954) makes a similar point as to the often myopic scope of the physicist and natural scientist. See Einstein, Preface.

Verschollene") is a good case in point. In this exemplary modernist text Kafka, who had been a secretary and lawyer at an accident insurance company for industrial workers, juxtaposes the restlessness and fast-paced rhythm of the modern bureaucratic state with an imaginary natural counter-space opaquely called the "The Nature Theatre of Oklahoma." Riding on a crowded train through the American West, the novel's picaresque hero conjures up a pristine fairyland untainted by both time and civilization, against which "everything [...] faded into comparative insignificance before the grandeur of the scene outside" (297). Kafka's naïve vision of the American West as "virgin" land clearly shares an effort of many writers to reverse the changing meaning of time and space in modern society.[4] If the juxtaposition of natural spaces of "being" (outside of time) vs. the cultural spaces of "becoming" (i.e., geared to historical progress) cuts through much of Western thought from Rousseau to Heidegger, there is also, however, a counter-current to the metaphysical tradition of writing nature off as the other of culture and society. As Cecelia Tichi pointed out, modern art could as well be seen as an effort to formally adopt and incorporate technological progress. According to this view much of modernist writing is marked by the authors' attempt to become an "engineer" of words and the new emphasis on space and spatial forms was but "a collaborative effort of the engineer, the architect, the fiction writer, and the poet" (16). Rather than avoiding the time-bound efficiency and functionalism of contemporary society, the machine-art of the Futurists, Dos Passos's urban novels or the minimalist poetry of Ezra Pound and William Carlos Williams translated the dynamic potential of the modern cityscape into the abstract, kinetic design of verbal construction. In doing so, these writers gleaned as much from the history of modern architecture, the introduction of high-speed trains, or Frederick Winslow Taylor's *Principles of Scientific Management* as from

---

4   The "myth" of the frontier as counter-image to American progress during the nineteenth century is well documented (cf. Smith; Slotkin). That it even served the fledgling writer from Prague, who has never been to America nor, for that matter, has traveled much in Europe either, as a foil onto which he could project his anxiety about the pressures of bureaucratic time lends ample proof to both the mythopoeic power of space and the role of myth in the cultural construction of ideal spaces. For Kafka's idiosyncratic writing style as a literary response to the modern recoding of social space and time by accelerated technological innovation, see Benesch and, more recently, Kwinter (104-211).

a literary tradition that privileged the search for ahistorical, immutable truths outside the sphere of cultural activity.

How, then, can we conceptualize the shifting experience of time-space relations in modern and postmodern societies? Obviously, we have to move away from the idea of a world "out there," a sense of space that is extrinsic and independent of the structure of our own thinking and perception. Because we live not only *in* but also *through* and *with* space, it affects every area of human existence. Living space, the German "Lebensraum," has always been a space of action, communication, and discourse; how we perceive it, appropriate it, or exploit it as resource is constantly being transformed by technological and scientific progress and its concomitant erosion of traditional worldviews. From this perspective, one can argue that time and space are in no way "objective" conceptions but are created by material conditions and social practices.[5] Put another way, under changed economic and technological conditions, definitions of time and space change accordingly.

Postmodern Architectures of Time

There is little doubt that today, while physical space is shrinking, virtual spaces proliferate. After the era of "spatiality," that is, the imperialist exploration, usurpation, and exploitation of geo-physical spaces during the nineteenth and much of the twentieth century (both on earth and in outer space), it seems as if we have entered a new stage where space is finally replaced by time, or rather "real" time. With the advent of the personal computer and the widespread establishment of electronic mass media, space, time, and movement have acquired a new meaning. If real space has become a limited resource, cyberspace, the World Wide Web and other global electronic networks at once expanded and subverted our traditional sense of space. While we exchange data via email, explore the ever-proliferating sites of the Internet, or do business online, as cybernauts we are everywhere and nowhere at the same time. As the German art historian Bernd Meurer recently observed in an essay on "The Future of Space," "the place

---

5   A comprehensive assessment of social practices and their impact on the changing role of space in modern and postmodern society can be found in Harvey 201-323.

which we perceive as telereality and the place where we do the perceiving are synchronous. Real proximity is replaced by the image of closeness. [...] Space and time disconnect" (15).

What are the consequences of this far-reaching switch from space to time? While modern architecture opened up a multitude of new spaces by reorganizing the urban centers of nineteenth-century industrial cities, the postmodern transformation of space into cyberspace seemed to have reduced architectural design and city planning to merely ornamental functions of global electronic networks. Advocates of the new electronic paradigm often argue on merely practical grounds. Thus, architect Martin Pawley points out that "the traffic density of a conventional urban street system is limited by its intersections. The traffic density of an optical [or electronic] road network would be unaffected by its intersections" (41). For Pawley, the arrival of the global city network marks a "catastrophic diminution of the cultural status of architecture." Similar to the fate of painting at the hands of photography, and the fate of cinema at the hands of television and video, urban space has become "no more than the detritus of consumption [...]. In the new global city system, the old static arts, literature, painting, music, sculpture and architecture, would have no place" (39). And yet, if we consider the fact that with the constant expansion of the World Wide Web both access time and the time necessary to navigate and exploit its rhizomatic structures have also increased (and thus limited the available cyber-spatial options), not to speak of aggressive commercialization (disk space cluttered with advertising and junk mail) and widespread electronic totalitarianism (surveillance, control, and manipulation of individual choices and movements), one may well contend the glib assertion that space has now been superseded by time as the dominant cultural category.

Significantly, if also somewhat paradoxically, the most striking blow yet to the current tendency of annihilating space has been wielded by the Moslem fundamentalists who attacked the World Trade Center on September 11th. I will keep my comments brief here on the obvious and tragic repercussions of these events with regard to the topic of space and spatiality. What turned 9/11 into a powerful statement against the ongoing downgrading of "real" space versus the "virtual" spaces of electronic networks has been pointed out many times. "A small group of men have literally altered our skyline," novelist Don DeLillo wrote in an editorial of *Harper's Magazine*, now "we have fallen back in time and space" (38). Apart and beyond the inherent iconoclasm of the events, however, the physical destruction of the world's most important concentration of economic power made visible in a cataclysmic *mis-en-scène* what Saskia Sassen, in a study of globalization and global cities, describes as the spatial grounding of postindustrial capitalism: namely, that there is still a "place" or real space attached to the international centers of economic and political power. We now know that these powers are both located and locked in space; rather than entirely made of bits and bites or run by administrators identifiable only through their email-addresses or account numbers, the global marketplace bustles with human capital. The thousands who died in the attacks had real names and were "real" people. What is more, they were not just representatives of power but also of what Sassen calls "the amalgamated other": lower-tier secretaries, the countless members of maintenance crews, service and technical staff or the Chinese street vendor and immigrant caterer who tend to be excluded from corporate culture and the dominant economic narratives.[6] If the "neutralization of distance through telematics," Sassen convincingly argues, "has as its correlate a new type of central place" ("Economy" 75), we can hardly neglect the socio-spatial implications of the emerging global megalopolis.

What 9/11 thus has brought home with utmost clarity is that "a house," as architectural critic Mark Wigley noted, "is never innocent of the violence inside it" (qtd. in Sassen, "Economy" 83). Architecture may be an effort to arrest time by wresting and shaping a livable place from space, yet its specific design is always shaped by particular cultural values and social norms. It is here that a central paradox arises, a paradox that can be traced throughout the history of modern aesthetics and, as readers will find out, informs many of the discussions in the present collection.[7] The dilemma is generic with spatial representations in general but has special relevance with regard to architectural space as a contact zone of both aesthetic and social concerns. In its simplest form, it can be formulated as follows: since architectural de-

---

6 For a more detailed analysis of this issue, see Sassen, *Global City*.
7 I here follow in part Harvey's discussion of time-space relations in postmodern society (206-7). His main concern, how different forms of spatialization inhibit or facilitate processes of social change, overlaps with the larger scope and range of topics to be discussed on the following pages.

signs are by their very nature spatializations of time, how can they adequately convey new ideas and insights vis-à-vis the flow of human experience and the change of social processes? As spatial constructs, how can they transcend their solid grounding in matter and engage in an organic relationship with their human environment? More specifically, how can architecture, as New York architects/philosophers Arakawa and Madeline Gins claim in their book *Architectural Body*, "actively participate in life and death matters" (1)?

*

Since we believe that space, place, and architecture both reflect and create the cultural specificity of any society (and thereby clearly participate in "life and death" matters) and that, when it comes to America, space, as Charles Olson noted, has been perhaps the most important single driving force not only to build a new nation but to imagine one, we invited in the fall of 2001 a number of eminent scholars, artists and political activists to an international conference at the University of Bayreuth (Germany), entitled "From Landscape to Technoscape: Contestations of Space in American Culture." Though not all participants in the conference were able to contribute to the larger project of the present collection, much of its scope and initial interdisciplinary fervor has been preserved in the selection of the following essays.[8]

As many of the contributions make clear, America's sense of space has always been tied to what Hayden White called the "narrativization" of real events. If the awe-inspiring manifestations of nature in America (Niagara Falls, Virginia's Natural Bridge, the Grand Canyon, etc.) were often used as a foil for projecting utopian visions and idealizations of the nation's exceptional place among the nations of the world, the rapid technological progress and its concomitant appropriation of natural spaces served equally well, as David Nye argued, to promote the dominant cultural idiom of exploration and conquest. From the beginning, American attitudes towards *space* were thus utterly contradictory if not paradoxical; a paradox that scholars tried to

---

8   While others, such as Arakawa, Madeline Gins, and Robin Collin, who, because of 9/11, could not join us then, actively supported and contributed to the book.

capture in such hybrid concepts as the "middle landscape" (Leo Marx), an "engineered New Earth" (Cecelia Tichi), or the "technological sublime" (David Nye).

Yet not only was America's concept of *space* paradoxical, it has always also been a contested terrain, a site of continuous social and cultural conflict. Many foundational issues in American history (the dislocation of Native and African Americans, the geo-political implications of nation-building, immigration and transmigration, the increasing division and "clustering" of contemporary American society, etc.) involve differing ideals and notions of space. Quite literally, space or, more accurately, its "warring" ideological appropriations formed the arena where America's search for identity (national, political, cultural) has been staged. If American democracy, as Frederick Jackson Turner claimed, "is born of free land," then its history may well be defined as the history of the fierce struggles to gain and maintain power over both the geographical, social, and political spaces of America and its concomitant narratives.

To be sure, all of the following essays reflect and add to earlier critical studies of the political, cultural, and aesthetic implications of space in America. While the pioneering works of Henry Nash Smith, R. W. B. Lewis, Perry Miller, Leo Marx, Annette Kolodny, Barbara Novak, and Cecelia Tichi drew attention to the ideological inscriptions and aesthetic representations of nature and landscape from the seventeenth to the late nineteenth century, historians of technology, sociologists, and critics of architecture such as Lewis Mumford, Thomas P. Hughes, Jane Jacobs, Langdon Winner, Stephen Kern, David Nye or Mike Davis examined the succeeding transformation of American concepts of space within the proliferating technological environments of the twentieth century. More recently, electronic extensions into cyberspace, on the one hand, and the successful exploration and "colonization" of the intra-human, microscopic spaces of genetic engineering, on the other, initiated a further, perhaps even more dramatic redefinition of space in American culture. If the present collection of essays unavoidably fails to cover the full trajectory of these critical and discursive shifts, we nevertheless hope that by the sheer number and range of topics, interests, and critical approaches the essays gathered here will help to open up further and exciting new avenues of inquiry into the tangled relations of space in America.

Works Cited

Arnold, Matthew. *Culture and Anarchy and Other Writings*. 1869. Cambridge: Cambridge UP, 1993.

Benesch, Klaus. "*Writing Machines*: Technology and the Failures of Representation in the Work of Franz Kafka." *Reading Matters: Narrative in the New Ecology of Media*. Ed. Joseph Tabbi and Michael Wutz. Ithaca, NY: Cornell UP, 1997. 76-95.

Carlyle, Thomas. "The Sign of the Times." *Edinburgh Review* 49 (1829): 439-59.

Davis, Mike. *City of Quartz*. London: Verso, 1990.

DeLillo, Don. "In the Ruins of the Future: Reflections on Terror and Loss in the Shadow of September." *Harper's Magazine* (December 2001): 34-40.

Einstein, Albert. Preface. *Concepts of Space*. By Max Jammer. Cambridge, MA: Harvard UP, 1954.

Frank, Joseph. "Spatial Form in Modern Literature." *The Widening Gyre: Crisis and Mastery in Modern Literature*. New Brunswick, NJ: Rutgers UP, 1968. 3-62.

Giedion, Sigfried. *Mechanization Takes Command*. Oxford: Oxford UP, 1948.

Gins, Madeline, and Arakawa. *Architectural Body*. Tuscaloosa/London: The U of Alabama P, 2002.

Harvey, David. *The Condition of Postmodernity: An Enquiry into the Origins of Cultural Change*. Oxford: Basil Blackwell, 1989.

Hughes, Thomas P. *Networks of Power: Electrification in Western Society, 1880-1930*. Baltimore: John Hopkins UP, 1993.

Jacobs, Jane. *The Death and Life of Great American Cities*. New York: Random House, 1961.

Jameson, Frederic. *Postmodernism Or, The Cultural Logic of Late Capitalism*. Durham, NC: Duke UP, 1991.

Jencks, Charles A. *Architecture 2000: Predictions and Methods*. New York/Washington: Praeger Publishers, 1971.

—. *The Language of Post-modern Architecture*. New York: Rizzoli, 1977.

Kafka, Franz. *Amerika*. Trans. Willa and Edwin Muir. New York: Schocken, 1974.

Kern, Stephen. *The Culture of Time and Space, 1880-1918*. Cambridge, MA: Harvard UP, 1983.

Kolodny, Annette. *The Land Before Her: Fantasy and Experience of American Frontiers, 1630-1860*. Chapel Hill: U of North Carolina P, 1984.

—. *The Lay of the Land*. Chapel Hill: U of North Carolina P, 1975.

Kwinter, Sanford. *Architectures of Time: Toward a Theory of the Event in Modernist Culture*. Cambridge, MA: MIT, 2001.

Leibniz, G. W. *Hauptschriften zur Grundlegung der Philosophie*. Ed. Ernst Cassirer. Leipzig 1904.

Lewis, R. W. B. *The American Adam: Innocence, Tragedy, and Tradition in the Nineteenth Century*. Chicago: U of Chicago P, 1955.

Marcuse, Herbert. *One-Dimensional Man*. Boston: Beacon Press, 1964.
Marx, Leo. *The Machine in the Garden: Technology and the Pastoral Idea in America*. New York: Oxford UP, 1964.
Meurer, Bernd. "The Future of Space." *The Future of Space*. Ed. Bernd Meurer. Frankfurt/New York: Campus, 1994. 13-36.
Miller, Perry. *Errand into the Wilderness*. Cambridge, MA: Harvard UP, 1984.
Mumford, Lewis. *The Myth of the Machine. Vol. II: The Pentagon of Power*. New York: Harcourt Brace Jovanovich, 1970.
—. *The Myth of the Machine*. Vol. I: *Technics and Human Development*. New York: Harcourt, Brace & World, Inc., 1967.
—. *Technics and Civilization*. New York: Harcourt Brace Jovanovich, 1934.
Novak, Barbara. *Nature and Culture: American Landscape and Painting, 1825-1875*. New York: Oxford UP, 1980.
Nye, David E. *American Technological Sublime*. Cambridge, MA: MIT, 1994.
—. *Narratives and Spaces. Technology and the Construction of American Culture*. Exeter: U of Exeter P, 1997.
—, ed. *Technologies of Landscape: From Reaping to Recycling*. Amherst: U of Massachusetts P, 1997.
Olson, Charles. *Call Me Ishmael. A Study of Melville*. San Francisco: City Lights Books, 1947.
Pawley, Martin. "The Redundancy of Urban Space." *Future of Space*. Ed. Bernd Meurer. Frankfurt/New York: Campus, 1994. 37-58.
Sassen, Saskia. "Economy and Culture in the Global City." *The Future of Space*. Ed. Bernd Meurer. Frankfurt/New York: Campus, 1994. 71-89.
—. *The Global City: New York, London, Tokyo*. New York: Princeton UP, 2001.
Slotkin, Richard. "Myth and the Production of History." *Ideology and Classic American Literature*. Ed. Sacvan Bercovitch and Myra Jehlen. Cambridge, MA: Harvard UP, 1986. 70-90.
Smith, Henry Nash. *Virgin Land. The American West as Symbol and Myth*. Cambridge: Harvard UP, 1971.
Taylor, Frederick Winslow. *Principles of Scientific Management*. 1911. New York: Harper & Row, 1947.
Tichi, Cecelia. *New World, New Earth: Environmental Reform in American Literature from the Puritans Through Whitman*. New Haven, CT: Yale UP, 1979.
—. *Shifting Gears: Technology, Literature, Culture in Modernist America*. Chapel Hill/London: The U of North Carolina P, 1987.
White, Hayden. *Tropics of Discourse: Essays in Cultural Criticism*. Baltimore: The Johns Hopkins UP, 1982.
Williams, Raymond. *The Country and the City*. New York: Oxford UP, 1973.
Winner, Langdon. *Autonomous Technology*. Cambridge: MIT, 1977.

Theory

Imaginary Space; Or, Space as Aesthetic Object

Winfried Fluck

Although there is an instinct in all of us to assume that space is simply there as a given of our perception of the world, we are, at the same time, quite aware of the fact that all perceptions of space are constructs, so that two viewers may look at the same object, room or landscape, and yet see something entirely different. Physically speaking, a room or a landscape consists of an aggregate of physical matter; experientially speaking, it consists of a number of sense impressions. In order to arrive at a meaningful shape, the viewer has to link these physical particles and sense impressions by means of an ordering principle, that is, a principle that provides it with some kind of meaning (if only that of representing a "chaotic" world). Or, to put it differently: in order to gain cultural meaning, physical space has to become mental space or, more precisely, imaginary space. It is, then, highly interesting to consider for a moment what processes take place when physical space is culturally appropriated as imaginary space.

The crucial issue here—crucial, I think, for literary and cultural studies in general—is that of representation, understood in the double sense of the German words *darstellen* and *repräsentieren,* which are often conflated in the use of the English term representation. One traditional claim in the discussion of the arts is that art should represent reality truthfully or, to include a more recent version of this mimetic aesthetics, that it should represent reality in a politically correct way. For an analysis of the literary representation of space, for example the artistic representation of a particular region, this would imply comparing image and reality in order to criticize distortions of reality. But it is also possible to argue that literary or pictorial representations will, by definition, always be distorting, because it is the whole point of their existence that they do not simply reproduce something that is already there but that they redefine (and thereby recreate) it in the act of representation.[1] Wolfgang Iser therefore calls representation a per-

---

1   See my essay on Kate Chopin and the representation of Louisiana in her work, "Kate Chopin's *At Fault*: The Usefulness of Louisiana French for the Imagination."

formative act ("Representation: A Performative Act"). This does not mean that we cannot and should not note the romanticizing tendencies in the representation of the American South in a movie like *Gone With the Wind*. But it does mean that such a critique should only be the beginning, not the end of our interpretation of the film, for if we merely register its failure to reproduce our current consensus on what the historical South was really like, we fail to deal with the object of interpretation as an aesthetic object. This, however, is only another way of saying that the nature and function of verbal or pictorial representation changes once an object is considered as aesthetic object.

By introducing the term aesthetic I do not want to evoke a traditional view of the aesthetic as a philosophy of art or of the beautiful. Such a traditional understanding of aesthetics is, at least partly, to blame for the fact that contemporary critics often resort to explicitly or implicitly mimetic models in interpretation, because they think that this is the only way in which the object can be assigned some political or social relevance. Properly understood, however, the term of the aesthetic describes not a quality of an object—so that some objects, called art, possess this quality and others do not—but a possible function of an object, so that, by taking an aesthetic attitude toward an object, any object or, for that matter, any spatial representation—building, subway map, landscape or a picture—can become an aesthetic object. This redefinition as aesthetic object changes the object's function: we do not look at it any longer in terms of its referential representativeness but regard it as a form of representation that has the freedom to redefine and transform reality or even to invent it anew.[2]

To the best of my knowledge, it was the American pragmatist John Dewey in his book *Art as Experience,* published in 1933, who first replaced a concept of the aesthetic as inherent quality of an object by the idea of the aesthetic as potential function of an object. Interestingly, Dewey makes the point in the description of a spatial object when he describes possible views from a ferry on which commuters approach the Manhattan skyline:

> Some men regard it as simply a journey to get them where they want to be—a means to be endured. So, perhaps, they read a newspaper.

---

2 For a more detailed outline of this "de-ontologized" view of the aesthetic in terms of the taking of an attitude, cf. my essay "Aesthetics and Cultural Studies."

> One who is idle may glance at this and that building identifying it as the Metropolitan Tower, the Chrysler Building, the Empire State Building, and so on. Another, impatient to arrive, may be on the lookout for landmarks by which to judge progress toward his destination. Still another, who is taking the journey for the first time, looks eagerly but is bewildered by the multiplicity of objects spread out to view. He *sees* neither the whole nor the parts; he is like a layman who goes into an unfamiliar factory where many machines are plying. Another person, interested in real estate, may see, in looking at the skyline, evidence in the height of buildings, of the value of land. Or he may let his thoughts roam to the congestion of a great industrial and commercial centre. He may go on to think of the planlessness of arrangement as evidence of the chaos of a society organized on the basis of conflict rather than cooperation. Finally the scene formed by the buildings may be looked at as colored and lighted volumes in relation to one another, to the sky and to the river. He is now seeing esthetically, as a painter might see. (140)

The problem with Dewey's—in all other respects remarkably advanced—redefinition of the aesthetic is that it is still based on a latent organicism. We only see aesthetically when we overcome heterogeneity and link our sense impressions in such a way that we have an experience of wholeness.[3] The Czech structuralist Jan Mukařovský, who develops his concept of aesthetic function at about the same time, goes one step further. Again, the case is made with reference to spatial objects. In an essay entitled "On the Problems of Functions in Architecture," Mukařovský argues, for example, that

> there is no object that could not become the carrier of an aesthetic function, just as, on the other side, there is no object which inevitably has to be its carrier. Even where objects are created primarily with the purpose of achieving an aesthetic effect, the object may completely lose this dimension in another time, space or social context.[4]

We can, in principle, look at any object of perception or experience as an aesthetic object. As Mukařovský claims: "The aesthetic is neither

---

3   For a more detailed discussion of Dewey's aesthetics, see my essay "John Deweys Ästhetik und die Literaturtheorie der Gegenwart" and my summary of the discussion in "Pragmatism and Aesthetic Experience."
4   Cf. Mukařovský, "Zum Problem der Funktionen in der Architektur" 224 (my trans.). In the essay, Mukařovský argues that wherever other functions, for whatever reasons, are weakened, dropped or changed, the aesthetic function may take their role and become dominant.

the property of an object, nor is it tied to particular qualities of the object" (29, my trans.).

In even more radical fashion than Dewey, for whom aesthetic experience marks a culminating moment in which fragmented elements of daily experience are successfully reintegrated, the aesthetic, for Mukařovský, is created by a temporary and, possibly, fleeting shift in a hierarchy of functions that is in constant flux, so that each of the functions remains present and can, at every moment, regain dominance.[5] Consequently, the aesthetic cannot be defined as separate sphere or ontologically separate object. Mukařovský's description is almost postmodern in this respect: "The border lines of the aesthetic realm are thus not firmly drawn in reality. On the contrary, they are highly permeable. [...] In fact, we know from our own personal experience, that the relations between the realm of the aesthetic and the non-aesthetic [...] may shift with age, health or even our current mood" (14, my trans.). In his essay on architecture, Mukařovský employs images of special plasticity in order to determine the shifting relations between aesthetic function and other functions. He describes the aesthetic function in terms of air and darkness which creep into an empty room and fill out the spaces that have been vacated by taking away an object or by switching off the light.

Referential and aesthetic dimension thus do not occupy ontologically separate planes. Or, to draw on Mukařovský's argument: as an—in comparison with other functions—"empty" function, the aesthetic function depends on other functions in order to manifest itself. Many forms of recent art, such as pop art, junk art or abject art, therefore declare everyday objects or, increasingly, thoroughly "profane" objects to be art objects in order to dramatize the redefining power of shifting attitudes that can transform even the "lowest"—the most vul-

---

5   Cf. the summary of Mukařovský's position by Raymond Williams in the chapter on "Aesthetic and Other Situations" in his book *Marxism and Literature*: "Art is not a special kind of object but one in which the aesthetic function, usually mixed with other functions is *dominant.* Art, with other things (landscapes and dress, most evidently), gives aesthetic pleasure, but this cannot be transliterated as a sense of beauty or a sense of perceived form, since while these are central in the aesthetic function they are historically and socially variable, and in all real instances concrete. At the same time the aesthetic function is 'not an epiphenomenon of other functions' but a 'codeterminant of human reaction to reality'" (153).

gar, junkiest or most repulsive—materials into aesthetic objects.[6] Similarly, to take a recent example from literature, in Donald Barthelme's experimental postmodern story "The Glass Mountain," the dogshit on the streets of Manhattan, in its subtle color shadings, can take on an almost sublime aesthetic quality.[7]

Taking an aesthetic attitude toward an object thus does not mean, or, at least does not necessarily mean, that we disengage the object or ourselves from reality. What exactly does it mean, then, to take an aesthetic attitude? The concept refers to the capacity of any system of signification to draw attention to itself as a form of expression and to refer to itself as a sign, thus foregrounding the organizing and patterning principles by which the object is constituted.[8] For this purpose, the object is temporarily depragmatized and dereferentialized. We do no longer insist that reality is truthfully represented, because only in this way can we concentrate on other aspects and possible functions of the

---

6   Harold Rosenberg was one of the first art critics to draw attention to this development. Cf. his description of the movement toward the "de-aestheticization" of art in the 1960s: "Ideally, art *povera* strives to reach beyond art to the wonder-working object, place ('environment'), or event. It extends the Dada-Surrealist quest for the revelatory found object into unlimited categories of strange responses. Redefining art as the process of the artist or his materials, it dissolves all limitations on the kind of substances out of which art can be constructed. Anything—breakfast, food, a frozen lake, film footage—is art, either as is or tampered with, through being chosen as fetish" (37). As Rosenberg indicates, de-aestheticization paves the way for re-aestheticization. It does not do away with aesthetics, it paves the way for a new aesthetics.
7   I am referring to fragment No. 30 of Barthelme's description of New York: "The sidewalks were full of dogshit in brilliant colors: ocher, umber, Mars yellow, sienna, viridian, ivory black, rose madder" (68).
8   In his essay "Die Bedeutung der Ästhetik" ("The Importance of Aesthetics"), reprinted in the collection *Kunst, Poetik, Semiotik,* Mukařovský provides the example of gymnastics. As long as our perception of physical exercise is dominated by practical functions (gaining strength, strengthening certain muscles etc.), we will focus on aspects which are helpful for achieving those goals and will judge the single exercise in relation to how well it helps to realize the desired result. Once the aesthetic function becomes dominant, on the other hand, the exercise takes on interest in itself as a performance or spectacle. The various movements, the sequence of movements, and even the "useless" details of the periods between different exercises may now become objects of attention for their own sake. The significatory dimension of reality is foregrounded and the sign is of interest *sui generis*. Even the "wrong" movements may now be of interest as movements with a logic of their own, not just as "wrong" movements.

object. In this sense, the aesthetic function can be seen as an "experimental and experiential epistemology" (Peper 296). At the same time, the dominance of the aesthetic function does not mean that the reference of the object is cancelled. On the contrary, the new perspective on the object can only be experienced in its various possibilities of revelation, criticism, intensification of experience or pleasure as long as the reference is kept in view, so that we are constantly moving back and forth between the newly created world and the reference which has served as a point of departure for this reinterpretation.[9]

In principle, I have argued, any object can become an aesthetic object where an aesthetic attitude is taken toward it and its aesthetic function becomes dominant. This shift to an aesthetic attitude can be encouraged by the object, however, in suggesting that we should take such an attitude. This is especially obvious in the case of fictional texts (in the broadest sense of the word as any form of "invented" representation, including literature, paintings or film). Once we classify a representation as fictional, we can no longer regard the object as predominantly referential. Rather, we have to recreate the object mentally. Since we have never met a character named Huckleberry Finn and do, in fact, know that he never existed, we have to come up with our own mental representation of him. We may take our cues from the literary description of the character but, inevitably, we also have to invest our own emotions, draw upon our own associations, and create our own mental pictures in order to imagine a character like Huck Finn and make him come alive, so that we can become interested in his fate. These imaginary additions can only acquire a *gestalt*, however, if they are connected with discourses of the real.[10] As Wolfgang

---

9   Peper thus states that "aesthetic effects can only unfold against and into the non-aesthetic. [...] The aesthetic pleasure in the free play of cognitive powers is most intense where—far from empty arbitrariness—it has to be gained within a given conceptual structure, making us aware of this level of cognition as the reflexive play of forces" ("Democratizing Principle" 314-315).
10 Cf. Rachel Brownstein's description of the doubleness of a novel heroine: "In one sense this doubleness of a novel heroine is perfectly obvious. Every good reader recognizes a heroine as a representation of an actual woman and, at the same time, as an element in a work of art. She does not regard a woman in a novel as if she were one of her acquaintances; she experiences how the context of the fiction limits a character's freedom and determines her style. [...] The reader identifies with Elizabeth, and as she does so accepts the rules involved in being Elizabeth, and at the same time she sees how the rules determine that

Iser argued, a fictional text comes into existence as a combination between the real and the imaginary: on the one hand, the imaginary—defined by Iser in a phenomenological sense as a set of diffuse, formless, fleeting moods, feelings, and images without clear object reference—needs a discourse of the real in order to manifest itself in a perceptible form, and, on the other hand, the discourse of the real requires imaginary elements in order to be more than the mere replication of something that already exists.[11]

Fictional forms of representation, including the representation of space, bring an object into our world but they are not identical with that object. They create an object that is never stable and identical with itself. Fictional representation is thus, to draw from Iser again, a performative mode: "Representation can only unfold itself in the recipient's mind, and it is through his active imaginings alone that the intangible can become an image" ("Representation" 243). This means that in order for a representation to acquire cultural meaning, a transfer has to take place and this transfer is intensified by fictional representations. As Iser puts it:

> In this respect the required activity of the recipient resembles that of an actor, who in order to perform his role must use his thoughts, his feelings, and even his body as an analogue for representing something he is not. In order to produce the determinate form of an unreal character, the actor must allow his own reality to fade out. At the same time, however, he does not know precisely who, say, Hamlet is, for one cannot properly identify a character who has never existed. Thus role-playing endows a figment with a sense of reality in spite of its impenetrability which defies total determination. [...] Staging oneself as someone else is a source of aesthetic pleasure; it is also the means whereby representation is transferred from text to reader. (244)

Iser's description of the fictional text as a mode of representation that only comes into existence by means of a transfer may appear plausible as far as fictive characters are concerned. But does it also apply to the representation of space? One could argue that, in contrast to character, space in fiction often functions as discourse of the real designed to

---

Elizabeth be as she is—not merely the rules of the society Jane Austen's novel represents, but also the rules that govern the representation of it, the novel" (xxiii).

11 For a short, succinct summary of his argument, see his essay "Fictionalizing Acts."

provide a context of plausibility or authenticity for an imaginary character. This argument, however, is concerned with instances in which space becomes a central source of meaning and aesthetic effect. Secondly, Iser's argument is not based on the possibility of recognition of an object, that is, on its reality effect. It refers to the mental processes that are necessary to translate abstract letters on a given page into an imagined world. This, in fact, is one of the problems of his approach, for in the way he presents the argument it only appears to work with literature, so that pictorial representations of space would not seem to qualify.

As I have tried to show so far, aesthetic experience is constituted by a transfer between the recipient and an aesthetic object (constituted as such by taking a specific attitude toward it). This transfer can become the basis for the articulation of otherwise inexpressible dimensions of the self. However, can this mode of explanation also be applied to our perception and experience of an image, such as, for example, the pictorial representation of space? It is at this point that we have to distinguish between two forms of images: mental constructs, for example of the literary character Huckleberry Finn, and pictures. Obviously, the image as mental construct forms an important part of aesthetic experience, because it plays a crucial role in the actualization of the literary text. The image as picture, on the other hand, seems to work exactly against such engagement, because it replaces mental activity by optical perception, as Iser himself points out in *The Act of Reading:*

> The image, then, is basic to ideation. It relates to the nongiven or to the absent, endowing it with presence. [...] This strange quality of the image becomes apparent when, for instance, one sees the film version of a novel one has read. Here we have optical perception which takes place against the background of our own remembered images. As often as not, the spontaneous reaction is one of disappointment, because the characters somehow fail to live up to the image we had created of them while reading. However much this image may vary from individual to individual, the reaction: 'That's not how I imagined him' is a general one and reflects the special nature of the image. The difference between the two types of picture is that the film is optical and presents a given object, whereas the imagination remains unfettered (in reading). Objects, unlike imaginings, are highly determinate, and it is this determinacy which makes us feel disappointed. (137-138)

Iser's contrast of an indeterminate form of literary representation and the determinacy of a picture or visual object appears plausible insofar as, in the perception of a painting or a film, the picture seems to precede mental construction. Before we can construct a mental picture we have already seen the image we are supposed to construct. But what do we actually see when we look at pictures? Gestalt theory and, more recently, constructivism have rejected naive empiricist notions of perception as the mere registering of sense impressions. In order to make sense of what we see, our perception has to have a focus that gives structure and meaning to the object. Landscape painting provides an obvious case in point. Not every piece of nature is a landscape. On the contrary, in order to qualify as landscape, certain iconographic and cultural criteria have to be met. In other words, we do not first register and then interpret what we see. Quite on the contrary, we already interpret what we see in the act of registering it.

On what grounds is this interpretation-in-the-act-of-perception based? Some critics refer to the role of schemata which help to order a bewildering array of sense impressions, so that what we are transferring to the image is a set of culturally inherited cognitive structures that successfully affirm their functionality. As David Bordwell puts it: "To recognize an object or event is to possess a schema for it and to have a procedure for judging it a member of some class" (146). However, theories of cognition and image comprehension can only explain why pictures are intelligible, not why they might be experienced as significant or provide an aesthetic experience. To be sure, picture comprehension depends on the recognition of the iconic dimension of the sign, but recognition is not yet the same as "making meaning," as Bordwell claims, and certainly not identical with aesthetic experience. Moreover, as Vivian Sobchack points out, vision is meaningless, "if we regard it only in its objective modality as visibility" (290). We must acknowledge subjective experience and the invisible as part of our vision—that part which does not "appear" to us, "but which grounds vision and gives the visible within it a substantial thickness and dimension" (290). In making her point, Sobchack, too, draws on a spatial example:

> The back of the lamp is not absent. Rather, it is invisible. It exists in vision as that which cannot be presently seen but is yet available for seeing presently. It exists in vision as an *excess* of visibility. [...] The most forcefully felt 'presence' of such invisibility in vision is, at one pole, the unseen world, the *off-screen space*, from which embodied vision prospects its sights and, at the other pole, [...] the *off-screen sub-*

ject, who enacts sight, revises vision, and perspectivally frames its work as a visible image. (292)

Vision thus emerges in an interplay between the visible and the invisible: "The visible extends itself into the visibly 'absent' but existentially and experientially 'present.' And the invisible gives dimension to the visibly 'present,' thickening the seen with the world and the body-subject's *exorbitance*. The visible, then, does not reveal everything to perception" (294-295).

This doubleness of perception is intensified in the perception of objects that we classify as aesthetic objects, because these objects invite us to emphasize their non-identity as representation and to reconstruct them mentally anew as objects, much in the same way that we have to construct literary characters like Hamlet or Huckleberry Finn in order to constitute them as objects of aesthetic experience. This description of the act of seeing may appear counterintuitive at first. How is it possible to say that we have to construct an object in order to give it meaning although we see the object represented right before our own eyes? The analogy to Iser's example of the actor may be of help here. The picture can be seen as equivalent of the actor in Iser's example whom we also see before our very eyes, whom we recognize, in many instances, as a familiar character easily to be identified as type, but whom we really do not know, so that the typical or familiar aspects of classification only become a resource for triggering and feeding our own mental activities.

Both, literary as well as pictorial, representations of space thus create not only a mental but an imaginary space; even where this representation may appear life-like, truthful or authentic, its actual status is that of an aesthetic object that invites, in effect, necessitates a transfer by the spectator in order to provide meaning and to create an aesthetic experience. Inscribed into the reception of a narrative or a picture is always a second narrative or a second picture constructed by the reader or spectator. This, in turn, raises the interesting question whether we can say a bit more about the nature of the transfer that takes place between recipient and aesthetic object. For what purposes can the fictional representation of space be used by the recipient? Or, to put it differently and more specifically, what is the usefulness of imaginary space for a reader or spectator? Why does it engage us, interest us, or even provide an aesthetic experience at times, although we know quite well that it is "invented"?

The crucial question arising at this point is what the recipient brings to the transfer that constitutes aesthetic experience. Is this transfer generated by the articulation of "internal otherness" which is then projected into "the other," as scholars such as Gabriele Schwab suggest who have tried to redefine Iser's concept of transfer as psychological transference in order to give Iser's reader an emotional and psychological dimension?[12] Schwab's concept of internal otherness remains a very broad term designed to characterize the psychological structure of a whole group, nation or period; hence, it cannot explain the fact that responses to fictional texts are varied and multi-faceted. In contrast, I have suggested to speak of a second narrative or a second image that is inscribed into the aesthetic object in the act of constituting it. This second narrative or image is both similar to, and different from, the representation by which it is generated. It is similar because it is based on a semblance between the text and the imaginary needs of the recipient; it is different because the emotion invested can have entirely different sources and can be causally unrelated to the representation itself. This is the only possible explanation for the fact that a narrative or an image which deals with issues far removed in time and thus may no longer have the same daring, explosive connotation which it might once have had, can nevertheless still fascinate and engage present-day audiences.

Why does the representation of the South in a movie like *Gone With the Wind* still have such amazing appeal today? The film's viewers have never met Scarlett O'Hara; in effect, most must be aware of the fact that she never existed. Moreover, most contemporary viewers may know little and care very little about the historical South and its regional identity. Ironically enough, however, this is exactly the point and the actual source of usefulness for the film's viewer. For in order to make the fictional representation come alive, a transfer has to take place in which the viewer invests her or his own emotions, for example, through affectation such as the experience of social humiliation, or a trauma of loss, to the film. We have, in fact, a recent example for this: the temporary identification of some East Germans with the fate of the American South right after German unification when historical

---

12 See Schwab's book *The Mirror and the Killer Queen. Otherness in Literary Language* and my discussion of her argument in "Pragmatism and Aesthetic Experience."

phenomena like the carpetbagger or the myth of a lost cause appeared as plausible concepts to make sense of present-day developments. Although the feudal social structure of the Old South and the ideology of socialist egalitarianism of the GDR are miles apart, the representation of the Old South in *Gone With the Wind* could thus function as host for the articulation of feelings of loss and historical defeat. This means that the aesthetic object, including the representation of space, is of interest exactly for what it does not represent but what, on the other hand, it permits to articulate. Or, to relate this insight to the issue of imaginary space: paradoxically, its major appeal rests not on what is visible but exactly on what is not visible. In both cases, the whole point of representation is to articulate something that cannot be represented itself and therefore has to find a host.[13] Fictional texts are wonderfully effective in mobilizing individual affects and, at the same time, in hiding them behind the immediate experience and sensuous impact of representation.

The immensely popular paintings of Edward Hopper can serve as an illustration of this point. Whenever critics or students try to explain their amazing appeal, they describe a world of alienation, melancholy or isolation, presented in paintings where isolated human beings are often placed in wide empty spaces and the viewer is placed in front of enigmatic surfaces. But why should the depiction of alienation or isolation have so much of an appeal that copies of these paintings have become almost ubiquitous? We find them not only in bars and cafés but also on calendars, picture postcards, in dentist's waiting rooms, university offices, business offices, and government buildings. The only possible explanation is that these paintings are not taken literally, but as an aesthetic experience, so that a thematic interpretation will fail to provide a convincing explanation of their appeal. This appeal is related to spaces or, more precisely, to the empty spaces of Hopper's pictures, because it is this empty surface, in its often colorful barren-

---

13   Of course, one may claim that the view that the collapse of the GDR presents a deplorable instance of defeat can also be expressed outside of fiction, but in order to give that defeat a grandiose dimension of tragedy, one needs narrative and fiction. Generally speaking, there is a broad spectrum of the "unsayable" that strives for articulation by means of fiction: on one end of the spectrum, there are—politically or culturally tabooed—ideas or feelings that can only be expressed under cover of fiction, on the other end, there are ideas or feelings that can gain an additional impact by transforming them into an aesthetic object.

ness, that is ideally suited to function as a host for aestheticized emotions or moods.[14]

In his study *Bewusstseinslagen des Erzählens und erzählte Wirklichkeiten*, as well as in subsequent elaborations of his theory of the dehierarchizing thrust of Western cultural history, Jürgen Peper has provided a useful sketch of this gradual liberation of space and time from moral, social, and other contexts to which they were originally subordinated. In their focus on the wide, empty spaces of nature, romantic philosophy and literature liberate space from typological meaning or from the illustration of universal laws of creation and transform it into a source of individual revelation. Space begins to take on a subjective dimension. At the turn of the century, impressionism's representation of space as primarily an effect of sense impression radicalizes this "subjectivation" of space. While nature in romanticism can become an aesthetic object only as a unified *gestalt* (called landscape), single impressions of space are now foregrounded in order to draw attention to themselves as components as well as constituents of sensuous experiences. And the more radical the liberation of time and space has become in modern and postmodern culture, the stronger the tendency to cut off representations of space from any semantic reference. In effect, this accelerating logic of liberation ("Verselbständigung") has by now gone beyond space as a self-contained entity of representation and has proceeded to dissolve this entity into single components such as line, color, shape, and, finally, mere canvas in order to foreground the potential of these components to become aesthetic objects in themselves. Starting with Abstract Expressionism, contemporary painting has constantly reminded us that we do not need characters or even faces to initiate the kind of transfer that makes aesthetic experience possible. Space, including empty space, can do the job as well, and, for certain purposes, even better.

One conclusion that can be drawn from this development is that the importance of space as a host for the transfer processes through which an object is constituted as aesthetic object is increasing. One

---

14 The phenomenon that space can represent something that is not visible is effectively illustrated in Otto Preminger's film noir *Laura* where the main character, who is trying to solve the riddle of the mysterious disappearance of the beautiful Laura, moves through her rooms and uses the objects he sees as triggers for the imaginary construction of an image with which he falls in love.

reason is that the importance of visual culture is growing. In reading a literary text, characters as well as descriptions of space retain a dimension of indeterminacy that has to be overcome by the reader through her own imagination. In paintings, photographs, and especially in film and television, this indeterminacy is reduced because of the iconic nature of the sign. We see the object in front of us and do not have to imagine it. Consequences are different, however, for character and space. The visual representation of characters also foregrounds their difference: whereas in reading a novel, we can create the image of a person along the lines of our own imaginary, a character in film is not entirely open to this kind of reinvention. The filmic character can invite identification but can also be a barrier to it: either we like what we see or we don't. Hollywood tries to neutralize this risk by choosing actors that either represent a mainstream consensus (and thus signify sameness) or are so attractive that they invite an upgrading identification (and thus make difference exotic and desirable). Upgrading identification is the easiest and most effective way of overcoming the possible barrier created by the physical appearance of characters on screen.

For space, on the other hand, the consequences of visualization are different. While the visualization of characters creates new possibilities but also new risks, space profits from visualization: on the one hand, it gains determinacy through visual representation and thereby achieves solid object-status; on the other hand, it retains a certain degree of indeterminacy, because its representation is not directly linked, as the representation of a character is, to a specific identity. A certain degree of semantic openness is preserved even in visualization. It is representation without focus on an identity, so to speak. Directors such as Douglas Sirk have taken advantage of this by employing space as externalization of their character's interiority. Whereas transfer processes with regards to characters may depend on sympathy for physical appearance etc., space invites a much more directly somatic—and therefore "unconscious"—transfer. This transfer can also be described as a form of embodiment. Because the transfer process does not have a human *gestalt* as its point of reference, it does not have to be mediated with another person's identity and personality profile and therefore can take place in direct, somatic fashion. As Peper, among others, has demonstrated, this move to ever more "embodied," somatic forms of reception is a general characteristic in the development of Western art. Hence, it is not surprising that (imaginary) space has become more and more important as a source of aesthetic experience. In effect, it has played a crucial role in paving the way for an aesthetics of embodiment.

Works Cited

Barthelme, Donald. "The Glass Mountain." *City Life.* New York: Pocket Books, 1976. 67-74.

Bordwell, David. *Making Meaning. Inference and Rhetoric in the Interpretation of Cinema.* Cambridge, MA: Harvard UP, 1989.

Brownstein, Rachel M. *Becoming a Heroine. Reading about Women in Novels.* New York: Penguin, 1982.

Dewey, John. *Art as Experience. The Later Works, 1925-1953.* Vol. 10: 1934. Carbondale: Southern Illinois P, 1987.

Fluck, Winfried. "Aesthetics and Cultural Studies." *Aesthetics in a Multicultural Age.* Ed. Emory Elliott, Louis Freitas Caton, and Jeffrey Rhyne. New York: Oxford UP, 2002. 79-103.

—. "John Deweys Ästhetik und die Literaturtheorie der Gegenwart." *Philosophie der Demokratie. Beiträge zum Werk von John Dewey.* Ed. Hans Joas. Frankfurt/Main: Suhrkamp, 2000. 160-193.

—. "Kate Chopin's *At Fault*: The Usefulness of Louisiana French for the Imagination." *Transatlantic Encounters. Studies in European American Relations.* Ed. Udo J. Hebel and Karl Ortseifen. Trier: Wissenschaftlicher Verlag, 1995. 218-231.

—. "Pragmatism and Aesthetic Experience." *REAL. Yearbook of Research in English and American Literature* 15 (1999): 227-242.

Iser, Wolfgang. *The Act of Reading. A Theory of Aesthetic Response.* Baltimore: Johns Hopkins UP, 1978.

—. "Fictionalizing Acts." *Amerikastudien / American Studies* 31 (1986): 5-15.

—."Representation: A Performative Act." *Prospecting: From Reader Response to Literary Anthropology.* Baltimore: Johns Hopkins UP, 1989. 236-248.

Mukařovský, Jan. *Kapitel aus der Ästhetik.* Frankfurt/M.: Suhrkamp, 1966.

—. *Kunst, Poetik, Semiotik.* Frankfurt: Suhrkamp, 1989.

—. "Zum Problem der Funktionen in der Architektur." *Zeitschrift für Semiotik* 5 (1983): 217-228.

Peper, Jürgen. "The Aesthetic as a Democratizing Principle." *REAL. Yearbook of Research in English and American Literature* 10 (1994): 293-323.

—. *Bewusstseinslagen des Erzählens und Erzählte Wirklichkeiten.* Leiden: Brill, 1966.

Rosenberg, Harold. "De-aestheticization." *The De-definition of Art. Action Art to Pop to Earthworks.* New York: Horizon Press, 1972.
Schwab, Gabriele. *The Mirror and the Killer-Queen. Otherness in Literary Language.* Bloomington: Indiana UP, 1996.
Sobchack, Vivian. *The Address of the Eye. A Phenomenology of Film Experience.* Princeton: Princeton UP, 1992.
Williams, Raymond. "Aesthetic and other Situations." *Marxism and Literature.* New York: Oxford UP, 1977. 151-157.

Where Are We? Some Methodological Reflections on Space, Place, and Postmodern Reality

Lothar Hönnighausen

> "No one lives in the world in general."
> Clifford Geertz

Clifford Geertz believes in the continuing importance of concrete places, but the number of voices deconstructing *place* seems on the increase (qtd. in Feld/Basso 10-11). One of the most popular locations, particularly for people shunning the practical problems of regional planners and urban geographers, is the "discursive" site where intertextual references are constantly being negotiated and *rewritten*. In this scheme, places have become intertextual sites. By the same token, new places are merely rewritten old texts. We no longer live in places but in *environments* and *ethnoscapes*. Some may say that this is nothing to worry about since environments are places anyway, others, such as Arjun Appadurai, note with satisfaction that the term *ethnoscape* makes us realize that "cultures" need not be seen "as spatially bounded" (183).

As for the metaphoric implications of the two terms environment and place, they do differ considerably, and if our generation has learned anything new about language, it is that metaphors matter. They appear to us no longer as rhetorical decorum but as quintessential modes of poetic thinking. For instance, the term environment, in contrast to place, makes us think of multiple relationships, of functions, of something volatile rather than fixed and stable. Furthermore, environments and ethnoscapes are stereotypically qualified as open, overlapping, and interacting. The terms liminality and boundary crossing, transgression or transgressiveness belong to the fashionable vocabulary gracing every second doctoral dissertation. However, instead of bemoaning this faddishness, I take the popularity of liminality or the invention of a placeless ethnoscape as indicative of the problematic nature of our contemporary spatial experience and as a starting point for some reflections on what architectural critic Paul Virilio has called the "aesthetics of disappearance" ("Interview" 180-187, 186).

Most western intellectuals tacitly assume that space and time are part of the essential human make up, that the experiences of space and time are interrelated, and that they are to be understood in the Kantian sense as a priori forms of human sensibility conditioning whatever is apprehended through the senses. In non-Kantian terms, space serves as a frame of reference for the apprehension of matter and, along with time, of motion. Space is what place is a realization and concretization of. Drawing its inspiration from anthropology and phenomenology, the notion of space in Maurice Merleau-Ponty and Edward S. Casey is by far more comprehensive than Kant's cognitive approach. This is not to say, however, that Kant's understanding of space and time as "a priori forms of human sensibility" is irrelevant or invalid; rather it responds to and is informed by the context of eighteenth century Enlightenment culture and, thus, needs to be modified in order to correspond with the changing conditions of human life in the twenty-first century. From an anthropological viewpoint, the experience of space is more concrete than the experience of time, as painting is a more concrete art than music. By the same token, most critics will probably find the anthropological view of space and time more directly useful in the study of art and literature than the one propounded in the transcendental aesthetics of Kant's *Critique of Pure Reason*.

Merleau-Ponty defines space holistically, as a bodily sense rather than as an a priori form of sensibility. Moreover, the experience of space is not a matter of the individual alone, but it is a social and socializing experience as well:

> Space and perception generally represent, at the core of the subject, the fact of his birth, the perpetual contribution of his bodily being, a communication with the world more ancient than thought [...]. The constitution of a spatial level is simply one means of constituting an integrated world: my body is geared onto the world when my perception presents me with a spectacle as varied and as clearly articulated as possible. (*Phenomenlogy of Perception* 80)

Casey elaborates on Merleau-Ponty's concept of *corporeal intentionality* and stresses the interdependence of body and place to mutually constitute each other. He speaks of "the dialectic of perception and place" and defines "human beings" as "ineluctably place-bound" (Casey 19).

Due to what Merleau-Ponty calls *corporeal intentionality*, the lived body integrates itself with its immediate environment, that is to say, its concrete place. This body itself serves as a "field of localization" (Casey 22). We need to recognize the crucial interaction between body, place, and "motion [...] staying in place, moving within a place, moving between places" (Casey 23). In keeping with this phenomenologist framework, Casey then outlines a philosophical tradition, that would include Aristotle as well as Bachelard and Heidegger, a tradition in which place has come to be the prime category (Casey 16), and he contrasts this tradition with that of Newton, Leibnitz, and Kant all of who foreground space (Casey 37). To emphasize the specificity of the experience of place, as opposed to that of space, Casey juxtaposes the German terms *Erlebnis* and *Erfahrung*: "The coherence of perception at the primary level is supplied by the depth and horizons of the very *place* we occupy as sentient subjects [...]. Such genuinely local knowledge is itself experiential in the manner of *Erlebnis* 'lived experience', rather than of *Erfahrung*" (Casey 18).

The full implications of Casey's argument are revealed when, informed by both Bourdieu's idea of *habitus* and Merleau-Ponty's concept of *corporeal intentionality,* he leaves the narrow arena of cognitive theory and situates the problem of place vs. space in the wider field of culture studies:

> To be cultural, to have a culture, is to inhabit a place sufficiently intensely to cultivate (culture from *colere-cultivate*) [...]. The common lesson of Merleau-Ponty and Bourdieu: the body that has incorporated cultural patterns into its basic actions. These actions depend on *habitus,* "history turned into nature [...]. No more than space is prior to place is the body prior to culture [...] the body is itself enactive of cultural practices by virtue of its considerable powers of incorporation, habituation, and expression. And as a creature of *habitus,* the same body necessarily *inhabits* places that are themselves culturally informed [...]. Bodies not only perceive but *know* places [...]. It is by bodies that places become cultural in character. (Casey 34)

Today, scholars are more interested in the different historical manifestations of space and time than in Kant's concept of space and time as a priori forms of sensibility. David Harvey is one of the authors who have opened new vistas by pointing out that "transformations of space, place, and environment are neither neutral nor innocent with respect to practices of domination and control."[1] In appraising the political and socio-economic dimension of space, he acknowledges Émile Durkheim's *The Elementary Forms of Religious Life* (1915) as one of his sources. Evidently, it was Durkheim who, maintaining that "different societies produce qualitatively different conceptions of space and time" (Harvey 210), first defined "space and time as social constructs." The idea of space as a cultural construct has proved a seminal concept and is now widely accepted. The function of the term social or cultural construct is to emphasize that space and time are not given essences but socio-culturally formed concepts. However, the term construct has the drawback of metaphorically suggesting a clearness and abstractness of purpose that is alien to the nature of collective images and the emergence of cultural patterns.

Apart from the content of time and space, the form of their interaction is of interest because the relationship between time and space in painting as well as in literature undergoes considerable changes from the Middle Ages through the Renaissance to Postmodernism. For instance, the relationship between time and space in a painting dominated by a central perspective such as John Constable's *Salisbury Cathedral* (1827) differs very much from that in David Hockney's multi-perspectivist paintings *A Bigger Grand Canyon* (1998) or *Going Up Garrowby Hill* (2000). Nevertheless, as the following quotations from David Hockney confirm, the interaction of time and space per se is undoubted. What changes is the *form* of their interaction:

> The longer you look at it, actually, the more you create space in your head because you're converting time to space. They are obviously interchangeable in our minds [...]. That's why we can't have a feeling of space without time. (Hockney 106)[2]

> Perspective is a theoretical abstraction that was worked out in the fifteenth century. It suddenly altered pictures. It gave a strong illusion of depth. It lost something and it gained something. That loss [...] was the passing of time. (Hockney 35)

---

1   "Spatial and ecological differences are not only constituted by but constitutive of what I call socio-ecological and political-economic processes." See Harvey, *Justice, Nature, & the Geography of Difference* (Oxford: Blackwell, 1996) 44.
2   I am indebted to Dr. Kay Heymer, curator of the Kunst- und Ausstellungshalle der Bundesrepublik Deutschland, Bonn, for helping me verify the Hockney quotations.

David Hockney, who has made the juxtaposition of the-not-contemporaneous and of the not-simultaneously visible one of his major themes, lends ample proof to what Michel Foucault has outlined in his essay "Of Other Spaces" (1986): "The present epoch will perhaps be above all the epoch of space. We are in the epoch of simultaneity: we are in the epoch of juxtaposition, the epoch of the near and far, of the side-by-side, of the dispersed" (22). If postmodernism is the epoch of space, then modernism may be termed the epoch of time (a particularly striking example of this is the numerous time shifts and the deconstruction of the sequentiality of time in the Benjy section of William Faulkner's *The Sound and the Fury)*. With this important epistemological shift in mind, one may well describe the simultaneity of sequential perspectives in Hockney paintings as a creative postmodern response to what amounts to a major change not only in the experience of space and time, but of reality as well.

This is also confirmed by Appadurai who, in his book *Modernity at Large: Cultural Dimensions of Globalization*, analyzes the shift from the modern to the postmodern in terms of a theory of rupture, taking "electronic mediation and mass migration" as its "two major, and interconnected diacritics" (3-4). In view of the issues discussed here, the chapter on the "Production of Locality" ("What is the place of locality in schemes about global cultural flow?" [Appadurai 178]) deserves particular attention. Like Deleuze/Guattari and other critics of the postmodern, Appadurai considers de-localization, deterritorialization, and "Ortslosigkeit" as distinctive characteristics of our time and, accordingly, raises the important question: "Can the mutually constitutive relationship between anthropology and locality survive in a dramatically delocalized world?" For Appadurai locality obviously does not denote fixed places, but "a structure of feeling concerning specific places" (180). In contrast to geographers, the sociologist Appadurai views "*locality* as primarily relational and contextual rather than as scalar or spatial," and he uses "neighborhood" as a contrastive term "to refer to the actually existing social form in which *locality,* as a dimension of value, is variably realized" (178-179).

The advantage of the term locality is that it makes us shift our attention from locale/place as something given and fixed to the creation of places as a fundamental cultural activity. While it has been generally accepted that such an activity is involved in the act of home or nation building, it has not been fully realized that this cultural act is a constituent in the creation of all places. Appadurai, like David Harvey, highlights the political dimension in this place-creating-activity ("All locality building has a moment of colonization" 183), and he discusses the present situation ("diasporic and transnational") as that of nation states destabilized by mass migrations.[3]

This process is further complicated by "the role of mass media, especially their electronic forms, in creating new sorts of disjuncture between spatial and virtual neighborhoods" (194). Appadurai's argument implies that today the actual places are less relevant than either forms of migration, displacement, and diaspora or the "projection of *virtual* neighborhoods" (195). His special interest in these "*virtual* neighborhoods, no longer bounded by territory, passports, taxes, elections" may be derived from the fact that as an Asian-American he has his own ideological and methodological ax to grind; as his definition of the term ethnoscape reveals, "[he] used the idea of *ethnoscape* to get away from the idea that group identities necessarily imply that cultures need to be seen as spatially bounded" (183). Yet Appadurai tends to overemphasize the element of "delocalization" and to ignore that there are equally strong forces favoring "re-localization." Moreover, the present situation seems to be characterized not so much by "delocalization" as by a crisis and a modification of our traditional experience of space and place.

If we look at contemporary fiction from Thomas Pynchon's *The Crying of Lot 49* and William Gibson's *Neuromancer* to Paul Auster's *Moon Palace* and Don DeLillo's *Underworld*, we are repeatedly told that contemporary life and fiction is neither space- nor placeless but that both are registered in new ways. In fact, there is mounting evidence that *locality*, our contemporary sense of place, is of a peculiar kind, and that several heterogeneous factors such as human expansion into both outer space and micro-space, global migrations, worldwide urbanization, and an increasingly globalized economy have affected it.

---

3   "All locality building has a moment of colonization" [...]; the transformation of spaces into places requires a conscious moment [...] [and] involves the assertion of socially (often ritually) organized power over [recalcitrant] places and settings" (Appadurai 183-84). "The isomorphism of people, territory, and legitimate sovereignty that constitutes the normative charter of the modern nation-state is itself under threat from the circulation of people" (Appadurai 191).

The most powerful single influence, however, is undoubtedly the emergence of virtual reality or cyberspace.

As of now, the most important new development, however, seems to be the simultaneous elimination of our traditional notion of time and space and their replacement by virtual reality and cyberspace. Even though cyberspace, a mathematically generated world, remains indirectly dependent on expectations initiated by our ordinary perceptions, digitalization necessarily implies that our spatial experience is no longer based on experience, but on abstract calculation. The decisive question for literary scholars and critics is therefore how the experience of cyberspace will affect artistic perception of the world. In anticipation of this new experience of place, Gibson writes in his novel *Neuromancer*:

> Cyberspace. A consensual hallucination experienced daily by billions of legitimate operators, in every nation, by children being taught mathematical concepts [...]. A graphic representation of data abstracted from the banks of every computer in the human system. Unthinkable complexity. Lines of light ranged in the nonspace of the mind, clusters and constellations of data. Like city lights, receding. (51)

Here is how the home of cyberspace cowboy Case is described:

> BAMA, the Sprawl, the Boston-Atlanta Metropolitan Axis. Program a map to display frequency of data exchange, every thousand megabytes a single pixel on a very large screen. Manhattan and Atlanta burn solid white. They start to pulse, the rate of traffic threatening to overload your simulation. (43)

Case's postmodern home is substantially unreal: "distanceless, transparent, 3D, chessboard extending to infinity" (52). Moreover, with regard to the impact of cyberspace on locality and the feeling of place it is worth noting that Gibson's cyberworld is predicated on both a transition from one person to another and from real to virtual space:

> The abrupt jolt into other flesh. Matrix was gone, a wave of sound and color [...]. She was moving through a crowded street, past stalls vending discount software, prices felt-penned on sheets of plastic [...]. Then he willed himself into passivity, became the passenger behind her eyes [...]. The transition to cyberspace, when he hit the switch, was instantaneous. He punched himself down a wall of primitive ice belonging to the New Public Library, automatically counting potential windows. Keying back into her sensorium, into the sinuous flow of muscle, senses sharp and bright. He found himself wondering about the mind he shared these sensations with. [...] Ghost impressions of

the software complex hung for a few seconds in the buzzing calm of cyberspace. (56-57)

In contrast to Gibson's science fiction vision of cyberspace, Don DeLillo's *Underworld* (1997) makes cyberspace the subject of postmodern irony. Instead of ascending to heaven, Sister Edgar finds herself on a parodic trip through cyberspace:

> Here in cyberspace she has shed all that steam-ironed fabric. She is not naked exactly but she is open—exposed to every connection you can make on the World Wide Web. [...] There is no space or time out here, or in here, or wherever she is. There are only connections. [...] But she is in cyberspace, not heaven, and she feels the grip of systems. This is why she's so uneasy [...]. She senses the paranoia of the web, the net. (824-825)

The impact of cyberspace is probably more profound and far-reaching than Gibson's and Don DeLillo's literary responses suggest. There is not only Appadurai, who seems delighted that cyberspace has become a virtual homeland for Indian immigrants, but also French architectural critic Paul Virilio, who refers to cyberspace in an apocalyptic tone as "this pollution of *life-size* [reducing] to nothing earth's scale and size" (*Open Sky* 58). While Gaston Bachelard welcomes these changes in the experience of space as innovating, Florian Rötzer, commenting on a manifesto by Newt Gingrich and the conservative *Progress and Freedom Foundation* ("Cyberspace and the American Dream: A Magna Carta for the Knowledge Age" [1994]), warns that the great ideal behind the so-called *cyberspace frontier* is the shoddy American Dream with its panacea of "deregulation, competition, privatization, decentralization," which, as Rötzer remarks, "can only mean commercialization, [...] reduction and homogenization of 'communities' [worldwide], [...] as if American social conditions could be used as an example for the whole world" (129).[4]

There is no doubt that "virtual space," in addition to its special function in the exploration of outer- and micro-space, as well as in engineering and city planning, will make a major impact on the entertainment industry. Fiction writers, too, switching back and forth be-

---

4 "By changing space, by leaving the space of one's usual sensibilities, one enters into communication with a space that is psychically innovating. For we do not change place, we change our nature" (Bachelard, *The Poetics of Space*, qtd. in Davies 145-155).

tween traditional and virtual reality, will experience not only reality but also their fictional worlds differently. The fact that they have to cope mentally and emotionally with two different coexisting modes of time and space is bound to have consequences although we cannot as yet anticipate them. In this regard it is of interest that Paul Virilio has registered a peculiar kind of evanescence in contemporary architecture: "the *disappearance* [of space] not only affects architecture but any kind of materiality [...]. Any kind of matter is about to vanish in favor of information." At the same time, he emphasizes that disappearance does not necessarily signify extinction:

> To me to disappear does not mean to become eliminated. Just like the Atlantic, which continues to be there even though you can no longer feel it as you fly over it [...]. The same happens with architecture: it will continue to exist, but in the state of disappearance. ("Interview" 186-187)

What Virilio calls "the state of disappearance" is a basic impulse of the postmodern world in which self-referential signs are replacing reality, and where art and architecture as well as literature are dominated by the urge and fascination of quoting. It is the same phenomenon which Mark C. Taylor, Venturi, and other contributors to the volume *Learning From Las Vegas* find so intriguing in the grotesque mimicry of styles and places in Las Vegas "from frontier villages to Mississippi riverboats, from medieval castles and the land of Oz to oriental palaces."[5]

In view of this fascination with Las Vegas, it is not surprising that for Jean Baudrillard Disneyland should become a key metaphor of the postmodern experience of reality. In *Simulacra and Simulations* (1988), a seminal text concerning the problem of virtuality vs. reality, Baudrillard parodically juxtaposes the postmodern principle of simulation and the venerable aesthetic concept of mimesis or representation. The real simulation consists not in the trashy architectural

---

5   Thus Taylor argues: "America cannot be understood today without understanding Las Vegas [...] the fastest growing city in the country [...] the way in which the real becomes virtual and the virtual becomes real in this desert oasis" ("Stripping Architecture" 195). And Venturi, in *Iconography and Electronics: Upon a Generic Architecture*, points out that "because the spatial relationships are made by symbols more than by form, architecture in this landscape becomes symbol in space rather than form in space" (196).

imitations of Disneyland, but in the substitution of America by its prettified, innocent Disneyland image:

> Disneyland is there to conceal the fact that it is the 'real' country, all of 'real' America, which *is* Disneyland [...] all of Los Angeles and the America surrounding it are no longer real, but of the order of the hyperreal and of simulation. ("Simulacra and Simulations" 151-162)

In *The Perfect Crime*, Baudrillard, who seems to have taken his inspirations from Nietzsche's philosophy of lying and role-playing, has playfully committed the "perfect crime" by deconstructing the traditional concept of reality. This process of de-realizing reality and its successive simulation as hyperreality seems to be at the core of the contemporary debate on *space* and *place*:

> It is not, then, the *real* which is the *opposite of simulation*—the *real* is merely a *particular case of that simulation*—but *illusion* [...]. There will always be more reality, because it is produced and reproduced by simulation, and is itself a model of simulation. (Baudrillard, *The Perfect Crime* 16-17)

It is perhaps a sign of continuity between the pseudo-revolutionary 1960s and the present that Baudrillard's inversion of the traditional hierarchy between "reality" and "image" had already been anticipated by Marshall McLuhan's dictum that "the medium is the message." In its terse oxymoron, McLuhan's famous image of the "global village" iconizes the contrast between global de-territorialization and cyberspace as an electronic idyll. On the other hand, Paul Auster's parodic merging of "travel, moon-landing, landscape painting" in his novel *Moon Palace* (1989), with its widespread spatial ramifications and counter-motifs, decidedly marks our distance from the 1960s. By ironically contriving ever so many crazy coincidences and by intentionally "overusing" spatial motifs, Auster clearly subverts the conventions of place in literature. Invoking space only to make it eventually disappear altogether, he creates concretized, fictional landscapes that confirm Geertz's observation that "no one lives in the world in general."

Works Cited

Appadurai, Arjun. *Modernity at Large: Cultural Dimensions of Globalization.* Minneapolis: U of Minnesota P, 1996.
Auster, Paul. *Moon Palace.* New York: Viking, 1989.
Baudrillard, Jean. "Simulacra and Simulations." *Selected Writings.* Ed. Mark Poster. Cambridge: Polity P, 1988.
Baudrillard, Jean. *The Perfect Crime.* Trans. by Chris Turner. London: Verso, 1996.
Beckmann, John, ed. *The Virtual Dimension: Architecture, Representation, and Crash Culture.* New York: Princeton Architectural Press, 1998.
Casey, Edward S. "How To Get From Space To Place In A Fairly Short Stretch Of Time. Phenomenlogical Prolegomena." *Senses of Place.* Ed. Steven Feld and Keith H. Basso. Santa Fe: School of American Research Press, 1996. 13-52.
Davies, Char. "Changing Space: Virtual Reality as an Arena of Embodied Being." Ed. John Beckmann. New York: Princeton Architectural Press, 1998. 144-55.
DeLillo, Don. *Underworld.* New York: Scribner, 1997.
Feld, Steven and Keith H. Basso, eds. *Senses of Place.* Santa Fe, NM: School of American Research Press, 1996.
Foucault, Michel. "Of Other Spaces." *Diacritics* 16 (Spring 1986): 22-27.
Gibson, William. *Neuromancer.* New York: Ace Books, 1984.
Harvey, David. *Justice, Nature, and the Geography of Difference.* Oxford: Blackwell. 1996.
Hockney, David. *Hockney on "Art:" Conversations with Paul Joyce.* Boston: Little, Brown & Co., 1999.
McLuhan, Marshall. *War and Peace in the Global Village.* New York: Bantam, 1968.
Merleau-Ponty, Maurice. *Phenomenology of Perception.* Trans. Colin Smith. New York: Routledge, 1962.
Pynchon, Thomas. *The Crying of Lot 49.* London: Picador, 1979.
Rötzer, Florian. "Outer Space or Virtual Space? Utopias of the Digital Age." *The Virtual Dimension: Architecture, Representation, and Crash Culture.* Ed. John Beckmann. New York: Princeton Architectural Press, 1998. 121-43.
Taylor, Mark C. "Stripping Architecture." *The Virtual Dimension: Architecture, Representation, and Crash Culture.* Ed. John Beckmann. New York: Princeton Architectural P, 1998. 194-203.
Venturi, Robert, Denise Scott Brown, and Steven Izenour. *Learning from Las Vegas: The Forgotten Symbolism of Architectural Form.* Cambridge, MA: MIT P, 1972.
Venturi, Robert. *Iconography and Electronics: Upon a Generic Architecture.* Cambridge, MA: MIT P, 1996.
Virilio, Paul. *Open Sky.* London: Verso, 1997.

Virilio, Paul. "Architecture in the Age of Its Virtual Disappearance." Interview with Andreas Ruby. *The Virtual Dimension: Architecture, Representation, and Crash Culture*. Ed. John Beckmann. New York: Princeton Architectural Press, 1998. 180-87.

The Subject-Object Paradigm: Conflict and Convergence in Theories of Landscape, Consciousness, and Technoscape since Emerson and Thoreau

Jochen Achilles

> The leaden twilight weighs on the dry limbs of an old man walking towards Broadway. Round the Nedick's stand at the corner something clicks in his eyes. Broken doll in the ranks of varnished articulated dolls he plods up with drooping head into the seethe and throb into the furnace of beaded lettercut light. "I remember when it was all meadows," he grumbles to the little boy.
>
> John Dos Passos, *Manhattan Transfer* (1925), 249.

> Tayo thought about animals then, horses and mules, and the way they drifted with the wind. Josiah said that only humans had to endure anything, because only humans resisted what they saw outside themselves. Animals did not resist. But they persisted, because they became part of the wind.
>
> Leslie Marmon Silko, *Ceremony* (1977), 27.

1. Introduction

As poststructuralist critics repeatedly pointed out, identity constitution on an individual as well as a national scale is never a unilateral procedure based on indisputable essences. It is rather a process of sense making and construction that involves relationships between a multiplicity of components.[1] In the case of American identity formations, the relation to space has always played a particularly prominent role. As Conrad Oswalt has demonstrated, for instance, the secularization of Western civilization can be traced back to American conceptions of

---

1   For a discussion of theories of identity, see, for instance, Henrich.

the environment from the Puritan sacralization of John Winthrop's "City upon a Hill" and the concomitant satanization of the wilderness through Romantic spiritualizations of landscape to the secular and urban wastelands of the late nineteenth and early twentieth century.[2] One might also add, to the virtual technoscapes of our own time. Thus, on the one hand, waning metaphysical horizons translate into disenchanted spaces. On the other hand, the image of the American Garden, although thoroughly weeded, as it were, by deconstructive efforts, is still considered an emblematic expression of a civilizational *terminus ad quem*, a perhaps utopian harmony between nature and culture, the subject and the object world: "The garden of America was sacred space in two different ways. It represented a sacred and paradisiacal natural world; however, it also symbolized a sacred social world where people could aspire to live without sin and in total harmony with one another" (Oswalt 26).[3] In the relationship to nature, the interests and selves of Americans were both forged and reflected. Lawrence Buell has distinguished three waves of these interpenetrations between Americans and their environment:

> First it was constructed in the image of old world desire, then reconstructed in the image of American cultural nationalism, then reconstructed again in a latter-day scholarly discourse of American exceptionalism. Thus the territorial facticity of America has always been both blatant and opaque. (*Imagination* 5-6)

The tension between the historically increasing marginalization of nature to an ephemeral and insignificant residual position on the fringes of civilization, on the one hand, and the ongoing search for a meaningful positioning of humans within their environment, on the other, informs both the writing *about* nature in the American tradition and the current critical debate *of* nature in which it is involved. Both American writing about nature and contemporary theories of nature approach the relationship between humans and nature from two alternative angles – either from the point of view of what the contempla-

---

2   Odo Marquard considers identity as a surrogate for lacking metaphysical rootedness.
3   Beyond the seminal discussions of the garden image by R.W.B. Lewis, Henry Nash Smith, and Leo Marx, see Fritzell. For one of these deconstructive efforts, which argues that adherence to the image of the American Garden is tantamount to an oppressive Anglo-Protestant monopoly of American civilization, see Noble.

tion of nature contributes to an understanding of ourselves or from the perspective of how we can do justice to a nature which we tend to obscure, if not obliterate. In traditional philosophical terminology one could say that the relationship between humans and nature is either subject- or object-oriented. Although these different approaches are two sides of the same coin, they lead to notably different accentuations of the same issues. I shall begin by describing these two approaches in contemporary theories of nature. Prominent representations of both these theoretical approaches converge in laying claim to the particular significance of what can be called the Romantic subject-object paradigm of nature as the groundwork of their respective positions. I shall then try to retrace these positions in philosophical thought from the Romantic period onwards. My focus here will be particularly on postmodern cybernetic reconstructions of this paradigm of nature as a subject-object.

2. Environmental Subject- and Object-Orientation in Contemporary Theory: Lawrence Buell, Charles Taylor, Joachim Ritter

Lawrence Buell's study *The Environmental Imagination: Thoreau, Nature Writing, and the Formation of American Culture* (1995) represents the object-oriented approach. It puts nature first and humans second. Buell's attitude towards the relationship between humans and nature, as expressing itself in his definitions of ecocentrism and the type of nature writing in which he is interested, emphasizes the necessity of reinforcing the dominance of the object—of nature—as the basis of human civilization. Buell holds that after the modernist revolution and the professionalization of American literary criticism, developing alongside the empowerment of women and ethnic minorities assisted by the New American Studies, nature has also to be reconsidered and re-empowered. Buell wishes to redirect and refocus the way that nature is observed: "What happens when we try to reread Euro-American literature with biota rather than homo sapiens as our central concern?" (*Imagination* 22; see 15-16), he asks. In addition, he intends to analyze writing that embodies this object-orientation and leads away from anthropomorphism—nature writing like the treatment of the Galapagos Islands in Darwin's *Journal of Researches into the Natural History and Geology of Countries Visited during the Voyage of HMS Beagle*, where the flora and fauna of the islands are discussed for their own sake, as opposed to Melville's in *The Encantadas*, where the same natural phenomena become the material of intricate homocentric metaphorization.[4] In a chapter entitled "Nature's Personhood," this decentering of subjectivism is seen as leading to a re-emergence of nature's subject status: "the [...] revival of the kinship between nonhuman and human. Its metaphysics withered in the last half of the nineteenth century; high modernism announced its death, modern ecologism has brought it back" (*Imagination* 180). It also leads to what Buell calls "The Aesthetics of Relinquishment" (143-179), which is not only an aesthetic, but also a Thoreauvian ethic of making it small, of parting with inessential civilizational gadgetry. Such gestures prefigure a more radical relinquishment, however, that consists of shedding "individual autonomy itself, to forgo the illusion of mental and even bodily apartness from one's environment" (144). The "revival of the kinship between nonhuman and human" (180) is to be achieved by a merging of the individual into the environment, of the subject into the object.

Charles Taylor's 1989 study *Sources of the Self: The Making of the Modern Identity* betrays its subject-orientation already by its title.[5] The rationality of the subject, the benevolence of the object world and of God—or, in Taylor's terms, theistic belief, "the dignity of disengaged reason" and "the goodness of nature" (316), as represented by religious traditions and Kant's and Rousseau's philosophies, respectively—emerge as trajectories of human self-definition (see 359-366). Taylor considers this triad of potential sources of the self as a field of contestation: "modern culture has diversified our moral sources and added two frontiers of exploration to the original theistic one: nature

---

4   This distinction constitutes nature writing as a genre, comprising texts such as Thoreau's *Walden*, John Muir's *My First Summer in the Sierras*, Aldo Leopold's *Sand County Almanac*, Edward Abbey's *Desert Solitaire*, Annie Dillard's *Pilgrim at Tinker Creek*; in any case, "texts that rely on nature's motions to provide the central organizing device. As such they shed further light on the central question of just how far the human imagination is prepared to be drawn away from anthropocentrism, to enter imaginatively into a realm where human concerns are no longer central" (Buell, *Imagination* 220).
5   Leo Marx's *The Machine in the Garden: Technology and the Pastoral Ideal in America* (1964) would perhaps be the more obvious choice to delineate a counterposition to Buell. But Taylor's study is chronologically and, therefore, also from the perspective of the background issues to which both writers respond closer to Buell.

and our own powers" (390). Whereas Buell suggests an exteriorization of the subject implicating him or herself in nature, Taylor delineates the development of an interiorization of nature which becomes a felt and sensed inner truth and thus a good constituting the self. In the eighteenth century, the "providential design of nature takes the place of the hierarchical order of reason as the constitutive good. This design becomes evident to us partly through our own motivations and feelings. The good is discovered partly through a turning within, consulting our own feelings and inclinations, and this helped bring about a philosophical revolution in the place of sentiment in moral philosophy" (361-362). In Taylor's view, the Romantic intuition of an interiorized nature provides both a feeling of oneness with the universe and a counterposition to utilitarianism and the mindset underlying and accompanying industrialization and urbanization. Alienation in a society increasingly built on what Taylor calls the "disengaged stance of calculating reason" (370) can be avoided by having recourse to our inner sources: "We must open ourselves up to the élan of nature within, as we had to open ourselves to God's grace on the orthodox theory" (370). But this opening up can only be known as well as felt if it is articulated. This is what Taylor calls the expressivist turn in Romanticism – a diagnosis which obviously lays emphasis on the activity of the individual in his or her relationship with nature and can be considered to stand in opposition to Buell's concept of relinquishment, the subject's surrender to nature. Taylor argues that expression does not simply mean manifestation, but also definition in the sense that what, in a Bergsonian phrase, he calls the élan of nature may perhaps not only be made manifest in its expression by somebody who senses it, but also generated in the act of such expression: "What the voice of nature calls us to cannot be fully known outside of and prior to our articulation/definition of it. We can only know what realizing our deep nature is when we have done it. [...] This has been a tremendously influential idea. Expressive individuation has become one of the cornerstones of modern culture" (376).

If Buell insists on the topicality of Thoreau's self-embedding, ecological projects in *Walden,* Taylor insists on the topicality of Romantic expressivism. The Romantics' epiphanic insights into the totality of nature may have been replaced by modernist epiphanies of disillusionment. These changes are, nevertheless, "changes wrought on the aspiration, which originates in the Romantic era, to recover contact with moral and spiritual sources through the exercise of the creative imagination" (490). Buell's object-oriented, ecological approach and Taylor's subject-oriented, identitarian approach meet in their opposition to an instrumentalist rationality, which silences the inner voice and cuts the bonds with nature. Buell and Taylor also share the common insistence on the validity of the traditions of human self-expression in philosophy, literature, and nature writing, which counteract this dominance of instrumental reason. In short, Buell and Taylor seem to agree on the battle between instrumental reason and an ecological spirit that can be reached through the reflection of nature as well as through self-reflection. Taylor describes this battle as follows:

> And so among the great aspirations which come down to us from the Romantic era are those towards reunification: bringing us back in contact with nature, healing the divisions within between reason and sensibility, overcoming the divisions between people, and creating community. These aspirations are still alive: although the Romantic religions of nature have died away, the idea of our being open to nature within us and without is still a very powerful one. The battle between instrumental reason and this understanding of nature still rages today in the controversies over ecological politics. Behind the particular issues about the dangers of pollution or resource depletion, these two spiritual outlooks are in confrontation. One sees the dignity of man in his assuming control of an objectified universe through instrumental reason. If there are problems with pollution or ecological limits, they will themselves be solved by technical means, by better and more far-reaching uses of instrumental reason. The other sees in this very stance to nature a purblind denial of our place in things. We ought to recognize that we are part of a larger order of living beings, in the sense that our life springs from there and is sustained from there. Recognizing this involves a certain allegiance to this larger order. The notion is that sharing a mutually sustaining life system with other creatures creates bonds: a kind of solidarity which is there in the process of life. To be in tune with life is to acknowledge this solidarity. But this is incompatible with taking a purely instrumental stance towards this ecological context. [...] This dispute between spiritual outlooks is deeply embedded in the inner conflicts of advanced industrial, capitalist societies. Instrumental reason plays such a large role in their institutions and practices that whatever shakes our confidence in it as a spiritual stance also causes deep malaise in contemporary advanced societies. There is a circular causal relation between the other crises and difficulties of capitalism and this spiritual malaise. (384-385)

Joachim Ritter's 1963 treatise on the functions of landscape, *Landschaft: Zur Funktion des Ästhetischen in der modernen Gesell-*

schaft, anticipates in several ways the ecological debate about the purposes of nature in the eighties and nineties and, at the same time, denies the irreconcilability of ecological awareness and instrumental reason also posited by both Buell and Taylor. Like Taylor, Ritter defines the aesthetic experience of nature and its moral implications in counterdistinction to the instrumentalist exploitation of nature on which modern societies are based. Insofar as the scientific view of nature becomes dominant and tends to reduce nature to its component parts which are being analyzed in isolation, the theoretical attitude loses its directedness towards the whole of nature. This holistic approach is then taken care of by the arts and by literature which express the harmony of the cosmos in terms of visual and emotional experience rather than in terms of conceptual cognition:

> Die ästhetische Natur als Landschaft hat so im Gegenteil gegen die dem metaphysischen Begriff entzogene Objektwelt der Naturwissenschaft die Funktion übernommen, in 'anschaulichen', aus der Innerlichkeit entspringenden Bildern das Naturganze und den 'harmonischen Einklang im Kosmos' zu vermitteln und ästhetisch für den Menschen gegenwärtig zu halten. [...] In der geschichtlichen Zeit, in welcher die Natur, ihre Kräfte und Stoffe zum 'Objekt' der Naturwissenschaften und der auf diese gegründeten technischen Nutzung und Ausbeutung werden, übernehmen es Dichtung und Bildkunst, die gleiche Natur – nicht weniger universal – in ihrer Beziehung auf den empfindenden Menschen aufzufassen und 'ästhetisch' zu vergegenwärtigen. (Ritter 20-21)

As theory orients itself towards the uses of nature and towards the segmentalized perspective of the scientific experiment, the whole of nature as a residue of cosmological harmony is handed over to the totalizing aesthetic perspective. Ritter speaks of "diese Gleichzeitigkeit wissenschaftlicher Objektivierung und ästhetischer Vergegenwärtigung im Verhältnis zur Natur" (Ritter 21).

Interestingly, Ritter does not share Taylor's and Buell's belief in the critical potential which this aesthetically mediated ecological awareness of a partnership with nature may have with regard to the societally sanctioned, instrumentalist domination of nature. Although he describes the dissociation of the totalizing view of nature, on the one hand, and the particularizing perspective of the modern sciences, on the other, Ritter suggests the option of harmonizing scientific instrumentalism and the disinterested contemplation of landscape. This attempt to make an omelette without breaking eggs opens up the all too realistic possibility of the totality of nature becoming a recreational commodity in the shape of the experience of national parks or prepackaged safaris, while the exploitation of nature goes on unhampered. In Ritter's view, this trajectory has a more positive accentuation: "Die zum Erdenleben des Menschen gehörige Natur als Himmel und Erde wird ästhetisch in der Form der Landschaft zum Inhalt der Freiheit, deren Existenz die Gesellschaft und ihre Herrschaft über die zum Objekt gemachte und unterworfene Natur zur Voraussetzung hat" (Ritter 27-29). In other words, the free and disinterested contemplation of nature glosses over its utilitarian instrumentalization. The aesthetic attitude towards nature compensates for nature's societal instrumentalization:

> Demgegenüber hat die geschichtliche Zusammengehörigkeit der objektiven Natur der Gesellschaft mit der Natur als ästhetisch vermittelter Landschaft allgemeine Bedeutung. An ihr zeigt sich, daß die gleiche Gesellschaft und Zivilisation, die dem Menschen in der Verdinglichung der Natur die Freiheit bringt, zugleich den Geist dazu treibt, Organe auszubilden, die den Reichtum des Menschseins lebendig gegenwärtig halten, dem die Gesellschaft ohne sie weder Wirklichkeit noch Ausdruck zu geben vermag. (Ritter 31)

Ritter neither sees the precarious nature of this coincidence nor the utopian potential that the totalizing view of natural harmony possesses vis-à-vis the fragmentation and alienation produced by industrial society. He is prescient, however, in unexpected and unintended ways. The postmodern collapse of all distinctions between natural and social realities in cybernetic technoscapes presupposes exactly the precarious balance of, on the one hand, the instrumentalization and, on the other, the disinterested contemplation of nature, as suggested by Ritter.

3. The Subject-Object Paradigm in Thoreau's and Emerson's Conceptions of Nature

The "revival of the kinship between nonhuman and human," pursued by Lawrence Buell, or Coleridge's "translucence of the eternal through and in the temporal," cited approvingly by Taylor (379), are obviously central Romantic notions of the relationship between nature and culture. William Blake's lines about the man and the fly, cited by Buell, pinpoint this mutual translucence of nature and culture, the ideal of a subject-object, in deceptively simplistic and concrete fashion: "'Am not I / A fly like thee? / Or art not thou / A man like me?'" (*Imagination* 185). Hegel's programmatic insight in his *Phänomenologie des Geistes* (1807) that truth is the process of the mediation and interpenetration of subject and object expresses the same desire for total harmonization in lofty abstraction: "Es kommt nach meiner Einsicht [...] alles darauf an, das Wahre nicht als *Substanz*, sondern ebensosehr als *Subjekt* aufzufassen und auszudrücken" (22-23). In American Romanticism, as in contemporary theories of nature and the self, these subject-object dialectics are approached from both angles, from the side of the object and from the side of the subject. Although subject- and object-orientation cannot always be neatly differentiated and sometimes coexist in the same text, Emerson develops the clearest conceptualization of subject-orientation, while Thoreau's work is the most pronounced expression of object-orientation. It is no accident, of course, that Buell's *Environmental Imagination* takes Thoreau's *Walden* as its point of departure. Instances in which the "nonhuman environment is present [...] as a presence that begins to suggest that human history is implicated in natural history" (*Imagination* 7) and which thereby fulfil Buell's definition of ecofiction and nature writing, abound in *Walden* (1854). Contemplating his famous bean field near Walden Pond, for instance, Thoreau expresses an acute awareness of both the provisional nature and limited importance of human efforts that form only a minute element in the development of creation as a whole. Why should the farmer's cultivation of the soil be considered more valuable than what nature itself produces, Thoreau asks, and proceeds to an answer which, at the same time, minimizes the human contribution and emphasizes the ecological prerogatives of nature: "Shall I not rejoice also at the abundance of the weeds whose seeds are the granary of the birds? It matters little comparatively whether the fields fill the farmer's barns" (*Walden* 212).

This attitude is also present in Thoreau's essays. In "Walking" (1862), the titular activity is defined as a process which increases the distance to civilization and to the alienated, fragmented social existence of laborers and bureaucrats. Walking away from this civilization leads to a holistic life in the woods. In Thoreau's eyes, the walker is the saunterer, a nature-worshipper who, like Christ's disciples, leaves behind his family and all his worldly possessions to lose himself in the forest whose ground he does not own and does not wish to own ("Walking" 1954-1955). Like Emerson in "Nature," Thoreau acknowledges the fact that the direct approach to nature will be restricted by civilizational encroachments, but he also believes that these encroachments will remain negligible: "Man and his affairs, church and state and school, trade and commerce, and manufactures and agriculture, even politics, the most alarming of them all,—I am pleased to see how little space they occupy in the landscape" ("Walking" 1957-1958). Considerable space will forseeably be partitioned off for private use, but this development, too, will remain manageable:

> At present, in this vicinity, the best part of the land is not private property; the landscape is not owned, and the walker enjoys comparative freedom. But possibly the day will come when it will be partitioned off into so-called pleasure-grounds, in which a few will take a narrow and exclusive pleasure only,—when fences shall be multiplied, and man-trapped and other engines invented to confine men to the public road, and walking over the surface of God's earth shall be construed to mean trespassing on some gentleman's grounds. To enjoy a thing exclusively is commonly to exclude yourself from the true enjoyment of it. ("Walking" 1960)

But Thoreau also believes that nature will be potent enough to hold its own, to unsettle the human property claims that are being made on it, and to retransform civilization into a part of nature: "Not a flock of wild geese cackles over our town, but it to some extent unsettles the value of real estate here, and, if I were a broker, I should probably take that disturbance into account" ("Walking" 1961). Financial speculation will be shaken off by the object of such speculation, Thoreau seems to think.

In "Walking," Thoreau's aesthetic standards for judging nature are dominated by considerations of nature's culture-resistance. The spaces that appear most attractive to Thoreau are those which are least likely to be integrated into civilization:

> Hope and future for me are not in lawns and cultivated fields, not in towns and cities, but in the impervious and quaking swamps. [...] Yes, though you may think me perverse, if it were proposed to me to dwell in the neighborhood of the most beautiful garden that ever human art contrived, or else of a dismal swamp, I should certainly decide for the swamp. How vain, then, have been all your labors, citizens, for me! (1966)

Contrary to swamps, the summit of Mount Katahdin, the highest elevation in Maine climbed by Thoreau in 1846 and described by him in "Ktaadn," a section of *The Maine Woods* (1857), radiates sublimity.

More importantly, however, Mount Katahdin is similarly impervious to civilization as swamps:

> Here was no man's garden, but the unhandselled globe. It was not lawn, nor pasture, nor mead, nor woodland, nor lea, nor arable, nor waste land. It was the fresh and natural surface of the planet earth [...] Man was not to be associated with it. It was Matter, vast, terrific,—not this Mother Earth that we have heard of, not for him to tread on, or be buried in,—no, it were being too familiar even to let his bones lie there—the home, this, of Necessity and Fate. There was clearly felt the presence of a force not bound to be kind to man. ("Ktaadn" 116)[6]

In dialectic perspective, Thoreau's concept of nature may be seen to be negatively defined by the civilization he pits it against, but his intention is a reform of this civilization on the basis of nature's standards. Nature provides the moral standards even for his vehement abolitionist argumentation against the consequences of the Fugitive Slave Law in his speech, entitled "Slavery in Massachusetts," delivered in Framingham on July 4th, 1854. Thoreau ends this speech by the unlikely gesture of holding a flower before the eyes and the noses of his listeners:

> But it chanced the other day that I secured a white water-lily, and a season I had waited for had arrived. It is the emblem of purity. [...] What confirmation of our hopes is in the fragrance of this flower! I shall not so soon despair of the world for it, notwithstanding slavery, and the cowardice and want of principle of Northern men. It suggests what kind of laws have prevailed longest and widest, and still prevail, and that the time may come when man's deeds may smell as sweet. [...] It reminds me that Nature has been partner to no Missouri Compromise. I scent no compromise in the fragrance of the water-lily. [...] I do not scent in this the time-serving irresolution of a Massachusetts Governor, nor of a Boston Mayor. ("Slavery in Massachusetts" 1953)

The moral quality of Massachusetts politicians' decisions to send fugitive slaves back into slavery is measured against the aesthetic quality

---

6 See Tichi 167. Buell discusses this passage as an object-oriented "reaction to the primordialness of Mount Katahdin" on the side of Thoreau which counteracts "Emerson's bookish homocentrism" (12). Even on top of Mount Katahdin, however, Thoreau's object-orientation is not complete. He also anthropomorphically defines the profuse clouds that surround the mountain's summit as "in fact, a cloud factory,—these were the cloud-works, and the wind turned them off done from the cool, bare rocks" ("Ktaadn" 112). For a more comprehensive discussion of Thoreau's position, see Lifton; Schneider; Schulz, *Amerikanischer Transzendentalismus*.

of the waterlily. Political action is to be the vehicle and natural beauty the tenor in this metaphorical relationship—not the other way round. Thoreau even goes as far as developing the water-lily's fragrance into the basis of a Kantian categorical imperative of political ethics: "So behave that the odor of your actions may enhance the general sweetness of the atmosphere, that when we behold or scent a flower, we may not be reminded how inconsistent your deeds are with it" ("Slavery in Massachusetts" 1953).[7] Literature should be based on similarly natural standards. In "Walking," Thoreau proposes a literature that does not suggest an Emersonian spiritual translucence of natural phenomena. It should rather be a form of minimizing the creative subjectivity of the writer and maximizing the sensual presence of nature, of making nature speak for itself thereby turning literature into an almost natural phenomenon, among others:

> A truly good book is something as natural, and as unexpectedly and unaccountably fair and perfect, as a wild flower discovered on the prairies of the West or in the jungles of the East. [...] Where is the literature which gives expression to Nature? He would be a poet who could impress the winds and streams into his service, to speak for him; who nailed words to their primitive senses, as farmers drive down stakes in the spring, which the frost has heaved; who derived his words as often as he used them,—transplanted them to his page with earth adhering to their roots; whose words were so true and fresh and natural that they would appear to expand like buds at the approach of spring, though they lay half-smothered between two musty leaves in a library,—ay, to bloom and bear fruit there, after their kind, annually, for the faithful reader, in sympathy with surrounding Nature. ("Walking" 1968)

By contrast, Ralph Waldo Emerson's epistemology is based on an idealistic and subject-oriented model of the correspondence between spirit and matter, the world and the soul. In his programmatic essay "Nature" (1836), Emerson develops the interpenetration of subject and

---

7   Again, as in the case of Mount Katahdin's "cloud-factories," the nature-orientation of Thoreau's political ethics is not entirely consistent. In the lines following the above quotation, Thoreau's argument exchanges vehicle and tenor so that the sweet-smelling water-lily turns into an allegorical representation of a moral principle: "[F]or all odor is but one advertisement of a moral quality, and if fair actions had not been performed, the lily would not smell sweet. The foul slime stands for the sloth and vice of man, the decay of humanity; the fragrant flower that springs from it, for the purity and courage which are immortal" ("Slavery in Massachusetts" 1953).

object in both directions. He romantically spiritualizes and subjectifies nature. And he seems to objectify a mode of human perception. In the most famous passage of "Nature," Emerson suggests that subjectivity tends to dissolve in the observation of nature:

> Standing on the bare ground,—my head bathed by the blithe air, and uplifted into infinite space,—all mean egotism vanishes. I become a transparent eye-ball. I am nothing. I see all. The currents of the Universal Being circulate through me; I am part or particle of God. The name of the nearest friend sounds then foreign and accidental. To be brothers, to be acquaintances,—master or servant, is then a trifle and a disturbance. I am the lover of uncontained and immortal beauty. In the wilderness, I find something more dear and connate than in the streets or villages. In the tranquil landscape, and especially in the distant line of the horizon, man beholds somewhat as beautiful as his own nature. (1075)

For the ecstatic moment when the observer totally surrenders to what he observes, he reduces himself to sheer perception and becomes one with his gaze—nothing but a transparent eyeball. This is an obviously momentary and hardly sustainable neutralization of subjectivity. Emerson elsewhere admits that perception is not neutral, that it even partially produces what it beholds. The Romantic gaze can shape the reality it beholds as well as be shaped by it: "The eye is the best of artists. By the mutual action of its structure and of the laws of light, perspective is produced, which integrates every mass of objects, of what character soever, into a well colored and shaded globe, so that where the particular objects are mean and unaffecting, the landscape which they compose is round and symmetrical" ("Nature" 1077). Contrary to the, at best transient and at worst illusionary, suspension of subjectivity in his Romantic gaze, Emerson's claim that nature is essentially spiritual—that, as Hegel has it, the substance is also the subject—is an axiomatic assumption about the nature of the universe: "The world is emblematic. Parts of speech are metaphors because the whole of nature is a metaphor of the human mind. The laws of moral nature answer to those of matter as face to face in a glass" ("Nature" 1083). The object of perception is in its deepest core what the perceiving subject also is—spirit. It is this that constitutes the comprehensibility of nature.[8]

---

8   This spiritual essence of nature is the fundamental tenet upon which Emerson's idealism rests. The dual thrust of Emerson's concept of nature makes clear that

Like Thoreau, Emerson is aware that the ideal fusion of mind and matter, nature and culture clashes with social realities that do not support it. In some passages of "The American Scholar," Emerson criticizes the fragmentation and alienation resulting from the progress of American civilization radically and in near-Marxian terms:

> Man is not a farmer, or a professor, or an engineer, but he is all. Man is priest, and scholar, and statesman, and producer, and soldier. In the *divided* or social state, these functions are parcelled out to individuals, each of whom aims to his stint of the joint work, whilst each other performs his. [...] The state of society is one in which the members have suffered amputation from the trunk, and strut about so many walking monsters,—a good finger, a neck, a stomach, an elbow, but never a man. Man is thus metamorphosed into a thing, into many things. [...] and the soul is subject to dollars. ("The American Scholar" 1102)

Thoreau trusts the power of nature to unsettle civilizational efforts, even to give shape to political morality and literary expression, or simply walks away from civilization to a hardly accessible terrain which he hopes it will not reach. Emerson uses different strategies to support his idealist view. He either minimizes the effects of civilization, or he uses the productive properties of his Romantic gaze as a method of systematic oversight. In the introductory passage of "Nature," the stamp humans have left on their environment is belittled as "a little chipping, baking, patching, and washing," which, "in an impression so grand as that of the world on the human mind," does not "vary the result" ("Nature" 1074). As, from this angle, the impact of civilization remains hardly noticeable, its conflict with nature's course all but disappears. In addition to such attempts to shrink the role of the division of labor, social inequality, and the exploitation of natural re-

---

his spiritualism contains an element of the subject's sublation in nature, which he shares with Thoreau. Both Thoreau's object- and Emerson's subject-orientation are not totally consistent and include gestures in the direction of the respective counterposition. But they remain clearly distinguishable on the basis of their different emphasis. My discussion of Emerson is based in part on my essay "Edgar Allan Poe's Dreamscapes and the Transcendentalist View of Nature." For Emerson's 'triumph of the subject over nature,' see Schulz, *Amerikanischer Transzendentalismus* 115-120. For Emerson's concept of nature, see also Burkholder; Cameron; Cascardi; *Emerson's Nature: Origin, Growth, Meaning*; Horstmann, "Mythos der Bemächtigung;" Levine; Quigley; Rao; Schulz, "Emerson's Visionary Moments;" Steele; and Wilson.

sources in nineteenth-century America, Emerson also hypostatizes his concept of the harmonization of nature and culture in order to be able to shut his eyes to those aspects of reality that contradict it. This usage becomes obvious when he defines his poetic view of nature against the background of the condition of New England:

> When we speak of nature in this manner, we have a distinct but most poetical sense in the mind. We mean the integrity of impression made by manifold natural objects. It is this which distinguishes the stick of timber of the wood-cutter, from the tree of the poet. The charming landscape which I saw this morning, is indubitably made up of some twenty or thirty farms. Miller owns this field, Locke that, and Manning the woodland beyond. But none of them owns the landscape. There is a property in the horizon which no man has but he whose eye can integrate all the parts, that is, the poet. This is the best part of these men's farms, yet to this their warranty-deeds give no title. ("Nature" 1074)

The problem with the unified and integrated perception of nature is that it can only be bought at the price of a dual vision. The "stick of timber of the wood-cutter" and "the tree of the poet" are, after all, the same thing. The philosopher's integrated view perceives the identical landscape which the segmentalizing and utilitarian perspective of the Millers, Lockes, and Mannings considers their separate farms. The holistic vision of a spiritualized nature exists only for those who decide to share the poet's Romantic perception. Nature turns into an aesthetic construct that depends upon the repression of divisive facts such as the simultaneous exploitation of nature, while the poet chooses to recollect its seemingly virgin state in tranquility. In some passages of "Nature," Emerson distances himself unambiguously from the practical and utilitarian viewpoint of farmers like the Millers, Lockes, and Mannings. He regrets that "you cannot freely admire a noble landscape if laborers are digging in the field hard by." He adds: "The poet finds something ridiculous in his delight until he is out of the sight of men" ("Nature" 1096). The poets and philosophers who specialize in the transcendentalist stance also belong to the members of society who "have suffered amputation from the trunk." Unwittingly, they become subject to the same division of labor which they try to ignore or evade. From the angle of this division of labor, the poets deal in holism as the woodcutters deal in timber. Escapism seems to be the price to pay for spiritual wholeness. Thoreau's materialist and object-oriented escapism is literal and consists in alternative environments and forms of living. Emerson's spiritualist and subject-oriented escapism consists in the distortions of his "transparent eyeball." The clash between the claim to general relevance and the specialized status of both philosophy and art become more and more problematic.[9]

4. The Subject-Object Paradigm in Modernist Conceptions of Consciousness: William James and Henri Bergson

Under the impact of increasing industrialization upon the American landscape, perhaps best epitomized by the advance of the railroad, the Romantic subject-object paradigm of nature dramatically loses credibility. Regionalist and realist fiction towards the end of the nineteenth century, for instance, covering the whole expanse of the United States from Sarah Orne Jewett's Maine via Hamlin Garland's Iowa to Samuel Clemens's Mid-West and California, radically questions and deconstructs this holistic view of nature. Yet, unexpectedly, the very technological advances which seem to deny its validity, have revitalized this Romantic holism on a new cybernetic basis, recreating it as a simulacrum. It is this trajectory that seems to allow for a re-evaluation of the utilitarian stance disclaimed by Romantics such as Emerson and Thoreau and contemporary theorists such as Taylor and Buell. On the level of a technologically reproducible nature—no longer a contradiction in terms—the conflicting attitudes discussed with regard to first-degree nature, including object- and subject-orientation, seem to recur. Modernist conceptions of consciousness represent an intermediate, subject-oriented stage in this process. William James's and Henri Bergson's modernist maps of the human mind eventually develop into the topography of external realities in postmodern technoscapes.

---

9 In statements by painters of the Hudson River School – for instance, Thomas Cole's "Essay on American Scenery" (1836) and Asher B. Durand's "Letters on American Landscape Painting"—similar artistic desires for "that sweet communion" with nature (Cole 339) and the expression of "the essence of the object seen" (Durand 367) are being articulated. Cole even fraternizes with waterfalls, notably Niagara Falls, "the voice of the landscape [...] In gazing on it we feel as though a great void had been filled in our minds—our conceptions expand—we become a part of what we behold!" (Cole 343). Both painters also strongly express the rift between such artistic interests and the utilitarian superficiality of American society. See also Novak.

Around the turn of the twentieth century, artists and philosophers register a paradigm change in the notion of what reality is and concomitant alterations of the concepts of time, language, truth, and the individual. This subject-oriented reorientation originates in studies of the interiority of the mind, its perceptions of the outside world. In retrospect, the American social philosopher Daniel Bell regards "the Cartesian turn from depicting *objects* as we know them to capturing *sensations* of perception" (*Cultural Contradictions* 111) as the criterion for the distinction between pre-modernity and modernism. In his view, modern art is a very expressive indicator of this Cartesian turn. It is characterized by the suspension of the notions of space and time originating in Newtonian physics and the invalidation of the mimetic relation between art and reality:

> In art and literature, the activity theory of knowledge becomes the agency for the transformation of the older modes of *mimesis* and given coordinates of space and time. And instead of contemplation, we find substituted *sensation, simultaneity, immediacy*, and *impact*. These new intentions provide a common, formal syntax for all the arts from the mid-nineteenth to the mid-twentieth century. (*Cultural Contradictions* 110-111)

One of the originators of this "formal syntax" is the American philosopher and psychologist William James, the brother of novelist Henry James, whose scientific insights into the processes of perception decisively influence this novel sense of reality. Emersonian subject-orientation develops a new, scientifically motivated foundation. In *Psychology: Briefer Course* (1892), which followed *The Principles of Psychology* (1890), James assumes the continuity of consciousness as one of its four basic characters. States of consciousness can become disordered and deranged by qualitative changes, but they can never be totally interrupted. Consciousness can indeed also be broken into fragments by scientific analysis, but as such it remains the unitary, continuous and infinite substratum of all individual states of consciousness. Therefore, James defines it by means of a metaphor which has become famous as the designation of a literary technique which tries to reproduce this inner reality:

> Consciousness, then, does not appear to itself chopped up in bits. Such words as 'chain' or 'train' do not describe it fitly as it presents itself in the first instance. It is nothing jointed; it flows. A 'river' or a 'stream' are the metaphors by which it is most naturally described. *In talking of*

> it hereafter, let us call it the stream of thought, of consciousness, or of subjective life. (James 159)

This interior world of consciousness is marked by a changeability and fluidity not attributable to the solid substantiality of the object world that pertains to traditional concepts of reality. It is not so much the specific perceptual impression and its concrete qualities which James's research concentrates on, but rather the relations of such impressions, the process of combination that makes them elements of one and the same consciousness in the first place.

James subdivides consciousness into substantive and transitive elements. The existence of the latter makes possible the streaming and flowing movement of the former. Viewed epistemologically, the transitive elements of consciousness correspond to the relations between objects in the external world; viewed linguistically, they correspond to functional or form words—those linguistic signs which connect other linguistic signs, but do not designate an object or quality. Reality thus resembles a language—or, as James also puts it, the movements of a bird—more than it resembles a configuration of solid objects:

> When we take a general view of the wonderful stream of our consciousness, what strikes us first is the different pace of its parts. Like a bird's life, it seems to be an alternation of flights and perchings. The rhythm of language expresses this, where every thought is expressed in a sentence, and every sentence closed by a period. The resting-places are usually occupied by sensorial imaginations of some sort, whose peculiarity is that they can be held before the mind for an indefinite time, and contemplated without changing; the places of flight are filled with thoughts of relations, static or dynamic, that for the most part obtain between the matters contemplated in the periods of comparative rest. *Let us call the resting-places the 'substantive parts,' and the places of flight the 'transitive parts,' of the stream of thought.* (James 159-160)

Every substantive impression is accompanied by a halo or fringe, indicating its movability, that is, its derivation from somewhere else, as well as its directedness toward yet another destination:

> Every definite image *in the mind* is steeped and dyed in the free water that flows round it. With it goes the sense of its relations, near and remote, the dying echo of whence it came to us, the dawning sense of whither it is to lead. The significance, the value of the image is all in this halo or penumbra that surrounds and escorts it,—or rather that is

fused into one with it and has become bone of its bone and flesh of its flesh. (James 164-165)[10]

Although formulated as a subject-oriented theory of human perception, James's notions in effect collapse the distinguishability between subject and object, the inner and the outer world. In James's eyes, the nexus of the substantive elements brought about by the transitive elements forms the only possibility to conceive of consciousness as unitary. James rejects any mediating element which is not identical with, but lies beyond, this nexus—for instance, the idea of a soul. The integration of the stream of consciousness is produced by its transitive, relational elements alone. They replace what has formerly been called the identity of the individual. Consistently, James deconstructs the concept of personal identity. Personal identity becomes a matter of aspect, of perspective; it dissolves in a multiplicity of protean selves:

> The past and present selves compared are the same just so far as they *are* the same, and no farther. They are the same in *kind*. But this generic sameness coexists with generic differences just as real; and if from the one point of view I am one self, from another I am quite as truly many. Similarly of the attribute of continuity: it gives to the self the unity of mere connectedness, or unbrokenness, a perfectly definite phenomenal thing—but it gives not a jot or tittle more. (196-197)

The dissolution of a recognizable subject is tantamount to the dissolution of a substantial object. The states of consciousness have no substantial, but only a functional unity, as they form a relational complex held together by the transitive elements. The elimination of personal identity goes hand in hand with the elimination of "any

---

10 Modernist writers such as Joseph Conrad and Virginia Woolf have given expression to a similar sense of dynamization. In *Heart of Darkness* (1899), Conrad makes a point of Marlow's unconventional mode of storytelling which coincides with James's insight into the dynamism of the modern perception: "[T]o him the meaning of an episode was not inside like a kernel but outside, enveloping the tale which brought it out only as a glow brings out a haze, in the likeness of one of these misty halos that, sometimes, are made visible by the spectral illumination of moonshine (9). In "Modern Fiction" (1924), Virginia Woolf famously argues that "[l]ife is not a series of gig-lamps symmetrically arranged; life is a luminous halo, a semi-transparent envelope surrounding us from the beginning of consciousness to the end" (106). The series of gig lamps aptly characterizes the segmentalization and juxtaposition on which traditional concepts of reality are based, while the "lumionus halo" and "semi-transparent envelope" almost literally echo James's imagery.

transcendent principle of Unity" (James 199). Subject- and object-orientation coalesce, as the distinctions between subject and object, imagination and reality, psychology and ontology blur. On the one hand, it becomes unclear whether the substantive elements in the stream of consciousness are indeed denotations of an objective world independent of consciousness, whether each of these substantive elements represents "a quality of our feeling" or rather "our feeling of a quality" (James 430). On the other hand, the negation of the notion that consciousness is necessarily the consciousness of an identifiable individual, that it is his or her consciousness, calls in question the psychic nature of consciousness and thereby the meaning of this concept as such: "It seems as if consciousness as an inner activity were rather a *postulate* than a sensible given fact, the postulate, namely, of a *knower* as correlative to all this known" (James 432). The stream of consciousness sets adrift any possibility to distinguish between subject and object. What remains is the stream itself as a relational complex of impressions, shaped in its configuration by its transitive elements.[11] Everything else is a part of this stream of consciousness. It transcends and determines everything else; nothing determines it. It extends in time but also encompasses it. It is therefore itself beyond the flow of time in what James calls a "specious present" and an "intuited duration": "Meanwhile, the specious present, the intuited duration, stands permanent, like the rainbow on the waterfall, with its own quality unchanged by the events that stream through it" (271). The specious present, the intuited duration of the stream of consciousness is that which holds together its substantive and transitive parts without being itself either a substantive or a transitive part.[12] It is that which synthesizes everything else without being itself subject to further synthesis. In Kantian parlance, it is the ultimate transcendental condition in that it does not in turn operate under another transcendental condition. James thus develops the concept of an all-pervasive and dynamic relational

---

[11] For the continuity of the stream of consciousness as its unifying principle, see Schmidt 16-23.

[12] For the connective and synthesizing power of James's stream of consciousness, see Schmidt 42-72.

complex that buries both subject and object in the folds of its weblike structure.[13]

This alleged pervasiveness of James's concept of the relational complex as governing the world of both subject and object—the comprehension of the psyche and the understanding of the world at large—is all the more surprising since, in James's time, the felt inner reality of the stream of consciousness began to be considered to be irreconcilable with the analytical and segmenting world view of the sciences. The rift between the sciences and the arts, which the British novelist and scientist C. P. Snow later described as "two cultures" in his lecture *The Two Cultures and the Scientific Revolution* (1959) began to open up. In the stream of consciousness, simultaneity is intuitively experienced but cannot be measured, whereas chronological time is measurable, but cannot be experienced. Chronological time allows for a quantitative determination of sense impressions and states of consciousness, but this is only possible if the experience of the stream of consciousness is given up in favor of scientific analysis, if the "inner" perspective of the specious present is exchanged for the "outer" perspective of chronology. From this angle, time can no longer be regarded as "duration," but as a construction more or less symbolic. The French philosopher Henri Bergson, whose theories, especially with regard to the structure of time, were taken up eagerly by many modernist novelists, replaces James's empirical analysis of human perception by a vitalistic approach. Bergson's central idea of a life force, *l'elan vital*, can be considered as a metaphysical interpretation of James's stream of consciousness stressing the irreconcilability with the world view of the natural sciences to a degree that James does

---

13   In this regard, James's stream of consciousness anticipates Jacques Derrida's concept of *différance*, developed in 1972, which also encompasses all differences and differentiations, including the ones between space and time. As James's stream of consciousness is demonstrable only in its myriad concrete materializations, Derrida's *différance* remains as ungraspable as it is claimed to be fundamental. While James takes his departure from the interiority of consciousness and is in this regard subject-oriented, Derrida takes his departure from the semiotic difference between the sign and what it signifies, the signifier and the signified, and is thus object-oriented. As James's interpretation of consciousness contributes to laying the groundwork for modernism, Derrida's *différance*-text is one of the cornerstones of postmodernism.

not.[14] Like James, Bergson foregrounds the dynamics of both consciousness and the external world. These dynamics can be intuitively experienced but not rationally dissected. Neither the conventional structures of language nor the sequentiality of astronomical time represent this flux appropriately.

Bergson does not tire of providing examples that demonstrate the inability of our scientific mode of thought to capture the essential dynamics of movement: Zeno's classical and mathematics-based paradoxes of the arrrow, motionless in mid-air, and of Achilles, unable to overtake a tortoise, as well as, on a more technological plane, the cinematograph, which creates the illusion of movement by unreeling static photographs in quick succession, are all used to show that what we feel or perceive in these cases is undivided movement, whereas mathematics and the natural sciences, just like the cinematograph, inappropriately conceive of these movements as a series of frozen moments which can then be measured. Thereby the dynamics of the original movement, the *élan vital*, is sacrificed on the altar of scientific and mathematical analysis:

> Instead of attaching ourselves to the inner becoming of things, we place ourselves outside them in order to recompose their becoming artificially. We take snapshots, as it were, of the passing reality, and, as these are characteristic of the reality, we have only to string them on a becoming, abstract, uniform and invisible, situated at the back of the apparatus of knowledge, in order to imitate what there is that is characteristic in this becoming itself. Perception, intellection, language so proceed in general. Whether we would think becoming, or express it, or even perceive it, we hardly do anything else than set going a kind of cinematograph inside us. We may therefore sum up what we have been saying in the conclusion that *the mechanism of our ordinary knowledge is of a cinematographical kind.* (Bergson, *Creative Evolution* 306)

It is impossible, Bergson argues, to retain the qualitative intensity of reality's movability—its transitivity, as James might say—in approaches to it that are based on quantitative analysis (see Bergson, *Time and Free Will* 106). Both the subject and the object, our inner intuitive feelings and the natural world in its waxing and waning, are

---

14 For the difference between James and Bergson with regard to the split between the reality of experiential continuity and that of the natural sciences, see Schmidt 98.

out of sync with the utilitarian knowledge produced by the scientific approach. Science "takes account neither of *succession* in what of it is specific nor of *time* in what there is in it that is fluent. It has no sign to express what strikes our consciousness in succession and duration. It no more applies to becoming, so far as that is moving, than the bridges thrown here and there across the stream follow the water that flows under their arches" (Bergson, *Creative Evolution* 338). And this scientific mode of knowledge pays tribute neither to our inner sensations of duration nor to the essence of natural phenomena: "So of the works of nature. Their novelty arises from an internal impetus which is progress or succession, which confers on succession a peculiar virtue or which owes to succession the whole of its virtue—which, at any rate, makes succession, or *continuity of interpenetration* in time, irreducible to a mere instantaneous juxtaposition in space" (Bergson, *Creative Evolution* 341).

The dichotomy in Emerson's thought between the utilitarian approach to nature by the farmer and the spiritual approach of the poet—between those for whom the woods are timber and those for whom they are an emblem of the spirit—recurs here, replacing the farmer by the scientist and, by implication, the industrialist. Scientifically segmentalized knowledge is useful for the mastering of nature and for dominating the earth, but not for capturing its essence. It "has the advantage of enabling us to foresee the future and of making us in some measure masters of events; in return, it retains of the moving reality only eventual immobilities, that is to say, views taken of it by our mind. It symbolizes the real and transposes it into the human rather than expresses it" (Bergson, *Creative Evolution* 342-343). By contrast, the intuited *élan vital* is useless but, like Emerson's gaze of the transparent eyeball, close to the essence of both subject and object, the human psyche and the cycles of nature: "The other knowledge, if it is possible, is practically useless, it will not extend our empire over nature, it will even go against certain natural aspirations of the intellect; but, if it succeeds, it is reality itself that it will hold in a firm and final embrace" (Bergson, *Creative Evolution* 343).

The concepts of reality, language, and time developed by James and Bergson objectify subjective experience. From the point of view of a physiology of perception and a metaphysics of intuition, respectively, the distinction between subject and object is dissolved by the reduction of both categories to elements of the all-pervasive flux of consciousness—a consciousness which appears coextensive with the individual's deepest feelings and the movements within nature. The development from a static and substantialist to a dynamic and relational conception of reality, initiated by James and Bergson, seems to overcome the traditional dichotomies of subject and object, materialism and idealism and pave the way for a new monistic world picture. Although both James and Bergson share a subject-oriented, consciousness-centered approach, both their findings tend to drain these terms of their meaning. Interiority and exteriority merge. Bergson interprets his own doctrine as a complement to scientific theories and hopes for a gradual convergence of both ways of thinking. But the dichotomies which dissolve in the stream of consciousness recur in the relation between the Jamesian stream of consciousness and the Bergsonian *élan vital* on the one hand and the rationalist descriptions and formations of reality by modern science on the other. The dual nature of intuited and measured time, central to both James and Bergson, is indicative of this unresolved discrepancy between intuition and intellect, physics and metaphysics. If, from this perspective, Bergson seems to have carried Emerson's subject-oriented approach to nature at least one step further, this also means one step further away from the world of science and industrialization.

The gap persists between the notions of the natural sciences and these Jamesian and Bergsonian conceptions of reality, language, and time, derived as they are from dimensions of consciousness. This gap translates into a new version of the conflict between the promise of technological perfection and an ecologically motivated desire for a return to a more natural life. The avant-garde trends of modern art, informed by the findings of both James and Bergson, frequently define themselves in marked contrast to a world increasingly dominated by the results of scientific research transformed into technological realities. Culture and technology are in danger of turning into spheres that are totally, irrevocably and irreconcilably alienated from each other. Not until the middle of the century does the chance for a synthesis of both spheres come into sight. This reintegration is rendered possible by technological innovations producing a hitherto unthinkable compatibility with the Jamesian and Bergsonian concepts of reality, language, and time.

5. The Cybernetic Totalization of the Subject-Object Paradigm: Norbert Wiener, Marshall McLuhan, and Donna Haraway

Recently, Bergson's cinematograph is being replaced by the computer which renders insignificant the discrepancy between the analytical character of its technical operations and the semblance of fluid and dynamic realities that it produces. The speeding-up of many formative social processes by the introduction of electronics in a wide variety of fields tends to render negligible the distinction between the simultaneity pertaining to consciousness and the segmental nature of chronological time, since electronic operations are so fast that they can be called synchronic for all earthly purposes. To the extent electronic technology permeates society, chronological time becomes a *quantité négligeable*. Developments in time turn into synchronic configurations. Thus, empirical reality, transformed by the nearly ubiquitous application of electronics, more and more resembles the originally psychic reality described by James and Bergson. Central notions associated with the sense of reality generated by this electronic technology can be considered as cybernetic reformulations of the Romantic subject-object paradigm of nature. In Emerson's Romantic conception, nature and the transparent eyeball of the beholder melt into each other. In James's and Bergson's modernist stance, nature and the object world at large become fused with a subject reduced to the stream of consciousness, or *élan vital*, of its myriad sense perceptions. In the cybernetic age, electronic technology lends support to this modernist fusion of subject and object by the creation of an exterior reality consisting largely of ensembles of impulses. Postmodern technoscapes can thus be viewed as a technological version of the translucent landscape perceived by Emerson's transparent eyeball.

In the late 1940s, Norbert Wiener, one of the first theorists of cybernetics to discuss his findings outside of the hermetic circle of specialists, emphasizes the correspondences between automata and human beings in two books, *Cybernetics or Control and Communication in the Animal and the Machine* (1948) and *The Human Use of Human Beings: Cybernetics and Society* (1950). Long before Marshall McLuhan and Daniel Bell were to use the same analogy, Wiener described computers as the central nervous system of cybernetic organisms: "It has long been clear to me that the modern ultra-rapid computing machine was in principle an ideal central nervous system to an apparatus for automatic control" (*Cybernetics* 26). Electronic machinery comes so close to imitating physiological processes that the distinction between the organic and the mechanical blurs. Machines can be described as possessing the physiological properties of organisms:

> [T]he many automata of the present age are coupled to the outside world both for the reception of impressions and for the performance of actions. They contain sense organs, effectors, and the equivalent of a nervous system to integrate the transfer of information from the one to the other. They lend themselves very well to description in physiological terms. It is scarcely a miracle that they can be subsumed under one theory with the mechanisms of physiology. (*Cybernetics* 43)

If matter becomes subject-oriented, as it were, and adopts characteristics of human organisms, humans become object-oriented and can, in turn, be conceived of as resembling machines in Wiener's technological version of James's and Bergson's dissolution of individuality:

> It is my thesis that the physical functioning of the living individual and the operation of some of the newer communication machines are precisely parallel [...]. Both of them have sensory receptors as one stage in their cycle of operation: that is, in both of them there exists a special apparatus for collecting information from the outer world at low energy levels, and for making it available in the operation of the individual or of the machine. In both cases these external messages are not taken *neat*, but through the internal transforming powers of the apparatus, whether it be alive or dead. The information is then turned into a new form available for the further stages of performance. In both the animal and the machine this performance is made to be effective on the outer world. In both of them, their *performed* action on the outer world, and not merely their *intended* action, is reported back to the central regulatory apparatus. (*The Human Use* 26-27)

Wiener's notion of the structural sameness of man and machine rests on the possibility of regarding both the human brain and the central nervous system as self-regulating systems for the processing of data. The common denominator of this computer-technology-based subject-object paradigm is the claim that the whole world, humans as well as nature and machines, must be considered as patterned entities, determined by dynamic interrelations similar to James's and Bergson's reality concepts of the relational complex and the dynamic flux:

> The metaphor to which I devote this chapter ["V: Organization as the Message"] is one in which the organism is seen as message. Organism is opposed to chaos, to disintegration, to death, as message is to noise.

> To describe an organism, we do not try to specify each molecule in it, and catalogue it bit by bit, but rather to answer certain questions about it which reveal its pattern [...]. (*The Human Use* 95)

From the viewpoint of informational technology, machines become virtual organisms and humans become encoded messages. Wiener claims that human beings function as cybernetic systems: "We are not stuff that abides, but patterns that perpetuate themselves" (*The Human Use* 96). The gap between subject- and object-orientation, mechanism and vitalism, science and art, the world of technology and that of the mind begins to close once again. The distinctions between the stream of consciousness and the realities outside it, the linearity of measurable astronomical time and the synchronicity of the intuited duration begin to fold entirely:

> Thus the modern automaton exists in the same sort of Bergsonian time as the living organism; and hence there is no reason in Bergson's considerations why the essential mode of functioning of the living organism should not be the same as that of the automaton of this type. Vitalism has won to the extent that even mechanisms correspond to the time-structure of vitalism; but as we have said, this victory is a complete defeat, for from every point of view which has the slightest relation to morality or religion, the new mechanics is fully as mechanistic as the old. (*Cybernetics* 44)

Wiener's caveat deserves recognition. His argument about the homology between the organic and the mechanical is strictly structural and not moral. The later enthusiasm about the closing of the gap between organicism and mechanism, voiced by theorists such as Marshall McLuhan, tends to overlook this limitation and to present the same diagnosis as if it were the solution to all problems and the advent of utopia. The debates about biomedical possibilities such as the cloning of humans and about the justifiability, as well as viability, of massive manipulations of the ecosphere fill precisely this moral void.

The homology of man and machine, suggested by Wiener, is taken up by the literary critic and media specialist Marshall McLuhan in his 1964 study *Understanding Media*. *Understanding Media* became a cult bestseller in the sixties, not least because of the utopian hopes for the harmonization of existential dichotomies with which McLuhan associates it. They are the same utopian hopes Wiener had warned the world against. McLuhan becomes the prophet of the total mediatization of society which dissolves materiality in the processing of information: "As automation takes hold, it becomes obvious that *information* is the crucial commodity, and that solid products are merely incidental to information movement" (McLuhan 220-221). As he considers all media to be extensions of human organs and abilities (the wheel, for instance, is an extension of the foot), electronic technology appears as the final of these extensions and the apogee of this development: "It is a principal aspect of the electric age that it establishes a global network that has much of the character of our central nervous system" (McLuhan 370-371). McLuhan emphasizes the global character of such electronic dematerialization that renders it possible to conceive of the whole world as entirely subject-oriented, as "a single unified field of experience" (371). Electronic technology removes all object qualities from the world and, thereby, fulfils the most ambitious human aspirations: "What emerges is a total field of inclusive awareness. The old pattern of psychic and social adjustment become [!] irrelevant" (McLuhan 115).

Expanding its own reach to the remotest parts of the world, electronic technology shrinks this world and makes it as transparent as individual consciousness. Emerson's romantic belief that nature is an emblem of the spirit has turned into a technological creed. The world becomes a brain. By the advance of the immensely complicated new cybernetic technology, mankind is, in McLuhan's view, paradoxically on the way back towards simpler, more manageable conditions. For these conditions, he finds an image that has become a byword of processes of globalization, the global village, a kind of electronic retribalization (see McLuhan 99-116). Because the heading of the first chapter in *Understanding Media*, "The Medium is the Message," which is also his best-known slogan, takes to extremes the emphasis on relation and configuration rather than on content and substance, McLuhan's depiction of the consequences of this convergence between psychic and technological reality appears over-optimistic. The paradox that the most advanced results of technological research are supposed to bring about the satisfaction of those basic human needs that have been alienated and repressed by this very technological progress justifies the suspicion that the all-embracing unification, which McLuhan sees achieved in the electronic era, may only be a new and different formation of conflicting forces.

In the 1970s, the social philosopher Daniel Bell less radically diagnosed that the trend towards a structural convergence of technological, perceptual, and cognitive processes is more than a utopian vision.

In his 1974 *The Coming of Post-Industrial Society*, Bell maintains that the axial principle of modern societies in the highly industrialized countries, i.e., the central axis of these societies around which social stratification is organized, is changing. Bell describes this alteration as one from a pre-industrial to an industrial and post-industrial society:

> Thus, the 'design' of pre-industrial society is a 'game against nature': its resources are drawn from extractive industries and it is subject to the law of diminishing returns and low productivity; the 'design' of industrial society is a 'game against fabricated nature' which is centered on man-machine relationships and uses energy to transform the natural environment into a technical environment; the 'design' of a post-industrial society is a 'game between persons' in which an 'intellectual technology,' based on information, rises alongside of machine technology. (116)

As data processing permeates society on all levels, its creed, informational theory, turns into the principle which structures society at large. While Bell agrees with McLuhan on the arrival of a postmodern, cybernetic subject-object paradigm which consists in the sublation of the material world in a web of consciousness, he also shares Wiener's scepticism as to the ability of such cybernetic configurations to provide meaning or moral guidance. Bell believes that nature survives in the shape of ineradicable destructive impulses and instincts:

> Will this changed experience create a change in consciousness and sensibility? For most of human history, *reality was nature*, and in poetry and imagination men sought to relate the self to the natural world. Then *reality became technics*, tools and things made by men yet given an independent existence outside himself, the reified world. Now *reality is primarily the social world*—neither nature nor things, only men—experienced through the reciprocal consciousness of self and other. Society itself becomes a web of consciousness, a form of imagination to be realized as a social construction. Inevitably, a post-industrial society gives rise to a new Utopianism, both engineering and psychedelic. Men can be remade or released, their behavior conditioned or their consciousness altered. The constraints of the past vanish with the end of nature and things. But what does not vanish is the duplex nature of man himself—the murderous aggression, from primal impulse, to tear apart and destroy; and the search for order, in art and life, as the bending of will to harmonius shape. (488)

Bell's post-industrialism leads to a stance which comes close to asking for an ecological, object- and nature-oriented moderation of the triumph of subject-orientation. The substitution of a relational and structural concept of reality for a substantial one is in danger of being accompanied by the substitution of functionalism as an end in itself for moral values and social norms. Here we have clearly reached the limits of the analogy between man and machine: Humans are not identical with organic self-regulation, but realize themselves in the framework of ethical value systems, which they establish, accept, or reject. The cybernetic equation seems to entail a reduction of human beings to physiological entities. Any aspirations to seek a meaning of life beyond this level have to be abandoned. This is also the point where the capacity of the cybernetic concept of reality to bring about the universal convergence and unification of heterogeneous spheres becomes doubtful. While the prevalent technological functionalism fails to provide solutions for the problems it raises, traditional values correspondingly fail to fill an ethical vacuum which raises questions incompatible with the old answers.

In her "Cyborg Manifesto" (1991), Donna Haraway tries to demonstrate that the cybernetic subject-object paradigm deserves a less sceptical attitude than Wiener's and Bell's with regard to its ability to redefine human identity in viable ways. In a more gendered fashion than McLuhan, Haraway celebrates the disappearance of traditional dichotomies as a chance to reorganize the human condition. All the "troubling dualisms [...] self/other, mind/body, culture/nature, male/female, civilized/primitive, reality/appearance, whole/part, agent/resource, maker/made, active/passive, right/wrong, truth/illusion, total/partial, God/man" (Haraway 313) tend to disappear in a technoscape rendering the distinction between the biosphere and the nonorganic, between matter and consciousness, fact and fiction questionable:

> High-tech culture challenges these dualisms in intriguing ways. It is not clear who makes and who is made in the relation between human and machine. It is not clear what is mind and what body in machines that resolve into coding practices. [...] we find ourselves to be cyborgs, hybrids, mosaics, chimeras. Biological organisms have become biotic systems, communications devices like others. There is no fundamental ontological separation in our formal knowledge of machine and organism, of technical and organic. (Haraway 313)

From the vantage point of object-orientation, technology emerges as an improved and perfected nature: "Our best machines are made of sunshine; they are all light and clean because they are nothing but signals, electromagnetic waves, a section of a spectrum [...]. Cyborgs are ether, quintessence" (Haraway 294). And a new, technology-inspired animism is in the offing: "The new machines are so clean and light. Their engineers are sun-worshippers mediating a new scientific revolution associated with the night dream of post-industrial society" (Haraway 294). From the perspective of subject-orientation, individual identity dissolves more radically than in James's and Bergson's modernist conceptions: "Our machines are disturbingly lively, and ourselves are frightfully inert" (Haraway 294). All fixed distinctions disappear in a Baudrillardian mesh of labyrinthine simulations:

> I am making an argument for the cyborg as a fiction mapping our social and bodily reality and as an imaginative resource suggesting some very fruitful couplings. [...] By the late twentieth century, our time, a mythic time, we are all chimeras, theorized and fabricated hybrids of machine and organism; in short, we are cyborgs. The cyborg is our ontology; it gives us our politics. The cyborg is a condensed image of both imagination and material reality, the two joined centres structuring any possibility of historical transformation. (Haraway 292)[15]

In Haraway's view, the prevalence of such structures not only redefines the relationship between nature and culture but also collapses manifold gender, ethnic, and social differences. The cybernetic subject-object paradigm cuts the ties to traditions, even mythical ones: "The cyborg would not recognize the Garden of Eden; it is not made of mud and cannot dream of returning to dust" (Haraway 293). But Haraway also concedes a dystopian as well as a utopian perspective of this development:

> From one perspective, a cyborg world is about the final imposition of a grid of control on the planet, about the final abstraction embodied in a Star Wars apocalypse waged in the name of defence [...] From another perspective, a cyborg world might be about lived social and bodily realities in which people are not afraid of their joint kinship with

---

15 Baudrillard focuses on the collapse of the semiotic distinction between signifier and signified, which is one of the distinctions Haraway also sees vanish. Representation is sucked up, as it were, by simulation. Representation does not represent anything anymore except for itself. It turns into "a gigantic simulacrum: not unreal, but a simulacrum, never again exchanging for what is real, but exchanging in itself, in an uninterrupted circuit without reference or circumference" (Baudrillard 152). Klaus Benesch has published articles and, recently, a book-length study on the development of the notion of the cyborg from the Romantic period onwards. See also my own articles on technology and the antebellum American short story and on the development from the modernist to the postmodernist aesthetic.

animals and machines, not afraid of permanently partial identities and contradictory standpoints. (Haraway 295)

Haraway tends to stress the utopian dimension and the chances furnished by both the digitalization of humanity and the creation of cyborgs. By contrast, computer scientist David Gelernter, for instance, emphasizes the unbridgeable gap between humans and electronic machines. In his treatise *Machine Beauty* (1998), Gelernter insists on the necessity of humanizing even the most advanced electronic machinery by designing it for our purposes as opposed to making ourselves compatible with machinery by turning ourselves into cyborgs. Object-orientation survives, as (human) nature is to be the yardstick for machine quality and machine beauty. Therefore, Gelernter describes the, in his opinion, excellent usability of the Java computer language as "computer science's latest return to Walden Pond" (Gelernter 46). In Haraway's and Gelernter's positions, the conflict between subject- and object-orientation re-emerges on a technologically advanced level as a reaction to a radically transformed world.

In *Writing for an Endangered World* (2001), his latest book to date, Lawrence Buell provides the last-ditch argument for the object-oriented stance so far. In *Writing*, Buell retains his object-oriented approach of embedding humanity within a larger environment on which it depends, but which does not depend upon it: "human beings are biohistorical creatures constructing themselves in interaction with surroundings they cannot not inhabit" (2). Like Emerson at the beginning of his essay "Nature," Buell tries to include civilization, the man-made material world, in his concept of nature. When Emerson speaks of *Nature* capitalized, he is talking about the object world in its entirety as it is opposed to the subject or, as Emerson says, the soul. Emersonian *Nature* comprises lower-case *nature*, i.e., the material world as untouched and unaltered by humans, and *art*, i.e., the human environment which consists of natural materials changed by human labor and technology into products or commodities. Although his all-embracing gesture clearly raises the question of the relationship between human civilizational developments (*Nature*) and the natural environment (*nature*), Emerson declares that the distinction between *Nature* capitalized and lower-case *nature* is not important at all. He does so on the grounds that human production and civilization do not change lower-case *nature* in any significant way (which, as contemporary readers know, has been a gross misjudgment):

Theories of Landscape, Consciousness, and Technoscape 85

> Philosophically considered, the universe is composed of Nature and the Soul. Strictly speaking, therefore, all that is separate from us, all which Philosophy distinguishes as the NOT ME, that is, both nature and art, all other men and my own body, must be ranked under this name, NATURE. [...] *Nature*, in the common sense, refers to essences unchanged by man; space, the air, the river, the leaf. *Art* is applied to the mixture of his will with the same things, as in a house, a canal, a statue, a picture. But his operations taken together are so insignificant, a little chipping, baking, patching, and washing, that in an impression so grand as that of the world on the human mind, they do not vary the result ("Nature" 1073-1074).

While Emerson conflates natural objects and material products on the basis of the allegedly negligible influence of human interventions in nature, Buell does so for the opposite reason, namely, that these human interventions have become so forceful and ubiquitous that nature proper is now all but indistinguishable: "By 'environment(al),' I refer both to 'natural' and 'human-built' dimensions of the palpable world. Though I shall also insist on the distinction, one must also blur it by recourse to the more comprehensive term. Human transformations of physical nature have made the two realms increasingly indistinguishable" (*Writing* 3). Although he grants this blurring of the boundaries of nature and civilization, Buell insists on the basic function and import of nature as the substratum of human life: "[T]he history of human modification of environment should not be taken as implying a comprehensive, irreversible transformation of 'nature' into artifact" (*Writing* 5). In the face of the overwhelming technological transformations of the environment outlined, among many others, by Wiener, McLuhan, and Haraway, Buell makes a case for object-oriented nature awareness. He basically argues that, as long as humans are remotely what they have hitherto been, they will depend more on the groundwork of nature than vice versa:

> On the one hand, the world's physical environment is being increasingly refashioned by capital, technology, and geopolitics, with so-called nature consumed or reproduced as lawns, gardens, theme parks, habitat zoos, conservancies, and so on. On the other hand, this process has made tracts of (relatively) unfabricated nature in some quarters more salient and, in general, all the more crucial both as concept and as term of value: as a way of designating what has not yet been greatly transformed by pollution, climate change, and the like; as a way of dramatizing the violence and excess of techno-transformation; and as a way of underscoring the importance of the however-modified non-human world to the maintenance of life. (*Writing* 5-6)

In Buell's interpretation, nature has become a liminal and peripheral entity which is nevertheless necessary as a yardstick for responsible environmental attitudes and conduct. Nature, and the value orientation derivable from it, fills the ethical void which Wiener and Bell see opening up underneath the simulacral surface of the postmodern technoscape. Contrary to theorists like Wiener, McLuhan, and Haraway, Buell does not believe in the change of the fundamental structure of human existence through technological progress:

> Even if people were to become as 'posthuman' as the bionic characters of cyberpunk fiction, they would likely remain physically embodied and permeable to the influences of water cycle, photosynthesis, macroclimate, seismology, bacterial resistance to pharmaceuticals, and the 'natural' advantages and disadvantages of regional habitats. [...] A version of the nature-culture distinction, then, will likely remain indispensable as a recognition of empirical fact as well as of human desire. (*Writing* 6)

Against the background of the oscillations between the indicated object- and subject-orientation, contemporary object-oriented actuations of a bioethical nature seem to counterbalance the subject-oriented cyber-spiritualism arising from technological developments. In an ongoing debate, the Thoreauvian object-oriented and Emersonian subject-oriented options are reformulated by eco-theorists such as Buell and neo-Romantics such as Taylor, by prophets of cyberculture such as Wiener, McLuhan, and Haraway, and sceptics such as Gelernter and, again, Buell. Even in a world that has largely become a cyberreality, Buell argues, nature remains essential as a term of value. Buell's sceptical argument is not exactly discredited by the publication of David Bell's and Barbara M. Kennedy's *Cybercultures Reader* (2000), which is a collection of essays on various aspects of cyberreality. Among other issues, these essays discuss "the discursive culture of cyberhate," "digital rage," "compu-sex," "queer 'n' Asian virtual sex," "pain and subjectivity in virtual reality," "aging and virtual reality," "the male criminal subject as biomedical norm," "feminism and the concept of home in cyberspace," and, finally, "racial passing on the Internet" (Bell and Kennedy vii-x). In view of such topics, the suspicion does not seem far-fetched that cyberrealities leave us with much the same problems we already had in other forms of reality, especially with problems of class, race, gender, sex and crime. It is not entirely unlikely either to assume that ecological problems will also stay with us.

Works Cited

Achilles, Jochen. "Von der Moderne zur Postmoderne: Zu den Entstehungsbedingungen einer neuen Ästhetik." *Der zeitgenössische amerikanische Roman.* Ed. Gerhard Hoffmann. Vol. 2. München: Wilhelm Fink, 1988. 7-30.

—."Edgar Allan Poe's Dreamscapes and the Transcendentalist View of Nature." *Amerikastudien/American Studies* 40.4 (1995): 553-573.

—. "The Technological Imagination and the Antebellum American Short Story." *Early America Re-Explored: New Readings in Colonial, Early National, and Antebellum Culture.* Ed. Klaus H. Schmidt and Fritz Fleischmann. New York: Peter Lang, 2000. 505-536.

Amerikastudien/American Studies. Special Issue: *American Transcendentalism.* 28.1 (1983).

Baudrillard, Jean. "From 'Simulacra and Simulations'." Ed. and intr. Peter Brooker. *Modernism/Postmodernism.* London and New York: Longman, 1992. 151-162.

Bell, Daniel. *The Coming of Post-Industrial Society: A Venture in Social Forecasting.* 1973. New York: Basic Books, 1999.

—. *The Cultural Contradictions of Capitalism.* 1976. New York: Basic Books, 1996.

Bell, David and Barbara M. Kennedy, eds. *The Cybercultures Reader.* London: Routledge, 2001.

Benesch, Klaus. "Romantic Cyborgs: Technology, Authorship, and the Politics of Reproduction in Nineteenth-Century American Literature." *Amerikastudien/American Studies* 41 (1996): 339-359.

—. *Romantic Cyborgs: Authorship and Technology in the American Renaissance.* Amherst, MA: U of Massachusetts P, 2002.

Bergson, Henri. *Creative Evolution.* Trans. Arthur Mitchell. Mineola, NY: Dover, 1998.

—. *Time and Free Will: An Essay on the Immediate Data of Consciousness.* Trans. F. L. Pogson. Mineola, NY: Dover, 2001.

Buell, Lawrence. *The Environmental Imagination: Thoreau, Nature Writing, and the Formation of American Culture.* Cambridge, MA: Harvard UP, 1995.

—. *Writing for an Endangered World: Literature, Culture, and Environment in the United States and Beyond.* Cambridge, MA: Harvard UP, 2001.

Burkholder, Robert E. "The Radical Emerson: Politics in 'The American Scholar'." *ESQ: A Journal of the American Renaissance* 34 (1988): 37-57.

Cameron, Kenneth Walter. *Emerson's Poem: The Structure and Meaning of Nature (1836).* Hartford, CT: Transcendental Books, 1988.

Cascardi, A. J. "Emerson on Nature: Philosophy Beyond Kant." *ESQ: A Journal of the American Renaissance* 30 (1984): 201-210.

Cole, Thomas. "Essay on American Scenery." *The American Landscape: Literary Sources & Documents*. Ed. and intr. Graham Clarke. Vol. I. Mountfield: Helm Information, 1993. 337-347.

Conrad, Joseph. *Heart of Darkness*. Ed. Richard Kimbrough. New York: Norton, 1988.

Derrida, Jacques. "Différance." Jacques Derrida. *Margins of Philosophy*. Trans. Allan Bass. Chicago: U of Chicago P, 1984. 1-28.

Dos Passos, John. *Manhattan Transfer*. New York: Houghton Mifflin, n.d.

Durand, Asher B.. "Letters on American Landscape Painting." *The American Landscape: Literary Sources & Documents*. Ed. and intr. Graham Clarke. Vol. I. Mountfield: Helm Information, 1993. 364-368.

Emerson, Ralph Waldo. "Nature." *The Norton Anthology of American Literature*. Ed. Nina Baym. 5th ed. Vol. I. New York: Norton, 1998. 1073-1101.

—. "The American Scholar." *The Norton Anthology of American Literature*. Ed. Nina Baym. 5th Edition. Vol. I. New York: Norton, 1998. 1101-1114.

Emerson's Nature: Origin, Growth, Meaning. Ed. Merton M. Sealts, Jr., and Alfred R. Ferguson. Carbondale: Southern Illinois UP, 1979.

Fritzell, Peter A. "The Wilderness and the Garden: Metaphors for the American Landscape." *Forest History* 12 (1968): 16-22.

Gelernter, David. *Machine Beauty: Elegance and the Heart of Technology*. New York: Basic Books, 1998.

Haraway, Donna J. "A Cyborg Manifesto: Science, Technology, and Socialist-Feminism in the Late Twentieth Century." *The Cybercultures Reader*. Ed. David Bell and Barbara M. Kennedy. London and New York: Routledge, 2001. 291-324.

Hegel, Georg Wilhelm Friedrich. *Phänomenologie des Geistes*. Georg Wilhelm Friedrich Hegel Werke 3. Frankfurt/Main: Suhrkamp, 1993.

Henrich, Dieter. "'Identität'—Begriffe, Probleme, Grenzen." *Identität*. Ed. Odo Marquard and Karlheinz Stierle. München: Fink, 1979. 133-186.

Horstmann, Ulrich. "Mythos der Bemächtigung: Anmerkungen zur Ästhetik des Ralph Waldo Emerson." *Amerikastudien/American Studies* 25 (1980): 175-197.

—. "The Whispering Sceptic: Anti-Metaphysical Enclaves in American Transcendentalism." *Amerikastudien/American Studies*. Special Issue: American Transcendentalism 28 (1983): 47-57.

James, William. *Writings 1878-1899*. Ed. Gerald E. Myers. New York: The Library of America, 1992.

Lawson-Peebles, Robert. *Landscape and Written Expression in America: The World Turned Upside Down*. Cambridge: Cambridge UP, 1988.

Levine, Stuart. "Emerson and Modern Social Concepts." *Emerson: Prospect and Retrospect*. Ed. Joel Porte. Cambridge: Harvard UP, 1982. 155-178.

Lewis, R.W.B. *The American Adam: Innocence, Tragedy and Tradition in the Nineteenth Century*. Chicago and London: U of Chicago P, 1955.

Lifton, Frederick C. "Henry Thoreau's Cultivation of Nature: American Landscape and American Self in "Ktaadn" and "Walking." *American Transcendental Quarterly* 12 (1998): 67-86.

McLuhan, Marshall. *Understanding Media*. London: Sphere Books, 1964.

Marquard, Odo. "Identität: Schwundtelos und Mini-Essenz – Bemerkungen zur Genealogie einer aktuellen Diskussion." *Identität*. Ed. Odo Marquard and Karlheinz Stierle. München: Fink, 1979. 347-369.

Marx, Leo. *The Machine in the Garden: Technology and the Pastoral Ideal in America*. Oxford: Oxford UP, 1964.

Noble, David W. "Revocation of the Anglo-Protestant Monopoly: Aesthetic Authority and the American Landscape." *Soundings* 78 (1995): 150-168.

Novak, Barbara. *Nature and Culture: American Landscape and Painting, 1825-1875*. New York: Oxford UP, 1980.

Oswalt, Jr., Conrad Eugene. *After Eden: The Secularization of American Space in the Fiction of Willa Cather and Theodore Dreiser*. Lewisburg: Bucknell UP, 1990.

Quigley, Peter. "Rethinking Resistance: Nature Opposed to Power in Emerson and Melville." *West Virginia University Philological Papers* 37 (1991): 39-51.

Poenicke, Klaus. *Dark Sublime: Raum und Selbst in der amerikanischen Romantik*. Heidelberg: Carl Winter, 1972.

—. "Nature's Gender: Zur Konstruktionsgeschichte des 'Schönen' und 'Erhabenen'." *Amerikastudien/American Studies* 37 (1992): 373-391.

Rao, Adapo Ramakrishna. *Emerson and Social Reform*. Atlantic Highlands: Humanities, 1980.

Ritter, Joachim. *Landschaft: Zur Funktion des Ästhetischen in der modernen Gesellschaft*. Münster: Verlag Aschendorff, 1963.

Schmidt, Hermann. *Der Begriff der Erfahrungskontinuität bei William James und seine Bedeutung für den amerikanischen Pragmatismus*. Heidelberg: Winter, 1959.

Schneider, Richard J. "Thoreau and Nineteenth-Century American Landscape Painting." *ESQ: A Journal of the American Renaissance* 31 (1985): 67-88.

Schulz, Dieter. "Emerson's Visionary Moments: The Disintegration of the Sublime." *Amerikastudien/American Studies* 28 (1983): 23-32.

—. *Amerikanischer Transzendentalismus: Ralph Waldo Emerson, Henry David Thoreau, Margaret Fuller*. Darmstadt: Wissenschaftliche Buchgesellschaft, 1997.

Silko, Leslie Marmon. *Ceremony*. New York: Penguin, 1977.

Smith, Henry Nash. *Virgin Land. The American West as Symbol and Myth*. Cambridge, MA: Harvard UP, 1950.

Steele, Meili H. "Romantic Epistemology and Romantic Style: Emerson's Development from 'Nature' to the Essays." *Studies in the American Renaissance* (1983): 187-202.

Tallmadge, John and Henry Harrington, eds. *Reading under the Sign of Nature: New Essays in Ecocriticism*. Salt Lake City: U of Utah P, 2000.

Taylor, Charles. *Sources of the Self: The Making of the Modern Identity.* Cambridge, MA: Harvard UP, 1989.

Thoreau, Henry David. "Ktaadn." *The American Landscape: Literary Sources and Documents.* Ed. and intr. Graham Clarke. Vol. II. Mountfield: Helm Information, 1993. 108-116.

—. "Slavery in Massachusetts: An Address, Delivered at the Anti-Slavery Celebration at Framingham, July 4th, 1854." *The Norton Anthology of American Literature.* Ed. Nina Baym. 5th Edition. Vol. I. New York: Norton, 1998. 1943-1953.

—. *Walden.* Ed. and intr. Michael Meyer. Harmondsworth: Penguin, 1986.

—. "Walking." *The Norton Anthology of American Literature.* Ed. Nina Baym. Fifth Edition. Volume I. New York: Norton, 1998. 1953-1976.

Tichi, Cecilia. *New World, New Earth: Environmental Reform in American Literature from the Puritans through Whitman.* New Haven: Yale UP, 1979.

Wiener, Norbert. *Cybernetics or Control and Communication in the Animal and the Machine.* 1948. Cambridge, MA: Massachusetts Institute of Technology P, 2000.

—. *The Human Use of Human Beings: Cybernetics and Society.* 1950. New York: Da Capo P, 1988.

Wilson, R. Jackson. "Emerson's 'Nature:' A Materialistic Reading." *Subject to History: Ideology, Class, Gender.* Ed. David Simpson. Ithaca: Cornell UP, 1991. 119-142.

Woolf, Virginia. "Modern Fiction." *Collected Essays.* Vol. 2. London: Hogarth Press, 1966. 103-110.

Multiplicity: Foldings in Architectural and Literary Landscapes

Hanjo Berressem

overture: crumpled space

Imagine me taking the title page of this essay and crumple it up. According to how one looks at it, the result would be either a piece of waste paper or an almost infinitely complex, multiply folded, unique|singular paper landscape [ill. 001]. [*Deleuzefold: "The atomistic hypothesis of an absolute hardness [order] and the Cartesian hypothesis of an absolute fluidity [disorder]" (Fold 6, my brackets) should be abandoned in favor of "a certain cohesion" (6). This 'stickiness of the object' [Freud talked of the 'stickiness of the libido'] produces a "continuous labyrinth" (3) that "resembles a sheet of paper divided into infinite folds or separated into bending movements, each one determined by the consistent or conspiring surroundings" (Fold 6)*]. In fact, such a gesture might be read as a micro-essay on the relation between ordered and disordered space, or, as Gilles Deleuze and Félix Guattari call it in *Thousand Plateaus: Capitalism and Schizophrenia*, between 'striated' and 'smooth' space. [*Koolhaasfold: "There are strong analogies between the topics of our work and those of Gilles Deleuze. In their book* A Thousand Plateaus *Deleuze and Guattari differentiate between two kinds of space—striated and smooth space. Striated space can be visualized as a landscape separated into fields, in which everything is measurable, straight and enclosed by defined lines. And smooth space can be compared to the sea and the desert, it is not tenable, fluid" (Arch+ 22)*]. In this context, crumpled space might be considered as the 'differential' of striated and smooth space; as a complex, mani*fold* site that is actualized from a virtual, infinite multiplicity and situated on a continuous scale between complete striation and complete smoothness, both of which are abstracted ideals. In actual fact, there are only mixtures of these ideal spaces, the world being, according to Michel Serres, a "pure multiplicity" which in turn consists of "ordered multiplicities [what we call 'order'] and pure multiplicities [what we call 'disorder']" (*Genesis* 111, my brackets). Deleuze and Guattari note that such aggregates of mixed multiplicities [in German: 'Viel*falt*,' something that is folded in many ways] are invariably in a state of '*n*-1'. "Subtract the unique from the multiplicity to be constructed; write at *n*-1 dimensions. A system of this kind could be called a rhizome" (*Plateaus* 6). [*Deleuzefold: "the multiple is not only what has many parts but also what is folded in many ways" (Fold 3)*]. The crumpled site thus might be said to mark a specific position|singularity within a continuum of more or less ordered multiplicities|foldings. [*Serresfold: "complex thus means [...] folded, crossed, entangled in terms of form and relation" (Hermes III 74)*].

Inherent continuity, in fact, is one of the essential characteristics of folded space. In opposition to other figures of movement in|of space like those defined by such terms as cut, jump or break, the fold implies a spatial continuity, which means that "for a first time perhaps, complexity might be aligned with neither unity nor contradiction but with smooth, pliant mixture" (Lynn 8). [*Cachefold: "digital machines and productive technologies in general allow for the production of an industrial continuum. From the mold we move toward modulation. We no longer apply a preset form on inert matter, but lay out the parameters of a surface of variable curvature [...] the design of the object is no longer subordinated to mechanical geometry: it is the machine that is directly integrated into the technology of the synthesized image*" (97)]. As Deleuze folds his text into that of Leibniz in his book *The Fold: Leibniz and the Baroque*, "the division of the continuous must not be taken as of sand dividing into grains, but as that of a sheet of paper or of a tunic in folds, in such a way that an infinite number of folds can be produced, some smaller than others, but without the body ever dissolving into points or minima" (6). [*Eisenmanfold: "in the labyrinth of the continuous ... the smallest element [is] not the point but the fold" (Unfolding 12)*]. In such an all-over folded space seemingly straight lines are invariably inflected and parts of larger folds.

But back to my crumpled site: Whatever one thinks of such a spatial arrangement|event, a classical theory of space would consider the result as an object embedded within a surrounding space that is defined as empty and infinite. It is only within this Cartesian space that the construct is characterized as folded|crumpled. What, however, if the surrounding space was also defined as folded? As John Rajchman notes, in such a multiplex, folded space there is nothing 'before' the fold|ing: "The multiple is thus not fragment or ruins which suppose a lost or absent Unity, any more than its incessant divergence is a dismemberment of some original organism" (28). In *Difference and Repetition* Deleuze calls such a continuous becoming|being folded a state of perplication, a "folding-through or folding across" (30).

The science that deals with such folded spaces is topology or 'projective geometry,' which understands space as no longer empty but as a dynamic field traversed by forces and thus as a constantly emergent space, an "'eventual space' of complex, sensitive, dynamic uncertainty and change" (Kwinter 72). In topological space, objects are no longer defined by metrical measurements within the Cartesian grid, but by immanent relations between objects|masses and forces|energies within the spatio-energetic field that they create. [*Cachefold: "a field of surfaces thus governs the object that has now become the set of possibilities of their intersection. But the surface of the object also becomes separated from its function when the latter is no longer mechanical but electronic. Just as Leibniz had conceived it, texts, information, images, and sounds are now all the object of numerical manipulation" (97-8)*]. In such an environment, the identity of objects does no longer lie in their specific form but in their spatial structure. In this space, it is no longer possible to abstract an 'original' from the object, because the 'essence' of the object does no longer reside in itself but in its relative positions within an inherently complex, dynamic spatial con*text*. This space defines the parameters within which the object can be modelled and as such it is, and will remain, an integral part of the object. [*Cachefold: "the primary image is no longer the image of the object but the image of the set of constraints at the intersection of which the object is created" (97)*].

As one of the possibilities of such a folded space, consider how two points that are far away can be folded onto each other not through a movement within space, but through a movement of space itself. [*Serresfold: "If you take a handkerchief and spread it out in order to iron it, you can see in it certain fixed distances and proximities. If you sketch a circle in one area, you can mark out nearby points and measure far-off distances. Then take the same handkerchief and crumple it, by putting it in your pocket. Two distant points suddenly are close, even superimposed. If, further, you tear it in certain places, two points that were close can become very distant. This science of nearness and* *rifts is called topology, while the science of stable and well-defined distances is called metrical geometry. [...] It is simply the difference between topology (the handkerchief is folded, crumpled, shredded) and geometry (the same fabric is ironed out flat). [...] As we experience time—as much in our inner sense as externally in nature, as much as* le temps *of history as* le temps *of weather—it resembles this crumpled version much more than the flat, overly simplified one" (Conversations 59-60). Koolhaasfold: "More and more English people buy or build houses in Lille because, purely in terms of time, Lille is nearer to London than the periphery of London" (Entfaltung 30)].

Inherently folded space is often related to the topo|logics of unilateral figures such as the projective plane, the möbius-strip or the Klein bottle. [*Eisenmanfold: Project for the Max Reinhard Haus, Berlin* [*ill. 002*]. *Koolhaasfold: "The center of the building* [*the Rotterdam museum*] *is the empty space of the ramp around which the continuous walkway winds* (*in the form of a möbius-strip*)" (*Arch+ 51, my brackets*)]. In *The Fold*, Deleuze refers specifically to the general unilaterality of the space of philosophy|thought:

> The monad as absolute interiority, as an inner surface with only one side, nonetheless has another side, or a minimum of outside. [...] Can topology resolve the apparent contradiction? The latter effectively disappears if we recall that the "unilaterality" of the monad implies as its condition of closure a torsion of the world, an infinite fold, that can be unwrapped in conformity with the condition only by recovering the other side, not as exterior to the monad, but as the exterior or outside *of* its own interiority: a partition, a supple and adherent membrane coextensive with everything inside. (111)

Deleuze describes the folding of opposites as a process in which the fold functions as a concept that allows to connect binary opposites and to think movements like the "internalization of the outside" (8) as continuous, because they take place within a fundamentally folded space: "the world must be placed in the subject in order that the subject can be for the world. This is the torsion that constitutes the fold of the world [outside] and of the soul [inside]" (26).

Deleuze develops this general fold from within an architectural register: "*The inside and the outside*: the infinite fold separates or moves between matter and soul ["the pleats of matter, and the folds of the soul" (3)], the façade and the closed room, the inside and the outside" (35) [ill. 003]. In this house of philosophy|perception, "the upper floor [soul] is folded over the lower floor [matter]" (119, my brackets), the result being a "montage that moves between the lower floor, pierced with windows, and the upper floor, blind and closed, but on the other hand resonating as if it were a musical salon" (4)]. *[Deleuzefold: "In the Baroque the soul entertains a complex relation with the body. Forever indissociable from the body" (Fold 11)]*. Within this general topology, the fold also comes to mark the continuity of "the conscious [soul] and the unconscious [matter]" (93, my brackets), with "perception straddl[ing] the micro-folds of tiny perceptions and the great fold of consciousness" (98). No wonder that Deleuze finds in the art of origami a metaphor for science: "The model for the sciences of matter is the 'origami,' as the Japanese philosopher might say, or the art of folding paper" (6).

But to return 'once more' to the crumpled site and to the question what it would mean if the space around it is defined as similarly complex and chaotic as that crumpled piece of paper? This question forms the basis of my essay, which maintains that, with notions of space constantly changing and in themselves contested sites, it might be helpful to delineate some of the contestations *about* space in order to negotiate contestations *of* space. In other words: how to think a folded world? *[Deleuzefold: "an organism is defined by endogenous folds, while inorganic matter has exogenous folds that are always determined from without" (Fold 7)]*. Can subjectivity be thought of as a biocultural folding sequence|routine? *[Deleuzefold: "the butterfly is folded into the caterpillar that will soon unfold" (Fold 9)]*.

architecture: multi:pli:city—a series of fast foldings

> ... the subject consists of the study of simplicity, complexity of various kinds, and complex adaptive systems, with some consideration of complex nonadaptive systems as well. To describe the whole field, I've coined the word 'plectics,' which comes from the Greek word meaning 'twisted' or 'braided.' The cognate Latin word, *plexus*, also meaning 'braided,' gives rise to 'complex,' originally 'braided together.' The related Latin verb *plicare*, meaning 'to fold,' is connected with '*simplex*,' originally 'once-folded,' which gives rise to 'simple.'
>
> Murray Gell-Mann

> "The geometrization of the event."
>
> Kwinter 73

Although *The Fold* is perhaps not Deleuze's most architectonic book, as Rajchman maintains, it is, in the 1990s, without doubt the most important reference for an already highly philosophized architectural theory. In this context, Jeffrey Kipnis notes "the sheer number of terms that the architectural literature has borrowed from the Deleuzian discourse (affiliation, pliancy, smooth and striated space, etc.), not to mention such fortuities as the shared thematization of folding" (44) [ill. 004]. As a motto for an essay on his project Frankfurt Rebstockpark: "unfolding events: Frankfurt Rebstock and the possibility of a new urban architecture," for instance, the American architect Peter Eisenman has chosen a quote from Deleuze's *The Fold*: "The entry of Germany on the scene of philosophy implicates the entire German soul which, according to Nietzsche, presents little that is deep but is full of foldings and unfoldings" (*Unfolding* 8). Eisenman adds the original Nietzschean reference which is not given in Deleuze's text: "The German soul is above all manifold [*vielfältig*] [...] the German is acquainted with the hidden path of chaos [...] the German himself is not, he is becoming, he is developing" (8).

Eisenman's project submits the model of a German pre-world war 2 settlement [*Vorkriegssiedlung*] to a chaotization|complexification by means of a series of foldings that are related to three models. As Eisenman notes, "from Leibniz, one can turn to the ideas of two contemporary thinkers concerning the fold; one is Gilles Deleuze, and the other is René Thom" (*Unfolding* 12). The crossover between these three models is not surprising, considering the complex discursive site that has developed around the concept of folding. [*Deleuzefold: "Rene Thom's transformations refer in this sense to a morphology of living matter, providing seven elementary events: the fold; the crease; the dovetail; the butterfly; the hyperbolic, elliptical, and parabolic umbilicus" (Fold 16)*]. In-between these references, Eisenman computes an architectural event that unfolds in time and space. Within this architectural event|space, the buildings are characterized as what Deleuze calls in *The Fold*, following the architect|designer Bernard Cache, 'objectiles,' objects|singularities "no longer designed but calculated" (*Earth Moves* 88) and produced on a mass-scale. Such a calculated mode of production differs essentially from earlier ones in which 'identical' objects were designed by building them up from simple, basic forms. In opposition to such modes, the new, "non-standard" (88) form of production produces singular objects because

> the modification of calculation parameters allows the manufacture of a different shape for each object in the same series. Thus unique products are produced industrially. We will call variable objects created from surfaces "subjectiles," and variable objects created from volumes "objectiles." (88)

This mode of production "allows complex forms to be designed that would be difficult to represent by traditional drawing methods [modes of plotting]. Instead of compositions of primitive or simple contours, we will have surfaces with variable curves and some volumes" (88, my brackets). Starting from the complex|folds—from a virtual multiplicity that is contained in the 'almost infinite' operations of the algorithmic machine; a virtual multiplicity from which the singular objects are actualized—rather than from the simple|points, such a process of production, creates objects that can be defined according to what Eisenman calls a "modulation in time" (*Unfolding* 13). [*Deleuzefold: an objectile is a "fluctuation of the norm replaces the permanence of a law; where the object assumes a place in a continuum by variation" (Fold 19)*].

The conceptual basis of Eisenman's design is René Thom's 'catastrophe theory' [a branch of chaos- or complexity theory] which deals with systemic events and systemic changes and in which folds function as figures of the passages|translations of one stable system [S1] into another stable system [S2]. In these dynamics, the morphogenetic, transitory event is defined as a spatial folding. At a specific moment [a temporal singularity], a system folds, like a breaking wave, into another system [ill. 005]. Thom calls this specific form of catastrophe the 'cusp-catastrophe.' In what he calls the 'butterfly catastrophe,' the moment of folding is expanded to a field of 'constant instability' [ill. 006]. Eisenman's project literally materializes 'in architecture' the phase-space [*Phasenraum*] of the butterfly catastrophe [ill. 007+008+009]. According to Eisenman—"architecture must now deal with the problem of the event" (*Unfolding* 9)—such a folding allows the conceptualisation of an eventual, momentary architecture in which singularities are directly related to an "unfolding in time" (*Einfalten* 23). If Goethe describes architecture as frozen music, Eisenman's project inscribes this frozen dynamics into the structure of an architectural site.

Yet, as Goethe's description shows, such a conceptual architecture moves only statically or metaphorically, and for other architects such as Rem Koolhaas, who maintains that "the more direct and unmediated the influence of theory is on architecture, the more devastating are the results" (*Arch+* 23), such abstractions of movement|folding are too immediately theoretical, too abstract [*Cachefold: "an alea puts form in a state of fluctuation that offers us a true image of the norm. [...] it is this quasi-object that is but a fragment of a surface of possibilities where each exemplum is different. Yet it is not a personalized object [...] it is an ordinary object that may well entertain singular relations with a user" (98)*] and indeed frozen. Koolhaas himself uses philosophical and scientific terms more loosely, noting that he has "a more cannibalistic relation to metaphors" (*Arch+* 23). Greg Lynn also suspects that Eisenman, as well as other architects like Carsten Juel-Christiansen with *Die Anhalter Faltung*, [ill. 010+011] and Bahram Shirdel with *Nara Convention Hall*, [ill. 012] might have used Thom's concepts as a purely "formal technique" (13). Whatever the ultimate judgement on that, one should note that Eisenman is well aware of the fact that what is at stake is no longer foldings *in* space, but foldings *of* space. As he notes,

> In one sense catastrophe theory can also explain abrupt changes in the state or form [...] by means of a complex fold that remains unseen.

This type of folding is more complex than Origami, which is linear and sequential and thus ultimately involves a frame. (*Unfolding* 14)

Eisenman thus acknowledges that origami still implies foldings taking place *in* and framed *by* Cartesian space. As Rajchman comments, "the Rebstock Fold is thus not only a figurative fold as in Origami—not simply a matter of folded figures within a free container or frame. Rather the container itself has been folded together, or complicated, with the figures" (*Unfolding* 48).

In his own work, Koolhaas also refers to theories of folding. The space of his design for the new library of Jussieu, for instance, is defined by "the cutting and folding of the floor levels" (*Arch+* 28) [ill. 013+014]. At the centre of the project lies an eminently Deleuzian concept: to create a space that is continuous but at the same time not unified. As Koolhaas states, "the spatial multiplicity does not rest on separating, partitioning and contrasting, but on *continuous transformations*. Space widens, contracts, rises and falls, bends, parts and unfolds" (*Arch+* 39).

What differentiates Koolhaas from Eisenman? For one, according to Koolhaas, the folded milieu invariably couples a spatial field to one or many other fields. In architectural terms, for instance, it couples space and inhabitants. [*Deleuzefold: "The inorganic fold happens to be simple and direct, while the organic fold is always composite, alternating, indirect (mediated by an interior site)" (Fold 9)*]. For another, Koolhaas couples a theory of foldings to a theory of emergence. Mixed architectural aggregates often show autopoietic behavior and thus they have an elective affinity to the science of non-linear dynamics. In fact, a mani*fold* cityspace can easily be described in terms of attractors, which "can become immensely important to clarify urban questions" (*Arch+* 23), or in terms of "turbulence" (23) which can be used, for instance, to delineate zones of urban condensations [the topic of Koolhaas' book *Delirious New York*]. Especially in Koolhaas' book *S,M,L,XL* complexity theory and non-linear dynamics are central references, which brings him into the vicinity of the work of Félix Guattari, who notes that

> perhaps it belongs to architects and urban planners to think both the complexity and the chaos along new lines. The equivalent of the "strange attractors" from the thermodynamics of states far from equilibrium (from the field of non-linear dynamics) could be sought here. (*Semiotext(e)* 119G2)

Both Koolhaas and Guattari in fact see the city as an "autopoietic system" (119G2) that should be approached by way of complexity theory: "the urban object is of a very great complexity and asks to be approached with the methodologies adapted and appropriate to its complexity. Social experimentation aims at particular species of 'strange attractors,' comparable to those of physics of chaotic processes" (120G3). Maybe, as Alejandro Zaera Polo maintains, urban planning is indeed the best example for "an investigation of random and complex, non-linear processes, which are defined by a multiplicity of interrelated factors" (*Arch+* 58). From this perspective, contemporary cityscapes open up questions of mobile architectures and, as Guattari notes, of architectural "re-singularisations" or "heterogeneses" (120G3). [*Cachefold: "the purpose of the norm is not to stabilize our movements; on the contrary, it is to amplify the fluctuations or aberrations in our behaviour. Changes are the mode of the norm" (96). Berressemfold: "Chaosmose: Von Psychischen Hypertexten und Chaotischen Ökologien"*]. Increasingly, then, architectural space is considered as an inherently dynamic, intrinsically folded space that shows the characteristics of emergent behavior and autopoiesis. [*Serresfold: "the main element of space is now multiplicity in a Riemannian sense, spatial manifoldedness" (Hermes V 57)*].

literature: notes towards a crumpled hermeneutics

From the mid-nineteenth century onwards 'projective geometry' began a crossover into other sciences and into the humanities. It is against this mathematical background, for instance, that Merleau Ponty developed his notion of a twofold body. As M.C. Dillon notes,

> the body, as flesh, is the inside of the outside; that is, the Flesh of the World is the same as the flesh of the body, it is *the outside of the inside*: the circuit is closed within Flesh, within the relation of Flesh to itself, within its selfsameness. The one Flesh incorporates the duality of its fission, its dehiscence, its folding back upon itself. (35, emphasis added)

In the 1950s, the American poet Charles Olsen found the direct inspiration for his poetics in projective geometry which is folded into the title of his essay "Projective Verse," but also into terms such as "composition by field" (*Projective* 16) and into his interest in "kinetics" and in "process" (16). Symptomatically, at the end of his argument about a projective, dynamic writing in "Equal, That Is, to the Real Itself," the essay itself becomes a figure of the projective, folded space that it describes, with the last sentence, which seems to end abruptly in the middle, twisting|folding back onto the title. "The structures of the real are flexible, quanta do dissolve into vibrations, all does flow, and yet is there, to be made permanent [in poetry], if the means are equal" (52). The sentence is only finished, of course, if the title is added to it: 'equal, that is, to the real itself.'

In this 'projective' twisting of beginning and end into each other—in fact, the essay might be said to follow the unilateral topology of the projective plane—Olson's poetics find their appropriate topological figure [ill. 015]. Interestingly, Olson also stresses, like Deleuze, the inherent continuity of topological, folded space:

> within five years, two geometers, Bolyai and Lobatschewsky, weren't any longer satisfied with Euclid's picture of the world, and they each made a new one, independently of each other, and remarkably alike. It took thirty-one years [...] for the German mathematician Riemann to define the real as men since have exploited it: he distinguished two kinds of manifold, the discrete (which would be the old system, and it includes discourse, language as it had been since Socrates) and, what took to be more true, the continuous. (*Equal* 46)

As with Deleuze [philosophy] and Koolhaas [architecture] this literary continuity does not imply a unity or an essence, because in this new definition of space, as Riemann himself has noted, "the metric field is not given rigidly once and for all, but is causally connected with matter and thus changes with the latter" (Riemann, qtd. in Weyl 86-7). Because such a space is not a "part of the static homogeneous form of phenomena, but of their ever-changing material content" (Weyl 87) it is no longer "opposed to things [...] like an empty vessel into which they are placed and which endows them with far-geometrical relationships. No empty space exists here" (172). Rather, the two registers are defined by a mutual influence in which "matter excites the field, [and] the field acts upon matter" (173).

What interests Olson in particular about topology is that the 'topological field' liquifies|smoothes space:

> Euclidean space may be compared to a crystal, built up of uniform unchangeable atoms in the regular and rigid unchangeable arrangement of a lattice; Riemannian space to a liquid, consisting of the same indiscernible unchangeable atoms, whose arrangement and orientation, however, are mobile and yielding to forces acting upon them. (88)

For Olson, this concept of a dynamic spatio-temporal field, in which quantity is no longer considered as a material substance, but defined as "intensive" (*Equal* 46), is especially liberating because it allows him to do away with the "rigidities of the discrete" (47). The concept of this dynamic field involved a change in the hermeneutico-epistemological position of man, who is no longer an objective observer, but finds himself "*folded in*" (48, emphasis added) into the forever changing, dynamic force-field through his very "physicality" (48), and thus *object*ivity, through which he partakes of the field's physical forces. Maybe statements like "get on with it, keep moving, keep in, speed, the nerves, their speed, the perceptions, theirs, the acts, the split second acts, the whole business, keep it moving as fast as you can, citizen" (*Projective* 17) and Olson's belief in speed and movement are too easily read into a politically liberatory rhetorics. In the first place, they are the result of a folding of mathematics onto poetics.

If topological space was used by Olson as a metaphor on the level of the signified, in the 1960s, topological space enters the realm of the signifier. Once again, the hinge between text and topology is provided by a theory of folding. Based on early experiments by Brion Gysin, William S. Burroughs begins to work with a 'fold-in method' in order to break up the linearity of the not only literary text [instead of 'flashbacks' there are now 'fold-backs']. In his essay "Fold-ins" [note the nearness to sit-ins, teach-ins, shop-ins and other political actions in the 1960s], [*Burroughs fold: "Alexander Trocchi [...] has said [...] If writers are to travel in space time [...] I think they must develop techniques quite as new and definite as the techniques of physical space travel" (Mind 95)*] he notes that the "fold-in method" is "an extension of the [more well-known] cut-up method" (95). To create a fold-in, a

> page of text—my own or someone else's—is folded down the middle and placed on another page.—The composite text is then read across half one text and half the other—The fold-in method extends to writing the flashback used in films, enabling the writer to move backward and forward on his time track—For example I take page one and fold it into page one hundred—I insert the resulting composite as page ten. (96)

The fold-in method is thus a means to make writing-space dynamic, and to move texts into each other; in fact, it is a means to 'crumple' writing space. Later on in the essay, Burroughs extends the method to a general theory of intertextuality—"I have made and used fold-ins from Shakespeare, Rimbaud, from newspapers, magazines, conversations and letters so that the novels I have written using this method are in fact composites of many writers" (96)—so that the folded writing space is not only that of a single work, but of the space of the whole of literature. [*Deleuze fold: "The issue is not one of relation, but of 'fold-in,' or of 'fold according to fold [...] the expression 'fold-in' is borrowed from Gysin and Burroughs, who designate thus a method of textual folding, in extension with the 'cut-up'" (Fold 163-164)*]. Ultimately, Burroughs uses the fold-in to create a dynamic spatial field of writing in which the near and the far as well as the inside and the outside are 'intertextually' enfolded.

kinetics: textual and cultural

In times of relentless virtualization and digitalization, the title of this collection—"from landscape to technoscape"—might evoke a trajectory that starts from the concept of a natural, material landscape [nature], proceeds first to a material technoscape [machine] and then to a virtual technoscape [digital machine], to come to a halt, having come 'full circle,' at a virtually simulated natural landscape [the buzzwords are 'full immersion,' or 'embodiment']. Although it is quite inviting, I have not followed this trajectory. Rather than foreclosing materiality in a vision of a 'full digital jacket,' my aim has been to once more link space and materiality: to fold virtual space back onto real space through the concepts of topological foldings, in which space and materiality are inextricably combined. This seems to me to be important not only for theoretical discussions, but for discussions of cultural spaces and for discussions of 'contestations of space' in general.

Contemporary space is never empty and it has never *been* empty. It is a dynamic, energetic field in which various forces, often oppositional ones, are operative. This means that ultimately everything, not only specific pieces of art, is 'site-specific.' If this is the case, then it might be time to think about the movement of space, objects, texts and images. It is here that this paper might be folded onto a paper on hypertext, which delineates how the text itself begins to move, how texts are folded onto the computer screen, and how a textual mobile is organized by 'code works.' [One line of tradition might be traced directly from Olson via the Black Mountain College and Cage to the electronic writing projects of Glazier or Bernstein]. Or, the paper might be folded onto a paper about moveable architecture; tents, nomadic houses and other 'foldable' habitations. Or, the paper might fold onto a discussion of performativity and the body and, in extension, onto the discussions about the 'third,' in-between spaces that define cultural studies. Instead, however, I will fold it once more onto *The Fold*, which ends with an acknowledgement of a continuous folding. Its final sentence shows once more Deleuze's belief that everything has to be thought of from within a theory of folded space because there is no outside position and no state of being once-for-all-unfolded. [*Deleuzefold: "Unfolding is thus not the contrary of folding, but follows the fold up to the following fold" (Fold 6)*]. In that sentence, he stresses that the world today consists of "divergent series" (137) which "do not allow the differences of inside and outside, of public and private, to survive" (137). The backdrop is to replace Leibniz' idea of unity and *con*vergencies by a theory of *di*vergencies. Leibniz' monadology, this implies, is replaced by a Deleuzian nomadology: "We are discovering new ways of folding, akin to new envelopments, but we all remain Leibnizian because what always matters is folding, unfolding, refolding" (*Fold* 137).

Works Cited

Berressem, Hanjo. "Chaosmose: Von Psychischen Hypertexten und Chaotischen Ökologien." *texte: psychoanalyse. ästhetik. kulturkritik*. Wien: Passagen, 2000. 35-55.

Burroughs, William S., and Brion Gysin. "Fold-Ins." *The Third Mind*. New York: Viking Press, 1978. 95-124.

Cache, Bernard. *Earth Moves: The Furnishing of Territories (Writing Architecture)*. Ed. Michael Speaks. Trans. Anne Boyman. Cambridge: MIT P, 1995.

Deleuze, Gilles. *The Fold: Leibniz and the Baroque*. Trans. Tom Conley. Minneapolis: U of Minnesota P, 1993.

Deleuze, Gilles, and Félix Guattari. *A Thousand Plateaus: Capitalism and Schizophrenia*. Trans. Brian Massumi. Minneapolis: U of Minnesota P, 1987.

Dillon, M. C. "Ecart: Reply to Claude Lefort's 'Flesh and Otherness'." *Ontology and Alterity in Merleau-Ponty*. Evanston, IL: Northwestern UP, 1990. 14-26.

Eisenman, Peter. "Unfolding Events: Frankfurt Rebstock and the Possibility of a New Urbanism." *Unfolding Frankfurt*. Berlin: Ernst & Sohn, 1991. 8-17.

—. "In Zeit Einfalten: Die Singularität dese Rebstock-Geländes." *Frankfurt Rebstockpark: Folding in Time*. Ed. Volker Fischer. Köln: Prestel, 1992. 19-24.

Guattari, Félix. "Drawing Cities Nomads." *Semiotext(e) Architecture*. Ed. Hraztan Zeitlian. New York: Columbia University, 1992. 118G1-125G8.

Ingraham, Catherine. "X...stasis." *Semiotext(e): Architecture*. Ed. Hraztan Zeitlian. New York: Columbia University, 1992. 3011-3314.
Kipnis, Jeffrey. "Towards a New Architecture." *Architectural Design: Folding in Architecture* 63/3-4 (1993): 40-49.
Koolhaas, Rem. Interview: "Die Entfaltung der Architektur." *Arch+* 117 (1993): 22-43.
—. "Kunsthalle Rotterdam." *Arch+* 117 (1993): 50-53.
—. *S,M,L,XL*. Ed. Jennifer Sigler. Rotterdam: 010 Publishers, 1995.
Kwinter, Sanford. "Die Neuerfindung der Geometrie." *Arch+ 117* (1993): 72-73.
Lynn, Greg. "Architectural Curvilinearity, The Folded, the Pliant and the Supple." *Architectural Design: Folding in Architecture* 63/3-4 (1993): 8-15.
Olson, Charles. "Equal, That Is, to the Real Itself." *Selected Writings*. 46-52.
—. "Projective Verse." *Selected Writings of Charles Olson*. Ed. Robert Creeley. New York: New Directions, 1966. 15-26
Polo, Alejandro Zaera. "Kapitalflüsse, Datenströme, Drive-Thru und andere Strömungen." *Arch+ 117* (1993): 56-58.
Rajchman, John. "Out of the Fold." *Architectural Design: Folding in Architecture* 63/3-4 (1993): 61-63.
—. "Perplications: On the Space and Time of Rebstockpark." *Unfolding Frankfurt*. Berlin: Ernst & Sohn, 1991. 18-76.
Serres, Michel (with Bruno Latour). *Conversations on Science, Culture, and Time*. Trans. Roxanne Lapidus. Ann Arbor: U of Michigan P, 1995.
—. *Genesis*. Ann Arbor: U of Michigan P, 1995.
—. *Hermes III: Übersetzung*. Berlin: Merve, 1992.
—. *Hermes. V: Die Nordwest-Passage*. Berlin: Merve, 1994.
Weyl, Herman. *Philosophy of Mathematics and Natural Science*. Princeton: Princeton UP, 1949.

Between, Beyond, Elsewhere: Mapping the Zones and Borderlands of Critical Discourse

Sabine Sielke

On September 11, 2001, at 8.46 am, Eastern standard time, time itself shifted to a different register, a new era, the 21st century began. These or similar assessments were hurriedly made by politicians, policy makers, and postmodern authors after the twin towers had vanished from the New York skyline. In some sense these claims reminded me of Virginia Woolf's famous remark that in December 1910 modernism was born. Of course, we all know that like the shift from Victorianism to modernism the recent shift from the post-modernist 1980s and 90s to a new time scale has been in process long before the two planes crashed into the World Trade Towers. We also know that this new focus on time—opposed as it is to the desire dominant in modernism to transmute history and narrative sequence into the "timeless world of myth" (Frank 60)—that this shift toward time is a "mere metaphor" within a rhetoric preoccupied with space; that space and time, as W. T. Mitchell insists, are by no means antithetical modalities; and that "we never talk about temporal experience without invoking spatial" measures, never apprehend space apart from time and movement (544). In fact, as Foucault underlines, "it is not possible to disregard the fatal intersection of time with space" ("Spaces" 22).

The questions that I am driving at here can thus be phrased like this: if September 11 ushered in a sense of the new millennium, has it also evolved new notions of space? And if time and space are not to be separated, what does a seemingly new concept of space suggest about our current sense of time and history? And more importantly has this post-9/11 sense of time and space impacted the actual accessibility and distribution of space? I am well aware that one can come up with no more than speculative answers to such speculative questions. Plus, before we can speculate about 21st-century conceptions of space, we need to look back at how space has been conceived at the end of the last millennium. In the main part of my paper I will therefore explore the borderlines and zones of critical discourse as well as the particular cultural work that has been achieved by this mapping of critical space, by the many "beyonds," "betweens," and "elsewheres" that were projected in the final decades of the twentieth century. However, at this point in time my inquiry into the spacial dimensions of contemporary critical discourse aims beyond an understanding of their cultural and political functions and effects. Meanwhile I rather wonder if the liminal spaces that current literary and cultural theory have projected are in any way connected with the sense of space mapped out by the 21st century 'new world order.' Accordingly, the third and final part of my paper is highly limited in its scope by the time at which this essay originally evolved, in October 2001, and should be read as a preliminary reflection for a project in process.[1]

Between, Beyond, Elsewhere: Privileged Spaces in Late Twentieth-Century Critical Discourse

It has long been a commonplace observation that the insights of deconstructivist and poststructuralist thought have tended to limit and minimize the arenas of effective individual and collective agency, thus to disempower, at least to a certain degree, the historical subject and to capitalize spaciality instead. The present epoch, Foucault famously wrote in his essay "Of Other Spaces," is "above all the epoch of space. We are in the epoch of simultaneity; we are in the epoch of juxtaposition, the epoch of the near and far, of the side-by-side, of the dispersed" (22) (accordingly, around the world we were able to collectively "share" the experience of the traumatic events of September 11.) At the same time, however, theories that have evolved on the margins, at the dawn of as well as in the aftermath of poststructuralism—and I am thinking in particular of various modes of feminist inquiry, cultural anthropology, and postcolonial criticism—have also effected a

---

[1] In agreement with the editors of this collection, I decided that this essay which evolved as a paper for an international conference in Bayreuth should not be updated and elaborated upon retrospectively. Instead we meant to preserve the sentiment of the particular historical moment. For the further development of the argument I refer the reader to my forthcoming essays "From Elsewhere to Ground Zero: Space, Transgression, and Critical Discourse at the Turn of the Millenium" and "West of Everything? The Frontiers and Borderlands of Critical Discourse."

shift within our modern sense of space, a shift more specifically from modernist notions of "text as space" to post-modernist conceptions of "space as text," a shift in the process of which the term space itself has been problematized and repoliticized in novel ways. This repoliticization, one may have to add though, rests on a sense of the political that is by no means undisputed.

More precisely, as theories of the post-modern, the post-colonial and, most particular, of performativity conceive of the political in terms of discursive space, they have frequently projected spaces of political momentum located in an indistinct, if not nebulous "inbetweenness," "beyond," or "elsewhere." These and related spatial terms like liminality and borderland have been incessantly deployed by late twentieth-century critical discourse, my own work being no exception. In my first book *Fashioning the Female Subject*, for instance, I argue—as I would still hold—convincingly that the poetics of Emily Dickinson and Marianne Moore work in a rhetorical and philosophical "in-between," a term that I borrow from the French poststructuralist Hélène Cixous. And there is yet no end to the privileging of the inbetween, the liminal, the spaces beyond dominant discourse. In 2002 the 26th Annual Conference of the International Association for Philosophy and Literature, for instance, set out to explore "Intermedialities" and featured sessions entitled "In the Between," "Liminal Spaces," "Inter-Esse: Beyond Borderlines," "The Third," "Hermes—The Intermediary," "Inter-Writing/Imaging," "Between the Cultures of Multiculturalism," and even one called "In-Between Jacques Derrida."

Significantly enough, this continued faith in the liminal, in a discursive space of inbetweeness involves a return, rather than the loss of subject and history Fredric Jameson has mourned. It is the return, however, of an other subject and history, one that had long been buried under the debris of Western cultural dominance. So as we moved from New Critical conceptions of a closural spatial aesthetics (as explored, for instance, by Robert Frank) to a post-modernist sense of space as an open intertextuality, critical discourse has evolved a previously marginal subject, another voice that is oftentimes resituated quite literally center stage. The projection of those betweens and elsewheres thus has been, to use the words of Héctor Calderon and José Saldivar, "a highly conscious, imaginative act of resistance" (5). At the same time, the space that was granted for this previously peripheral—female, African American, or Third World subject—his or her speaking position and agency, have been highly limited and contested by pretexts and discursive conventions from the start. In the works of theorists as diverse as Victor Turner, Julia Kristeva, Luce Irigaray, Derrida, Judith Butler, Linda Hutcheon, Henry Louis Gates, Hector Calderon, and Homi Bhabha, to mention but a few prominent names, the inbetweens, beyonds, and elsewheres correspond to realms of subtle discursive liminality, parody, and subversion, realms whose actual political impact is rather minute. Accordingly, critical discourse aggrandized this very limitation into a politically effective potential. In fact, from Kristeva who developed the concept of intertextuality from Bakhtinian dialogism across Turner's work that thrives on liminality to Gates's position on signifyin(g) and Bhabha's notion of mimicry we find plenty of faith in the powers of repetition, parody, and pastiche, of the subtle spaces of ironical distance.[2]

In this context I cannot explore these subtle spaces of subversion in depth and would like to refer the reader to my essay on "Spatial Aesthetics, Ironic Distances, and Realms of Liminality." What is significant for my argument here is to underline that those theories which invest the liminal and the realms of intertextuality and ironic distance with subversive power seem to have revitalized modernist utopias in post-utopian times. By proposing a borderland or an elsewhere located "between" or "beyond" the modes of dominant discourse, a significant part of current critical discourse to my mind remembers and salvages the central utopias of modernism—and most prominently the desire for difference without hierarchy, utopias which seemed to have had their final heyday in the late 1960s and early 70s. Since the effect of parody and pastiche is significant, yet hard to measure, they have easily opened up toward utopian spaces, into "borderland[s] between art and the world" (Hutcheon 23), a realm within what others dismiss as the aestheticized post-modern condition or a body politic turned thea-

---

2   Jameson conceptualizes the difference between modernism and post-modernism as parody versus pastiche, reading post-modernism as a culture of citation that has done away with the quotation marks and in the process creates a kind of "blank parody" (114). I myself would object, however, that post-modernist citation as deployed by contemporary popular culture, for instance, frequently historicizes and even authorizes itself in modernist cultural practices, thereby engaging in the significant work of memory and subject formation. Jameson's distinction between parody and pastiche therefore cannot be drawn all that clearly.

ter. And whereas the heterotopias envisioned by post-modernist fiction are mostly disturbing, this utopian realm of cultural and literary criticism is soothing, even if it does not open up into the easily accessible lands that have dominated the utopian imaginary. Thus rather than facing "the end of utopia," as Russell Jacoby phrases it, post-modern culture and its critique has attempted to salvage the utopias of aesthetic modernism for the new millennium.

Ground Zero or: The Spatiality of a New Era?

The futility of this attempt to salvage a modernist utopia for the new millennium seems blatantly obvious once the economic and military centers of the United States, represented by the World Trade Center and the Pentagon, were literally deconstructed. (It is worth noting that the Towers were built by Minoru Yamasaki, in the years 1969 to 1973, the very time when social utopias thrived, the very time also when the US was at war in Vietnam.) No marginal voice or group came playfully into power on September 11 or after. Quite the opposite: There has been utter silence or even denial on the part of those who are deemed responsible, those whose culture seems to work just as brilliantly in oral expression as in writing (Osama bin Laden has produced TV announcements, not confessional letters). Thus while critical discourse—like post-modernist novels that explore the "between-worlds space" of zones (McHale 58)—meant to rediscover and open up intertextual spaces, realms of historical difference and ironic distance where multiple texts and voices join in polyphony with each other,[3] while Chicano/Chicana criticism located itself in the borderlands and proposed to "travel between first and third worlds, between cores and peripheries, centers and margins," the developments that followed the terrorist attacks of September 11 so far seem to redraw the boundaries, leaving little space for intricate differences, fine discriminations, and, least of all, ironical distance.

In fact, whereas Turner defines liminality as "a betwixt-and-between condition often involving seclusion from the everyday scene" and a shift to what he calls the "subjunctive mood," the "as-if" mode

---

3   McHale himself finds most effective the borrowing of a character from another text, the transmigration of characters from one to another fictional universe that overruns world boundaries (58).

that characterizes rituals as well as theatrical performances, both of which function as meta-commentaries on human relatedness (22), September 11, by contrast, involved a shift from the "as if" to the everyday, a shift, however, that took its detour through well-traveled American utopias of freedom and democracy. The experience, made by so many—no matter whether they were present on the scene or watched the events on television from a safe distance—, the experience that the image of a plane crashing into the World Trade Tower, on the one hand, recalled scenes familiar from Hollywood movies and thus seemed entirely unreal, while, on the other, our acknowledgment of these scenes as real depended on their incessant repetition, the loop of that image on our TV screens, this apparently paradoxical experience testifies to the power of representation and the construction of reality through media technologies. At the same time, however, the seeming identity of familiar—inferno-film—imagery and traumatic experience appears to minimize the inbetween spaces opened up by a critical discourse highly conscious of representation and mediation. And while life seemed to be imitating art in the most uncanny manner, art was stalled in its track: the opening of *Collateral Damage*, for instance—a film in which Arnold Schwarzenegger impersonates a fire fighter who claims justice after his family was subjected to a terrorist attack—was postponed; the production of several Hollywood movies was cancelled as if their cinematic enterprise and subject matter amounted to a terrorist attack. The events of 11 September 2001 have thus, for a short while, diminished the realms of ironic distance, the spaces of subtle difference, the inbetweens, beyonds, and elsewheres (see Sielke, "Das Ende der Ironie"). And as we opt for literal readings the space previously populated by marginal voices is emptied out, the mobility and processional dynamic critical discourse has privileged comes to a halt. For some interpreters, such as David Cook, scholar of religious studies at Rice University, the modernist utopias of difference without hierarchy crumble under an apocalyptic vision which clearly separates good from evil, believers from infidels, the familiar from the foreign, a vision that, according to Cook, claims "no less than world supremacy" (15). Others offer a different reading. So far "it is open," Slavoj Žižek wrote on September 20, "what kind of acts the events will eventually legitimate. Yet there are bad omen already such as the return of Cold War terminology like the talk of a 'free world': the conflict apparently is," Žižek remarks, "between the 'free world' and the powers of darkness. The question that arises is: Who belongs to the world that is not free? Are China and Egypt, for instance, part of this free world? The message is, of course, that the old division between Western democratic states and all the others is being reinforced" (48).

And yet: As the US caved in on itself, dressed their wound, and mourned their loss of innocence once again, they also reached out for foreign territory in ways that were as novel as they were short-lived. Or as a commentator of the WDR 5 "Morgenecho" claimed on 5 October 2001: On September 11 America became aware of the existence of the "Ausland," of a space abroad, beyond its own borders, elsewhere. Thus while America gathered around and reclaimed ground zero as a place of mourning, memory, and making it new, while certain lines were redrawn, other lines shifted, opening up new vistas. Or who would have imagined—in 1980, 1990, or even in the year 2000—that NATO would seriously contemplate making Russia its member? A few years ago, we may have deemed such an idea, voiced by a minister of defense of the Rumsfeld caliber, a joke, or maybe, an ironic remark. And meanwhile, as NATO has lost at least part of its former significance, the Eastern extension of NATO has gotten an ironic twist indeed. Moreover, as the catastrophic events of September 11 turned into a site, a tourist attraction, a kind of mecca, those who have been marginal to dominant American culture have joined in the pilgrimage. New spaces thus tended to rapidly transform into rather familiar realms.

Let me phrase my point yet another way and thus readdress the questions I raised in the first part of this argument: The post 9/11 deployment of temporal terms, first and foremost the claim that the new century or millennium had begun, does not mark the arrival of a new era, but a shift in emphasis within what Foucault called the "fatal intersection of time and space." Accordingly the shifts and changes in the climate of American political cultures and cultural climates that seemed to evolve from and have repeatedly been legitimated with reference to 9/11 have been on their way for almost a decade (see Glatz). Still they do underline why the intersection of tropes of time and space can be fatal indeed. After all the insistent rhetoric of time deployed after the collapse of the World Trade Towers ushered in a revitalization of timeless American myths, myths which we are supposed to read literally, without irony and which in turn have indeed effected an increasingly restrictive politics of (real) space (see Sielke, "Das Ende der Ironie"). And this politics meanwhile informs plans for the reconstruction of Ground Zero as well as immigration policies and established practices of border crossing around the 49th parallel. Thus while the American "mission" has transgressed many borderlines, including those of so-called rogue territories, new borders have indeed been erected.

Works Cited

Bhabha, Homi. "Of Mimicry and Man." *Modern Literary Theory: A Reader.* Ed. Philip Rice and Patricia Waugh. London: Arnold, 1989. 234-241.
Butler, Judith. *Gender Trouble: Feminism and the Subversion of Identity.* New York: Routledge, 1990.
—. "Performative Acts and Gender Constitution: An Essay in Phenomenology and Feminist Theory." *Performing Feminisms: Feminist Critical Theory and Theory.* Ed. Sue-Ellen Case. Baltimore: Johns Hopkins UP, 1990. 270-82.
Caldiron, Héctor, and José David Saldivar. *Criticism in the Borderlands: Studies in Chicano Literature, Culture and Ideology.* Durham: Duke UP, 1991.
Foucault, Michel. "Of Other Spaces." *Diacritics* 16.1 (1986): 22-27.
—. *Die Ordnung der Dinge: Eine Archäologie der Humanwissenschaften.* Frankfurt: Suhrkamp, 1989.
Frank, Joseph. "Spatial Form in Modern Literature." *The Widening Gyre: Crisis and Mastery in Modern Literature*: Bloomington: Indiana UP, 1969. 3-62.
Glatz, Anne-Kathrin. "A New Grand Strategy in U. S. Foreign Policy? The 2002 National Security Strategy in Comparative Perspective." Master thesis, University of Bonn, 2002.
Hönnighausen, Lothar, ed. *Space: Place, Environment, and Landscape.* Tübingen: Francke Verlag, 2003.
Hutcheon, Linda. *The Poetics of Postmodernism: History, Theory, Fiction.* New York: Routledge, 1988.
Irigaray, Luce. *This Sex Which Is Not One.* Trans. Catherine Porter. Ithaca: Cornell University Press, 1985.
Jacoby, Russell. *The End of Utopia: Politics and Culture in an Age of Apathy.* New York: Basic, 1999.
Jameson, Fredric. "Postmodernism and Consumer Society." *The Anti-Aesthetic: Essays on Postmodern Culture.* Ed. Hal Foster. Port Townsend: Bay Press, 1983. 111-25.

Kolodny, Annette. "Feminist Criticism in the Wilderness." *The New Feminist Criticism: Essays on Women, Literature, and Theory*. Ed. Elaine Showalter. New York: Pantheon, 1985. 243-70.

Kristeva, Julia. *La révolution du langage poétique: L'avant-garde à la fin du XIXe siècle: Lautréamont et Mallarmé*. Paris: Édition du Seuil, 1974.

MacAloon, John J., ed. *Rite, Drama, Festival, Spectacle: Rehearsals Toward a Theory of Cultural Performance*. Philadelphia: Institute for the Study of Human Issues, 1984.

McHale, Brian. *Postmodernist Fiction*. New York: Methuen, 1987.

Mitchell, W. J. T. "Spatial Form in Literature: Toward a General Theory." *Critical Inquiry* 6.3 (1980): 539-67.

Mukherjee, Arun. *Oppositional Aesthetics: Readings from a Hyphenated Space*. Toronto: TSAR, 1994.

Sielke, Sabine. "Das Ende der Ironie? Zum Verhältnis von Realem und Repräsentation zu Beginn des 21. Jahrhunderts." *Der 11. September 2001: Fragen, Folgen, Hintergründe*. Ed. Sabine Sielke. Frankfurt: Lang, 2002. 255-73.

—. *Fashioning the Female Subject: The Intertexual Networking of Dickinson, Moore, and Rich*. Ann Arbor: U of Michigan P, 1997.

—. "Post-Modernists or Misfits? Nonsynchronism, Subjectivity, and the Paradigms of Literary History." *Making America: The Cultural Work of Literature*. Ed. Susanne Rohr, Peter Schneck, and Sabine Sielke. Heidelberg: Winter Verlag, 2000. 215-33.

—. *Der 11. September 2001: Fragen, Folgen, Hintergründe*. Ed. Sabine Sielke. Frankfurt: Lang, 2002.

—. "Spatial Aesthetics, Ironic Distances, and Realms of Liminality: Measuring Theories of (Post) Modernism." *Space: Place, Environment, and Landscape*. Ed. Lothar Hönnighausen. Tübingen: Francke Verlag, 2003. 74-87.

—. "West of Everything? The Frontiers and Borderlands of Critical Discourse." *Polish Journal for American Studies* 1 (2004): 19-29.

Turner, Victor. "Liminality and the Performative Genres." *Rite, Drama, Festival, Spectacle: Rehearsals Toward a Theory of Cultural Performance*. Ed. John J. McAloon. Philadelphia: Institute for the Study of Human Issues, 1984. 19-41.

Žižek, Slavoj. "Willkommen in der Wüste des Realen." *Die Zeit* (20. September 2001): 48.

Landscape / Nature

Foundational Space, Technological Narrative

David E. Nye

This paper has five parts. First, I will sketch the subject my book *America as Second Creation*, in particular, the various technological narratives by which Americans construct and narrate their culture. Second, I will suggest the more general outline of such technological narratives, when taken as a group. Part three will explore a conception that underlies these narratives, the American conception of space that was expressed in the National Survey, commonly known as the grid system. Fourth, I will provide characteristic examples of a technological narrative about railroads that is inseparable from that spatial system. The final section will then examine a number of counter-narratives written against the dominant story.

I

Second Creation is about the American version of that fundamental narrative which every society must construct to make sense of its existence. I speak of the narrative that explains how a people came to live in a particular place and legitimates their presence there. Native Americans provide an instructive contrast to European Americans, for their stories of origin express a sense of primeval oneness with the places they inhabit. Native Americans can imagine that they have always been present on the land. In their creation stories, the first people are *sui generis*. They emerge out of the local earth or come into the world through the intervention of spiritual beings. One tribe, for example, believes their ancestors emerged out of the earth at a sacred location near the junction of the Little Colorado and Colorado Rivers, at the northern end of the Grand Canyon.

Anthropologists have found that the Navajo have an average of one sacred place in every twenty-six square miles. While some of these are man-made sites, including Anasazi ruins, most are "features of the natural landscape" including "mountains, hills, rock outcrops, canyons, springs and other bodies of water, natural discolorations on rocks, areas where certain plants grow, mineral deposits, isolated trees, places where rocks produce echoes, air vents in rocks, sand dunes, flat open areas, lightning-struck trees and rocks" (Kelley and Francis 38-39). These natural sites were not apprehended as isolated spots but rather as part of a larger integration with the landscape, expressed through story telling. Although the anthropologists asked about places, the Navajo frequently organized their answers as stories, and these tales linked sacred spaces both to rituals and to the central myths of their society (see Graham 15-17, 29, 45, and passim).

For European Americans, however, such sacred places and local stories of origin were impossible. Instead, white Americans constructed stories of self-creation in which the mastery of particular technologies played a central role. In these technological foundation stories, the mythic status of the stories is usually effaced, so that they are widely taken to be factual accounts. The Native-American self-conception was inseparable from the first creation of the world; Europeans imaginatively projected a second creation. They started without a detailed knowledge of the land itself, and they could never imagine away their belated arrival. Instead, they constructed stories that emphasized self-conscious movement into a new space. One cluster of stories was the frontier epics that emphasized the hardships of the pioneers and the conflict with Native-Americans. Their central technologies were firearms, particularly the rifle and the six-gun, and these tales of what Richard Slotkin persuasively called "regeneration through violence" have received a great deal of scholarly attention. However, my subject is another important cluster of stories that also deserve study. These are narratives about the settlements that came after Native-Americans were swept aside. These stories seldom mention the original inhabitants, and they usually treat the New World as an uninhabited region. In these foundation stories, an unknown and unused abstract space is transformed into a technologically defined place. Particular man-made objects are valorized, because they offer the means to transform this space.

Technological stories about the foundation of new American communities began to emerge at the end of the eighteenth century, and they were unlike those of settlers and explorers during the colonial period. When Europeans first began to colonize the New World, some imagined themselves to be returning to the bower of paradise.[1] Others saw themselves as conquerors of a pagan land that needed Christian redemption (Savelle). Early settlers in New England believed that they had embarked on what Perry Miller called an "errand into the wilderness" to create a better Christian community than had been possible in Britain. The Puritans gradually came to understand their relocation in Biblical terms; they were a new chosen people, and the New World was a new Promised Land. This way of thinking about America by no means disappeared in 1776, and derivatives of such ideas can be traced to the present. However, after the Revolution and particularly in the nineteenth century, Americans developed another way to understand their settlement of the Western Hemisphere, as the story of transforming a new space with powerful technologies. This secular story, which I call the technological foundation narrative, was projected back in time as well as forward into the immediate future. In the American beginning, after 1776, the former colonies re-imagined themselves as a self-created community, and wove these technologies into this narrative of second creation. A few technologies assumed particular prominence, among them the axe, the mill, the canal, the railroad, and the irrigation dam. *Second Creation* is thus about an American story of origins, conceived as a second creation built in harmony with God's first creation.

II

While no fixed structure lies "beneath" the many technological creation stories, there are clusters of recurrent features. My purpose is not to establish the existence of a fixed pattern (or "deep" structure) underlying hundreds of individual examples, nor is it to suggest an idealized form which individual foundation stories ought to "live up to." Yet, American technological foundation stories often do contain similar elements that unfold in a sequence along the following lines.

---

1 These early narrative conceptions of the settlement of America have been frequently analyzed, and are not my subject. See, for example, Jones, *O Strange New World*; and Marx, *The Machine in the Garden*.

1. A person or group enters an undeveloped region.
2. They have one or more new technologies.
3. Using them, they transform a part of the region.
4. The new settlement prospers, and more settlers arrive.
5. Land values increase and some settlers become wealthy.
6. The original landscape disappears, replaced by a second creation largely shaped by the new technology.
7. The process begins again, as some members of the community depart for another undeveloped region.

The order of these elements and their meaning varies depending upon both author and audience. The pattern is abstracted from the many individual cases and presented as an introduction, and not as a conclusion. Not every story contains all of these elements, their order may vary, and the meaning given the whole changes over time. Yet, a few generalizations are possible. A foundation narrative is usually not about an individual hero. Often it is told in the passive voice and emphasizes the technologies themselves. In such cases it is the axe, the mill, the canal, the railroad, or the irrigation ditch that "causes" the chain of events. While a particular person or a corporation is acknowledged to have initiated the process or to have profited from it, the story is presented as a typical case of what "inevitably" will take place.[2] The narrative is less a story about a hero than an example of a developmental process. It is an exemplary tale of progress in which human will is conflated with natural forces (Emerson, "Wealth" 698).

Such a story is progressive and optimistic. Its champions included Alexander Hamilton and early industrialists, bankers, businessmen, land agents, canal companies, railroads, politicians, and town boosters. Millions of farmers had to believe in such a story in order to act it out. It was not merely a description written after the fact, but a story that encouraged settlers to give up a familiar life, move west and put new lands into production. The narrative needed to have a powerful hold on the imagination; it had to convince people to risk a leap into the unknown.

---

2   When technologies are quite new, however, they will often be described as wonders in terms of the sublime. Thus some writers believed, as one Charles Caldwell put it in 1832, that the railroad had a morally uplifting influence, and nineteenth-century Americans celebrated in turn their canals, railroads, bridges, and skyscrapers in these terms. See Nye, *American Technological Sublime* 58.

Foundation stories had to appear to be both a sober matter of fact and a promise of betterment. They had to exist in the past as a guarantee of their probable re-enactment in the immediate future. Because a story had to appear to be repeatable, the action itself did not emphasize the struggles and triumphs of an extraordinary individual hero but rather the movement of a people as a whole. The narrative of second creation was about the unfolding of "destined" processes. Despite the fact that the foundation narrative told a story of national transformation, it minimized the state's role to that of a guiding influence. For if the state were to play a decisive role, then the repeatability of the narrative would come into question, and it would become a tale of political intrigue rather than a matter of manifest destiny. The narrative thus implicitly was based on laissez-faire economics and a whigish sense of history, assumptions that a majority of nineteenth-century Americans shared.

III

What sense of space underlies these technological creation stories? They take certain things for granted about the structure of their world.

The envelope of assumptions that supports a foundation narrative usually is un-voiced and remains scarcely visible. As Pierre Machery put it in *A Theory of Literary Production,*

> the [literary] work is articulated in relation to the reality from the ground of which it emerges: not a 'natural' empirical reality, but that intricate reality in which men—both writers and readers—live, that reality which is their ideology. The work is made on the ground of this ideology, that tacit and original language: not to speak, reveal, translate or make explicit this language, but to make possible that absence of words without which there would be nothing to say. We should question the work as to what it does not and cannot say, in those silences for which it has been made. [...] The order which it professes is merely an imagined order, projected on to disorder, the fictive resolution of ideological conflicts [...]. (155)

The ideological ground was shifting at the time of the American Revolution, transforming the possibilities of narrative at the same time that a new structure for society was embodied in new laws and social practices. While the transformations wrought by the Revolution were many, the second creation story rested particularly on a shift in perception, as Americans abandoned traditional land divisions in favor of an abstract grid.

The anthropologist Edward Hall once observed a striking difference between France and the United States visible in their road systems (146-147). The French roads radiated out from towns, forming clear centers and peripheries. The cathedral stood in the middle of town, often as the literal focal point of most highways, and its spire was the first object visible from a distance. Looking at a road map, a star-like pattern of lines flows out from the heart of older European cities and towns. The origin of the pattern is ancient, and the location of each road is a combination of local topography, history, and convenience. In contrast, most of the United States west of the Alleghenies was laid out in a vast checkerboard pattern, imposing a design on the contours of the land without regard for its topography and without reference to any prior history or land use.

This landscape was based on a new sense of space invented immediately after the American Revolution. During the 1780s and after Americans formally embraced a new sense of space that found expression in a National Survey, dividing all federal land into perfect squares.³ The grid was a fundamental change, literally putting a new frame around stories of migration and settlement.

The imposition of the geometrical pattern of the grid on much of North America was central to the imagined order that made possible stories of technological creation. In the Colonial period, not the individual but the community had been central. The theocratic order of the first settlers was visible in the layout of the land, as Americans reproduced the European village, with the church at the center and the roads radiating outwards. The local governments of first settlers did not conceive of land as being generic. A family's land was not all in one location but divided into woodlots, pasture, and farmland. These lots were not contiguous, the shape of each lot was by no means regular or square. In contrast, the new grid system erased hierarchy and centrality from the landscape, substituting the values of individuality and equality.

---

3   This was first tried on a smaller scale in several states. Notably, the year before the new system was enacted into federal law, New York State had successfully introduced it in its western areas.

Considering this contrast between pre- and post-revolutionary American land use, it seems particularly significant that George Washington, before he commanded the American army, had been a surveyor, and that Thomas Jefferson introduced and promoted the idea of the grid in Congress. The two most popular founding fathers were particularly well-qualified to understand the decision to impose the grid on the new nation's western territories. It is tempting to assume that the creation of the grid expressed an immediate and fundamental shift in consciousness. But a look at the discussions surrounding the adoption of the Ordinance of 1784 and the later revisions of the grid scheme demonstrates that the legislation was a practical program as well as a reconception of space. It expressed the Enlightenment values of rationality, equality, and order, but the survey also was intended to facilitate selling western land to pay off the national debt. The "policy makers faced an immediate, practical problem in linking supply to demand. They had to create a market for a commodity, unimproved frontier land" (Onuf 208). To do this they needed a system to survey it and guarantee title. The grid hastened that process. It was not an ideal solution for most localities, since the grid ran roughshod over topography (Jackson 4). But it could be put into effect immediately, because it used longitude and latitude as the basis for all land divisions. This made it possible to survey any location, no matter how remote, and demarcate its boundaries, without necessarily having surveyed all the land around it.

Some geographers have defended the system down to the present. John Fraser Hart recently argued that "it may be the best system of land division ever invented. It provides an excellent frame of reference for orientation, and it conveys a sense of neatness, order, and stability." Perhaps even more important, the grid system "has obviated an enormous amount of litigation by facilitating a brief but precise description of the exact location of any tract of land" (155). But if the National Survey made land transactions easily comprehensible to all, it also encouraged farmers to ignore the contours of the land. The grid became the basis for a system of roads and power lines that followed north-south or east-west boundary lines and defied the actual landscape of hills and valleys. Such roads fatigued horses, which had to work much harder than they would have in a road system based on topography. American roads also frustrated the traveler seeking to move diagonally rather than according to the four cardinal points of the compass.

Nevertheless, during the nineteenth century Americans accepted and naturalized the geometrical ordering of the land, as the grid moved from the Appalachian Mountains to California. Accepting this land division affected not only the sense of space but also the sense of the past. The grid, like the technological creation story that it underpinned, represented a radical break with the colonial story of the settlement of the New World. That story had represented colonists as the carriers of European spatial patterns to a new place. The early settlers were often compared to the ancient people of Israel. In this encodation of events, the immigrants to America were bringing to perfection the religious and social ideals of Europe. Significantly, before the Revolutionary period there seem to be no fully worked out examples of the technological narrative, with its radically different assumptions about the relationship to the land. Only people who self-consciously saw themselves not as colonists but as *Americans* were ready to reinvent their sense of space.

The grid was not a scientific solution, however. Mathematically speaking, the idea made no sense. As some legislators realized at the time, demanding that surveyors carve up land into squares based upon the lines of latitude and longitude was theoretically impossible. Such a plan assumed the earth was flat, whereas the "squares" surveyed on a globe were really trapezoids, slightly narrower at the top than at the bottom. As Timothy Pickering vainly explained to anyone who would listen in 1784, meridians converge near the poles, and as surveyors laid out thousands of contiguous "squares" they would have to be shorter on their northern boundary, or they would soon be out of alignment (qtd. in Stilgoe 103). Thus when surveyors went out and attempted to carve up the land in accord with Congress's wishes, compromises and approximations were inevitable. Over time they learned to establish correction lines at regular intervals (Johnson 127-132, and passim).

This method of land division made it easier for white Americans to define the west as essentially empty space, a *tabula rasa*, a "virgin land" waiting to be appropriated.[4] This expansive sense of space is

---

4 The classic work is Smith, *Virgin Land*, while Annette Kolodny contributed to a revision of his work with *The Land Before Her*.

still visible in the layout of fields and roads if one flies in a plane over the Middle West. The system not only called for the division of lands into a checkerboard of 640 acre squares, or sections of one square mile each, but it also assembled 36 sections to define a perfectly square township.[5] The grid system expressed philosophical ideas that Americans literally inscribed on the land.[6] Most obviously, the grid asserted human dominion. As Denis Cosgrove noted, "Confidence that nature had been nailed down by geometry was shared by both railroad boosters in New York and Chicago and isolated homesteaders on their quarter or half-quarter sections that stretched across Oklahoma and the Texas Panhandle with only the rail line to measure the endless horizon" (9). Surveying the land into squares was, in Macherey's terms, part of the underlying and unarticulated ideology that was a necessary precondition for a technological narrative. Surveying was a kind of writing on the land, turning it into a free market landscape. Its endlessly interchangeable units articulated an egalitarian sense of space that had no center and no past. The new geography made land into an abstraction, a commodity, and an item of speculation.

Furthermore, this conception of space was atomistic. It assumed that in each place the same social reality could be replicated, creating a society that was at once homogeneous and at the same time made up of self-reliant parts (Fisher 47). Such a space had no limitations; it was conceptually unbounded, and it was perpetually open to new people and new technological systems (Fisher 48). Given the grid's uniformity, this social space seemed to be transparent and intelligible, as though there were no coding to experience. With only one geographical system, Americans soon felt that their land division was not at all arbitrary. Philip Fisher observed, "such a Cartesian space provides for no observers, for no oppositional positions. There are no outsiders." To be an "observer is a symptom of a divided social space" (50). The grid was a totalizing system, making it difficult to write, and even more difficult to win an audience for, a counter-narrative.

---

5   For an overview, see Meinig, *The Shaping of America* 341-343, or Daniel Boorstin, *The National Experience* 241-248. Boorstin points out that part of Georgia was laid out into square mile sections as early as 1717.
6   This inscription is beautifully visualized in Corner and MacLean's *Taking Measures Across the American Landscape*.

The grid also ignored and dispossessed Native Americans. Its endless squares declared that the land was unused, empty, and waiting for settlers. The adoption of the grid made it easier to believe in Manifest Destiny; filling in the "empty" and "undeveloped" spaces of the grid became an automatic historical process. The grid naturalized America's second creation.

The implications of this change in perception are immediately obvious in the famous Currier and Ives print, Frances Palmer's "Across the Continent: Westward the Course of Empire Takes its Way" (1867). It represents an unambiguous relationship between the railroad, the telegraph and the landscape. These technologies are rapidly developing the American West. Human creations transform the landscape, which in the distance remains vague and unformed, in contrast to the foreground where a new town has sprung into existence, impelled into life by the railroad. The caption itself is a quotation from Bishop Berkeley's often-repeated declaration, made already in the 1720s, that "Westward the Course of Empires Takes Its Way" (364). This notion that human history records a continual westward shift in power, from the Middle East, to Greece, to Rome, to Northern Europe, and then to the New World, had become a staple of the American self-conception by the time this image was crafted and sold to a large public in 1868. By that date the first transcontinental railroad to the Pacific was nearing completion. The Currier and Ives image was both a vision of the recent past and a prediction of the future. It uses space to represent time: the new community in the foreground is the present, the empty land ahead of the train is the future, which extends to the vanishing point of perspective. This painting is also rather unselfconsciously imperialistic. The land ahead is presented as empty space awaiting the coming of white civilization. A few Native Americans on horseback are literally on the margins, watching, and the smoke from the train blows over them, obscuring their view of the land, and thus of the future.[7]

The geometrical vision was expressed in the thousands of new towns that nineteenth century entrepreneurs and railroad companies laid out. Through forested tracts, open prairie, and unpeopled swamps,

---

7   The place of this lithograph in a larger ideology of technological transformation is discussed in my book, *Second Creation: Technological Creation Stories in the United States, 1776-1920*, 156-159.

surveyors marked off farms, streets and lots, almost always in uniform, rectilinear patterns. By mid-century the grid had been fully naturalized. As the cultural geographer J. B. Jackson noted, "whereas in the older states of Ohio and Indiana and Illinois (where the heritage of the colonial farm lingered) the straight lines of the grid were valued as an efficient and democratic way of organizing individual landholdings, west of the Missouri the grid played a much more decisive role: it was the *only* practical and speedy method of organizing space." In the western half of the country, the grid's "long-range effect was to eliminate, once and for all, the impact of tradition and traditional spaces, in the forming of the new High Plains landscape. A composition of identical rectangular squares extending out of sight in every direction, ignoring all inherent differences, produced a landscape of empty, interchangeable divisions [...]" (Jackson 154). As one of Willa Cather's narrators put it, when first confronted with the empty spaces of Nebraska, "There was nothing but land: not a country at all, but the material out of which countries are made" (7). In most foundation narratives there is no mention of any previous inhabitants, as though the continent had been completely raw and undeveloped, waiting for the axe, the sawmill, and the arrival of the first railroad.

IV

Through narrative, nineteenth century Americans understood the creation of their landscape as a dynamic technological process. They did not conceive of either landscapes or technologies as abstract things in themselves. Rather, they naturalized them through storytelling. Stories of building national roads and railroads did not come after the fact. Rather, story telling anticipated and promoted the emergence of each new technology and its landscape. In 1846, a generation before the first transcontinental railroad was completed in 1869, the geologist Charles Lyell visited the United States. He heard "much characteristic conversation in the [railroad] cars, about constructing a railway 4000 miles long from Washington to the Columbia river' and some of the passengers were speculating on the hope of seeing in their lifetime a population of 15,000 souls settled in Oregon and California" (357). These passengers saw the railroad as the spearhead of settlement, literally opening the empty west to them.

Both in the North and in the South, the railroad was central to similar technological creation stories. The New Orleans newspaper, the *Picayune* expressed it well in 1860. American railroads created a new society, which the newspaper visualized as a new landscape:

> Nine-tenths of our roads when first traversed by steam pass through long ranges of woodlands in which the axe has never resounded, cross prairies whose flowery sod has never been turned by the plow, and penetrate the valleys as wild as when the first pioneers followed upon the trail of the savage. They connect distant centers of population, and open markets for an agricultural population in the very heart of the continent. But no sooner is the great work achieved, then population pours into the rich wilderness, is scattered over the wide sweeping prairies, and settles in the fertile vales, and away business springs up destined to increase each year for centuries to come. Villages soon dot the margin of the road. Factories turn to service the water power of the little streams it crosses [...] and golden grain covers the lands that since the primeval time have been overshadowed by the dark forest. ("English and American Railways" 926)

The New York newspaper editor Horace Greeley told a similar story, emphasizing that "Railroads in Europe are built to connect centers of population; but in the west the railroad itself builds cities. Pushing boldly out into the wilderness, along its iron track villages, towns, and cities spring into existence, and are strung together into a consistent whole by its lines of rails, as beads are upon a silken thread" (Greeley, *Industries* 1032). The same idea was visualized in "Across the Continent," shown earlier.[8]

It was not possible for nineteenth-century Americans to conceive of the settlement of the American west without thinking of the railroad and the dynamic process of building it and using it. By the 1840s the expansion of railways into new regions seemed to be the same thing as the spread of civilization itself.

V Counter-narratives

Not all Americans shared this view of the railroad. Particularly after mid-century, an increasing number of counter narratives reconfigured the same events. Hayden White has argued that differences between

---

8   For discussion, see Kasson, *Civilizing the Machine* 178-179.

Foundational Space, Technological Narrative

historical interpretations of events arise through the different techniques of encoding facts as parts of a larger design:

> [...] the primary meaning of a narrative would then consist of the destructuration of a set of events (real or imagined) originally encoded in one tropological mode and the progressive restructuration of the set in another tropological mode. As thus envisaged, narrative would be a process of decodation and recodation in which an original perception is clarified by being cast in a figurative mode different from that in which it has become encoded by convention, authority, or custom. And the explanatory force of the narrative would then depend on the contrast between the original encodation and the later one. (96)

To apply White's terminology to the technological creation narratives, each selected and emphasized a set of events, structured in a narrative that served most white, middle-class Americans as a conventional account of their history. This story of the railroad seemed to be an unproblematic account of "the facts." Indeed, the same story would later be told by economic historians, such as Schumpeter (1:303). In contrast, other groups, such as Native Americans, farmers, fishermen, striking workers, or environmentalists challenged or inverted these dominant technological creation stories. They constructed counter narratives cast in a different figurative mode. These are stories of conflict, rather than of the harmonious unfolding of events. While second creation stories treat the land as empty space, ignoring the original inhabitants, the counter narratives are told from the point of view of the indigenous community and/or emphasize the ecological effects of technological change.

The possible ways to recode the foundation narrative are many and can be extremely complex. There is no ideal form for the counternarrative, but to provide a sense of how a dominant form night be challenged, consider the following inversion of the earlier example.

1. Outsiders enter an existing biotic and/or human community.
2. They acquire its land and assets by force or legal trickery.
3. The newcomers possess powerful new technologies.
4. They begin to use these technologies to transform the landscape, undermining the existing community's way of life.
5. The old and the new communities come into conflict.
6. The new community wins this conflict.
7. As additional settlers arrive, they complete the transformation of the landscape.
8. The original community loses population and goes into decline.

9. Its people become marginal, and they disappear or move away.

Unlike the technological foundation story, which traces an inevitable working out of "manifest destiny" and the free market for middle-class white Americans, the counter-narrative is a tragic tale of struggle and defeat, which often begins with treaty violations or other illegalities. For example, Native Americans on the Great Plains told of how the railroad destroyed the buffalo herds that were the material basis for their way of life.

Among whites as well, the story of the American railroad creating cities and populating the West with settlers came under sharp critique after 1860. The same Horace Greeley, who imagined the railroad as the creator of the west, soon found that railroads were swindling the public by abusing the land grants given to them by state and federal governments. He was surprised to find, when traveling a new line through Missouri, "infinitely less population and improvement" than he had expected. "Of course," he ironically noted, "this road was run so as to avoid the more settled districts, and thus to secure a larger allotment of the public lands [...]. I had not believed it possible to run a railroad through northern Missouri so as to strike so few settlements" (*Overland Journey* 14). Greeley found one section of level prairie fifty miles long virtually uninhabited, and he thought it "incredible that such land, in a state forty years old, could have remained unsettled till now" (15). Railroads often refused to serve towns that did not grant them special subsidies. In the 1870s the Southern Pacific "did not hesitate to change its route to avoid towns which refused it subsidies. Many of these deserted settlements were thus doomed to stagnation" (Dumke 20-21). New railroads actively avoided or undermined towns that already existed, in order to promote towns that they had designed and built themselves.

Furthermore, railways often forced early settlers off the land or kept land off the market, waiting for its value to increase. During the boom in railway construction of the 1870s "memorials and petitions poured into Congress from dispossessed settlers" of the West and from their legislatures (Robbins 257). They complained that people who settled a territory ahead of the railroad often found their land claims invalidated. The railroad, rather than fostering settlement, drove settlers away and seized their lands. Furthermore, the railroad did not open the west to poor settlers, because they could not afford to pay the higher prices that property suddenly fetched along its routes. Worst of all, from the western point of view, the railroads transformed settlement from an individualistic process to a centralized corporate practice. The railroad brought not free market development and prosperity, but immediate economic disaster for some and long-term economic control for all (see George Miller; Gates 171-175).

Railroads and steamboats were used to stimulate land speculation from Pennsylvania to California. Promoters of new towns in the northern plains described cities with "great parks, opera houses, churches, universities, railway depots and steamboat landings" that "made New York and St. Louis insignificant in comparison. But if the newcomer had the unusual wisdom to visit the prophetic city before purchasing lots," he soon found that "The town might be composed of twenty buildings; or [...] perhaps a tent and an Indian canoe on the river in front of the 'levee.' Any thing was marketable." It seemed that all of the Great Plains would become urban, and "Wags proposed an act of Congress reserving some land for farming purposes before the whole Territory should be divided into city lots" (Richardson 59). A contemporary concluded, "It was not a swindle, but a mania. The speculators were quite as insane as the rest" (Richardson 59). They continually reinvested their inflated profits only to lose them in the end. The apparent truth of that railroads created prosperity and expansion was too strong for mere facts of geography.

Aside from over-stimulating land speculation, many critics realized that the railroads had become a dangerous economic power. As interstate corporations the railroads at times were beyond control of state legislative control, and they threatened the democratic system of politics. As the largest businesses and the main form of transportation in the country, they could dictate shipping costs to farmers, purchase the entire output of steel mills to supply their rails and consume the wood of entire states to replace their trestles, bridges, and ties. Accordingly, there were counter-narratives that focused on political and economic abuses.

In addition, early environmental critics of the railroad complained that in practice it destroyed the landscape it claimed to make available to tourists. The naturalist John Muir journeyed through much of the West by train and was shocked at the enormous areas carelessly set alight by the sparks from steam engines. The railroad builders typically cleared away trees and brush and left it lying near the tracks.

When sparks set this dry wood on fire, "nobody was in sight to prevent them from spreading [...] into the adjacent forests and burn the timber from hundreds of square miles" (155). He wrote a parody of the advertisements of the transcontinental lines whose "gorgeous many-colored folders" each described its "scenic route." The advertisements should instead read, he declared,

> 'The route of superior desolation'—the smoke, dust, and ashes route—would be a more truthful description. Every train rolls on through dismal smoke and barbarous melancholy ruins, and the companies might well cry in their advertisements: 'Come! travel our way. Ours is the blackest. It is the only genuine Erebus route. The sky is black and the ground is black, and on either side there is a continuous border of black stumps and logs and blasted trees appealing to heaven for help as if still half alive, and their mute eloquence is most interestingly touching. The blackness is perfect. On account of the superior skill of our workman, advantages of climate, and the kind of trees, the charring is generally deeper along our line, and the ashes are deeper, and the confusion and desolation displayed can never be rivaled. No other route on this continent so fully illustrates the abomination of desolation.' Such a claim would be reasonable, as each seems the worst, whatever route you chance to take. (154)

Thus, by the end of the nineteenth century the technological creation story of the railroad had been debunked. There could be no doubt that the railroad improved transportation, but it had stimulated wasteful land speculation, created ghost towns, undermined and destroyed existing communities by denying them service, driven early settlers off their claims, and slowed settlement of some areas by charging high prices for both freight and land.

Conclusion

By the 1920s technological creation stories no longer described the future, or even the present, but primarily referred to the past. Yet, they by no means disappeared. Like the captivity narrative or the Puritan jeremiad, which had also emerged long before, technological foundation narratives continued to be rewritten and to circulate as part of the repertoire of stories Americans told themselves to make sense of their migration and settlement. If the details varied, the pattern remained much the same whether the creation stories were based on the American axe, the mill, the canal, the railroad or irrigation. For most Americans, the meaning of these technologies was contained in and inseparable from these foundation stories. In each case, they assumed that the land was empty and undeveloped. European Americans surveyed and sub-divided this space and sold it to private individuals. Using one or more new technologies, they developed the land and increased its value to themselves. Agriculture flourished, the population grew, and the land was transformed. European-Americans had made a second creation, they believed, not by exploiting but by improving nature. The new order seemed essentially in harmony with first creation. Indeed, they believed the improvements were latent within the land. Far from violating an original perfection, the settlers worked in partnership with nature. The clearing in the forest, the mill in the valley, the canal and the railroad toward the west, or the irrigation ditch in the desert, were designed to enhance the bounty of the earth and to help mankind to follow the Biblical injunction to "increase and multiply." Each completed a providential design, fulfilled divine intentions, and manifested the destiny of the nation. Each improvement seemed to justify taking land that had "lain idle." Second creation stories legitimized white expansion into the "empty" space of the continent; they made private development of land and resources seem to be inevitable processes.

This technological creation story has by no means disappeared. On television, pioneers still enter the empty space of the American west. Children play computer games such as Sim City, which invite them to create new communities from scratch in an empty virtual landscape where the grid defines the contours of roads and the arrangement of houses, factories, and commercial districts. Nor are such visions limited to children's games. At the New York World's Fair of 1964, General Motors told 29 million visitors that Americans could "improve" any location, whether on earth, under the sea, or in outer space, and build a comfortable second creation there (*Official Guide* 201-202). Its "Futurama" exhibit became the most popular exhibit on the fairgrounds, for it expanded the technological creation story to embrace underwater communities, air-conditioned utopias in the jungle, and lunar colonies.

Many Americans continue to imagine colonizing outer space. In March 1998, newspapers in the United States carried excited stories about the discovery of ice on the moon—between 10 and 100 million tons (Carlin 20). The mainstream media assumed that the water was there for the taking, to be used to make rocket fuel, irrigate green houses, and supply tourist hotels. Preliminary market studies suggested that up-market lunar travelers would want condominiums, tennis courts, and even golf courses.

The "conquest" of "empty" space appeals to many as a future scenario, as the technological creation story continues into its third century.

Works Cited

Berkeley, George. "Verses on the Prospect of Planting Arts and Learning in America." *The Works of George Berkeley, D. D.* 4 vols. Ed. Alexander C. Fraser. Oxford: Oxford UP, 1901.

Boorstin, Daniel. *The National Experience.* New York: Random House, 1965.

Carlin, John. "Fly Me to the Moon." *Independent on Sunday* (8 March 1998): 20.

Cather, Willa. *My Antonia.* Boston: Houghton Mifflin, 1918.

Conzon, Michael P. *The Making of the American Landscape.* New York: Harper Collins, 1994.

Corner, James, and Alex S. MacLean. *Taking Measures Across the American Landscape.* New Haven: Yale UP, 1996.

Cosgrove, Denis. "The Measures of America." *Taking Measures Across the American Landscape.* Ed. James Corner and Alex S. MacLean. 3-14.

Dumke, Glenn S. *The Boom of the Eighties in Southern California.* San Marino: Huntington Library, 1944.

"English and American Railways." Repr. in *American Railroad Journal* XXXIII (1860): 926.

Emerson, Ralph Waldo. "Wealth." *Selected Writings of Emerson.* Ed. Brooks Atkinson. New York: The Modern Library, 1950. 693-716.

Fisher, Philip. "Democratic Social Space." *Still the New World: American Literature in a Culture of Creative Destruction.* Cambridge, MA: Harvard UP, 1999. 33-55.

Gates, Paul Wallace. *Fifty Million Acres: Conflicts over Kansas Land Policy, 1854-1890.* Ithaca: Cornell UP, 1954.

Graham, Loren. *A Face in the Rock: The Tale of a Grand Island Chippewa.* Berkeley: U of California P, 1998.

Greeley, Horace. *An Overland Journey from New York to San Francisco in the Summer of 1859.* New York: Saxton, Barker & Co., 1860.

Greeley, Horace, et. al. *The Great Industries of the United States.* 2 vols. Reprint. New York: Garland Publishing, 1974.

Hall, Edward. *The Hidden Dimension.* New York: Doubleday, 1966.

Hart, John Fraser. *The Rural Landscape.* Baltimore: Johns Hopkins UP, 1998.

Jackson, John Brinckerhoff. "The Accessible Landscape." *A Sense of Place, a Sense of Time*. New Haven: Yale UP, 1994. 1-12.
Johnson, Hildegard Binder. "Towards a National Landscape." *The Making of the American Landscape*. Ed. Michael P. Conzon. New York: Harper Collins, 1994. 127-145.
Jones, Howard Mumford. *O Strange New World*. New York: Viking, 1964.
Kasson, John F. *Civilizing the Machine*. Harmondsworth: Penguin, 1977.
Kelley, Klara Bonsack, and Harris Francis. *Navajo Sacred Places*. Bloomington: Indiana UP, 1994.
Kolodny, Annette. *The Land Before Her*. Chapel Hill: U of North Carolina P, 1984.
Lyell, Charles. *A Second Visit to the United States*. Vol. 2. London: Murray, 1849.
Macherey, Pierre. *A Theory of Literary Production*. London: Routledge & Kegan Paul, 1978.
Marx, Leo. *The Machine in the Garden*. New York: Oxford UP, 1964.
Meinig, D. W. *The Shaping of America*. Vol. 1. New Haven: Yale UP, 1986.
Miller, George H. *Railroads and the Granger Laws*. Madison: U of Wisconsin P, 1971.
Miller, Perry. *Errand into the Wilderness*. Cambridge: Harvard UP, 1956.
Muir, John. "The American Forests." *The Atlantic Monthly* 80 (August 1897): 145-57.
Nye, David E. *American Technological Sublime*. Cambridge, MA: MIT P, 1994.
—. *Second Creation: Technological Creation Stories in the United States, 1776-1920*. Cambridge, MA: MIT P, 2002.
Official Guide, New York World's Fair, 1964/1965. New York: Time Incorporated, 1964.
Onuf, Peter S. "Liberty, Development, and Union: Visions of the West in the 1780s." *William and Mary Quarterly* 43.2 (1986): 179-214.
Palmer, Frances. "Across the Continent: Westward the Course of Empire Takes its Way." Currier and Ives, 1867. Copy in Library of Congress.
Richardson, Albert D. *Beyond the Mississippi*. Hartford: American Publishing Company, 1867.
Robbins, Roy M. *Our Landed Heritage: The Public Domain, 1776-1936*. Lincoln: U of Nebraska P, 1962.
Savelle, Max. *Empires into Nations: Expansion in America*. Minneapolis: U of Minnesota P, 1974.
Schumpeter, Joseph. *Business Cycles*. Vol. 1. New York: McGraw-Hill, 1939.
Slotkin, Richard. *Regeneration Through Violence*. Middletown: Wesleyan UP, 1973.
Smith, Henry Nash. *Virgin Land*. Cambridge, MA: Harvard UP, 1950.
Stilgoe, John. *Common Landscape of America, 1580-1845*. New Haven: Yale UP, 1982.
White, Hayden. *Tropics of Discourse: Essays in Cultural Criticism*. Baltimore: Johns Hopkins UP, 1978.

Waste and Race: An Introduction to Sustainability and Equity[1]

Robin Morris Collin and Robert W. Collin

> TO J.Q.
> What are the things that make
> life bright?
> A star gleam in the night.
> What hearts us for the coming
> fray?
> The dawn tints of the day.
> What helps to speed the weary
> mile?
> A brother's friendly smile.
> What turns o' gold the evening
> gray?
> A flower beside the way.
>
> —Paul Lawrence Dunbar

Societal concern about sustainable development masks issues of racism and environmental inequity. What do race and sustainability really mean? We explore these terms in the US context of unequal environmental benefits and burdens.

The history of environmental injustice in the United States can be traced back to the colonization efforts of Western European nations. Before their arrival, the North American continent was sparsely populated with other humans, and ecosystems flourished. As the Colonialists and subsequent settlers searched for natural resources, the land, lives, and livelihoods of indigenous peoples were taken and often destroyed. Natural resources were transformed into the commodities of a newly global trade, and the people themselves were converted to labor commodities as colonies began to use slaves to provide labor to grow

---

[1] The authors thank Willamette University College of Law for its support of their work through the Summer Writing Stipend program.

agricultural commodities such as indigo, rice, cotton and tobacco.[2] This was the beginning of the extract, consume and pollute economies that continue to devastate poor and indigenous peoples and ecologies throughout the world.

Slavery in the United States was among the most oppressive forms of slavery in the long history of this institution in the world (see Patterson). Slaves in the United States had no protection of the laws of this country. In the Dred Scott decision, Chief Justice Taney of the United States Supreme Court said that slaves in his country had no rights which any white man was bound to honor. He meant specifically, no right to live, to marry, to protect and maintain families, to read or learn, to vote, to participate in government or the systems of justice. These prohibitions and disabilities, and more were institutionalized by law and perpetuated in US social institutions. After Emancipation, racial oppression continued in education, housing, land use, municipal service provision, and employment. The impact of imperial/colonial agriculture on the land was nearly as devastating; tobacco is legendary for ruining the soil in which it is grown leaving it unfit for the cultivation of other crops. Indigo plantations were abandoned as the international demand shriveled due to new technologies of color and dye production, and the slaves used to produce it were left in a kind of blessed isolation to reconstruct their own cultures and livelihoods as documented in the popular film, *Daughters of the Dust*. Cotton crops require some of the most toxic herbicides, insecticides and fungicides to grow, leaving a toxic soup of agricultural runoff from the cotton fields of Mississippi that poisons all downstream waters and the soil of the Delta. And now, the Gulf of Mexico has an ominously expanding Dead Zone at the base of the Delta.

This example repeated itself throughout the conquered New Worlds and Africa from Brazil to Mombasa, from Canada to Australia, as the modern economy established itself on the foundations of extraction of mineral and agricultural resources, development of consumer cultures, tastes, and dependence upon these conscripted re-

---

2   The contemporary slave trade continues to fuel the global economy contributing 13 billion dollars of uncompensated wealth per year. Andrew Cockburn delivers a compelling description of the structure and participants in the current global traffic in human suffering in the *National Geographic* magazine for September 2003.

sources, and obliviousness to the pollution, toxicity, and devastation that are the consequences for land and the people closest to the land. The foot print of colonialism, and slavery lead directly to the current landscape of environmental injustice in the US and globally. The current generation of toxic colonialism, garbage imperialism, and environmental racism exists on a scale which now threatens the underlying systems on which all life depends (see Bullard). Retracing these footprints reveals the simple fact that all of the environmental problems which now threaten species, human health, air and water quality, and the viability of the land have their roots in economic, industrial, agricultural, and trade policies of the industrial age. Our contemporary environmental problems are not independent of these political, social and economic judgments exercised upon nature, and on other people during the preceding ages. The consequence of this history is that even though the patterns of extraction, consumption and pollution are recognized as instrumental in degrading both Nature and people, our economies force daily choices and activities that perpetuate degradation though few individuals actually intend or wish to harm either Nature or the people closest to Nature. This is the awesome power of institutionalized values; they normalize a bloody, brutal past by cloaking it in the banality of everyday behavior. To extract, consume and pollute has become normal, and the pattern of degradation and pollution leaves our environment, people of color, and all future generations impacted.

The most insidious legacy of these extract-consume-pollute economies is their values; profit as a proxy for social good, consumption for its own sake, externalizing pollution onto Nature or vulnerable people, and racism as an justification for power and privilege.[3] These values guided the policies of exploitation for profit, rationalized and absolved the guilty, and wrapped its beneficiaries in spiritual obliviousness to the suffering of others. They continue to guide, rationalize, and absolve environmental and ecological injustices even when they threaten the systems upon which all life depends—the privileged as well as the burdened.

The ripples from accumulated degradation of bioregional watersheds, and air sheds are spreading to affect ecological systems. The bioaccumulation of toxins in the bodies of human babies and mother's

---

3   See Posner, *Economics* ch. 3, "Wealth," and "Utilitarianism."

milk is affecting new generations of wealthy and poor alike. Gross environmental inequities affect disenfranchised communities first with sites so toxic that the carrying capacity of a bioregion is affected threatening human life, with alarming statistics on childhood cancers, asthma related illness, and the phenomena of estrogenization including decreased sperm counts and early onset of menses. National concern for environmental justice is simply the recognition that wealth and privilege will postpone but not prevent the spread of these pollution-based health hazards. What money and privileges can purchase now is only time.

Human communities and human bodies are the terminuses where complex policy decisions and their environmental consequences have come to rest. Communities are where the waste streams join, where development pressures for increased power generation and water usage continue, and where population growth is most visible. Current environmental decision making can exacerbate environmental pressure on communities already burdened by environmental injustices of the past. For example, it is easier and less expensive to expand a current waste site than to find a new site for waste. Human bodies, especially those of children born into communities where synthetic chemicals and toxins have become ubiquitous since World War II, carry the detritus of industrial development in their tissue and bones. Women's bodies and children's bodies, for whom safe dose responses are not calculated, are the human counterparts to urban sacrifice zones where industrial pollution and costs have been externalized, dumped, covered up, ignored, and ultimately denied. These are the politics of waste, race, and hate.

Too often solutions to the complex environmental and social problems left in the wake of industrial development are posed as false choices: nature or people, environment or jobs. These false choices operate once again to externalize the costs of clean up and abatement onto either nature or poor communities, and communities of color, victimizing them once again. When solutions are offered which poison workers to benefit neighboring communities, no sustainable solution has been found; when communities are destroyed and nature is blamed, the real culprit may be technology which destroyed employment, not endangered species. These false choices blackmail the politically vulnerable into choices that preserve privilege and wealth built over the preceding centuries of industrial and capital growth, but continue to poison both nature and the people who live, work, and play closest to nature.

Sustainability is often defined in the abstract as meeting the needs of the present without compromising the ability of future generations to meet their own needs. Definitive values tie together the entire concept of sustainability. First, there is an explicit concern for future generations. The major documents on sustainability all refer to a principle of resource use that protects the interests of future generations of humans and nonhuman species as well. The central defining characteristic of sustainability is its concern that contemporary humans conduct themselves in a way that protects the interests of future generations of humans; a very specific kind of intergenerational equity. In this way, intergenerational equity is the central core value of sustainability as a philosophy, and this is reflected in a variety ways, including the concept of carrying capacity, sustainable development, and resource management.

As compared with other ideologies, the concern of sustainability with future generations is unique. This new value orientation ushers in the emerging ecological paradigm. It implies human duties to future generations of human and nonhuman life. This new value orientation ushers in the emerging ecological paradigm. Simple justice to succeeding generations lies in acknowledging that they will need the systems that nature provides to support all life, including,

> as noted by the Dutch scientist Rudoph S. deGroot, oxygen production, purification of water and air, regulation of atmospheric chemistry, protection against cosmic and ultraviolet radiation, solar energy, regulation of local and global warming, maintenance of biological and genetic diversity, maintenance of wildlife migration and habitat, storage, detoxification and recycling of human waste, natural pest and weed controls, immense medicinal resource production, prevention of soil erosion, sediment control, regulation of runoff and flood prevention, regulation of chemical composition of the ocean, formation of topsoil, maintenance of soil fertility, nutrient storage and recycling, fuel and energy production. (Hawken, "Natural Capitalism" 1997, 42)

Since we don't have technology to replace these systems, and we know that the people with whom we share this planet, and those beings who will come to dwell here in the future depend upon them, it is incumbent upon us to preserve those life systems. Simple equity demands that we show the same degree of care to contemporary strangers as we hope to show to future strangers. We must not infringe upon their future environmental liberties by ignoring contemporaneous constituents. In this way, the environment is a Commons without time. In order to achieve sustainability we must learn to live within the limits of the remaining natural resources. This idea raises all kinds of political, social, and economic questions related to the equitable distribution of these natural resources.

Different iterations of the term sustainable development can become vague when removed from Nature. The term sustainability implies many things to many people, prompting concerns that the term is used to "greenwash" practices and programs without real content. But the policies that led to social conditions from segregation to sprawl sprang the separation of resources and needs between communities based upon their privilege and wealth, and they are not sustainable. While sustainable development generally calls for constraints on unlimited economic growth, to some it implies a degree of uncritical continuation of current wealth and power. Sustainable development is generally seen as requiring industry to internalize its waste and pollution and pay true costs for resource use. Real sustainable social policy in the US will require substantial changes in consumption and production patterns; changes in values, including redefining wealth and prosperity, and fair distribution between current and future generations as well as between contemporaries. Change must follow the solemn reality that privilege buys time for a future that may not promise much for any living thing. False choices, secret decision making, lying, and suppression environmental information cannot preserve privilege forever. Authentic sustainability is grounded upon equity; we must first find out what is just and do that first, finding ways to make that sustainable.[4]

Sustainability and environmental equity require that ecosystems be dealt with as an undivided whole, with no part being unsustainable. The interrelated nature of our environment creates complex and dynamic ecologies. To the extent that sustainability means sustaining the natural environment and its systems, we must deal with nature as an undivided whole, with no part being unsustainable. Sustainability also requires that we deal with the human population as an undivided whole. Sustainable communities are only as strong as their weakest

---

[4] See also *Our Common Future*; *Rio Declaration on Environment and Development*; *Stockholm Declaration*; Elder; Riddell.

link. A poisoned air shed or aquifer that poses an unacceptable risk to human health threatens all the people who live, work and play there. Those people most exposed to these hazards by their work or by the location of their housing will suffer health effects first, but their concerns may soon be all of ours. Increases in our population, technological prowess in natural resource use, patterns of consumption, and accumulated environmental impacts must be met with an equal commitment to include every single community. Sustainability and social policy also require the human population be treated as an undivided whole. To treat any one point of a bioregion as acceptably unsustainable, or to treat any group of people as acceptably unsustainable contradicts any policy of sustainability because of the fundamentally interconnected natures of bioregions and communities. In the sustainable global community we are only as strong as our weakest link, or our most toxic community. The historical bias of environmental decision making is too painfully clear in terms of who was not included in the decision making process. When communities are not included in the environmental decisions that affect them where they live, work, and play, they will distrust and oppose them. Environmental decisions stand the best chance of being implemented when there is little local opposition to them. Historically, local opposition to a land use can be avoided by avoiding notice to the local community about the environmental decision, and the community's lack of information about the potential risks posed to the community. The new context for environmental decision making in the US will be eco-civics, including actual notice of environmental decisions that affect communities, increased knowledge of potential risks to all populations and their exposure routes, and a reengagement with urban form. This is particularly true in land use planning processes. Communities of color are engaging in land use planning processes in a way that helps them from continuing to bear the overwhelming burden of our incomplete and unenforced environmental decisions. Sustainability, and environmental justice are overtaking environmental thinking, and the canaries in our bioregional coal mines are the true pioneers of grassroots sustainability. Although environmental groups in the US have been strong advocates in courts and legislatures for environmental protection, the leadership of the mainstream environmental movement in the US is overwhelmingly white, upper class, educated males. This privileged class has led mainstream environmentalists to exclude concerns of communities of color. This dynamic creates distrust from these communities who are demanding that they speak for themselves. The failure of the US environmental movement to embrace land use planning or zoning in its advocacy or planning efforts has led it to ignore or minimize important decision making forums for communities. The inescapable dynamics of development, expanding right to know laws, and federal targeting of the worst pollution hazards, have brought mainstream environmental activists and environmental regulators squarely into communities of color because race is the best predictor of the sites of controlled and uncontrolled hazardous waste (see United Churches). Sometimes these encounters have been acrimonious. Original siting decisions regarding the placement of hazardous and noxious uses did not consider environmental factors such as hydrology. Siting of these locally unwanted land uses followed the path of least political resistance into politically marginalized communities. The larger the concentration of people of color, the greater the likelihood a hazardous waste site exists. Now, with the increased engagement of communities in environmental decisions we will begin to have some type of social foundation for developing sustainable practices.

The cost of exclusion is a "downward spiral" of depletion of resources, and toxicity to the extent that it changes what it may mean to be human on this planet. If we make decisions about sustainability as we have made other environmental decisions, we will continue to make certain bioregions and human populations sacrifice zones. These are land areas that are forsaken because of the people who live there. This happens because of artificially imposed limits in our thinking about the nature of bioregions, and because of the systematic exclusion of marginalized people and communities in political decision making about land, environment, and even voting. We cannot afford to ignore the U.S. political and economic realities that often drive decisions in our society.

There are many difficult challenges and barriers to implementing concepts of sustainability in the current landscape of environmental decision making. A bridge surmounting these differences may be found in shared perceptions of risks. A number of barriers to sharing perceptions of risk must be overcome in order to implement concepts of sustainability successfully. As a society, we are divided into different groups by race, class, education, age, and gender. Different groups often have different perceptions regarding the degree of risk, the amount of risk that is dangerous, and the amount of risk that is acceptable for them, as well as for others. Some groups in our society may have privileges that remain unacknowledged, and other groups may have suffered generations of life-diminishing environmental injustices. We must overcome our differences and pool our knowledge and perception of risk. The risk posed to an individual or a community may emanate from the workplace, the home, or school. Presently, risk assessment tends to focus on single agent causation. Communities need to know the full range of risk they encounter in their day to day existence, and this requires multiple risk assessment. Unknown risks should be borne equally, or decided on by those that may bear them. New technologies constantly are being developed, and unlike past generations, we must also assess the risk they pose and to whom the risk is the greatest whether the vulnerable are women, children or the elderly. As new vulnerable populations emerge, they provide a new demographic context for assessing risk. Past methods of risk determination aggregate risks and populations in such a way as to disguise actual exposure of any one person or subpopulation. But neither risk assessment nor cost/benefit analysis should assume any longer that the greatest good for the greatest number defines sound environmental policy making.

A fundamental rule of equal treatment necessary for the acceptance of sustainability concepts by everyone is that since we are all equal, no group should involuntarily assume a greater degree of environmental risk. This requires that everyone at least know about the risk, and this in turn requires the community capacity to thoroughly and accurately know about risks to them personally and society as a whole. It is important to individuals to know about the risks posed to themselves, and important that we all know the risks we ask other groups collectively to assume.

The divisions between some groups in our society are very strong, and in some instances, irreconcilable. Perhaps chief among these barriers in contemporary U.S. society is a pervasive lack of trust in government that is uniquely American. This lack of trust in governmental leadership has contributed to the failure of leadership to motivate necessary changes in vision, values, and behavior. The failure of leadership can also be traceable to a failure to broadly embrace the constituencies that make up a popular society and contribute to behavioral and attitudinal realities which have made our society unsustainable at present. This lack of trust is greatest among those most oppressed, and makes their inclusion under government auspices more challenging.

Another core barrier to sustainability in our contemporary society can be found in a lack of identification with place. This is often described as a lack of sense of a community. Ethnocentrism often prevents an identification with a loss of community other than one's own. Cultures that experienced limited mobility, such as African Americans, may identify with a particular neighborhood. People know each other in a neighborhood that lacks mobility because of the greater role of mutual assistance. However, the majoritarian culture suffers as many impediments to mobility and therefore may not be as reliant on mutual assistance, and may not self identify with his or her neighborhood. One of the factors that contributes to the organic ability of indigenous people to express a concern for future generations and for the integrity of their environment may well lie in their identification with place over a period of generations extending both backwards in the past and forward into the future. Contrast this with our contemporary society and its policies encouraging rapid and continuous movement of the labor force. It is very difficult to conduct a dialog that expresses concern for place and future generations across splintered communities, splintered ideologies, splintered ethnicities, and a changing community base. Inadequate notice as to important environmental decisions that affect one's place make it impossible for even long term community residents to meaningfully participate. Added to this barrier of ethnocentrism of place is the whole political economy of land itself. Ownership and control of land is directly related to political and socioeconomic power, not the necessities of a particular bioregion.

Another major barrier to sustainability is the ethos of development and growth, especially as it applies to natural resources. Another barrier to achieving sustainability may well lie in the inability of present day leadership and communities to address the present day effects of historic inequity. This results in continued exclusion from environmental decisions. Finally, a serious barrier to building sustainable communities in contemporary U.S. society may be our heterogeneity of values of identity. These barriers to sustainable development are important because to continue to ignore them will increase risk for already overburdened communities and for everyone in those natural systems.

Environmental Reparations

The general arguments for reparations for African Americans are well developed. Besides the glaring material inequality linked explicitly to slavery and its unremedied injustice, there is a gap in both wealth and income that is structural and that prevent African Americans from meeting present and future needs. It is a sign of the deep and pervasive character of United States racism that many other groups have received reparations and the descendants of slaves have not.

Our premise, supported by nearly four centuries of African experience in the New World, is that the places where our waste has accumulated now has a human face on it. Reparations to some communities may be environmental reparations for an entire region. For example, in a community with a history of dumping toxic and hazardous chemicals in an African American community, the location of those sites is of key importance to a regional water quality program, especially if the wastes have migrated into the water table. Making environmental reparations to that African American community for waste site detection, clean up, adaptive reuse, and environmental monitoring will benefit the water quality of the region. In a city such as Portland, Oregon, the water quality in the Willamette River is such that many returning salmon die when they return to spawn. Water quality issues can benefit everyone, and water quality in urban areas is directly related to cleanup. Who better than the local neighborhood and community to include when tracking waste sites? Underground storage tanks, either never regulated or conveniently forgotten, are remembered by both the environment and the people who have lived, worked, played, and learned there. The location and contents of waste storage and transfer sites are fundamental components to establishing any type of environmental baseline. As waste and population increase as fast as citizen knowledge about risks we can expect a rise in citizen monitoring of the environment and especially of land uses. If we do not develop inclusionary urban environmental planning processes that incorporate urban community monitoring, capacity building, and equal power positions, then we lose the human testimony of our oppression of Nature. We also lose the ability to know the ecosystems that are necessary to sustain all of us.

We propose Environmental Preservation Districts as a form of reparations. Land as reparations, not capital, is not a new idea, as former colonies have recently reasserted these types of claims at the World Conference Against Racism.[5] Parks are separate land uses and often banked as land to develop later and are not adequate. Preservation Districts themselves are not a radical concept, and an entire legal and policy framework at the local, state, and federal level exists to implement them. Environmental Preservation Districts would be modeled on current Historic District land use ordinances. There are over 35,000 historic listings on the US National Register of Historic Places. Federal law requires federal agencies to take historic resources into account in Environmental Impact Statements. Historic District programs are widespread at the state and local level.

Environmental Preservation Districts would ecologically and culturally restore ecosystems and communities, and the purposes and goals that would animate these processes would be community inclusion and precautionary development. US legally articulated social policies with respect to human interests and ecosystem needs in land use planning will require these processes. Environmental Preservation Districts will still increase wealth over time for private property owners. Just like Historic Districts, Environmental Preservation Districts would not allow the property owner to demolish her land so she can put it to a more profitable use, would require her to restore the ecosystem, and would require her to go through an Environmental Review Board similar to the Architectural Review Board required in Historic Districts.

Environmental Preservation Districts would help establish urban environmental baselines, which are sorely missing from US cities. Environmental benefits and burdens of a land use regulation raise questions about the carrying capacity of the land. Just as in a land use plan where build-out occurs when every zone has its maximum allowed density, carrying capacity analyses would examine the build-out of an ecosystem. While it is probably a good policy to know ecosystem capacity, to plan to grow to the point of capacity may violate

---

5   See Itano. The United States withdrew from this conference when the African delegates called upon the United States to make restitution for the slave trade.

precautionary principles. Reparations will help create trust between city and suburb by demonstrating an observable and long lasting commitment to truly end sprawl for all. In this way we can help to eliminate some of the historical bias of environmental decision-making, and begin to make environmental decisions that are truly sustainable over the long term.

The land doesn't lie; it exists in an integral and inescapable relationship with all. The law of the land is not a document that lets us call it ours. The law of the land is a demand for including all beings impacted by past and present acts of environmental degradation. The law of the land is that it be forever wild, and that will be true to the extent people are truly forever free.

>
> ONE WAY TICKET
> [...]
> 'I am fed up
> With Jim Crow laws
> People who are cruel
> And afraid
> Who lynch and run,
> Who are scared of me
> And me of them.
> I pick up my
> life
> And take it away
> On a one-way ticket—
> Gone up North,
> Gone out West
> Gone!
>
> —Langston Hughes

Works Cited

Bullard, Robert D. *Confronting Environmental Racism: Voices from the Grassroots.* Boston, MA: South End Press, 1993.

Cockburn, Andrew. "21st Century Slaves." *National Geographic* 204.3 (September 2003): 2–20.

Dred Scott v. Sandford. 60 U.S. 393 (1856).

Dunbar, Paul Laurence. "To J.Q." *The Complete Poems of Paul Laurence Dunbar.* New York: Dodd, Mead, & Co., 1913. 238.

Elder, P.S. "Sustainability." *McGill Law Journal* 36 (1991): 831.

Hawken, Paul. "Natural Capitalism." *Mother Jones* (March/April 1997): 42 (inset).

—, Amory B. Lovins, and L. Hunter Lovins. *Natural Capitalism: The Next Industrial Revolution.* London: Earthscan, 1999.
Hughes, Langston. "One Way Ticket." *Selected Poems by Langston Hughes.* New York: Vintage, 1974. 177.
Itano, Nicole. "Former Colonies Calling For Reparations." *Christian Science Monitor* 93.198 (9/5/2001): 1 Op, 1c.
Our Common Future: World Commission on Environmental Development. Ed. G. Bruntland. Oxford: Oxford UP, 1987.
Patterson, Orlando. *Freedom.* New York: Basic Books, 1991.
Posner, Richard A. *The Economics of Justice.* Cambridge, MA: Harvard UP, 1981.
—. "Utilitarianism, Economics and Legal Theory." *Legal Studies* 8 (1979): 103-140.
—. "Wealth Maximization Revisited." *Notre Dame Journal of Law, Ethics, and Public Policy* 2 (1985): 85-106.
Riddell, Robert. *Ecodevelopment.* New York: St. Martin's P, 1981.
The Rio Declaration on Environment and Development. U.N. DOC. A/CONF.151/-5/REV. 1 (1992). [Reprinted in 31 I.L.M. 876 (1992)]
The Stockholm Declaration. U.N. Doc. A/CONF. 48/14 & CORR./(1972).
United Churches of Christ Commission for Racial Justice. *Toxic Wastes and Race in the United States.* New York: Public Data Access, 1989.

The Cultural Spaces of Southern California: From Colonial Conquest to Postborder Region

Hellmut Fröhlich

Introduction to the Southland

> LA is a place we should know more about, since it is paradigmatic in some regards, exaggerated in others, and in some ways unique among American cities.
>
> Cuff 28-29

Over the last 25 years, the Los Angeles (LA) region has received increasing attention from urban scholars of various disciplines, including geography, urban planning, sociology, political sciences, and cultural studies. Turning the so-called "Southland" from the "most understudied major city in the United States" (Dear, "Los Angeles" 6) into a paradigm of urban development in the late 20th century, the so-called "LA School of Urban Studies" has addressed a wide range of issues such as the post-Fordist restructuring of the region's industrial agglomeration, LA's role as "global city," the physical structures of its sprawling urban landscape, or the struggles and conflicts inherent to LA's political realms. Among the central topics of urban discourse in/about LA are the ongoing ethnical diversification of the region's increasing population and the resulting complex processes of cultural and spatial reconfigurations.[1]

In this section of my paper I trace the history of cultural-spatial changes in Southern California over the last 150 years as they mirror the different stages of immigration into the region. In LA's colonial epoch, as well as in its most recent development, structural changes in the population have both created struggles over cultural spaces and have triggered new ways of cultural interaction. In recent inquiries into the cultures of Southern California, a "postborder condition" has

---

1   For an introduction to the LA School, see Fröhlich.

been identified that has its origins in the re-latinization of LA. The LA region as "postborder city region" may be regarded as one of the prime examples of a culturally and spatially hybridized metropolis, in which identities that are both "Northern" (U.S.-American) and "Southern" (Latin-American) are formed and find their expression in a complex spatial-cultural dynamic.

The LA region is most commonly defined by the five counties Los Angeles, Orange, San Bernardino, Riverside, and Ventura, which together form the "Los Angeles-Riverside-Orange County Consolidated Metropolitan Statistical Area" (CMSA) used by the U.S. Bureau of Census. With a population of 16.3 million (2000), the LA region is the second-largest metropolis in the U.S., second only to the New York metropolitan area (21.2 million). The recent population development shows a sustained high level of population growth from 1990 to 2003, with LA County adding 1.1 million people (+12.6%) and the LA region growing by almost 19% or 2.76 million [ill. 016]. While LA County continues to add the largest population increase in total numbers, it is the Inland Empire (Riverside and San Bernardino) that grows at the fastest rates of up to 46% since 1990, indicating the shift of the urban edge to the outer periphery of the LA region. Within the last three years since the 2000 Census, the LA region grew by 917.000 people or 5.6%, roughly adding a population the size of Detroit. This increase in population is due to both international immigration and natural increase, and both factors are effective in changing the ethnical composition of LA's population.

LA's role as major agglomeration is largely a result of its strong economic position developed throughout the 20th century. The completion of transcontinental railways, the opening of San Pedro Harbor in 1899, and the water supply delivered to LA from the Sierra Nevada by the Owens Aqueduct since 1913 enabled the development of a large-scale industrial complex in Southern California. Prior to the early 20th century, LA's prime industries had been agriculture (cattle, citrus fruits), tourism and real estate speculation based on a promotional machine marketing LA as Mediterranean heaven for wealthy Midwesterners (Soja 123-127).

The most visible of LA's 20th-century industries took its course in 1909, when the first motion picture was shot in Hollywood. The LA landscape and its climatic benefits soon made Hollywood the pseudonym for U.S. film production and, by 1914, no less then 70 studios had been established in the LA region. The exploitation of LA's oilfields at an industrial scale started in the 1920s and became the initial stimulus for the development of LA's industrial landscape. Petrochemical industries, car assembly plants, and, starting in WW II, the largest military-industrial complex in the U.S. that specialized in aviation and aerospace technology became the leading industrial branches of LA's economy. When the end of the cold war lead to reduced defense-related spending, the region's industrial base had diversified to include a wide range of High-Tech industries, machinery, apparel and other design-oriented manufacturing, and food processing. Besides this still important manufacturing sector, business and private services, especially international trade, health services, education and retail trade provide for a large share of the region's total employment of 6.7 million (1997). With a GDP of $600 billion in 2002, the LA region would rank 11th among national economies, close behind Spain ($655 billion) and Mexico ($636 billion) and well ahead of nations like India ($486 billion), Australia ($399 billion), or Russia ($347 billion) (LAEDC).

An illustration shows the population distribution in the LA region according to the 2000 Census [ill. 017]. It demonstrates the highly differentiated settlement patterns within the region, with zones of very high population density in the central cities such as LA, Long Beach, San Fernando, Santa Ana. Other areas of high density are the San Fernando Valley, the axes connecting downtown LA, Long Beach and northern Orange County, and stretching from LA eastward into the Inland Empire of San Bernardino and Riverside counties. The Inland Empire has recently seen the strongest increase in population together with other areas on the periphery of the LA region such as southern Ventura County, the Santa Clarita area and the desert region of the Antelope Valley, with Palmdale and Lancaster as two of the LA region's fastest growing cities. The settlement patterns in the LA region are in large parts determined by the area's natural landscape: Limited in the West by the Pacific Ocean, the LA basin and San Fernando Valley as central parts of LA's built-up environment are delineated by regional mountain ranges and semi-desert areas. Some of these areas, such as the cañons of the Santa Monica Mountains, are among the most desirable residential areas for the region's upper 10,000, and substantial development has occurred in the semi-desert areas of the Antelope Valley and the Inland Empire. However, other parts of the natural surrounding of the LA basin, like the San Gabriel Mountains or the Santa Ana Mountains on the border of Orange and Riverside counties, still function as natural limits to urban development.

Compared to the history of European urban development, the LA region is a very young agglomeration. Founded in 1791 as Spanish colonial settlement, the City of Los Angeles was initially a small agricultural colony of 44 inhabitants and was placed on the banks of the Los Angeles River a few miles southwest of San Gabriel Mission. When the City of Los Angeles was first surveyed by the U.S. Census in 1850, its population was a mere 2,000; thirty years later, its population had grown very moderately to 11,000. However, even before the first boom of the LA region boosted its population to 250,000 by the year 1900, the ethnic changes and cultural dynamics among its population had resulted in major modifications of the cultural and spatial patterns and practices in Southern California. In the following section, a short overview of the history of immigration into the LA region will provide the framework for a more detailed analysis of the cultural-spatial dynamics of the last 150 years of Southern California's history.

Different People, Different Cultures: Immigration into Southern California

> [...] nowhere can one detect the shape of emerging America better than in L.A., where newcomers [...] have set the region on a new course sure to be followed by other urban areas.
>
> Waldinger/Bozorgmehr 4

As Michael J. Dear notes in "Peopling California," the LA region had been settled by Native Americans for more than 10,000 years, and, by the time of European contact with the Americas, was "occupied by diverse groups of migrants and settlers later referred to as "Indians" (49). Anton Wagner estimates the number of Gabrielino Shoshones settling in the LA area by the time of Spanish contact at 5,000, noting that the benefits of LA's natural landscape had resulted in a comparatively dense settlement of the region (42). In this paper, though, I will omit the long history of Native American settlement in the region and focus on the development that started with the European colonial period. As I discuss below, the colonial conquest of Southern California marks the beginning of a series of demographic restructurings in the region as the earliest and arguably most violent spatial-cultural turning point in LA's modern history.

After the first European contact with present-day California had been made by a Spanish expedition led by Juan Rodríguez Cabrillo in 1542, the territory of Alta California was neglected by the Spanish Crown and experienced what Dear calls "almost two centuries of colonial indifference" ("Peopling California" 49). This indifference ended as Spain reacted to British and French colonial acquisitions in the eastern parts of North America and to Russian expeditions along the American west coast by increasing their interest in using Alta California as buffer state between its holdings in New Spain and rivaling colonial territories.

Beginning with an expedition led by Gaspar de Portolá in 1769, the Spanish established a chain of 21 missions along the "Camino Real," using both missionary influence and military power to co-opt the indigenous people of Alta California. Although Father Junípero Serra, the chronicler of Portolá's expedition, had described the banks of the Los Angeles River as most suitable for settlement and agriculture and thus providing supplies for the nearby San Gabriel Mission, the settlement of Los Angeles did not commence until September 4, 1781. Shortly after a revision of Spanish colonial policies in California had shifted power significantly from the church towards political authorities, Governor Felipe de Neve of Spanish California decreed that the new "Pueblo de Nuestra Señora la Reina de Los Angeles de Porciúncula" be built near present-day Olvera Street in downtown LA. During the Spanish colonial epoch, which ended with Mexican independence in 1822, the LA region, and Alta California in general, remained relatively underdeveloped and experienced only moderate growth. The presence of Spanish missions and military personnel, however, was the driving force for the steady decline of California's Native American population. Characterizing Spanish (and later) Mexican Alta California as a "violent and unruly" colony, Dear points out that open rebellion and out-migration of indigenous groups, as well as negative influences of missionary efforts (relocations, exposure to new diseases, punishment according to colonial law) resulted in a decrease of California's native population from about 300,000 to 100,000 between 1769 and 1846 ("Peopling California" 50).

The transition from Spanish to Mexican rule in 1822 was followed by the first large-scale redistribution of regional real estate in Southern California. Seizing mission lands in accordance with Mexican secularization acts, the Mexican administration did not redistribute land to native groups, but rather sold it into private hands. Hence, the Mexican era in Southern California saw the establishment of large ranches and the formation of a Mexican agricultural elite called "Californios." By the late 1820s, Anglo Americans who immigrated into the LA region started to gain influence in the region, some by marring into Californio ranching dynasties, some by adjusting to Californio culture. In general, however, growing Anglo-American access to power and land was paralleled by increasing tension between newcomers and the established Californio elites. These dynamics continued over the second half of the 19th century, the period in which LA experienced what Soja calls the "WASPing of Los Angeles" (123). The immense surge in regional population—from 20,000 in 1870 to 250,000 by 1900—was mainly due to a "flood of White Anglo-Saxon Protestant American migrants," who were drawn to Southern California from the northeastern states and the Midwest. Soja attributes this first major boom in parts to LA's role as the richest agricultural region in the U.S. by the end of the 19th century, and in parts to the benefits of its Mediterranean climate attracting retirees, tourists, and health-seekers. The most important factors in LA's early boom, however, were the promotional skills of its real estate agents and the effectiveness of LA "boosterism" among its business clite. Land speculators and developers cooperated with municipal officials in advertising the regional attractions throughout the U.S., and contemporary popular literature praising Southern California's beauties added to the urban mythology that "Los Angeles would continue to define the American Dream more than any other real or imagined place" (Soja 126).

For more than 50 years, migration by native-born Whites from the Northeast and Midwest continued to be the dominant force in the steady growth of LA's population. With its Mexican heritage reduced to invisibility and the share of foreign-born residents decreasing to an all-time low reached in 1960, the WASPing of LA's political and economic elites and the absolute majority of its White population had turned LA into an "American" city by the mid-20th century. Although the relatively hospitable climate of race relations and the economic opportunities of LA started to attract substantial numbers of African-

Americans from the South during WW II, LA remained a predominantly White city with an 82% White majority in the 1960 census. The mid-1960s marked a turning point for international immigration into the U.S., and the effects of the Hart-Celler Act passed by Congress in 1965 were most visible in the LA region. After the U.S. Congress had virtually closed the gates for immigrants in 1924, the Hart-Cellar Act of 1965 reopened the U.S. for a large number of international immigrants, and the regulations it provided for immigrants to legally enter the U.S. produced entirely different results than those intended by the advocates of Hart-Cellar (Waldinger/Lee 31-32). Abolishing the old country-of-origin quotas, which had allotted only small quotas to southern and eastern Europe and almost prohibitively small ones to Asia, the Hart-Cellar Act established two main criteria for admission of a substantially increased number of immigrants to the U.S.: family ties to citizens or permanent residents of the U.S., and possession of wanted professional skills. Aiming at Central and Western Europe as major regions of origin for new immigrants, and hoping for a very selective influx of individuals according to workforce considerations, the results of Hart-Celler proved to be quite different. The "new immigration" into the U.S. since 1965 has been dominated by Latin America and Asia as regions of origin and is very heterogeneous with regard to the educational level and occupational status of immigrants (Waldinger/Lee 33-38, 50-53). While immigrants remain urban-bound due to family ties and employment opportunities, LA rather than New York or any other eastern city has been the prime immigrant region of the U.S. for the last four decades. According to the 2000 Census, more than 5 million (30.9%) of LA's 16.4 million residents were foreign-born, with Latin America (62.1%, 3.15 million) and Asia (28.9%, 1.46 million) being by far the dominant regions of origin. The dominant national backgrounds among LA's immigrants is Mexican, which alone contributes about half of the region's foreign-born, and El Salvador and Guatemala, which together comprise another 10% of foreign-born population in LA. Over the last twenty years, the LA region has averaged about 100,000 legal immigrants per year, with LA County adding about 75,000 immigrants annually. Within the last two decades, the mid-1980s and late 1990s saw the relatively weakest influx of legal immigrants into Southern California with 80,000 to 90,000 annually, whereas the early 1990s (about 130,000) and the years since the millennium (150,000 to 160,000) set the records for international immigration into the LA region (California Dept. of Finance, *Legal Immigration*).

The "new" immigration into the Southland is characterized by an enormous degree of heterogeneity regarding the education and professional skills of immigrants. In contrast to previous generations of newcomers to the U.S., some groups of recent immigrants are very likely to acquire managerial or professional occupations, starting at middle-class or even upper-middle class income levels. While this holds especially true for well-educated individuals from Asia or certain Middle Eastern countries, most immigrants from Latin America—both legal and illegal—still face the challenge of starting at the very bottom of the socio-economic scale.

An illustration shows LA region's ethical composition according to the 2000 Census racial categories [ill. 018]. It clearly expresses the fundamental shifts of Southern California's population during the last decades. According to the 1960 Census, the LA region had an 81.9% White majority, with Latinos (9.8%) and Afro-Americans (6.4%) as largest minority groups. Within forty years, this White dominance, which had existed since the mid-19th century, ended as LA's population changed from White majority to what could be called "majority of minorities." The City of LA and LA County are at the forefront of latinization, with a relative Latino majority of 46.5% and 44.6%, respectively, and Whites at under one-third of the total population. For the five-county LA region, Whites and Latinos hold equal shares of about 40%, and Asians (10.3%) have outnumbered Blacks (7.33%) as leading "small minority." Orange, Riverside, and Ventura counties show the most "traditional" ethnic compositions, with an absolute majority of Whites, Latinos at about one-third of the total population, and relatively small African-American communities. Orange County, however, is home of a large Asian-American population, including Little Saigon as the largest cluster of Vietnamese immigrants in the U.S.

The U.S. Census data on major ethnic groups can only provide a first glance of the diversification processes that have reshaped the LA region since 1965. Among the more detailed information provided by the U.S. Census, the data on the languages spoken in everyday use by immigrant populations can be recognized as one indication of the perseverance of ethnic identities among immigrant groups. While the use of native languages is strongest among first-generation immigrants, the development of permanently bilingual immigrant groups of the second and third generations can be linked to increased contact levels between immigrants in the U.S. and contact persons in their countries of origin as well as to the formation of stable immigrant communities in the LA region. The 2000 Census data on language use for the LA region indicates a predominance of English (53%) and Spanish (34%) as major languages, and Asian languages such as Chinese, Tagalog, Korean, and Vietnamese as most important smaller language groups. Although languages other than English and Spanish account for less then 14% of the region's relevant population over five years, the total numbers of individuals speaking these languages in everyday use underline the strength of LA's various ethnic communities. At under 1% of the region's population, language groups such as Armenian (147,000 speakers), Persian (95,000 speakers), German (52,000 speakers), or Arabic (51,000 speakers) still represent substantial ethnic groups with a population of over 50,000 individuals that use their native languages in everyday communication with family and friends [ill. 019].

The changed demographics of the LA region result in complex reconfigurations of the settlement patterns of ethnic groups. While major U.S. cities have long been adequately described as "Chocolate Cities, Vanilla Suburbs," the distribution of ethnic groups in the LA region has developed far beyond the Black-and-White dichotomy of modern city regions. The complex pattern displayed in the illustration [ill. 020] mirrors the profound demographic and spatial changes occurring in the LA region. Showing the strongest ethnic group per census tract in 2000, this illustration [020] indicates a majority of Latinos, Asians, Blacks, or Whites in a given tract, and, by different color shades, reflects the degree of relative or absolute predominance.

The large areas in dark green indicate that census tracts with clear predominance of Whites (>70%) include more expensive low-density outer suburbs and mountain areas. While the Westside of LA (the foothills of Santa Monica Mts.) and the Pacific coast areas remain predominantly White, the central parts of the LA basin stretching from downtown LA to Long Beach and into Orange County are dominated by a non-White population.

The central dynamic of LA's changing ethnic landscape is the growth of its Latino population and the expansion of residential areas that are predominantly Latino. Far beyond the traditional Latino barrio of East LA, residents of Latin American origins are now the dominant ethnic groups in most of LA's central region and in many suburban areas which had only a very small minority population until the 1970s. Especially in the San Fernando Valley, the paradigmatic post-WW II suburb of LA's White middle-class, as well as in parts of the San Gabriel Valley and northern Orange County, traditional White suburban census tracts have changed into ethnically heterogeneous mosaics with absolute Latino majorities. According to James P. Allen and Eugene Turner, the relatively small size of most Latino-dominated tracts indicates the higher population densities and urban character of these areas—a strong indicator for the low- to middle-income economic status of many Latino families (46). This is also true for the areas with a predominantly Black population, which have rapidly decreased in size over the last decades. With the expansion of Latino-dominated areas from East LA into South Central, traditionally Black neighborhoods east of Interstate 110 (e.g. Watts, East Compton) have now turned into areas with clear Latino majorities.

According to the California Department of Finance, this dominant trend in LA's population dynamics will remain constant for a considerable amount of time [ill. 021]. While LA in the 1970s was still a predominantly white region, this situation had been reversed by the turn of the millennium. With a slight decline in the total White population (dropping from 7 to 6.5 million by 2040), the relative position of Whites will continue to weaken within the next decades. By 2040, less than one quarter of LA's population is projected to be White. A similar development is expected for the region's Black community, whereas the total number and relative share of Asian-Americans will continue to increase to 3.8 million or 13.7% respectively. Becoming the absolute majority in the early 2000s, the Hispanic population will continue to grow due to immigration and natural increase over the coming decades and will reach a total number of about 16 million (57.7%) by the year 2040.

This continuous strong increase in Latino population is the latest example in a series of complex cultural and spatial reconfigurations of the LA region. In the following, I will highlight some of the central elements of socio-cultural and spatial dynamics that have continued to reshape Southern California's cultural spaces over the last 150 years.

Conflicting Cultures and Struggles over Spaces in LA

Omitting the long history of indigenous settlement in Southern California, I will first focus on the colonial period, which saw Spanish and Mexican influence in the region last for less than a century before White Anglos gained power in LA. While most of the political structures and the logics of the American land development processes established by White Americans during LA's era as "American" city remain effective, the demographic shifts of LA were instrumental in the creation of new, hybridized forms of cultural processes and in forming a spatial mosaic of ethnic and cultural groups.

Conquering Space: Colonial Strategies in Southern California

> Los Angeles was a tough cowtown.
>
> Modarres 135

The initial conquest of Spanish Alta California was, as indicated above, driven by military interests and missionary efforts. The intention to use California mainly as a buffer state against rivaling colonial territories led to an isolationist policy that prevented non-Spanish civilians from settling in the LA region. The number of Spanish colonists settling in the area was kept small by a discouraging land grant policy based on the central role of the Franciscan missions in seizing land from the native groups and using them as mission estates. Although the Spanish mission system brought with it all the negative effects of European colonization for the native groups that lost many members to diseases or in conflict, or lost control over their territories and were forced to adopt to the "culture" imposed on them, its spatial limitedness left most of California uninfluenced. This limited scope of European hegemony ended soon after Mexican independence in 1822, as the colonial conquest of Southern California was almost completed due to the spatial impact of a simple cultural difference: private property rights.

Within the short period between Mexican independence in 1822 and the 1880s real estate boom, the LA region saw two major shifts in real estate ownership, and, alongside with control over space, shifts in political power and cultural dominance. The first redistribution of land was the result of Mexican secularization acts, which were intended to reduce the influence of the church by seizing mission lands and redistribute them among native groups and colonial settlers (Dear, "Peopling California" 50). While it may not be surprising in retrospect that the initial intention of reinstating the native groups' pre-colonial control over their territories in Southern California was soon to be lost in the practice of selling land to *rancheros*, Wagner notes that a few Native Americans actually were given small parcels near the former San Gabriel mission that were unsuitable to become part of any of the newly established large-scale ranches in the area (56). However, both the Native groups in control of some parcels and the Californio *rancheros* were soon to lose most of their lands after the LA region became part of the U.S. as a result of the U.S.-Mexican War (1846-1848).

The territorial expansion of the U.S. finally reached the "natural boundary" of the Pacific Ocean after the Mexican War, and setting up an "American order" in the new southwestern states followed the same rationale that dominated U.S. expansion throughout the 19th century. As Dear points out, the prosperity of newly incorporated American territories was seen to be closely linked to the ability of authorities to assure the perfect security of land titles (*Postmodern Urban Condition* 103). According to this priority, one of the first measures taken by U.S. authorities after the U.S. Navy had taken control over LA was an accurate land survey of the entire LA region. This survey soon sparked controversy between the new authorities and Californio ranchers, who were often neither capable of delineating, with the same high level of accurateness of the land surveys, the lands granted to them by Mexican authorities, nor to ultimately prove clearly their title to the land. This requirement of the California Land Act of 1851, and the enormous efforts Californios faced in the task of proving their land titles, was one main factor in the decline of the Southern California ranch economy and eventually led to the end of the first Spanish-Mexican period in LA's history. With their land titles constantly subjected to legal battles and their political influence and cultural heritage reduced to marginality, most remaining Spanish-Mexican ranches additionally became victims of a devastating drought during the Civil War and had to face competitors from the San Joaquin Valley. The LA region, however, should soon thereafter experience an unprecedented real estate boom, in which a strikingly "American" cultural logic of space was adopted in Southern California.

Prior to the period of LA's rapid "Americanization" between 1850 and 1890, several distinct stages can be identified in the cultural interpretations of "space" in Southern California. For the native groups who had settled in the LA region, the human species and its natural environment were inseparably connected elements of one holistic eco-cultural system. Some features of the natural environment were used as sources for food and clothing, but even as natural spaces and animals were "used" as resources, they remained primarily spiritual entities with close links to their human counterparts. In a second stage of the cultural interpretation of space, the Spanish authorities regarded Southern California primarily as fulfilling military purposes, and their native populations were turned into subjects of Christianization. In many regions of the Spanish empire, colonial territories were also used as natural resources. Colonies other than Spanish California served as sources of valuable goods such as precious stones and metals or spices and were thus seen as a source of wealth for the crown and for privileged individuals.

The notion of a primarily private utilization of space started with the Mexican system of land grants to Californio ranching dynasties. However, their system of extensive cattle ranching left the natural landscapes of the LA region largely untouched, and cattle, not the land it grazed on, was the focus of business and the main commodity of the period. The "Americanization" of the cultural logic of spaces initially added to the Mexican privatization of real estate the idea of land speculation as a major branch of LA's regional economy. Before LA boosters were successful in realizing major infrastructure projects and in attracting industrial enterprises to the area, a real estate boom hyped-up by developers and officials turned the natural and cultivated landscapes of Southern California into a commodity to be sold as the Californian version of the American Dream. Initiated as the first Anglo-American settlers gained influence in the LA region by the 1840s, the cultural logic of space as commodity and the mechanisms of LA's subdivision and housing industry as established in the first real estate boom of the 1880s remain effective until today. However, both the disastrous ecological impacts—as discussed by Davis in his ecological history of LA, *Ecology of Fear* (1998)—and the social and political implications of LA's spatial logic have been increasingly addressed by academic criticism and became subject of political controversy.

Spaces and Cultures in the "American" City

> Obviously the poly-centered complexity of the contemporary system of elites is no longer susceptible to the diktat of any single dynasty or Mr Big.
>
> Davis, *City of Quartz* 101

LA's period as an "American city" saw continuing struggles over space throughout most of the 20th century. On the one hand, large-scale urban development projects and the formation of LA's sprawling post-WW II suburban landscape can be analyzed with regard to their inherent cultural and political dimensions. These spatial politics of "white privilege" can, on the other hand, be contrasted with the socio-spatial dynamics originating in LA's central city areas. Many different strands of "oppositional" cultural and political practices have developed in the minority-dominated areas of LA's inner city areas. They range from incidents of civil unrest like the 1965 Watts riots to the formation of a variety of community activism organizations addressing issues of concern for LA's marginalized groups.

The interpretation of land in an urbanizing area as a commodity was brought to the industrial scale in LA as urbanization became dominated by large-scale urban development projects. To argue that the notion of LA-style urban development as largely "unplanned" series of chaotic and incremental urban developments is seriously shortsighted, Hise's *Magnetic Los Angeles* and Cuff's *Provisional City* illustrate that large-scale urban development projects were results of a close cooperation between city planning agencies and housing developers rather than "chaotic" sprawl. A first major boom of housing projects with thousands of single-family houses was realized during WW II when housing companies like Marlow-Burns or Kaiser Community Homes developed and marketed sites in close proximity to the locations of defense and aircraft industries, such as Westchester, Westside Village, and Toluca Wood (Hise 138). After WW II, the continuing growth of LA's industrial agglomeration and the financial benefits for veterans buying homes led to a massive expansion of the housing economy in LA's suburban areas. Locations in the San Fernando Valley, northern Orange County, and the eastern parts of LA County were developed at an astonishing pace. In many of these projects, several square-miles of farmland had to be converted into small cities of up to 5,000 single-family homes, supermarkets, schools, and recreational facilities within a few years. Such achievements were possible only by using an integrated and fully industrialized development and construction scheme. A single developer would acquire the entire lot, negotiate the master plan and infrastructure construction with city authorities, construct the pre-fabricated standardized homes and sell them through an aggressive marketing machine to home-seekers.

While the cultural logic of urban space as commodity was perfected during this era, the social politics of early post-WW II suburbanization remained relatively simple. The target group for standardized suburban homes were white middle- and upper-class citizens, who sought to realize the suburban American dream of a tranquil living environment, away from the crowdedness of inner-city residential areas, the industrial zones of the central city, and, in many cases, away from the higher taxes of the city. This latter consideration was central to the formation and political activism of homeowners' associations, which Davis regards as the "most powerful 'social movement' in contemporary Southern California" (*City of Quartz* 153). Especially during the mid-1950s, these groups of affluent homeowners were instrumental in advocating the incorporation of small suburban communities, who could contract out many municipal services with LA County, thus benefiting from economies of scale in public services and, at the same time, being able to keep their taxes low. Following the incorporation of Lakewood in 1954 as first "minimal city" or "city by contract," 25 suburban communities in LA County were incorporated by 1960. While arguments of public services efficiency were central in the public discourse about the minimal cities, Miller identifies another central motivation: the intention of homeowners to keep their tax payments low and to secure the values of their homes by keeping their communities "homogeneous." Thus, the spatial politics of many suburban areas focused on the homogeneity of race, class, and income status, contributing to a strict separation between white and minority residential areas. In addition to these new communities, other measures such as discriminatory zoning ordinances, the exclusion of minorities as potential buyers by housing developers, and the enormous lobbying influence of affluent homeowners' associations resulted in a highly segregated pattern of residential areas by the 1960s.

The period of the 1950s and 1960s was also marked by efforts of city planning authorities to address the problems of neglected inner-city areas with large-scale urban renewal projects. Often resulting in the displacement of large numbers of low-income and immigrant residents, this attitude of simply erasing urban "problem areas," and the fact that some of the most intensely debated renewal projects in LA failed to create dwelling units available for the displaced groups, contributed to the heated social and political atmosphere of the mid-1960s. Among LA's urban renewal projects, the Chavez Ravine and Bunker Hill projects stand out with regard to the intensity of public debate they sparked and their symbolic character for LA's treatment of space.

Chavez Ravine was an immigrant community in the hills north of downtown LA, a substandard housing area clearly categorized by official standards as urban slum. Records and photographs about life in Chavez Ravine where a large Mexican community lived together peacefully with various other groups of recent immigrants tell a different story of a poor, but stable community with strong family and neighborhood ties and functioning social networks (Cuff 272-279; Normark). The initial plan for Chavez Ravine put forward by the City Planning Department sought to replace the slum with 3,360 units of public housing on a 254 acre site to be renamed "Elysian Park Heights." This plan soon became the subject of intense opposition from a coalition of anti-public housing interest groups including private developers, the *LA Times*, the Chamber of Commerce, and homeowners' associations like CASH (Citizens Against Socialist Housing). Interpreting the use of tax money for the creation of adequate housing for lower-income groups as a "socialist" policy, and fearing the higher population densities of the proposed large-scale housing development could negatively impact real estate values and taxes, the coalition finally reached their goal and the plan to start construction of public housing on the already virtually cleared Chavez Ravine site was dropped in 1953 after two years of intense political battles. Ironically enough, the City of LA voters agreed in 1958 to a deal giving a 315-acre Elysian Park Heights site along with $4.7 million worth of infrastructure to Brooklyn Dodgers' owner Walter O'Malley in exchange for the nine-acre Wrigley Field. Instead of using public money to the benefit of low-income groups by replacing substandard homes with over 3,000 units of public housing, the city used tax money to attract a professional, privately-owned baseball team.

Similar conflicts arose from the Bunker Hill project approved by the LA city council in 1954. In this case, the neighborhood in which 10,000 people, mainly poor people of color, were replaced was in close proximity to downtown LA and consisted of dilapidated and subdivided Victorian homes. The City of Los Angeles Community Redevelopment Agency (CRA) played a central role in the Bunker Hill redevelopment and similar projects. Although community redevelopment was the central mission of CRA, which should have included housing, economic development, and the creation of new jobs for all qualification levels, many of CRA's large-scale projects resulted in massive displacement of residents and mainly catered to downtown business interests. The Bunker Hill project was especially remarkable in that it not only erased the living environment for 10,000 low-income people, but it also used public funds to create some of downtown LA's corporate citadels which now form part of the "Fortress LA." The area's former residents remain excluded from both the employment "created" on Bunker Hill and, by physical, regulative, and mental barriers created by the downtown lobby, from the urban spaces that once were their neighborhood.

The perceived injustices in many events and projects of LA's urban development throughout the 20th century have not remained unopposed by those groups suffering from LA's politics of space. Unfortunately, the most violent forms of opposition, such as the 1965 Watts riots or the civil unrest following the 1992 Rodney King case, dominate the collective memory and imagination of "struggles over urban spaces in LA." Together with the media-driven images of LA's South Central as a paradigmatic late-20th century mega-ghetto of gang crime, drug trafficking, and open street warfare, the violent explosions of collective aggression form a powerful but highly inadequate and selective meta-image of LA.

Throughout the Southland, various grassroots and non-profit organizations have created a vital source of community activism addressing issues of social and spatial justice, i.e. injustice. One of the initial movements formed in the late 1970s to mid-1980s in South

Central and East LA, where plans to construct waste incinerating plants added to the already heightened concerns of local residents about the concentration of hazardous industrial plants. The keyword "environmental justice" pointed to the fact that residents of lower-income and immigrant neighborhoods were exposed to air, water, and soil pollution to substantially higher degrees than Whites. Not only the placement of new hazardous facilities, but also the structural dynamics of "White privilege" that allowed Whites to move farther away from industrial zones to suburban areas at a time when suburban living was almost exclusively available to Whites contribute to what is called "environmental racism," which, of course, raised strong opposition among community activists. With the post-Fordist restructuring of LA's industrial base greatly reducing stable blue-collar employment in the region, the focus of new social movements has shifted from single-purpose agendas to a broader horizon based on the idea of spatial justice. The new social movements advocate better low-income housing, improved educational and job opportunities for inner-city youths, better public transportation for those unable to afford a car, and propagate ways to include the millions of non-citizens in the political discourses of LA. Analyzing the "Lived Spaces" of LA after the 1992 civil unrest, Soja concludes that new forms of community mobilizations are likely to play a central role in the reformulation of LA's politics of space (407-415). Although their present political influence may still be limited, Soja hopes that new social movements will have the potential to achieve a more responsible political representation of the LA region's large working poor and marginalized immigrant populations. While the future will show whether or not LA moves towards greater spatial justice—equality in individual opportunities regardless where one lives—the marginalized groups among which new social movements frequently emerge have been the central focus of some of the most interesting analyses of the new cultural spaces in Southern California, some of which will be discussed in the following section.

The New Cultural Spaces of Southern California

> Our belief is that cosmopolitanism and hybridity are the constitutive elements of the postborder condition.
>
> Dear/Leclerc 10

Architectural critic Charles Jencks, in his examination of LA-style architecture, identified LA's immense heterogeneity as its most important characteristic. Besides its natural landscape, it is mainly the diversification of ethnic groups and cultural identities that leads Jencks to call LA a "heteropolis," a place where heterogeneity of people and cultures is appreciated and reflected in architecture (46). The LA region has over the last four decades become a heterogeneous spatial mosaic, in which traditional notions of the social urban makeup have become as obsolete as the concept of assimilation. Although LA's suburban development in the first post-WWII decades resulted in the typical "bipolar" separation of white suburbs from the predominantly minority inner city areas, the recent processes of ethnic and socio-economic diversification have turned LA into a spatial mosaic, a city of enclaves. This process of diversification and heterogeneity has two main effects: among many residents, increased diversity and spatial proximity to "the others" leads to increased feelings of insecurity and threat. Thus, many enclaves such as gated communities, shopping malls, office buildings or downtown plazas are designed to form spaces protected from the allegedly dangerous outside. Second, the enormous ethnic diversification of LA's population has created a multiplicity of cultural spaces, among which the latinization of Los Angeles has received the highest attention by urban scholars.

The last two decades of urban development witnessed what Davis calls the formation of "Fortress LA" (*City of Quartz* 220-263). In reaction to the perceived levels of violence and crime in LA, private residences and businesses as well as "public" buildings and spaces increasingly try to seal off a protected inner space from the "threats" on the outside. Although LA, as Steven Flusty notes in *Building Paranoia*, has never had public spaces in the European sense of one or few common urban arenas for social interaction, cultural expression and political activity, the new division between private spaces and the dangerous outside reveals a new dimension of spatial paranoia (12-

15). This is most drastically visible in the increase of gated communities in the LA region. Traditionally a hallmark of very few residential areas for the upper 10,000, the "gatedness" of residential developments—from medium-range two bedroom apartments to luxurious mansions—has become a selling factor in the real estate and housing market for almost all income levels.

In the business districts of downtown LA or in one of LA's "edge cities" the tendency towards the privatization of space was dominated by the creation of "corporate citadels," i.e. office buildings with sophisticated surveillance technology and private security that are more or less autonomous from their urban environment. While many of these citadels offer recreational spaces for their white-collar workforce in internal or rooftop plazas, some have outdoor plazas that form a very specific kind of public space. These plazas form quasi-public spaces (Flusty, "Thrashing Downtown"; Davis, *City of Quartz* 226-236). Though accessible to all potential users, these private spaces are regulated by codes of conduct defining the proper uses accepted in these plazas. The codes enforced by private and public security personnel result in the exclusion of many "disturbing" groups of individuals, including the homeless population of downtown LA, skaters, youths, street musicians, or even tourists unfamiliar with the codes of conduct.

The "New Plaza" [ill. 022] illustrates the proliferation of another type of quasi-public sphere: the state-of-the-art combination of shopping, entertainment, and dining for LA's suburban consumers. With shopping mall architects adopting some of the stylistic principles of new urbanism, village-style shopping malls grow more and more similar to what pedestrian areas in European cities might look like. Their version of a public sphere, however, remains strictly regulated by "codes of conduct" and controlled by security guards. The chances of the individual to participate in this quasi-publicity are determined by a person's ability or willingness to consume, and by the willingness to accept the fact that security-oriented design has turned many urban settings into worlds of surfaces and facades.

The cultural logics of a "built paranoia" are contrasted by a variety of cultural and spatial dynamics forming "outside" of the post-public spaces of shopping malls and gated communities. Urban scholars of the LA School have addressed various cultural phenomena among the region's heterogeneous ethnic minority groups in the wake of the so-called "cultural turn" that geography and other disciplines central to urban inquiry have experienced since the 1990s. Structural analysis of the impacts of immigration into Southern California used to address issues such as residential patterns of recent immigrants, language usage, educational attainment, or criminal activity among immigrants. Another major focus of structure-oriented work on LA's immigrants is their integration into the official and informal labor markets, occupational strategies and niches, and the economic effects of immigrant businesses (e.g. Waldinger/Bozorgmehr; López-Garza/-Diaz). Closely related to the socio-economic situation of the immigrant communities—and mostly focusing on low- and middle-income Latin American and Asian immigrants—are studies of the social policy issues related to the large number of recent immigrants.

More recently, these approaches to the ethnic diversification of LA have been supplemented by an increasing body of literature dedicated to the everyday cultures of Asian and Latin American immigrants. In the following paragraphs, I shall discuss three approaches to the investigation of everyday cultures that have been pursued by urban scholars of the LA School over the last couple of years, with a special emphasis on the discussion of the latinization of LA's cultural spaces.

First, several authors have focused on various aspects of youth culture among immigrant youngsters. Some central elements of a hybridized Latino-American spatial identity can be traced in clothing styles or the Chicano/a music scene, in the variation on American car cult in Latino youths' low-rider culture, or in Latino comics such as Lalo Alcaraz' *L.A. Cucaracha* (Leclerc et al.). This formation of a territorial and collective group identity through self-stylization and group rites is also the main focus of the studies about street gangs in the LA region (Maxson/Klein; Vigil). Mirroring the difficulties of ethnic communities in everyday life, the street socialization of youngsters in their gang replaces families and schools as central institution of youth socialization. Forcing their young members into a system of "multiple marginality," i.e., outside educational institutions, labor markets, sometimes even outside both legality and their families, street gangs often remain the central means by which a member relates to the social and spatial environment (Vigil 8-17). By their explicitly territorial character, that is, by the fact that street gangs are organized spatially by claiming and defending their "turf," gangs are also central to the ways their members as well as other youths experience the urban landscape—the segmented geography of gang turfs defines which areas are safe, neutral, or off limits for gang members and other youths alike.

Besides the special situation of immigrant youths trying to adjust to and, at the same time, recreating the cultural and spatial settings of LA, a second group of scholars deals with everyday cultural-spatial changes initiated by LA's latinization. James Rojas' contribution to *La Vida Latina en L.A.*, for example, analyzes the differences in the use of urban space between Anglo LA and Latino East LA. He discusses how neighborhood interaction is facilitated in East LA by the use of movable furniture on the sidewalks, or how murals illustrate the history of Latino immigrants and of political opinions or religious beliefs. Using the example of the spatial arrangements of the front yards of residences, Rojas also shows how fundamental the social implications of cultural differences in the use of urban space can be. While the typical suburban home of Anglo LA has a lawn without fence out front, thus relying of the front door as threshold between private and public spheres, the typical Latino arrangement has a front yard with a fence determining a privacy-publicity dividing line close to the sidewalk. This spatial arrangement allows for the enclosed yard, on the one hand, to be used as private realm designed according to the residents' taste and ideas. On the other hand, the fence functions as a "social catalyst" as it becomes the central social meeting place for neighborly chats and the like. A wide array of topics adds to the depiction of the vitality and scope of LA's everyday re-latinization. The influx of Latin American immigrants initiated changes in every aspect of urban life, ranging from the resurgence of (Latin American) Catholicism as major denomination in LA through the founding of a large Spanish media conglomerate redefining the imagery of Latino America to the replacement of the Americanized Mission-style architecture of LA's villas by Mexican vernacular architecture of Mexican-owned homes.

Finally, the most recent scholarly contributions to understanding the cultural-spatial changes triggered by LA's re-latinization investigate forms of cultural production such as poems, TV formats, film, music, painting and sculptures as well as theater pieces (Dear/Leclerc). In all these forms of artistic expression, Latino artists create representations and re-interpretations of life in Southern California, but they not only reflect the conditions prevalent in the metropolis LA, but they also redefine them. As opposed to the "hard" facts of the U.S.-Mexican border as a barrier between the First and Third Worlds, the "soft borders" of cultural identification between North and South have become increasingly fuzzy and permeable. The constant to-ing and fro-ing of migrants, tourists, goods, capital, and personal interactions between Mexico and Southern California have generated a specific version of cosmopolitanism, making cultural hybridity the central feature of personal identifications and artistic expressions.

Underlying all approaches to everyday (Latino or immigrant) cultures in contemporary LA is the notion that LA has entered a postborder urban condition. With millions of residents who have developed a cultural identity "in-between" the poles of "America" and "the other" (predominantly "the South"), with Spanish being the second official language of LA, and with the perspective of turning into a clearly Latino-dominated metropolis within the next decades, Los Angeles has definitively experienced the end of its period as a traditional "American" city by now. Despite political struggles, economic hardships, and structural discrimination recent Latino immigrants as well as U.S.-born Chicanos/as still have to face, the demographic changes and cultural dynamics of LA strongly indicate a powerful continuing latinization for LA and probably for most of urban America. In the case of Los Angeles, it is a path ahead into the region's Spanish-Mexican history. Thus, the cultural and spatial configurations of Southern California's metropolis are about to be profoundly redefined once again.

Works Cited

Allen, James P., and Eugene Turner. *Changing Faces, Changing Places—Mapping Southern Californians*. Northridge: The Center for Geographical Studies, 2002.
California Department of Finance. *E-1 City/County Population Estimates, with Annual Percent Change*. Sacramento, 2003. Dec. 03. 2003
  <http://www.dof.ca.gov/HTML/DEMOGRAP/E-1text.htm>.
California Department of Finance. *Legal Immigration to California by County, Federal Fiscal Year 1984–2002*. Sacramento 2003. Dec. 05, 2003
  http://www.dof.ca.gov/HTML/DEMOGRAP/LegImmCounty01.htm.

California Department of Finance. *Race/Ethnic Population with Age and Sex Detail, 1970–2040*. Sacramento, 1998. Sept. 22, 2003 http://www.dof.ca.gov/HTML/DEMOGRAP/Race.htm
Cuff, Dana. *The Provisional City*. Berkeley: University of California Press, 2000.
Davis, Mike. *City of Quartz—Excavating the Future in Los Angeles*. New York: Vintage Books, 1992.
—. *Ecology of Fear—Los Angeles and the Imagination of Disaster*. New York: Metropolitan Books, 1998.
Dear, Michael J. "Los Angeles and the Chicago School: Invitation to a Debate." *City and Community* 1 (2002): 5-32.
—. "Peopling California." *Made in California. Art, Image, and Identity, 1900–2000*. Ed. Stephanie Barron et al. Los Angeles: Los Angeles County Museum, 2000. 49-63.
—. *The Postmodern Urban Condition*. Oxford: Blackwell, 2000.
—, and Gustavo Leclerc. Introduction. *Postborder City: Cultural Spaces of Bajalta California*. Ed. Michael J. Dear and Gustavo Leclerc. New York: Routledge, 2003. 1-30.
Flusty, Steven. *Building Paranoia: The Proliferation of Interdictory Space and the Erosion of Spatial Justice*. Forum Publication 11. West Hollywood: Los Angeles Forum for Architecture and Urban Design, 1994.
—. "Thrashing Downtown: Play as Resistance to the Spatial and Representational Regulation of Los Angeles." *Cities* 17 (2000): 149-158.
Fröhlich, Hellmut. *Learning from Los Angeles—Zur Rolle von Los Angeles in der Diskussion um die postmoderne Stadt*. Beiträge zur Stadt- und Regionalplanung 5. Bayreuth: Universität Bayreuth, Abteilung Raumplanung, 2003.
Hise, Greg. *Magnetic Los Angeles—Planning the Twentieth-Century Metropolis*. Baltimore: Johns Hopkins University Press, 1997.
Jencks, Charles. "Hetero-Architecture and the L.A. School." *The City—Los Angeles and Urban Theory at the End of the Twentieth Century*. Ed. Allen J. Scott and Edward W. Soja. Berkeley: University of California Press, 1996. 47-75.
LAEDC—Los Angeles County Economic Development Corporation. *2003–2004 Economic Forecast and Industry Outlook, Midyear Update*. Los Angeles: LAEDC, 2003. Dec. 05, 2003. http://laedc.info/pdf/Forecast-2003-07.pdf
Leclerc, Gustavo, Raul Villa, and Michael J. Dear, eds. *La Vida Latina en L.A.—Urban Latino Cultures*. Thousand Oaks: Sage, 1999.
López-Garza, Marta, and David R. Diaz, eds. *Asian and Latino Immigrants in a Restructuring Economy—The Metamorphosis of Southern California*. Stanford: Stanford UP, 2001.
Maxson, Cheryl L., and Malcolm W. Klein. "'Play Groups' No Longer—Urban Street Gangs in the Los Angeles Region." *From Chicago to L.A.—Making Sense of Urban Theory*. Ed. Michael J. Dear. Thousand Oaks: Sage, 2002. 239-266.

Miller, Gary J. *Cities by Contract—The Politics of Municipal Incorporation.* Cambridge: MIT Press, 1981.

Modarres, Ali. "Putting Los Angeles in Its Place." *Cities* 15 (1998): 135-147.

Normark, Don. "Chávez Ravine." *La Vida Latina en L.A.—Urban Latino Cultures.* Ed. Leclerc, Gustavo, Raul Villa, and Michael J. Dear. Thousand Oaks: Sage, 1999. 19-22.

Rojas, James. "The Latino Use of Urban Space in East Los Angeles." *La Vida Latina en L.A.—Urban Latino Cultures.* Ed. Leclerc, Gustavo, Raul Villa, and Michael J. Dear. Thousand Oaks: Sage, 1999. 131-138.

Soja, Edward W. *Postmetropolis—Critical Studies of Cities and Regions.* Oxford: Blackwell, 2000.

Vigil, James Diego. *A Rainbow of Gangs—Street Cultures in the Mega-City.* Austin: U of Texas P, 2002.

Wagner, Anton. *Los Angeles—Werden, Leben und Gestalt der Zweimillionenstadt in Südkalifornien.* Schriften des Geographischen Instituts der Universität Kiel 3. Kiel: Geographisches Institut der Universität Kiel, 1935.

Waldinger, Roger, and Mehdi Bozorgmehr. "The Making of a Multicultural Metropolis." *Ethnic Los Angeles.* Ed. Roger Waldinger and Mehdi Bozorgmehr. New York: Russell Sage Foundation, 1996. 3-37.

Waldinger, Roger, and Jennifer Lee. "New Immigrants in Urban America." *Strangers at the Gate—New Immigrants in Urban America.* Ed. Roger Waldinger. Berkeley: U of California P, 2001. 30-79.

Simulated Safaris:
Reading African Landscapes in the U.S.

Kirk A. Hoppe

> In a tropical landscape one's eye takes in everything
> except human beings [...]. He is the same colour as
> the earth, and a great deal less interesting to look at.
>
> George Orwell (189-190)

There is a telling politics to George Orwell's observation that Westerners see Africa as landscape without people. This is certainly true in the present day U.S. where every year millions of people spend hundreds of millions of dollars to drive their own cars or take amusement park rides through pretend African lands stocked with African wildlife. In the last 20 years the simulated African adventure industry has exploded into a cultural and financial powerhouse that plays a central role in tourism in the U.S. and in defining what Africa means to millions of North Americans. These carefully structured controlled spaces produce profits and generate meanings and politics that legitimize and naturalize those profits. Corporations market these spaces as both exciting and educational, in a term from their own publicity, as "edutainment." According to safari park advertisements, tourists will learn about animals in nature, and as animal nature reflects human nature, they will learn about themselves. And drawing on the cultural currency of wildlife conservation, park promotions argue that for visitors to participate in Africa edutainment is for them to participate in a real way in the global politics of protecting African wildlife.

I am interested in a common cultural sequence of experiences with African animals in the U.S. that begins locally with children and their parents watching the animated Disney film *The Lion King* at home or in theaters and consuming in various other forms the mass marketed images and ideas from this film and other animal documentaries. Lured by the ideological meanings of African animals, families then travel to drive-through African safari parks and African animal amusement parks within the U.S. to consume "the real thing." I argue that in these filmic and tourist spaces, people do indeed participate in global politics. By naturalizing human behavior and anthropomorphizing animal behavior in film and in parks, these corporate texts reflect, generate, and legitimize specific hierarchies of race, class, gender, and nation that reinforce global order and corporate power. This essay explores some of the relationships between public experiences of corporate edutainment and the ideological meanings of African wildlife encounters in simulated safaris in the contemporary U.S.

I. Ecotourism and the Personal Politics of African Wildlife

The colonial and postcolonial politics of nature conservation and ecotourism intersect in powerful ways through the African safari. A component of modernity is the construction of ur-essential nature as separate from, alienated from, and threatened by modernity itself. Modern men and women invent, recover and defend the authentic natural self supposedly lost through processes of modernization by commodifying and accessing authentic nature as external object (Wang 46-71). According to this process, we know our authentic selves better by experiencing and understanding nature. Urban life and office work defeminizes modern women and demasculinizes modern men by alienating them from processes of production and reproduction and thereby from themselves. So modern people seek to reconnect with their human nature by hiking or canoeing through unchanging and essential natural places. The production and consumption of ecotourism is then only possible in a world where global culture fetishizes and commodifies nature both as ahistorical eternal truth and as truth threatened by history (see Bandy). Accordingly, western discourses about nature conservation present access to authenticity in nature as a human right to self-knowledge, and the protection of nature as a global civic obligation to the eternal real.

While the ideological power of accessing nature operates on an experiential level, a correct understanding and conserving of nature rests on the ideological meanings of modern science. The twentieth-century shift in the history of safaris in Africa from elite colonialist hunting trips to journeys for the drawing, filming, counting, and observing of animals in nature reflects a gendering, professionalization, and empowerment of natural science. Ideologically, modern people present and understand science as by definition not exploitative but impartial, absolute and humanitarian as it serves the greater human good simply by revealing universal truth; it is non-ideological (Pratt 38-39). By embracing nature conservation, people imagine that they remove themselves from the aggression, violence and imbalances of current global relationships, and that their actions and intentions become located within the universal moral good of keeping nature "natural." The culling, darting, capturing, measuring, and doctoring of animals that conservationists do to African animals reflects the tough paternalism of the white man's burden to keep the natural order in order. Positioning themselves as a naturally dominant and scientific group, Westerners give themselves the global obligation to protect African animals.

The politics of Western viewings of African animals links ideas of social Darwinism, global order, and animal conservation. Since the 1930s, when paleoanthropologists began to locate the origins of the human species in East Africa, a "dawn of man" in Africa discourse centers African nature as ur-nature and emphasizes the idea of African animal nature as a reflection of timeless and pure primordial human nature. Drawing from this discourse that all people are part of nature, cultural texts about nature naturalize political relationships as "human nature" by anthropomorphizing animal behavior. Hierarchies of animal nature, for example, in relationships between predators and prey and in territorial dominance, reflect and legitimize colonialism and capitalism as natural. Dominant male behavior, male competition, marking, defending and patrolling territory, animal family groups, and maternal "instinct" prove what is moral and immoral and what is natural and unnatural, in human interactions. Texts about animals present animals acting out true human politics as men and women, parents and children, soldiers and civilians living together (naturally) as families, communities, races, and nations.

In American popular culture, the conservationist arguments about bio-diversity also intersect with political ideas about the values of racial and cultural diversity. The problematic politics of the "family of man" and the "global village" extend to a "family of all living things." In this cross-species system, animal species have distinct and equally legitimate race, culture, and class identities and by extension certain human rights—to life, liberty, and the pursuit of happiness perhaps. People have obligations to promote and assure these human/animal rights, and a human right to act on these obligations. Conservation texts present species extinction as a form of genocide. The idea of human genocide inscribes culture as race as sub-species identity. Thus genocidal violence against Armenians, Jews, Tutsi, and Palestinians are particularly abhorrent historical examples of human rights' crimes against humanity not just because they are racist mass murders but also because they reduce species diversity. Likewise, the extinction of a species of animals takes on overtones of race murder and human rights' violations both against the animal group and against us all.

So more than just a potentially revolutionary and revitalizing inward journey, the value and power of the safari are that it is imagined sacrifice for the good of the human and animal family. The eco-tourist is advocating and demonstrating for racial diversity and correct race relations. As modernity has demasculinized modern men, the African safari promises to remasculinize men through visions of primeval and primal nature and the masculine struggles necessary to access and protect this nature. As modernity has defeminized modern women, exposure to African animals can refeminize women through the witnessing and midwifing of the eternal maternal. The African eco-safari has cultural meaning as a politically and personally constructive leisure activity. The safari reconfirms the essential natural self of eco-tourists as they can see and be part of imagined real nature. It is a journey of global self-discovery across time and space. And it should be a challenging journey. The eco-safari combines Western values of physical fitness, environmental education, action, and adventure (Bandy 554). The money spent is politically moral money transforming tourists into scientist-adventurer-activists working for the good of themselves and for the good of the world even while on vacation.

II. Disney's *Lion King* and the Animal Order of Naturalized Capitalism

An extremely popular filmic depiction of African space is a touchstone in the edutainment industry. The economic success and cultural power of the 1994 animated Disney film *The Lion King* both adds to the cultural meanings and financial success of other displays of African animals in North America and reflects the ideological meanings of African nature for North Americans. Because the film is a parable of patriarchy, heterosexual monogamy, and racial hierarchy, and because images and ideas from the film are so often directly referenced in African-animal parks in North America, I see *The Lion King* as often the initial and at-home ideological partner to the drive-through safari parks and African animal amusement parks discussed later in this essay. The film is a powerful text for children and their parents, which, along with footage from the Discovery Channel and National Geographic, reinforces the meanings of the imaginary African spaces in Disney's Animal Kingdom and Busch Gardens in Florida and Wild Safari Animal Park in New Jersey.

Marketed as a family film, *The Lion King* is a phenomenon. In 2003 it was the 10th most successful film ever in terms of gross ticket receipts worldwide, the most successful animated film and the best selling video in home entertainment history.[1] This does not include Disney profits from video sales of the original film, from two direct video sequels (*Simba's Pride* in 1998 and *Hakuna Matata* in 2004) and from Lion King clothes, toys, games, and music recordings. There are web-site organizations where people share their Lion King-inspired fan-art, Lion King-inspired fan-fiction, and Lion-King inspired fan-music.[2] Fifteen million people worldwide have seen a Broadway musical version of the story since it opened in 1997.[3] Characters and themes from the film provide the organizing structure to Disney's Animal Kingdom in Orlando, Florida, with its central "Tree of Life" and "Rafiki's Education Center." The Lion King Celebration was the daily afternoon parade from 1994–1997 in Disneyland with no human characters but only, as one reviewer put it, animals dressed in "African-themed tribal costumes" (Lancaster). Recent generations of working and middle class children and their parents, influenced by this overlapping nexus of images and sounds, know the Swahili words *simba* and *hakuna matata*. Children wear pictures of Simba on their t-shirts at T-ball. Their parents carry *hakuna matata* coffee cups to boardroom meetings.

The Lion King depicts distinct kinds of African natural spaces each with corresponding moral orders. There are no people in the film or references to people thus rendering Africa a purely animal realm. The animal characters represent natural and unnatural gender, class,

---

1 See "The Lion King Production Notes."
2 See "The Lion King Fan-Art Archive."
3 See "The Lion King WWW Archive."

and ethnic relationships and the correct triumphs over the incorrect to assure peace and productivity (see Gooding-Williams; Morton). Natural moral order is based on the patriarchal heterosexual nuclear family (the awkward polygamy of the lion king notwithstanding) with political power passed down from elite family father to son. The space of utopian peace and beauty is maintained through the rule literally on high of lions over all other animal species. The grateful and content subjects of this society include the lions' herbivore prey that graze under blue skies in green well-watered pastures.

In contrast, the hyena mob represents the rising power of the boneyard ghetto. Hyena voices are done in lower class and non-white race specific tones by Whoopi Goldberg and Cheech Marin. The hyenas live in a place of poverty, hunger, violence, and environmental disorder. This underclass mob, led by a fey lion pretender to the throne named Scar, kill the lion king and bring the ghetto to the suburbs. The revolution ushers in an era of environmental devastation, carnage, suffering, and poverty for the many. Skies are gray, the land is parched and citizens live in fear. The natural heir to the throne, the lion prince Simba returns to defeat Scar and the hyenas, reclaim his throne, marry his girlfriend, and reassert correct class, gender, and race order. The African savanna is again a luxuriant green and well-watered place and the herbivore subjects of the new king gather to sing his praises.

The film assigns African animal species distinct class and race positions. Lions are a white ruling class. As in most animal display spaces, lions have particular pride of place. This draws from the exotic and erotic thrill of the danger of predation, but also naturalizes a specific capitalist, masculinist, racialized, and hierarchical order. *The Lion King* presents a natural correctness to certain kinds of competition, pursuit and killing reflected in the savanna relationship between predators and prey. In a correct social order, there is justice to who eats and who is eaten and competition and hierarchy are necessary for healthy natural order. Such clichés of Darwinism and natural science pervade explanations of U.S. global capitalism. As reflected in predation, financially strong corporations consume weak ones, and weak national economies rightfully suffer the dictates of strong national economies. A global hierarchy of racialized continents is reflected in a racialized hierarchy of animal species. And although some cooperation is good, strong genetically-proven male leadership is always important.

What exactly do the hyenas do wrong in the film? They rise to power through organization and a will to power. They follow a charismatic leader. They dominate and predate according to a class system. They transform the African environment to serve their needs. They would seem to be good capitalists. But we as viewers enter the teleology of the fable. We know the good is natural and the natural is good. We know the hyenas are out of place and have subverted natural order. We know this because their pallor is dark, their homes are poor, and their accents and gang-behaviors are threatening. In the natural order Scar as a usurping uncle, Whoopi Goldberg as a black female gang leader, and hyenas as a racialized underclass class naturally are not meant to hold power.

Indeed in *The Lion King* the good are naturally good and the bad naturally bad. The hyenas are not acting against their nature. What is at the heart of the parable, as was at the heart of the colonialist idea of White Man's Burden, is the obligation of each class, race and gender to acknowledge and maintain their rightful place in the global order of things or face the consequences.

III. Simulated Safaris and the Politics of Edutainment

The Lion King helps lead North Americans in search of living African animals. In 1997, 40% of all adults in the U.S. visited a zoo, aquarium or wild animal park (Desmond 153). A higher percentage watched a televised nature documentary about Africa. While safaris in Africa have recently become more affordable and therefore cross-class accessible, a weak dollar, fear of flying, fear of anti-Americanism, and fear of chaos abroad are making profits at Africa-in-America venues soar. Private drive-through safari parks are proliferating in the U.S. and African animal-centered amusement parks are centers of the American tourism industry.

In the drive-through form of the simulated safari, tourists act out the politics of the African safari in diverse corners of North America—Ohio, Ontario, Florida, New Jersey, and Oregon—by experiencing "free roaming" African wildlife from the familiarity of their own cars. These privately owned parks range from 100 to 400 acres in size with miles of paved roads snaking through various species display areas. Most of these parks began in the 1960s and 1970s as animal breeding centers for zoos and are affiliated with breeding and conservationist organizations. The two largest, Lion Country Safari Park in Florida and Wild Safari Animal Park in New Jersey, each have over 1000 animals representing over 100 species. Over 500,000 people visited each park in 2002 and attendance is growing annually.

The drive-throughs are organized onto world regions, although Africa regions predominate. In Lion Country Safari, 5 of 7 world areas are African. In this park, the animal organizers divide African species to recreate specific African national parks and places: Ruaha National Park (Tanzania), Kalahari Buschveld (Southern Africa), Gorongose (Mozambique), Serengeti (Tanzania), and Hwanye (Zimbabwe). Within specific world areas, some herbivore species are mixed, in particular to recreate a cliché East African savanna multispecies vision, for example, of antelope, zebra, ostriches, and warthogs. Strong high fences or other structural divides separate predators from other species and separate world regions.

According to Jane Desmond, the establishment of modern zoos in the West beginning in the second half of the nineteenth century was part of a larger movement to reform urban public spaces, to assimilate and civilize the working class, and to construct the modern citizen. Desmond quotes H.F. Osborne, the president of the American Museum of Natural History, that zoo visitors "become more reverent, more truthful [...] and better citizens of the future through each visit" (159). According to Osborne, exposure to animal nature somehow turns people into better human beings. It is unclear what Osborne meant in 1922 by "citizens of the future," but the Western ideological organization of global nature does train people as imperial citizens. Viewing animals from around the world is only possible through a system of global power that includes the public in the process of global ordering, as animal parks bring together and display the global family of animals in a compact yet "realistic" manner. Zoos and drive-through parks are articulations of capitalist access with specimen-subjects brought from all corners of the world. These spaces organize animals according to correct continents and regions thus essentializing and segregating the world into African, Asian, South American, and North American animals paralleling racially and culturally specific continental groupings of people. Part of the ideology of this organization of nature is an affirmation of multi-culturalism and a condemnation of miscegeny. It is important that distinct groups coexist but do not mix. Either groups of animals not present at all or groups improperly mixed together would be unnatural for and unfair to animals and people alike.

In her history of western zoos, Desmond examines changing animal exhibition styles. The "bar-and-shackles" style emphasized the modern contradiction of freedom through captivity. The next most recent phase of spatial organization emphasizes bar-less naturalism without visible fences and large habitat spaces. The idea behind expansive animal habitat is that it allows animals to express their natural behaviors, to fulfill powerful behavioral and social needs (160-166). Since human audiences do not see fences or obvious barricades in these places, at least tourists are free to imagine the animals acting in nature.

In a second form of simulated safari, Busch Gardens and Disney's Animal Kingdom in central Florida combine animal viewing with amusement park rides. They both advertise massive open-range animal spaces without fences. These amusement parks are large-scale capital-intensive enterprises that bring nature conservation to a postmodern pinnacle. Ecotourism merges with amusement park rides, combining the thrill of the roller coaster or water slide with the thrill of the controlled and artificially constructed viewing of nature, topped-off with shopping in a native market.

The Busch Corporation inaugurated Busch Gardens in the 1960s as a 15-acre wildlife sanctuary to promote a nearby brewery. In the 1990s the now over 100-acre park included amusement park rides like the Congo River Rapids boat ride, the Ubanga-banga bumper cars and the Lion and the Tiger roller coasters, above and through its wildlife areas. The park is divided into African geographical locations such as Egypt, Nairobi and Timbuktu, each with its own group of fast food stands, shops, rides, and animals. Brochures invite you to "immense yourself in the culture of the African Continent as you experience its majestic wildlife."[4] People can access the 70-acre Serengeti Plain by railway, skyway, truck, and on foot. A thirty minute open truck tour hosted by an education specialist costs extra as does the two hour walking and open-truck Animal Adventure Tour, which comes with an accompanying professional photographer as well. Over three mil-

---

4   See "Vacation Services Orlando."

lion people visited Busch Gardens in 1982 and over five million in 2000.[5]

Nearby, Disney's Animal Kingdom is perhaps the ultimate safari simulacrum, with concrete shaped to resemble mud and carefully hidden physical barriers between humans and animals (more for the protection of the animals than of people). The 500-acre 800 million dollar park opened in 1998. It houses over 100 animals and 300 different species. As at Busch Gardens, the park combines amusement park rides, stores, and animals. Visitors access the park through a 140-foot high synthetic "tree of life" carved with all species of animals. They enter the over 100-acre Kilimanjaro Safari area through Harambi Village and past the Duka la Filamu (film store in Swahili). Between 7 and 10 million people have visited the park each year since its opening.[6]

These two amusement parks promote themselves as educational and as moral. Indeed here and in drive-through safari parks, education is overt and omnipresent. There are two sides to the educational components of edutainment. On the one hand, there is natural science. Busch Gardens has an animal nursery station. Drive-through safaris offer lectures and veterinary theater shows. Disney has the Pangani Forest Exploration Trail Research Center, and Rafiki's (the wise old Rastafarian monkey mentor to Simba from *The Lion King*) Animal Watch. Disney promotes the Disney Species Survival Plan and the Disney Wildlife Conservation Foundation. Everywhere guide books, guides and informational plaques address natural life cycles, food, family organization, reproduction, and territory. As in *The Lion King*, these are tales of animal parents and children for human parents and children, of the inevitability of patriarchal power in the public sphere and maternal power in the home, of correct sex and maternal care, of the necessity of hierarchy, predation and ownership. This knowledge is conveyed to us through the structure and personnel of the edutainment parks representing themselves as middlemen. It is therefore not politicized information being presented through edutainment, but as in Rafiki's Animal Watch, lessons of nature taught to us by the anthropomorphized animals themselves.

---

5   See "Busch Gardens Tampa Bay: A Blueprint for a World-Class Theme Park."
6   See "Disney World Orlando Attendance Figures."

On the other side of the education of edutainment are carefully managed messages about the politics of conservation. Lectures and plaques might tell of threats to a species by poaching and destruction of habitat by local people. There are lessons of the need to protect African animals from Africans or to help Africans become better protectors of their natural environments. But certainly African animals occupy the moral crucible of Africa and non-Africans, such as Disney in alliance with its customers, are best equipped to manage the continent. Edutainment does not link destruction of the rainforest, for example, to multi-national corporations and World Bank investments in ranching or to Western demands for beef and lumber, and does not link poaching to civil wars generated and financed by colonial histories and Western foreign policies. It is essential to the meaning of simulated safaris that African nature is outside of global history.

Indeed scholars have noted the corporate erasure of history. Disney attempts to tame, control, cleanse, and anthropomorphize nature (Kunzle 21). According to Ariel Dorfman and Armand Mattelart:

> Disney exorcises history, magically expelling the socially (and biologically) reproductive element, leaving amorphous, rootless, and inoffensive products—without sweat, without blood, without effort, and without the misery they inevitably sow in the life of the working class. (Dorfman/Mattelart 64)

So there can be no Africans in The Animal Kingdom or in Busch Gardens hunting for food or previously occupying the Serengeti. And there can be no signs of the nature in these edutainment parks as being produced by industrial labor and technologies. The ideological power of African nature in the U.S. depends on a representation of essential timeless relationships.

For the history of national parks is a history of colonial violence against local people, of land alienation, and of restructured human-animal and animal-animal interactions. On the site of national parks, colonial and post-colonial states have removed local people and curtailed their economic activities. As local people moved out to areas of higher settlement density, animals moved away from human settlement and into areas of higher bio-density. There is nothing natural about national parks. But if nature has history, then the supposedly timeless ideas and relationships that nature affirms become unstable. Simulated safari spaces present simulacra of nature yet circumvent the variety and unpredictability of nature. Nature is recreated into technological order to protect it from the history of the past and change in the future (Gitlin 295-297). Corporations thus present themselves as the best safeguard to preserving and presenting essential nature. Todd Gitlin observes that new architectural spaces in the U.S. enshrine the principle that the corporate space can and should appropriate nature by enclosing it (292). Corporate private property then becomes sacrosanct. Because corporations protect nature and nature conservation is a public right and duty, corporate private property becomes public property. Corporate profits that fund the Disney Wildlife Conservation Foundation, for example, become globally beneficial for all.

Conclusion

> The utopia that subsumes nature kills the life of it.
>
> Todd Gitlin (297)

On Disney's Kilimanjaro Safari ride, each open-truck load of 40 tourists drives by various populations of wildlife. Tourists then participate in a poaching drama of freeing an illegally captured baby elephant named Little Red (as opposed to the legally captured or bred elephants in the park) and scaring off poachers. Tourists hear over the truck radio that the mother elephant Big Red has been injured and that poachers have taken Little Red. As the ride continues, everyone sees the poachers' vehicle speed off. Appearing around a corner, a park ranger reassures each group that they have scared off the poachers and that the baby elephant has been found. The group then hears the cries of Little Red. Tourists arrive at the end of the ride to find a mechanical mold of an elephant's trunk gesturing for freedom from inside a plastic version of a slatted wooden crate. The entire experience lasts twenty minutes.

An irony of Little Red, and of all African animal edutainment in North America, is the drama of the evils of taking African animals from the wild played out by African animals who themselves (or their ancestors) were taken from the wild. It is a question of who is doing the stealing. As Donald Lazere writes, it is "[...] corporations' ingenious capacity to sell back to the consumer a nostalgic replica of everything they have contributed to destroying in nature and in society, and to reap praise for their civic mindedness in the bargain" (103). Disney tells us that corporations and consumers working together can protect Little Red as moral consumerism and corporate power reinforce one another.

The ideology behind and within African animal edutainment parks in the U.S. is that in form and function they represent themselves as protecting for the public what belongs to the public and conserving for humans what it is to be naturally human. The nature they present reflects and reifies the natural correctness of the current global capitalist order. Within these simulated African environments, animal examples of family, sex, class, race, and nation-state orders naturalize particular human politics for good parents and happy children.

Works Cited

Bandy, Joe. "Managing the Other of Nature: Sustainability, Spectacle, and Global Regimes of Capital in Ecotourism." *Public Culture* 8.13 (1996): 539-567.

Desmond, Jane. *Staging Tourism: Bodies on Display from Waikiki to Sea World*. Chicago: U of Chicago P, 1999.

Dorfman, Ariel, and Armand Mattelart. *How to Read Donald Duck: Imperialist Ideology in the Disney Comic*. 1971. London: I.G. Editions, 1975.

Gitlin, Todd. "Domesticating Nature." *Theory and Society* 8 (1979): 291-297.

Gooding-Williams, Robert. "Disney in Africa and the Inner City: On Race and Space in The Lion King." *Social Identities* 1.2 (1995): 373-379.

Kunzle, David. Introduction. *How to Read Donald Duck*. Ed. Ariel Dorfman and Armand Mattelart. New York: International General, 1975. 11-21.

Lancaster, Cory. "Live Skunks Onstage." *Orlando Sentinel* (April 3 1998).

Lazere, Donald. Introduction. *American Media and Mass Culture*. Berkeley: U of California P, 1987.

Morton, John. "Simba's Revolution: Revisiting History and Class in The Lion King." *Social Identities* 2.2 (1996): 311-317.

Orwell, George. "Marrakesh." *Essays*. New York: Doubleday, 1954. 189-190.

Pratt, Mary Louise. *Imperial Eyes: Travel Writing and Transculturation*. London: Routledge, 1992.

Wang, Ning. *Tourism and Modernity*. Amsterdam: Pergamon, 2000.

Webpages

"Busch Gardens Tampa Bay: A Blueprint for a World-Class Theme Park." www.atlasmc.com/bgse/faq1.htm. 16.11.03.

"Disney World Orlando Attendance Figures." www.wdisneyw.co.uk/attend.htm. 12.01.04
"The Lion King Fan-Art Archive." www.fanart.lionking.org. 12.01.04.
"The Lion King Production Notes." www.cinemareview.com. 12.01.04.
"The Lion King WWW Archive." www.lionking.org. 12.01.04.
"Vacation Services Orlando."
    www.vacationservicesorlando.com/themeparks/BG.htm. 12.01.04.

Water and "the land's disease": Poetics and Politics of Muriel Rukeyser's "The Book of the Dead"

Gerd Hurm

I

> Water celebrates, yielding continually
> sheeted and fast in its overfall
> slips down the rock, evades the pillars
> building its colonnades, repairs
> in stream and standing wave
> retains its seaward green
> broken by obstacle rock; falling, the water sheet
> spouts, and the mind dances, excess of white.
> White brilliant function of the land's disease.
>
> ("The Dam" 95)[1]

Water is central to Muriel Rukeyser's poetic investigation of the "land's disease" ("The Dam" 95) in "The Book of the Dead," the 20-poem sequence published in 1938 in her second poetry collection *U. S. 1*. It is central because it serves as a polyvalent discursive spatial figure in Rukeyser's exploratory voyage to a hydroelectric power plant near Hawk's Nest and Gauley Bridge, West Virginia, the site of death of about seven hundred miners in the "worst industrial disaster" in American history (Cherniack iii).[2] Investigating the ways in which the power of American nature could have been misused against its people, Rukeyser makes her poems' journey assume the shape of a "national allegory" (Davidson 146). Her trip to West Virginia is intended to

---

1   The quotes refer to the most accessible version of "The Book of the Dead" in Muriel Rukeyser's *Collected Poems*.
2   In subsequent references, this essay will use for reasons of brevity Hawk's Nest as the sole reference point for the events. Prior to Martin Cherniack's definitive study, which established Hawk's Nest as the key site by its title, it was common to refer to either Gauley Bridge or Hawk's Nest as the place of the incident.

function as a poetic voyage to the center of things: "These are roads to take when you think of your country" ("The Road" 71).[3]

The following will critically examine the discursive uses of water as a means to indicate some of the sources of power in Rukeyser's portrait of events and to explain some of the reasons why "The Book of the Dead," now critically acclaimed as "one of the major poem sequences of American modernism" (Nelson 2294), was for a long time overlooked and neglected. It will assess in particular the various dimensions of Rukeyser's discourse on water in order to improve understanding of the uniqueness of her poetic vision in the 1930s and to underline its continued relevance today.

II

> But it was always the water
> the power flying deep
> green rivers cut the rock
> rapids boiled down,
> a scene of power.
>
> ("West Virginia" 72)

Prior to the publication of Martin Cherniack's groundbreaking study *The Hawk's Nest Incident* in 1986, the immensity and monstrosity of the West Virginia industrial disaster was virtually forgotten by the general public.[4] It also took quite some time until a host of literary scholars noticed the astuteness of Muriel Rukeyser's poetic response

---

3   Throughout her poems, Rukeyser creates explicit connections between her journey and the path of West Virginian waters. The second poem "West Virginia" develops the road image as follows: "Coming where this road comes, flat stones spilled water which the still pools fed. / Kanawha Falls, the rapids of the mind, / fast waters spilling west" (72).
4   In 1986, Cherniack summarized the reactions to the scandal as follows: "This, then, was the totality of what the American public was to know of the disaster at Gauley Bridge: nine days of inconclusive hearings within a subcommittee of Congress. A score of ill-researched, sensationalized, or dismissive articles in the press and a few fleeting images on the movie screen. A perfunctory gesture of concern for human suffering. An unnoticed novel, a song briefly heard" (88). The following sketch of events is deeply indebted to Cherniack's account.

to the events of the 1930s.[5] Doubly neglected, the disaster and its consequences have in recent years assumed an important place in the political and cultural history of 1930s industrial America.[6] In order to see the nature of Rukeyser's accomplishment more clearly, it will be useful to sketch the course of events that roused her interest and that made her investigate the scandal in person in West Virginia in 1936.

The story of the disastrous construction of the Hawk's Nest hydroelectric plant begins in the late 1920s when proposals were made to use West Virginia's natural resources industrially to boost the regional economy. For this purpose, the Union Carbide and Carbon Corporation founded the New Kanawha Power Company, which then received permission to erect a power plant. In March 1930, under the guidance of Union Carbide engineers, a Virginia contractor, the Rhinehart and Dennis Company, started to drill two tunnels to divert water from the New River to the hydroelectric power house. As they began the tunnel construction, the contractors found silica, a highly valuable—but also highly dangerous—mineral. Inhaled with rock dust in drilling the tunnels, silica could cause silicosis, a severe and potentially lethal infection of the lungs.[7]

The ensuing problems arose with the company's decision to mine the rich deposits, selling the silica for the electro-processing of steel to a nearby Union Carbide plant in Alloy, West Virginia. Even though the company knew of the dangers of handling silica, they had the mineral deposits mined without proper precautions and safety equipment (Cherniack 79). The workers in the hydro tunnel, the majority of them African-American migrant workers, initially drilled silica without protective respiration gear.[8] In order to maximize profits, the company

---

5   The first study to have given the poem sequence a prominent position was Louise Kertesz's monograph in 1980. In the 1990s it became a chief focus in Rukeyser studies with key essays by Davidson, Hartmann, Kadlec, Kalaidjian, Minot, Thurston, and Wechsler.

6   Cherniack points out that this neglect is also based on the intentional erasure of evidence. He argues that "a deliberate and impressively successful attempt by the corporations involved to obliterate all traces of the occurrence have frustrated attempts to produce an account that could claim either authority or completeness" (2).

7   Silicosis leads to a shortness of breath. Though sharing some symptoms with tuberculosis, the disease was known at the time and could be diagnosed (Cherniack 79).

8   The racial dimension to the scandal is discussed most fully by Kadlec (23-25).

had the workers mine the mineral through dry drilling: this increased the pace of the operation considerably in comparison with water-based drilling methods, but also produced much more of the lethal dust (Kadlec 23).

As miners grew ill and began to die in large numbers as a consequence of the irresponsible mining policies, the people in charge did not take the responsibility for the improper working conditions. Instead of correcting safety breaches and compensating miners affected by the disease, the company took measures to cover up the causes for the disease. For instance, the death of workers was related primarily to other infections, blaming sickness on bad weather and the worker's loose leisure and drinking habits (Cherniack 3). Company doctors misdiagnosed silicosis as tuberculosis and pneumonia, denying workers any chance to claim compensation. To top all other measures, a local undertaker was paid a large sum of money to bury quickly and clandestinely unclaimed corpses. At times there were so many migrant miners killed by silicosis that these were simply stuffed in canvas bags and buried in an unidentified field at some distance from Gauley Bridge (Cherniack 59, 111).

When the surviving infected miners filed suits against the company and used labor organizations to assist them in their cause, the public slowly began to take notice of the scope of the scandal. Eventually, an article in the labor tabloid *People's Press* came to the attention of the New York congressman Vito Marcantonio, a politician with an interest in labor issues, who managed to establish a series of hearings in a Congressional subcommittee (Cherniack 75-80). With the involvement of Congress and the resulting coverage of hearings in leading newspapers and magazines such as the *New York Times*, *New Republic*, *Time*, and *Newsweek*, the regional affair briefly gained national attention. Still, the economic crisis and the election campaign made the Hawk's Nest affair but a transient issue in 1936. In Congress, Marcantonio failed to get a full-scale investigation into the incident.

For surviving infected miners and families of deceased miners, the brief national interest was almost to no avail. While a law for worker's compensation in the case of silicosis was passed by the West Virginia legislation, there were so many loopholes that only a few employees received the meager compensation (Cherniack 86). Even worse, those local workers who survived drilling the tunnel found it difficult to get new jobs in the region. Other employers knew of their increased chance of falling ill and thus would decline to hire them (Cherniack 104).

Roused by the news of the political scandal and by fundraising activities for affected families, Rukeyser decided to look into the matter herself. Together with her photographer friend Nancy Naumberg she traveled to West Virginia in 1936. While commentators would later try to make a case of inadequacy due to Rukeyser's gender and youth, she seemed predestined to take on the complex issue (Thurston 62). In the early 1930s, she had attended the Scottsboro trials in Alabama as a cub journalist and thus possessed first-hand experience of a major political scandal. Moreover, her strong interest in science and technology, evident in her training as an aviator and the focus in her first poetry volume *Theory of Flight*, rendered her a congenial investigator who could master the technical complexities of the incident competently.[9]

Given her journalistic background it is important to note that Rukeyser decided against publishing her response to the Hawk's Nest outrage in the form of a newspaper or magazine article. Instead, she deliberately chose the genre of poetry, making "The Book of the Dead" the centerpiece of her second poetry volume *U. S. 1*.[10] For the Hawk's Nest material she wanted to use the specific power of the poetic, arguing in a concluding note to *U. S. 1* that "poetry can extend the document" (*U. S. 1*. 146).

As may be seen from an examination of the ways in which she transforms water and Virginian waters in "The Book of the Dead," her poetic practice went beyond the customary 1930s stance of using documentary material for political purposes. Transcending the specific Hawk's Nest issues, her poetic response intends to address a larger sickness, the "land's disease" ("The Dam" 95).[11] As she would write a

---

9 In his review of *U. S. 1*, William Carlos Williams compared Rukeyser's skill in using scientific material for poetic purposes with that of Ezra Pound (141-142).
10 As her career showed, the multi-talented poet could have selected various forms. Being skilled in many genres, she has written plays, novels, and children's stories like *Houdini*, *The Orgy*, and *Bubbles*, researching and composing biographies like that of the physicist Willard Gibbs and the Renaissance astronomer and ethnographer Thomas Hariot.
11 Her note at the end of *U. S. 1* also argues such a broader project. "Book of the Dead" is "a summary poem of the life of the Atlantic coast of this country, nourished by the communications which run down it" (146).

few years later in her book about poetics, *The Life of Poetry*, it is poetry that provides the "fullness," the "total" response necessary "in time of crisis" (*The Life of Poetry* 1, 21).

III

> Down the reverberate channels of the hills
> the suns declare midnight, go down, cannot ascend,
> no ladder back; see this, your eyes can ride through steel,
> this is the river Death, diversion of power,
> the root of the tower and the tunnel's core,
> this is the end.
>
> THE DAM
>
> All power is saved, having no end. Rises
> in the green season, in the sudden season
> the white the budded
>   and the lost.
>
> ("Power," "The Dam" 95)

Throughout "The Book of the Dead," Rukeyser intends to evoke a strong sense of poetic and political totality. She therefore presents the places and events involved in the Hawk's Nest scandal as a spatial *pars pro toto* for American society. The town of Gauley Bridge stands for a prototypical American community: "any town looks like this one-street town" ("Gauley Bridge" 75). Its bus station relates to all sections of the nation, posting a "coast-to-coast schedule on the plateglass [sic] window" ("Gauley Bridge" 75). Above all, Rukeyser's investigative journey, following "rivers back," will take readers to the central arteries of their "country" ("The Road" 71):

> Here is your road, tying
>
> you to its meanings: gorge, boulder, precipice.
> Telescoped down, the hard and stone-green river
> cutting fast and direct into the town.
>
> ("The Road" 71)

Through her selection of materials and her choice of focal points in the poems, Rukeyser makes clear that the Hawk's Nest sequence addresses a totality of American society. The people portrayed in the poems provide a representative picture of the groups involved: Rukeyser includes the diversity of workers on the project (drillers in "George Robinson: Blues," miners "Absalom," and an engineer "Arthur Peyton"), friends and family members ("Absalom," "Juanita Tinsley," "Mearl Blankenship"), town people ("Gauley Bridge," "Statement: Philippa Allen"), and professionals connected with the construction site ("The Doctors," "The Disease," "Cornfield," "Power," "The Dam"). The poems feature men and women, locals and outsiders, African-American migrant workers and Appalachian miners.[12] In addition to these personal portraits, the poems address the crucial facets of the incident. They describe the technical and statistical side to the project ("Statement: Philippa Allen"), explain the medical aspects of the disease ("The Doctors"), document the local struggle for recognition and compensation ("Mearl Blankenship"), depict the effect on federal politics ("The Bill"), and highlight the historical dimension of the affair ("West Virginia," "The Book of the Dead").

Throughout the poems, the discourse on water and water imagery serves the function of establishing, sustaining, and underlining this impression of totality. Conceived as a central medium, water fuses the various strands that appear in the poems.

One of its key functions in the beginning is to remind readers of the powerful natural resources available to the community. Time and again, Rukeyser celebrates the beauty and power of West Virginian waters. There is the mention of the "proud gorge and festive water," presenting a show of "immense and pouring power" ("The Face of the Dam: Vivian Jones" 77). Water is seen as a "perfect fluid," which is "willing to run forever to find its peace" ("The Dam" 97). Water flows, connects, and proves powerful in overcoming obstacles.

In the hands of the company and its stockholders, however, the people's resource is turned into a threat, doing "its death-work in the country" ("The Face of the Dam: Vivian Jones" 77).[13] The "misuse of land" ("The Cornfield" 89) turns water into a poisonous fluid for the people: "The water they would bring had dust in it, our drinking wa-

---

12   Hartmann emphasizes the "strikingly inclusive terms" of selection for a 1930s poet (209).
13   Rukeyser reproduces in the poem a newspaper clip noting the actual value of Union Carbide stocks ("The Dam" 97).

ter" ("George Robinson: Blues" 85). The silica dust produced is so pervasive and strong that it cannot be cleansed by water: "it stayed and the rain couldn't wash it away" ("George Robinson: Blues" 85). The polluting fluid invades all areas of living, even affecting the domestic sphere where it leaves lethal traces. The account of Mrs. Jones, the mother of three sons killed by silicosis, highlights this poisonous presence:

> I first discovered what was killing these men.
> I had three sons who worked with their father in the tunnel:
> Cecil, aged 23, Owen, aged 21, Shirley, aged 17.
> They used to work in a coal mine, not steady work
> for the mines were not going much of the time.
> A power Co. foreman learned that we made home brew,
> he formed a habit of dropping in evenings to drink,
> persuading the boys and my husband—
> give up their jobs and take this other work.
> It would pay them better.
> Shirley was my youngest son; the boy.
> He went into the tunnel.
>
> *My heart my mother my heart my mother*
> *My heart my coming into being.*
>
> My husband is not able to work.
> He has it, according to the doctor.
> We have been having a very hard time making a living since
>   this trouble came to us.
> I saw the dust in the bottom of the tub.
>
> ("Absalom" 81)

In a larger perspective, the exploitative misuse of land and water are shown as an attack on the American body politic. Silica stops the flow of life:

> It sets up a gradual scar formation;
> this increases, blocking all drainage from the lung,
> eventually scars, blocking the blood supply,
> and then they block the air passageways.
> Shortness of breath,
> pains around the chest,
> he notices lack of vigor.
>
> ("The Disease: After-Effects" 99)

In the vein of Walt Whitman, Rukeyser uses the imagery of the body politic to indicate a larger pattern of disempowerment: "Mr. Griswold. 'A corporation is a body without a soul'" ("The Dam" 95).[14] The entire American body politic is consequently shown in a state of paralysis: "Bill blocked; investigation blocked" ("The Disease: After-Effects" 99).[15]

Rukeyser enhances these images with instances of enslavement, imprisonment, and crime in American and western culture in order to suggest an additional historical and mythical dimension to the contemporary affair. For instance, she emphasizes West Virginia's link with the Civil War and uses the popular reference to John Brown for her purposes: "dead John Brown's body walking from a tunnel / to break the armored and concluded mind" ("The Bill" 102). On a different level, she ties the events to the biblical story of the Egyptian enslavement and to Christian narratives of plight. The buried migrant workers and miners thus assume a mythic status: "Abel America, calling from under the corn, / Earth, uncover my blood!" ("The Cornfield" 90).

As much as the water used in the construction of the hydroelectric plant presents a repressive power for the workers, the poem sequence celebrates water as a force that ultimately will not tolerate enslavement, containment, and paralysis. For instance, water is related to images that will provide insights to counter the disease:

> But planted in our flesh these valleys stand,
> everywhere we begin to know the illness,
> are forced up, and our times confirm us all.
>
> (The Book of the Dead" 104)

It is also connected with the chance for a beginning, for a rebirth:

---

14   For an account of Whitman's use of the discursive figure of the body politic, see Erkkila. The image of a paralyzed political body is prepared and assisted by other examples of miners unable to move their bodies: "I wake up choking, and my wife / rolls me over on my left side; / then I'm asleep in the dream I always see: / the tunnel choked / the dark wall coughing dust" ("Mearl Blankenship" 80).
15   Hartmann argues that the "model of the body as a fluid, dynamic system is central to Rukeyser's work" (221).

> *I open out a way over the water*
> *I form a path between the Combatants:*
> *Grant that I sail down like a living bird,*
> *power over the fields and Pool of Fire.*
> *Phoenix, I sail over the phoenix world.*
>
> ("The Dam" 95)[16]

Since water is often blocked, yet strong enough to overcome barriers, it serves ultimately as an image of an uncontainable, liberating force.[17] The construction of the hydro tunnel and the dam play a crucial role in Rukeyser's hope of a victory over paralysis.

> Effects of friction: to fight and pass again,
> learning its power, conquering boundaries,
> able to rise blind in revolts of tide,
> broken and sacrificed to flow resumed.
> Collecting eternally power. Spender of power,
> torn, never can be killed, speeded in filaments,
> million, its power can rest and rise forever,
> wait and be flexible. Be born again.
> Nothing is lost, even among the wars,
> imperfect flow, confusion of force.
>
> ("The Dam" 97)

Despite the unresolved political issue and the evident plight of the people affected by the corrupt uses of power, Rukeyser ends the poem sequence on a note of hope. The eternally regenerating force of water is central to her stance. Widening the scope of vision to include all ills of colonial repression and enslavement, she concludes the final, the title poem, "The Book of the Dead," with the belief that "Down coasts of taken countries" one may still envision the victory of "seeds of unending love" (105).[18]

---

16 Another instance of Rukeyser's aspiration for totality, Egyptian religion is pervasively alluded to in the poem sequence. Its key document, *The Book of the Dead*, provides the title for the poems. Davidson sees Rukeyser as a "modernist Isis" (147).
17 Thurston relates water and its "uncontainable energy" to an anarchic impulse in Rukeyser's sequence (76).
18 Hartmann sees Rukeyser's optimism in "The Book of the Dead" as a belief in the possibility of agency in the modern world (221).

IV

How many feet of whirlpools?
What is a year in terms of falling water?
Cylinders; kilowatts; capacities.
Continuity: $\Sigma Q = 0$
Equations for falling water. The streaming motion.
The balance-sheet of energy that flows
passing along its infinite barrier.

It breaks the hills, cracking the riches wide,
runs through electric wires;
it comes, warning the night,
running among these rigid hills,
a single force to waken our eyes.

("The Dam" 96)

Viewed from the dominant competing perspectives in literary criticism in the 1930s, Rukeyser's poems must have seemed flawed and contradictory. For those hoping to find an engaged, revolutionary account of events, the poems appeared to be too aesthetically experimental and romantic.[19] For those hoping to find texts purged from all non-literary concerns, the poems were too fact-ridden and politicized (Kertesz 112-113). Equally reductive in their approaches to literature, the dominant discourses in criticism could not capture Rukeyser's complex fusion of strands. Her unique documentary poems simply were not poetically and politically correct (Flynn 264-265).

Examined from a distance, however, disregarding the outmoded tenets of dogmatic Marxism and New Criticism, Rukeyser's implicit poetics in "The Book of the Dead" make more and more sense. A closer look at her aesthetic principles in *The Life of Poetry*, the book of poetics that she conceived in the decade following her Hawk's Nest sequence, may reveal more clearly the innovative potential behind her approach. In *The Life of Poetry*, Rukeyser attempts to deduce from her practice as a poet a new relation between politics and poetics. Challenging the reductive approaches to poetry in the 1930s, she intends to found a poetics of "fullness" and "growth" (21, 56), fusing rational

---

19 Kalaidijan shows that Rukeyser consciously avoids employing universalizing leftist vocabulary (65-88).

and intuitive modes of understanding in an innovative merger of scientific and mythic, realist and romantic elements.[20]

The ideas developed in *The Life of Poetry* may be said to be already present *in nuce* in the ways in which the discursive figure of water is treated in "The Book of the Dead."[21] The "Atlantic seaboard" ("Praise of the Committee" 77), the West Virginian rivers, and the Hawk's Nest water resources invoke the relational holism and dynamic process Rukeyser celebrates in her poetics (*The Life of Poetry* 159-172). As a matter of fact, the impulse to conceive of a new poetic politics is explicitly related to water and the beginning of a sea journey in *The Life of Poetry*. Rukeyser places the account of how she was caught in a refugee boat in Barcelona in 1936 and forced to flee from the fascist violence in the Spanish Civil War right at the beginning of her book. There and then on the water, she listens to the "deep fertile sea of night" in order to recount to the others caught in the boat the reasons why poetry matters for humanity, particularly "in time of crisis" (*The Life of Poetry* 1).[22] She then proceeds to enlist the necessary steps of a new poetics that will challenge and overcome the paralysis of a degenerate American and western culture.

As she shows at length in *The Life of Poetry*, the power of poetry lies in its open and dynamic character. All elements in poetry are in motion, all elements are related and affect one another:

> I have attempted to suggest a dynamic of poetry, showing that a poem is not its words or its images, any more than a symphony is its notes or a river its drops of water. Poetry depends on the moving relations within itself. It is an art that lives in time, expressing and evoking the moving relation between the individual consciousness and the world. The work that a poem does is a transfer of human energy, and I think

---

20 As has been pointed out by other critics, Rukeyser's modernist poetics anticipates many facets associated with postmodernism. Herzog notes that Rukeyser is a poet "with strong affinities for postmodernism in ways singular for her generation" (32).
21 Kertesz also emphasized this close relation between water imagery and certain properties of the poems: "The effect of the lines' movement and content is a healing, like the self-healing of a river" (109).
22 The boat trip, with some stops in between, actually becomes the journey back to the U.S. to finish the publication of *U. S. 1*. The collection includes two poems that explicitly relate her project to sea journeys, namely "The Cruise" (126-136) and "Mediterranean" (136-143).

human energy may be defined as consciousness, the capacity to make change in existing conditions. (*The Life of Poetry* xi)

For Rukeyser both cybernetic and ecological models are among the best analogies to explain her new conception of poetry.[23] Since modern scientific theories suggest that truth does not derive from a single source, but must be conceived as "an agreement of components" (*The Life of Poetry* 167), she looks to this relational pattern as a spatial model upon which to base her own poetics. Following Henri Poincaré, she sees poetry like science primarily as a "system of relations" (*The Life of Poetry* 165). In this system, all elements are connected and constantly "in motion" (*The Life of Poetry* 51).

Taking but this brief survey of Rukeyser's key concepts in *The Life of Poetry* as a yardstick, it becomes obvious why the medium of water would prove fruitful as a dominant image cluster in "The Book of the Dead." Its capacities as fluid allow Rukeyser to merge the various strands that constitute her total vision of reality. She thus may integrate a scientific-formulaic conception of water ("Continuity: $\Sigma Q = 0$," "The Dam" 96) with a religious-mythic one ("this is the river Death," "Power" 95). Her ecocritical celebration of the regenerative power of water may thus serve as a politically viable reminder of the need to keep cultural and historical processes open.

Since she fuses the rational exploration and intuitive grasp of nature in new ways, she may make her praise of the hydroelectric plant—as a great technical achievement and as a sign of human progress—compatible with her criticism of its builders as criminals who pollute an entire region.[24] Her relational holism in which conflicting facets may fruitfully coexist as signs of a productive friction explains

---

23 Relating it to key principles of natural history, Rukeyser defines ecology as follows: "In our time, we have become used to an idea of history in which process and relationship are stressed. The science of ecology is only one example of an elaboration of the idea, so that the life of land may be seen in terms of its tides of growth, the feeding of one group on another, the equilibrium reached, broken, and the drive toward another balance and renewal" (*The Life of Poetry* 12).

24 Wechsler stresses that Rukeyser is aware of her dual responsibility to science and technology. Rukeyser knows that "the damage done by the mining of silica ore could not have been exposed without silicon-based photomechanical technology and the representational fields it supports" (228). For the importance of photographic metaphors, see Minot.

why one of the most destructive images of industrial production in American modernism:

> This is the most audacious landscape. The gangster's
> stance with his gun smoking and out is not so
> vicious as this commercial field, its hill of glass.
>
> Sloping as gracefully as thighs, the foothills
> narrow to this, clouds over every town
> finally indicate the stored destruction.
>
> Crystalline hill: a blinded field of white
> murdering snow, seamed by convergent tracks;
> the travelling cranes reach for the silica.
>
> ("Alloy" 92)

may stand next to a celebration of the beauty of the power plant:

> This is the midway between water and flame,
> this is the road to take when you think of your country,
> between the dam and the furnace, terminal.
> The clean park, fan of wires, landscapers,
> the stone approach. And seen beyond the door,
> the man with the flashlight in his metal hall.
> Here, the effective green, grey-toned and shining,
> tall immense chamber of cylinders. Green,
> the rich paint catches light from three-story windows,
> arches of light vibrate erratic panels on
> sides of curved steel.
>
> ("Power" 93)

Rukeyser's poem sequence challenges an easy assignment of her criticism along the conventional dichotomies of natural/cultural, literary/scientific, mythic/modern, and right/left. Seen from this perspective, the misperception and rejection of Rukeyser's achievement in "The Book of the Dead" by rigid and reductive critical discourses seems a logical consequence.

In addition to fusing discourses of science and art in unexpected ways, Rukeyser's poetry also challenges customary notions of autonomous and engaged art. As she repeatedly admonishes in *The Life of Poetry*, art should not be conceived outside of social and political concerns. At the same time, her decidedly engaged poetics argues that people will "not be saved by poetry" (*The Life of Poetry* 213). Literature only prepares for life and politics; it cannot replace them. In this sense, poetry remains autonomous in its engagement. What poems may achieve is that they change attitudes toward life, demanding a total response to the fullness of life. In Rukeyser's eyes, poems function as a "meeting-place" (*The Life of Poetry* xi) where a complete sense of totality may be prepared for and envisioned. This holistic interaction with life is conceived as an open-ended process.

The images of water in "The Book of the Dead" serve this key function. As Rukeyser argues in the final section, the meaning of a poem will have to remain open. Later generations of readers will find new significance in her lines: "and you young, you who finishing the poem / wish new perfection and begin to make" ("The Book of the Dead" 104). Running dialectically "forever to find its peace" ("The Dam" 97), water is the vital force and discursive figure in the "The Book of the Dead" to keep history, its meaning, the search for truth and fullness in poetry open.

The road to Hawk's Nest, staged as a trip that intends to make American readers "think" of their "country" ("The Road" 71) turns out to be more than an engaged commitment to American miners and their right to life, work, and dignity. It portrays their situation as a paradigmatic one: it represents their case as an example of an incomplete, yet ultimately obtainable unity and fullness (Gardinier 104). In sum, the power of Rukeyser's poetic vision is best captured by the discursive figure of water. At the end of the poem "The Dam," Rukeyser imagines its historical dynamic congenially as follows: "It changes. It does not die" (98).

Works Cited

Cherniack, Martin. *The Hawk's Nest Incident. America's Worst Industrial Disaster.* New Haven: Yale UP 1986.
Davidson, Michael. *Ghostlier Demarcations: Modern Poetry and the Material World.* Berkeley: U of California P, 1997.
Erkkila, Betsy. *Whitman the Political Poet.* New York: Oxford UP, 1989.
Flynn, Richard. "'The Buried Life and the Body of Walking': Muriel Rukeyser and the Politics of Literary History." *Gendered Modernisms: American Women Poets and Their Readers.* Ed. Margaret Dickle and Thomas Travisano. Philadelphia: U of Pennsylvania P, 1996. 264-279.

Gardinier, Suzanne. "'A World That Will Hold All the People': On Muriel Rukeyser." *Kenyon Review* 14 (1992): 88-105.

Hartmann, Stephanie. "All Systems Go: Muriel Rukeyser's 'The Book of the Dead' and the Reinvention of Modernist Poetics." *How Shall We Tell Each Other of the Poet?: The Life and Writing of Muriel Rukeyser*. Ed. Anne F. Herzog and Janet E. Kaufman. 209-223.

Herzog, Anne F., and Janet E. Kaufman, eds. *How Shall We Tell Each Other of the Poet?: The Life and Writing of Muriel Rukeyser*. New York: St. Martin's P, 1999.

Herzog, Anne F. "'Anything Away from Anything': Muriel Rukeyser's Relational Poetics." *How Shall We Tell Each Other of the Poet?: The Life and Writing of Muriel Rukeyser*. Ed. Anne F. Herzog and Janet E. Kaufman. 32-44.

Kadlec, David. "X-Ray Testimonials in Muriel Rukeyser." *Modernism/Modernity* 5 (1998): 23-47.

Kalaidjian, Walter. "Muriel Rukeyser and the Poetics of Specific Critique: Rereading 'The Book of the Dead.'" *Cultural Critique* 20 (1991): 65-88.

Kertesz, Louise. *The Poetic Vision of Muriel Rukeyser*. Baton Rouge: Louisiana State UP, 1980.

Minot, Leslie Ann. "'Kodak As You Go': The Photographic Metaphor in the Work of Muriel Rukeyser." *How Shall We Tell Each Other of the Poet?: The Life and Writing of Muriel Rukeyser*. Ed. Anne F. Herzog and Janet E. Kaufman. 264-276.

Nelson, Cary. "Muriel Rukeyser 1913–1980." *The Heath Anthology of American Literature*. Ed. Paul Lauter et al. Boston: Houghton Mifflin, 1998. 2:2294-2295.

Rukeyser, Muriel. *Bubbles (for children)*. New York: Harcourt Brace, 1967.

—. *The Collected Poems of Muriel Rukeyser*. New York: McGraw-Hill, 1978.

—. *Houdini*. Produced by Lenox Arts Center, 1973

—. *The Life of Poetry*. 1949. Ashfield: Paris P, 1996.

—. *The Orgy*. New York: Coward McCann, 1965.

—. *Theory of Flight*. New Haven: Yale UP, 1935.

—. *The Traces of Thomas Hariot*. New York: Random House, 1971.

—. *U.S. 1*. New York: Covici, Friede, 1938.

—. *Williard Gibbs*. New York: Doubleday, 1942.

Thurston, Michael. "Documentary Modernism as Popular Front Poetics: Muriel Rukeyser's 'Book of the Dead.'" *Modern Language Quarterly* 60 (1999): 59-83.

Wechsler, Shoshana. "A Ma(t)ter of Fact and Vision: The Objectivity Question and Muriel Rukeyser's 'The Book of the Dead.'" *How Shall We Tell Each Other of the Poet?: The Life and Writing of Muriel Rukeyser*. Ed. Anne F. Herzog and Janet E. Kaufman. 226-240.

Williams, Carlos Williams. Rev. of *U. S. 1*." *New Republic* (March 9, 1938): 141-142.

Technoscape / Architecture / Urban Utopia

A Brief Introduction to *Architectural Body* by Madeline Gins and Arakawa

Klaus Benesch

If the reorganization of space has been a pressing concern of late-twentieth century culture, the ongoing collaboration of New York based artists-architects-poets Arakawa and Madeline Gins, that culminated in 1994 in the construction of a seven acre "Reversible Destiny" site in Yoro, central Japan, added to and, simultaneously, extended this concern about space into the realm of philosophy, psychology, and cognitive science. Arakawa and Gins have long been relentless thinkers and re-thinkers of concepts of space and its numerous aesthetic and philosophical ramifications. Their monumental work clearly testifies to the need for a spatial reconfiguring of the human body in postmodern, posthuman society. Rather than merely creating works of art, Arakawa and Gins have worked outside the often narrowly construed definitions of art production, exploring instead existential issues such as the "mechanism of meaning," the decoding and recoding of different types of signs, or the spatial conditioning of human perception, as exemplified in the architectural concept of "landing sites."

Arakawa's and Gins' re-conceptualization of space as a fundamental parameter of subjectivity, an idea that can be traced throughout their artistic and written work, is rooted in the belief that to say "I" is already an architectural assertion, because it creates spatial relations and establishes a fiction of place. "To reform perception," as one critic succinctly summarizes their architectural project, "is to transform the architecture of the I. Since the world is not merely a given but is constructed by the activity of the subject, the recoding of the I is the recreation of the world" (Arakawa/Gins, *Reversible Destiny* 32). Spatial relations, according to this logic, are seen as the driving agents of human perception. When a person enters a symmetrical octagonal structure, s/he confronts an array of what Arakawa and Gins have come to call "landing sites," that is, visual, tactile, aural, olfactory, kinesthetic, and imaging spaces that allow for the establishing and maintaining of distance, volume, and a sense of place. Arakawa and Gins distinguish between three levels of landing sites: perceptual, imaging, and dimensionalizing; taken together these levels mark the place or, to use Heidegger's term, the "Urgrund" where space is formed and the world is created. "A heuristic device for mapping how a person forms the world and situates herself within" (Arakawa/Gins, *Architecture* 19), the tripartite concept of landing sites reconfigures the subject-object relation as essentially anchored in and determined by space.

"If the basic unit of concern is the body," Arakawa and Gins write in an open letter to Francois Lyotard, "then will not the concepts most central to the living of a life be those formed—no matter how fleetingly—through architectural encounters?" (Arakawa/Gins, *Reversible Destiny* 12). It is important to note, however, that their view of the world and the way in which we perceive it, though largely informed by architectural surrounds, does not gives in to neither postmodern solipsism (that it is us who shape the world around us) nor materialist determinism (that we are "made" by and through our surrounds); rather it conceives of the human mind and body as continually engaged by and, at the same time, engaging the creation and contestation of new spaces. One could also say that we experience space by "using" it as a landing site for the self's physical interacting with the world.

In a very literal sense, then, architecture is instrumental in achieving what Arakawa and Gins think is a primary purpose of life in our time, that is, "to not to die." A paradoxical contention that, at first sight, seems to run counter to common sense and established views of the human condition, the proclaimed wish "to not to die" expresses, at one level, simply a desire to not to acquiesce in regard to the abysmal fate of human life in posthuman society. It is a call to arm oneself with the perceptional tools to figure out the existential linking between the body and the world outside. On yet another level, it is also an attempt to reverse human destiny not by changing the world, but rather by asking questions, architectural questions, about the positioning of the "I" in space: "How does the human body—together with its environment—accomplish what it manages to? How is it possible that she who is a body walks and talks? How much does the body avail itself of its environment [...]" (Gins/Arakawa, *Architectural Body* xv). Architecture, Arakawa and Gins argue, is a tool that can be used as writing has been, except that it can have a far more extensive range of application. It teaches us that the bodily and mental processes it has set in motion within the beholder or inhabitant of an architectural construct are more important than the structure itself. "Might not an architectural surround set up to cooperate with the gathering of intelligence," they ask, "increase, at the very least, ones feeling of connection with and sense of responsibility to the world?" (Arakawa/Gins, *Reversible Destiny* 12).

Arakawa's and Gins' project of the "architectural body" emphasizes the solid grounding of human life in real spaces. If the investigative work necessary to solve the puzzle of human life has to be focused on architectural surrounds, that is, the relations between the subject and the environment in which it quite literally "comes" to life, this investigation cannot be done in the abstract, "it must, on the contrary, be done on-site where living happens" (Gins/Arakawa, *Architectural Body* xv). Procedural architecture, as realized in the "Site of Reversible Destiny" at Yoro, thus reconfigures the human body as physically rooted in and constantly imaging new spatial surrounds of its own making. If the testing of this renewed "architectural body" as a powerful statement against the down-grading of body-space relations in posthuman society necessitates, as Arakawa and Gins point out in their "Introduction" to *Architectural Body* that "an entire house (or a city) be constructed, why worry over the expense?" (Gins/Arakawa xxii).

Selected Works by Arakawa and Madeline Gins

Arakawa and Madeline Gins. *Architectural Body*. Tuscaloosa: The U of Alabama P, 2002.
—. *Architecture: Sites of Reversible Destiny*. London: Academy Editions, 1994.
—. *For Example (A Critique of Never)*. English/Italian. Trans. Aldo Tagliaferri. Milan: Alessandra Castelli, 1974.
—. *Helen Keller or Arakawa*. Santa Fe: Burning Books, 1994; and New York: East-West Cultural Studies, 1994.
—. *Mechanism of Meaning*. 2nd ed. New York: Harry N. Abrams, 1979. Also published in French as *Le Mécanisme du sens* (trans. Serge Gavransky. Paris: Maeght Editeur, 1979); in Japanese, as exhibition catalogue, Osaka: National Museum of Art, 1979; and in German: *Mechanismus der Bedeutung*. 1st ed. Trans. Carlo Huber. Munich: Bruckmann, 1971.
—. *Pour ne pas mourir/To Not To Die*. Paris: Éditions de la Différence, 1987.
—. *Reversible Destiny: We Have Decided Not To Die*. New York: Guggenheim Museum Publications, 1997.
In 2004 the French-American journal *Interfaces: Image—Texte—Langage* dedicated a two-volume special issue to the work of Arakawa + Madeline Gins: "Architecture Against Death—Architecture Contre la Mort," *Interfaces* 21/22 (2004).

The Architectural Body—Landing Sites

Madeline Gins and Arakawa

Were nothing being apportioned out, no world could form. What is being apportioned out, no one is able to say. That which is being apportioned out is in the process of landing. To be apportioned out involves being cognizant of sites. To be cognizant of a site amounts to having greeted it in some manner or to having in some way landed on it. There is that which gets apportioned out as the world. There is an apportioning out that can register and an apportioning out that happens more indeterminately. A systematic approximating of how things are apportioned out should be possible.

The body is sited. As that which initiates pointing, selecting, electing, determining, and considering, it may be said to originate (read *co-originate*) all sites. Organism-person-environment consists of sites and would-be sites. An organism-person, a sited body, lives as one site that is composed of many sites. One can, for example, consider one's arms and legs to be part of a single site (the body) or elect them to be two sites (an upper-appendages realm and a lower-appendages one) or four (two upper and two lower appendages) or twenty-four or more sites (two arms having a total of ten fingers, and two legs with ten toes in all).

*

"If persons are sited, why do philosophers inquiring into what constitutes a person, or, for that matter, into the nature of mind, rarely, if ever, factor this in?"

"Philosophers considering persons as sites would be obliged to develop a person architectonics. They would, I am afraid, have to turn themselves into architects of sorts."

"First off, might not the world exist so that everyone may turn into an architect? Contemporary philosophers who insist on remaining within the narrow confines of their discipline risk not being able to frame questions as broadly as necessary and thus jeopardize the logical basis of their inquiry. Does anyone really believe that a person could ever be figured out as such in the abstract?"

*

Designating the "coming alive" for sentience—as sentience?!—of anything whatsoever, including even the most fleeting sensations, a landing site is but a neutral marker, a simple taking note of, nothing more. When how the world is apportioned out is translated into landing sites, all stays the same, touched but untouched. A person parses the world at any given instant into particular distributions of landing sites, or better, an organism-person-environment can be parsed into these distributions; it is of great use, we hope to demonstrate, to think of the world as reduced to these distributions, these parsings, these arrays, and nothing more. This way what goes on as the world, the world taken all together, all inhabitants included, can be kept track of and looked into with a minimal amount of speculation as to what's in play. If we don't know what is being distributed, let us simply stay with the fact that distributions of some order are underway. We may not yet know how we are connected to the world, but we do know that we are. Let us be precise or suitably imprecise about what we do know so far.

Adopting as a theoretical posit the concept of a landing site, we seek to make and keep explicit an otherwise hidden-in-plain-sight constant of awareness: all things and events have specific positionings. Intent on tracking a person's apportioning out of thinking-feeling to form a world that she then interacts with, and wondering whether it is at all valid to think of a "depositing" of sited awareness everywhere around one, we establish a schematic domain of *landing sites*.

A multiple, complex siting process or procedure would seem to be in effect as organism-person-environment; or posing it more neutrally, the world one finds in place lends itself to being mapped by means of a multiple, complex siting process or procedure. Human action depends on an attributing of sites and takes place in large part through sequences of sitings. In determining her surroundings, a person proceeds by registering a "this here" and a "that there" and a "more of this here" and a "more of that there". In fielding her surroundings, she makes use of cues from the environment to assign volume and a host of particulars to world and to body, complying with what comes her way as best she can. Her fielding of her surroundings never ceases, continuing even in sleep. Whatever comes up in the course of this fielding should be considered a landing site.

We start off by thinking of world-construction as involving three different ways to land as a site. Every landing-site configuration—that is, every instance of the world—involves all three ways of landing as a site. A *perceptual landing site* lands narrowly as an immediate and direct response to a probable existent, a bit of reporting on what presents itself. An *imaging landing site* lands widely and in an unpinpointing way, dancing attendance on the perceptual landing site, responding indirectly and diffusely to whatever the latter leaves unprocessed. Apeing a perceptual landing site's direct response to a probable existent, it keeps faith with and firms up a reporting impetus underway. Usually this mimicking landing site, a gloss instrumental in its coming to seem that nothing has escaped attention, simply goes about indirectly coming up with more of the same, making it appear that direct responding to probable existents covers a wider area and has a longer-lasting effect than it actually does. But an imaging landing site can also, absent perceptual landing sites, when a sensory modality has closed down, suggest itself to be a direct response that initiates a report, thus turning itself for all intents and purposes into a perceptual landing site (witness the Karl Dahlke report a few pages further along). Imaging landing sites can also, in response to an indeterminate probable existent, simply come forward as a portion of sited awareness that remains diffuse, thus presenting areas of world without mimicking anything at all; to demonstrate this look off into thin air. A *dimensionalizing landing site* lands simultaneously narrowly and tightly and widely and diffusely, combining the qualities of a perceptual landing site with those of an imaging one, coupling and coordinating direct responses with indirect ones, the formed with the formless. Attaching a grappling hook of a perceptual landing site to a vaguely sketched-in rope of an imaging landing site, a dimensionalizing landing site, in landing, hooks onto the environment to gain traction on it. With the hook-and-rope ensemble flung out and availing surface caught hold of, there comes to be an as-if-tugging-back-to-the-body that conveys a sense of (kinesthetic) depth.

Defining features (perceptual landing sites), plus all the imaging that bounces off that which surrounds a person (imaging landing sites), plus guesses and judgements as to how elements of the surroundings are positioned (dimensionalizing landing sites) fabricate a world or suffice to map one. Landing sites dissolve into each other, or abut, or overlap, or nest within one another.

Every square foot or every square nanometer of organism-person-environment occasions a landing site. Surroundings are for a person what comes of her ubiquitous siting; that is to say, they exist as a result of her having dispersed landing sites ubiquitously within a circumscribed area, leaving no square nanometer uncovered. Fielding the surroundings, distributing sentience in specific ways to do this, one lets loose ubiquitous sitings or landing-site configurations which permeate and supplant one another in rapid succession. Every surroundings elicits from those within it a characteristic series of ubiquitous sitings or landing-site configurations.

Landing sites abound within landing sites. Anything perceived can count as both a landing site in and of itself and as part of a larger landing site. The corner of a desk can be taken as a full-fledged landing site, even while subsisting as part of the landing site holding and portraying the desk as a whole. The taking of a particular expanse or event to be a landing site happens in a flash; over in a flash; these events that are decision-like but far from being decisions yield to whatever can come next. A bit of substance, a segment of atmosphere, an audible anything, a whiff of something, whatever someone notices can be declared either a whole landing site or part of one, or both of these at once. Through landing-site configurations, organism-person-environment takes hold and holds forth.

Accepting that the world can be sorted out, at each instant, into only a limited number of landing sites that can readily be kept track of and maneuvering with this information without trying to overreach it amounts to taking a neutral stance. A landing-site configuration can, then, be thought of as a heuristic device with which to leaf through the universe, never mind that it is unpaginated. This heuristic device, a set of apportionings-out capable of reading what else has been and is being apportioned out, leafs through the universe to determine its arrangement and its contingencies. Leafing through a universe turns it into the world.

Perceptual Landing Sites

Theoretically, what counts as the world might be divided into an infinite number of specific locatings or focal areas of awareness, but various studies have shown that, at any given moment, the world consists, for a person, of only a limited number of activated regions or focal hubs of activity.[1] The continual, albeit episodic, designating of this or that as here or there is not routinely included in this small limit-group of focal notings, but inasmuch as we have in this the originator, or more accurately co-originator, of all regions and hubs, it—this that apportions out—merits inclusion as a member. In any event, one finds a constant selecting of discrete groups of designated areas, with yet other groups in the offing. All points or areas of focus, that is, all designated areas of specified activity, count as perceptual landing sites (visual, aural, tactile, olfactory, proprioceptive, kinesthetic, somaesthetic [pain]).

Perceptual landing sites occur always in sets—a flock of birds flying in formation. With every move she makes, a person disperses her perceptual landing sites differently. Resting within or overlapping one another, they are hard to pin down as to size. Should, however, there be a fairly continual distinguishing of a focal area of activity, a definite size might provisionally be accorded a member of the set. Upon this happening, there would surface the illusion that one had met with that rare, nonexistent bird: the lone perceptual landing site.

Perceptual landing sites pop up on demand, converging upon whatever is around to be landed on. All singled-out elements of surrounding surfaces: perceptual landing sites. Even a mere intimation of a singling-out equals having been landed on and sited. Repeated singlings-out bring the world into existence in all its features. I assign a perceptual landing site to this. Or does it take shape by means of many sites of this type? A shape may be formed first as one perceptual landing site and then considered to be defined by ten, after which it might be judged to have been defined by one hundred or any number of such sites, landing sites that are "direct hits." Because sites abound within

---

1 George A. Miller, "The Magical Number Seven, Plus or Minus Two: Some Limits on Our Capacity for Processing Information," *Psychological Review* 63 (1956): 81-97; Zenon W. Pylyshyn, "Visual Indexes reconceptual Objects, Situated Vision," *Cognition 80* (June 2001): 127-58.

sites, and because any X that is not a site is a would-be one, the assigning of perceptual landing sites can only be carried out hazily and tentatively. That is not possible to determine the number of perceptual landing sites involved in something's coming to be perceived may be viewed as a drawback to the system we propose, yet it need not be a matter of great concern. Regardless of the softness of numbers assigned, despite the inevitable imprecision, perceptual landing sites, whatever their number, always, by definition, register accurately enough features and elements of the circumstances they have been dispersed to record.

Were there no perceptual landing sites, there could be no organism-person that is a body. Perceptual landing sites serve up the initiating site of all sites, the basically fixed but constantly changing kinesthetic-proprioceptive schema of body that keeps a person always kinesthetically grounded and figured and configured. Nothing happens without kinesthetic instigation, corporeal proddings. All events have palpably active starts, stops and turnabouts and kinesthetic repercussions. A mobile and sculpted medium of locatings or of events composed of kinesthetic- and proprioceptive-preceptual landing sites animates the show from within and in great measure runs it.

Imaging Landing Sites

To honor and mark that it is unquestionably the case that landing–site dispersal occurs within the context of an imaging capability, as well as to account for this capability within the information management system that landing-site theory, still in its infancy, apparently engenders, we have taken to referring to ubiquitous emissaries of this capability as imaging landing sites. An area not captured by perceptual landing sites, accorded no points of focus or touchdown points of awareness, does not simply go blank or vanish; instead, it—a looming non-focused-upon area—far from bowing out of the picture or leaving great gaps in it, gets continually supplied, or roughed in, or approximated, by imaging landing sites.

Imaging, integral to a person's forming of the world, gets staked out and maintained by landing sites that fill in gaps in the world or "generalize" it. Imaging landing sites hover around, pick up on, and emulate qualities or features that perceptual landing sites highlight. Taking off from perceptual landing sites (actual points of focus), imaging landing sites (generalizing factors) extend and diffuse surfaces and volumes. Imaging landing sites enlarge the areas over which qualities hold sway. In the course of producing what they produce, they bruit this about: "Have there be more of this here and around here." The picture that emerges is a far cry from the mosaic of empiricists, with its standard same-sized tiles of sensation. Instead of a mosaic of registerings, we have a shifting-about patchwork quilt of registerings and quasi-registerings. We have a patchwork quilt that never stays the same. Palimpsests of quilts of patchworked registerings and quasi-registerings on the move; registerings and quasi-registerings slipping under and over one another, replacing one another. Imaging landing sites: quasi-registerings.

Amorphous accordings of more information than is directly supplied, imaging landing sites exist as even less discrete patches of world than perceptual landing sites. Blending the surroundings and blending into the surroundings, they have hardly any shape at all and perhaps had best be spoken of as shapeless; even so, they help define the shapes of the objects of the world. Imaging landing sites are not even of an indeterminate size; they are, instead, possibly without scale. This does not mean that they have no part in recording scale. They fall in line with whatever perceptual landing sites (and dimensionalizing landing sites) determine the measure of things to be. What they mete out in this regard gets abundantly meted out in the spirit of a grand, continual, cooperative gesture toward getting a world to form (out of the universe).

And where might imaging landing sites lie? Where do any landing sites lie? Might not all landing sites lie within (or throughout) an imaging domain of sorts? If so, how what transpires originates in imaging has yet to be determined. Surely imaging capability derives from a mobile and sculpted medium of locatings composed, for a start, of kinesthetic and tactile landing sites, the human body. In any event, a part of the whole exists as imaging. Imaging landings sites eventuate not only in patches that fill in and finish the world but also in all manner of figural event. We believe that the resolving of these matters requires the construction of complex measuring and tracking devices, constructions by which to gain perspective on human functioning and separate out its component factors.

Persons, then, field their surroundings kinesthetically, tactilely, visually, aurally, olfactorily, and gustatorily all at once, with each modality having a direct or perceptual component and an indirect or imaging one. For example, within the perceptual array, objects that are not touched have no immediate tactile component; these might be said to have, instead, a mediate one, a tactile-*imaging* component that portrays how objects are *likely to feel* to the touch. Tactile-imaging landing sites confer on the world a sense of texture or of nascent texture. All perceptual landing sites have corresponding imaging landing sites; visual landing sites have corresponding sets of visual-*imaging* landing sites, aural landing sites have corresponding sets of aural-*imaging* landing sites, and so on. We have taken to referring to kinesthetic-*imaging* landing sites as ambient-kinesthetic landing sites or as ambient kinesthesia. We plan to study in a later work the extent to which sited awareness is imbued with an ambient kinesthesia.

Not only do imaging landing sites extend perceptual landing sites, continually providing "more of the same" as they hover about them and emulate qualities and features they incarnate as or capture, they can unprompted imitate these direct responses to probable existents well enough to act as stand-ins for them. Although much about the following account remains unresolved, it being after all an isolated case, anecdotal and un-followed-up-on, we present it here for three reasons: it demonstrates well the stand-in capacity of an imaging landing site; it has something to contribute to our difficult-to-put-together concept of a dimensionalizing landing site; and it gives an undistorted view of imaging capacity, leaving it untouched, an open question, even as it shows how in some way all depends on it.

Recounting how he was able to perform the amazing feat of solving the polyomino puzzle, a mapping puzzle about bordering territories that had gone unsolved for several decades, Karl Dahlke, the blind mathematician, reviewed the steps he had taken. He remembers having cut a piece of cardboard into twenty identical pieces, polyominos, and then having spent time positioning them in relation to one another. Next, he left off working with the physical pieces and began instead to visualize a large, brown board that stood right in front of him ready to have shiny, white polyominos placed upon it. Choosing a corner from which to begin, he affixed piece after piece to the board, finding how best to position each one so as to come up with a solution; he continued doing this until the number of pieces affixed to the board exceeded his capacity to remember—that is, until he began, as he put it, "to run out of memory"—at which point, using Lego blocks, he con-

Architectural Body—Landing Sites

structed a model of what he had visualized. When questioned about the elements of his visualization, he replied as follows:

> Come to think of it, the puzzle pieces were three-dimensional or had some three-dimensionality to them ... and this was so despite the fact that I was seeking to solve a puzzle of two-dimensional space. This is a false artifact, I guess, having to do with the way my touch can be of use in positioning pieces. Memory also plays a part in it. My early memories of three-dimensionality during the years when I still had sight.... And you ask about the density of the visualized pieces? I would say they have the same density in the visualization as I feel them to have when I touch them—now that of the cardboard pieces and now that of the Lego blocks, at times turning out to be a mixture of the two. And how thick is the board to which I affix the puzzle pieces? It needs to be as thin as possible, for it is there only as a...what shall I say, I put it to use only as a memory expander. But I cannot repeat often enough: Choosing carefully the corner from which to begin is critically important.[2]

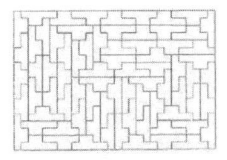

POLYOMINO PUZZLE

Dahlke recalls having spent hour upon hour placing shiny, white polyominos into position upon a thin, brown board. Working in this way, he could try polyominos out in various positions within the group he had assembled, even while he was strolling across campus, soaking in a tub, or resting in bed. He would go on deliberating and, in his words, "seeing-touching along," until he grew tired, at which point he would promptly shut off the lights as it were and go to sleep. Remarkably, when he awoke, the puzzle pieces were exactly as he had left them. The puzzle was always there as he had thus far worked it out.

There can be no doubt that Dahlke's picturing of the polyomino puzzle involves no visual perceptual landing sites. He is certainly not

---

2   Karl Dahlke, interview, April 21, 1989.

issuing direct responses to probable existents. Even so, puzzle pieces need to be given definite shapes and precisely positioned, and both these tasks are, by definition, specific to perceptual landing sites. This leads us to conclude that imaging landing sites act, for Dahlke, as stand-ins for visual perceptual ones. We find these mimics keying polyominos or salient features of polyominos into position in ways more in keeping with events and actions of a seen world than an imaged one. How do Dahlke's imaging landing sites succeed in plausibly presenting themselves as direct responses to puzzle pieces?

It is only in special circumstances that an imaging landing site can take on all of, or nearly all of, the characteristics of a perceptual landing site, and Dahlke would seem to have instinctively arrived at having fashioned such circumstances for himself. One thing we can be certain of is that Dahlke's imaging landing sites that parade as perceptual landing sites could never field the external world as the latter do. Nonetheless, he is able to sharpen their focus and get them to deliver up to him results most people can only get from perceptual landing sites. He does this, we believe, by being willing to reduce the whole of his surroundings down to a thin, brown board—a focused-in world to which to attend. He reduces ambient light and air and the whole field of probable existents to but a single object with minimal breadth and expanse that has been, it appears, apportioned out to hold precisely twenty polyominos of a particular yet hard-to-specify size. Dahlke puts this object, which we would be tempted to call a critical holder,[3] in place as a memory expander. Is it only in a context as limited as this, one as pointedly reined in as this, that imaging landing sites can perfectly mimic perceptual one?

When Dahlke reduces his surroundings, at least as far as visual perception is concerned, to a thin, brown board, what makes his imaging landing sites able to come alive as perceptual ones? An imager of a puzzle or of, for that matter, anything at all usually has a wide-open choice as to where within sited awareness to place what is imaged. Imaging thus comes with a whole host of would-be sites to be imaged. The more ambiguous the surroundings, the greater the number of imaging landing sites that will be needed for making determinations and giving things shape. Ambiguous surroundings tap an imager's resources or energy supply on two counts: first, because a large number

---

3   See Ch. 8 of Gins/Arakawa, *Architectural Body*.

of imaging landing sites will need to be churned out, and second, because a great deal of short–term memory will have to be used to keep track of what these landing sites have surfaced as.

While for computers—and Dahlke's term, "memory expander," does seem to have originated in computer lingo—memory expansion can be effected through the deletion of data, the insertion of additional hardware for increased storage capacity and more processing power, or the swapping out of different storage or processing areas; in human beings, memory (short-term) expansion can be effected only through a provisional striking out of data that translates into a freeing up of memory space, that is through reducing memory requirements for one task so that the requirements of another task can be met. A certain over-allness, what might otherwise be seen to take up most of short-term memory, and which even in ordinary circumstances must be seen to put an enormous strain on imaging or generalizing power, has been cut short, reduced back to a thin, brown board—a board that conveniently stays parallel to the imager's forehead no matter which way he moves. Now Dahlke can concentrate on imaging-remembering what polyominos he put where. A great reduction in one area has made it possible for there to be a great expansion (of imaging power) in another.[4]

When queried further, Dahlke does admit there to be a bit of ambient distance between the part of himself that initiates the thing-like events he uses as puzzle pieces, his landing sites, and the board upon which he will, by means of imaging landing sites, place polyominos and to which he will find himself, again by means of imaging landing sites, frequently returning. He also remembers there to have been now and then a vague hand-like event affixing the pieces to the board.

The external world, which is always there to supply what one might otherwise feel obliged to remember, and thus frees memory for matters other than keeping track of the immediate surroundings, might qualify as a memory expander for the sighted. Memory is freed up when one no longer needs to remember what is perceived because one is simply able to revisit it, and this, by most accounts, is what the external world has to offer. Upon entering a room, a person begins dis-

---

4   For more on how reduction leads to expansion, see Arakawa and Madeline Gins, "Expansion and Reduction—Meaning of Scale," subdivision no. 6 of *The Mechanism of Meaning* (New York: Abbeville Press, 1988).

persing perceptual landing sites to record its features. One may not know what one first noticed, where one's reading of one's surroundings began, but one of course must and does begin somewhere. It is, in any event, in the nature of actions within surroundings to have beginning, middle and end points and for chosen beginning, middle and end points to be places that are stable enough to invite return visits. That it is able to be returned to makes something's existence more probable. Hence, Dahlke speaks of how critically important choosing where to begin is. His careful constructing of a starting point would seem to be a way for him to transform his drastically reduced surroundings into an as-if external world. We think this would remain true even if upon further questioning Dahlke were to reveal that it was not the whole setup for the polyomino puzzle but the puzzle itself that required a focused beginning. We can unhesitatingly assert this because we have come to see that to carry imitating of a perceptual landing site to exquisite lengths, that which disperses mimicking sites needs first of all to mimic a probable existent on which to land; if he is to make his world be as-if external, endowing it with probable existence, Dahlke must boldly mark a beginning place that can be revisited.

It is fair to say that Dahlke has never seen a polyomino. It should probably be assumed that for the solving of this puzzle he "sees" the polyomino in whatever form it is most convenient for him to have it. It is a compromise solution whose startling accuracy is sufficient to allow the puzzle to be solved. He manufactures polyominos out of the whole cloth of his sited awareness; we will bring up more of what goes into their manufacture when, in the next section, we discuss dimensionalizing landing sites; neither we nor anyone else is prepared at this time in history to go into the whole of this whole cloth. But what are these polyominos? What is a polyomino of Dahlke's manufacture made of? An imaging landing site that suddenly has a sharp face, a face suddenly in focus, all of a sudden a new facet? Or is this polyomino that he can affix to the board a sculpted flake of the crust of some cloud that has grown to be bread-like? Whatever else this is, it is a class of long-lasting imaging landing site able to remain in place long enough for other imaging landing sites to visit it. When Dahlke thinks he has solved a section of the puzzle, say, one-fourth of it, that group of polyominos, those several imaging landing sites parading as perceptual ones, coalesce into a single larger imaging landing site that can, in its guise of probable existent, be revisited. We leave it to the reader to imagine the sound with which imaging landing sites assume their positions upon the thinnest of thin boards to which they flock even as their source models perceptual landing sites.

The most highly probable existent or landing site in all that Dahlke recounts would have to be Dahlke himself. In any event, although Dahlke's marvelously intensified or souped-up image, his precise picturing of the polyomino puzzle, a special order or precision-held image that marvelously permits shifting-about and change, takes place through imaging, and can therefore be said to exist in the realm of imaging, it certainly cannot be said to be completely without perceptual landing sites. In addition to having locatings and notings throughout his body (kinesthetic perceptual landing sites) and sounds and odors coming at him from every direction (aural and olfactory perceptual landing sites), Dahlke feels feet in shoes and shoes on terrain, clothing wherever it touches his skin; sitting upon a chair, he feels it along his back and arms and across his bottom, or lying upon a bed, his head upon a plumped pillow, he feels the cushioning surface along his back, neck, and head, or along the front of his body, or along one side of his body (tactile perceptual landing sites all). Any tactile landing site stirs up around itself kinesthetic flickerings, nudgings, and push-pull-cracklings. Dahlke's precisely positioned puzzle that would seem to be all made of imaging landing sites has, then, a firm basis in perceptual landing sites as well. Never to be overlooked: there is a great deal more to imaging than imaging alone.

Dimensionalizing Landing Sites

Acknowledging that a person experiences not only sites but also depths, we posit a composite landing site (a landing-site "molecule" formed of the two landing-site "atoms" we have named perceptual and imaging). A dimensionalizing landing site registers location and position relative to the body. Building, assessing, and reading volume and dimensions, dimensionalizing landing sites "engineer" depth and effect the siting of sites. These sites register and determine the bounds and shapes of the environment.

A chair as pictured or held in place by perceptual landing sites (direct perception) with the assistance of imaging landing sites (indirect or imitative perception) has for its perceiver a distinct position in relation to everything else in the room—the work of dimensionalizing landing sites (part direct, part indirect perception).

Think of the part that judgments of dimension play in Dahlke's surprisingly precise picturing of the polyomino puzzle. He uses tactile and kinesthetic perceptual landing sites to add depth to a visualized image. Transposing how, in sum, the puzzle pieces felt to his touch as he held them at various angles and moved his fingers over them, he endows the imaged pieces with some solidity, a burgeoning hint of three-dimensionality. Dimensionalizing is conducted cross-modally, as are all the actions of a person. It has been shown that the illusion generated by the Ames room—giant boy, tiny adult—vanishes when the viewer, armed with a stick so as to probe the room's interior, learns tactilely and kinesthetically that the floor slopes, and gathers that what she has imaged to be an ordinary room is anything but ordinary.

The best way to get a sense of how dimensionalizing landing sites function is to think of what happens when they are missing or insufficiently arrayed. Everyone has had the experience of feeling like an idiot when stubbing her toe. The necessary dimensionalizing landing sites were not in place, depth was not inserted where it needed to be.

A Neutral Zone of Emphasis

Think of a nod of recognition to position and substance, a nod that recognizes where and what and nothing more. A dispersion of landing sites: a scattering of nods that everywhere notes positionings. A landing-site configuration forms, as a heuristic device, when the continual symbolizing of a symbolizing creature—when that which can, in effect, make a metaphor or symbol of anything—becomes slightly muted or is put on hold for a bit; the symbolizing creature becomes a landing-site coordinating creature. The tense of landing sites holds as that split second of muting whose instantaneous time span lasts only long enough for basic positionings to be registered. Providing a neutral zone of emphasis, landing sites simply bypass subject-object distinctions. Landing site: a muted symbol, or one—but inseparable from all others—event-marker in and of the event-fabric that is organism-person-environment.

A neutral stance asks that nonresolvable issues be kept on hold—fluidly and flexibly on hold—right out there in the world where they occur; it asks as well that they be held open and be made to open still further to yield additional information about what is at issue. Landing sites deliver an on-the-spot data management system. Information management—that is what landing sites are set up to do. On-the-spot data managing is now within everyone's reach.

Procedural Architecture

What Counts as Architecture? What Counts as Bioscleave? What Counts as Architectural Body?

Start by thinking of architecture as *a tentative constructing toward a holding in place*. Architecture's holding in place occurs within and as part of a prevailing atmospheric condition that other routinely call *biosphere* but which we, feeling the need to stress its dynamic nature, have renamed *bioscleave*.

All species belonging to bioscleave exist only tentatively (which remains true whatever turns out to be the truth about natural selection, whether it happens randomly or with directionality), with some species, all things being unequal, existing on a far more tentative basis than others. Additionally, bioscleave stays breathable and in the picture only so long as elements take hold of each other in particular ways, only so long as there can be a cleaving of a this to a that and a cleaving of a this off of a that. So that there might be new and different link-ups, fresh points of departure, ever renewed *tentative constructing toward a holding in place*, a firm and definite taking hold, which gives one sense of the term to cleave, must also readily entail cutting apart, cut-off, relinquishment, the other sense of the term. Should a crucial element fail to hold its own, bioscleave would go missing, collapsing into untempered atmosphere, leaving (but no one would be there to tell) an uninhabitable planet in its wake. A single missing element (carbon or oxygen) or an aberrant formation of a molecule, to say nothing of a large-scale cataclysmic event, could make bioscleave vanish, bringing an abrupt end to millennia of *tentative constructing toward a holding in place*. In studying so tenuous and elusive an event-fabric as bioscleave, the making of cut-and-dried separations, such as distinguishing between subject and object, should be avoided.

Because bioscleave itself occurs as a demonstrably *tentative constructing toward a holding in place,* architectural works constructed into it cannot be anything but tentative; furthermore—and it is for this reason that we have chosen tentativeness as an organizing principle in our practice—it is not enough to know that in deep time all architectural works are fleeting things: it is necessary to construct architectural works that reflect bioscleave's intrinsic tentativeness. An architectural work that will serve the body well will maximize its chances of drawing on and blending with bioscleave, positioning the body in such a way that it can best coordinate itself within its surroundings. Simply, pretending that architecture is not tentative is just that, only a pretense. Architecture will come into its own when it becomes thoroughly associated and aligned with the body, that active other *tentative constructing toward a holding in place,* the ever-on-the-move body. The tense of architecture should be not that of "This is this" or "Here is this" but instead that of "What's going on?"

Staying current with bioscleave, remaining alive as part of it, involves keeping pace with the tentativeness it brings to bear, staying focused on the elusiveness as such of this tenuous event-fabrix or event-matrix. Everything is tentative, but some things or events have a tentativeness with a faster-running clock than others. So that there can at least be a keeping pace with bioscleave's tentativeness, it becomes necessary to divine how best to join events into an event-fabric, which surely involves learning to vary the speed at which one fabricates *tentative constructings toward a holding in place.*

Architecture occurs as one of many ways life sees fit to conduct and construct itself, a form of life, and all forms of life have, without doubt, as of this date, but a limited and uncertain existence. Even so, thus far only nomads have held architecture to be as a matter of course tentative.

Life—Bios—would seem to be constituted by interactions between *tentative constructings toward a holding in place,* with the body, the body-in-action, surely the main fiddler at the fair. Bodily movements that take place within and happen in relation to works of architecture, architectural surrounds, are to some extent formative of them. Those living within and reading and making what they can of an architectural surround are instrumental in and crucial to its *tentative constructing toward a holding in place.* We do not mean to suggest that architecture exist only for the one who beholds or inhabits it, but rather that the body-in-action and the architectural surround should not be defined apart from each other, or apart from bioscleave. Architectural works can direct the body's *tentative constructing toward a holding in place,* its forming in place. But it is also the case that how the body moves determines what turns out to hold together as architecture for it.

What is authoritative in human life: a person's tentativeness—a totally constructed tentativeness—surefooted rightful hesitation, on-the-hesitating-mark. Persons need to be rescued from self-certainty, but they also need to put their tentativeness in precise order in relation to works of architecture. The hypotheses of procedural architecture query how it is possible—what *tentative constructing toward a holding in place* entails—to be a knowing body in a bioscleave—the ins and outs of viability.

*

What stems from the body, by way of awareness, should be held to be of it. Any site at which a person finds an X to exist should be considered a contributing segment of her awareness.

Architectural Body Hypothesis/Sited Awareness Hypothesis

This supposition would seem to state the obvious were it not for the fact that the historical record reveals awareness to have rarely, if ever, been defined as sited, or studied as such. Recognize, this supposition urges, that awareness sites itself all over the place at once; or better, that a person positions herself within her surroundings by taking her surroundings up as her sited awareness. Sites of sited awareness are, of course, landing sites of the moment. Put in evidence in this hypothesis is the disparity that exists between the world as it happens—awareness as indeed sited—and the world, reduced and distorted, made to appear as other than what it happens as—awareness abstracted out of any surroundings.

Putting two seemingly discrete *tentative constructings towards a holding in place* forward as one, the Architectural Body Hypothesis/Sited Awareness Hypothesis, a supposition that guides procedural architecture, would have it that a person never be considered apart from her surroundings. It announces the indivisibility of seemingly separable fields of bioscleave: a person and an architectural surround. The two together give procedural architecture its basic unit of study, the architectural body. The Architectural Body Hypothesis/Sited

Awareness Hypothesis puts forward the idea that embodied mind, a current way of referring to mind or awareness so as to give body its due, extends out beyond the body-proper into the architectural surround; the surrounding bioscleave needs to be weighed in as part of awareness's body. This hypothesis would have us never forget that we are babies of bioscleave and are therefore only comprehensible (to ourselves) in term of it.

*

What Counts as Procedural?

Bioscleave—people breathe it, it sustains them—has parts and elements, many of which exhibit an order, even as it presents itself as an enormously confused mass with operative factors that cannot be distinguished. Who moves through this mass of chaos, this massive mix of order and chaos, has sited awareness buried there within it. People are forced to abstract in order to proceed, but any abstracting requires that not as much be taken into consideration as ought to be. A person can never get to the bottom of her own alertness. Having to abstract in order to proceed, an organism that persons is half-abstracted from the start. She behaves as if she were on her own recognizance, never quite sure that it is valid to assume this. People get drawn off in this direction or that. In a world of persistent inexplicability, everyone will be fairly directionless, even those appearing to have chosen a definite course of action. The world as one finds it: a concatenation of partial procedures or procedure-like occurrences, diffuse or defused procedures, incomplete or bedeviling ones.

Calculated measures that have distinct and purposeful steps do take shape under the aegis of some agency. But because what (if anything) authorizes agency within bioscleave lies hidden, agency, all agency, remains suspect. Defining procedure as a process that is the work of an agent, or that at least implies agency, we attempt to smoke out hidden agents or agency or to grow (the basis for) new ones.

People interact with bioscleave largely through what has come to be called *procedural knowing*, a term covering both instinctual sequences and encoded knowing, that is, habitual patterns of activity. Perceiving, walking, talking, and eating, for example, happen as procedural knowing. Acquiring a skill involves integrating all steps needed for skillfully performing a task and then reducing them to a procedure. Whatever has come to be know-how has been cast as procedural; the many activities and considerations that subsist as procedural knowing within or to one side of sited awareness, taking up fewer of its sites now than they had need of before they were thus reduced, free it to be active elsewhere. With steps and nuances of coordinating skills handled apart from awareness, a person can go on to acquire still other coordinating skills. The instinctual and the newly ingrained get played back through operations lying outside awareness—as procedurally triggered occurrences. Learned behavior equals procedures that can automatically, minus awareness, be set in motion. Steps are performed outside awareness.

Landing-site dispersal, that which transpires as sited awareness, is coordinated beneath awareness. If thinking is thought of as a subroutine of this siting procedure, it too must be regarded as procedural. Even thinking as traditionally defined—that is, thinking taken as a single course of action, which, we suggest, is an outrageously reductive definiton—would seem to depend on procedures. In any case, when sets of instructions are carried out and tasks performed, one is tempted to speak of procedure; shall we categorize thinking as a body-wide, no, biocleave-wide, mixture of procedures belonging to different realms, a thus far ineffable and unexplainable series of procedurally conducted occurrences?

Procedures do and do not walk up to one to introduce themselves as existing. Processes linked, no matter how briefly, to awareness: procedures, procedural. Rather than flat-out knowing, there is a continual anticipating, self-guarding, accommodating, allowing, bypassing—all of which can be counted as procedural. All bodily dynamics: procedurally orchestrated. The unconscious: the procedural. Innate functions, defense mechanisms, built-in and built-up tendencies, hidden knowing: procedures at the behest of someone or something—procedures born of procedures?

That which counts as procedural will need to be enlarged and made to exist so that it can be entered wittingly. Only once the procedural can on its own account be entered, only once the procedural has been writ large, will members of our species have it in them to complete centuries-old procedures that, having remained unfinished, have left them in the lurch, bereft and doubly bereft. A constructed world that has, with great forethought, been tactically posed and thus been given its procedural due will instruct people in brand-new coordinating skills and in the compounding of skills attained. Ability to coordinate a greater number of skills leads to a freer and wider-ranging and more perspicacious intellect.

*

This brings us to the second of the three hypotheses underpinning procedural architecture:

> It is because we are creatures of an insufficiently procedural bioscleave that the human lot remains untenable.
>
> Insufficiently Procedural Bioscleave Hypothesis

Within an insufficiently procedural bioscleave, members of the human species have neither the wherewithal to figure out the nature of their agency nor the requisite skill to engineer for themselves what would amount to a reversible destiny. Although it has plenty of processes and procedures in place, bioscleave consistently lets us down, that is, drops us one by one—we are mortal—because procedures through which we could sustain ourselves indefinitely are lacking to it.

The Insufficiently Procedural Bioscleave Hypothesis does not give the universe and its bioscleave a failing grade, only an incomplete.

Those who are of bioscleave need to come to its aid. Procedures woven, carpentered, poured, or cantilevered into bioscleave might lead to nurture life without end, or at least to articulate its lacks and needs, perhaps by delivering them (but does it already do this?) as not-to-be-missed sharp insights.

*

Adding carefully sequenced sets of architectural procedures (closely argued ones) to bioscleave will, by making it more procedurally sufficient, reconfigure supposed inevitability.

Closely Argued Built-Discourse Hypothesis

We thus hypothesize that an important recourse available to those living within an insufficiently procedural bioscleave is to add procedures back into it. Simply, our species needs to devise and build whatever bioscleave does not spontaneously provide.

Surely it is plausible to think that if people build into their surroundings procedures in which to immerse themselves, bioscleave will grow more procedurally ample. Supplying bioscleave with missing procedures will make it more coherent to itself and to the members of our species. How shall our species set about making the bioscleave sufficiently procedural? "Sufficiently procedural for what?" did someone ask? Listen to that crying. It would be better not only to construct the procedural, but also to have it become one's home ground, one's training ground. At which point, we trot out our hard-won notion of an architectural procedure.

Architectural surrounds stage architectural procedures. A surround constructed to constrain a sequence of actions presents a procedure to be followed; and as soon as someone sets foot into an architectural surround that constrains action, the architectural procedure it stages gets going. The constraining we are speaking of is so light that it is better thought of as constructive guiding.

Tactically positioned constructed procedures would appear to be those corrective maneuvers bioscleave has need of to make it more fully procedural. In a world in which processes and procedures naturally compound, it is hardly a far reach to think of architectural procedures responding to and expanding on the consequences of other constructed procedures. At such time that the human species will be genuinely able to augment bioscleave, life will have come to be lived on a new basis.

Within tactically posed surroundings (hereafter referred to as tactically posed surrounds) a territory of mediation gets described or suffuses or flourishes in/as place through movements and activities of individuals or groups, or of singles or "withs," as sociologists put it with lovely professional succinctness. Movements and the sited awareness they modulate and that enfolds them mediate architecture; responding to tactically posed surrounds, joining forces with them, actions complete the architectural procedures that put (the) procedural into procedural architecture. Mediating for a person much of what hitherto existed for her as procedural or unconscious, movements and the sited awareness they modulate turn groups of walls and room features, lifeless material, into a more focused, higher level of the procedural. Think of the procedural as having been enlarged to life-size and as now taking place throughout the sited awareness bounded by an architectural surround; the procedural having thus been brought into palpable view, its fixed sequence of actions can be altered. Can it be, then, that in architecture we have the means to construct awareness on a new basis? Oh yes, that is what we have begun to believe.

*

What Counts as a Closely Argued Built-Discourse? What Counts as an Architectural Procedure?

It is by relying on juxtaposed repeatable and re-combinable items that verbal discourse, with great sleight of mouth (or hand), encompasses and presents sequentially considered events. Modularly constructed areas and the architectural procedures they engender will be the juxtaposed repeatable and re-combinable items of a built discourse.

An architectural procedure resembles its predecessor, a word, in two respects for a start: first, it is a repeatable item that readily lends itself to discursive use; second, charged with conveying a specific experience or range of experiences, it can be evaluated as to how well it serves its purpose or how effectively it has been put to use.

Architectural procedures used only for studying interactions between body and bioscleave have an observational-heuristic purpose, while those devised for transforming body and bioscleave have a reconfigurative one. Architectural procedures and the tactically posed surrounds that structure and institute them often incorporate both purposes at once, with one purpose grading into another.[5]

If architectural procedures serve as the words of a built discourse, then tactically posed surrounds, combining these procedures as they do, are its phrases, sentences, paragraphs, and texts. Surely, as well, tactically posed surrounds will factor out as those poems that have ever eluded poets, poems through which those of us who wish to can save our own necks, poems that could only heretofore be intimated by an insufficiently procedural biocleave. An architectural procedure that helps a person observe more precisely how landing sites disperse may be thought of as an observational-heuristic one, but if, when she performs this procedure, it also provides her with a critical edge on biocleave, it may be classified as transformational or reconfigurative as well; similarly, if a reconfigurative procedure successfully transforms biocleave and in the process pinpoints an indistinguishable constituent factor of the person performing it or evinces evidence in support of, for example, the architectural body hypothesis, it serves an observational-heuristic purpose as well. In tactically posed surrounds set up primarily to observe events, houses and towns are constructed as laboratories in which a person's every move can be surveyed, assessed, and reflected upon. Surrounds that run primarily reconfigurative procedures through which to transform biocleave are more training grounds than laboratories. Ideally, tactically posed surrounds should be laboratories that double as training grounds.

If continuity could be maintained across tactically posed surrounds, a built discourse would start up; sequences of tactically posed surrounds would have to be able to be not only consequent on previous sequences but also consequent to ones slated to be built later. Information states produced when someone moves through the slightly different layouts and features of paired tactically posed surrounds would naturally reflect—and inflect and deflect—built-in closely comparable differences; gradations would thrillingly yield a spectrum of body-wide knowing capable of physically manifesting cause and result or warrant and inference.

---

5 See Ch. 7 of Gins/Arakawa, *Architectural Body*, for a more detailed discussion, including descriptions of the first architectural procedures to have come into existence, of what we next allude to only in passing.

Not all well-organized enclosures weigh in as the highly structured architectural surrounds we term tactically posed surrounds. Space capsules, for example, despite housing purposefulness aplenty, do not merit the term and therefore do not qualify as works of procedural architecture. An architectural surround that is functional, such as a space capsule, and such as the greater part of the built world of our day, facilitates an organism that persons in its actions, extending the senses no questions asked, whereas an architectural surround that is procedural, a tactically posed surround, fills an organism that persons with questions by enabling it to move within and between its own modes of sensing.

Discursive sequences of tactically posed surrounds, constructed as built propositions, marshal existing logical connectives and position newly invented ones into the "real," steering, regulating, and guiding interactions between body and bioscleave through three-dimensional THEREFOREs, BUTs, ORs, ANDs, and built-up WHATEVERs. What will need to be studied is which types and combinations of bodily movements are most conducive to an optimal *tentative constructing toward a holding in place,* and which constructed discursive sequences best constrain them.

A built record of measures taken for remedying bioscleave's insufficiency will rise up with corners and edges, and windows and doors, and hallways and rooms, and streets and crossroads. It will be truly astonishing for someone entering a town to realize that she has set foot within what has been intuited, surmised, and reasoned through, all for the purpose of augmenting her as a member of her species and so that sited awareness (read *architectural body*) can come into its own. Walking along will be discoursing along through an argument of strategic allocations and reallocations. When it stands up to be counted and entered, this built argument or discourse will manifestly turn us inside out, imbuing the ever receptive bioscleave with more of what it is like to be us. We will officially and for all time have put our ruminative selves on view for bioscleave. This will be a depiction in three dimensions (and counting) of how members of our species have fielded what has come to them—what came upon them—as a consequence of their having wielded sited awareness (read *architectural body*) in a coordinated manner. The body moves through a tactically posed town puzzling itself out of focus and then back into it, now with a wider yet sharper focus. Merely by stepping into one's own apartment or that of a friend, one starts the on-the-spot testing of procedural architecture's hypotheses.

A town can be constructed to register the effect a neighboring town has had on the body. This happens to some degree even in nonprocedural towns: Los Angeles has a lot to say to your body about what Chicago or Paris or Singapore has led it to become. But in towns that are closely argued built-discourses, the interchange between body and biocleave proceeds by means of shaped atmospheric denotations and connotations. One town's assembled constructed statements, its tactically posed surrounds, take up where another's left off, for procedural architecture's subject matter is always the same, with the discussants remaining in all situations body and biocleave.

Activating an architectural procedure, a person comes alive to her own tacit knowing; body-wide and wider, occurrent tacit knowing goes explicit. A built world, designed with foresight peering through forethought, and that will have been, with great deliberation, arrayed as a communal project, will frame the formation for "the human." In the shadow play of beauty and the beast as one, organism and person, the implicit shines out explicitly. A person stays alive to how she is dispersed and then to how she is again and again dispersed through and into that dispersal. Tacit knowing (knowing how) can then begin to be directly addressed, directly mapped, propositionally, even as propositional knowing (knowing that) can be investigated in regard to how it is bodily—yes, biocleave, in rapport with you—coordinated to occur.

It arrives to a newcomer moving through town to wonder, "Of the many ways that I could *tentatively construct a holding in place,* which might serve me best in the long run?" The architectural procedures that tactically posed surrounds are set up to run help those enacting them pull together an otherwise all-over-the-map sited awareness. They elicit specific landing-site dispersals, thereby sculpting or molding sited awareness, thereby changing, degree of awareness. The subject matter: staying alive/coming alive to/staying alive to. She contrasts in slow motion, or in odd motion, her intricate sitings of herself in terms of this town and the previous one, examining effect and upshot of landing-site dispersal, savvy to the need to identify constituent factors that knit, explode, and weave the world's occurrence. The town has been prepped to recognize and expand on, affirm or negate, in part or in full, what other towns have led her to be able to feel and know. At issue always: what the body can come to know on its own behalf and what the body comes to be able to say to itself.

Because issues of viability are everyone's concern, as are too epistemological conundrums, procedural architecture, a populist architecture of hypothesis, should be approached as a community-wide collaborative initiative. Together the members of our species will exponentially increase the tremendous amount of forethought that is needed for town planning. Exhorted and cajoled by their town, by virtue of being gently constrained by its features and elements, to perform architectural procedures, people work and play at figuring out what in the world they could possible be. Hypotheses put forward through built form will be predictive of built hypothesizing to come. In a rephrasing of the hypothesis under discussion here, a closely argued built-discourse can foster fundamental reconfigurings of bioscleave that will constitute or lead to a restructuring of viability, to be translated immediately into life on new terms.

It can be argued, of course that the world has, to some extent, always existed as a built discourse, with people making use of juxtaposed artifacts to address each other. But for a group of constructions—a series of nothing more than inert enclosures, after all—actually "to converse" as a built discourse, systematic conveying will have had to be reasoned through and put in place. An organism that can person is a symbolizing creature that casts thoughts and images upon the faintest anything that gives the slightest indication of being able to in some guise be gotten hold of. Such a creature will easily get traction on and come to think itself through in terms of a world built in a discursive order sequenced to raise existential questions.

*

A prescriptive supposition, the Closely Argued Built-Discourse Hypothesis presents architecture as the supreme context for the examined life, a stage set for body-wide thought experiments. With architectural procedures prodding the body to know all that it is capable of, this becomes an intrusive and active stage set. The body must either escape or "reenter" habitual patterns of action—habitual actions that have customized life into only a few standard patterns. Upon the body's mastering new patterns of action, bioscleave emerges reconfigured.

Notes for an Architectural Body

Architectural bodies have everything to do with what a person makes of the fact, the soft but sure-enough fact, that she perceptually subtends, and as-if palpates, architectural surrounds as wholes.

*

Not a series of actions taken on this scale of action or that but the *coordinating* of several scales of action makes a person able to construct a world. Some scales of action, such as operations that take place in nanoseconds or femtoseconds, are too tiny even to stand up and be counted as scales of action. That which routinely gets coordinated so that a world forms must, even if fleeting, even if immeasurable, continue to be so coordinated, or no actions can be initiated and nothing will form. The coordinating of different scales of action needs to be cut some slack, a great deal of slack—assume it to be the work of all the surroundings and call it an architectural body. Begin by thinking of coordinating one bodily action in conjunction with and in anticipation of another. The coordinating that goes on across a variety of scales of action, a criss-crossing between different world-sizes, continues within and as part of what goes on as basic human-scale bodily coordination. The general phenomenon in muscle control that goes by the name of co-articulation gives a snapshot view of the coordinating of actions or events. A saucer sits on a table at a distance of nearly a foot from its matching cup. A person asked to touch the saucer and pick up the cup at the same time will most likely reach to touch the saucer at the edge nearest the cup while she moves her fingers to be as-if holding the cup's handle even before they reach it. It is through coordinatings such as these that life receives its plausibility. An architectural body might be said to live as a summation of coordinatings of this order.

*

There is that which prompts (architectural surround) and that which gets prompted (organism-person). Features of the architectural surround prompt the body to act. Actions and maneuvers secure a general taking shape of the surroundings, determining for the body the structure and characteristic features of an architectural surround. In responding to the ubiquitous call that comes from nooks, crannies, and non-nooks and crannies of an architectural surround—most observers feel that they ought eventually to get around to noting everything around them—a person assembles and takes on an architectural body, half-knowingly piecing it together into a flowing whole. The harkening to any feature or element of the architectural surround, bodily stirrings and promptings included: an articulation of the architectural body.

*

Until a significant number of tactically posed surrounds are in use, the architectural body we hypothesize to exist cannot but make itself scarce. It will be hard to come by except as a heuristic device. Architectural bodies do exist outright in surroundings that are not tactically posed.

*

An organism casts itself onto the world as a person, and wavers continually between existing as organism and existing as person. Say that all of this casting onto the world and wavering of an organism that persons defines into existence an architectural body.

*

Above all, an organism-person critically holds in place its assembled "behavings as a person" as a located tentativeness on the move. Architectural body: the dispersing and juxtaposing and culling of landing sites in respect to an architectural surround; a super-convening of many convenings; messenger-like—in rapport with all there is; that which revs as momentum—revved and revving; an amassing of the provisional; a ubiquitous piecing together.

*

An organism that persons articulates itself and its surroundings through its movements and its landing-site configurations.

*

Features of the surroundings call forth from organisms-persons the actions and gestures that architect them into persons. On all occasions and any, an organism that persons disperses landing sites, and, by so doing, turns itself into a person having an architectural body.

*

Through a continual assembling of convened-on sites, an architectural body takes shape near and far. Sectors of the event-fabric interpenetrate in landing embrace, sidling into position. Convened-on sites tremble on the brink as the brink. The world is the brink ... at the rim. As the architectural body coordinates landing-site activity, sites-on-the-move divide into those that were once landed on and those now being landed on. Incessantly suddenly surfacing or coming around the corner yet once again, penumbral and subliminal landings animate the ubiquitous site of a person within an architectural surround. Ricocheting landings surge up and swoop down, articulating segments of an architectural body. Landing sites land or form not only in the conventional sense of "to land," lowering down to a destination, but also just as often by rising up to one. The sum of all landings convening along the axes of the triad of elemental paired opposites (front-rear, above-below, left-right) that the body continually generates is what formerly went by the name of spacetime.

*

If organisms form themselves as persons by uptaking the environment, then they involve not only bodies but domains, spheres of activity and influence.

*

What emanates from bodies and what emanates from architectural surrounds intermix.

*

A person as a moving body describes an ever-changing sequence of domains, associating herself with some more closely than with others. Surely personing is preferable to person—in the name of accuracy and in the name of tentativeness.

*

All that emanates from a person as she projects and reads an architectural surround forms an architectural body that moves with her, changing form depending on the positions she assumes. A person's capacity to perform actions is keyed to layout and composition of her architectural body.

*

Playing to and playing off of that which surrounds it, an organism behaves as a person, and in the process forms now this, now that momentary architectural body.

*

At its ever-on-the-move edges, the architectural body we hypothesize instantaneously presents itself as shell-like. Within this hint of shell or this enclosing atmosphere that smacks of shell, an organism, pressing against all manner of offered resistance, persons.

*

If the architectural surround indeed equals nothing more than how it takes shape for the person within it, then the architectural body might be seen as synonymous with it. However, people tend to distinguish between where they are or that within which they are and what they are or what they consider themselves to be subtending.

*

A summing and rounding up of a person's occurrent landing sites or a grand tour of all a person subtends, the architectural body is of value to us as a heuristic device derived from a heuristic device (landing-site: landing-site configuration).

*

To be faithful to occurrent tentativeness.

*

The architectural body is a body that can and cannot be found. Boundaries for an architectural body can only be suggested, never determined.

*

We speak of an architectural body, rather than an architectural field or an architectural context simply because, to begin with, what we want to describe originates from and joins up with the physical body. Think of the body-proper as lending some of its body to the architectural surround, which, in turn, lends some of what characterizes it as architectural to the body-proper. In addition, the word *body*, used to indicate a collection or quantity of information (as in the expression "a body of evidence"), is descriptively apt for indicating the amassing of landing-site configurations formative of an architectural body. We also find the denoting by the word *body* of a mass of matter that is distinct from other masses (as in the expression "a body of water") useful for conveying all of what belongs to that which we wish to describe, that is, all of what fills an architectural surround, whether that "filling" be counted as "thin air" or "sited awareness."

*

As well as having to it some of the body of "human body," architectural body has about it some or much of the body of "student body." Have it that "body of sited awareness" parallels not only "body of water" but also "body of work" and "body of thought."

*

Indeterminate. A mass of indeterminacy. Is there, in fact, an it to this it. Sizeless, or many different sizelessnesses at once. Perspectiveless.

*

We want to say this body's territory weighs in as a huge ambient kinesthesia, an endowing of the rest of the world with some of the feel of the body-proper's kinesthetic activated (and activating) organismic thickness.

*

Everywhere one turns: *tentative constructings toward a holding in place;* many *tentative constructings*—and holdings within holdings as latencies and phases—*toward holdings in place.*

Tentative constructings toward holdings in place on many scales of action at once require skillful coordination. An architectural body critically—ever examining and always assessing—holds possibilities in place. The architectural body consists of two *tentative constructings toward a holding in place:* body-proper and architectural surround.

*

For the purposes of a direct mapping, have symbolic activity or symbolizing—a close relative of imaging capability or derived from it (Construct architectural surrounds through which to investigate this relation!)—be provisionally considered a variety of critical holding. An organism's forming of itself as a person equals its permeating itself with symbolizing. If an organism is knocked off its feet while it is behaving as a person, a person falls; she falls symbolizing, as best she can, herself as a person falling; the landing sites that hold her in place as a person tumble with her, sometimes unable to hold her anymore as a person. Each instant, a person has the ability to handle only a limited amount of critical holding and only a certain amount of symbolizing. The sum of each instant's critical holding: an architectural body.

*

How to hold onto that which ought not to be allowed to disappear? How to observe and adjust attention's grip on itself? Insert into the world, or into the sequences of landing-site configurations that form it, the edges of a pliable and tentative architecture. Have an architectural surround as the least fragmentary form of sculpture elaborate awareness (landing sites) out into the open. Architecture in the tentative mode can envelop and define a flexible field of knowing.

*

The drawing out of an organism-person into its personhood is effected within architectural surrounds, which have been fabricated by those whose own personhoods also formed in respect to architectural surrounds.

*

In cooperation with other organisms, not only synchronically but also in some respects diachronically, the architectural body mediates the body proper and the architectural surround, and it therefore ought to be viewed as communal.

*

Architectural surrounds have distinct neargrounds, middlegrounds, and fargrounds. Landing-site configurations will articulate at least this many positions: nearnearground, nearmiddleground, nearfarground, middlenearground, middlemiddleground, middlefarground, farnearground, farmiddleground, farfarground; nearmiddlefarground, nearfarmiddleground, middlenearmiddle-ground, middlenearfarground, farnearmiddleground. But these positions can just as well be thought of as areas of an architectural body, which takes its ubiquitous cue and command from the form and features of an architectural surround, subtending all positions within the surround's confines.

*

Assigned positions of course quickly lose ground: one moment's nearground slips into the next's farground. Proceduralists insist on taking note of even the most transient of positionings.

*

In dreams one wields one's body within one's world in an analogous manner to how one positions them in relation to each other in waking life. Think of the famous dream of a woman named Rose who dreamed on the night she succumbed to the deadly 1914 flu of a climbing rose bush clinging to a stone tower only to find upon waking that she, Rose, having fallen victim to paralysis, was clinging for dear life to a stone-like body. In an informal survey of dreams, we found: a hotel in which the dreamer's room cannot easily be returned to because it is on a floor at which the elevators never stop; a hotel elevator that deposits the dreamer on the first floor of a department store at the other end of town or one that shoots right up past the roof into the starry sky; an apartment that is of a distinctly different shape and size from the one the dreamer inhabits in waking life, but in which, she comes to realize, she has been residing for days on end; a narrow, ten-storey high brick tower in which the dreamer is imprisoned, but through whose skylight roof sunlight splendidly pours in; a huge house in Northern Italy to which, a decade ago, the dreamer paid a two-week visit in waking life and in which now, many years later, she, a surprise guest of hosts who are off traveling, plays havoc, in this her recurring dream, with the setting's features and elements even as she fears all the while the imminent return of the missing hosts; rooms that extend the dreamer's waking-life apartment while she sleeps but that with daylight are nowhere to be found. These dreams and countless others should be taken as evidence of how deeply committed to, and intermixed with, its surroundings the body is.

Illustrations

023 Site of Reversible Destiny, Elliptical Field, Yoro Park, Gifu Prefecture, Japan (1993-1995)
024 Ubiquitous Site, Nagi's Ryoanji, Architectural Body; Nagi Museum of Contemporary Art, Nagi, Japan (1992-1994)
025 Ubiquitous Site House, poster
026 Infancy House, poster
027 Landing Site Study I
028 Landing Site / Architectural Body Study II
029 Landing Site / Architectural Body Study III***

030 Ubiquitous Site House Study I
031 Ubiquitous Site House Study II
032 Inside a Room Full of Trenches: Arakawa and Madeline Gins
033 Reversible Destiny Village / Museum of Living Bodies

***Notes on Captions

In 1994, in Architecture: Sites of Reversible Destiny (Architectural Experiments after Auschwitz-Hiroshima), *Landing Site / Architectural Body Study III* was paired with the following caption:
— "Each designated area of specified activity within the event-fabric is a set of perceptual landing sites."
— Although an image ought generally to be, for simplicity's sake, contextualized and elucidated by means of one caption at a time, surely the contextualization and elucidation of a particular image can be achieved by quite a number of different captions, each with its own points of emphasis and overall organization of attention space.
— It will probably be best not only to allow but indeed to prepare for the possibility that, with time, new captions would come along to replace earlier ones.
— With the articulation and palpation of the architectural body the overarching goal, the more captions the merrier, as long as they palpate the architectural body. In the spirit of "communal figuring-out," invite others to submit caption-candidates.
— The artic articulation and palpation of the architectural body is the goal, and the more captions that can work to this effect the merrier. In the spirit of a "communal figuring-out" invite others to submit caption-candidates.
— As we read Beebe and Lachman's Infant Research and Adult Treatment the following caption candidates for *Landing Site / Architectural Body Study III* suggested themselves:

> √ Variations in face, voice, and orientation provide an essential means of sensing the partner. Moment-to-moment shifts can be considered to be the smallest unit, nested within larger units that are more prolonged, such as discrete verbalizations. [210]
>
> **A & G's comment: Landing sites abound within landing sites, nesting within one another.**
>
> √ Lyon-Ruth has defined **implicit relational knowing** as 'rule-based representations of how to proceed, of how to do things... with others... such as knowing how to joke around, express affection, or get attention... as much affective and interactive... as cognitive... [I]t begins to be represented long before the availability of language and continues to operate implicitly throughout life.' [215]
>
> √ The patterns of mother-infant interaction described in this book are examples of **repetitive action sequences organized procedurally.** An implicit "knowing how to proceed" can be illustrated by attention regulation patterns, such as who initiates looking, whether or not the partners mutually gaze at each other, how long it is comfortable to

hold a mutual gaze, who looks away first, and how reactive either partner is to the other's looking away. [216]

√ It is at the implicit procedural level, on a moment-to-moment basis, that powerful interactive "emotional schemes" (Bucci, 1997) of face gaze, vocalization and orientation are organized, shifts in degrees of coordination are played out, and disruption and repair are negotiated. [216]

A & G's comment: Dwelling on this paragraph and opening it up further should prove useful.

√ In the constructivist view, actions contain information as an objective property, in contrast to the former view that information has no psychological reality until it is symbolically represented. [217]

√ Interactiveness can be defined as "a system whose processes are its essence" (Kulka, 1997). Rather then conceiving of self as interacting with other, we conceptualize an ongoing co-construction of processes of self- and interactive regulation. Interactiveness is emergent, in a constant process of potential reorganization. [224]

√ The quality of interpersonal communication is related to the degree of coordination between the partners. Various theorists have suggested that high coordination is either optimal (Chapple, 1970) or not optimal (Gottman, 1979) for communication. Currently, nonlinear models of degree of coordination provide a more general view of its varying meaning (Cohn and Elmore, 1998; Lewis and Feiring, 1989; Thelen, 1998; Warner 1988a; Watson, 1994). This nonlinear view argues that the person and the environment (partner or inanimate environment) are always coordinated in time; and that the tightness of the coordination is flexible, changing according to the context (Thelen, 1998). In a situation of danger, such as speeding down the Los Angeles Freeway, we better be tightly coupled to the road. [231]

√ Thelen (1998) suggests that **flexibility in the ability to change the strength of coordination** provides one definition of adaption. [231]

Lengthy Caption (March 12, 2004)

Most probably these people have agreed to be subjects in an experiment which requires of them that they position themselves as they like and then stay put no matter how else they get shifted about. Alternatively, it might either be by order of an expanding universe or by virtue of actions taken by someone or something not pictured here that of a sudden, and then of a sudden again, the same positionings of people and chairs bloom into full-fledged existence in a series of distinctly different removes from the table.
As they cease to be any longer seated at the table, the people depicted here lose those tactile-perceptual landing sites that were their points of contact with it. But mostly, by

not varying one bit how, across this set of pictures, they sit or stand, they pretty much maintain at each of the different several removes from the table the same areas of immediate physical contact with the world, that is, the same array of tactile-perceptual landing sites.

Do kinesthetic-landing sites and proprioceptive ones follow the lead of tactile-landing sites? If so, then they too will be nearly the same from one placement of the group to the next, across each of the different removes from the table. This will, of course, not be true for all other landing sites (visual- and aural- perceptual landing sites as well as imaging landing sites and dimensionalizing landing sites).

The architectural body assumes its shape, its heft, its potency, depending on how landing sites are dispersed.

Urban Exodus? The Future of the City[1]

Florian Rötzer

Cyberspace imposes itself onto the real world, its access points and power bases, with ever increasing speed. The trend is clear: the progressing miniaturization of technology is accompanied by the webbed integration of our everyday lifeworld—ranging from the 'intelligent' home with its interconnected and computerized refrigerators and garbage cans to robots and cars as well as to animals and human beings themselves. Microchips, sensors, effectors, transmitters, cables, and satellites envelop the earth like a second skin in a gigantic tide of circulating data. There is a considerable danger that everything which up until now has benefited from the advantages of centralization and spatial concentration will lose in importance. Global competition plays a crucial role in this process since the world has become 'smaller' as a consequence of new and faster means of transportation. More importantly, computer networks threaten traditional spatial hierarchies. What so far determined and made localized urban concentrations attractive, i.e., spatial proximity, will be replaced by the ease and speed with which cyberspace transmits information. The exodus of commerce, of business and banks, of offices and bodies of administration, of schools and universities, of libraries and museums, has already begun and will continue with greater intensity as more broadband connections are introduced, that is, the more the capacity of computers increases to send and transfer ever larger amounts of data within ever shorter periods of time.

Human beings will increasingly come to live in two worlds simultaneously: two worlds that are interconnected and interpenetrating. This will, however, also spawn new conflicts and give rise to a number of far-reaching changes. In one of the possible scenarios the spatial structures of the city as a 'machine of compression and acceleration' will dissolve and will be replaced by the scattered struc-

---

1 Translated by Matthias Freidank.

tures of a 'digital urbanism' that provides access to the virtual realm and is thus not tied to a particular place or location in the material world. At the same time, the traditional cities, which suffer from growing budget problems, will receive the socially marginalized and poor. 'Digital urbanism' thus refers to the fact that people in the future will live predominantly in decentralized, metropolitan landscapes where the traditional lines of demarcation between the city and the country will be even more blurred than today.

The importance of cities and of spaces that are characterized by a high density of people, institutions and buildings is not going to change as rapidly as some commentators have predicted a few years ago; rather these transformations will take place slowly and gradually. The attacks of 9/11 are likely to be conducive to such a development. The terrorist attacks on the metropolis New York, and especially on such symbols of urbanity as the World Trade Center, not only destroyed an emblem of urbanism but also demonstrated the great risk posed by a means of mass transportation, the airplane. Eventually, mass transportation and concentrated urban spaces, where masses of people work and live together, have become a threat.

Since the invention of gun-powder, and thus of long-range weaponry, cities, despite their fortifications, have no longer been able to provide protection from outside attacks. With the possibility of destroying cities through air-strikes and the dangers posed by weapons of mass destruction cities have been turned into deadly traps because, in contrast to rural areas, they offer a maximum number of possible points of attack. They usually accommodate the crucial sectors of the political, economic, and social infrastructure of a nation. A mass of people concentrated within a densely populated area has thus become itself a potential risk and a genuine target not only for terrorists but also for conventional military attacks. Nevertheless, the city also allows small groups of people to go into hiding, for big cities resemble in this respect spaces that are difficult to survey and control such as a jungle or mountainous landscapes. After the terrorist attacks, anthrax letters appeared demonstrating that every letter and every parcel potentially prove dangerous for its receiver; finally, due to unfathomable reasons another airplane crashed into a residential area of New York City, thus increasing the insecurity of the inhabitants of the metropolis.

In the near future, these events will provide the backdrop for deliberations over whether it is absolutely necessary to travel from one place to another when there is also the possibility to carry out transactions and exchanges in other ways, for instance, through video hook-ups or video conferences. Surely, we still want other people to be bodily present, but we are as yet only at the beginning of the age of telesociety even if we have already become used to operating the telephone and watching other people on screens. The sudden emergence of the cell-phone as the harbinger of a society of boundless mobility and an all-pervading integration of information technologies has shown that communication with people who are distant often seems to be more important than with people who are physically present. The permanent capacity to communicate and also the possibility of mutual control and surveillance demonstrate that cyberspace and reality pervade each other more and more—a development that will undoubtedly have consequences for the construction of the real.

If the images of hijacked airplanes crashing into the emblems of global capitalism symbolically herald the slow disappearance of the skyscrapers and thus of the concentrated and centralized character of the cityscape, then the dangers posed by letters transformed into deadly messages will probably not only lead to the triumph of the virtual email over the traditional letter; they will also be conducive to the further 'virtualization' of society, even if this development triggers new dangers such as hacker-attacks, cyber-sabotage or simply computer viruses attached to emails. Yet the risks of virtual reality are still relatively harmless in contrast to the threats to corporeal life itself that are posed by terrorist attacks; a devastating cyber-terrorist attack has in any case not yet occurred. Nevertheless, the American government has already considered to set up a computer-network totally independent from the World Wide Web in order to ensure the functioning of sectors crucial to society as a whole. The disadvantages of such a project, however, can be seen in the fact that this would lead to a wholesale retreat form the public as well as to the necessity of operating two networks side by side. The attention that contemporary media society pays to particular subjects or images can quickly be incited, but its memory is also relatively short. Thus in situations of an impending terrorist threat, to which virtually everybody can fall prey, security measures and defensive fantasies proliferate, which in all probability are of short duration, provided that the threat does not materialize.

This process, however, can intensify developments that have already been unfolding for a longer period of time, such as the transition from spatial centrality to a greater decentrality, from professional meetings in the real world to those taking place in the virtual world, as well as from large buildings to decentralized networks.

To give only one example of such possible changes: as a consequence of the anthrax letters the U.S. congress had already been closed once. This led the Democratic Leadership Council to entertain the idea that in the face of future threats—whatever their kind—at least the possibility should be available to hold sessions via the World-Wide-Web in order not to bring political life to a standstill. To back up its move, the Council referred to an incident during the American Revolution when the members of the House of Representatives had to flee from the advancing British troops and to continue their sessions at a pre-arranged meeting place.

Allegedly, the White House had already asked the Congress in November 2001 to take over government for up to thirty days if the legislators were not able to come together. Even though there are a number of buildings in the vicinity of Washington where meetings could be held, the level of technological sophistication makes an "electronic Congress" feasible as well. The Council imagined that all of the House of Representatives' daily proceedings, from discussions to votes, could also be managed via the internet. The members of the House of Representatives would thus access a website located securely on a server somewhere in the US, but geographically distant from the place they convene; certainly, measures would then have to be taken for authentication and identification. One can think, for instance, of an identification based on biometric data; or, when they can log on only at specific access points, the representatives would have to be searched in person. A result of such a development for the average American citizen could perhaps be a greater transparency since they would then have the opportunity to follow the proceedings of the House of Representatives via the internet—on the basis of "read only."

So far Congress has not implemented what is technically feasible anyway. Though it is praiseworthy that, in the face of terrorist threats, the representatives intend to go about their business as usual, terrorists can, however, not be defeated solely by such courageous behavior; intelligence and technology are at least just as important. This means that at least a technological infrastructure should be put into place which allows the holding of sessions over the internet. Because of concerns about possible protests by anti-globalization activists, just in June 2001, the World Bank had held a conference over the internet, which was originally scheduled to take place in Barcelona. The subsequent assessment of this retreat into cyberspace closed with the conclusion that virtual conferences cannot only provide a viable alternative to the traditional conference, but they also enable a larger number of people from around the globe to participate. Though activists had announced to disrupt the conference via virtual sit-ins, it seems in retrospect that no such problems occurred. Yet the potential risks inherent in the use of the internet are not considered worth mentioning by the Council. To disrupt or sabotage a parliamentary debate would certainly be a tempting target for hackers and cyber-terrorists as well as for the secret service of another country.

The destroyed skyscrapers in the center of Manhattan made it at least temporarily necessary for those firms and companies whose offices were located in these towers to move their offices to another location. The business premises that were destroyed in the six towers that collapsed comprise a space of 1,2 million square meters. Just the same amount of office space is currently vacant in Lower Manhattan, that is, fifty percent more than before 9/11. The firms have probably only moved within the N.Y.C. area, but what was initially conceived as only a temporary solution is likely to turn out to be a lasting arrangement, for not only are the prices for real estate lower and the danger posed by terrorist attacks smaller at other sites; it could also become apparent that, due to new information technologies and means of communication, it is no longer a requirement to be present in concentrated, densely populated urban areas. The attack on the "civilized world" therefore represents an attack on both the metropolis and on urban centrality. As a response to allegedly worldwide terrorist networks, military action (apart from long-distance wars with unmanned tactical and reconnaissance airplanes) relies more on small, secretly operating, decentralized, and flexible structures; what is more, the very structure of life in geographical space will be reorganized accordingly. The future probably holds a digital de-urbanization in store: the metropolis is re-built in cyberspace.

Gradually it will become easier to separate access to information and communication from concrete places. The information-city migrates—as far as possible—to cyberspace in order to constitute a truly global metropolis which will then be accessible from every location that is connected to computer networks. Most authorities, companies, organizations and many individuals are already present in the virtual metropolis, which comprises more than 400 million inhabitants and is hence by far bigger than the biggest urban metropolis. The virtual metropolis grows on the basis of urban infrastructure, culture and life, but it bursts their confines and incorporates them in the same way as traditional cities once expanded from a core settlement and subsumed surrounding villages. The centralized structure of cities, which used to be an advantage because it accelerated the circulation of commodities and information, now turns into a barrier to further development. While the means of mass transportation still required a network of geographically scattered urban centers, the passage from societies whose infrastructure was geared to the requirements of heavy, large-scale industry to societies based upon the new information technologies makes the production, processing, and distribution of information independent from transportation in geographical space.

Of course, the densely populated urban areas will in no way disappear; what will become obsolete is the dependence of the economy and society at large on urban centers. Yet our imagination is still dominated by the notion of the city as a space with a commercial district at its center. As Saskia Sassen has repeatedly pointed out, the infrastructure of global cities—that is, the close physical proximity of specialists and companies and thus of techno-scientific know-how—still offers a competitive advantage that must not be underestimated. Equally important, lively cities are very attractive with respect to the standard of living and the choice between leisure activities. At the same time, the new centrality brought about by the concentration of information technology infrastructures enables companies to extent their radius of operation to the global level since the new technologies facilitate management and control of all business activities. Yet the leading position that cities, especially urban centers, occupy in this respect is likely to be of limited duration. For quite some time fast means of transportation as well as communication technologies such as telephone, television, and radio have initiated a development that will lead to the leveling of these differences. Being present in a city center does not necessarily constitute a strategic advantage over being connected to highways, airports or the railroad.

Also because of population growth, a majority of people will continue to live in densely populated urban areas. Cities will not only continue to grow gradually; rather, they will—especially in the so-called Third World—spread with explosive rapidity to unprecedented scales and thus transform the very *gestalt* of the traditional city. This process of urban growth is usually referred to as 'sprawling,' that is, a mainly uncoordinated overflowing of the—at least in Europe—clearly demarcated city borders into the hinterlands, eventually leading to the formation of new urban areas. These new urban spaces are still closely connected to the old core-cities, which served in many ways as the catalyst of these developments, yet they separate themselves more and more from them and gain economic power until they finally even surpass the core-cities in terms of financial power. The result of these processes is the emergence of new spatial structures that combine urban and rural elements and functions and that—for lack of better terminology—are often, somewhat awkwardly, referred to as 'agglomerations,' 'metropolitan areas,' 'megalopolis' or 'conurbation.' Thus, the claim that in the highly industrialized countries ninety percent of the population live already in cities eclipses the fact that they actually inhabit such mixed, hybrid spaces.

Though it borders on exaggeration, one could argue that what we are currently witnessing is the 'ruralization' of the city, or conversely, the 'urbanization' of the rural hinterland. Urbanity as a form of life can hardly be found in such novel hybrid spaces, which incorporate villages, towns, and small cities; this holds also true for the rural communities and their specific modes of living, even in the case of those new urban spaces that are designed on the model of the 'garden cities,' that is, as relatively autonomous areas with traditional centers built for homogeneous communities with the same class and/or ethnic background. Centers and sub-centers can no longer gain autonomy or independence in such far-flung spaces, because their specific character is still largely determined by the spatial connection to the transportation system characteristic of traditional cities; they are increasingly shaped by the flow of information and commodities in contemporary mobile information society.

Once the possibilities opened up by tele-work, tele-shopping, tele-education or tele-medicine as well as by the virtualization of institutions have been fully explored, we can expect this development to contribute further to the fragmentation of society and homogenization of social groups. Moreover, these possibilities will diminish or even obliterate certain social constraints and requirements arising from particular social situations: going to work, getting along with colleagues, confronting strangers in shops or in public buildings, or simply the need to live close to where you work. As a consequence, the number of options to choose from will increase as we are no longer dependent on the traditional community in which solidarity among its members was indispensable for the functioning of the community. Replacing constraints with options will result in establishing still closer ties between people with similar interests or from the same ethnic background or social class. Ultimately, those virtual communities are only the mirror image of the ghettos or the fortified medieval towns with their controlled entrance-ways, whose populations were relatively uniform and homogenous. It can already be observed that the disintegration of communities held together by networks of solidarity also undermines the state whose duty it is balance diverging interests and appeal to all people regardless of class and social group in order to maintain peace and stability. In the face of this disintegration, one possibility to re-establish social unity, at least temporarily, is still and has always been a war or any other kind of threat to society as a whole.

Being surrounded by computers connected to the internet enables us as citizens, employees, and consumers to participate in a global public that has been inconceivable until recently; at the same time, theses circumstances also make constant surveillance possible, anywhere and anytime. The more intelligent the machines become, the more interactive and integrated, the more sensors and effectors they have, the more recordable traces we leave of our various activities, inclinations, and emotional investments. Cell phones, for instance, allow us to communicate with other people and to access the internet from almost any place; at the same time, they enable a third party to trace our geographical movements and to eavesdrop on our conversations. Surveillance cameras increasingly infiltrate public spaces and become more 'intelligent' so that they are capable of identifying people as well as certain behavioral patterns; moreover, biometric identification programs are employed, satellites with high-definition cameras move in the orbit above us, secret services—as in the case of the Echelon program—tap all worldwide communication that is sent over satellites. When we work on computers linked to larger networks, surveillance software can record all our movements in meticulous detail—the keys we press, the programs we use, the content of the emails we send and the websites we access. All environments that are meant to react to us also control us at the same time. These developments range from computers, as in the case of affective computing, that not only react to the movements of identified persons but also to physiological data, through robots or virtual agents designed to communicate with us, to intelligent homes.

These cataclysmic changes that have taken place in the once clearly demarcated public and private spheres will modify urban space. By the use of mass media in the formerly private sphere we are already part of a public that is immeasurably larger than that of the largest urban metropolis. Not only do people expose themselves to the public gaze on TV, but they are even exposed in their homes and during work via web cams. At the same time, anonymity in the public spaces of the cities disappears with the intensification of video surveillance.

To conclude I would like to discuss the intelligent house and its implications for the future of human life in environments created by the new information technologies.

The Intelligent House: Living under Surveillance

Though it is hard to predict the future shape of our homes, we can already observe a tendency for houses—at least for the houses of those who have the necessary financial resources—to resemble the Big-Brother Container, even if these houses are designed for the well-being of their occupants and react to their needs and wants. As to the owners of these new personalized intelligent homes, in all likelihood they will be prosperous, old people—at least according to the constructors of the "Aware Home," a prototype thoroughly equipped with computers and sensors.

Scientists of the Georgia Institute of Technology are currently designing a future model home, which can see and hear its occupants as well as "sense" their movements by way of multiple motion and contact sensors and video- and audio-technologies. The computers are kept out of sight, hidden in rooms and pieces of furniture so that the house becomes an intelligent environment. The prototype of the Aware Home is a two-storied house with four rooms, equipped with sixty computers, twenty-five video cameras and an equal number of microphones, forty pressure sensors, four DSL and a two-gigabit broadband ISDN connection as well as a wireless internal eleven megabits network.

With such a "perceptive" home scientists plan to lay the foundation for the future by going beyond conventional intelligent homes where the computers only switch the lights on and off or regulate the heating. Their objective is to program the house in such a way that it can identify the people in the house at a particular time, monitor their activities and anticipate their needs and wants. Yet, at the same time, the occupants must not be inundated by information and any infringement of their privacy has to be avoided; a goal that can hardly be reconciled with the overall objective of the project: to establish all-round surveillance on as many levels as possible.

The "intelligent floor," i.e. pressure sensors installed underneath the floor, can not only ascertain when and where a person moves within the house, but also determine the identity of that person, for intelligent homes can identify the occupants by their respective patterns of movements. Moreover, the house should be able to discern and interpret a person's gestures and facial expression. If the house were additionally able to observe individual preferences and predilections and establish a model of individual behavior based of this information, then the house could also anticipate the personal wishes and needs of the occupants.

Future occupants—other than scientists and students testing the intelligent house—will probably be elderly people rather than technophile nerds. There are obvious reasons for this: the number of old people increases steadily, and old people often have more money at their disposal so that they can probably better afford these houses in which they can live relatively independently from the help and care of others. It is likely that in the near future the technical equipment of such "Aware Homes" will become cheaper than nursing staff. These houses thus seem to provide a new alternative in changing demographic conditions, the dwindling willingness of children to care for their parents in their own homes or the lack of relatives altogether. Japanese scientists, by contrast, prefer the less costly observation robot to the intelligent home. While the intelligent home may successfully keep watch over its occupants, it does not yet seem sufficiently equipped to actually nurse and care for old people.

As part of the project "Aging in Place," scientists are about to design a house that will not just automatically call for help in cases of emergency but also serve as mnemonic aid for aging people. Also, relatives will be assured of the occupants' well-being. Scientists have already proposed the following features: for example, when the door bell rings, cameras take pictures of the activities the occupants were performing before the bell rang. These pictures also serve to remind them later of the activities that were interrupted.

To monitor the occupants of the house scientists have designed "digital family portraits": flat screens on which the individual members are represented. On these screens, certain age-related icons indicate the senior's recent activities and social behavior. These icons should not only express moods and behaviors on a particular day, but chart a whole series of days. By reading the color of the icons, relatives can learn about the condition and possible improvement or deterioration of the intelligent home's inhabitants. These digital family portraits provide an update on the situation of occupants at least once a day, if not several times a day. The use of alternative technologies other than webcams seems to be an attempt to make surveillance as unobtrusive as possible.

While scientists are mainly interested in installing as many computers and high-tech devices as possible and, at the same time, in concealing the continuous surveillance, the intelligent house may well trigger a discussion of the extent to which our lives should be invaded by technology. With the intelligent home, it is not so much the actual exposure to the public that is at stake, but a vague, yet agonizing feeling of lost privacy.

Envisioning Progress at Chicago's White City

Astrid Böger

Judging by its overwhelming success with contemporary visitors and also the fascination it has held for scholars as well as amateur devotees for well over a hundred years, it appears that many would agree with Chicago writer George Ade that "the world's greatest achievement of the departing century was pulled off in Chicago—the Columbian Exposition was the most stupendous, interesting and significant show ever spread out for the public" (qtd. in Miller 488). And considering that the exposition, more popularly known as the White City, drew about twenty-seven million visitors and was hence one of the greatest tourist attractions in American history, it is hard to argue with Ade's praise for it. But why is it that this particular exposition continues to engage people's imaginations to this day? In part, its great appeal can be explained by the fact that the Columbian Exposition was the first world's fair in the United States that reconciled local, national, and international interests within the space of one singular *Gesamtkunstwerk*, whose brilliant displays of scientific progress, art and entertainment inspired myriads of critical as well as artistic responses. Ideally situated along the scenic shores of Lake Michigan, the fair put Chicago—less than sixty years old at the time and often ridiculed for its cultural backwardness—literally on the map of the United States as the second most important metropolis emerging on the eve of the twentieth century.

However, this feat could not have been achieved without the combination of various architectural and technological innovations that has become typical of the most successful world's fairs (and conversely, those were undoubtedly the weaker fairs that failed to present such an innovative mix, as was last the case in Hannover, Germany, in 2000). Here, I will focus on those areas that gave visible shape to the idea of progress, and whose central role at the fair was particularly relevant to Americans' changing perceptions of their culture: These are its architecture, that actually paved the way for the "City Beautiful Movement"[1] of the early twentieth century, electricity and especially electrical light, as well as photography. In combination, these innovative fields provided the technological means for a projected vision of American progress and power as well as an opportunity for the individual visitor to envision that progress in concrete, tangible ways, with his or her own strained eyes.

In fact, so stunning were the sights and the seemingly endless displays of technological wonders that at times visitors could hardly believe what they saw in Jackson Park in the summer of 1893. To many, the fair appeared more like an enchanted fairyland or a beautiful dream than simply a large exhibition of the arts and products as well as the peoples from around the world. Especially when compared to the ultramodern look of downtown Chicago with its recent addition of skyscrapers and ever-growing industrial landscapes, the neoclassical look of the fair rather surreally invoked "the presence of an ancient city in contemporary time," as Arnold Lewis put it (179). Despite their ephemeral and hence, some would contend, inconsequential nature, and regardless of their uncertain relation to the actual cities hosting them, one can argue that the so-called 'heavenly city fairs' of the turn of the century, such as the one in Chicago, offered an ideal environment for negotiating what was desirable in the way of technological as well as social progress in the face of actual urban conditions.[2] Following Émile Durkheim, what is considered ideal and what is real should not be seen in opposition but rather as a continuum of social experience:

> The ideal society does not stand outside the real society: it is part of it. Far from being torn between two opposite poles, we cannot be part of the one without being part of the other. A society is not simply consti-

---

1   "The term derived from the title of a book by Charles Mulford Robinson (1869-1917), *Modern Civic Art, or the City Made Beautiful* (1903), and used in the USA for a nationwide endeavour to dignify city centres with boulevards, squares and monumental Beaux Arts style public buildings, usually financed by public subscription. [...] The buildings and layout of the World's Columbian Exposition, Chicago 1893, were products of these ideas and the main source of inspiration for the following two decades." (Fleming, Honour, and Hugh 114-115).
2   The others took place in Buffalo (1901), St. Louis (1904) and San Francisco (1915).

tuted by a mass of individuals who compose it, by the territory they occupy, by the things they use and the actions they perform, but above all by the idea it has about itself. (153)[3]

*

In early 2001 I first visited the former exhibition grounds in Jackson Park, which borders on Lake Michigan approximately seven miles south of downtown Chicago. Surveying the landscape from the distance, I could easily imagine what the group of landscape architects, future fair managers and local businessmen saw upon arriving at the site for one of the initial inspections back in 1890: not much of anything, except for a somewhat swampy, flat landscape with occasional oak trees and park benches placed at irregular intervals throughout the vast and rather deserted-looking area. I should add that getting across the park was not as easy as one might expect considering its convenient access by CTA, the city's public transportation system which is arguably the greatest remnant of its first world's fair. About to exit the train station and turning to the service personnel for directions to the park entrance less than a mile away, I was warned that I should not attempt to walk there because it was considered quite unsafe to do so. While registering the ambivalent feelings that such well-intentioned advice can cause the in uninitiated outsider, due to the highly problematic underpinnings of such demarcations of mostly ethnic neighborhoods as potentially dangerous 'problem zones', I politely thanked the CTA staff and heeded their advice by taking a nearby bus directly to the only remaining and rather magnificent building of the 1893 fair, the former Fine Arts Building, which is now Chicago's renowned Museum of Science and Industries. Having turned away from the outside realities—whatever they really were—and finding myself safely surrounded with the impressive merger of educational and

---

3   Also qtd. in Nye, *Sublime* xiii. Warren Susman also used Durkheim's ideas, in a piece on the ideological functions of world's fairs, and makes a related point: "Doesn't the visit to the fair mean for those who attend a separation from the world as they lived it, an opportunity to regroup and rethink the world from a vantage point somewhere between past, present, and future—a vantage point that leads to an acceptance and participation in a new social order that is emerging technologically, socially, culturally, politically?" (6).

commercial spectacle typical of such museums, I could not help but marvel at some of the historical continuities. More specifically, there continues to be a sharp divide between the splendor of certain cultural institutions such as the Museum of Science and Industries and the University of Chicago nearby (the latter was built along what had been the Columbian Exposition's amusement area called the 'Midway Plaisance') and their underdeveloped surrounding areas. Today as in 1893 access to such prestigious cultural institutions is by entrance admission or academic merit, respectively, and thereby restricted. Consequently, these privileged educational sites stand out in a landscape that is otherwise perceived as disorderly and even dangerous, access to which, while theoretically open, is considered a bad idea.

*

The guiding idea behind The World's Columbian Exposition was to build an harmonious and orderly model city, in many ways the exact opposite of the urban space that was the day-to-day reality Chicagoans negotiated at the time, and which they frequently experienced as chaotic, overcrowded, full of vice, and therefore dangerous.[4] By contrast, the fair would offer a respite from such turmoil. As Neil Harris explains:

> The Columbian Exposition and others like it demonstrated that it was possible to take hundreds of acres and buildings and place them under effective control. Specially organized police and fire forces, new water and electrical systems, novel transport devices, all supported the visitor surges. There was an obsession with demonstrating the orderly management the exposition enforced on the perils of social congestion. These fairs were designed to be safe, clean, peaceful, and easy to move through. (*Cultural Excursions* 117-18)

When placed in their historical context, these "obsessive" measures appear even more significant. For if the fair's official purpose was to

---

4   A similar dichotomy is at the core of a recently published book by Erik Larson, which captures the enlightened values behind the White City, on the one hand, and their nemesis, or irrational violence, on the other. He does this by opposing throughout Daniel Burnham with a real-life serial killer, Henry H. Holmes, who made it his preoccupation to abduct and gruesomely kill scores of young women during the fair.

celebrate—one year late—the four hundredth anniversary of Columbus's arrival in the New World, it is hard to miss its rootedness in its own, and rather precarious, historical moment. Thirty years after the devastations of the Civil War, there was a deeply-felt need to demonstrate the nation's unity and renewed economic strength, made all the more urgent by the severe financial panic of 1893. Undaunted by even the most adversary conditions, "White City would display just how wonderful America had become," writes Alan Trachtenberg in his landmark essay (209).[5] However, Chicago's reputation as an emerging industrial, commercial as well as cultural center was at stake after the prolonged period of labor unrest culminating in the Haymarket riot of 1886, in which dozens of protestors as well as several police were maimed or killed. In response to that crisis and the growing fear of anarchist mayhem, the city's business and cultural elites had expressed the need "to create order out of chaos," and out of this impulse several important cultural institutions were created. As Robert Rydell points out:

> In the years after Haymarket, civic leaders built libraries, the Art Institute [prominently located in the central Loop area in downtown Chicago], and the University of Chicago as examples of high culture [...]. The World's Columbian Exposition was the culmination of this cultural renaissance. (*Fair America* 32)

Whereas some architects proposed building the fair in several locations spread around other downtown landmarks, the influential landscape designer Frederick Law Olmsted convinced the building committee headed by Daniel Burnham to build the entire fair in Jackson Park, then (as now again, in certain areas) an unimproved park site. Apart from the advantages of closeness to the lake and good possibilities for infrastructural development, this choice also allowed for the contained-yet-spacious and coherent architectural scheme the Columbian Exposition is famous for. Concerned that the exposition should not be dismissed as a 'cattle show on the shores of Lake Michigan', the planners consciously designed the White City to make the previous Paris Universal Exposition (1889) look pale in compari-

---

5   Alan Trachtenberg's "White City" is still the most persuasive effort to date to situate the Columbian Exposition between the Haymarket crisis and the Pullman railroad workers' strike in the year following the fair.

son.[6] At the same time, they implicitly acknowledged the aesthetic influence of the then-fashionable French Beaux Arts style that the eastern architects around Burnham favored: The Chicago Exposition would be the first world's fair to use for its central buildings the harmonious, neoclassical look that would dominate American fairs for the next two decades [ill. 034]. The White City received its name for the monumental court area also referred to as the Court of Honor, with the main exposition buildings surrounding a Grand Basin, which was overlooked, on one end, by the impressive Statue of the Republic by Daniel Chester French, "a classical allegory of the United States" (Rydell, *Fair America* 37), and by the golden-domed Administration Building and the Columbian Fountain by Frederick William MacMonnies on the other.[7] Thus framed, the Court of Honor provided imposing vistas from various heights and vantage points (perhaps the most popular being the roof of the Manufactures and Liberal Arts Building, reached by a state-of-the-art elevator), and awed visitors with its brilliant layout (cf. Hollweg 93-99).[8] Also, as this was where most people entered the fairgrounds, "the Court of Honor became not only the focal point but also the spectacular 'entrance hall' to the World's Columbian Exposition" (de Witt 81). Beholding the Court of Honor for the first time, many felt moved to resort to religious pathos to express their feelings, that is, if they could express them at all.[9]

---

6   On the Chicago Exposition see, for example, Harris, *Cultural Excursions* 115. For a detailed account of the sense of anxious competition the Chicago architects felt vis-à-vis the 1889 fair, see, for example, Findling, *Chicago's Great World's Fairs* 12-15.
7   The main buildings were Manufactures and Liberal Arts, Electricity, Mines, Transportation, Administration, Machinery, and Agriculture. For a thorough discussion of the national and imperial symbolism of the Court of Honor structures, see, for example, Wim de Wit.
8   In a Foucauldian turn, Hollweg compares the visual layout of the fair, especially of the Midway, to Jeremy Bentham's *Panopticon* (1791) (95).
9   Though the Court of Honor was generally admired by the public for the impression of symmetry and order it conveyed (the effect can best be compared to San Francisco's Civic Center or the Mall in Washington, D.C., as all three structures express the ideals of The City Beautiful Movement—see fn. 1), it was not altogether uncontroversial. Many thought it did not fit the energetic modernity of America as symbolized by the skyscrapers then erected in downtown Chicago. For a critical evaluation of the World's Columbian Exposition's architecture see Giedion: "Public, artists, and literary people believed themselves to be witnessing a splendid rebirth of the great traditions of past ages. The immense appeal of

Others experienced a failure of vision altogether, as witnessed by William Dean Howells's *Altrurian Traveller*, whose temporary inability to see upon arrival is compensated by the deeply-felt patriotic pathos of home-coming:

> The tears came, and the pillared porches swam against my vision; [...] the liquid notes of our own speech stole to my inner ear; [...] I was at home once more, and my heart overflowed with patriotic rapture in this strange land, [...]. (22)

By all accounts, such lofty feelings were greatly heightened still at night, when spectacular illuminations changed the landscape to a magical dreamscape, and thereby "made it possible to display two landscapes in one space, one by day and another by night", as David Nye explains ("Electrifying Expositions" 113; [ill. 035]). While nighttime photographs of these illuminations are rare (and no black-and-white still photograph could adequately capture the choreographed effects of color lighting, moving spotlights, fireworks and water fountains combined into one great visual symphony), narrative descriptions of the spectacle by awe-struck visitors are not. Brenda Hollweg discusses the following account by one visitor who published his or her astounded reaction to the night illuminations in *Harper's Bazaar*:

> One is spellbound, altogether entranced, floating on a sea of splendor, living in a land of strange enchantments, where everything beautiful ever thought of or dreamed of by men has suddenly been bestowed upon them as realities by some gracious divinity, who would thus atone to them for all the delights and pleasures missed by mortals who do not dwell among the gods.[10]

Hollweg focuses on the obvious religious rhetoric of the passage, which, she argues, points to the realm of the immaterial beyond concrete appearances (142-44). However, it is equally possible to read the text in the opposite way, namely, as anchoring dreamy visions of the nightly illuminations safely in the domain of material progress. After all, these illuminations were only made possible with the latest developments in electrical power and intricate lighting and sound mechanisms, as everyone watching the spectacle must have been aware—or

---

this re-created past in 'the White City' can only be laid to a quite unnecessary national inferiority complex" (394).

10 L.H.F., "Night Scene in the Court of Honor," *Harper's Bazaar* 9 (September 1893) 749; qtd. in Hollweg 143.

made aware of, through corporate advertising—at the time. Using state of the art technology to such a striking effect, the illuminations are therefore a good example of what David Nye has defined as the 'technological sublime', "that typical American amalgamation of natural, technological, classical, and religious elements into a single aesthetic" (*Sublime* 23).

An inherently sublime science if not an art or even pure magic in the eyes of many visitors experiencing the latest inventions in the field for the first time, electricity particularly lends itself to such an aesthetic amalgamation because on the one hand, it stands for some of the most ancient problems humankind had to solve to ensure its survival—generating and maximizing power—while also serving as a symbol of enlightenment in both concrete and metaphorical terms. "Here can be seen all the advances made in the field of electricity since Franklin first succeeded in bringing that element from the clouds to be the agent and servitor of mankind," claims one official portfolio advertising the displays in the Electricity Building, thereby effectively substituting a religious and mythological (Promethean) image with a scientific one, i.e., of the lightning conductor Franklin had invented (see *Portfolio of Photographs of the World's Fair*).

In fact, electricity and electrification have played a central role at world's fairs ever since their development reached a point in the 1860s when public display of electricity became possible, and can indeed be considered the driving force behind them—especially when considering that such mass events depended more and more on electrical appliances for their newly developed systems of mass transportation as well as lighting (cf. Nye, "Electrifying Expositions" 117).[11] But it is important not to lose sight of the deeper meaning and the symbolism of electrical power beyond such practical uses. As Nye explains:

> Electrification quickly became more than a mere expedient that permitted the fairgrounds to remain open in the evening. It was an elusive concretization of abstract qualities that could be known only by its effects: light, heat, and power. Spectacular lighting was dramatic, non-utilitarian, and universalizing. Its introduction did not detract from other exhibits, but rather provided a brilliant canopy, connecting diverse elements in one stunning design. [...] Electricity became more

---

11 For a detailed account of the importance of electricity to all parts of the World's Columbian Exposition, including a discussion of the earlier fairs, see Barrett. Barrett was the Chief of the Department of Electricity at the exposition.

than just the theme for a major exhibit; it provided a visible correlative for the ideology of progress and abundance through technology. ("Electrifying Expositions" 117)

Faced with the problem of having to visualize something so significant yet invisible, exhibitors in the Electricity Building found various creative solutions using a total of about 30,000 incandescent light bulbs to brilliant effects, and some of their displays proved to be among the most popular on the fairground (see Barrett 12). For the Western Electric and the General Electric Companies, the display of choice was a 'Column' or 'Tower of Light', respectively, whereas the Westinghouse Electric & Manufacturing Company, apparently reluctant to produce yet another towering structure, instead installed an ingenious display of its own company name juxtaposed to a portrait of Columbus and the anniversary dates 1492–1892, all made up of incandescents and prominently visible on the building's southern wall. "As a whole the decoration was one calculated to charm the beholder," one contemporary expert notes (Barrett 13), but at the same time it impressively set the stage for large-scale corporate advertising in America [ill. 036].[12] Generally speaking, the exhibitors of the Electricity Building seemed to have followed a 'more is more' approach, resulting in an unprecedented amount of candle power, or intensity of light.[13] As Nye points out, "[s]ome visitors saw more artificial light at the fair than they had previously seen in their entire lives," and some, it turns out, were not prepared for the experience ("Electrifying America" 38). In at least one novel about a visit to the fair, a character even temporarily loses his mind at the overwhelming sight of the General Electric Company's Tower of Light exhibit:

> He stood gazing at the column for fully three minutes after the light had been turned off and his countenance betrayed overwhelming bewilderment. Once or twice he raised a hand and drew it across his forehead. Then he was seen to press his temples with both palms, all the while gazing in an awe-stricken way at the great pillar. The attention of several visitors was attracted to the farmer, and one of them stopped to his side to inquire if anything was wrong with him. As the

---

12 On the role of corporate advertising at the Columbian Exposition, see Rydell, "The Culture of Imperial Abundance" 198-204.
13 Barrett gives the grand total of 1,804,000 candle power of lighting in the Electricity Building, "by far a greater amount of lighting than has ever before been confined for lighting purposes within a like area" (12).

gentleman reached his side the latter threw his arms upward and, with a shriek that started the echoes, fell forward upon his face. Two or three guards rushed to the prostrate man's assistance, but before they reached his side he leaped to his feet and, screaming at the top of his voice, ran through the aisle toward the entrance facing the lagoon. (Stevens 73)

This passage illustrates a truly Burkean experience of sublime astonishment, caused by the simple physiological phenomenon of an afterimage created by staring into bright lights for an extended period of time, which becomes a source of horror to someone clearly unaccustomed to artificial light (a likely scenario as rural electrification in the United States took place several decades later). A significant number of accounts by fair visitors contain similar narratives of the inability or the refusal to comprehend what they saw, or else the frustrations of attempting to take it all in, albeit rarely rendered in such drastic terms.

Regardless of such individual moments of crisis due to the failure to make sense of it all, the World's Columbian Exposition was overwhelmingly successful in projecting an image of abundance and seemingly unlimited energy. While the electric displays served as visual metaphors for energy and progress, material abundance was the overall impression everywhere on the fairground and has, in fact, been the core theme of all world's fairs, which are in essence large-scale competitions between different nations based on their technological, industrial, and artistic output. By the massive proportions of the Manufactures and Liberal Arts Building alone, which was the largest building in the world at the time, it was immediately apparent to anyone visiting the fair that the United States economy of 1893 relied mostly on manufacturing goods. As was generally the case with the Columbian Exposition, the building's neoclassical exterior did not suggest its quite modern and even minimal construction principles using a steel frame, which allowed for huge glass surfaces and required no supporting outer walls, and gave the interior a spartan but expansive appearance.

This dual approach to fair architecture has at times been discredited as somehow insincere or simply fake, especially when compared to the 'form follows function' aesthetic then visibly gaining momentum in the context of the Chicago School of architecture. But Neil Harris draws attention to the fact that it merely "mirrored a set of conventions about appropriate urban appearance" (*Cultural Excursions*

120). Moreover, the look of the Manufactures and Liberal Arts Building and the other main exposition buildings as well suggests a close connection with the department store aesthetic developing at around the same time in urban centers in America and Europe. According to Russell Lewis, "[e]ach offered an array of comforts, conveniences, and entertainment, and together they defined a new urban ideal based on consumption" (28).

For the White City to successfully embody this urban ideal of the emerging consumer society, a new vision or, rather, many different new visions were required giving people a concrete idea of what such an urban society would look like. Not surprisingly, photography and other visual technologies were of central importance in this regard, and virtually omnipresent on the fairgrounds (something that has not changed since 1893, as witnessed by the overwhelming reliance on video technology at the Hannover exposition in 2000). In Chicago, photographic displays dominated in all major exhibits, often serving to 'frame history' from a particular point of view. In the U.S. Government Building, for instance, images of Native Americans showed traditional tribal dances and sacred rituals before some of these were outlawed in government-controlled reservations; others documented the overseas exploits of the colonial powers or presented a visual record of important archeological finds, to give but a few examples.[14] So ubiquitous was photography at the Columbian Exposition that its planners no longer felt that there was a need for a separate building displaying nothing but photographs, as there had been at the previous American world's fair, in Philadelphia in 1876.

Moreover, the tightly controlled visual representations of the exposition itself were a step in the direction of making world's fairs spectacles of consumer culture and mass marketing. Souvenir books and other collectibles with images of the world's fair on them, such as paper fans, plates, spoons, commemorative coins, etc., were produced in unprecedented numbers and, by all accounts, found ready buyers. As most of the officially commissioned photography of the fair was done by the same photographic company headed by Charles Arnold, the look of the fair was homogeneous and instantly recognizable, even to those who had not been there in person but relied on the print me-

---

14 For a more thorough discussion of the uses of photographic exhibits at the World's Columbian Exposition, see Brown 17-34.

dia to see the fair. So influential was the White City aesthetic of Arnold and his staff that those amateurs who spent the steep fee of two dollars a day for bringing in a hand-held camera in addition to the general admission fee of 50 cents tended to imitate the professional look in their own picture-taking, for instance by taking photographs from the same vantage point they had seen in the professional images.[15]

When the official photography of the Columbian Exposition is discussed, typically a distinction is made between images of the main exposition sites around the Court of Honor and those taken at the Midway Plaisance (see Gilbert 121-26). And in many ways this distinction is well-founded. While the Court of Honor images tended to be taken from great distances and rely on symmetrical framing underscoring the impression of order and great visual harmony, photographs of the Midway generally suggest a closer relationship between the photographer and his subjects. Perhaps the most striking difference is that these latter images focus on people on the Midway, whereas the more formal pictures rarely emphasize the presence of human subjects. Finally, while the Court of Honor images have stirred much enthusiasm and little debate, the opposite is the case with the photographs of Midway subjects.

In particular, the photographs of foreigners on the Midway, who were frequently part of so-called 'living exhibits' and engaged visitors in song and dance routines presumed typical of their native culture, have been the cause of great debate for the past several decades, as they blatantly expose certain ideological and frequently racist underpinnings. Moreover, they have been seen as reflective of a hegemonic worldview ultimately legitimizing Western dominance over other cultures. Robert Rydell has been the most persistent in critiquing what he states was "the overriding characteristic of America's turn-of-the-century fairs," namely, their imperial gesture. Taking his leads from Trachtenberg and Walter Benjamin, he argues that "[f]airs promised material abundance and made the promise of abundance contingent on the acquisition, maintenance, and growth of empire" ("Imperial

---

15   Cf. Brown 93-113. James Gilbert's "Fixing the Image: Photography at the World's Columbian Exposition" also includes a detailed discussion of amateur photography at the fair and its tight regulation by the fair officials. In: *Grand Illusions* 101-132.

Abundance" 192). The displays of foreign peoples on the Midway, Rydell argues, served to affirm again and again the Western cultures' inherent superiority over others: "On the Midway at the World's Columbian Exposition, evolution, ethnology, and popular amusements interlocked as active agents and bulwarks of hegemonic assertion of ruling-class authority" (*Fair America* 41).[16] Seen in this way, the White City is indeed synonymous for white supremacist values. And some historical facts make it difficult to challenge this position, such as the exclusion of African Americans at the Columbian Exposition, which famously led to Frederick Douglass's renaming it a 'White Sepulcher'.[17]

With the near-complete absence of African-American representation at the fair—excepting the highly controversial "Colored People's Day," where Douglass delivered his well-known address calling for the recognition of the contributions African Americans had made to U.S. history, especially as soldiers in the Civil War[18]—images of Africans gained further significance. They also caused many African Americans, including Douglass himself, considerable anguish as they tended to show Africans as primitive and uncivilized savages, in other words, the precise mirror image of White City—as well as what Reed terms Afro-Saxon—values (cf. Reed 142). A portrait of a "Group of Dahomeyans," showing about thirty representatives of the West African Fon people engaged in a staged war dance, is a case in point [ill. 037]. With nothing detracting from the semi-naked bodies of the performers, the eye lingers on their expressive poses and the fierceness of their gestures.[19] The scene appears to be quite lively, as nearly everyone in the image holds up weapons as if about to attack, but at the

---

16   See also Rydell's groundbreaking earlier work, All the World's a Fair. Visions of Empire at American International Expositions, 1876-1916.
17   For a detailed discussion of the African American contribution to the White City, or lack thereof, see Reed.
18   The speech by Douglass held on August 25, 1893 is reprinted in full in Reed 193-194.
19   Apparently with respect to Victorian sensibilities, the image was 'retouched' for publication in *Midway Types. A Book of Illustrated Lessons About the People of the Midway Plaisance, World's Fair 1893* by painting clothes on the nine women whose bare breasts showed in the original photograph. Absurdly, the accompanying caption still manages to deplore "a regretful absence of tailor-made clothes, and a leaning toward a plethora of black skins" (n.p.).

same time the image is strangely static. Anyone familiar with the conventions of still photography of the time the picture was taken immediately recognizes the staged character of the scene, realizing that any shaking movement such as the gestures suggest would have made the image blurry (and in fact the expressionless faces of the performers seem to betray the artificiality of the extended 'frozen' moment before the camera shutter finally closed). All of the subjects in the image face the camera—and therefore, the audience—directly, which gives the photograph a certain intensity despite appearing static and frozen.

The 'Dahomeyans' were a great Midway attraction, but at the same time they were considered to be representative of the lowest level of civilization, according to the quasi-Darwinian evolutionary view of superior versus inferior species underlying the presentation of natives on the Midway. This view is reflected, for instance, in the account by one of the official historians of the fair, Hubert Howe Bancroft:

> As the concert opens, the men and women crouching in the center of the floor, some 30 in number, are aroused from sleep or stupor, and rising to their feet, begin to beat time to the music. When all are ready the war-dance or march begins at a signal from their leader. Forward and backward passes this motley crew, brandishing war-clubs and grinning as only Dahomeans can grin. Louder and yet more loud grow the beating of a drum, the blast of horn, and the clash of a cymbal. Then the posturing begins; but in this there is nothing of the graceful or sensuous; simply a contortion and quivering of limb and body, with a swing of weapons as though nothing would more delight than to kill and destroy. (qtd. in Reed 159)

The 'description' minimizes the artfulness of the war dance, and reduces it instead to the racist stereotype of the grinning primitive who enjoys killing for mere pleasure, a notion which appears to have held great fascination for contemporary audiences despite its rather obvious unfoundedness. Depictions such as the ones above advanced the notion of the unbridgeable otherness and inherent inferiority of certain foreign cultures to one's own.[20]

---

20 For a critical discussion of performances of otherness, and in particular the relationship between bodies and spaces in performances of ethnicity, including a brief review of the human exhibits at late 19th century world's fairs, see the work of Reinhold Görling.

The rhetorical nature of Midway portraiture becomes all the more obvious when compared to a less formal—and in this regard unfortunately quite rare—photograph telling a different story. In a picture taken in front of the 'Encampment of Bedouin and Arabian Tribes', we recognize two Arab men engaged in a concentrated but friendly exchange with two American or European males, presumably fair visitors. In contrast to the official ethnographic descriptions according to which Arab culture was seen as barely above level of the Dahomeyan 'savages', this image suggests otherwise: In its center, we see a confident-looking Arab man, taller than the others, who appears quite in control of the moment as he coolly considers the matter at hand (see *Portfolio* [ill. 038]). While it would be going too far to claim that this photograph shows the 'real', somehow more democratic Midway and that the turn-of-the-century world's fairs have unfairly been depicted as racist, imperial affairs, it does indicate that it might be too facile to completely discredit the world's fairs as having been *only that*. All the highly justified criticism notwithstanding, the world's fairs of the late 19th century were, among many other things, an attempt to think of the world as a space of many cultures engaging in various forms of exchange. Often such exchanges took the shape of ritualized performances put on for ever-curious audiences, but there was also some space for direct and spontaneous engagement with people not from one's own culture, which took place under the watchful eyes of a veritable army of quasi-military 'Columbian Guards'. Hence, one could argue that the strict boundaries between one's own culture and others were at times made somewhat fluid, especially on the Midway, where representations of cultures foreign and exotic to Americans of the late 19th century stood side by side with those of large immigrant populations such as the Irish or German Villages, much more familiar—and a source of great national pride—to many visitors.

Moreover, it is often overlooked that the visitors of the fair were very much part of the world's fair spectacle, thus complicating the assumed clear-cut divide between performers and spectators. In addition to directly contributing to the financing effort through entrance fees and consuming goods and services on the fairground, they were also themselves part of the display and the attraction. Many visitors acknowledged that they had gone to the fair as much for the formal exhibits as for the entertainment derived from watching people (cf. Hawthorne 34-44). And it seems that Americans were at least as interested in seeing other Americans as they were in seeing foreigners, as there were more novels written about people from rural areas going to the big city to see the fair than there were about foreigners on the Midway.[21] Much like the depictions of foreign natives on the Midway, it is up to the reader to decide if such intracultural encounters, frequently rendered quite humorously, were done in a sympathetic or condescending, or even voyeuristic and derogatory fashion.

The main motivation behind world's fairs has always been the bringing together of diverse social groups and cultures, to visualize the world as one. Different though they were, perhaps it is helpful in this respect to think of the Columbian Exposition's Court of Honor and Midway not so much as opposites, but as complimentary aspects of a unified picture of the world on the verge of the century that would see the emergence of increasingly globalized markets, unprecedented waves of immigration, the birth of international mass travel and tourism as well as two devastating world wars, among many other things. The fair tried to reflect such 'mass movements' (including the rise of militarism, as evidenced by the imposing Krupp gun exhibit), by creating a coherent picture of many of the scientific and technological innovations that would make them possible, especially in the fields of manufacturing, transportation and communication. Seen from this perspective, the world's fair presented a vision of the world held together above all else by commercial interests. But its vision went beyond the merely material level. "Together," writes Richard Hughes Seager, the White City and the Midway "created a complete *imago mundi*, a universal world picture, based on a set of interrelated religious, cultural, and racial assumptions that, in the worldview of the Columbian myth, could serve as the ideological foundations for a common discourse about global community" (24).

It is hardly doubtful that the turn-of-the-century expositions were hegemonic and even imperial affairs. However, the vision they projected of technological progress and of the commodification of all areas of life was truly encompassing, and cannot be accounted for by aggressive imperial ambitions alone. Remarkably, the White City was the first American world's fair that worked itself like a perfect machine, and was as much admired for its ground-breaking solutions to

---

21 Two good examples are the studies by Charles McClellan Stevens and Marietta Holley.

mass transit, public hygiene and crowd control as it was for the beautifully lit up buildings around a lagoon. Its imposing vision was efficiently captured by already established visual conventions such as the photo portrait and the more formal architectural views; moreover, there were exciting innovations in photography that would serve to keep up with the accelerating pace of the dawning machine age, such as Muybridge's movement studies and Edison's kinetoscope first introduced at the fair. Especially the latter invention would revolutionize how we experience the world and in due course, some would argue, make mass events such as world's fairs superfluous. The former, perhaps a bit less conspicuously, and rather more educational than entertaining, would teach equally important lessons: that movement could be measured, objectified, and carried out to maximum efficiency and work output. In the following decades, when Ford and others pioneered in the introduction of assembly line work, these studies would prove profitable indeed.

*

The White City consequently represented corporate interests. Visitors could learn a lot about the model town Pullman had built for his workers outside of Chicago, but nothing about Jane Addams's effort to house and educate poor African American and immigrant children at Hull House on the city's South Side. One hundred years after the White City, a third world's fair was going to be held in Chicago to honor and repeat the success of the Columbian Exposition, named the 1992 Age of Discovery fair. America at this time was painstakingly coming to terms with everything that the Columbian myth had stood for in its history, and this time around, the causes for celebration were increasingly overshadowed and finally dwarfed by those for controversy and conflict. The planning, already far advanced, fell apart in the summer of 1985 due to a failed financial scheme, but also—and perhaps more importantly—for distinctly political reasons.[22] Enor-

---

22 For a detailed account of the failed 1992 fair effort, see Hutchins. Dorfman gives a brief and somewhat more informal summary, For a discussion of some of the larger philosophical issues behind the 'controversies surrounding the 1992 Columbiad', see Seager 144-148.

mous pressure had been used by organized groups such as Chicago's African American, Mexican and Polish communities and several other neighborhoods as well as anti-corporate activists to achieve what they felt was once again missing, namely, a fair representation of the various communities' contributions to the cultural and economic success of a city and a region (cf. McClory). In the end, they could not be accommodated. The failed fair effort is all but forgotten today. What caused it, however, is still all too clear: the absence of a vision of a common culture.

Works Cited

Bancroft, Hubert Howe. *The Book of the Fair*. Chicago: Bancroft, 1893.

Barrett, J. P. *Electricity at the Columbian Exposition, Including an Account of the Exhibits*. Chicago: R. R. Donnelley & Sons Company, 1894.

Bronner, Simon J., ed. *Consuming Visions. Accumulation and Display of Goods in America 1880-1920*. New York and London: Norton, 1989.

Brown, Julie K. *Contesting Images. Photography and the World's Columbian Exposition*. Tucson and London: U. of Arizona P, 1994.

de Wit, Wim. "Building an Illusion: The Design of the World's Columbian Exposition." *Grand Illusions. Chicago's World's Fair of 1893*. Neil Harris, Wim de Wit, James Gilbert, and Robert Rydell. Chicago: Historical Society, 1993. 41-98.

Dorfman, Ron. "Chicago Politics and the World's Fair of 1992—The Old Establishment Meets the New." *World's Fair* 4.1 (Winter 1984): 1-4.

Durkheim, Émile. "The Elementary Forms of the Religious Life." *Durkheim on Religion*. Ed. W. S. G. Pickering. London: Routledge & Kegan Paul, 1975. 102-166.

Findling, John E. *Chicago's Great World's Fairs*. Manchester and New York: Manchester UP, 1994.

Fleming, John, Hugh Honour and Nikolaus Pevsner, eds. *The Penguin Dictionary of Architecture and Landscape Architecture*. 5th ed. London and New York: Penguin, 1998.

Giedion, Sigfried. *Space, Time and Architecture. The Growth of a New Tradition*. Cambridge, MA: Harvard UP, 1967.

Gilbert, James. "Fixing the Image: Photography at the World's Columbian Exposition." *Grand Illusions. Chicago's World's Fair of 1893*. Neil Harris, Wim de Wit, James Gilbert, and Robert Rydell. Chicago: Historical Society, 1993. 101-132.

Görling, Reinhold. "Rahmen—Zeuge—Körper: Das Feld der Performance." *Wechselspiel: KörperTheaterErfahrung*. Ed. Florian Vaßen, Gerd Koch, and Gabriela Naumann. Frankfurt a M.: Brandes & Apsel, 1998. 50-62.

Hawthorne, Julian. *Humors of the Fair*. Illustrated by Will E. Chapin. Chicago: E.A. Weeks & Company, 1893.

Harris, Neil. *Cultural Excursion: Marketing Appetites and Cultural Tastes in Modern America*. Chicago and London: U of Chicago P, 1990.

Harris, Neil, Wim de Wit, James Gilbert, and Robert Rydell. *Grand Illusions. Chicago's World's Fair of 1893*. Chicago: Historical Society, 1993.

Hollweg, Brenda. *Ausgestellte Welt. Formationsprozesse kultureller Identität in den Texten zur Chicago World's Columbian Exposition (1893)*. Heidelberg: C. Winter Universitätsverlag, 2001.

Holley, Marietta. *Samantha at the World's Fair*. New York: Funk & Wagnalls, 1893.

Howells, William Dean. *Letters of an Altrurian Traveller, 1893-94*. Gainesville: Scholars' Facsimiles & Reprints, 1961.

Hutchins, Robert. "The Planning of the 1992 Chicago World's Fair." *Central Papers on Architecture* 3 (winter 1987): 75-92.

Larson, Erik. *The Devil in the White City. Murder, Magic, and Madness at the Fair that Changed America*. New York: Crown, 2003.

Lewis, Arnold. *An Early Encounter with Tomorrow. Europeans, Chicago's Loop, and the World's Columbian Exposition*. Urbana and Chicago: U of Illinois P, 1997.

Lewis, Russell. "Everything Under One Roof: World's Fairs and Department Stores in Paris and Chicago." *Chicago History. The Magazine of the Chicago Historical Society* 12.3 (Fall 1983): 28-47.

McClellan Stevens, Charles. *The Adventures of Uncle Jeremiah and Family at the Great Fair, their Observations and Triumphs*. Chicago: Laird & Lee, Publ., 1893.

McClory, Robert. *The Fall of the Fair: Communities Struggle for Fairness*. Chicago: The Chicago 1992 Committee, 1986.

Midway Types. A Book of Illustrated Lessons About the People of the Midway Plaisance, World's Fair 1893. Chicago: The American Engraving Company, 1894.

Miller, Donald L. *City of the Century: The Epic of Chicago and the Making of America*. New York et al.: Simon & Schuster, 1996.

Nye, David E. *American Technological Sublime*. Cambridge and London: MIT, 1994.

—. "Electrifying Expositions, 1880-1939." *Narratives and Spaces. Technology and the Construction of American Culture*. Exeter: U of Exeter P, 1997.

Portfolio of Photographs of the World's Fair. Chicago: Published by the Werner Company, 1893.

Reed, Christopher Robert. *All the World is Here! The Black Presence at White City*. Bloomington and Indianapolis: Indiana UP, 2000.

Rydell, Robert. *All the World's a Fair. Visions of Empire at American International Expositions, 1876-1916*. Chicago: U of Chicago P, 1984.

—. "The Culture of Imperial Abundance. World's Fairs in the Making of American Culture." *Consuming Visions. Accumulation and Display of Goods in America 1880-1920*. Ed. Simon J. Bronner. New York and London: Norton, 1989. 191-216.

Rydell, Robert, John E. Findling, and Kimberly D. Pelle. *Fair America: World's Fairs in the United States*. Washington and London: Smithsonian Institution Press, 2000.

Seager, Richard Hughes. *The World's Parliament of Religions. The East/West Encounter, Chicago, 1893*. Bloomington: Indiana UP, 1995.

Stevens, Charles M. *The Adventures of Uncle Jeremiah and Family at the Great Fair, their Observations and Triumphs*. Chicago: Laird & Lee, 1893.

Susman, Warren. "Ritual Fairs." *Chicago History. The Magazine of the Chicago Historical Society* 12.3 (Fall 1983): 4-7.

Trachtenberg, Alan. "White City." *The Incorporation of America: Culture & Society in the Gilded Age*. New York: Hill and Wang, 1982. 208-234.

Vaßen, Florian, Gerd Koch and Gabriela Naumann, eds. *Wechselspiel: KörperTheaterErfahrung*. Frankfurt a M.: Brandes & Apsel, 1998.

Where Every Woman May Be a Queen: Gender, Politics, and Visual Space at the Chicago World's Fair, 1893

Tracey Jean Boisseau

Although political and even social historians can often pinpoint foundational events or key institutions that provide originary explanation, it is not often that cultural historians can point to specific moments—and even less commonly to specific places—that constitute clear turning points in the history of the formation of an identity. The 1893 Chicago World's Fair represents an exception as it permits historians of American feminism to depart from this general rule.[1] Although disparate features of American "new womanhood" can be glimpsed prior to 1893, it was at the Chicago World's Fair and during its aftermath in the middle years of that decade that the full-fledged figure of the "new woman" appeared in public discourses in the United States media and print culture.[2] In keeping with its modern ethos, the exposition presented an opportunity to invent a model of modern womanhood specifically illustrating the chief characteristics of an idealized modern America, one that rejected the sequestration of "true women" in their homes and challenged the ban on public roles for women. Although other historians of the fair have noted the relatively conservative nature of women's participation at this event, I believe that the temperate tones of much of the fair's rhetoric on women should not obscure the historic importance of the shift that the official inclusion of women in the exposition alone signified (see Trachtenberg 221; Bederman 32-5).

---

1   In this essay I mean to discuss feminism as a set of inter-related identities rather than a group of organizations or a series of political battles. Much of this material has been excerpted or reprinted from my article "White Queens at the Chicago World Fair, 1893."
2   "New woman" first appeared in the British press in the mid-1890s as a derogatory label for middle-class women who seemed to violate the doctrine of "separate spheres." Middle-class women who aspired to professionalism, engaged in athleticism, critiqued the institution of marriage, decried the sexual double-standard, or eschewed confining clothing on semi-political grounds were vulnerable to the charge of being "new women."

For the first time the national government had invited millions of Americans to celebrate American women's participation at a public event as evidence of their nation's global stature and cultural preeminence. Never before had the United States government positioned women as national representatives at an international event and never before had government appointees so forcefully joined the advancement of civilization with the advancement of women. However vague and open to interpretation the phrase "advancement of women" certainly was, in the official literature, speeches, and reports on the fair it clearly augured a more than chivalric protection or "republican motherhood" (see Kerber).

Inclusion in the fair was not accomplished without significant arm-twisting and effective organizing on the part of elite and well-connected women (see Weimann; Grabenhorst-Randall; Pohl). Both their fight with men for official inclusion and the fight between women for control of this inclusion (as well as the near whole-sale exclusion of non-white women) from the fair has been examined elsewhere (Bederman 31-40; Massa). However, little about the fair's gendered orientation of space has appeared in the scholarly literature—this, despite the abundance of analyses of the spaces of the fair as venues for racial and nationalist articulations of ideology.[3] In fact, women's official contributions to the fair largely hinged on, and often faltered over, their deliberate attempts to reorganize the space of the fair. Public and often acrimonious debates over the logic of segregation versus integration as well as the appropriateness of particular spatial and visual metaphors for modern American womanhood were covered extensively in the local and national media in the months preceding the fair and through the entire five months that it ran. If an examination of women's internecine skirmishing reveals the stakes of their struggle to stretch the fair's modernist vision to include a new relationship between women and the nation-state, a close look at the visual spaces the fair presented illuminates the extent to which the fairgrounds themselves were newly interpreted by female fairgoers within a feminist framework of meaning.

---

3   An early exception to this is a brief essay by art historian Snyder-Ott. More recently, film historian Lauren Rabinovitz has taken a close look in *For the Love of Pleasure* at what she calls female flanerie and looking relations at the fair (47-67).

Oddly enough, as a result of women's demands that Modern Woman be appropriately situated within the iconography of the White City, white, middle-class female fair organizers grasped hold of the figure of the medieval queen, explicitly white in some cases but generally implicitly so, to draw attention to themselves and to affirm their commanding presence. As I will show, the "fair women"[4] rhetorically and visually declared themselves the modern "queens" of the fair, and, by extension, of the world. The ubiquitous image of the American woman as modern queen and queen of the modern world at this event not only signaled a change in American women's relationship to the public sphere and the nation-state, it reveals new womanhood's reliance upon class, racial, and national hierarchies for its expression and specifically upon primitivism as a foil. In this essay, after establishing the literal and symbolic significance of women's presence at the fair, I demonstrate the centrality of the queen as metaphor to female fair organizers' strategies and examine their attempts to control the public's interpretation of their use of queenly iconography. I conclude that white queen rhetoric and visual iconography made lasting impression on visitors to the 1893 Columbian Exposition and thus had an important impact on the ideology of modernity the fair helped forge.

---

4   The expression belongs to Weimann and is meant to refer to both the female fair organizers and exhibitors.

Woman's Place at the Fair

> In the Colombian Exposition, which celebrates a fifteenth century fact, the Board of Lady Managers stands for a nineteenth century idea. The Act of Congress authorizing the commemoration of the 400th anniversary of the discovery of America, declares that the great event shall be celebrated by "an exhibition of the progress of civilization in the New World." Now, the creation of the Board of Lady Managers of the World's Colombian Commission may surely be considered a signal illustration of progress in the New World.
>
> Virginia C. Meredith, 1893

Alongside technological innovation and industrial output, the status of Woman in the late nineteenth century constituted a prevalent gauge of a people's relative cultural advancement along an imaginary path of human progress.[5] Charles C. Bonney, who organized the Congresses held in conjunction with the exposition, cited women's official participation at the fair as evidence of the fair's contribution to "women's progress," and further argued that such progress was the clearest sign that the human race had just made a large leap forward along the evolutionary path. Bonney argued that "woman's progress" represented "the substitution of the law of love for the law of force," and foretold that the "higher and better civilization of the race" would come only in proportion to women's advancement (qtd. in Sewall 8). Such rhetoric is a powerful indicator of the significance attributed to this event and to women's participation in it. The fair itself would complete this instruction, fleshing out its multi-layered meanings and implications in accordance with the many other "great object lessons" it had to teach (Rydell 40).[6]

---

5 This theme was repeatedly stressed; for instance, an explicit statement of just this idea was made by Lucinda Stone in her speech, "Higher Lessons of the World's Fair," reprinted in Eagle.

6 The prevailing view of the fair among scholars follows Rydell in seeing it as "an exercise in educating the nation on the concept of progress as a *willed* national activity toward a determined, utopian goal" and as successfully compelling "mil-

Of course, there were many lessons to be learned at that memorable exposition: about other places, other peoples; about how railroad engines worked and large buildings were constructed; about new scientific theories, such as evolution. But the overall lesson that the fair communicated concerned the very "order of things."[7] Indeed, national ranking was among the most important hierarchies the fair imparted to its over twelve million ticket holders. The United States Congress allocated special funds for the Columbian Exposition, expressly in the interest of international cooperation and to mark the United States' ascendancy to great-nation status; the two purposes appeared indistinguishable in Chicago that summer (Burg xiii). In fact, the federal government, state and municipal institutions, and more middle-class Americans than any national movement or organization had heretofore aggregated exerted a massive effort to venerate the entrepreneurial and industrial achievements of a nation barely a century old. The national, racial, and class-specific import of the 1893 fair has been insightfully examined by Robert Rydell, among other scholars.[8] But, perhaps because so much of what was exhibited at the fair was the work of men, the Woman's Building and the foregrounding of women in 1893 has been all-too-infrequently acknowledged and inadequately considered

---

lions of Americans [to] understand the ensuing decades of social struggle and imperial adventure as an integral part of the evolutionary process that accompanied progress" (46; 71). Contemporaries articulated such ideas openly and forcefully. G. Brown Goode, Assistant Secretary to the Smithsonian Institution at the time and in charge of overall classification of exhibits at the fair, wrote for instance that the fair would illustrate "the steps of progress of civilization and its arts in successive centuries, and in all lands up to the present time," that it would become, "in fact, an *illustrated encyclopedia of civilization*," that its very essence was to educate and "formulate the Modern" (qtd. in Rydell 44-45, emphasis his).

7   The phrase "the order of things" is meant to remind readers of Michel Foucault's formulation of power/knowledge in his *The Order of Things: An Archaeology of the Human Sciences* and to acknowledge that it is this theorization of power and ideology which underlies my thinking regarding ideological production at the fair. More to my point, my use of this phrase refers to the fact that many architects and organizers of the fair viewed it thusly and that many historians since have utilized the notion of an "object lesson" as a framework for understanding the fair's most basic themes.

8   An important primary source for the fair is the Official Directory of the World's Columbian Exposition May 1 to October 30.

by historians.[9] This oversight has obscured the degree to which women's participation at the fair was noted by contemporaries as a historic, and uniquely American, achievement.

With the legitimacy that the federal government could proffer hanging in the balance and the exposure that such a massive undertaking presented, the Columbian Exposition comprised a tremendous chance to intervene in popular conceptions of American womanhood. The elite women charged with determining the shape and substance of the vision of American womanhood to be enshrined at the fair strove to capitalize on the opportunity. At the Congress of Women and in the design and organization of the Woman's Building, the fair women fused visions of modern women unfettered by constraints on their professional ambitions and public lives with traditional images of respectable women as mothers and hearth-tenders. Indeed, the phrase "true woman," so reminiscent of the earlier nineteenth-century "cult of true womanhood" which had revolved around an idealization of middle-class women's domesticity, cropped up frequently in fair organizers' speeches and private writings.[10] Female fair organizers wielded

---

9   Official historical records of the fair do not overlook the Woman's Building as much as they give brief, condescending accounts of it. These include Truman et al.; Ade et al.; Johnson. However, several informative official histories specifically concern the Woman's Building, the Board of Lady Managers, and the Congress of Women. These include Elliot; Eagle; Sewall; Wright; *Official Record of the Board of Lady Managers of the World's Columbian Commission.* Unlike Robert Rydell's Ph.D dissertation, in which he discusses the Woman's Building, Rydell's published chapter on world's expositions omits mention of the Woman's Building and the role that gender played at the 1893 fair. This is also true of Gilbert's work. Although Badger and Burg include significant treatments of the Woman's Building, gender does not play a central role in their analyses. Trachtenberg goes so far as to state that "images implied and stated of blacks and Indians served the total pedagogy. No social image served more significantly, however, than that of women. This was the moment, as the Fair proclaimed, when women (like artists) came into their own." Despite such statements, Trachtenberg only devotes two paragraphs to demonstrating his point and circumscribes the importance of gender politics at the fair in the process. Trachtenberg concludes that "the prevailing note" of the Woman's Building "was domesticity" and that this undercut any political "militancy" otherwise imparted at the Congress of Women (221-22).

10 A "cult of true womanhood" among white, middle-class women of the nineteenth century was first identified by Welter. According to Welter, the "cult" idealized middle-class women, restricting them to a wholly domestic and private sphere and attributing to them an exclusive relationship to the morality and pu-

this phrase often and seemingly self-consciously as they sought to impress on fair visitors a continuity between modern woman's talent for public service or capacity for individual achievement and her maternal or domestic virtues. Organizers of the Women's Congress and the Woman's Building, primarily wives of the Chicago business elite, attempted to accommodate the sensibilities of conservatives as well as those of women reformers and their supporters who had, for a generation or more, collectively posed an implicit challenge to the prescribed containment of respectable women in their homes.

Far less politically experienced or active than the latter, the otherwise conservative Chicago socialites who supervised women's exhibits at the fair and controlled the administration of the Woman's Building searched for common ground with male fair officials and the general public even as they expanded the boundaries of (white, middle-class) woman's domain to include the professions, political involvement, and public roles. While I agree that it would be a mistake to view women's official participation at the fair as a sign that Victorian bourgeois gender ideologies were moribund by 1893, still, a commitment on the part of the state to celebrate certain women as active agents of modernity deserves more scholarly attention than it has thus far received. Juxtaposing images of freedom enjoyed by modern emancipated American women with the patriarchalism endured by "primitive" women of colonized or soon-to-be-colonized lands drove home the point that American women's emancipation from the home and formal entrance into the public halls of power signaled the triumph of a uniquely American civilization, white supremacy, and bourgeois culture. To the extent that this new twist to Americans' sense of "manifest destiny" linked woman's emancipation with the advancement of American civilization, it also tied the emerging set of new womanhood reforms to imperial attitudes.

Yet, women's official presence at the Columbian Exposition held more than symbolic value. The exposition had tangible effects on the

---

rity associated with that sphere. The cult demanded respectable women's near-total exclusion from the public domain (where market forces and character traits such as avariciousness, aggression, and individualism predominated). Cott noted the capacity of this doctrine of separate spheres, based on an even earlier "canon of domesticity," to enshrine a "unifying, leveling common identity of the domestic 'American lady' (not the aristocratic lady)," providing many middle-class American women with a sense of "solidarity with their sex" (99).

development of a woman's movement in the United States.[11] The Woman's Building acted as a headquarters for women's ambitions at the fair and even as a clearing house for women's organizational activities which were extraneous to it. No one recognized the possibilities engendered by this situation more clearly than President of the Board of Lady Managers, Bertha Palmer. According to Palmer, the "official" character that government recognition and funding lent to the Woman's Building would alter the way that middle-class women's associations operated and the way the "woman movement" could be documented and publicly discussed:

> Government recognition and sanction give to these committees of women official character and dignity. Their work has been magnificently successful and the reports which will be made of the conditions found to exist will be placed on record, as public documents, among the archives of every country. (qtd. in Truman 177)

Palmer made no attempt to obscure the fact that a political agenda lay behind the organization of the Woman's Building. She declared:

> The absence of a just and general appreciation of the truth concerning the position and status of women has caused us to call special attention to it, and to make a point of attempting to create, by means of the Exposition, a well-defined public sentiment in regard to their rights and duties [...]. (qtd. in Truman 177)

"Creating a public sentiment" was what the fair did best and forms the primary focus for this essay. But the Columbian Exposition also generated concrete gains for the new women of the 1890s. What was left in place once the fair had been burned to the ground in 1894 was an organizational infrastructure of women's clubs which would prove indispensable in the fight for women's suffrage, temperance, protective labor legislation, and women's civil liberties and educational opportunities—that is, for the construction of a tangible, multi-pronged feminist movement. In her final speech before the Board, President Palmer proudly announced that the institutionalization of organizational structures was the finest accomplishment of women that the fair would re-

---

11 For the impact that national women's clubs organized as a prelude and an aftermath of the 1893 World's Fair had on the suffrage movement and progressive reform, see Blair; Bordin; Buhle; Freedman; Weimann 487-521; Scott 128-35, 142.

veal; by extension, she suggested, it would prove to be one of the most significant achievements of Woman that the world had ever known:

> That we have been successful in creating an organization through the world, and in interesting the governments of the world in the condition and position of their women, is of incalculable benefit. A community of interests has been created among women in every part of the world, such as has never heretofore existed. [...] It was the proudest moment of my life, when I was told last Saturday with a heartfelt hand-shake and with accents of deepest sincerity by one of our visitors, that seeing me had given her more pleasure than anything at the fair, except the Ferris Wheel. (qtd. in Burg 247)

For those middle-class women who had not contributed to the organizing of the fair as well as for the millions of lower middle-class and working-class women who attended the fair simply as elated spectators, the organizational scaffolding behind the Woman's Building may not have been as apparent as was the embodied presence of authoritative, power-wielding women. Such women claimed the public space as their own; their voices rang with indignation, pride, and ambition. To their audience of white, middle-class women from the United States and Europe, the fair women presented themselves at the Congress of Women as the clear spokeswomen and best representatives of an American woman's movement.

It is no coincidence that the same decade which saw Chicago's World Exposition also saw the coining of the term "feminism" and the founding of women's national organizations which a generation later would permit the adoption of several reform measures, notably woman's suffrage in 1920. The fair not only helped crystallize turn-of-the-century discussions of the woman question; by constructing the organizational apparatus upon which political reform would rest, it also helped facilitate the incorporation of new woman reformism into mainstream U.S. society and culture. The fair introduced the precepts of new womanhood as though they were intrinsic aspects of American-ness, effectively linking the proto-feminist tenets of new womanhood to national identity. An examination of the spectacle that women made of themselves at perhaps the most spectacular event of the nineteenth century reveals the extent to which their enlargement of woman's sphere relied upon a particular visual and figurative device: the queen.

New Womanhood Enthroned

> Mrs. Barker, South Dakota: I remember when the International Convention of Women convened [...] I took up a Minneapolis paper [...] and I read that they were going to have a "hen" convention. But when the reports of the papers came back [...] the Minneapolis paper came out and said, "The Queens of the World have just closed their convention in Washington." (Soon, they) will be ready to say that the Queens of America have been in session in Chicago.
>
> "Minutes of the First Session," *The Official Manual of the Board of Lady Managers*, 1891 (149)

In these minutes from the first organizing session of the Board that would oversee the choosing and placement of women's exhibitions at the fair, a member reported that the public was already being prepared to view the Lady Managers as queenly. Indeed, female organizers, speech-makers, and observers at the exposition seemed unable to resist honoring various female individuals by referring to them as queens: "We are all doubtless aware here that Columbus discovered America. America's uncrowned queen, Miss Frances E. Willard, once said the greatest discovery of the nineteenth century is the discovery of woman by herself" (Eagle 817). Indeed, queen metaphors abounded at the Chicago World's Fair of 1893, and at the many events held in and around the Woman's Building especially, often interwoven as they are here within the many pithy comments comparing Columbus's discovery of a new world and modern woman's discovery of an autonomous and public self. In their introductory speeches, formal papers, and bulletins, women repeatedly drew a parallel between the emergence of a modern world and the birth of modern woman. This mantra was quickly adopted by visitors and echoed by sympathetic journalists throughout the six months that the fair lasted. No female image was more conspicuous than that of Queen Isabella of Spain. The exposition claimed in its title to be a monument to Columbus and his vast achievement, but rarely was the Italian explorer invoked apart from his patroness. Isabella held great symbolic value as an example of a woman at the helm of state and empire, and bore particular currency at the Columbian Exposition as a primary player in the historic feat of colonization, which the fair specifically commemorated. In the eyes of many women who attended the fair, Queen Isabella came to symbolize American women's long-overdue claim to public recognition of their rights to participate on the national level. Such tendencies were so widely noted that spoofs on the theme began to appear in print. Marietta Holley, author of *Samantha at the World's Fair—by Josiah Allen's Wife*, which was published the same year as the fair, entertainingly exaggerated female fairgoers' tendency to sentimentalize Isabella by imagining her as a four-hundred-year-old champion of women's rights. After viewing the exhibits in the Woman's Building, the thoughts of Samantha Allen, the untutored narrator in Holley's story, turned toward the Spanish Queen:

> to think mine eyes had been permitted to gaze on the marvels and wonders my own sect[12] had wrought. And then I thought of Isabelle [...] thinkses I, if it hadn't been for her we wouldn't have been discovered at all, as I know on, and then where would have been the Woman's Buildin'? I thought I would love to talk it over with her; how, though she furnished the means for a man to discover us, yet four hundred years had to wear away before men thought that wimmen wuz capable of takin' part in any International Exposition. I wanted Isabelle there that day—I wanted her like a dog. (279)

Here colonialism is celebrated as the requisite precursor to the dawn of the modern age, an age characterized, in large part, by women's recognition as public actors. Despite Holley's humorous hyperbole, the target of this send-up was not the fanciful imagination of the average American woman whom this character was meant to represent. Samantha is presented in the tale as a wiser-than-thou folkswoman who accurately perceives the underlying messages of the fair, which elude her truly simple and hopelessly sexist husband, Josiah.

In her depiction of Samantha and Josiah Allen, Holley implies that men and women viewed the fair and absorbed its gendered ornamentations differently, with women determinedly interpreting the many female symbols as signs of their own sex's emancipation. There was a plethora of queenly images to spark the imagination of women like Holley's narrator. Samantha was frequently rent by paroxysms of joy and identificatory bliss at the sight of the many depictions of crowned women representing Art or Justice or Progress which were

---

12 By "sect," Samantha meant her own sex—the use of dialect makes a punning allusion to religious groups.

dribbled into friezes, splayed across walls as murals, and propped up in the center of courtyards or fountains in three-dimensional form throughout the White City. Apparently, the accent that female fair organizers placed on women's accomplishments at the exposition transformed for some what might have remained typical neo-Greco-Roman abstractions into potent symbols of modern women's prowess. Frances Willard, one of the most famous and respected "uncrowned queens" in nineteenth-century America, refused to acknowledge the level of abstraction usually accorded such statuary when she substituted the term *women* for the more ideational (and prevalent) term *woman* in her official description of some pediment statuary. She bluntly declared that, "the pediment represents women as the genius of civilization" (452-453).

Even the queenly carriage of the Statue of Liberty, a reproduction of which graced the White City's lagoon, was reinterpreted by women at the fair as a sign of American womanhood's rightful ascendance to a position of importance and public authority. The rural narrator of *Samantha at the World's Fair* was inspired by the majestic display of Liberty "on her marble pedestal" and declared herself just as "sot" and "solid" on the "firm and solid foundation of my love, and admiration and appreciation for my own sect" [sex] (244-45). Samantha's sentiments reveal the degree to which women's official participation at the fair prompted a pleasurable collective identification among women and inspired political sensibilities in female visitors. After listing the many contributions made by European royalty to the Woman's Building and the many images of queens within its halls, Samantha concluded: "you see from what I have said that there wuz a great variety of Queens a-showin' off in that buildin' [...] you felt real familiar with 'em" (284). Holley implies that the profusion of queenly images in the Woman's Building and elsewhere encouraged female visitors to reimagine themselves as queenly and encouraged them to associate this new self-image with political struggle: "connected with this great work is not only the hull caboodle of our own wimmen, fur or near—American wimmen, every one on 'em a queen, or will be when she gits her rights" (281).

Holley's narrator explicitly differentiated between the meaning of the statuary at the Columbian Exposition and the usual practice of displaying female figures to adorn public buildings with no regard for or implicit endorsement of the advancement of women:

> It is enough to make a stun woman, or a wooden female, mad, to see how the nation always dipicters wimmen in statutes, and pictures, and things, as if they wuz a-holdin' the hull world in the palm of their hand, when they hain't, in reality, willin' to gin 'em the right that a banty hen has [...]. (307)

Unlike such statuary, the Woman's Building, the statues of Liberty and Columbia, and so many other grandiose images of women viewed collectively seemed to promise a new day for modern American women. In case the relationship between women's interests as a "sect" and the fair's celebration of the United States as a premier nation among nations went unacknowledged by her reader, Holley drove home the point that Americans should be able to expect their own nation to set a strong example of "liberty and justice for women":

> Havin' such feelin's as I have for our own native land—discovered by Christopher Columbus, founded by George Washington, rescued, defended and saved by Lincoln and Grant. [...] Bein' so proud of the Republic as I have always been and so sot on wantin' her to do jest right and soar up above all the other nations of the earth in nobility and goodness—havin' such feelin's for her, and such deep and heartfelt love and pride for my own sect—what wuz my emotions, as I see that statute riz up to the Republic in the form of a woman, when I went up clost and paid particular attention to her! A female, most sixty-five feet tall! Why, as I looked on her, my emotions riz me up so, and seemed to expand my own size so, that I felt as if I, too, towered up so high that I could lock arms with her, and walk off with her arm in arm, and look around and enjoy what wuz bein' done there in the great To-Day for her sect, and mine; and what that sect wuz a-branchin' out and doin' for herself. (305-6)

The neo-classical female allegorical figures resplendent in the White City were most numerous in and around the Woman's Building, where their allegorical nature most clearly merged with an exultation of women and an advocacy of women's right to pursue achievement in the public sphere. On the Woman's Building's roof garden, where so many women relaxed at the fair in each other's company (the *American Architect* peevishly dismissed it a "hen-coop for petticoated hens, young and old"), eight groups of allegorical female figures guarded the four corners (Weimann 261). From the roof, women reputedly had one of the best views of the fair and especially of the Midway Plaisance, which stretched for a mile behind it. Over the course of the months that the fair ran, millions of women may have looked out towards the ignoble midway from between tall, glorious figures of crowned and enthroned women representing "The Enlightenment" or "The Spirit of Civilization" (Weimann 263). The very layout of the fair implied an order within which white, middle-class fair women located themselves.

Ideas linking modernity, woman's emancipation, and human progress were further demonstrated by murals strewn throughout the building. Lining the great hall were two long rows of portraits of historical queens and biblical figures heralding women as important historical actors. Most of the interior walls sported immense, didactic murals replete with similar female allegorical figures; the great rotunda was etched with four such panels, and giant murals erected at either end of the central court of the Woman's Building provided an ultimate schematic representation of the relationship of woman's advancement in the public sphere to modernity and American national identity. At one end of the great hall, Mary Cassatt painted "Modern Woman" dancing and playing music, plucking the fruits of "Knowledge and Science," and pursuing "Fame." At the other, "Primitive Woman" could be seen plowing fields, lugging water, and attending to "Man as Hunter." Encumbered by large water-jars balanced on heads and babes balanced on hips, primitive women appeared as the "bearer of burdens, the toilers of the earth, the servants of man, and more than this, being without ambition, contented with their lot," according to the muralist, Mary MacMonnies. After considering costumes which would signify to visitors that the women depicted in her mural were either "savage" or "prehistoric," like the "slave" or the "Oriental woman," MacMonnies said she chose to portray this "abstract and universal idea" of primitive womanhood apart from any "special type or costume, in a landscape background that might be of any time or country and is certainly not in America" (Pohl 302). In Macmonnies's view, images invoking colonized or yet-to-be colonized women provided the most pertinent foil for Modern Woman, that is, for American womanhood. Critics and visitors agreed, finding Macmonnies's reassuring depiction of primitive women as "other" the more satisfactory of the two murals (Pohl 302).

The racist and colonialist implications of the symbol of the queen are most evident in the disjuncture between the attention and adulation showered upon white queens and princesses and the condescension and even embarrassment that brown, yellow, or black queens encountered in their white American hostesses. White queens, princesses, duchesses, and countesses from Europe who attended the Columbian Exposition were met with an excess of fanfare, receptions, and newspaper coverage.[13] Their handicrafts were featured prominently in the Woman's Building as a sign of woman's collective talents and abilities. In contrast, exhibits offered by non-white noblewomen were accepted most patronizingly by the Board of Lady Managers. According to President of the Board of Lady Managers, Bertha Palmer,

> The orient has not been behind in its efforts to co-operate with us, although it has succeeded in doing so only on a limited scale and in many cases unofficially. We have received the most pathetic[14] letters from those countries, in which women are only beginning to learn that there is a fuller development and a higher liberty of action permitted their sex elsewhere. Japan, under the guidance of its liberal and intelligent Empress, has promptly and cordially promoted our plans. Her Majesty, the Queen of Siam, has sent a special delegate with directions that she put herself under our leadership and learn what industrial and educational advantages are open to women in other countries, so that Siam may adopt such measure as will elevate the condition of her women. (Great Applause.) (qtd. in Truman 182)

Japan, a significant colonialist power in its own right, was at least imagined "liberal and intelligent" enough to permit its empress to execute the plans put forth by the American Board of Lady Managers. The Queen of Siam and other women of the Orient could be congratulated only for looking to America for examples of women's progress. It is clear that women from outside the West, despite their royal status, were thought of and were depicted as unlike American women, especially on the key question of woman's emancipation.[15] As MacMonnies's giant mural insinuated, such women could only represent that which Modern (American) womanhood had left behind.

Though aristocratic women outside the West were sometimes welcomed as interesting anomalies, they were barely acknowledged by the Board of Lady Managers and were not regarded as representatives of the modern womanhood whatever their prominent status as

---

13 In fact, according to Weimann, all of the European commissions sent to the Woman's Building were royal ones.
14 Palmer's use of the term "pathetic" to indicate the letters' ability to elicit sympathy would not have carried the extremely pejorative implications we associate with the term today.
15 For the seminal work on the notion of time as anthropological othering device, see Fabian.

public figures in their home countries. The devastatingly flat tone of President Palmer's diary record of a reception given to a noblewoman from India poignantly reveals the racialism which fostered such logic: "Monday July 10, the NY Building where I met the Princess—from Bombay [...] to me simply a negro woman, wearing a singular type of dress, yet having a gentle voice and good English accent—I do not know why New York was giving her a reception" (Weimann 564). A small reception to honor a "negro" princess comprised a gaffe in protocol, in the view of this most influential fair organizer. Such an exception proves the rule of the fair: an untitled bourgeois white woman, if only she donned a "singular type of dress" and could place herself within a distinctly colonialist frame of reference, might be legitimately celebrated by female fair organizers as queenly, but the racist and imperialist assumptions of the fair precluded venerating women from non-Western societies, even when they were actual royalty.[16] Honoring non-white women as queenly risked leveling the distinction that Palmer intended the image of the queen at the fair to help establish. The racism revealed in her diary discloses that the fair's reverence for queenliness should not be mistaken for literal adulation of title. Queenliness was a convenient vehicle to communicate the prestige white women at the fair both hoped to acquire and to announce as theirs by right.

Not surprisingly, since the white queen was more a symbol than a literal goal, the queenly image to which female fair organizers made most frequent reference was not a living queen but a historic one. Even so, utilizing queen imagery as proto-feminist iconography was a complicated matter, considering the contrariness of aristocratic symbolism in the context of the fair's celebration of America as a republic. In fact, fair organizers's determination to celebrate Isabella for her queenliness was nearly curtailed by the U.S. Mint. While mint officials agreed to arrange for an Isabella coin as part of the mint's support of the exposition, they failed to appreciate the significance of Isabella's rank to the goals of female fair organizers. A letter from a di-

---

16 The clearest evidence of this contrast can be found in Williams' article, which declares May French-Sheldon, a middle-class American woman who participated at the fair, as a veritable "White Queen" purely on the basis of her racialized presentation of self. See my "White Queens at the World's Fair" for a more complete discussion of French-Sheldon's performance of queenliness.

rector of the mint discloses his displeasure with the design Palmer chose for a coin commemorating the queen's contribution to the discovery of America, inasmuch as it emphasized Isabella as queen:

> You notice that the Director desire[s] that you should model a head of Queen Isabella from the best portrait you can obtain. This head should be without a crown, as a crowned head on an American coin would, in my judgment be exceedingly unpopular and offensive to the teachings of our republican institutions. Isabella should be represented as the patron of Columbus and not as a Queen, according to my notion.[17]

The bureaucrat who made these remarks in a letter to the sculptor commissioned by the Board of Lady Managers to design a commemorative quarter for the fair was seemingly unaware of the importance of queen imagery to female fair organizers' strategies. An uncrowned head failed to express the very queenliness Isabella was meant to convey. Shorn of a crown, Isabella's visage might fail to be recognized, worse, it might fail to communicate the public power she had so forcefully wielded. Clearly, it was the crown as much as the historic woman who seemed to symbolize the imperial puissance of American new womanhood. Palmer held out for the crown and, in the end, the mint abandoned its insistence that a crowned head was unsuitable for an American coin. Under severe pressure from Palmer, its director approved the minting of the coin so adorned, making the Isabella quarter the first U.S. coin to display the image of an actual female historical figure as well as the first to bear the image of a crowned head.[18] Thus, fair women's contention that powerful and historical female public actors were queenly, and the queen was not an inappropriate American symbol of womanhood, was solidified.

Perhaps even more illustrative of the importance of the symbol of the queen in general, and Isabella in particular, is the tug-of-war that erupted between the Board and a rival organization of women called

---

17   This quotation is taken from an enclosure in a letter from E. C. Leech, Director of the Mint, to Caroline Peddle, the young sculptor whom President Palmer of the Board of Lady Managers favored to design the Isabella Commemorative Quarter (April 8, 1893). See Records of the Mint, National Archives, Washington D. C. The quotation also appears in Weimann 482. See also "Isabella Coins."
18   The next U.S. coin with a face of a woman upon it would be the Susan B. Anthony quarter. This fact supports my point that the fair marked only the beginning of a period when feminist heroines were to be designated national symbols by the U.S. government.

the Queen Isabella Association.[19] The Isabella Association was made up of influential reformers and professional women from across the country. Many of these women had been in the forefront of the pressure groups that had pushed for women's inclusion on the executive committees proposed to oversee the organization of the fair and its exhibits. However, once Chicago was chosen as site of the exposition, this loose association of nationally active organizers was outflanked by a local group, made up chiefly of wives of prominent Chicago businessmen. The local women, led by the influential Bertha Palmer, proceeded to exclude all but their associates from the governing council of the Board of Lady Managers, a separate organization from the fair's all-male National Commission and executive committees. The Isabellas (as they came to be known) and their supporters never relinquished their resentment against what they saw as the Board's monopolization of power and self-segregating decisions. In turn, President Palmer of the Board of Lady Managers never forgave the Isabellas as a group or as individuals for dogging the preparatory months before the fair opened with bitter condemnations and repeated leaks to the press disclosing internal fissures and mismanagement in the organization of the Woman's Building.

Because the Board had had to endure months of opposition from the members of the Isabella Association, President Palmer, once firmly in the saddle, set out to eliminate the Isabellas' presence at the exposition and strenuously opposed the Isabellas' one firm resolution—to construct a pavilion apart from the Woman's Building in order to house a statue of Queen Isabella being sculpted by Harriet Hosmer especially for display at the fair. Palmer cited the fact that the Board of Lady Managers was charged with overseeing all women's exhibits and implied that the Woman's Building was the most appropriate place for any such display. Her stonewalling of the Isabellas' efforts to erect a separate pavilion provoked them into a renewal of their attack on the management of the Woman's Building. The war of

---

19 Weimann has painstakingly chronicled the many rifts within the Board of Lady Managers and the Isabellas in *The Fair Women*. Weimann's research showcases the fair women's abundant use of queen imagery without attempting to analyze their striking reliance upon it. In fact, Weimann unironically repeats the theme of queenliness throughout her work. For example, her first chapter is titled "Queen of the West" in reference to Chicago as an appropriate venue for the fair, in asmuch as it comprised the "seat of empire."

words waged in the press between the two groups of women so infuriated Palmer that she urged the Board to drop all plans to house the statue and attempted to conduct the business of the Woman's Building without any mention of the Spanish sovereign at all in order to avoid inadvertently drawing attention to the association bearing her name.

Although Palmer succeeded in preventing a woman's pavilion from diverting female fairgoers from the Woman's Building and Hosmer's statue was never displayed at the fair at all, Palmer eventually relinquished her plan to avoid all references to Queen Isabella. Such an action would have left too much of a void in the iconography available to her and the organizers of the Woman's Building. Palmer had attempted to substitute for the illustrious empress another historical female figure related to Columbus's discovery of America. Before the fair began, Palmer gave serious consideration to erecting Felipa Monez Perestrello, Christopher Columbus's wife, in Queen Isabella's stead. The preliminary research, which the historian Jane Mead Welch performed for Palmer indicated that Columbus's wife might be even more suitable as a historical model of modern womanhood than the Queen. Felipa Monez Perestrello, according to Welch, had been highly educated, was well-traveled, and had supported her husband's voyages with her own geographical drawings and charts. Still, there was no grandeur or mastery associated with Perestrello; her significance rested on her position as a wife. Without an obvious and official relationship to the nation-state or to empire, as Queen Isabella bore, or women like May French-Sheldon suggested, Perestrello did not seem to comprise an adequate symbol of modern woman's new-found public power. The self that the Board meant to exhibit as exemplary of modern womanhood had to be able to convey power in the world and command over others, as well as possession of oneself.[20] An empress fit this bill as no other female figure could. Queenliness in the form of Isabella proved too evocative of the sensibility Palmer wished to lend new womanhood to forsake. It proved simpler to appropriate the image than to relinquish it. Once the combative Isabellas's bid for a pavilion had been firmly defeated, Palmer abandoned the idea of championing Perestrello and threw her considerable weight behind the reinstatement of Queen Isabella in particular and queenliness in gen-

---

20 Class-specific reasons for Palmer's dismissal of Perestrello are evident in Maney's article.

eral as a most appropriate and effective metaphor for modern American womanhood at the fair. At the urging of the Board of Lady Managers, the fair's official celebration of Isabella assumed multiple forms, including the coining of an Isabella memorial quarter along with the Columbian half-dollar. The United States Post Office even issued an Isabella postage stamp.

The Isabella Association responded to its complete elimination from the fair grounds and Palmer's re-appropriation of Queen Isabella with a reversal of rhetorical strategy that makes manifest the contradictions embedded within fair women's use of queen iconography as well as the tenacious hold queenliness had on new women's imaginations of themselves at the fair. In the late spring of 1893, just as the Board of Lady Managers under Palmer's leadership fully adopted Queen Isabella as its symbol and instituted their planned celebrations of various visiting queens or their handiwork, public questions emerged regarding the legitimacy of enshrining nobility and of grafting queenly symbolism onto a fair originally intended as a celebration of the achievements of a republic. A member of the Isabellas leaked rumors to the press that the Board's elitism was manifesting itself in the form of an exclusive highlighting of royal women. In print, just prior to the start of the fair, queen imagery drew forth the charge of anti-Americanism from the very group, which had named itself for a queen:

> When the Lady managers were assembled in Chicago, they declared positively and unequivocally against any form of special or separate exhibit of women's work, and now we are told that a building is to be erected for the display of special exhibits of women's work, and *O dei immortales!* these exhibits are to be confined to the work of royalty [...] how could such an idea as that or a building to especially exhibit and protect the work of royal women emanate from an American brain? What a spectacle to present to the gaze of the civilized world! (qtd. in Weimann 56)

The Isabellas attacked the Board by stressing the autocracy associated with queenliness rather than its worth as a symbol of modern woman's public power and capacity to represent the nation-state. Perhaps vulnerable themselves on this point, they knew just how to apply the pressure. The disjuncture between the fair's emphasis on a break with a feudal, authoritarian and distinctly patriarchal past and the evidence of queenly imagery all around could easily rankle, if not taken in the proper spirit. The article laid out the paradox succinctly, if rather incompletely: "a body of ladies called into existence by the hard work and quick wits of an organized body of working women erecting a building to especially exhibit and protect the work of royalty [...]?" Left to dangle as a sign of the board's estrangement from professional middle-class women as well as women of the working classes, this rhetorical question challenged the board's efforts to heighten the drama and majesty of the moment as an un-American gesture and exposed the autocratic nature of new womanhood iconography at the fair.

The turnabout of the Isabella Association on the suitability of the queen as symbol of American women's modernity highlights the degree to which fair women were reaching past traditional American symbols to reinvent American womanhood in the 1890s. Even more illustrative of its significance, perhaps, is the fact that even a direct attack upon queen rhetoric and iconography did not render white queenliness unfit for the model of modern American womanhood that female fair organizers advanced. Once the fair was underway, expressions of outrage at the excess of queenly iconography subsided entirely. As an examination of Holley's narrator Samantha reveals, the board's celebration of modern woman as queenly was met with enthusiasm, producing intense feelings of identificatory pleasure in the largely female crowds, which jammed the Woman's Building from morning to night. Female fair organizers had successfully tied American prowess and progress to white queenliness through sheer repetition of this theme. Palmer's speech at the opening ceremonies, for instance, countered the Isabellas' eleventh-hour strategy, claiming that the flaw in likening a modern American woman to a queen was not that "the pleasures and powers and duties" American women shouldered were not tantamount to a queen's, but that women all too often were denied their rights as modern women; indeed, that all of America's womanhood did not enjoy sovereignty even domestically, or (as she put it) "that each is not 'dwelling in a home of which she is the queen'" (qtd. in Truman 182).

Palmer presented the queen as a republican standard that not only entitled American women to a life of bourgeois security and domestic dominion but rationalized and facilitated their participation in the public life of the nation as well. In the Board's wielding of queenly imagery, the tenets of true womanhood and new womanhood did not conflict. Speeches made at the reception held for President Palmer at the end of the fair reveal female fair organizers's self-consciousness on this point and regarding the potentially feudal and anti-republican associations queenliness could carry. Yet these speeches also reveal a successful maneuvering around such aspects in order to appropriate the national and public power white queenliness provided:

> We covet not titles of rank in this land of ours, where every woman may be a queen, and when the women of America choose a leader and representative she is not only a queen, but queenly. [...] If we can not crown Our Queen we will present to you Our Queen, already crowned.[21]

This pronouncement, including an astonishing number of queenly references, preceded the dramatic unveiling of a portrait of President Palmer at a ceremony held in late October to mark the closing of the Woman's Building and the fair of 1893. Out from under a dark wrap emerged a stunning portrait of the platinum-blond Palmer, showing her dressed in an elaborate white gown, donning a pointy jewelled tiara, and wielding something that looked like a scepter or a fairy's wand in her right hand. The darkened background and dramatic lighting created an impression of glowing majesty, purity, and whiteness. In her speech and in her person, President Palmer, Chicago's "jeweled queen who had widened her realm and drawn attention to the American woman" (as one biographer described her), did not shy away from invoking the white queen in much the same form that French-Sheldon's personification of the image had taken earlier that summer (Ross 100).[22] Palmer's dressing as a white queen at the closing ceremonies, and her enshrinement of that self-image in a portrait, points to just how central queenliness was to the new feminine identity that female fair organizers helped to forge and promote.

---

21 Comments made by Eagle upon the occasion of the unveiling of President Palmer's portrait at the closing ceremonies. Quoted in Eagle, *The Congress of Women* 817.
22 Queen imagery continues to echo even in twentieth-century accounts of Palmer and the Board of Lady Managers. See Ross.

Conclusion: A Fair Spectacle of Womanhood

> The Board [...] drew upon it the attention of the world. It was an unprecedented spectacle. An executive body composed wholly of women, acting with government authority, was a sight to fix the gaze.
>
> Frances Willard, "Women's Department of the World's Fair" (448)

What the fair accomplished, it did by way of spectacle.[23] The Woman's Building and the Board of Lady Managers were among the most intensely regarded of spectacles at the fair.[24] Female fair organizers took advantage of the opportunity such attention afforded them, doing their utmost to tailor a new standard of American womanhood to complement and augment the fair's promotion of the United States as preeminent modern nation. With the Columbian Exposition serving as a sort of mass coronation ceremony, female fair organizers set about to construct a vision of middle-class, white, American women as the queens of a modern world. The theme of queenliness pervaded the exhibits and events the Board of Lady Managers orchestrated. Literary and journalistic accounts of the fair confirm that queenly iconography and rhetoric encouraged identification with and celebration of white American women as queens of a modern world—a modernity measured, in part, by the presence of emancipated American women. Tussles over Queen Isabella among female organizers not only betray how entrenched queen imagery was at the fair as a symbol of woman's right to participation in the public sphere, they also disclose the self-conscious struggle to wed such iconography to a model of modern womanhood appropriate to the United States' national identity. Idealizations of American womanhood underwent revision at the World's Fair of 1893, as the "Queens of America" deftly wielded queenliness

---

[23] Trachtenberg argues that the "White City implied not only a new form of urban experience but a new way of experiencing the urban world: spectacle" (231).

[24] In Truman's opinion, a disproportionate number of visitors attended the Woman's Building events and "no event of the Exposition except the official opening produced more transport than the formal dedication of the Woman's Building" (173).

in order to appropriate the powerful discourses of progress and modernity and to locate white, middle-class American women advantageously within them.

Works Cited

Ade, George et al. *The Chicago Record's History of the World's Fair.* Chicago: Chicago Daily News Com., 1893.
Bederman, Gail. *Masculinity and Civilization: A Cultural History of Gender and Race in the United States, 1880-1917.* Chicago: U of Chicago P, 1995.
Blair, Karen. *The Clubwoman as Feminist: True Womanhood Redefined, 1868-1914.* New York: Holmes and Meier, 1980.
Boisseau, Tracey Jean. "White Queens at the World's Fair." *Gender and History* 12.1 (April 2000): 33-81.
Bordin, Ruth. Women and Temperance: The Quest for Power and Liberty, 1873-1900. Philadelphia: Temple UP, 1981.
Buhle, Mari Jo. *Women and American Socialism, 1870-1920.* Urbana: U of Illinois P, 1981.
Burg, David F. *Chicago's White City.* Lexington: U of Kenntucky P, 1976.
Cameron, William E. *The World's Fair, Being a Pictorial History of the Columbian Exposition.* Chicago: Chicago Publication and Lithograph Company, 1894.
Cott, Nancy. *The Bonds of Womanhood: 'Woman's Sphere' in New England, 1780-1835.* New Haven: Yale UP, 1977.
Eagle, Mary Kavanaugh Oldham, ed. *Congress of Women.* Chicago: Bezeley, 1894.
Elliot, Maud Howe, ed. *Art and Handicraft in the Woman's Building of the World's Columbian Exposition, Chicago, 1893.* Chicago: Rand-McNally, 1894.
Fabian, Johannes. *Time and the Other: How Anthropology Makes Its Object.* New York: Columbia UP, 1983.
Foucault, Michel. *The Order of Things: An Archaeology of the Human Sciences.* New York: Vintage Books, 1973.
Freedman, Estelle B. "Separatism as Strategy: Female Institution-Building and American Feminism, 1870-1930." *Feminist Studies* 5 (1979): 512-29.
Grabenhorst-Randall, Terree. "The Woman's Building." *Heresies* 1 (1978): 44-46.
Holley, Marietta. *Samantha at the World's Fair—by Josiah Allen's Wife.* New York: Funk & Wagnalls, 1893.
n.a. "Isabella Coins." *American Journal of Numismatics* 27.4 (April 1893): 80.
Johnson, Rossiter, ed. *A History of the World's Columbian Exposition.* New York: Appleton & Co., 1898.
Kerber, Linda. "The Republican Mother—Women and the Enlightenment: An American Perspective." *American Quarterly* 28 (1976): 187-205.

Maney, Regina. "The Wife of Columbus." *The Columbian Woman*. Ed. Mrs. Rollin A. Edgerton. Archives of the Chicago Historical Association, 1894. n.p.

Massa, Ann. "Black Women in the 'White City.'" *Journal of American Studies* 8 (1974): 319-37.

Meredith, Virginia C. "Woman's Part at the World's Fair: The Work of the Board of Lady Managers." *American Review of Reviews* 7 (May 1893): 417-419.

Official Directory of the World's Columbian Exposition May 1 to October 30, 1893. Chicago: Conkey, 1893.

Official Manual of the Board of Lady Managers of the World's Columbian Commission, September 19, 1890 to September 9, 1891. Chicago: Rand, McNally & Company, 1891.

Pohl, Frances K. "Historical Reality or Utopian Ideal?" *International Journal of Women's Studies* 5 (1892): 289-311.

Rabinovitz, Lauren. *For the Love of Pleasure*. New Brunswick: Rutgers UP, 1998.

Records of the Mint. National Archives. Washington D.C.

Ross, Ishbel. *Silhouette in Diamonds: The Life of Mrs. Potter Palmer*. New York: Harper and Bros., 1960.

Rydell, Robert. *All the World's a Fair: American International Expositions, 1876-1916*. Diss. U of California, 1980.

Scott, Anne Firor. *Natural Allies: Women's Associations in American History*. Urbana: U of Illinois P, 1991.

Sewall, Mary Wright, ed. *World's Congress of Representative Women*. 2 vols. Chicago: Rand-McNally, 1894.

Snyder-Ott, Joelynn. "Woman's Place in the Home (that she built)." *Feminist Art Journal* 3 (1974): 7-8.

Trachtenberg, Alan. *The Incorporation of America: Culture and Society in the Gilded Age*. New York: Hill and Wang, 1982.

Truman, Ben C. et al. *History of the World's Fair*. Philadelphia: H. W. Kelley, 1893.

Weimann, Jean Madeleine. *The Fair Women*. Chicago: Academy Press, 1981.

Welter, Barbara. "The Cult of True Womanhood, 1820-1860." *American Quarterly* 18 (Summer 1966): 151-174.

Willard, Frances. "Women's Department of the World's Fair." *The World's Fair, Being a Pictorial History of the Columbian Exposition*. Ed. William E. Cameron. Chicago: Chicago Publication and Lithograph Company, 1894. 448-70.

Williams, Fannie C. "A White Queen at the World's Fair." *Chautauquan* 18 (1893): 341-45.

Wright, Mary, ed. *World's Congress of Representative Women*. 2 vols. Chicago: Rand-McNally, 1894.

Literature

Charles Sealsfield's and Ferdinand Kürnberger's Spatial Constructions of America

Joseph C. Schöpp

"I take SPACE to be the central fact to man born in America," Charles Olson emphatically declares at the beginning of *Call Me Ishmael*; he spells space "large because it comes large here. Large, and without mercy" (11). Ranging from the Atlantic to the Pacific, from the Great Lakes to the Gulf of Mexico, 'America' (to use Olson's term) appears as a large geographic space indeed. Such a space, measurable and subject to the "estimates of the surveyor," is one thing; how this measurable space affects and informs the mind and how the mind, in turn, reconceives and restructures it imaginatively is quite another. A space "seized upon by the imagination," Gaston Bachelard argues, "cannot remain indifferent space," since it is one "lived in, not in its positivity, but with all the partiality of the imagination" (xxxvi). Space is so central a fact that to this very day it has seized the American imagination in manifold ways. Writers as different as Alexis de Tocqueville, Frederick Jackson Turner or Gertrude Stein have tried to determine the uniqueness of the American spatial experience. For Tocqueville it is "the continual movement" that characterizes it, a movement "which agitates a democratic community" (144). Frederick Jackson Turner sees the space of the frontier with "its striking characteristics" impressed upon "the American intellect," an intellect which he defines as practical, inventive, energetic, expansive, restless, in motion, and "continually demand[ing] a wider field for its exercise" (57). Gertrude Stein's conception of the American space concurs with that of both Tocqueville and Turner; in her opinion it is "something strictly American to conceive a space that is filled with moving, a space of time that is filled always filled with moving" (286). It is, as it were, a temporal space in motion, always in the making, as she so impressively demonstrates in *The Making of Americans*. Both Stein and Turner, William Gass points out, "thought that human behavior was in great part a function of the amount of free land [...]. The human mind went on like the prairie, on and on without limit" (11). John Dewey's concept of the democratic mind as one always "incomplete and in the making" sounds remarkably similar. For Dewey "any notion of a perfect or complete reality, finished, existing always the same without regard to the vicissitudes of time, [is] abhorrent" (50). Not even the Great Depression could shatter such a position, as Louis Adamic in *My America, 1928-1938* testifies: "America is a continent, a thing-in-process, elemental, ever-changing, calling for further exploration, for constant rethinking, for repeated self-orientation on the part of its citizens. It cannot be caught or imprisoned in words of finality" (xiii).

Philip Fisher in his recent book *Still the New World* subsumes these arguments under the concept of America as a "democratic social space" with its essential features of openness, internal mobility and an absence of limits (44). He sees America as a country of permanent "newness and nextness" (18), of a continuous "creative destruction" which reminds one again of John Dewey's concept of a "creative democracy" as an "ongoing process" of self-renewal, "continually open[ing] the way into the unexplored and unattained future" (229).

American painters, poets, and prose writers have enacted this "space of time" in the making. Asher B. Durand's painting *Progress* (1853) or George Inness' *The Lackawanna Valley* (1855) show landscapes under "creative destruction." To make newness possible primeval nature has to be destroyed. Thus Durand can remove the Indians, barely visible, to a dark corner of his otherwise sunsplashed canvas while Inness foregrounds the tree stumps as emblems of a cleared space that makes room for a new age of steam. William Cullen Bryant, in his poem "The Prairies," imagines "the sound of that advancing multitude which soon shall fill" the vast, silent solitudes of the Great Plains (53). N. P. Willis' *American Scenery* predicts a future of "villages that will soon sparkle on the hill-sides, the axes that will ring from the woodlands, and the mills, bridges, canals, and railroads, that will span and border the stream that now runs through sedge and wildflower" (2). Such a democratic social space is first and foremost a dynamic space, continuously transforming itself, ceaselessly making and unmaking, structuring and restructuring itself. "In Europe," Tocqueville argues, "people talk a great deal of the wilds of America, but the Americans themselves never think about them [...]. Their eyes are fixed upon another sight; the American people views its own march across the wilds,—drying swamps, turning the course of rivers, peopling solitudes and subduing nature" (181). Europeans, due to their different cultural conditions, were obviously more hesitant to accept such spatial constructions while a new country saw it practically as a necessity to invent and envision itself anew in what Fisher calls the democratic social space.

The following discussion will largely center on the spatial constructions of two European writers of the first half of the nineteenth century, now largely forgotten, yet of some renown in their time. Both wrote in German but, due to their different political orientation, generated very different spatial constructs of America. The one, Charles Sealsfield, "the celebrated Seatsfield [sic]," "a real man of flesh and blood [who] had his earthly domicile in Germany," as Hawthorne somewhat ironically characterized him in "A Select Party" (953), was an ex-monk with a somewhat mysterious past. Born in the Moravian town of Popitz, he had joined the Kreuzherren order in Prague. In 1823 the freedom-loving monk fled both his monastic cell and his country groaning under an authoritarian regime and via Switzerland and France escaped to the United States where he established his literary reputation as a journalist, travel writer, and novelist. The other, Ferdinand Kürnberger, a Viennese forty-eighter, had fled from Austria to Dresden, then to Hamburg where he saw some of his fellow-fighters off en route to America; from Hamburg he went to Frankfurt where he completed his novel *Der Amerikamüde* without ever having set foot on American soil. Though representing two different generations with different political agendas, both, like so many of their German contemporaries, saw the vast spaces of America as a grand canvas onto which they could project their utopian and/or dystopian anxieties and desires. Thus the American landscapes which they created were first and foremost political landscapes. Not unlike the painters represented in Martin Warnke's book *Politische Landschaft*, Sealsfield and Kürnberger painted literary landscapes in which nature became one with politics and the aesthetic, as it were, merged with the political.

*

Charles Sealsfield's first literary attempt was a two-volume treatise of the geographical, political, social, and religious conditions of America entitled *The United States of North America As They Are* and *The Americans As They Are,* published in 1827/28 in both German and English. While the first volume discusses the American political system the second volume describes the author's journey from Pennsylvania down the Ohio and Mississippi Rivers to New Orleans. Despite his reputation as a master of poetic landscapes in nineteenth-century German literature, Sealsfield's first publication presents itself as surprisingly flat and prosaic. The impressive landscape scenes of his later novels which Alexander Ritter and Günter Schnitzler have discussed in great detail, are almost entirely absent from the travel book. Only occasionally the reader witnesses the author's mastery as a landscape artist. The confluence of the Ohio and the Mississippi, a classic site for many travel writers of the time, provides one of these rare occasions:

> The deep silence which reigns [here], and which is interrupted only by the rushing sound of the waves, and the immense mass of water, produce the illusion that you are no longer standing upon firm ground; you are fearful less the earth should give way to the powerful element, which, pressed into so narrow a space, rolls on with irresistible force. [...] The immense number of streams which empty into the Mississippi, and caused it to be named, very appropriately, the *Father of Rivers*, render it powerful throughout the year. (II:81)

The traveler suddenly loses the solid ground under his feet; he is literally carried away by the magnificent spectacle of nature. What Sealsfield generates here is an American space in motion, a "Bewegungslandschaft," as August Langen calls it (184), a descriptive convention popular in the eighteenth century which in Sealsfield's time had more or less grown out of fashion. Yet the American spatial experience, dynamic rather than static, may have inspired Sealsfield to choose this dynamic (*bewegt*) form of representation.

What we observe on the microstructural level of such a single scene also characterizes Sealsfield's textual macrostructure. His construction of the American space which he traverses on his journey is clearly one in motion. Therefore he foregrounds scenes of the so-called middle landscape, "located in a middle ground" between civilization and the wilderness (Marx 23) where everything is in a continuous process of transformation, a space marked by a "mania for change [...] perpetually amending and altering" (I:165). "From forty to fifty axes resound in the wood; the timber is prepared in a few days, and the log-cabin is erected" within a short time (I:199); farmland is carved out of the wilderness, interstate roads like the one from Washington to New Orleans are built, canals are dug out, coal-mines are operated by "aspiring, energetic, shrewed, and intelligent" entrepreneurs (I:239). The whole land is literally in the making. Since "similarity," according to Fisher, is another characteristic of the new democratic social space (44), the scenes here strikingly resemble one another; a fact that accounts as much for the stylistic flatness and the almost monotonous repetitiveness of Sealsfield's book as it underscores the egalitarianism characteristic of a democratic space. Traveling through Ohio, Indiana, and Illinois, Sealsfield time and again portrays industrious and enterprising merchants, plowing, sowing, and reaping farmers, flax spinning and weaving housewives. It is a highly metamorphic space; its agents are always in motion and on the move. To be an American for Sealsfield means as much as to be "adventurous, restless, and erratic," a disposition frequently misunderstood by Europeans traveling in America. "Did the American yield to excessive sensibility either in personal or local attachments," he counters the critique of a British traveler, "the beautiful plains of the west would remain unoccupied and deserted" (I:205). Roads, canals, and one day railroads would not be built. Steam is already one of the major sources of power; steamboats on the Ohio and the Mississippi, "the steam mill on the river [...], several steam engines, iron and nail manufactories, all on the steam principle" (II:3) begin to invade the garden: the American landscape transformed into an early nineteenth-century technoscape.

Such a space lacks, as Fisher points out, the traditional poetic qualities. Unlike many contemporaneous landscape painters and nature poets Sealsfield constructs a rather prosaic America of farmers, boatmen, storekeepers, merchants, mechanics, and manufacturers. Court-houses, banks, churches, wholesale and retail stores, libraries, newspapers, printing offices (II:102) he lists as the pride of nearly every town, a listing technique that Walt Whitman in his democratic chants would later lead to poetic perfection. Sealsfield's construction of America as a democratic social space may also explain why he could devote over one third of the book to a city like New Orleans, the destination of his journey. The fact that he knew the city best, since it was his temporary home, and that Andrew Jackson, his political hero, in 1815 had won here the decisive victory over the British which—in the German edition—provides the material for a grand finale, only in part explains the rather unbalanced structure of the book. With his description of New Orleans as a city of progress that, not too long ago, had "groaned under the yoke of the most wretched tyranny" (II:163), Sealsfield pays his high respect to political progress in a liberal democracy. "A totally different sensation possesses the mind on entering an American city," he observes. In a city like New Orleans "man beholds what he can contend with, and what he can accomplish, when his strength is not checked by the arbitrary will of a despot" (II:144). While scenes of natural sublimity and beauty are remarkably rare in the book, Sealsfield, in great length, celebrates an urban sublimity and beauty:

> The view is splendid beyond description, when you pass down the stream, which is here a mile broad, rolls its immense volume of waters in a bed above 200 feet deep, and as if conscious of its strength, appears to look quietly on the bustle of the habitations of man. Both its banks are lined with charming sugar plantations, from the midst of which rises the airy mansion of the wealthy planter, surrounded with orange, banana, lime and fig trees, the growth of a climate approaching to the torrid zone. (II:145)

The city that had pulled down the French "circumvallations," once the impediments of commercial progress, can now fully enjoy its prosperity. Approaching the harbor with its flat boats, keelboats, steamboats, merchant vessels, brigs, and "the elegant ships appearing like a forest of masts," New Orleans, an urban *Bewegungslandschaft*, so to speak, offers a truly dynamic and "enchanting prospect" to the eye (II:146). Like the majestic scene at the confluence of the Ohio and the Mississippi, the urban sublime once more enchants and carries the author away—this time into a great future. He envisions this "most elegant and wealthy city of the republic" as "the emporium of America," if not "the most important commercial point on the face of the earth" (II:164). Sealsfield's urban euphoria is part of his promotional strategy. As a refugee from a *régime* "checked by the arbitrary will of a despot"—not unlike New Orleans a few years ago—he clearly sees the benefits and blessings of democracy and therefore creates a counterspace, "fiercely economic" (Fisher 38), energetic, on- and upwardly mobile: America a magnet, as it were, which would lure people into the country and "enable the future emigrant to follow the prescribed track" of prosperity and happiness (II:v).

Sealsfield's spatial construct, however, has one major defect that disqualifies it as a democratic social space in the true sense of the word. The egalitarian ideal, characteristic of such a space, is surreptitiously undercut by a rigid socio-ethnic hierarchization. Thus the pride of the respectable farmer and merchant forbids them "to mix with the [poor white] rabble" (II:105) and the black slave. A distinct ethnic hierarchy with the Anglo-Saxon on top of the ladder followed by the German and the French as "the least valuable acquisition for a new state" (II:174) is established. A democratic social space would need frugal, ascetic, hard-working Anglo-Saxon farmers and merchants rather than lazy French hedonists "passing the greater part of their time in grog-shops, or in dancing-companies" (II:95). The major defect, however, is that of slavery. For Fisher "the spatial structure of slavery [...] is clearly the most radical contradiction possible for a society constructing a democratic social space" (51) and Sealsfield seems unable to resolve this contradiction. As a political refugee from an authoritarian *régime* and as a fierce advocate of individual liberty he cannot but reject slavery as a truly peculiar institution which, in his opinion, "contributes not a little to the aristocratic notions of the people" (II:96) who may publicly profess their democratic beliefs while they privately act in a most inhumane way. Traveling on the Ohio with the free states of Ohio, Indiana, and Illinois on the one side and the slave-holding state of Kentucky on the other, Sealsfield becomes an eye-witness of the "baneful influence" that slavery has on the development of the country. Between Ohio and Kentucky he constructs a sharp contrast to make the reader aware of the damaging effect of slavery: "elegant farms, orchards, meadows, corn and wheat fields carefully enclosed" mark the free north-side while the gardens on the south-side of the Ohio River look blighted and "neglected" (II:19); slaves, "secured by a rope fastened to an iron collar," are driven like animals to the auction block; a "tremendous horsewhip" reminds them "to quicken their pace" (II:28). For Sealsfield Kentucky is therefore not "a country that could be recommended to new settlers." Due to its slave practices and its "insecure titles to land" he feels that he has to discourage and dissuade "every lover of peace and tranquility" from settling there (II:51). The Southern states, in his opinion, were politically less secure than the North. Their instability could only in part be explained by slavery as an institution; the slaves themselves, "vicious [...], treacherous and barbarous" by nature, were also to be held responsible for the unstable situation. They will one day, he feared, "subject their former masters to certain destruction and death" (II:177). In full accordance with the racist jargon of the time, Sealsfield could construct the black slave as sensuous, easily excitable, passionate, and of a "malignant and cruel disposition" (II:176).

The further Sealsfield travels southward, the more he adopts the dominant racial views of the South, the more slavery changes from a peculiar to a necessary institution. The plantations with their "high degree of prosperity and comfort" (II:142), "the airy mansion of the wealthy planter" (II:145) could hardly exist without slave labor. All too readily Sealsfield succumbs and subscribes to the stereotypical views of the slave-holding mistresses and masters:

> The fatigue and labor in these hot and sultry climates, can only be borne by slaves; a white man who should attempt the same labor which kept him stout and hearty in the north, would soon be overcome by the heat of the climate. (II:140)

The refugee of a despotic *régime* now suddenly an advocate of an even more despotic and inhumane system? What may appear as a conversion to Southern social beliefs must, at least in part, be explained by an unresolved inner conflict. Sealsfield speaks, as I believe, with two tongues: on the one hand, as a refugee and an apologist of political liberty guaranteed most effectively in a democratic social space and, on the other hand, as the defender of what Fisher calls "free enterprise capitalism" (37) which also thrives best in a liberal society and which Sealsfield so forcefully propagates in his book to promote immigration from Europe. There is still another unresolved conflict that characterizes Sealsfield's American space. As a propagator of a liberal democracy, he repeatedly exhibits a deep-seated admiration of stern authoritarian leader and father figures who, as he phrased it in *Austria As It Is,* with "an honesty, a good faith, a paternal hand" could inflict wounds, but could also cure them (129). Andrew Jackson, the Napoleon *des bois,* and Emperor Joseph II were among them. When such paternal figures, however, lacked honesty, good faith, and a warm fatherly hand, they often enough turned into dangerous despots with a "cold ambitious mind." Count Metternich had to be counted among them and John Quincy Adams, Jackson's political adversary, in Sealsfield's eyes exhibited traits of pride and arrogance characteristic of a "heartless diplomatist" à la Metternich. He therefore considered him "a most dangerous man to the freedom of the Union, and if he had been sent by Metternich himself, he could not pursue more closely the principles of the Holy Alliance" (I:19-21). Sealsfield's fear that America might one day turn into another Europe is latently present, yet his belief in America as a space in motion that constantly reinvents itself always gets the upper hand.

*

In his novel *Der Amerikamüde: Amerikanisches Kulturbild* (1855), Ferdinand Kürnberger approaches America from the opposite end of the spectrum. Unlike Sealsfield, with whose writings he was familiar, he had never set foot on American soil nor had he ever hatched any plans to seek political refuge in 'the land of the free' as so many of his fellow 'forty-eighters' had done. Despite its lack of first-hand knowledge, *Der Amerikamüde* is nevertheless, as Winfried Fluck remarks, "a very knowledgeable book about America" (189). Kürnberger had, in his own words, "set himself the task to study the nation from the best sources" available (Fluck 172). He could indeed rely on excellent publications ranging from travel books and political analyses to letters and newspaper reports, sources which he meticulously studied and which helped him paint a remarkably authentic picture of 'America.' The protagonist, Dr. Nikolaus Moorfeld, a romantic poet in search of "the urshades of the backwoods" (19), untouched and undefiled, is fashioned after Nikolaus Lenau, the Austrian romantic poet, whose travel letters from America served Kürnberger not only as a valuable source of information; they, above all, determined his point-of-view from which he was to construct his American space.

Upon his arrival in New York, Dr. Moorfeld, the freedom-loving forty-eighter, is full of enthusiasm: "Amerika!" he exclaims, "Welcher Name hat einen Inhalt gleich diesem Namen!" (9). The excessive rhetoric of the opening paragraphs, however, gives rise to doubts. Is it perhaps a kind of manic euphoria that will imperceptibly slide into a more depressive state? The city at first presents itself as vividly dynamic, a space in perpetual motion, incomplete ("unfertig" 33) and limitless; "wo ist sein Ende? Wo nur ein Ruhepunkt?" (24). The poet's delicate ears, however, perceive the urban hustle and bustle as increasingly chaotic and cacophonous. A group of African-American street musicians producing strangely chopped, syncopated rhythms whose measures seem to hover in the dark ("ein seltsam zerhackter Rhythmus, dessen Taktart in einigem Dunkel schwebt" 20), offend Dr. Moorfeld's musicality. As a violin expert he snatches the first violinist's instrument to teach him how to play his tunes correctly. The Black 'disharmony' deeply disturbs the poet's "klangreiche Seele" (52), a soul attuned to more harmonious sounds. Wherever he casts his glance he sees uniformity and an offensive pursuit of mammonism which Tocqueville had already diagnosed as characteristic of an egalitarian system. While Tocqueville analyzed them dispassionately, Kürnberger regards them as utterly offensive. Small wonder that Dr. Moorfeld, deeply disgusted, decides to flee this prosaic urban space and in the second half of the novel removes to a more poetic America in the backwoods of the West.

Pennsylvania at first presents itself as a place that seems to deserve the epithet "Garden of the Union":

> Wohin man blickt, ist der Gesichtskreis voll von Bildern des Wohlstandes und der Zufriedenheit. Farm an Farm reiht sich unabsehbar über die hügelige Bodenfläche eines Landes, dem es nirgends an Wald, Wasser, Weide und, wie es scheint, an Fruchtbarkeit gebricht. [...] Wie die Flüsse schweifen, die Täler ziehen, sanfte Abhänge, bewaldet oder bebaut, sich durch die Ebene mischen, zerstreute Bauernhöfe nach Ost und West ihre Fronten ins Land kehren, so gibt es auf jedem Hügel von ein paar Ellen Höhe eine freundliche, anmutige Umschau. Kurz das Land ist nicht eben malerisch, aber heiter behaglich.

The land is serene, affluent, content, and cozy, yet, Moorfeld asks himself, where is its picturesqueness ("malerisch") which a romantic poet so desperately seeks? The wilderness, though everywhere, does not affect his German "Gemüt" (320); it lacks 'the expression of quiet greatness and sublimity' ("Ausdruck der ruhigen Größe und Erhabenheit" 389). Nature is in a deplorable state of degeneracy and desolation:

> Heute fiel mir das Herz wie nie. Ich sah den ersten Hinterwalds-Anbau. Grausenhaft! Ich finde kein Wort, das Unversöhnliche eines solchen Anblicks für das europäische Gefühl zu beschreiben. Ist's denn möglich? (356)

Wherever he looks he sees a countryside disfigured by ugly zigzag fences, burnt trees and tree stumps. America's natural space is marked by absences. Where is the German oak? Where are the birds and the butterflies, the sylvan songs and fragrances? Where the precious, 'highly romantic' rock formations of the sonorous melaphyre, the augite porphyry, the trachyte or the dolomite (345)? What the traveler finds instead are such prosaic natural resources as 'soft coal, iron, gypsum, and marl' ("Braunkohle, Eisenstein, Gips, Mergel" 347) that fail to captivate his imagination. The Jeffersonian husbandman who, according to the national creed, cultivated his piece of land, content and happy, is also strangely absent. The farms of New Lisbon in Eastern Ohio, where Moorfeld plans to settle and where Lenau had already miserably failed in 1832, are far from independent units; a net of dependencies ties them to the banks of New York, Baltimore or Philadelphia (399); the so-called free-holders are either 'free-booters' (347) who mercilessly exploit the land, or victims of speculators who, with their invisible tentacles, control the land, an image reminiscent of Sealsfield's spies and secret police who weave, spider-like, their "net over the whole of Europe" (*Austria* 153).

Whatever Moorfeld perceives in the new world, he measures against the standards of the old. He has, as Jeffrey Sammons argues, "an absolutely inflexible mental set that is impervious to new experience" (48). America's "incomparable materials," its "barbarism and materialism," its "banks and tariffs, the newspaper and caucus, methodism and unitarianism" which Emerson hails as America's poetic assets, Moorfeld, the European cultural elitist, regards as flat and dull. For Emerson they are dull only "to dull people [and] rest on the same foundations of wonder as the town of Troy and the temple of Delphos" (465). Walt Whitman, in Fisher's eyes the true chanter of a democratic social space, could capture what Moorfeld fails to grasp. In his poems he could envision America as a space in which nature and technology, lilacs and locomotives, live oaks and steamboats, prairies, oceans and telegraphs would harmoniously blend into each other. What Moorfeld in his elegiac mood bemoans as repulsive, formless, *unfertig*, Whitman in a poem like "Years of the Modern" celebrates as "unperform'd" with "tremendous entrances and exits, new combinations" (489). Whitman can accept this ceaselessly metamorphic process, this "wearing out of reality and its replacement" by newer, more modern forms of the real (Fisher 73). The "turbulent democracy of America," would indeed require, as Ritchie Robertson argues, "not [Kürnberger's] classical harmony, but Walt Whitman's 'barbaric yawp'" (33).

Kürnberger's American cultural image (*Amerikanisches Kulturbild*) is informed by a concept of culture as an instrument of elevation and ennoblement. American money is pitted against European mind, utilitarian flatness against cultural depth. Moorfeld, assured of himself and his own culture, is not able "to redefine the concept of culture itself in more democratic terms" (Paul 370). Neither can he stand the chopped-up rhythms of the 'wild' Negro orchestra nor can he, a typical European monoculturalist, bear what little children, recognizably natives, quite obviously enjoy. They eagerly run to a scene and suddenly stand in the middle of two orchestras listening not just to one but "zwei Musik" (21), while Moorfeld flees from this scene of disharmony in disgust. With his concept of an elitist monoculture he not only misinterprets American multicultural phenomena; he is also unable to see that Americans in the first half of the nineteenth century still shared, as Lawrence Levine has pointed out, "a public culture less hierarchically organized, less fragmented into relatively rigid adjectival boxes" (9).

The spatial constructions of Sealsfield and Kürnberger could hardly be more different. While Sealsfield, the political refugee with a firm belief in liberty, constructs a vast space of free entrepreneuring people, Kürnberger's counter-image is one of a dense net of dependencies that belies the notion of America as a land of independent individuals. The book tellingly ends on an image of turmoil when a nativist mob terrorizes honest German settlers. As so often before, the disillusioned Dr. Moorfeld flees the scene in utter disgust and returns to Europe. As a book about America, *Der Amerikamüde* would, as Jeffrey Sammons puts it, "make a likely candidate in a competition for the silliest German novel of the nineteenth century" (48). Yet it is perhaps "not so much a book about America but about Germany" (Fluck 205). It can be read as an attempt at defining a national German culture when the nation was still in the making. As a political tract, a piece of German "Tendenzliteratur" (Meyer), however, it served its purpose. Disillusioned by the political ideals of 1848, Kürnberger formulates new ideals of a unified German *Kulturnation* with at times dubious nationalistic undertones. While America, in Kürnberger's eyes, could serve as a model for a political unity, it sorely lacked a deeply rooted cultural coherence. Thus for Sealsfield and Kürnberger, America, with its vast spaces, could become the vacant canvas unto which the deepest political desires of both the pre- and postfortyeighters could be effectively projected.

Works Cited

Adamic, Louis. *My America, 1928-1938*. New York: Harper, 1938.
Bachelard, Gaston. *The Poetics of Space*. Trans. Maria Jolas with a new foreword by
    John R. Stilgoe. Boston: Beacon P, 1994.
Bryant, William Cullen. *Poems*. New York: Thomas Y. Crowell, 1893.
Dewey, John. "Philosophy and Democracy." *The Middle Works, 1899-1924*. Ed. Jo
    Ann Boydston, et al. Carbondale: U of Southern Illinois P, 1976-83. XI: 41-53.

—. "Creative Democracy—The Task Before Us." *The Later Works, 1925-53*. Ed. Jo Ann Boydston, et al. Carbondale: U of Southern Illinois P, 1981-90. XIV: 224-230.

Emerson, Ralph Waldo. *Essays and Lectures*. New York: Library of America, 1983.

Fisher, Philip. *Still the New World: American Literature in a Culture of Creative Destruction*. Cambridge, MA: Harvard UP, 1999.

Fluck, Winfried. "The Man Who Became Weary of America: Ferdinand Kürnberger's Novel *Der Amerika-Müde* (1855)." *German? American? Literature? New Directions in German-American Studies*. New York: Lang, 2002. 171-206.

Gass, William, ed. *Gertrude Stein: The Geographical History of America or The Relation of Human Nature to the Human Mind*. New York: Vintage, 1973.

Hawthorne, Nathaniel. *Tales and Sketches*. New York: Library of America, 1982.

Kürnberger, Ferdinand. *Der Amerikamüde: Amerikanisches Kulturbild*. Frankfurt/Main: Insel, 1986.

Langen, August. "Verbale Dynamik in der dichterischen Landschaftsschilderung des 18. Jahrhunderts." *Landschaft und Raum in der Erzählkunst*. Ed. Alexander Ritter. Darmstadt: Wiss. Buchgesellschaft, 1975. 112-191.

Levine, Lawrence W. *Highbrow/Lowbrow: The Emergence of Cultural Hierarchy in America*. Cambridge, MA: Harvard UP, 1988.

Marx, Leo. *The Machine in the Garden: Technology and the Pastoral Ideal in America*. New York: Oxford UP, 1964.

Meyer, Hildegard. *Nordamerika im Urteil des Schrifttums bis zur Mitte des 19. Jahrhunderts. Eine Untersuchung über Kürnbergers 'Amerika-Müden'*. Hamburg: Friederichsen, 1929.

Olson, Charles. *Call Me Ishmael*. San Francisco: City Lights, 1947.

Paul, Heike. "Multilingualism and Metaphors of Musicality: Israel Zangwill, Jeanette Lander, Ferdinand Kürnberger." *German? American? Literature? New Directions in German-American Studies*. Ed. Winfried Fluck. New York: Lang, 2002. 359-382.

Ritter, Alexander. *Darstellung und Funktion der Landschaft in den Amerika-Romanen von Charles Sealsfield (Karl Postl)*. Diss. Kiel, 1969.

Robertson, Ritchie. "German Idealists and American Rowdies: Ferdinand Kürnberger's Novel *Der Amerika-Müde*." *Gender and Politics in Austrian Fiction*. Ed. Ritchie Robertson and Edward Timms. Edinburgh: Edinburgh UP, 1996. 17-35.

Sammons, Jeffrey L. "Land of Limited Possibilities: America in the Nineteenth-Century German Novel." *Yale Review* 68 (1978): 35-52.

Schnitzler, Günter. *Erfahrung und Bild: Die dichterische Wirklichkeit des Charles Sealsfield (Karl Postl)*. Freiburg: Rombach, 1988.

Sealsfield, Charles. *The United States of North America As They Are. The Americans As They Are*. 1828; Hildesheim: Olms, 1972.

—. *Austria As It Is*. 1828; Hildesheim: Olms, 1972.

Stein, Gertrude. *Writings 1932-1946*. New York: Library of America, 1998.

Tocqueville, Alexis de. *Democracy in America*. Ed. Richard D. Heffner. New York: Mentor Books, 1984.
Turner, Frederick Jackson. *The Significance of the Frontier in America*. Ed. Harold P. Simonson. New York: Frederick Ungar, 1963.
Warnke, Martin. *Politische Landschaft—Zur Kunstgeschichte der Natur*. Munich: Hanser, 1992.
Whitman, Walt. *Leaves of Grass*. Ed. Sculley Bradley and H.W. Blodgett. New York: Norton, 1973.
Willis, N.P. *American Scenery*. 2 vols. London: G. Virtue, 1840.

"Man Is Not Himself Only": Senses of Place in American Nature Writing

Heike Schäfer

Place is inevitable. No matter what else we are or strive to be, we are always somewhere in particular, faced with specific situations, enmeshed in particular spaces. Ceaselessly, we engage in conversation with our surroundings. How we participate in the world around us affects the texture and course of our lives. We cannot exist out of context. The experience of place indeed is such an elemental part of our daily lives that we hardly notice or mention it. Place, Clifford Geertz recently has pointed out, is so ubiquitous that it usually "goes without saying" (259). Though our sense of place often remains submerged, taken for granted, and unexpressed, we continuously align ourselves with the places we build, traverse, and inhabit. On a physical and psychological level, our interactions with the environment sustain and change us. They inflect who we are and inform who we become. As Eudora Welty notes, "Sense of place gives equilibrium; extended, it is sense of direction too" (792).

If indeed our sense of place and sense of self are fundamentally linked, the processes through which we come to know and interact with the places we inhabit may prove to be an intriguing field of study. How do we physically encounter and aesthetically make sense of our environments and how does this engagement with place shape our sense of self? Rather than leave my desk for an extended field trip now, I will explore some aspects of environmental experience in what follows by sampling the detailed narratives of place that the American nature writing tradition yields. I will take a closer look at the work of Henry David Thoreau, Mary Austin, and Annie Dillard—three writers who probe the dynamics of environmental perception and representation as they describe the animals, plants, and human residents, the ecological organization and cultural history of their respective places. These writers share the conviction that "man is not himself only," that our emplaced lives render us continuous with a more-than-human world that not only provokes our speculations but that also resists us and that, therefore, continually challenges our understanding of who we are and what it means to be human (Austin 437). For Thoreau, Austin, and Dillard, sense of place entails the awareness that one is part of what one is not. But before I discuss in more detail how these authors dramatize in their writing the reciprocal relations between our sense of self and sense of place, let me briefly characterize the literary tradition they are working in.

"Nature writing" as a generic marker denotes in current scholarship a specific tradition of nonfictional writing, which developed out of such diverse sources as the study of natural history, travel writing, and the pastoral tradition. Most critics trace the beginnings of the genre back to *The Natural History and Antiquities of Selbourne*, published by the British clergyman Gilbert White in 1788, and to William Bartram's *Travels*, published three years later in 1791.[1] In the nineteenth century, when nature writing increasingly established itself as a literary genre, the pivotal figure working in the field was Henry David Thoreau. His work has extended such a powerful influence on later writers that some critics consider him the progenitor of the genre or speak of the Thoreauvian tradition of nature writing.[2] During the genre's formative phase in the late nineteenth century, female authors significantly contributed to the tradition. Yet when the canon solidified in response to the professionalizing of the conservation movement and the wilderness cult at the turn of the century, they lost their prominent position (Norwood 48, 53; Buell 44-45). As a result, the lineage appears in most surveys of the genre as male-dominated. It usually continues in the early twentieth century with such writers as John Muir and John Burroughs. Later authors include Aldo Leopold, Edward Abbey, Barry Lopez, and Terry Tempest Williams.

Although the tradition draws on various sources and comprises the work of diverse authors, some identifiable characteristics exist that allow us to differentiate nature writing from other kinds of environmental literature. On the level of content, nature writing essays typi-

---

1 The first extensive study of the nature writing tradition is Tracy's *American Naturists*. Recent studies include those by Fritzell; Lyon; O'Grady; Scheese; and Slovic.
2 Thoreau's contribution to the nature writing tradition is thoroughly examined by Buell.

cally focus on the description of a particular locality—Walden Pond, for instance, Owens Valley, or Tinker Creek. They describe the natural phenomena of this place, the nesting habits of birds, the dispersion of seeds, or the intricate design of a cactus, to name a few examples. Yet nature writing usually lists not only things and events that could be perceived by any attentive observer. It also includes ecological and natural history information that requires some scientific training and that the authors themselves often draw from library research rather than from their observation of their natural surroundings. As Gary Snyder asserts: "It is not enough just to 'love nature' [...]. Our relation to the natural world takes place in a *place,* and it must be grounded in information and experience" (39).

Most nature writers share a sustained interest in the natural sciences. Darwin's *On the Origin of Species* (1859) provided Thoreau, for instance, with a major impetus to systematize his extensive observations and field notes into such essays as "The Succession of Forest Trees" (1860)—essays with which Thoreau in turn contributed to the study of natural history.[3] Likewise, Austin corresponded avidly with a desert biologist, Daniel MacDougal, as she worked on her biocultural history of the Southwest, *The Land of Journey's Ending* (1924). And Dillard disclosed that she drew on hundreds of index cards, writing her book *Pilgrim at Tinker Creek* (1974) mostly at a library desk (Major 363).

What distinguishes nature writing from other forms of natural history writing, then, is how these texts frame the scientific information they present. Typically, they are constructed as first-person narratives that recount the narrator's exploration of a given place. As readers, we are asked to join the narrator on excursions into the woods, along creeks, up mountains, or at least into the garden. As we follow the narrator's movement through space and observe his building sense of place, his sensations, thoughts and emotions, we become aware of the role that the perceiving subject plays in creating the described scene. We cannot read *Walden,* for instance, without noticing that the pond, cabin, railroad track, and fields only cohere and acquire significance—that is, begin to form a literary landscape—because they are perceived and described by one observer, Thoreau's narrator. *Walden*

---

[3] Thoreau was one of the first writers to describe the principle of forest succession (cf. McGregor 190-94).

is typical in this respect. The format of the nature-writing essay is designed to balance the presentation of factual information about a place's natural history with reflections on the ways in which we read and experience our environments. As Thomas Lyon has defined the genre, nature writing is characterized by the intersection of "natural history information, personal responses to nature, and philosophical interpretation of nature" (3). A representative example of this confluence can be found in Thoreau's essay "Autumnal Tints" (1862).

In "Autumnal Tints," Thoreau describes the changes of the vegetation around Concord as fall sets in. In the following passage, he portrays one of the region's prominent kinds of grasses:

> [...] near the end of August, a to me very interesting genus of grasses, andropogons, or beard-grasses, is in its prime: *Andropogon furcatus*, forked beard-grass, or call it purple-fingered grass; *Andropogon scoparius*, purple wood-grass; and *Andropogon* (now called *Sorghum*) *nutans*, Indian-grass. The first is a very tall and slender-culmed grass, three to seven feet high, with four or five purple finger-like spikes raying upward from the top. The second is also quite slender, growing in tufts two feet high by one wide, with culms often somewhat curving, which, as the spikes go out of bloom, have a whitish, fuzzy look. These two are prevailing grasses at this season on dry and sandy fields and hillsides. (143-44)

Thoreau proceeds in his description from a taxonomic classification of the grasses to a detailed portrait of the plants' build and areas of growth. His account is meticulous, and we may feel tempted to read this paragraph as evidence of his sometimes pedantic obsession with the exact recording of details. Yet, the wealth of botanical information which he offers here does not seem gratuitous once we consider the passage in context. Then it becomes apparent that Thoreau seeks to present his study of botany, both at the desk and in the field, as the appropriate experiential basis for his reflections on the nature of perception and knowledge, which are part of his lifelong inquiry into the correspondence of natural facts and moral truths, of particulars and principles. For he goes on to present the grass as an epitome of wild nature—of wildness in the sense that he develops the idea in his essay "Walking." Since it offers him relief from the demands of the human community, a "refuge" from "college commencements and society that isolates!" (145), the contemplation of the grass yields a different perspective on his place in the world and thus grants him a new standpoint from which he can consider the moral order of the world. This process reassures him, or as Thoreau says, he feels "blessed" by the grasses, his "purple companions" (145).

Thoreau's description of the grass can be considered representative of the tendency in American nature writing to synthesize scientific, aesthetic, and symbolic readings of the natural world to stress the situated character of environmental perception. Thoreau's description neither reduces the grass to a taxonomic specimen—classified, but taken out of context and seen from nowhere in particular—nor does it render the grass primarily as a sign or, as Walt Whitman put it, as a "uniform hieroglyphic" (34). Instead, Thoreau joins in his account the scientific ordering and detailed description of the vegetation to a symbolic reading of the grass' significance to emphasize that the observer's intentions and cultural training significantly influence how he perceives and interprets his environment. Thoreau contrasts, for instance, his present preoccupation with the grass with his prior lack of attentiveness and the disinterested attitude of his neighbors. He points out, "A man shall perhaps rush by and trample down plants as high as his head, and cannot be said to know that they exist, though he may have cut many tons of them, littered his stables with them, and fed them to his cattle for years" (145). Thoreau notes that it is the attitude of the observer that guides his perception of his surroundings and that determines what kind of local knowledge he acquires. While the mentioned farmer knows the properties of the grass intimately well as far as its use as fodder is concerned, he does not know the grass in Thoreau's sense because he pays merely instrumental attention to the plant. His purely resource-oriented approach allows him neither to appreciate the grass on its own terms nor to assign symbolic meaning to it. According to Thoreau, only scientific training combined with a physical exploration of the natural world in a contemplative state of mind can facilitate the broad range of observations, emotions, and thoughts that are necessary to grasp the "beauty" and "true wealth" of the natural environment (145), which for Thoreau always includes a correspondence between the actual and the ideal.

As contemporary readers, we may readily agree with Thoreau's assertion that our readings of the world are situated and culturally mediated. We know that numerous factors, such as our cultural background, our social standing, and our practical and ideological motivation, come to bear on our perceptual habits and aesthetic practices. We are not surprised that Thoreau notices different things than the neighboring farmer. And we anticipate that Thoreau will focus on different aspects of his environment when he takes to the field as a surveyor, makes an excursion as a natural history student, or goes walking as a transcendentalist poet. What we frequently forget in our concern with the cultural production of nature and the social inscription and structuring of space, however, is that environmental perception is an interaction and that the direction of this interaction tends to be reversible. It is a dialogue between experiencing or narrating subject and the environing world. As Thoreau oscillates between botanical, moral, and literary concerns, his narrative not only enacts "the different departments of knowledge" and the "different intentions of the eye and the mind" that they require (174), but it also alerts us to the relational and processual character of environmental experience.

In Thoreau's account, self and place seem to mutually constitute each other. Consider the following example: "Heaven might be defined as the place which men avoid" (145), Thoreau quips, only to exempt himself from the charge: "But I walk encouraged between the tufts of purple wood-grass over the sandy fields, and along the edge of shrub oaks, glad to recognize these simple contemporaries. With thoughts cutting a broad swathe I 'get' them" (144). Thoreau here pictures himself as moving through the narrated landscape, harvesting both sensual experiences of place and the larger truth that the grass signifies for him. Mindful perception and firsthand experience coupled with botanical study allow him to appropriate the place as his own. He describes the autumnal landscape as perceived, experienced, and interpreted by him. Yet, at the same time, he insists that it is not only his intellectual disposition or aesthetic preference that determines what he sees but also certain biophysical properties of the natural world that attract his attention, that elicit a particular response while they exceed signification. In his words: "I may say that I never saw them before," but since "I came to look them face to face [...] It is the reign and presidency of the andropogons" (145).

Nature writing thus can serve to remind us that our perception is culturally as well as environmentally mediated. It invites us to consider not merely how our sense of place may be an effect of cultural forces but also how our observations and conceptions are literally emplaced. It prompts us to ask how the environment affects our readings of it. For the natural world surely not only solicits our response but also resists our grasp. As Donna Haraway points out: "Accounts of a 'real' world do not, then, depend on a logic of 'discovery,' but on a power-charged social relation of 'conversation.' The world neither speaks itself nor disappears in favor of a master decoder" (198).

How have nature writers described these conversations between experiencing subject and environing world, then? How does the encounter with a natural world that invites yet exceeds their readings affect the narrator's sense of self? How do they define themselves in relation to their natural environment? If one reads a fair amount of nature writing, one gains the impression that most authors alternate between a sense of insuperable difference and a desire to merge with their environments. As they recount their experiences of place, they often move from descriptions of nature's radical otherness to the evocation of moments of mystical union. This alternation between a stance of "disjunction and conjunction" is so persistent that Scott Slovic described it as one of the major characteristics of the genre (6).

In oscillating between a sense of separation and belonging, nature writing alerts us to the intricate and sometimes surprising negotiations between self and world that our simultaneous existence in natural and cultural contexts requires of us. It reveals that the realization that human life unfolds within both a cultural and a natural matrix may give rise to a conflicting sense of selfhood—a sense of being other, of not wholly belonging to the natural world, while also being made of it, sustained, and eventually reabsorbed by it. We find this perplexing sense of being alien to and yet part of the natural world, for instance, in Austin's *The Land of Journey's Ending*. In the following passage, Austin recounts a moment that occurred during one of her walks in early spring in New Mexico, when she found the juniper trees arrest her attention. She writes that the trees engaged her senses in a way that made her feel as if she entered into a conservation with them:

> [...] first one and then another pricks itself on your attention. As if all the vitality of the tree, which during the winter had been withdrawn to the seat of the life processes underground, had run up and shouted, "Here I am." Not one of all the ways by which a tree strikes freshly on your observation,—with a greener flush, with stiffened needles, or slight alterations of the axis of the growing shoots, accounts for this flash of mutual awareness. You walk a stranger in a vegetating world; then with an inward click the shutter of some profounder level of consciousness uncloses and admits you to sentience of the mounting sap. (39-40)

The description carefully links Austin's epiphany to her embodied experience of place. The detailed account reveals her attentive perceptual engagement with her environment. Her careful observation of the tree's build—her alertness to botanical details, such as the "slight alterations of the axis of the growing shoots,"—also suggests that scientific training has sharpened her powers of observation. Still, it is only for a moment, when her observation of the concrete juniper expands into a mystical experience, that Austin ceases to feel like an intruding "stranger." She apprehends the tree's basic mode of existence, its very *treeness*, so to say, or as the narrator puts it, she becomes sentient of its "mounting sap." The sensation of "mutual awareness" reduces but does not erase her overall sense of difference. The experience allows her to perceive the tree as an "alien and deeply preoccupied" (40) life form, which actively reaches out to her while pursuing its own purposes. Austin thus shows that environmental perception and the experience of place may best be conceived as an interaction between the world and ourselves, a world from which we are neither fully separated, nor by which we are entirely absorbed. It is an exchange in which we participate as neither entirely active nor entirely passive forces. It is an interaction that changes and to a certain extent thus also produces self and other.

Austin, like Thoreau before her, describes environmental experience, then, as a seemingly paradoxical movement in which the focus on the other leads to a heightened comprehension of the self. She suggests that paying attention to what lies outside the human ken returns us to ourselves with a clearer sense of identity. This dynamic is also the subject of Dillard's essay "Living like Weasels" (1974).

In "Living like Weasels," Dillard describes how she once encountered a weasel and found herself transformed through the experience. She begins to recount the incident in deceptively innocuous terms: "I startled a weasel who startled me, and we exchanged a long glance" (123). As Dillard and the weasel look at each other, the boundaries between them start to dissolve, however. Dillard experiences the unchecked exchange of glances as a moment of unrestricted contact: "I tell you I've been in that weasel's brain for sixty seconds, and he was in mine. [...] for a sweet and shocking time" (125). The sensation of merging with the weasel unsettles the moral categories and perceptual habits that usually structure her vision. Seeing the weasel see her, the world starts to be in flux. A violent upheaval of established order and certainties ensues:

> Our look was as if two lovers, or deadly enemies, met unexpectedly [...] a clearing blow to the gut. It was also a bright blow to the brain, or a sudden beating of brains, with all the charge and intimate grate of rubbed balloons. It emptied our lungs. It felled the forest, moved the fields, and drained the pond; the world dismantled and tumbled into that black hole of eyes. If you and I looked at each other that way, our skulls would split and drop to our shoulders. But we don't. We keep our skulls. (124)

Dillard's encounter with the weasel destabilizes her prior sense of reality and self. She enjoys the experience and responds to it with a desire to live like a weasel in attentive physical engagement with the occasions of life as they unfold before her, unhampered by preconceptions and in recognition of her mortality and calling (125-26).

Issuing into an intense yearning for a simple life of "necessity" in unison with "the given" order of the world (125), Dillard's account continues an established mode of rhapsodic nature writing. The celebratory tone of her portrait of human nonhuman relations brings to mind Thoreau's rapturous salute to the radical otherness of nature in "Ktaadn."[4] Like Thoreau, Dillard portrays her epiphany as an experience of contact with something radically different which nonetheless is not experienced as entirely discontinuous with the self. Like Thoreau, she identifies with the wild—an initially disconcerting shift in consciousness that produces not only fear but also awe and an overall exhilaration and excitement.

The penchant of nature writers for epiphanic experiences has caused some writers and critics to recoil from the tradition. In an essay that ironically appropriates the genre's conventions, Joyce Carol Oates mockingly complains that the natural world "inspires a painfully lim-

---

4   Defying the conventions of sublime landscape representation, Thoreau describes in "Ktaadn" not an aesthetic experience of cosmic order on the mountain top but an epiphany he had during his descent from the mountain. As the distance between Thoreau as observer and the scenery implodes, he first experiences nature as alien and other, then comes to realize that he also belongs to this "hard matter in its home." Suddenly aware of his embodied and emplaced existence, he exclaims: "Talk of mysteries! Think of our life in nature,—daily to be shown matter, to come in contact with it,—rocks, trees, wind on our cheeks! the *solid* earth! the *actual* world! the *common sense! Contact! Contact! Who* are we? *where* are we?" (95).

ited set of responses in 'nature writers'—REVERENCE, AWE, PIETY, MYSTICAL ONENESS" (236). Though one may construe the persistence with which nature writers have articulated a desire for mystical union and simple living as evidence of a narrow emotional register, I find the recurrence of this theme suggestive of a desire to reconceptualize human identity as part of a unified world unfolding in differences. The encounter with the weasel, for instance, changes Dillard's sense of self because it allows her to experience herself as participating in a world that extends beyond human concerns. As she sees the weasel react to her and perceives in its response a reflection of the otherness that she represents for it, in this moment, she suddenly discerns that she lives simultaneously as a sensing individual in a biocultural world and that she exists anonymously among the things that are perceivable for others. Realizing that she is both sensing and sensed, perceiving and perceived, acting and acted upon, Dillard becomes aware that her sense of herself as a "sensible sentient," as Maurice Merleau-Ponty would say, always depends on who or what she encounters, where and when she finds herself, what she concentrates on, how she focuses. As a result, she regards herself and the confronted other, the weasel, as neither entirely distinct from nor completely merged with but as participant in this world.[5]

Accordingly, Dillard concedes that despite her overwhelming sensation of mutual awareness during her perceptual encounter with the weasel, the weasel's thoughts remain inaccessible to her. She writes: "What does a weasel think about? He won't say. His journal is tracks in clay, a spray of feathers, mouse blood and bone: uncollected, unconnected, loose-leaf, and blown" (125). In imagining a nonhuman

---

5   Merleau-Ponty articulates this idea and its ramifications for our perception of our environment as follows: "That means that my body is made of the same flesh as the world (it is a perceived), and moreover that this flesh of my body is shared by the world, the world *reflects* it, encroaches upon it and it encroaches upon the world (the felt [*senti*] at the same time the culmination of subjectivity and the culmination of materiality), they are in a relation of transgression or of overlapping." It follows that, "if there is a relation of the visible with itself that traverses me and constitutes me as a seer, this circle which I do not form, which forms me, this coiling over of the visible upon the visible, can traverse, animate other bodies as well as my own. And if I was able to understand how this wave arises within me, how the visible which is yonder is simultaneously my landscape, I can understand a fortiori that elsewhere it also closes over upon itself and that there are other landscapes beside my own" (248, 140-41).

mode of communication and signification, Dillard manages to assert at the same time that reality is intersubjectively produced and that there are nonhuman texts, which are not dependent on human readers. Her portrait of the weasel suggests that the realization that we not only perceive others but that we are also perceived by others may foster an awareness of the larger context of human life and facilitate an environmentally grounded sense of self.

To conclude, Thoreau's, Austin's, and Dillard's accounts of their experiences of place direct our attention to the dynamics of environmental perception and representation. They remind us that we participate not only in social but also in ecological relations. In Thoreau's words: "The poet says the proper study of mankind is man—I say to forget all that—take wider views of the universe" (Journal, April 2, 1852). While this will sound like an eminently sensible approach to critics concerned with an ecological redefinition of human identity, Thoreau's, Austin's, and Dillard's narratives of place alert us to both the joys and difficulties along the way.[6] They reveal that such a reconceptualization has far-reaching psychological and epistemological implications. It requires us to conceive of our identity as processual, reciprocal, and emplaced rather than as stable, self-contained, and autonomous.

By combining diverse modes of perception and inquiry—scientific, aesthetic, philosophical, spiritual, and corporeal—and by alternating between a sense of detachment and belonging, Thoreau, Austin, and Dillard dramatize the interactions on which our shifting sense of self and place depends. They show that we constantly adjust ourselves to a more-than-human world that actively engages our senses. Although their nature writing suggests that our natural surroundings can only be experienced subjectively and rendered discursively, their texts do not cast the described landscapes solely as a product of the perceiving subject but present them as the result of participatory relations between self and world. The human observers appear not only as interpreters of nature but also as "a backdrop to all the landscape's occasions" (Dillard, *Holy the Firm* 431). By alerting us to the environmental matrix of our lives, nature writing reminds us that

---

6   Neil Evernden, for instance, asks: "How can the proper study of man be man if it is impossible for man to exist out of context?" (95).

we are not ourselves only and invites us to think of our identity as a relational process unfolding in place.

Works Cited

Austin, Mary. *The Land of Journey's Ending*. New York: Century, 1924.
Buell, Lawrence. *The Environmental Imagination: Thoreau, Nature Writing, and the Formation of American Culture*. Cambridge, MA: Harvard UP, 1995.
Dillard, Annie. *Holy the Firm*. In: *The Annie Dillard Reader*. New York: Harper, 1994. 425-55.
—. "Living like Weasels." *The Annie Dillard Reader*. New York: Harper, 1994. 123-26.
Evernden, Neil. "Beyond Ecology: Self, Place, and the Pathetic Fallacy." *The Ecocriticism Reader: Landmarks in Literary Ecology*. Ed. Cheryl Glotfelty and Harold Fromm. Athens: U of Georgia P, 1996. 92-104.
Feld, Steven and Keith Basso, eds. *Senses of Place*. Santa Fe: School of American Research P, 1996.
Fritzell, Peter. *Nature Writing and America: Essays upon a Cultural Type*. Ames: Iowa State UP, 1990.
Geertz, Clifford. "Afterword." *Senses of Place*. Eds. Steven Feld and Keith Basso. Santa Fe: School of American Research P, 1996. 259-62.
Glotfelty, Cheryl and Harold Fromm, eds. *The Ecocriticism Reader: Landmarks in Literary Ecology*. Athens: U of Georgia P, 1996.
Haraway, Donna. *Simians, Cyborgs, and Women: The Reinvention of Nature*. New York: Routledge, 1991.
Lyon, Thomas. *This Incomparable Land: A Book of American Nature Writing*. Boston: Houghton Mifflin, 1989.
Major, Mike. "Annie Dillard: Pilgrim of the Absolute." *America* 138 (May 6, 1978): 363-64.
McGregor, Robert Kuhn. *A Wider View of the Universe: Henry Thoreau's Study of Nature*. Urbana: U of Illinois P, 1997.
Merleau-Ponty, Maurice. *The Visible and the Invisible*, Ed. Claude Lefort. Trans. Alphonso Lingis. Evanston: Northwestern UP, 1968.
Norwood, Vera. *Made from this Earth: American Women and Nature*. Chapel Hill: U of North Carolina P, 1993.
O'Grady, John. *Pilgrims to the Wild: Everett Ruess, Henry David Thoreau, John Muir, Clarence King, Mary Austin*. Salt Lake City: U of Utah P, 1993.
Oates, Joyce Carol. "Against Nature." *On Nature: Nature, Landscape, and Natural History*. Ed. Daniel Halpern. San Francisco: North Point P, 1987. 236-243.
Scheese, Don. *Nature Writing: The Pastoral Impulse in America*. New York: Twayne, 1996.

Slovic, Scott. *Seeking Awareness in American Nature Writing: Henry David Thoreau, Annie Dillard, Edward Abbey, Wendell Berry, Barry Lopez.* Salt Lake City: U of Utah P, 1992.

Snyder, Gary. *The Practice of the Wild.* San Francisco: North Point P, 1990.

Thoreau, Henry David. "Autumnal Tints." *The Natural History Essays.* Introd. and notes Robert Sattelmeyer. Salt Lake City: Peregrine Smith, 1980. 137-77.

—. "Ktaadn." *The Maine Woods.* New York: Penguin, 1988. 1-111.

Tracy, Henry Chester. *American Naturists.* New York: Dutton, 1930.

Welty, Eudora. "Place in Fiction." *Stories, Essays, & Memoir.* New York: Library of America, 1998. 781-96.

Whitman, Walt. "Song of Myself." *Leaves of Grass.* Oxford: Oxford UP, 1990.

Interior and Exterior Spaces: Versions of the Self in the American Novel around 1900

Ulfried Reichardt

In his novel *Libra* (1988), Don DeLillo at one point describes the moment that Lee Oswald's Russian wife Marina sees herself for the first time on a TV screen: "One evening they walked past a department store, just strolling, and Marina looked at a television set in the window and saw the most remarkable thing, something so strange she had to stop and stare, grab hard at Lee. It was the world gone inside out. There they were gaping back at themselves from the TV screen. She was on television" (227). In this important scene, self-perception and perception of the external world seem to merge; the self can be observed from the outside, "the world gone inside out." The boundaries between the self and its representation on the screen, between interior and exterior, are blurred in a cultural context in which, as Frank Lentricchia points out, the "environment-as-electronic-medium radically constitutes consciousness and therefore (such as it is) community" (195). Even though electronic media are a more recent phenomenon, a similar dissolution of the distinction between subject and object, between the self and its physical environment can already be observed around the turn from the 19th to the 20th century.

Cultural debates of the last few years have centered on issues of globalization and the Internet. Both are seen as having led to a dramatic dissolution of traditional limitations through space and also to a shift *within* conceptions of space. Because of the fast flow of information between the stock exchanges in New York, Tokyo, London, and Frankfurt, economic "empires" are dissolved and created within hours. Moreover, the Internet allows people to "be," at least virtually, not only at distant places on the globe, but also, more importantly, at several of them at the same time. Even more dramatically, as Sherry Turkle argues, people who participate in Multi-User-Domains create different identities for the different virtual spaces in which they live: with real life being only one option among many and, as Turkle dryly remarks, often the least exciting one (13).¹ With regard to television, Joshua Meyrowitz has traced how individuality in the age of electronic media has changed. In particular, the distinction between the public and private spheres shifted with what he claims has been an ongoing reorganization of private space by the media. In the 1960s, Marshall McLuhan had already announced the emergence of a global village and its concomitant, the retribalisation of the world population. Media theorists argue that historically the old European notion of individuality and, more philosophically, of subjectivity as an autonomous force was linked in many ways to the era of the book, of printing, and of solitary reading.² Self-reflection, reading and writing go together, and with the spreading of print culture a wider spectrum of people engaged in these activities. What is common to all these diagnoses, therefore, is not only that distances have shrunk, but also that the form of individuality and, particularly, the boundaries between the private and the public, between self and community, have changed.

In what follows I want to show that the notion of an autonomous subject has already been dissolving for at least a century and that, therefore, the appearance of the postmodern self is in important ways not an entirely new phenomenon. To shore up my argument I will examine some of the changes in American culture, philosophy, and fiction noticeable around the turn of the nineteenth century. My literary examples include Edith Wharton's *The House of Mirth* and Henry James's *The Ambassadors* both of which attest to a change in the division between the public and private sphere and between interior and exterior spaces. My suggestion is to conceive of the transformations at the beginning of the twentieth century as a folding-out of consciousness into the external world, which simultaneously renders the outer world significant mainly in regard to its effects on the self, to what the self makes of it and how it can situate itself within the external world. The relation between the inner and outer spheres thus becomes functional for the construction of subjectivity and simultaneously, since the latter is predicated on the very notion of "interpenetration," makes a clear division between the two spheres increasingly precarious. I

---

1   Turkle quotes Doug, a college student, who admits that "RL [Real Life] is just one more window [...] and it's not usually my best one" (13).
2   See, for instance, Martin Jay, *Downcast Eyes* 67 who refers to Walter J. Ong, *The Presence of the Word* (1967).

have chosen these novels because they seem to operate at opposite ends of this development: Lily Bart in Wharton's novel can be regarded as the prototype of a performative self, a character who constantly redesigns her identity in view of the conventions and expectations of society to the point of extinction of an independent inner self. In contrast, Lambert Strether, the protagonist of *The Ambassadors*, constitutes James's famous center of consciousness. Since almost everything we get to know about the world, as depicted by the novel, is filtered through his perspective, his mind appears to have what might called an *a priori* status with regard to the external world. Yet this privileging of Strether's point of view also involves the dissolution of his consciousness by a process in which interior and exterior world are intricately intertwined and the latter increasingly depends on the external world. Put another way, I argue that Wharton's sociological analysis of social character and James's phenomenological depiction of the nuances of consciousness are complementary attempts to describe the staggering fragmentation of the modern self at the turn of the century.

Immanuel Kant had defined space as "Anschauung a priori" (87), yet his view of space as a given of human life was clearly repudiated at the end of the nineteenth century, in particular by the American philosopher William James. James materializes and psychologizes the conception of space and regards it as a construction dependent on human psychology and physiology, specifically vision, and on one's respective constructions of space. Space, in the contemporary view, is neither an objective dimension out there in the world nor a property of the mind, but rather an experience and construction dependent on biological make-up and the socio-cultural context in addition to the physical environment. In doing so, James implicitly acknowledged that conceptions of space change over time and that they are historically contingent. One of the most important aspects here is the way that a person experiences him- or herself as being situated in social space. The ways in which the boundary between the self and the outside world is experienced determine to a large degree the ways in which an individual engages social interactions, how he or she interprets encounters, conflicts, and perceptions of other individuals. If there are three major forms of space, i.e. physical, mental, and social, and if these three forms are always interrelated and overlap, then mental space is intricately linked to historically specific social constructions of the mind. As Edward Soja emphasizes:

> The presentation of concrete spatiality is always wrapped in the complex and diverse re-presentations of human perception and cognition, without any necessity of direct and determined correspondence between the two. [...] But [...] the social production of spatiality appropriates and recasts the representation and signification of mental space as part of social life. (121)

What is more, social relations are simultaneously "space-forming and space-contingent" (126), thus underscoring the doubleness of being situated and being constantly involved in constructing one's own location. Put differently, social and mental spaces are closely linked. Even if not in a direct and linear fashion, social change and the change of conceptions of the self are mutually dependent and connected.

Before considering the two novels in more detail, I would like to briefly sketch the changes in society and, in particular, the notion of the public during the last decades of the nineteenth and the beginning of the twentieth century in America. The main factors of change were urbanization, industrialization and immigration, the rise of mass journalism as well as a strong shift to market relations and an acceleration in the development of new technologies, especially the new media of communication and transportation. As an English traveler wrote in 1900: "Life in the United States is one perpetual whirl of telephones, telegrams, phonographs, electric bells, motors, lifts, and automatic instruments" (qtd. in Mowry 1-2). Change was everywhere; the word "new" occurred with astonishing frequency. Due to the fast changing times, "reality itself began to seem problematic, something to be sought rather than merely lived" (Lears, qtd. in Rieke 12; see also Lears, *Grace*). As new developments can only be understood within earlier paradigms, the widespread experience of crisis took hold of the American public. Among some of the reasons were the growing heterogeneity, anonymity and abstractness of ordinary life. Moreover, the increase in information and the speed with which it could be obtained through the press considerably changed the structure of public life. More importantly, personal contact within a familiar environment, a world in which one knew almost everybody and his or her social position, gave way to a public that was made up to a large degree of persons one did not personally know, to abstract and functional relations and an exchange of information which was conducted by the press.[3]

The increasing complexity of urban life, therefore, necessitated new versions of perception and new social roles. As Emerson already remarked in a journal entry: "In New York City, as in cities generally, one seems to lose all substance, and becomes surface in a world of surfaces. Everything is external and I remember my hat and coat, and all my other surfaces, and nothing else" (qtd. in Ickstadt 197). A new flexibility and context-sensitive strategies of behavior were necessary in order to react and adapt to the constantly changing situations and expectations one encountered. As many critics have argued, this led to an insistence on performative qualities.[4] If the public is understood as a market, persons offer their characteristic features like a commodity and compete as to who is most successful.[5] The reorganization of the structure of personality can thus be understood also as an adaptation to a changing social reality and to a changing social space.

However, the ensuing changes of forms of individuality and the self have been interpreted in radically different ways. Two influential sociological interpretations of the relationship between interior and exterior space are David Riesman's *The Lonely Crowd* and, more recently, Richard Sennett's *The Fall of Public Man*. Whereas Riesman detects a development towards a social character who acts in accordance with the expectations of society, but who, in contrast to an earlier static notion of the self, is also dynamic and flexible, Sennett diagnoses an opposite development, a retreat into private and intimate worlds.

---

3   Robert Huddleston Wiebe claims that "individualism" and "casual cooperation" which were central values in small villages and towns were substituted by the new values of "regularity, system, continuity" (qtd. in Rieke 90).

4   Cf. Philip Fisher, "Appearing and Disappearing in Public," and, among others, Georg Simmel, "Die Großstädte und das Geistesleben."

5   As Hans-Joachim Rieke argues, "under these conditions performative capabilities become not only the central category of the construction of reality, but also of the experience of reality" (141, my translation). Jackson T. Lears traces these developments to the shift from Puritan self-discipline to a culture of consumption based on immediate wish-fulfilment (XIV).

Riesman distinguishes between three historical stages which he calls tradition-directed, inner-directed and other-directed.[6] What concerns us here is the transition from the inner-directed to the outer-directed type that begins to come to the fore in the late nineteenth-century. The inner-directed type is characteristic of the modern era. Through the increasing functional differentiation of society, tradition loses its grasp on the individual, and a person needs a "greater degree of flexibility in adapting himself to ever changing requirements and in return requires more from his environment" (16). As a result, a new psychological mechanism develops that Riesman aptly calls a "psychological gyroscope": "This instrument, once it is set by the parents and other authorities, keeps the inner-directed person [...] 'on course' even when tradition, as responded to by his character, no longer dictates his moves" (16). The crucial feature of the gyroscope's structure––which is a nautical instrument—is that the compass is located within several independent spheres, so that it can function even in a storm. Structurally, therefore, such a self is seen as allowing navigation and activity relatively independent from immediate contact with and disturbances by the environment. The inner-directed type implies a concept of a distinct and fixed inner space with boundaries which are understood as being permeable only to a small degree; exchanges with the external world are controlled by the gyroscope-like inner self that pivots in response to changes in the environment, but, as the metaphor implies, remains balanced from within.

As society became more complex and abstract, gyroscopic control was no longer flexible enough. "What is common to all the other-directed people," Riesman writes, "is that their contemporaries are the source of direction for the individual [...] it is only the process of striving itself and the process of paying close attention to the signals from others that remains unaltered throughout life" (21). Conformity is thus achieved through "an exceptional sensitivity to the actions and wishes of others" (22). Riesman's metaphor is now the "radar" (25), indicating a scanning of the exterior for responses to one's behavior, which are then integrated into one's personality in complex and mediated ways. The center of action, nevertheless, lies outside.

---

6   Riesman defines "social character" as "that part of 'character' which is shared among significant social groups and which [...] is the product of the experience of this group" (4).

Sennett, in contrast, diagnoses the reverse process when he claims that western societies are *en route* from outer-directed to inner-directed relationships. He detects a devaluation of public roles and a concomitant higher evaluation of the psychological, intimate level of personal relationships. And as a consequence of an increasing abstractness of social relations, "isolation in the midst of public visibility and the overemphasis on psychic transactions are complementary" (30). Because of the process of secularization, horizontal relations within society govern our views of the world. If role-distance in modern society increasingly dissolves the sense of a fixed place within a hierarchically structured social pyramid, personal and intimate relationships take on the function of guaranteeing identity: the self becomes the only vehicle with which to navigate within abstract relationships. Yet the retreat from the public sphere, which was formerly based on personal contact and fixed social positions, does not necessarily forbid, I would argue, a simultaneous extension of the public sphere or the intrusion of the external into interior spaces of the private self. Stephen Kern, for example, regards Riesman's and Sennett's diagnoses as complementary: "As the public became more intrusive, the individual retreated into a more strongly fortified and isolated private world. That is why we can observe in this period [1880-1918] both a greater interpenetration and a greater separation of the two worlds" (191).[7]

How were these developments represented in fiction? Edith Wharton's *The House of Mirth*, published in 1905, evokes a social space divided by marked social distinctions, which are, however, on the brink of dissolution. The sense of self of the protagonist, Lily Bart, rests on a continuous exchange between conventions and expectations of society, that is, external space, and a vague inner feeling of something beyond her social role, yet which is never fully realized. Using Philip Fisher's definition of social space in the late nineteenth century

---

7 Brook Thomas has pointed to Brandeis' and Warren's famous 1890 intervention for privacy legislation, which also responds to the increasing intrusions into the private sphere, in particular by journalists, but also by advertising and the market in general. The more the public sphere intrudes into the private one, the greater the pressure to create sanctuaries for privacy becomes—a concern that had direct effects on the family and domestic sphere. In a paradoxical reversal, however, this private sphere then folds back into and re-enters the public again with its needs and conflicts (56-58).

as a space of performance (157), Lily's self can thus also be described as essentially "performative." It is worth noting here that the notion of performance implies that the self is seen as acting in response to and in accordance with the social scene rather than reacting to it from a self-identical or gyroscopic position. The self thus becomes context-dependent in the extreme.

At the beginning of the novel, Lawrence Selden observes Lily Bart among the crowd in Grand Central Station: "it was characteristic of her that she always roused speculation, that her simplest acts seemed always the result of far-reaching intentions" (3). Lily's gestures are staged for others who interpret them as signs of calculation. However, she herself is aware of her need to create such an appearance, which she controls by observing herself in a sequence of mirrors, yet also by responding to how others see her. Lily constantly has to be conscious of her gestures and looks, as these are her only capital accepted by the high society she feels naturally to belong to. By the same token, she acts towards others in a strategic way, for example, when she plans to marry the rich but dull Percy Gryce: "The system might at first necessitate a resort to some of the very shifts and expedients from which she intended it should free her; but she felt sure that in a short time she would be able to play the game in her own way" (64). The emphasis on spectatorship, on acts of observation and on adjusting one's behavior to the response of others, is linked to the shift from a social structure based on tight family relations and traditions to a market society based on money and exchange. Wharton's metaphor here is the "marriage market."

In order to illustrate the paradox involved in Lily's desire to present herself according to her refined aesthetic sensibility, on the one hand, and her need to do so in order to meet the expectations of society, on the other, I will focus on a scene in which she appears in a *tableau vivant*. The Welly Brys, a rich family not yet recognized by the old aristocracy, tries to break into society by staging an evening of expensive music and *tableaux vivants*. The latter were common social events in which fashionable women represented scenes taken from old paintings and arranged carefully by a portrait painter. Lily has selected "a type so like her own that she could embody the person represented without ceasing to be herself. It was as though she had stepped, not out of, but into Reynolds's canvas [...]" (178). It is at this moment that Selden, the man Lily really loves, believes to see "the real Lily Bart"

(179). What is important about this scene is that it can be read as a paradoxical reversal of the performance upon which Lily's place in society is based. It is precisely when she performs a role, when she copies somebody else explicitly, that she does not have to hide the fact that she is performing. Only when she is on stage, rather than playing a role in real life, does she appear as the authentic Lily.

Placed within literary history, this scene takes on further contours. It is well known that the novel criticizes feudal society by depicting courtly manners as artificial and theatrical. As readers of sentimental novels are well aware, these texts often had recourse to the body to make sure that no calculated behavior on the part of their characters was involved: at significant, decisive moments, the heroines tend to faint. The reason for such theatricality is simple: physical expression was understood as being more expressive of the real self because it could not be interpreted as merely a rhetorical device. Yet Wharton seems to deconstruct this conception by de-authenticating the body as well. As indicated above, the impression of physical authenticity only emerges when Lily is "performing" and the expressive and the performative coincide. In this scheme the expressive refers to a behavior regarded as an expression of an inner self, whereas the performative refers to an external role. The double reversal, then, is that Lily's inner self only emerges when she does not have to fake a congruence of inner self and outward appearance, that is, when she is explicitly outside of herself. Nevertheless, her gesture remains a copy.

Because Lily is situated at the periphery of Old New York society, its stability and security of behavior do not apply to her. She is thus a transitional figure: since she is on the marriage market and her beauty is her "last asset" (44), she has to adapt swiftly to new and changing social situations. Even though she has learned but to perform, her vague idea of a realm of identity beyond social rules and conventions lets her occasionally fail to act adequately. Moreover, her acting appears to be constantly monitored by the media. After the *tableau vivant* evening, the yellow press criticized her for what is believed to have been an overly erotic exposure, thereby turning this "authentic moment" into an act of sheer sensationalism and improper role-playing. Even this paradoxically "authentic moment," then, conveys a sense of imposture and the trappings of a socially constructed self. With no clearly defined identity outside of her performance, Lily aptly foreshadows both Riesman's outer-directed character and the increasing interpenetration of interior and exterior spaces.

While Wharton's analysis of Lily Bart and the changes within New York society at the end of the nineteenth century is thoroughly sociological, Henry James provides us with a close-up view of the processes of consciousness and experience as constituted in and through perception and communication. He takes the conventions of his upper-class protagonists as a given and stages instead the oscillations and processes occurring within their consciousness as an exchange between the allegedly indissoluble unities of external and internal, other and self. This focus on consciousness in James's later novels, however, does not necessarily signify a retreat from society; rather, James focuses on mental space as it is linked to social space. His is a microanalysis of a mind in action, which, by necessity, is also a social process.

In *The Ambassadors* James renegotiates the relationship between interior and exterior spaces. The protagonist Lambert Strether (and his companions) appears to be entirely focused on the Parisian environment, with its streets, gardens, and interiors. The degree to which Strether's mind is linked up with the novel's setting may best be described as the "interpenetration" of the internal and the external, although the term is somewhat awkward.[8] To shore up my reading of a new notion of the self in the novel, a brief discussion of William James's (the author's brother) model of consciousness may be appropriate. In his essay "Does Consciousness Exist" (1904), William James questions the existence of any such thing as a consciousness; "rather," he claims, "there is a function in experience which thoughts perform, and for the performance of which this quality of being is invoked. That function is *knowing*" (4). Consciousness is temporalized as thinking, which itself is reconsidered as a "performance," as being functionally related to what is thought and perceived, i.e. the phenomenal world. Consciousness is thus reconceived as the term for an activity that cannot be described by reference to a dualism between representing and being represented. As James states: "In its pure state, or when isolated, there is no self-splitting of [...] [experience] into consciousness and what the consciousness is 'of.' Its subjectivity and objectivity are [...] real-

---

8 The concept of 'interpenetration' has been frequently used by sociologists Talcott Parsons and Niklas Luhmann (see "Interpenetration," *Soziale Systeme* 286-345).

ized only when the experience is 'taken,' [...] by a new retrospective experience [...]" (13). In James's view, consciousness loses its interior quality, its distance from the phenomenal world, and thus its autonomy. As he asserts, and this is crucial with respect to considerations of space, "consciousness connotes a kind of an external relation, and does not denote a special stuff or way of being" (14).[9] The ambiguous status of experiences, the double dimension of, as he puts it, 'being' and 'being known' lies in their relations between one another. Consciousness thus becomes a mental activity that cannot be separated from what is processed. In a similar vein, John Dewey claims that the "mind is primarily a verb" (qtd. in Levin 79). As consciousness is thus increasingly seen as a process (rather than a thing that *is*), the dualism between mind and matter, between subject and object dissolves.

The same dynamic model of self can be found in Henry James's later fiction where "the process of development utterly overtakes the narrating and the narrated selves" (Levin 118). James's characters *are* the processes of perception, reflection and communication in which they engage. The context has entered the self, boundaries become permeable; the self becomes a flexible entity that is always in transition by way of its exchanges with the external world, a process which is now seen as constituting consciousness in the first place. What, among other things, distinguishes William James's philosophical from Henry James's "dramatic method," is the latter's focus on perception *and* communication. With communication, however, the social sphere necessarily (if only implicitly) enters consciousness.

The fact that almost everything we get to know about the environment and the other characters is reflected in Strether's mind might be seen as James's insistence on the independence of consciousness. Yet to prevent the reader from becoming too much assured of the character's personality, James's narration always also introduces a moment of "vagueness." This vagueness emphasizes the fluid process of thinking in contrast to the treacherous clarity of finished thoughts and can thus be read as proof that Strether is by no means a detached observer but is himself in need of response and exchange. His thoughts, perceptions or interventions remain unfinished and thus call for further exchange, that is further *seeing* (which is both active and

---

[9] Pure experience, for James, "is made of [...] just what appears, of space, of intensity, flatness [...]" (14).

passive) and speaking/hearing. Because of the novel's underlying narrative vagueness no thought, perception or statement is independently conclusive, that is, independent of other, external sources of information. Though the flow of Strether's consciousness and the exchange between thinking, perceiving, and speaking/listening can, in all its complexity, only be grasped by looking at longer passages, I will briefly discuss a scene in which these exchanges are unusually condensed. I am referring to the moment when Strether meets Chad face-to-face for the first time in Paris:

> Chad again fell back at this and, his hands pocketed, settled himself a little; in which posture he looked, though he rather anxiously smiled, only the more earnest. Then Strether seemed to see that he was really nervous, and he took that as what he would have called a wholesome sign. The only mark of it hitherto had been his more than once taking off and putting on his wide-brimmed crush hat. He had at this moment made the motion again to remove it, then had only pushed it back, so that it hung informally on his strong young grizzled crop. It was a touch that gave the note of the familiar [...] to their quiet colloquy; and it was indeed by some such trivial aid that Strether became aware at the same moment of something else. The observation was at any rate determined in him by some light too fine to distinguish from so many others, but it was none the less sharply determined. [...] He saw him in a flash as the young man marked out by women. [...] It affected Strether for thirty seconds as a relevant truth; a truth which, however, the next minute, had fallen into its relation. "Can't you imagine there being some questions," Chad asked, "that a fellow—however much impressed by your charming way of stating things—would like to put to you first?" "Oh yes—easily. I am here to answer everything. I think I can even tell you things, of the greatest interest to you [...]." (97-98)

The narrator describes Chad's behavior as perceived by Strether at this moment, in a very nuanced way. While Strether observes Chad, he immediately evaluates his movements ("seemed [...] nervous") and interprets them as "a wholesome sign" with regard to what he wants from Chad. While Chad's attitude gives Strether the impression of a familiar situation, that he is at ease at this moment when speaking with Chad, he nevertheless recognizes as the crucial dimension of Chad's character that he is a favorite with the ladies. As Strether has been sent to Paris to lure him back to Massachusetts and away from the supposedly bad influence of a Parisian lady, this observation is decisive with regard to his project in France as well as to the further development of his sojourn there. Yet this impression does not remain conclusive; it is not a fixed and stable insight with which he will then continue his dialogue with Chad. Rather, as the narrator comments, what Strether briefly saw as 'truth' "had fallen into its relation" immediately afterwards. It is a provisional insight that is tested again during his further exchanges with Chad, in which Strether has to respond with a revised version of what he came to tell Chad, now that he sees him in a different light.

There is no resting place. Instead, preconceived notions, new impressions, dialogical exchanges merge into a continuous process of emergence, while Strether's consciousness oscillates between the inner and outer world. Neither stays fixed, and both spheres are constantly readapting themselves to the nuances of a slowly shifting new situation and its respective interpretation. What is more, the above-quoted passage attests nicely to the provisionality of this 'flow' of exchanges because none of the impressions conveyed has a definite, semantically fixed description or shape ("The observation was at any rate determined in him by some light too fine to distinguish from so many others, but it was none the less sharply determined.") For James, knowing consists of the process of thinking *and* perceiving, yet both are tentative and temporary at best and will lead to even further tangled acts of knowing.

Significantly, if somewhat paradoxically, Strether's unique point of view does not necessarily contradict my argument that what we encounter here is a folding-out of the inner self. True, the outside world is mirrored in the inner world, and it is only there that we can observe the 'real' in James' later work; yet perhaps more important, Strether's mind is occupied to such a degree with the constant understanding, decoding, sorting out of external material that we are confronted with the paradoxical presence of the exterior in the interior world; moreover, what has been processed within is then mirrored back onto the outside, a narrative sleight of hand that readers experience as an extreme form of self-involvement. As interior and exterior spaces interpenetrate, consciousness in James's later novels ceases to be a perceivable entity and instead turns into an unresolved and reciprocally dynamic process.

The changing concept of the mind that I have sketched above and its corollary, the waning autonomy of the subject, force the reader to follow the movements of the characters and their constant readaptations and exchanges throughout the text. While this procedure enacts aesthetically a new interdependence of social actors and their minds, both novels are transitional with regard to American literary realism. Strether, although receptive to surfaces and commodities, remains a mere spectator and flaneur. It is Chad who leaves Paris and goes into the thoroughly modern profession of advertising. And Lily Bart has to die, as Elaine Showalter claims, only to make room for the "new woman" who affirms and accepts the new fluidity of the self (142).[10] Both novels implicitly point beyond the literary conventions of their time, without having fully arrived yet in the succeeding era of modernism.

As we have seen, Riesman's and Sennett's diagnoses may indeed be complementary: the development towards an outer-directed character type is often correlated with a greater emphasis on the self, even if this self is no longer predicated on pre-given roles and positions alone. However, if the self increasingly turns into a flexible instrument to navigate social change, the notion of a clear-cut, independent identity is also at stake.[11]

Works Cited

DeLillo, Don. *Libra*. New York: Penguin, 1988.
Fisher, Philip. "Appearing and Disappearing in Public: Social Space in Late-Nineteenth-Century Literature and Culture." *Reconstructing American Literary History*. Ed. Sacvan Bercovitch. Cambridge, MA: Harvard UP, 1986. 155-188.
Ickstadt, Heinz. "Kommunikationsmüll und Sprachcollage: Die Stadt in der amerikanischen Fiktion der Postmoderne." *Die Unwirklichkeit der Städte: Großstadtdarstellungen zwischen Moderne und Postmoderne*. Ed. Klaus R. Scherpe. Reinbek: Rowohlt, 1988. 197-224.
James, Henry. *The Ambassadors*. Ed. S. P. Rosenbaum. Norton Critical Edition. Sec. ed. 1964. New York: Norton, 1994.
James, William. "Does Consciousness Exist?" *Essays in Radical Empiricism*. Cambridge, MA: Harvard UP, 1976. 3-19.

---

10   We may think of Carrie Meeber who makes her performative self her profession and becomes an actress. See Dreiser, *Sister Carrie* (1900).
11   As Stephen Kern sums up: "The breakdown of old forms, together with the affirmation of perspectivism and of positive negative space, levelled hierarchies. These changes in the experience of space contradicted the notion that convention and habit could dictate privileged points of view, places, or forms" (210).

Jay, Martin. *Downcast Eyes: The Denigration of Vision in Twentieth-Century Thought*. Berkeley: U of California P, 1993.

Kant, Immanuel. *Kritik der reinen Vernunft*. Ed. Ingeborg Heidemann. 1787. Stuttgart: Reclam, 1978.

Kern, Stephen. *The Culture of Time and Space. 1880-1918*. Cambridge: Harvard UP, 1983.

Lears, Jackson T. J. *No Place of Grace: Antimodernism and the Transformation of American Culture 1880-1920*. New York: Pantheon Books, 1981.

Lentiricchia, Frank. "*Libra* as Postmodern Critique." *Introducing Don DeLillo*. Ed. Frank Lentricchia. Durham, NC: Duke UP, 1991. 193-215.

Levin, Jonathan. *The Poetics of Transition: Emerson, Pragmatism, & American Literary Modernism*. Durham, NC: Duke UP, 1999.

Luhmann, Niklas. *Soziale Systeme: Grundriß einer allgemeinen Theorie*. 1984. Frankfurt/Main: Suhrkamp, 1987.

McLuhan, Marshall. *Understanding Media: The Extension of Man*. New York: New American Library, Times Mirror, 1964.

McLuhan, Marshall, and Bruce R. Powers. *The Global Village: Transformations in World Life and Media in the 21st Century*. New York: Oxford UP, 1989.

Meyrowitz, Joshua. *No Sense of Place: The Impact of Electronic Media on Social Behavior*. New York, Oxford: Oxford UP, 1985.

Mowry, George E. *The Era of Theodore Roosevelt and the Birth of Modern America 1900-1912*. New York: Harper Torchbooks, 1962.

Rieke, Hans-Joachim. *Strukturwandel der Öffentlichkeit: Der Viktorianismus als Formationsperiode der Moderne*. Würzburg: Königshausen & Neumann, 1991.

Riesman, David. *The Lonely Crowd: A Study of the Changing American Character*. With Nathan Glazer and Reuel Denney. New Haven: Yale UP, 1977.

Sennett, Richard. *The Fall of Public Man*. 1975. London: Penguin, 2002.

Showalter, Elaine. "The Death of the (Lady) Novelist: Wharton's *House of Mirth*." *Edith Wharton: New Critical Essays*. Ed. Alfred Bendixen and Annette Zilversmit. New York: Garland, 1992. 139-154.

Simmel, Georg. "Die Großstädte und das Geistesleben." *Aufsätze und Abhandlungen 1901-1908*. Bd. I. Ed. Rüdiger Kramme, Angela Rammstedt, and Otthein Rammstedt. Frankfurt/Main: Suhrkamp, 1995. 116-131.

Soja, Edward W. *Postmodern Geographies: The Reassertion of Space in Critical Social Theory*. London, New York: Verso, 1989.

Thomas, Brook. *American Literary Realism and the Failed Promise of Contract*. Berkeley: U of California P, 1997.

Turkle, Sherry. *Life on the Screen: Identity in the Age of the Internet*. 1995. London: Phoenix, 1997.

Wharton, Edith. *The House of Mirth*. New York: Macmillan, Collier Books, 1987.

Moving Earth: On Earthquakes and American Culture in Arthur C. Clarke's SF-novel *Richter 10*

Florian Dombois

"What's natural about an earthquake?" Crane asked.

Sitting on a rocking chair, looking out the window and watching rural life in the open country, one would assume that landscape is a solid setting. Perhaps we would see a horse cantering over the meadow, or a shepherd and his flock wandering slowly through the stable scenery. If we were to come back here often enough, we would see how the seasons affect the color of the landscape, and it would most likely seem appealing to us to follow these variations while the shape of the terrain remains unchanged. Landscape is very much a visual, "viewing" experience, as the term, introduced first as a technical term used by painters, readily suggests ("Landscape" 53-54). It literally evokes the act of painting, thereby stressing the static and scenic aspects of a particular environment. If we go by its literal meaning, landscape becomes a way of seeing 'land' as a 'scape', much like a pedestal on which a statue may be placed. In this sense, then, landscape also provides a stage for performance, yet it does not perform itself. This aspect of invariability coincides perfectly with the cliché of technological space as an embodiment of progression and change. The impression of an unchanging landscape, and the impression of an unstoppable progression of technology, can be viewed as two sides of the same coin. Furthermore, the juxtaposition of these aspects intensifies the experience of calmness or action on both sides. The action and power of a factory, for instance, becomes more obvious when surrounded by quiet, scenic land. The more idyllic the landscape, the more powerful the technospace appears, and vice versa. For similar reasons, many people gain satisfaction from switching between these diverse and diverging spaces: they live and work, say, in San Francisco during the week and, then, on the weekend, they go to Oregon or Yosemite to experience the countryside.

What happens, however, if the landscape of Oregon is no longer in keeping with the above-mentioned idea of scenery as a stable form of background? What happens if it becomes unstable and moves more powerfully than even the fast-paced rhythm of city life? And how does it affect the basic opposition of nature and culture when landscape shakes technospace and not the other way around? In what follows I address these questions by focusing on earthquakes and how they cause not only physical but also cultural disorientation. I use Arthur C. Clarke's and Mike McQuay's science-fiction novel *Richter 10* (1996) as a backdrop for my discussion, because it turns on an extreme vision of technological control against natural forces. *Richter 10* proposes to overcome the seismic disaster with nothing less than the stopping of the earth's movement and the freezing of all tectonic activity. To illustrate this radical position, the novel contrasts previous efforts to cope with earthquakes with a scientist's dream of a fully technologically controlled landscape. Since the story is set in the United States, I will also address specific aspects of American (techno-)culture.

"Fingertips tingling and toes numb, pyjamas damp with sweat, Lewis Crane came wide awake. Every one of his worst night terrors was real!" Lewis Crane, the protagonist of *Richter 10,* experiences the Northridge earthquake of January 17 in 1994 as an animation of his nightmares of "monsters" and "dragons": "the Wild Things did live in the back of his closet" (7). Both of his parents die in the collapsing house and his left arm is permanently injured. Following this prologue, the actual plot of the novel begins thirty years later in 2024. In the meantime, Lewis Crane has become a famous seismologist and a Nobel-prize winner. Driven by the aim to simulate earthquakes, he develops—along with his co-worker Dan Newcombe and Lanie King—a virtual globe for precise prediction and analysis of geotectonic activities. The technology allows him to reproduce successfully the origin of the Earth and to simulate future seismic events. Given his calculations, he predicts for 2058 a gigantic seismic disaster— magnitude 10 on Richter scale—that will break California off from the American continent. Crane is obsessed with the idea to prevent not only this particular earthquake, but also all future earthquakes; hence he develops the idea of stopping tectonic activity by fusing the plates with huge atomic explosions. After quarrels with Newcombe about this project, the latter leaves to join an Islamic revolution party. Crane marries Lanie King, with who he has a son, Charles. Lanie and Charles eventually die during an attack organized by Newcombe in order to destroy the underground atomic deposit, installed by Crane to test the bomb-fusion. Another of Crane's co-workers, Sumi Chan, takes on different roles in the story: first, she is a colleague, then a traitor, later a mentor, when, finally, she becomes the second spouse of Crane. In 2038, Crane buys a large property on the moon and founds the city 'Charlesville'. The novel reaches its climax with the big quake of 2058 that brings Crane and Newcombe back together only to leave them both killed in the natural disaster. With their brains digitally backed-up they appear again in the epilogue as ghostlike, virtual guardian angels in the brave new world of Charlesville—along with Lanie King, Charles, Sumi Chan and another co-worker, Burt Hill, whose brains have also been digitally saved.

Clarke and McQuay clearly push for the limits in their representation of earthquakes and disasters. The novel's title, *Richter 10*, obviously refers to the magnitude scale of Charles Richter and assumes an event that is more powerful (magnitude 10) than any earthquake that has ever been measured. Just consider that the largest earthquake in the history of quantitative seismology (roughly, during the last 130 years) occurred in 1960 off the coast of Chile and reached a magnitude of 8,6. Even before the invention of the seismograph, there is no report of any event that can be assumed greater than magnitude 9. The Richter scale is logarithmic and the extrapolation to number 10 means not only an increment of 1/9 but a multiplication. An earthquake of magnitude 10 has 31 times more energy release than an earthquake of factor 9, which is, from a geophysical point of view, next to impossible.

Even though the big quake referred to in the novel lacks both scientific probability and historical authenticity, there is one earthquake in Western culture to which it could be conceptually compared: the apocalyptic quake described in the Book of Revelation. In chapter 6, John prophesizes an ultimate earthquake that moves mountains and islands and—with regard to the novel—would have been able to break California off from the continent:

> I watched as he opened the sixth seal. There was a great earthquake. The sun turned black like sackcloth made of goat hair, the whole moon turned blood red, and the stars in the sky fell to earth, as late figs drop from a fig tree when shaken by a strong wind. The sky re-

ceded like a scroll, rolling up, and every mountain and island was removed from its place. Then the kings of the earth, the princes, the generals, the rich, the mighty, and every slave and every free man hid in caves and among the rocks of the mountains. They called to the mountains and the rocks, "Fall on us and hide us from the face of him who sits on the throne and from the wrath of the Lamb! For the great day of their wrath has come, and who can stand?" (12-17)

As in *Richter 10*, the vision of John describes a seismic catastrophe that exceeds everything in the past, and, if quantified, certainly comes close if not surpasses magnitude 10. Yet the biblical story is not only important here in terms of magnitude; it evokes a number of connotations that can also be identified in *Richter 10*: whereas the apocalyptic earthquake kills those who are evil and have strayed from the service of god, the 2058 quake ends all life on a polluted and corrupted earth. The biblical earthquake figures as a turning point towards a New Jerusalem—the place of ultimate destiny—, while the California break-off marks the beginning of the new city of Charlesville, a city that Crane calls "the last best hope for the human race" (303). Since Crane has elected only the 'good' people to join his utopia, there is no crime, no police, and no prison in Charlesville. It is a peaceful utopia, a place situated on the far side of the moon, from where the earth can no longer be seen, so that Crane and his congregation will eventually lose sight of the past, of the old world. Its inhabitants live on eternally in the digital back-up of their brains, without physical bodies, reminiscent of the surviving souls—not bodies—of the New Testament's prophecy. What is more, the appearance of Jesus, who sacrifices his life to save mankind, is somehow mirrored by Crane's role as a visionary hero and political *Führer*.[1]

Throughout the Bible, the meanings of earthquakes vary. They range from negative, that is the wrath of God, to positive, namely a sign of holiness.[2] Thus, the apocalyptic earthquake signifies, on the one hand, a catastrophe used by God to punish evil. On the other hand,

---

1 There is yet another relation between the novel and the Bible: the title, *Richter 10*, alludes to the German word "Richter," which means "judge" and is also used as an attribute of God, the ultimate judge. The title raises questions of law and penalty and, indeed, earthquakes are present in the Bible as one of the Judge's principal tools of punishment for disbelievers (cf. for instance the story of Korah at Numeri 16).
2 For descriptions of biblical earthquakes, see Dombois, "Über Erdbeben. Ein Versuch zur Erweiterung seismologischer Darstellungsweisen" 67-78.

the Earth, which is also victimized by the apocalyptic quake, figures as a scared space where God's power becomes manifest. During the quake the Earth trembles with both fear of and admiration for God's power. The dependence on God that the Bible ascribes to both mankind and earth, is glaringly absent in *Richter 10*. Of the three biblical referents, Man, Earth, and God, only two survive. In the novel, earthquakes and humankind have ceased to be complementary forces to execute the will of God and instead have become antagonists. Crane is not able to talk about the natural phenomenon without aggression and feelings of revenge, caused apparently by his losses during the 1994 Northridge quake. He repeatedly points out that "we're entering the fight of all time, Man against Nature. [...] I will slay this beast!" (144). In *Richter 10* the complex interpretation of earthquakes is scaled down to the aspect of disaster and negative fate; its message, finally, is as straightforward as it is simple: earthquakes are natural disasters that need to be prevented, once and for all.

In modern technological societies there are two general approaches to minimize if not avoid the disastrous effects of earthquakes: for one, researchers and engineers focus on the fragile aspects of buildings and technical appliances and improve their resistance to the effects of an earthquake; and, for the other, scientists try to develop an earthquake prediction theory. In current seismology the second approach has become less important because of the lack of substantial improvement and reliability in predicting earthquakes. In glaring contrast with these facts, *Richter 10* introduces a scientist who develops a new epoch-making theory both to predict and, ultimately, prevent earthquakes altogether. His path-breaking computer model allows him to chart the earth's motions in detail and to accurately predict their magnitude, time, and epicenter. Crane's theory is so precise that he is able to calculate ground oscillations of every square meter. This ability gives him the opportunity to identify calmer areas in an earthquake from where he and other visitors then can watch an event with relative safety.[3] This is an eerie but fascinating idea (even if not too plausible from a geophysical point of view). For all we know, earthquakes affect large areas when they hit, and there appears to be

---

3   "Ladies and gentlemen! As you see, yellow lines have been painted on the plain. For your protection, stay within the lines. I cannot guarantee your safety otherwise" (30).

only little spatial differentiation. A thunderstorm or a lava-flow, with their geographical trajectory, predetermines the direction of escape. An earthquake, however, offers no way out. In terms of escape and prevention, a reliable prediction becomes an absolute requirement.

Apart from its preventive function, prediction theories also influence the cultural and aesthetic reception of earthquakes. The possibility of experiencing a major quake without physical danger invests seismic events with an element of the sublime; according to Kant's idea of the so-called "dynamic sublime," to call forth an aesthetic pleasure while observing a powerful, often disastrous natural phenomenon, the viewer has to be in a position of relative safety.[4] Sheer helplessness dissolves and gives way to a feeling of aesthetic delight. Since the eighteenth century, people have traveled to natural disasters such as the eruption of mount Etna to watch their destructive power. In *Richter 10*, this curiosity and desire for the sublime has been directed towards earthquakes. There is a veritable tourism of fear, and earthquake watching is widely advertised as a fashionable tourist sensation. The crowds, who indulge in the controlled exposure to the immensity of geo-physical force, are aptly called "Seismos" (331).

Seen or rather felt from an identified "safe" site, the tremors provoke thought, which in turn provokes the idea of resistance (what Immanuel Kant calls "Widerstand") to an overwhelming natural phenomenon. In *Richter 10* Clarke and McQuay reflect upon this crucial role of the sublime even further. If earthquakes can be modeled and foreseen, can they also be avoided? Crane's ambitions actually reach beyond the ability to predict coming events: he wants to geologically stabilize the earth and thus prevent it from moving once and for all. He proposes to fuse the tectonic plates with each other and transform the crust into one continuous skin. This would stop, he believes, the action along fault lines and ridges and, consequently, end all major seismic activity. Technically speaking, Crane wants to spot-weld the earth's crust with subterranean atomic bombs of enormous proportions at specific locations that are pre-calculated by his virtual globe. From a geophysical perspective, this concept is, of course, not very plausible. Tectonic plates do not behave like a rigid metal sheet,

---

4   As Kant points out in *Critique of Judgment*: "Aber ihr [the natural phenomena] Anblick wird nur um desto anziehender, je furchtbarer er ist, wenn wir uns nur in Sicherheit befinden" (5:333).

and any kind of welding would seem to be impossible. If one fault zone could be held back, a new rift would force a break nearby. What is more, it is questionable if at all and how a heat source could melt and, then, fuse a major volume of geologic strata. A regular atomic explosion would certainly not be sufficient. The energy release of the Hiroshima bomb, for example, was not more than an earthquake of magnitude 6 and even the world's largest nuclear tests had approximately only the energy of the 1906 San Francisco quake (i.e. magnitude 7,9).

If *Richter 10* does not comply with today's scientific knowledge, its general concept is nevertheless worthy of consideration. What would it mean if Crane could and would weld tectonic plates? What would the consequences be? Stopping the earth from moving would surely affect more than just seismic activity. For instance, the process of orogeny, i.e. tectonic mountain-building, would come to a halt and, as a result, oceans and continents would begin to level out. It would also influence volcanic activity and, by the same token, all heat flow and energy transport from the inner earth through these valves. The global effects would be devastating and it is questionable whether these would be worth the prevented seismic-caused losses.

Crane's gigantomaniac approach makes us forget that the disastrous effects of earthquakes are not just caused by geophysical movement. As Jean-Jacques Rousseau pointed out in a famous letter to Voltaire, written on August 18, 1756, it is human architecture that actually transforms an earthquake into a catastrophe. In a desert, both its immediate and long-term consequences are miniscule. It is the falling roof tiles that cause harm, not the trembling ground. And it is absurd to "blame" the Earth for the damage caused by a quake, like Lewis Crane does. Earthquake disasters are primarily related to people and the way they build their houses. From an engineer's point of view, it is the rigidity and inflexibility of urban installations that resist seismic waves and, therefore, are likely to break. Significantly, if somewhat paradoxically, Crane's plan to permanently resolve the problem of earthquakes is based on the idea of solidity and stability. In this scheme, breaks may be avoided by hardening the crust; instead of adapting architecture to the inherent rheologic qualities of the earth, the latter is made to adapt to the logic of human settlement. Rather than creatively wedding architecture and its geophysical foundations, the earth is turned into an architectural monument in her own right.[5]

Crane employs huge computational and atomic power to stop nature from changing or, put another way, he uses technology to contain nature in a stable, unchangeable state. By subduing tectonics to technological control, he creates nothing less than a global landscape architecture. His project clearly adds a new twist to the opposition of an active technospace and a static landscape, as claimed earlier in this paper. In *Richter 10* we witness how a "moving" earth is transformed, by engineering know-how and technological power, into a passive, unmoving background position. When Crane finally fails to "freeze" the landscape, he moves on to the moon, where no "quake" can shake his obsession with a planet that is calm and un-moving.[6]

It needs faith to move a mountain; but certainly it needs even more faith to stop a mountain from moving. Crane, the architect of nature as technoscape, acts very much like a demiurge or, to use his own words, he is "playing God" (333). His is no longer the descriptive, analytical labor of science but a visionary and technocratic design to "master-mind" the world. He is not interested in understanding natural forces, but in controlling them. From a psychological point of view, Crane takes earthquakes personally and his seismological research is driven more by combativeness than by observation. To provide himself with an enemy, he personalizes the earth and makes it his rival. His demonizing attitude becomes obvious when he uses expressions such as "the monster of the Earth" or "the Beast" (31; 305). The projection of his deep-rooted fears and anxieties onto dead material serves as proof that the earth should indeed be stopped from moving. Obviously, the prospect of saving a few victims would not justify the atomic-bomb-surgery of the planet. Consequently, much of the novel is dedicated to Crane's psychological struggles with the earth rather than to actual disasters. Seismic research thus is staged as a mythical

---

5   Note the analogy to Piero Manzoni's land art piece "Socle du Monde," realized in 1961 at Herning, Denmark. Manzoni, in a similar train of thought, turns the whole earth into a monument by setting up a pedestal 180° upside down and naming it "Socle du Monde."

6   There is no tectonic activity on the moon. Seismic instruments have measured only very small moon-quakes caused by earth tides and, occasionally, a trembling caused by the impact of meteorites.

fight against dragons and ogres, comparable to Hercules' struggle, rather than as social drama.

Richter 10 also evokes aspects and images specifically pertinent to American culture. Thus Charlesville, the new village on the moon, appears to mirror the "New Jerusalem" of early American settlers. Crane and his people conquer the moon with a pioneering spirit similar to the settlers who came to the New World. It is an attempt to leave behind the Babylon of an imperfect earth and Crane takes great pains to insure that only the righteous will join his extra-terrestrial community. Furthermore, Crane is an American 'self-made man'. He metamorphoses from a scientific nobody into a Noble-prize winner and, later, a statesman. Driven by his visionary power, he is financially successful and spends his newly accrued fortune on what he believes is a charitable cause. And finally, Crane's manner of research and his final 'showdown' with earth and earthquakes calls forth the violent pattern of numerous Western movies. Crane's is an attempt to push beyond the limits of physics and to extend the frontiers of scientific research even at the cost of total destruction.[7]

Crane's naive bend on improving nature by technology is spelled out by his megalomaniac plan to violently change the entire planet. While earthquakes appear as a flaw or a stigma of nature, Crane wants to preserve the beauty of an unchanging landscape; to achieve this goal, he does not hesitate to make use of the most destructive nuclear forces. Yet is it psychologically plausible—even for a science-fiction story—that someone wants to punish the earth for shaking? Why does Crane reaction to earthquakes verge on panic and hysteria? Could it be that the novel also wants to comment on something particularly 'American' in Crane, a cultural disposition to rebel against the forces of nature and to reshape the planet according to one's own beliefs and convictions?

There is no doubt that earthquakes change and affect buildings as much as human beings. Yet they are also catastrophes in the sense of Greek drama, where 'catastrophe' designates the turning point of a story. Within a few seconds the world has changed. Earthquakes reshape everything: land, history, biographies. This is probably why the Book of Revelations describes the ultimate earthquake as a decisive

---

7   For the meaning and historical repercussions of the term 'frontier,' see F. J. Turner's *The Frontier in American History*.

turn in man's history, the Apocalypse. If we interpret the American Dream as an attempt to reverse the fate of mankind from apocalypse to a New Jerusalem on Earth, John's vision can also be revealing with regard to American history and culture. By using a nuclear device to change the geophysical make-up of the earth Crane apparently follows the apocalyptic plot. According to the biblical story, an earth-shattering turn-around event is needed to achieve the ideal state. Yet Crane's dream of a man-made and controlled apocalypse clearly also interferes with this ultimate and destructive moment. The novel thus proposes a rival apocalyptic master, an Armageddon that, in a final, apocalyptic showdown, pits man's ingenuity and hubris against the forces of nature. As Crane points out, "We're entering the fight of all time, Man against Nature. [...] I will slay this beast!" (144)

There is yet another, more 'down-to-earth' reading of Crane's project. Since his approach is largely predicated on emotions, he is unable to accept his defeat for what it is: the fate of a human being vis-à-vis the overwhelming power of nature. The story is marked by the glaring absence of anything even close to sportsmanship, an attitude otherwise highly valued in American culture. If viewed with a competitive spirit, earthquakes may be rightly called 'unfair'. Contrary to other natural disasters such as floods or volcanic eruptions, that give us time to prepare and brace ourselves against their destructive effects, earthquakes are unpredictable and so fast-hitting that it is almost impossible to react. One may even quip that earthquakes are a kind of hit-and-run disaster. They strike out of the blue and then disappear just as quickly. And since earthquakes extend over large areas and spaces, evacuation is often not an option. They follow no rules and, therefore, allow no defense, no control. Given the erratic ways in which seismic events unfold, they leave most people mostly helpless and, of course, any sportsman frustrated.

Works Cited

Clarke, Arthur C., and Mike McQuay. *Richter 10*. London: Gollanz, 1996.
Dombois, Florian. "Über Erdbeben: Ein Versuch zur Erweiterung seismologischer
    Darstellungsweisen." Diss. Humboldt Universität Berlin, 1999.
Kant, Immanuel. *Critique of Judgement*. Vol. V of *Werke*. Ed. by Ernst Cassirer. Berlin: Cassirer, 1922.

"Landscape." *The Oxford English Dictionary*. Vol. 6. Oxford: Clarendon P, 1970. 53-54.

The NIV Study Bible. New International Version with Study Notes and References, Concordance and Maps. 6th ed. London: Hodder & Stoughton, 1991.

Rousseau, Jean-Jacques. Letter 424: "Rousseau à François-Marie Arouet de Voltaire." *Correspondance complète de Jean Jacques Rousseau*. Ed. R. A. Leigh. Vol. 4. Geneva: Publications de l'Institut et Musée de Voltaire, 1967. 37-50.

Turner, Frederic J. *The Frontier in American History*. New York: Holt, 1920.

'Just driving': Contemporary Road Novels and the Triviality of the Outlaw Existence

Ruth Mayer

"He and I suddenly saw the whole country like an oyster for us to open," writes Sal Paradise, one of the two protagonists of Jack Kerouac's *On the Road*, about their trip to the American South, "and the pearl was there, the pearl was there" (138). His description echoes Walt Whitman's earlier insight in "Song of the Open Road" that "[o]nly the kernel of every object nourishes" and that "divine things [are] well envelop'd" (119-120). Both authors, as different as they are, hint at a deep truth hidden somewhere 'out there', truth to be found by means of experience and movement, rather than through expression and meditation. "You express me better than I can express myself, / You shall be more to me than my poem" (188), Whitman says about the "public road" (188), while Kerouac, who believed that experience supersedes expression, compares the road to the "manuscript of the night we couldn't read" (157). In Kerouac's adaptation of the road theme, perhaps even more than in Whitman's, being on the move spells out a form of in-betweenness that cannot be grasped by means of conventional expression and thus calls for a new provisional and tentative language, a new aesthetics of indeterminacy.

This excitement over the theme of the road seems no longer warranted today, even if countless postmodern travel narratives keep retelling Kerouac's insight that to be on the road is to perform the "one and noble function of the time, *move*" (134; cf. Atkinson, Laderman, Primeau). But while to get going is still so much more important than getting there, the notion that to be on the road produces never-ending novelty, excitement, and change has certainly undergone revision. It seems that today the road genre no longer turns on stylistic innovation and experimentation, a radical break with literary conventions; on the contrary, it has become a genre that traces its own roots and themes perhaps more obsessively than any other genre. In a reflection that could be easily extended to the entire realm of contemporary road narratives, film critic Timothy Corrigan speaks of a "repetition compulsion" that haunts the road movie, a compulsion which exemplarily brings to the fore the "overdramatized redundancy" of genre film by and large (142; 139). While the narratives of the sixties and early seventies relentlessly acted out the urge to rebel and to innovate, the films that followed, he claims, are obsessed with their predecessors:

> In the mid-seventies and eighties, the genre has made its very action and subject its own historical hysteria: if genre is the prototype of classification and interpretation, it now becomes the *mise-en-abyme* reflection of an audience that can no longer imagine a naturalized history. The environment, conditions, and actions of the road movie have become a borderless refuge bin, limning the state of contemporary perception, both in- and outside the movie theatres. (152-153)

As the genre folds in unto itself, the deepest recognition, the "kernel" of knowledge, as Whitman put it, or the "pearl" of experience in Kerouac's terms, is no longer sought on the road, but comes to be associated with the virtual space of the written road or cinematic screen: "The list could go on," writes Bennet Schaber, "but is finally very much summed up in *Lost in America* (1985) when Albert Brooks proposes to Julie Hagerty that they hit the road 'just like Easy Rider.' Here the entrance to the road and the entrance to the cinema have finally joined [...]" (34).

In the early 1990s, the vogue of ironic self-referentiality had reached a stage, as David Laderman put it, at which the genre threatened to "self-reflex itself into oblivion" (53). It was at the same time that a marginal subgenre came to suddenly take center stage: the outlaw-couple story and psycho-killer narrative in the tradition of films like *Bonnie and Clyde* (1967) or *Taxi Driver* (1976). Road film after road film that made it into the movie theaters turned out to be about people running wild, about drive-by shooters, highway killers, freaks, outlaws, and psychopaths on the road. Films such as *Kalifornia* (1993), *True Romance* (1993), *Natural Born Killers* (1994), or *The Doom Generation* (1995), to name just a few, had one recurrent theme—random violence on the highway. The Republican presidential candidate of 1995, Robert Dole, sourly warned about a "mainstreaming of deviancy" emanating from Hollywood (Leong, Sell, and Thomas 70). He was right, of course, since non-conformity and crime certainly do come across as cool in these films. But still, Dole's critique misses the point. To denounce the films' violence means to interpret them too literally and to miss their ironic stances of distancing and pastiche. As becomes especially evident in *Natural Born Killers*, Oliver Stone's take on the genre, violence is displayed in a blatantly stylized, artificial, and highly 'edited' fashion that relies heavily on quotation, repetition, and parody. His film is constantly a step ahead of its critics, enacting violence, relishing in its display and then immediately supplementing the alternately ironic or critical gesture of distancing (cf. Leong, Sell, and Thomas). In a complex maneuver, the symbolic repertory of simulation is put to work in order to achieve an effect of authenticity against all odds. The self-referential style of this film thus makes it almost impervious to the kind of critique ventured forth by Dole and others.

In what follows I want to investigate the literary repercussions of the phenomenon of aestheticized road rage. In particular I will focus on two novels, Stewart O'Nan's *The Speed Queen* (1997) and Stephen Wright's *Going Native* (1994). Both are replete with intertextual references, thereby attesting clearly to the fact that the road has become increasingly important as cinematic space in the last decades. "The night burns away and Monument Valley comes up like a cowboy movie, like the sequel to *Thelma and Louise*," we are told at a dramatic moment in *The Speed Queen*, and in Wright's *Going Native* somebody watches an accident as if at the movies: "several thousand pounds of white Camaro [flying] through the clear liquor of a late desert afternoon, a movie image really, trailing the usual streamers of ragged unreality [...]" (177). The latter example especially may sound as if the novel fits right into the formula of the genre, which easily combines the rhetoric of inauthenticity with the spectacular effects of shock and horror. And yet, both authors insist that they were trying to tell a different story than their cinematic colleagues: "My sense of life and of all these problems is much more complicated than what I get out of a movie like *True Romance*, for example," Wright declared in an interview, "much more complicated than this. So I think a lot of my impulse in doing this was to address this in several levels at once" (Kushner n.p.). And Stewart O'Nan, when asked about the filmic predecessors for his novel *The Speed Queen*, says "'Natural Born Killers' is the most stupid film that has ever been made. It is almost comically bad" (Kaiser n.p.). In another interview he elaborated: "This is the American fantasy of getting into a bigass muscle car, getting completely fucked up on drugs, having great sex, killing a bunch of people, driving west into the night as fast as you can. We've seen that story so many times that we almost buy into the idea that it might be a fun thing to do" (Hogan n.p.).

Admittedly, both authors remain somewhat vague. And then, Oliver Stone was not exactly propagating moral irresponsibility in the interviews he gave after the release of *Natural Born Killers*. Still, I would argue that O'Nan's and Wright's literary takes on the theme of being on the move reflect more than a mere reorientation within the road genre. Their novels reconsider the very elements of the road aesthetics that were most fascinating to a writer like Kerouac and that then took center stage in the 1990s road movies: the openness and indeterminacy, the physical and moral in-betweenness of the state on the road. In these texts, the spatial metaphors which are so fashionable in current critical and pop cultural discourses, gain quite interesting— and far from altogether positive—connotations. For the purpose of my argument I will first discuss Stewart O'Nan's *Speed Queen* and then, counter-chronologically, turn to Wright's *Going Native*.

The Speed Queen: This Road is Closed

"We've seen that story so many times that we almost buy into the idea that it might be a fun thing to do" (Hogan n.p.), Stewart O'Nan wrote about the psycho-killer road movie. Given this insight, we might expect his contribution to the genre of the road novel to be just another instance of media bashing.[1] Yet there is more to the novel than merely a critique of sensationalist media and spectacular Hollywood films and it certainly does not subscribe to Bob Dole's lament about the mainstreaming of 'deviancy'. If its protagonist appears to be influenced by films such as *Natural Born Killers* (or rather, its famous predecessor, explicitly mentioned in the novel, Arthur Penn's *Bonnie and Clyde*), the novel as a whole is just as deeply steeped in the symbolic repertory of the family film, pulp melodrama or the soap opera. In a highly creative mix of filmic and pop cultural references and the first-person narrative perspective, the logic of cause and effect is quickly lost.

---

1   Referring more specifically to *The Speed Queen* O'Nan also notes that the heroine "takes on models from the media that aren't good for her" (Hogan n.p.).

The novel's plot revolves around Marjorie Standiford who tells the story of her life on the night she is awaiting execution on death row in an Oklahoma prison. Speaking into a tape recorder, she works through a list of questions, sent to her by an unnamed famous author who wants to write a novel based upon her life. She relates how she came to hit the road together with her husband Lamont and her best friend Natalie. They did drugs, loved driving fast cars, and ended up committing a series of increasingly violent crimes, culminating in murder. Eventually, eight people were killed, Lamont is dead, Natalie badly wounded, and Marjorie put on death row. The media are fascinated; there is much talk about 'killer sprees' and 'highway killers' and Marjorie, with reference to her favorite drug, is renamed the 'speed queen.'

Although the novel seems to map out familiar territory, stylistically it clearly takes a different course. This effect of repetition (of the formula) and deviation (of style) is further enhanced by the strong suggestion that the anonymous author at whose request Marjorie records her story is Stephen King. Marjorie, who repeatedly refers to King's style of writing, knows, or believes to know, why he is interested in her life: "I was normal," she says about her childhood, "I liked school, especially geography. [...] You can check up on all of this and everyone will tell you it's true. It wasn't like *Carrie* at all. My shoes were new, no one laughed at my clothes" (15). Towards the end, she tends to assign the very task of meaning-making to the writer: "And then the whole thing gets stupid because I try to do a three-point turn and get stuck and when I finally rock myself out, I follow the wrong tracks and get lost. Cattle are wandering through my headlights. This could be funny or sad or me just getting what I deserve. It's your choice" (205).

Marjorie's story provides plenty of material for a thriller or splatter film; yet if the stuff is there, it refuses to fall into the right pattern. Her story, though often mediated by the narrator's interpretation and evaluation, is far from smooth. This effect has much to do with the over-determined referentiality of the novel, the fact that there are so many different themes and stereotypes that are indiscriminately evoked. Thus Marjorie describes her love story with her later husband Lamont in terms of road movie references ("You ever see *Bonnie and Clyde*? It was just like that" [O'Nan 10]), and at times tries to fashion her entire life after the model of spectacular kiss-and-kill films:

> It's like that movie *Vanishing Point*, the guy out there in the desert in that big old Challenger, just hauling around with Cleavon Little on the radio. In the end, he hits the blade of this bulldozer and the car just rips into flames, little pieces of sheet metal falling in slow motion like snow. That's the kind of life I wanted back then. I guess I got it, huh? (O'Nan 7)

Marjorie is right about the dramatic course of her life. At the same time, however, she could not be more mistaken. With respect to style and enactment, her life story differs markedly from the breathtakingly spectacular thriller road movie. After all, Marjorie does not stick consistently to the technique of casting herself as the tough movie heroine, whenever it comes to scenes of violence and cruelty; rather she tends to project a radically different image of herself, often posing as the perfect mother and good wife, that is well known from soap operas and family movies. Reminiscing about her love story with Lamont, she suggests to her invisible addressee: "You could start here and show how much we were in love and how normal we were and then how everything went wrong. That's what I'd do" (9). Time and again, she emphasizes how 'normal' she was, how deeply in love with her husband and how anxious about her son's well-being:

> The way it was planned, I would have been with Gainey the whole time. We'd even stopped at the Dairy Kurl up the street and gotten him junior hot fudge sundae. [...] The whole thing took ten minutes, and except for maybe two minutes in the walk-in fridge, I could see him the whole time. But in the paper they make it sound like I just left him there. I don't care what they say—a mother worries. (O'Nan 45)

The 'whole thing' mentioned in this passage is the brutal slaughter of five people which Marjorie either witnessed or participated in—but the memory of the event seems submerged in petty complaints and quibbles about the media and their opinion on what happened. But then, media images play a defining role in Marjorie's life, because it is the media—TV, film, and cheap magazines—that have shaped her self-perception. In her narrative, media references take on a life of their own and her mood during the events depicted seems to depend on what film or TV show comes to her mind momentarily. Marjorie certainly is not 'wild at heart,' to allude to another road movie of the nineties, but rather deficient of deep-set motivations because it has all been said and felt and expressed before in the movies.

If in films such as *Natural Born Killers* the mechanisms of sensational thrill and media critique are so intricately linked that one no longer notices where critical distancing and irony turns into spectacular display; in *The Speed Queen,* the garbled and convoluted juxtaposition of incompatible genre conventions does not allow for such logic anymore. Even though Marjorie casts herself in terms of spectacular abandon (in the mode of *Vanishing Point*), her narrative veers into a different direction. The overall effect of the story is not one of dislocation, indeterminacy, and openness, but, on the contrary, of an almost unbearable groundedness, if not in a geographical location then in the hybrid space of pop culture.

If Marjorie refrains from relating the murder scenes in detail, this is certainly no indication of delicacy or remorse. She is just not interested enough in the gruesome details of what she witnessed. In an interesting move, the novel manages to communicate a sense of horror without allowing for the kind of spectacular thrill that emanates from so many of the films with the same plotline: what is really shocking, it turns out, is precisely that the murder scenes are *not* related in detail, that time and again other activities and interests take center stage. Just consider the scene of the first "highway killings;" the victims are an old married couple. The event takes place shortly after Marjorie has discovered that her husband, Lamont, had an affair with her best friend Natalie—with whom she was, at the same time, busily exploring her own bisexual inclinations.

> I followed [Lamont] into the dining room, where he did Mrs. Close. Her nightgown went gray where [the kerosene] spilled. [...] When he was done, he threw the can against the hutch, breaking some plates. He took out a pack of matches.
> "Can we talk for a minute?" I asked him. "About me and Natalie."
> "Why?" he said, and then he saw that I wasn't going to let it go.
> "Okay," he said, and we sat down on the couch. [...]
> "I'm all done with her," I said. "It's over."
> "So?"
> "I mean I'm committed to you."
> "It's a little late for that, isn't it?"
> "Is it?" I said.
> "I don't know."
> "I love you." I said.
> "I know that," he said, "I love you too," but he didn't sound happy about it.
> "We should get going," I said. " I just wanted you to know that."
> "Okay," he said.
> And he kissed me then, I don't know why. I didn't expect it.
> I held the front door open while he flicked matches at Mrs. Close. It

took him a few tries. Every time a match scratched, she jumped. (O'Nan 165-166)

Cinematic memories of violence and spectacular passion do come up in Marjorie's tale, but not where one might expect them. In this gruesome scene, the reference is not to the well-known genre of splatter movies but to a soap opera-style relationship drama. The various associations and conventions she evokes here have one common denominator: they all work perfectly at keeping reality at bay. While spouting stereotypical declarations of regret and pity for her victims, she never faces what actually really happened. It seems as if she was not really there. Stereotypical genre references envelop her so completely that to describe her actions in terms of spontaneous impulses such as passion, madness, or savagery is completely beside the point.

The entire story evolves from spontaneous association rather than relying upon spectacular events, a technique that clearly bespeaks the influence of Kerouac. Yet in O'Nan's narrative, to be on the road is not to find yourself, much less to find some larger truth. Marjorie's road is a virtual space, a space already completely mapped out by the media images revolving in her head. "You express me better than I can express myself," wrote Whitman about the public road, and this insight also holds true with respect to Marjorie: the mix of mass cultural fantasies and popular stereotypes about the road indeed manages to express her completely. Her story no longer provides us with a "kernel of truth" or a "pearl of revelation;" for Marjorie, as well as for the reader, this road is closed.

No Exit. *Going Native*

"Sometimes he imagined he could even feel the media microwaves bombarding his skin, as if he were being literally baked by encoded clichés" (Wright 282), we learn about the protagonist of Stephen Wright's novel *Going Native* (if protagonist is the correct word for the detached and largely voiceless character that shows up or drifts by in the novel's loosely connected episodic chapters). Like O'Nan's Marjorie, Wright's Wylie Jones is a product of the media, and similar to *The Speed Queen*, filmic and TV references are crucial for an understanding of *Going Native*.² Moreover, Wright also takes a critical stand on the media-driven heteronomy of modern life. Even though his crimes and their presentation take a markedly different guise, Wylie also ends up as a highway killer. True, the two novels differ in terms of style and form: O'Nan adheres to a neo-realist mode of representation, while Wright has been counted among the more experimentally inclined so-called 'avant-pop' group of contemporary authors. Yet both novels trace similar themes, with similar critical implications.

Wright's protagonist also is a 'normal' guy who comes to steer an abnormal course. Wylie Jones (his first name is an allusion to the coyote character that chases the cartoon figure Road Runner) first comes into view as the all-American suburban dad, returning from a workday in the city to a little barbecue in his backyard. But things are not what they seem. It may have been the sight of a dead body in front of the local supermarket that prompts Wylie to leave his family and to go on the road: as another highway killer and drive-by shooter on the loose.

The reader never learns about Wylie's true motivation; only in the final chapter, Wright allows us some insight into the protagonist's mind. Even then, however, the impression remains vague, and Wylie's actions continue to look unmotivated and strange. Seen that way, Wright's protagonist is the extreme opposite of O'Nan's wordy narrator.

Yet Wylie is not exactly the epitome of the madcap road killer, either. In fact, it is unclear what he gains from his deviant time on the road. In the last chapter he is living with a girlfriend and a child in a Californian beach house. He ended up where he set out from, and does not even seem to be disturbed by the effect of repetition. If the predominant reading experience with this novel is thus one of disjunction, disjunction is also the basic condition of Wylie's life. The disjointed bits and pieces, the moments on the road or the various fake scenarios of domestic bliss never actually add up to a closed, consistent concept of selfhood. Driving from his new home into town, he undergoes a characteristic crisis:

> Who was he? What was his name? Where was he now? Because it had happened before (everything had happened before), he knew enough to ignore the questions and stay with the car, maintain control of the machinery, because when a moment splintered like this into a million

---

2   For the novel's intertextual layout, see Griem.

riddles, every ? was a doorway into another world, and the experienced traveler kept a firm hand on the wheel, secure in the knowledge that eventually he would catch up with himself. (Wright 283)

Where Marjorie seemed almost uncannily grounded, Wylie appears spaced-out. But as different as the two may feel and react, both seem to drift from one stage of being into another. They are not stable selves but lost causes, refashioning their identity at the spur of a moment and on the basis of whatever random reference might cross their mind at the time. Wylie Jones just 'keeps driving' in order to experience some kind of coherence again, and thus echoes Marjorie's restless credo at the end of *The Speed Queen*: "I didn't know what I was doing. Just driving" (O'Nan 207).

If such statements call to mind the Zen rhetoric of the Kerouac-inspired road novel and the cool sense of dislocation in the highway killer movie, the lost souls of Wright and O'Nan are no longer able to gain any deep awareness or passionate release against all odds from their road trips. Not even death presents a way out: Marjorie is unperturbed by the impending death sentence, and Wylie, who commits suicide at the end of the novel, does not present a tragic perspective either. Quite fittingly, the final chapter is titled: "No Exit."

Early on in the novel, the differences between *Going Native* and popular filmic versions of the road narrative are made apparent. A hitchhiker, who turns out to be Wylie's alter ego, is suddenly seen stabbing the truck driver who gave him a ride; it is an act of random violence, seemingly devoid of any rationale or motivation. When Wylie later picks up the juvenile psycho killer, the two men, who both look just "like any other guy" (84), start swapping stories, which increasingly reveal their weird and violent dispositions. Yet far from any violent denouement, a showdown of killers, or at least an eerie bonding of two equally deviant personalities, the scene ends with the hitcher telling of a dream that could have been Wylie's: "'I'm in a car. What kind? Don't know. How'd I get there? Don't know? Where am I going? Don't know but there's no one to answer to, no one-in-my-way.' 'Like this car, Ray?'," Wylie asks and the hitcher agrees (88).

Nothing happens. The hitchhiker eventually gets out of the car, deeply disgusted with life and people: "People everywhere were always, ultimately, a profound disappointment" (89). No fight or bonding ensue; as in *The Speed Queen* we are again confronted with a narrative technique that is predicated on the deferral of action and the denial of thrill, which forces us to reconsider our expectations and, by implication, the very rules and logic of the genre at hand.

Coda. *Underworld*

In one episode of *Going Native* which is set in the jungle of Borneo, two American tourists on the lookout for authentic savagery suddenly encounter a native tribe watching a video of *Batman*. In her reading of this scene, Julika Griem came to the conclusion that at the same time that literary criticism was still celebrating the concept of cultural hybridity Wright's novel is already one step ahead, because it shows that "the concept of hybridity [...] has already been petrified into just another 'formula of authenticity' the historical effect of which is just as limited as the one of its modernist predecessors" (44, my translation; cf. Lethen). The novels discussed here might well serve to show that still another paradigm of postmodernity, namely, the notion of in-betweenness and displacement, is currently undergoing a similar revision, and again it may not come as a surprise that the revision takes place in the experimental realm of fiction rather than in the more systematic realm of theory. In texts such as O'Nan's and Wright's the notion of in-betweenness, which has drawn considerable critical attention with regard to both road novels and road movies, has almost become commonplace. Rather than depicting their protagonists' drifting in terms of a contrast to the boring and complacent establishment, their novels describe the status quo in terms of drifting. There is nothing provocative and nothing spectacular in outlaw figures like Marjorie or Wylie; they are horrifying precisely because they can be seen as perfect representatives of the normal, the average, and the ordinary. If both *The Speed Queen* and *Going Native*, as stylistically different as these novels are, avoid adopting the attitude of the 1990s highway killer movies to display spectacular disruption for its own sake, they also avoid retelling the earlier road narrative and its celebration of rebellion and the cool.

In concluding my remarks I will briefly mention another contemporary novel, Don DeLillo's *Underworld* (1997), a text that is not exactly a road novel, at least not by the conventional standards of the genre. While the novel is too complex and too multi-layered to be discussed in full here, one strain of action clearly reflects some of the themes addressed before. During the first part of the novel, reports of the so-called Texas Highway Killer repeatedly interrupt the narrative. Of the ten or eleven murders, "the number is uncertain because the police believe that one of the shootings may have been a copycat crime" (159), only one is actually discussed in the novel. While the circumstances, a random drive-by shooting on the highway, are similar to most of the other incidents, this one stands out because a little girl, quickly named the 'Video Kid' by the media, had accidentally filmed it from the back seat of a passing car.

Matty, whose brother has shot another man years before the incident, becomes increasingly fascinated with the endless re-runs of the video clip on TV stations throughout the nation. Much of his fascination derives from the repeatability yet irreversibility of the scene. He becomes obsessed with the triviality of seeing this event played out time and again on the TV screen, and with the momentousness of the random, violent act that irrevocably changes the lives of those who become involved in it. There is nothing spectacular or exciting about the killing itself; on the contrary, it is shocking only because of the amateurish character of the tape that lends it a "jostled sort of non-eventness" (156), and thus makes it appear "more real, truer-than-life than anything around you" (157). As DeLillo never tires to point out, the effect of the real arises out of collective acts of representation and reception.[3]

At first sight, DeLillo's depiction of the drive-by killing does not really differ from filmic representations of the theme such as *Natural Born Killers*. In both cases, media images are being used to evoke a spectacular and exploitative context and, simultaneously, to create a sense of presence and reality against all odds. But here analogies end. Even though DeLillo insists upon the paradoxically immediate quality of the televised image ("There's something about the nature of the tape, the grain of the image, the sputtering black-and-white tones, the starkness—you think this is more real, truer-to-life than anything around you. [...] There's something there that speaks to you directly [...]" [157]), his literary representation of these images never quite produces the spectacular thrill of the same image in an Oliver Stone

---

3   As Heinz Ickstadt remarks with respect to DeLillo's earlier novel *Libra*, "[The] sense that the relation between reality and fantasy has been somehow inverted, that the shared image of the real is more real than reality itself [...] is a persistent motif in DeLillo's work [...]" (307).

film. What is more, DeLillo takes great care to avoid the mythologizing and aggrandizement that often threaten to override critical approaches to violence in film.

Given the power ascribed to images in DeLillo's work, it is not surprising that the Texas Highway Killer remains unseen in the novel. Much of his power over the public imagination derives precisely from his portrayal as an invisible, impersonal, and irrational force. The amateur video also focuses on the victim, and never pans to the side to catch the killer's face. It is thus only when Matty turns on the TV to witness the killer's live call-in to a TV show and his chat with the anchorwoman about his ambitions and plans, that he enters the narrative on more concrete terms. Similar to O'Nan's Marjorie, DeLillo's Texas Highway Killer cuts a tragic figure in this scene. As he is talking, the station runs the often-seen tape. Yet his comments do not add anything new or personal to the already familiar images. He appears to be as much obsessed with the representation of his crimes in the media and as determined by contemporary media speak as his female predecessor in *The Speed Queen*:

> "[...] People write things and say things on air that I don't know from day one where they're coming from. I feel like my situation has been twisted in with the profiles of a hundred other individuals in the crime computer. I keep hearing about low self-esteem. They keep harping about this. Use your own judgment, Sue Ann. How does an individual with this kind of proven accuracy where he hits targets in moving vehicles where he's driving with one hand and firing an handweapon with the other and he's not supposed to be aware of his personal skills?" (216)

This man insists on being approached as an individual, even as his own scheme and self-fashioning almost entirely depends on prefabricated media images and popular clichés. By the same token, he does not want to address the issue of the copycat killer ("You are aware, are you not, that one of these crimes is said to have been the work of a copycat killer. Can you comment on that for us?" [217]); after all, he is far from original and might thus well be considered a copycat himself. After making this one appearance, he drops out of sight (or out of hearing), until the ending of the novel, when he is finally dismissed into oblivion: "No one talks about the Texas Highway Killer anymore" (807).

If the novel does not allow for identification with the killer, neither does it encourage identification with the victim, who is presented only in generic terms. Similarly, the 'Video Kid,' the anonymous recorder of the killing, remains flimsy and ephemeral. Yet it is the person behind the camera, I would argue, that introduces a new element into the road killing narrative, an element that might take the genre to a new level of expression:

> She wandered into it. The girl got lost and wandered clear-eyed into horror. This is a children's story about straying too far from home. But it isn't the family car that serves as the instrument of the child's curiosity, her inclination to explore. It is the camera that puts her in the tale. (157)

True, this passage is no longer about the car, but about the revelatory power of the camera. However, DeLillo is not just adding another facet to the by now trivial insights on simulation and virtuality, the power of images to make reality. Even though the 'Video Kid' remains as opaque as the killer and the victim, the camera is capable of capturing something about her that reaches beyond the image itself, something that invests the recording with a deeper significance:

> Here it comes all right. He is shot, head-shot, and the camera reacts, the child reacts—there is a jolting movement but she keeps on taping, there is a sympathetic response, a nerve response, her heart is beating faster but she keeps the camera trained on the subject as he slides into the door and even as you see him die you're thinking of the girl. At some level the girl has to be present here, watching what you're watching, unprepared—the girl is seeing this cold and you have to marvel at the fact that she keeps the tape rolling. (158)

Here, as so often in DeLillo's writing, the force of personal experience and feeling momentarily overrules the impersonal and mass-produced power of the media, the "image-power" as Heinz Ickstadt called this phenomenon in a different context.[4] Or rather, by way of an immedi-

---

4   Ickstadt uses the term 'image-power' with reference to DeLillo's novel on John F. Kennedy's assassination, *Libra* (1988). In this text, DeLillo reflects on the power of mediated and all-too-familiar images to create an immediate, visceral, and communitarian sense of reality, although triggered by a trite spectacle with foreseeable effects. In *Underworld*, the Kennedy murder is mentioned in passing, in a scene that depicts one of the first public screenings of the Zapruder recording. Significantly, DeLillo chooses a public setting for the screening: "The footage started rolling [...] and it was filled with slurs and jostles, it was totally jostled footage, a home movie shot with a Super 8, and the limousine came down the street, muddied by sunglint, and the head dipped out of the frame and reappeared and then the force of the shot that killed him, unexpectedly, the

ate, visceral response, the power of media images is transformed, inverted. Identification is always already textualized, linking the man who watches the same video over and over again to the girl that recorded it.

It is important to acknowledge the tenuousness of the moment is presented in terms of a projection or transference; clearly, the above-quoted passage is not really about the child, the 'Video Kid', 'seeing it cold,' but about the man who watches the child's recording and projects his own reactions onto her, thereby managing to both watch the recording and to approximate the 'real thing' (through and by means of the recording).

If this move explodes the Kerouac-style road narrative and its insistence on immediacy and authenticity, it also helps to resurrect its central motif, the motif of random encounters, unexpected alliances, and intense, if fleeting, contact. In O'Nan's and Wright's narrative, as in many recent road narratives (filmic or literary), the American road has become a virtual space, a space which has been represented so often that it ceased to leave an impression on its own. The characters in the novels of O'Nan and Wright move around in a mediated rather than an immediate space, a space that has lost its novelty, openness, and coolness, and thus seems uncannily grounded and mapped out. In *Underworld* the sense of immediacy and bonding is clearly also based on projections, simulations, make-believe, yet it nevertheless figures as a vital alternative to the world of mass-produced images and remote-controlled emotions in which it is located. The open road has turned into a media space, but this media space may, at times, function like the open road.

---

    headshot, and people in the room went ohh, and then the next ohh, and five seconds later the room at the back went ohh, the same release of breath every time, like blurts of disbelief, and a woman seated on the floor spun away and covered her face because it was completely new, you see, suppressed all these years, this was the famous headshot and they had to contend with the impact—aside from the fact that this was the President being shot, past the outer limits of this fact they had to contend with the impact that any high-velocity bullet of a certain lethal engineering will make on any human head, and the sheering of tissue and braincase was a terrible revelation" (488-489). See also Ickstadt (309).

Works Cited

Atkinson, Michael. "Crossing the Frontiers." *Sight and Sound* 4.1 (1994): 14-17.
Corrigan, Timothy. *A Cinema Without Walls. Movies and Culture After Vietnam.* New Brunswick: Rutgers UP, 1991.
DeLillo, Don. *Underworld.* New York: Scribner, 1997.
Giamo, Ben. *Kerouac, the Word and the Way. Prose Artist as Spiritual Quester.* Carbondale: Southern Illinois UP, 2000.
Griem, Julika. "Das weiße Rauschen im Herz der Finsternis. Stephen Wrights Reise durch die Wildnis der Medienkultur." *Rowohlt Literatur Magazin* 39 (Der neue amerikanische Roman) (Spring 1997): 34-51.
Hogan, Ron. Interview with Stewart O'Nan. Beatrice Interview. http://www.beatrice.com/interviews/onan/
Ickstadt, Heinz. "Loose Ends and Patterns of Coincidence in Don DeLillo's *Libra.*" *Historiographic Metafiction in Modern American and Canadian Fiction.* Ed. Bernd Engler and Kurt Müller. Paderborn: Schöningh, 1994. 299-312.
Kaiser, Johannes. Review of Stewart O'Nan, *The Speed Queen.* http://www.dradio.de/cgi-bin/user/fm1004/es/neu-lit-buch/2208.html.
Kerouac, Jack. *On the Road.* 1957. Harmondsworth: Penguin, 1991.
Kushner, David. Interview with Stephen Wright. http://www.altx.com/int2/stephen.wright.html
Laderman, David. "What a Trip: The Road Film and American Culture." *Journal of Film and Video* 48.1-2 (1996): 41-57.
Leong, Ian, Mike Sell, and Kelly Thomas. "Mad Love, Mobile Homes, and Dysfunctional Dicks. On the Road with Bonnie and Clyde." *The Road Movie Book.* 70-89.
Lethen, Helmut. "Versionen des Authentischen: Sechs Gemeinplätze." *Literatur und Kulturwissenschaften. Positionen, Theorien, Modelle.* Ed. Hartmut Böhme and Klaus R. Scherpe. Reinbek: Rowohlt, 1996. 205-231.
O'Nan, Stewart. *The Speed Queen.* New York: Ballantine Books, 1997.
Primeau, Ronald. *Romance of the Road. The Literature of the American Highway.* Bowling Green: Bowling Green State U Popular P, 1996.
The Road Movie Book. Ed. Steven Cohan and Ina Rae Hark. London: Routledge, 1997.
Schaber, Bennet. "'Hitler Can't Keep 'Em That Long.' The Road, the People." *The Road Movie Book.* 17-44.
Whitman, Walt. "Song of the Open Road." *Leaves of Grass.* 1856. New York: Airmont, 1965. 116-124.
Wright, Stephen. *Going Native.* New York: Delta, 1994.

Sites of Community, Sites of Contest:
The Formation of Urban Space in the American West

Brigitte Georgi-Findlay

When people think or talk about the American West, especially the nineteenth-century West, they rarely associate it with urban space. Since at least the 1950s, however, historians of the American West have repeatedly emphasized that the region has been, especially since the Civil War, more consistently shaped by technology, industrialization, and urbanization than was previously assumed. Western historians such as Earl Pomeroy, Patricia Limerick, Richard White, and Donald Worster have argued that the nineteenth-century West was less provincial and backward than the image of the "wild West" suggests, and that, in fact, the region was at the forefront of economic development and was therefore never able to escape the resulting consequences (Worster 7-8). As Richard White has pointed out, by 1880 "the West had become the most urbanized region of the United States" (White 184).

Although the urban character of the West was established by both Western and urban historians for quite some time, it seems to have taken a bit longer until studies of western cities took cultural diversity into account as a potentially powerful factor defining urban development. While early urban historians focused on town building, boosterism, and growth, the more recent urban history has begun to foreground social issues (family, gender, ethnicity, race) as well as economics and politics (Dippie 235). Today we have learned to think of the West as a culturally very diverse place, a meeting ground of cultures in the sense of Mary Pratt's contact zone "where disparate cultures meet, clash and grapple with each other, often in contexts of highly asymmetrical relations of domination and subordination" (Pratt 4), a place where lines are drawn and a contest is held for dominance and legitimate control over its development, but also a place where space needs to be shared and where everyone "became an actor in everyone else's play" (Limerick 292).

Considering that the formation of western urban space took place in the context of high, although varying, degrees of national, ethnic, and/or racial diversity, one begins to wonder how processes of urban formation may have been shaped by the co-presences of so many different people: Americans of various descent, Native Americans with a multitude of cultures and languages, an established Hispanic population, African Americans, people of foreign nationality, including Europeans, Canadians, Latin Americans, Asians, Hawaiians, and people of mixed descent. How have these processes of urban formation and community-building included or excluded people? How have these processes been narrativized, and which identities have people of various cultural affiliations tied to these urban spaces? In the following I will explore some of the contexts and ways in which western urban space formed a ground that was shared and/or contested.

1. Patterns of Urban Formation

Although western urban development has characteristically not followed any uniform pattern, historians have identified a set of properties that have shaped the emergence and formation of western cities. One of these characteristics is the connection between town-building and growth. Tied as it was to economic growth, nineteenth-century western urban development was very much accompanied by boosterism and thus also connected to speculation, promotion, and image-creation.

A second set of characteristics includes the rapidity, instability, and demographic imbalance of western towns. Urban development does not seem to have conformed to Frederick Jackson Turner's theory of the linear, regular progression of a frontier line proceeding in various stages from the frontiers of the fur trader and the farmer to the urban frontier. Instead, many western towns developed, sometimes rather spontaneously, around certain economies, technologies, and industries: agriculture, mining, manufacturing industries, tourism, or military industries. Towns developed along the overland trails, the railroad lines, later around the car and along highways. Cattle towns sprung up where the cattle trails connected with the railroad. Other towns appeared simultaneously with the famous mineral rushes of the nineteenth century. Tied to these boom-and-bust economies, western urban development was thus generally characterized by rapidity (especially in the case of "instant cities" [Barth 1975] such as San Francisco and Denver), instability, and by a population that tended to be (especially in the case of mining camps which developed into towns) overwhelmingly young, male and often highly mobile (White 302-303).

A third set of characteristics of western urban development is connected to the high degree of cultural diversity. As Patricia Limerick explains, Western America

> shared in the transplanted diversity of Europe. [...] To that diversity, the West added a persistent population of Indians, with a multitude of languages and cultures; an established Hispanic population, as well as one of later Mexican immigrants; Asians, to whom the American West was the East; black people, moving west in increasing numbers in the twentieth century; and Mormons [...]. Put the diverse humanity of Western America in one picture, and the 'melting pot' of the Eastern United States at the turn of the century begins to look more like a family reunion. (Limerick 260)

Limerick's list is a reminder that the rush of Eastern Americans and European or Asian immigrants to newly created towns was not the only source of cultural diversity in the urban West. In fact, the focus on "instant" cities denies the existence of some of the oldest towns in the American West: the Spanish, then Mexican pueblos (Santa Fe 1609, Albuquerque 1706, Tucson 1776, Los Angeles 1781), which were already culturally diverse before the arrival of "Anglos" and whose histories were shaped by complex combinations of conquest, migration, and immigration. Whether in the case of "instant" cities or in that of Mexican pueblos transformed into American towns, cultural diversity must have posed serious challenges to urban community-building efforts in terms of the allocation of space, property, economic and political power. It also must have put a strain on the definition of a common ground. To quote Patricia Limerick again: "If Hollywood wanted to capture the emotional center of Western history, its movies would be about real estate. [...] Western history is a story structured by the drawing of lines and the marking of borders" (55).

While some of these lines were those of class based on property and moral authority, often reinforced by gendered discourses of the middle-class home, others were based on kinship, ethnic descent, or definitions of race. Obviously, Western towns often contained several distinct communities, which "tended to fall into distinct constellations separated by location (rural or urban), class, religion, and race" (White

316). While some of these divisions could be bridged, for example, by cooperative associations, others remained in place or were reinforced at particular times, leading to the exclusion of whole groups from particular spaces. Clearly, the claiming and allocation of space, or what Henri Lefebvre dubbed spatial practices (Lefebvre 50), are central to the production and reproduction of social relations in the nineteenth-century urban West.

2. Western Urban Space as Contested and Shared Space

Personal accounts of life in the West often register the highly diverse populations found in towns and mining camps. Records of life, for example, in California mining camps, regularly include lists of nationalities and ethnicities. Thus Mary Ballou tells her son in a letter from Negro Bar, a California mining settlement along the American River, in 1852: "I am among the French and Duch and Scoth and Jews and Italions and Sweeds and Chinese and Indians and all manner of tongue and nations but I am treated with due respect by them all" (qtd. in Zanner 10). In her 1852 letters from the California mining camp of Indian Bar, Louise Amelia Knapp Smith Clappe, better known as Dame Shirley, reported in 1852 of overhearing English, French, Spanish, German, Italian, and Kanakan (Hawaiian), as well as various languages she identified as American Indian (Clappe 109). She also noted the increasing tensions that arose between American and "Spanish" miners and that led to the exclusion of foreigners from some mines, causing them to move to others (126-127). Another writer, Sara Lippincott, better known as Grace Greenwood, noted in 1871 the remarkable variety of people in Virginia City, Nevada, particularly "more Chinese than I had before beheld, and more Indians" (Lippincott 175-176). In addition, Maggie Brown, a Virginia woman who had followed her husband to Colorado and New Mexico, wrote a letter in 1884 from Rincon, New Mexico, saying that her little girl played with Mexican children, that an Arab brought her "an egg of olive wood made in Jerusalem" and that "a Chinaman is doing my washing" (Schlissel, Gibbens, Hampsten 145).

Although some narratives point to the problems that may have arisen from the presence of a multinational and multiethnic population, stories of frontier communities, especially those written from the perspective of the pioneer generation, tend to underscore the impression that in the early frontier years an egalitarian network of relations was predominant and that social and racial stratification emerged much later. For example, in her memoir of a childhood in Deadwood, a former mining camp in Dakota Territory, in the 1880s, Estelline Bennett describes the spatial lines drawn through the frontier town, which, however, do not yet appear to reflect lines of class, ethnicity, or race. The most visible line is the one cast between the respectable and the scarlet world of Deadwood, between the world and values of families "in the secluded hollow of Ingleside" and those of the people in the "Badlands," the outlaws, gamblers, and prostitutes (Bennett 4-6). Urban space is additionally divided into female and male spheres (with unequal social power) and is characterized by social hierarchies. But the social mapping of Deadwood is incomplete without mentioning the presences of Chinese and Native people on the opposite ends of Main Street. Bennett remembers that at the "other end of Main Street, the Indians who used to come from the Pine Ridge and Rosebud reservations to attend United States court pitched their tepees and received their guests." Bennett's Western hyperbole creates the image of a tolerant society, although it also may mask distinctions of race: "We were a friendly people in Deadwood. We went to see everybody who came to town." On one of these visits, Estelline is asked to join the Sioux women's dance

> and we shuffled and hopped around the fire to the wailing music one of them made on a queer little instrument, and we were just as chummy and happy as though we spoke the same language and our forefathers had not believed that the West was too small for two races. We had come so far in the late nineteenth century as to believe that Deadwood Gulch was wide enough for as many races as could find it. (31)

Both urban histories and personal accounts of life in western towns (diaries, letters, travel narratives, memoirs) all tend to tell the story of urban development as that of a multicultural common ground that was shared at some time in the past but that was lost at a later point in time. Initial coexistence and cooperation, these (hi)stories often suggest, were replaced towards the end of the nineteenth century by urban fragmentation, the economic and social subordination of minorities (especially Asians, Hispanics, and African Americans), and residential as well as social segregation. This is especially the case in the histories of formerly Mexican pueblos (Los Angeles, Santa Barbara) and of the Mexican communities that underwent processes of "Americanization" as well as "barrioization" in the late nineteenth and early twentieth centuries (see Fogelson, Camarillo, Romo). Albert Camarillo has coined the term "barrioization" to denote "the formation of residentially and socially segregated Chicano barrios and neighborhoods" (53) that emerged with varying speed in many towns and cities across the American Southwest.

The most thoroughly researched urban history in this respect is probably that of Los Angeles. The transformation of Los Angeles from a Spanish, then Mexican, pueblo into an American city entailed a complex reordering of space in terms of economic, social, and residential activities. Many Hispanic towns of the West—some of them, like Santa Fe, the oldest in North America—had been carefully planned. Many were typically made of a grid pattern of streets and plazas, implying certain conceptions of social order, of public and private space, and of the role of towns and cities that may have conflicted with the conceptions of space the newcomers (a heterogeneous group in itself) brought with them. For example, as in other Latin American towns of the early nineteenth century, the Los Angeles plaza served as the center of economic and social activity (Romo 21). On their part, the Anglo newcomers were increasingly dissatisfied with patterns of water distribution, land use, the layout of the pueblo and the Mexican system of landholdings, which contained a combination of private and communal property. Economic, residential and social activities were gradually moved away from the central plaza (Fogelson 25-26). Ricardo Romo has shown that shortly after Anglo-American takeover, Hispanic residents concentrated increasingly in a section adjacent to the original site of the pueblo's plaza (vii). Towards the end of the nineteenth century one can observe, in Los Angeles as in other towns of the Southwest, the emergence of barrios, a development that was linked to a complex mix of Hispanic land loss, legal discrimination, political disempowerment, economic subordination (in the context of an emerging dual labor system), and cultural denigration of Mexicans, combined with new demographic realities. Barrio residents in early twentieth-century Los Angeles, for example, were, for the most part, newcomers from Mexico whereas the earlier Californian residents had either moved away, 'melted' into the Euro-American (not necessarily only Anglo-American) mainstream, or acted as the "Spanish" links to the glorious past of the missions and the ranchos in fiestas and other celebrations (Camarillo 69-71). The economic and social subordination of Hispanic Westerners was also connected to the arrival of the railroad in western towns which was accompanied by economic, demographic and cultural change—i.e., by an increased need for cheap labor, by unprecedented population growth due to migrants from the Midwest, the East, Mexico, and Europe, and by new "Anglo" majorities held responsible for the decline of Hispanic-Anglo intermarriage. In addition, city boosters appropriated and capitalized on their cities' "Spanish" heritage while ignoring the growing presence of Mexican immigrants and other ethnics in that landscape (Camarillo; McClung).

Yet the history of barrioization is only one chapter in a much more complicated story of urban social relations within a context of cultural diversity. It therefore makes sense to take a closer look at the stories of shared spaces, of interactions and exchanges between diverse individuals and groups in western towns. Before the conquest of ethnic "minorities" by an "Anglo majority" can be denounced, one first needs a better idea of the relations between "majority" and "minority" in western urban contexts. For example, George Sánchez has suggested that "racially mixed areas in which the dynamics and hierarchies of racial power and differentiation were played out in neighborhood politics and personal relationships" have been more widespread in urban America than racially exclusive communities such as ghettoes or barrios (Sánchez 3-4). In fact, memoirs and personal narratives of life in the urban Southwest often point to the predominance of ethnically mixed neighborhoods, which lasted until long into the twentieth century. Some of these memoirs were written by people of mixed Anglo-Hispanic ancestry whose large-scale presence in many formerly Mexican pueblos such as Santa Fe, Albuquerque, and Tucson complicates any idea of clear-cut ethnic hierarchies. An offspring of one of these mixed families, Consuelo Bergere Mendenhall, offers a closer look at ethnic relations in early twentieth-century Santa Fe: "Some of our best friends were Jews. [...] And they were all in high society. They never thought anything of it. We had very few Negroes. We had two families, the Slaughters and the Kerrs. When Poppa would have a dinner, Mrs. Slaughter would come and help in the kitchen. Mr. Kerr had the only barber shop. [...] you see, there was never any prejudice" (qtd. in La Farge 31). Katherine "Peach" Mayer, another Santa Fe resident, remembers that there "was much more socializing between the Anglos and the Spanish Americans than you think" (50). Anglo and Hispano children went to school together. According to Anita Gonzalez Thomas, 85% of the students at her school were Hispanic, although she admits that, in general, "the Anglos went further in their education," while the Hispanic children had to go to work at an earlier age (92). She claims that the "Anglos and the Spanish got along just fine. In fact, some of those McCrossen kids got so they spoke English with a Spanish accent" (91). Adding to the diversity were African Americans:

> There were very few blacks back then. When I was growing up, there were just two families. The Slaughters were one, Ernie was the mailman. They were real nice. [...] The other family, the mother was a seamstress. I suppose they attended some of the churches here; they were not Catholics. But everybody was real nice to them, treated them real well. And of course, the Millers. He was a mulatto and had been a cook at the Palace Hotel the one that burnt. Then he married a Spanish woman, I think she was a Lovato.

The children of this African Hispanic American couple, "since the mother had been Spanish, [...] were just part of the Hispanic world here." In school there was only one black child, "and she was such a novelty to those kids" that one time they even tried to undress her "to find out if she's black all over" (90). Charles "Chuck" Barrows, an artist newcomer to Santa Fe in 1928, confirms this picture of apparent racial harmony (despite clear acknowledgment of difference) accompanied by racial mixing: "When I was first here, we had a colony of blacks in Santa Fe. They first came up with the Texans, servants of Texans. They all lived around the street that goes west from Johnson Street, parallel to and north of San Francisco. They even had their own colored church there. [...] They had mixed dances at what later became the Line Camp at Pojoaque." In sum, he concludes, "I seldom saw any evidence of ethnic or racial prejudice" (qtd. in La Farge 139-140).

The group that, however, was excluded—or, in the perception of established residents, secluded itself—from social and marital intermixing, were the Chinese. Gonzalez Thomas remembers:

> well, *they* didn't mix with anybody, see? When those kids grew up, they brought more Chinese over. So if any of those Chinese kids had any notions of intermarrying with anybody else, they didn't get a chance because they all stayed pretty much family. Then—I never knew how come—but for some reason, they were Episcopalians. [...]

> But everybody liked them. My dad was a good friend of Henry Park. (qtd. in La Farge 88)

The Hispana Fabiola Cabeza de Baca remembers a similarly harmonious constellation in her narrative of childhood in late nineteenth-century Las Vegas, New Mexico. She describes a heterogeneous group of residents who "merged into one big family. There was no discrimination as to color or race. One of the best liked families was that of Montgomery Bell. He and his wife were mulattoes and I have never known finer persons. We had German, Jews, Spanish and plain American neighbors, but we all played together as one big family and we all loved the Bells" (Cabeza de Baca 84).

These reminiscences (some of them oral histories) suggest that until at least the early twentieth century ethnic interaction and cooperation were the norm and that mixed neighborhoods predominated in many western towns. Of course, the way the story is told also depends on who is telling it. Thus, whereas a white resident of Boulder, Colorado remembers the town (before 1870) as a haven of ethnic harmony, a black pioneer of the same place remembers the opposite: "We who (were Negroes, coming) from Cripple Creek, which was perfectly wide open, found that Boulder was absolutely closed" (qtd. in Rogers 58). There was hardly any employment for black people, except as shoeshine men, railroad laborers, laundresses, or domestic workers. African Americans could only rent or buy a house "in what was called a little rectangle. […] It wasn't a ghetto. It was a very small piece of land, but it was not a ghetto, because everybody owned his or her land" (59). Another black woman, Helen Washington, relativizes this statement somewhat: "Really […] I don't think we had too hard a time. We got along with the whites, and they got along with us. They would come down to the house" (59).

Some reminiscences even suggest that ethnic harmony and cooperation were possible especially in (what people remember as) "the early years," since there was no identity politics (yet) by which communities were polarized. Samuel Adelo, the son of a Lebanese immigrant, claims that "the Hispanic and Anglo communities began to pull apart" in Santa Fe only in the 1960s: "This is a phenomenon of the era when politics began to identify ethnic minorities. […] In Santa Fe some of that polarization was caused by militant Latinos coming in; less the locals because they always participated in politics: they held offices, they owned businesses, they pulled themselves up by their bootstraps" (qtd. in La Farge 269). As the Anglo-Hispana Anita Gonzalez Thomas remembers: "We never thought of ourselves as different. When you grow up, you think everybody is like you are. For one, we weren't conscious that we're a minority" (367).

It is significant that some of these personal narratives challenge the narrative of an ever-increasing progress in American race relations culminating in the cultural awakening of minorities during and after the 1960s. One may pass their statements off as 'oldtimers' nostalgic glorification of a simpler pre-modern past. One may also note critically that especially the references to African Americans show that this group was integrated into the urban community only at its lowest level. Even so, I think that these memories of an earlier, more integrated urban life should be taken seriously as visions of an America beyond identity politics.

The image of ethnic cooperation created in personal reminiscences is underscored by Henry J. Tobias and Charles E. Woodhouse's social history of Santa Fe which focuses on Anglo-Hispanic economic and political interdependence in an urban economy that always depended more on business and service than on industry. Tobias and Woodhouse suggest that in the late nineteenth century, economic and occupational diversification was a reality and a challenge for both Anglos and Hispanos in New Mexico. After 1850, the Hispano labor force increasingly entered into non-farming, urban occupations such as skilled crafts (shoemakers, tailors, blacksmiths) or unskilled labor. By 1880 there were also Hispano lawyers, nurses, Catholic teaching sisters, grocers, saloonkeepers, government workers (such as policemen), and clerks. The increasing shift to a cash economy in Hispano lives was also reflected in a growing number of grocery stores in the hands of Hispanos (Tobias and Woodhouse 8-10). Tobias and Woodhouse acknowledge that the two groups had, from the beginning of their encounter, operated in two distinct economic cultures and had developed distinct types of occupation. While Anglos were proprietors, managers, and officials, Hispanos were clerical workers—admittedly a hierarchical division of labor (120-121). Nevertheless, in contrast to studies of barrioization, Tobias and Woodhouse underscore the predominance of interdependence and common interests in Anglo-Hispano relations. One should not, they warn us, underestimate the extent and political strength of farming interests, which were for a long time largely dominated by Hispanos.

They also point to political power sharing based on economic and political interdependence: "While Anglos most totally dominated the small number of federal positions (including the territorial governorship), Hispanos were beginning to appear in local positions and they dominated the territorial legislature" (11).

According to Tobias and Woodhouse, Hispanos' political clout did not decrease in Santa Fe after New Mexican statehood in 1912 (111). Both Anglos and Hispanos found work in the new state government. Katherine "Peach" Mayer confirms this in her reminiscence: "you'll find most of the police, the city employees, or the state, are of Spanish extraction. So it was not a question of anything except education and money" (qtd. in La Farge 51). Tobias and Woodhouse find many indications that point towards an increasing equalization of Anglo and Hispano economic and social status in the first decades of the twentieth century (122-124; 135). They find this tendency also reflected in the residential distribution of ethnic groups in Santa Fe. Although there are some clearly diverging directions in the residential expansions of Anglos and Hispanos in Santa Fe by the 1930s, the pattern of mixed neighborhoods based on similarities in occupational status still dominates (134-135).

These observations on work, ethnicity and residential distribution in Santa Fe cannot, of course, be generalized, since they are related to that city's particular history and economy. Due to promotional strategies and Santa Fe's geographic setting, the arrival of the railroad did not cause a dramatic change in the city's economic orientation, as it did, for instance, in Albuquerque, El Paso, and Los Angeles. Neither did it result in the creation of a "new town" as was the case in Albuquerque. Rather, local citizens here were reluctant to modernize the infrastructure of their urban community, which was based on business and service. Moreover, ethnic heterogeneity was still largely limited to three groups: Anglos, Hispanics, and Native Americans (Wilson).

Nevertheless, there are other Southwestern cities whose histories were similarly shaped by interethnic cooperation rather than by barrioization. In Tucson, for example, Hispanics were in the majority and continued to exercise considerable economic and political power into the twentieth century. Comparative studies have suggested that Hispanics in Tucson gained higher social acceptance and upward mobility than those in Phoenix, Los Angeles, or El Paso (Sheridan 2-3; Luckingham, *Minorities* xiii; Sonnichsen 88). Although Anglos and Hispanics clearly drifted apart geographically and economically and were established in ethnic enclaves by 1920, some personal reminiscences emphasize the prevalence of multicultural life in early twentieth-century Tucson. This occurs as an example in Roy P. Drachman's memoirs. A well-known personality in Tucson's political and social life, Drachman is a descendant of a Jewish family from Poland whose roots in the town go back to the 1850s. Born in the early twentieth century, he still remembers the wood wagons driven by Indians from the nearby reservations that delivered mesquite to private homes, and the Chinese stores that provided groceries, vegetables, and bakery goods to most Tucson families (Drachman 2-3). Drachman also remembers Steinfeld's as Tucson's largest department store. He points out that "there were two or three good restaurants. Some were run by Chinese or Greeks, others by Mexican families" (44). His memories of childhood concentrate on life on the south side, "or the wrong side of the tracks," in the 1920s when most of his friends were "Mexican-American kids with whom I had grown up" (12). Within this context, this Jewish boy (whose father was born in Tucson and whose mother was born in France) seems to have fashioned himself as a "Mexican."

Nonetheless, despite patterns of widespread ethnic coexistence, interaction, and cooperation in the late nineteenth- and early twentieth-century urban West (which are not always registered clearly enough by urban historians), most histories of western cities come to one overwhelming conclusion: by the early twentieth century, residents in western cities had drifted apart geographically, economically, and socially, distributing themselves across urban space along (albeit flexible) lines of ethnicity, race, or class. This development seems to have been most dramatic in industrializing urban centers (Los Angeles, El Paso, Albuquerque, Denver) and almost always followed the arrival of railroads (see Luckingham "Urban Frontier;" Simmons). At the same time, the commercial and largely non-industrial nature of Tucson's and Santa Fe's economy seems to have delayed the proletarianization of the ethnic work force in these cities.

3. Conclusion

The history of urban communities in the American West appears to have been defined by increasing social and ethnic fragmentation, a process that was set in motion by forces of modernization and industrialization and that was supported by prejudice and racial ideologies that often relegated minorities (especially Asians, Hispanics, and African Americans) to a subordinate status in urban economies and societies. However, the story of a homogeneous group of Anglos asserting power over helpless, subjected minorities is, to say the least, misleading. Anglos often were a minority in western cities long into the twentieth century. They were also a heterogeneous group including Americans of various descent as well as immigrants of various nationalities, ethnicities, and religions. Neither Anglos nor Hispanics or European immigrants were necessarily tightly clustered groups but internally divided along lines of class, wealth, or date of arrival. Moreover, the culturally diverse nature of life in the urban West entailed more cooperation, interdependence and interaction than is commonly registered in studies of barrioization and ethnic segregation. This also means that, at least until the early twentieth century, mixed neighborhoods appear to have been the norm rather than the exception in many western cities. Finally, Western cities were characterized by dynamics of movement, which continuously changed and blurred the lines between neighborhoods and groups.

This being said, one cannot deny that the trend toward coexistence and cooperation has been persistently counteracted by a movement towards residential and social segregation that entailed refusals to interact—a refusal, I suggest, that goes both ways. Although these refusals, especially on the part of racialized minorities, were rooted in the mistrust, pain, and resistance created by discrimination, they were not always completely involuntary. In a recent study of the history of race in American culture, Scott L. Malcomson has addressed this issue by asking Americans to confront the fact that they have persistently given in to the desire to segregate themselves into groups, a tendency that applies to both "majority" and "minorities." To acknowledge this tendency toward segregation and self-segregation, especially in urban space, provides one path to understanding the workings of western urban society. We should not, however, close our eyes to the countervailing pulls toward interaction, cooperation and mixing, which have also persistently operated in western urban communities.

Works Cited

Barth, Gunther. *Instant Cities: Urbanization and the Rise of San Francisco and Denver.* New York: Oxford UP, 1975.
Bennett, Estelline. *Old Deadwood Days.* New York: J.H. Sears&Co., 1928.
Cabeza de Baca, Fabiola. *We Fed Them Cactus.* Albuquerque: U of New Mexico P, 1954.
Camarillo, Albert. *Chicanos in a Changing Society: From Mexican Pueblos to American Barrios in Santa Barbara and Southern California, 1848-1930.* Cambridge, MA: Harvard UP, 1979.
Clappe, Louise Amelia Knapp. *The Shirley Letters from the California Mines, 1851-1852.* Salt Lake City: Peregrine Smith Books, 1954.
Dippie, Brian W. "American Wests: Historiographical Perspectives." *Trails: Toward a New Western History.* Ed. Patricia Nelson Limerick, Clyde A. Milner II, and Charles E. Rankin. Lawrence: UP of Kansas, 1991. 112-136.
Drachman, Roy P. *From Cowtown to Desert Metropolis: Ninety Years of Arizona Memories.* San Francisco: Whitewing P, 1999.
Fogelson, Robert M. *The Fragmented Metropolis: Los Angeles, 1850-1930.* Berkeley: U of California P, 1967.
La Farge, John Pen. *Turn Left at the Sleeping Dog: Scripting the Santa Fe Legend, 1920-1955.* Albuquerque: U of New Mexico P, 2001.
Lefebvre, Henri. *The Production of Space.* Oxford: Blackwell, 1991.
Limerick, Patricia Nelson. *The Legacy of Conquest: The Unbroken Past of the American West.* New York: W. W. Norton, 1987.
Lippincott, Sara. *New Life in New Lands.* New York: J.B. Ford, 1873.
Luckingham, Bradford. *Minorities in Phoenix: A Profile of Mexican American, Chinese American, and African American Communities, 1860-1992.* Tucson: U of Arizona P, 1994.
—. "The Southwestern Urban Frontier, 1880-1930." *The Urban West.* Ed. Gerald D. Nash. Manhattan, KS: Sunflower P, 1979. 40-50.
McClung, William Alexander. *Landscapes of Desire: Anglo Mythologies of Los Angeles.* Berkeley: U of California P, 2000.
Malcomson, Scott L. *One Drop of Blood: The American Misadventure of Race.* New York: Farrar Straus Giroux, 2000.
Pratt, Mary. *Imperial Eyes: Travel Writing and Transculturation.* London and New York: Routledge, 1992.
Rogers, Maria M. *In Other Words: Oral Histories of the Colorado Frontier.* Golden, CO: Fulcrum Publishing, 1995.
Romo, Ricardo. *East Los Angeles: History of a Barrio.* Austin: U of Texas P, 1983.

Sánchez, George. "Working at the Crossroads: American Studies for the Twenty-First Century. Presidential Address to the American Studies Association November 9, 2001." *American Quarterly* 54.1 (March 2001): 1-23.

Schlissel, Lillian, Byrd Gibbens, and Elizabeth Hampsten. *Far From Home: Families of the Westward Journey*. New York: Schocken Books, 1989.

Sheridan, Thomas E. *Los Tucsonenses: The Mexican Community of Tucson, 1854-1941*. Tucson: U of Arizona P, 1986.

Simmons, Marc. *Albuquerque: A Narrative History*. Albuquerque: U of New Mexico P, 1982.

Sonnichsen, C.L. *Tucson: The Life and Times of an American City*. Norman: U of Oklahoma P, 1982.

Tobias, Henry J., and Charles E. Woodhouse. *Santa Fe: A Modern History, 1880-1990*. Albuquerque: U of New Mexico P, 2001.

White, Richard. *'It's Your Misfortune and None of My Own.' A New History of the American West*. Norman: U of Oklahoma P, 1991.

Wilson, Chris. *The Myth of Santa Fe: Creating a Modern Regional Tradition*. Albuquerque: U of New Mexico P, 1997.

Worster, Donald. "Beyond the Agrarian Myth." *Trails: Toward a New Western History*. Ed. Patricia Nelson Limerick, Clyde A. Milner II, and Charles E. Rankin. Lawrence: UP of Kansas, 1991. 3-25.

Zanner, Phyllis. *Those Spirited Women of the Early West: A Mini History*. Sonoma, CA: Zanel Publ., 1989.

Borders and Catastrophes: T. C. Boyle's Californian Ecology

Elisabeth Schäfer-Wünsche

> I've imagined quite a few disasters, because then I hope they won't happen.
> T. C. Boyle, Cologne, 13 October 2003

Global time, public voices insist, was indelibly marked by the destruction inflicted on New York on September 11, 2001.[1] In symbolic Manhattan, the erased architecture of the Twin Towers evoked the loss of human lives and dramatically visualized the vulnerability of a superpower to acts of terrorism. The project of rebuilding the site was thus placed under enormous weight. At the same time, it has been argued that the initial reaction of a global public, that is, a public with access to mass media, was intensified by a perceived dislocation. The televised images of September 11 seemed to have left their established place in the realm of fiction, suddenly representing a "real" world where destroyed bodies signify pain and deaths. The distinction between the "real" and the imagined, declared obsolete in concepts of hyperreality, was therefore reclaimed as a necessity.[2] Implicitly or explicitly, these debates about reality and representation called up the film studios of Hollywood as the place where imagined disasters are produced. What was rarely mentioned, however, is that many Hollywood narratives actually choose California, especially metropolitan Los Angeles, as their primary locus of destruction.

Fictional disaster tends to be triggered by a variety of causes, among them invasions by aliens and virus attacks—themes loaded

---

1 Current dissonances on both sides of the Atlantic are often explained through their attachment to historical dates. For many continental Europeans the historical marker is declared to be the fall of the Berlin Wall on October 9, 1989. For supporters of U.S. foreign policy it is supposed to be September 11, 2001.
2 CNN's broadcasting and its strategies of remembering, however, also produced counterclaims focusing on the generative power of representation.

with implications after September 11—but also ecocatastrophes: earthquakes, floods, volcano eruptions, and firestorms. Evidently, this representational project competes with the booster image of California as the Golden State and of Los Angeles as its quasi-capital. In a lopsided way it also competes with the cultural hegemony of New York. For if some disaster narratives do not tell about imagined futures and instead focus on the present, Los Angeles, the "Edge City," tends to be credited with the nimbus of already containing immediate American and, I would claim, global futures.[3] Los Angeles seems to stand in for an urban world to come.[4] However, as Mike Davis claims in *Ecology of Fear*, disaster narratives are rather ambivalent as to the representation of the city's downfall, opting for irony and the absurd rather than tragedy.[5] In Southern California the concept of *translatio*, the inevitable westward movement of empire and civilization, seems to have been fulfilled and subverted at the same time (see Freese, "Westward").

In the following I discuss the fictionalization of Californian spaces in the work of T. C. (Thomas Coraghessan) Boyle, and while I do not intend to categorize the selected texts as disaster narratives, disaster, irony, and the absurd do loom large here. Boyle's novels *The Tortilla Curtain* (1995) and *A Friend of the Earth* (2000) are highly aware of critical discourse on ecology and urban space.[6] They situate

---

3   The "Edge City maxim," according to Edward Soja, implies that "every American city is growing in the fashion of Los Angeles" (*Postmetropolis* 401). The term itself was coined by Joel Garreau, see 243-46. Cf. also Soja's term *Exopolis*, "a new urban form that challenges the very foundations of contemporary urban studies" (154-55). It was Soja's famous essay "It All Comes Together in Los Angeles" that shaped urban debates of the 1990s (*Postmodern Geographies* 190-221).

4   Cf. also Jean Baudrillard's prediction: "In years to come cities will stretch out horizontally and will be non-urban (Los Angeles). After that, they will bury themselves in the ground and will no longer even have names" (21).

5   Cf. the chapter "The Literary Destruction of Los Angeles" 273-355. Soja criticizes Davis' argument as reverting to "older stereotypes." Despite his own critical stance, he speaks of the city as a "still exemplary postmetropolis" (*Postmetropolis* 401). One may claim though that for Davis stereotypes are powerful agents of representation.

6   According to the MLA bibliography, there is, as of now, comparatively little secondary literature on *The Tortilla Curtain* in the U.S. For close readings of the novel, see Freese, "T. Coraghessan Boyle's *The Tortilla Curtain*: A Case Study in the Genesis of Xenophobia" and Paul, "Old, New and 'Neo' Immigrant Fic-

themselves, albeit ironically, within the tradition of American nature writing and canonical texts such as Ralph Waldo Emerson's "Nature" and Henry David Thoreau's *Walden*.[7] In addition, *The Tortilla Curtain* provokes a dialogic reading with Davis' urban histories *City of Quartz* and *Ecology of Fear*, texts that participate in the *noir* tradition of debunking Southern California's self-advertising capitalism.[8]

With its title, *The Tortilla Curtain* takes up a polemical border-metaphor that draws on boundary-making through reference to food as a marker of ethnic and racial groups. Unlike the metaphor of the "Iron Curtain" with its connotations of total rigidity and hermetic closure, "Tortilla Curtain" suggests permeability and border-crossing (through consumption). Yet if migration as an ongoing movement of bodies across national borders provides a major impulse for the novel's plot, border-crossing tends to become synonymous with border clashes, clashes that are intensified by and conflated with apocalyptic ecocatastrophes.

A brief excursus on Mike Davis' work—itself highly ironic—may be useful here. The city, Davis points out, dominates an "urban galaxy" ranging from Santa Barbara in the north to a heavily guarded national border in the south where it encompasses Tijuana in Baja California, Mexico (*City of Quartz* 6-7). There is also, one should add, another, much larger geo-morphological and economic space where Los Angeles has gained increasing weight: the Pacific Rim, connecting East Asia as it borders on the Pacific as well as the islands of South East Asia to the West Coast of the Americas (see also Soja, "It All Comes"). Drawing on the discourses of geography and geology, Davis stresses that Los Angeles is embedded in an explosive ecosystem comparable to the Mediterranean region. Single events may have enormous ecological consequences, and "average" as a term of measurement becomes a dubious abstraction (*Ecology of Fear* 16). The

---

tions in American Literature: The Immigrant Presence in David Guterson's *Snow Falling on Cedars* and T.C. Boyle's *The Tortilla Curtain*." While I am indebted to both readings, I also intensely draw on responses of my students in seminars at the Universities of Düsseldorf and Bonn.

7   I will not include a close reading of the short story "After the Plague." In many ways this dense satire, a post-apocalyptic tale of survival, is a variation of the novels' themes.

8   An earlier, fictional text that has informed my reading of Boyle's novel is Nathaniel West's *The Day of the Locust*.

landscape providing the space for the city and its sprawling developments may thus be categorized as revolutionary rather than reformist, and catastrophe theory plays an increasing role in explanations provided (16-17). Yearlong droughts and resulting wildfires, intense rain accompanied by mudslides and, of course, the fault lines and blind folds considered responsible for earthquakes make for disaster that classifies as ordinary. Moreover, the city's layout and its proliferation, its tenement constructions in flood areas and its luxury homes in wildfire corridors apply the stamp of natural disaster to the effects of urban development.

Public readings of the political through metaphors of an uncontainable nature perhaps most drastically manifest themselves in the commentary on social upheavals such as the Rodney King riots of 1992. Davis therefore includes the riots in the cluster of disasters that took place in the first half of the 1990s (8). Other metropolitan areas of the West Coast, especially the San Francisco Bay Area, but also Southern Florida, he claims somewhat partially, "face comparable risks of natural disaster over the next generation, but none bear Los Angeles's heavy burden of mass poverty and racial violence" (54). While Los Angeles has a history of repressive labor relations and segregationist settlement patterns, it is undoubtedly the proximity of the national border with Mexico that has intensely shaped its contours and changed its demographic makeup during the previous decades. As a consequence of immigration, the white population—and white still tends to connote Anglo/WASP—lost its majority status, first in the southern counties and eventually in the State of California.

Boyle's novel opens with an epigraph from John Steinbeck's *The Grapes of Wrath*: "They ain't human. A human being wouldn't live like they do. A human being couldn't stand it to be so dirty and miserable." In Steinbeck's narrative local Californians consider the poverty and unbearable living conditions of the rural immigrants from the Dust Bowl to be a proof of the latter's sub-humanness. Class as a powerful category of distinction evolves into race. In *The Tortilla Curtain*, however, it is race—an unbridgeable barrier of bodily markers—that seems to determine class and, in case of contact, creates inexorable forces of disruption. At the very beginning of the novel, contact is established as accidental collision, a motif that keeps resurfacing:

> Afterward, he tried to reduce it to abstract terms, an accident in a world of accidents, the collision of opposing forces—the bumper of

his car and the frail scrambling hunched-over form of a dark little man with a wild look in his eye—but he wasn't very successful. (*Tortilla Curtain* 3)

"He" is Delaney Mossbacher, one of the four protagonists through whose perspectives the three-part narrative emerges. Delaney is of German-Irish descent and very much aware of the status of immigration in U.S. history. He is a dedicated conservationist with fixed ideas of species behavior and "liberal-humanist ideals" (13) who, as the story unravels, watches himself turn into a vocal defender of white privilege. He is also an emancipated home-maker and care-taker of Kyra Menaker-Mossbacher's son. The "dark little man with a wild look in his eye" is Cándido Rincón, an illegal Mexican immigrant who stumbles through the world as a quintessential loser, one who attracts failure and trouble as if by magic. Cándido clearly evokes Voltaire's Candide, a hapless picaro traveling in search of the best of all possible worlds.[9] Cándido has led the life of an illegal Mexican migrant, crossing and re-crossing the national border. Utterly failing patriarchal expectations at home, his life deteriorated until he convinced a young woman named América to return to "El Norte" with him. Against the backdrop of Voltaire's satire, Boyle's novel establishes a highly politicized postcolonial setting where the forces colliding are truly unequal. In the first, symbolic contact it is bumper against body, and the body is almost destroyed.

Collision, the clashing of forces, is also a paradigm employed in a post-cold-war vision that reemerged as another explanatory text after September 11, Samuel Huntington's "The Clash of Civilizations."[10] Civilizations, which Huntington defines as clusters of cultures, act like tectonic plates bound to clash because of the determining forces of history. Perhaps one of the reasons why *The Tortilla Curtain* caused such an immense response and was claimed and condemned by opposing political camps, is the novel's formulaic representation of cultures as self-contained and sharply delineated, asymmetrical worlds. If this may well be part of the novel's didactics, the determinism that keeps

---

9   See the author's explanation quoted in Freese "*Tortilla*" 228, n. 8.
10 Huntington's influential essay was expanded into a best-selling book, published in 1996: *The Clash of Civilizations and the Remaking of World Order*.

emerging through Delaney's Darwinian reasoning remains, in its basic assumptions, unquestioned.[11]

Delaney is a nature writer, author of a monthly column entitled "Pilgrim at Topanga Creek" that is published in a magazine called *Wide Open Spaces*. If the title of the column—and the reader is ironically lectured here—pays homage to Annie Dillard's *Pilgrim at Tinker Creek*, the name of the magazine is of course loaded with multiple significations. Replicating suburbs, species-oriented conservationism, questions of national sovereignty and border control as well as the fetish of property value leave no doubt that Southern California is anything but a wide open space. Enjoying the scattered stars that are able to compete with the city's "light pollution," Delaney describes the vista from the hills: "To the north and east lay the San Fernando valley, a single endless plane of parallel boulevards, houses, mini-malls and streetlights, and to the south lay the rest of Los Angeles, ad infinitum" (63). Another description of Los Angeles at night, Baudrillard's famous view from the plane, is evoked: "There is nothing to match flying over Los Angeles by night. A sort of luminous, geometric, incandescent immensity, stretching as far as the eye can see [...]. Only Hieronymus Bosch's hell can match this inferno effect" (51). Yet for Delaney there is nothing grandiose about any spectacle the city might generate; to the naturalist, the grandiose and sublime reside in nature alone.

In the narrative, landscapes are mapped through Spanish words such as "arroyo," "canyon," "chaparral." Spanish words also name the built environment, the urban developments that have reshaped those landscapes. Delaney lives in Arroyo Blanco Estates, where the prescribed architecture is "Spanish Mission style" with optional "Navajo trim" (30). Implicitly, the text evokes a nostalgic architectural movement of the past, the Mission Revival, as well as a history of multiple expropriations.[12] Anglo settlers had taken the land of Spanish missions, that in turn had colonized coastal California and forced parts of the indigenous population into servitude. Moreover, the "Navajo trim"

---

11 Cf. also the author's insistence in an interview on a "biological imperative." Qtd. in Freese, "*Tortilla*" 231.
12 Davis' discussion of Charles Fletcher Lummis and the "Arroyo Set" of the 1890s and his mentioning of the Mission Revival craze of the 1980s is illuminating if provocative. See *City of Quartz* 24-30; 90; n. 16.

exoticizes Southern California as part of a multicultural South West. Arroyo Blanco thus reduces its historical Others to style and decoration that can be readily consumed. Most importantly, Spanish words belie rigidly segregated residential patterns, Arroyo Blanco is indeed *blanco*, that is, all-white. No Spanish is spoken here, except by maids and construction workers, and the latter get to build the gate and the wall that are supposed to keep them out. Private communities, the text suggests, rule out spatial justice.

Just as ironically, the unwanted also do the gardening, literally, the landscaping of Arroyo Blanco, providing the development with a lushness that competes with the arid spaces surrounding it. Materialized in the architecture and the amount of space per lot, the semantics of community signal commodification and sameness, a "homogeneity of race, class and, especially, home values" (Davis, *City of Quartz* 153). Their servant status has rendered the (im)migrants invisible, and it is only after repeated collisions with Cándido that Delaney realizes: The aliens have long arrived, and they are many.

In addition to the perspectives of Delaney and Cándido, the reader is introduced to the worlds of two women, Kyra and América. Gender may complicate but does not challenge the fault lines of race and class, of immigrant poverty and white affluence. The rigid binaries of the story remain intact despite many ironically inverted analogies between the two couples. Kyra Menaker-Mossbacher, the chief-breadwinner of the Anglo-family, is in the line of business that propelled the expansion of Los Angeles. She is a highly successful real-estate agent who caters to what Davis calls "the mythology of managed and eternal growth" (*City of Quartz* 83). If the environment becomes part of her considerations at all, hers is a Southern Californian environmentalism, "a congenial discourse to the extent that it is congruent with a vision of eternally rising property values in secure bastions of white privilege" (159). As opposed to her husband who suffers diminishing bouts of guilt about the walling in of their private community, Kyra fully accepts that the success of her trade is caused by anxiety and fear. While the 1992 riots are never openly alluded to, numerous and rather explicit statements make it obvious that urban protest has intensified white flight, and for Kyra white flight has meant business.[13] The exodus to an ever-receding and increasingly fortified suburbia is, as Kyra knows perfectly well, further politicized by the unaccustomed minority status of a white citizenry, one that feels embattled by the "Browning of America."[14]

The landscape surrounding Arroyo Blanco is not presented through Delaney's detailed descriptions alone. Cándido and América camp in the canyon, since they cannot afford to pay rent. To América, Delaney's romanticized, well-ordered nature, his best of all possible worlds—at the beginning of the narrative he distinctly evokes Dr. Pangloss, Voltaire's caricature of Leibniz—is simply hostile, is a curse. The canyon is a prison, and América wishes for a modest share of the North's civilization, such as a flush toilet. If the white residents of the luxurious hillside developments have fled the city (i. e. the inner suburbs), América would like to make one of the Spanish-speaking neighborhoods her home. In the many border clashes in the novel, América emerges as an allegorical figure of hope. Her name subverts the synechdochic use of 'America' as simply a reference to the U.S.: spelled with an accent it is hispanicized without, I would like to suggest, claims to a *reconquista*.

As an immigrant dreaming of a better life, the mestiza América affirms and simultaneously reinvents U.S. tradition, bridging the Americas, the Anglo North and Latina/o South. But if Delaney, Kyra and the nativists of Arroyo Blanco are stereotypically drawn as representatives of a sometimes blatantly racist white upper middle-class, Cándido and América seem to exist beyond any social context. While Cándido is the universal luckless migrant/traveler, always in search of a better life, América allegorically embodies a feminized continent—a space for male projections (see Paul 261). Boyle's drawing of charac-

---

13 Davis' argument seems to comment literally on Boyle's novel: "The real impetus of this movement to the hills is no longer love of the great outdoors or frontier rusticity, but [...] the search for absolute 'thickets of privacy' outside the dense fabric of common citizenship and urban life" (*Ecology of Fear* 141). However, while Davis mentions black affluence and very much stresses the importance of Latino/a immigrants for an urban Los Angeles, Boyle's morality tale focuses on the rigid binaries of rich/white vs. poor/of color.

14 Freese discusses the novel in the context of Proposition 187, which asked for the denial of basic public services such as schooling to illegal immigrants ("*Tortilla*" 221). The proposition was passed in 1994, carried by a vote of almost 59%, but it has been challenged in California courts.

ters thus clearly re-inscribes the asymmetry of postcolonial power relations.

A theme that connects both of Boyle's novels is the vulnerability of (im)migrant bodies, bodies that have very limited control over what is done to them. In *The Tortilla Curtain* they again and again become bodies in pain, a pain also caused by hunger. Concepts of hyperreality, that perfectly describe the media-generated world view of the Arroyo Blanco home-owners, appear out of place in the physical concreteness of an existence that is declared to be illegal. Cándido's body is not only injured by the Anglo car, but also by those who speak his own language and know him to be a newcomer. He is robbed and beaten in the neighborhood where he had thought to find support.[15] América's pregnant and nursing body is soft and swollen, putting her in drastic opposition to slender, perfectly toned and sharply contoured Kyra, to whom absolute body control is everything. When América finds temporary work in Arroyo Blanco, she is exposed to toxic liquids, and the baby she eventually gives birth to is blind. She had been attacked at the border in Tijuana and is raped on her way down into the canyon by two men, one of who, as Cándido puts it, spoke "the border Spanish of the back alleys and *cantinas* of Tijuana" (88). The history of the New World, a history replete with exploitation and conquest that turned rape into a powerful trope, is both repeated and changed in América's story.[16]

Borderlands as spaces of in-betweenness have been celebrated as locations of culture. The language of national borders has been hailed as transnational and subversive. In Boyle's novel, however, the quintessential border town Tijuana is less a space of cultural production than a dump, a place that breeds poverty and violence. Hybridity, as embodied by the light-skinned Mexican, is merely a threatening, almost monstrous mixture, a menace to any society. Few of the characters are actually bilingual, the many italicized Spanish or *Spanglish* words notwithstanding. Most importantly, the representative of the

---

15 Boyle's novel thus does not quite speak to Davis' later work, *Magical Urbanism*, where Davis claims a reinvention of U.S. cities by Latino immigrants.
16 See also Freese "*Tortilla*" 240. The novel eschews, however, the foundational story of Malinche, Mexican allegory, daughter of Moctezuma, lover of Hernán Cortés, translator and supposed traitor, but also, increasingly, a Mexican figure of hope.

border, the rapist with the accent of the cantinas of Tijuana, is certainly not engaged in translation, he disrupts and destroys.

There is yet another disruptive figure that dwells on the border and constantly crosses it: the coyote. Twice a coyote climbs the chain-link fence around the Mossbacher's lawn, and twice it escapes with one of Kyra's expensive little dogs as its prey. The trickster figure of Native American tales, initially celebrated by Delaney for its refusal to be contained and its immense capacity to adapt, has intruded into the luxurious homes of Arroyo Blanco. Significantly, it is Delaney, the expert on the local flora and fauna, who starts asking for control. White fear readily conflates an encroaching, undomesticated environment with uncontrolled immigration. Coyote is of course also the designation for those who smuggle people across the border, and when Delaney, the Darwinian, speaks about migrant species or, worse even, "introduced" species, the semantic ambiguities are more than obvious.

The boundary between human and animal becomes increasingly porous, and the text makes this all too clear: To many inhabitants of Arroyo Blanco the immigrants from the south are the fast-breeding species that threaten to take over by way of sheer demographics. Moreover, the constant references to the danger caused by the endless streams of cars evoke yet another iconography of the borderland: the traffic signs warning motorists of immigrants crossing the highway. Yet the text's border clashes lend themselves to more than an allegorical reading of the border-crossing immigrant as animal. In the novel's rigid dichotomy of an uncontainable/wild outside vs. an ordered/domesticated inside, the Mossbachers also strikingly resemble those whom they seem to identify with most, their fenced-in, overprotected and entirely dependent (pet) dogs.[17]

Cándido accidentally causes a fire in the canyon, thereby literally becoming "THE INCENDIARY 'OTHER'" (Davis, *Ecology of Fear* 130). The fire blows up into a full-fledged firestorm, comparable to the one that ushered in "the coming of the Apocalypse" (Boyle, *Tortilla Curtain* 274), and the residents of the hills are evacuated. If fires—even those caused by human intervention—are part of the local ecology, a form of "natural" disaster, they are also perceived as attacks on privileged living. White fear is thus superimposed on ecological disaster, and fighting fire and fighting crime are conflated. As De-

---

17 I thank Gerrit Kemmings for this suggestion.

laney's liberal humanism lapses into a reactionary pose that tips over into racial violence, his personal, self-avowed apocalypse, catastrophes double: the man-made fire is followed by torrent rains and sliding landscapes. I will only shortly hint at the biblical implications here, they are manifold and have been pointed out.[18] América gives birth in a shed, magically saved from the inferno. When the hillside houses start to slide along with the ground underneath them, evoking Davis' metaphor of a "sloping suburbia" (*Ecology of Fear* 141), the baby drowns, and Delaney is forced to take the only hand extended to save him, which is Christ-like Cándido's.

In the 1990s it seemed that the cluster of disasters hitting metropolitan Los Angeles and its surroundings became denser than ever, provoking Davis to ask the semi-ironic question "whether this vicious circle of disaster is coincidental or eschatological" (*Ecology of Fear* 8). The end of *The Tortilla Curtain*, despite its much-maligned gesture of reconciliation and rebirth, might rather hint at the latter. Yet, the eschatological in Boyle's work is tied to satire, which subverts, I hope, the conclusion that only singular acts of individuals can overcome border clashes and save the world from going under.

Considered by Boyle "a logical outgrowth of *The Tortilla Curtain*" (*T.C. Boyle*), *A Friend of the Earth* takes up the earlier novel's binary structure.[19] Yet, this structure does not emerge through paradigms of race, class, and culture, but through time lines or time segments created in the act of remembering. The years 2025/26 are marked as the present, and the protagonist and first person narrator of this futuristic present introduces himself as "half an Irish Catholic and half a Jew" (7). Tyrone O'Shaughnessy Tierwater—again names are highly suggestive—is a member of the fastest-growing segment of the U.S. population, the so-called "young-old" (9). Reluctantly, he allows himself to remember the past, and the reader eventually learns that the story or rather the stories told about the late 1980s and the 1990s emerge as a blueprint for the biography of his daughter. Sierra Tierwater had died at the age of twenty-five as a "martyr to the cause of the trees" (12), and it is the project of recreating her biography as a public commodity which Tierwater objects to.

---

18 Cf. Freese, "Tortilla" 239-240 and Paul 261.
19 'Friends of the Earth' is the name of a transnational network of environmentalist groups. See http//:www.foe.org.

While the future as present takes place in Santa Ynez, close to Santa Barbara, the past is largely set in Northern California and Southern Oregon. The segments of time that structure the narrative thus parallel segments of space.

In the space of the past, Tyrone Tierwater had joined a radical environmentalist group called *Earth Forever!*. With his daughter Sierra, he had made the fateful move from the East to the West Coast, a move that keeps being repeated in the life-histories of Boyle's protagonists and ironically evokes the *translatio* concept as individual biography, including the author's own. As Tierwater recalls rather cynically, his conversion from an unsuccessful Eastern shopping-mall owner to a fervent West Coast environmentalist was mostly inspired by his love for an attractive *Earth Forever!* activist, Andrea, who became his second wife and who he blames for all the misfortunes that befell him. *Earth Forever!* included among its members serious activists, treesitters who protected ancient redwood trees from logging companies. At least in its beginnings, *Earth Forever!* also practiced "[e]cotage" (8), eco-sabotage, such as cutting fences and pouring sand into the gasoline tanks of heavy machinery. In retrospect, to Tierwater even radical environmentalism looks just like "another career" (238), especially since the leading members started to develop a liking for BMWs and Bordeaux.

The droughts and El Niño-induced rainfalls of the 1990s, the reader learns, prefigured a much larger catastrophe, a global warming of apocalyptic proportions. Even in 2025 the catastrophe still keeps spiraling upward, since the earth's population continues to explode. The Los Angeles-dominated urban conglomerate has fused into "Los Andiegoles," and urbanity in the San Francisco Bay Area has melted into "San Jose Francisco" (2). There are "forty-six million in Mexico City" and "New York doesn't even rank in the top twenty" (42), another quip on New York's obsoleteness. Everything is grown indoors under huge domes, and the concept of environment and therefore any environmental activism has become meaningless. The slogan *Earth Forever!* sounds like a joke. Yet, an apocalypse that is not triggered by a cluster of sudden, dramatic events lacks pathos, is deprived of meaning. The stage reached is not (yet) entropy, the slow disappearance of all dynamics.[20] Rather the current 'end of the environment' implies an excess of dynamics, a general increase: "And people thought the collapse of the biosphere would be the end of everything, but that's not it at all. It's just the opposite—more of everything, more sun, water, wind, dust, mud" (8).

Water and howling winds have reshaped surfaces and drastically altered the consistency of things. The Southern Californian landscape is now marked by flooded and torn-up streets, by dislocated objects and mud. Even for the former middle-class, pond-raised catfish sushi and cheap sake have replaced the eclectic Pacific Rim cuisine and the Chardonnay lifestyle of the 1980s and 1990s—a lifestyle that marked the 'Arroyo Set' in *The Tortilla Curtain*. Bodies now run the risk of being smashed or pierced by flying objects or of dissolving after being infected with deadly viruses. Both the materiality of the body (including the medically enhanced body) and the materiality of space are powerfully foregrounded in this ecocritical dystopia.[21]

With *A Friend of the Earth* and its specter of overpopulation the author joins ranks with the so-called "Ecodoomsters" (Birnbacher 364) and becomes a satirical prophet of a long-term ecological doomsday. In 2025 specific geography and, one assumes, borders, seem to have lost their former relevance. As Tierwater declares condescendingly: "The whole world is Africa now, and India, Bloomington, Calcutta and the Bronx, all wrapped in one" (232). The sharp divides between the first and the third world, between country and city, that generated the clashes in *The Tortilla Curtain* have been leveled. Still, as the novel's set-up suggests, it is in Southern California where catastrophe and absurdity come together most convincingly, where the banal aspects of an excessive end that simply keeps repeating itself, reach their most bizarre proportions. The place is not metropolitan Los Angeles though. Things start to slide in the formerly pristine hills above Santa Barbara, hills that Baudrillard had called "aromatic," but whose villas he had described as "funeral homes" (30),

---

20 Cf. also Freese, *From Apocalypse to Entropy and Beyond* and Dieter Birnbacher, "Wärmetod oder nuklearer Winter? Die zeitgenössische Apokalyptik in ethischer Perspektive." For a general discussion of the apocalypse in the context of American Studies, see Gysin.

21 The materiality of body and space is a theme in much of Boyle's fiction. See also his short story collection *After the Plague* and his novel *Drop City*.

as part of a "resort-style civilization [that] irresistibly evokes the end of the world" (31). It comes as no surprise that the environmental activism of the past had been located in the north, that is, in Northern California and in Oregon. *Earth Forever!* had fought the logging industry, a concrete and visible enemy, as opposed to the quasi-immaterial real estate conglomerate of the Californian south.

After prison terms for eco-sabotage and, most importantly, after the death of his daughter who broke all records of tree-sitting and then simply fell from the platform, Tierwater was taken in by the immensely rich Maclovio Pulchris. He now manages a menagerie that is a haven for survivors of otherwise extinct species, and, the reader is assured, is vital for zoo-cloning. Mac, and the text is rather unambiguous here, is a fictionalization of age-defying Michael Jackson, whose success has long vanished. In 2025 Mac is still a remarkable if no longer a singular example of a heavily reconstructed face and body. "[P]ersonal DNA codes and telomerase treatments and epidermal rejuvenators" (8) have made medical progress in the realms of the functional and the aesthetic accessible for all who can pay for it. The collapse of the biosphere has leveled many differences; class has survived as a sharp division between a few super-rich and the nondescript multitudes. Still, there is the resolve to live. The dilemma experienced in 2025 is perfectly captured in Dieter Birnbacher's argument that in contemporary visions of the apocalypse the "alternative to survival is simple nothingness" (362, my transl.). The world of 2025, one might ironically conclude, consists of too many survivors.

The politics of conservationism and the ethics of radical environmentalism, an aging society, gender and parenting are among the themes that propel the narrative. Less controversial because less overtly political than *The Tortilla Curtain*, *A Friend of the Earth* no longer attempts to switch perspectives, to see through the eyes of others. There is only one perspective left in this satire: that of the aging, ethnocentric white male. As a friend of the earth he is a friend to all living beings, except to people. "Because to be a friend of the earth, you have to be an enemy of the people" (44). If *The Tortilla Curtain* adapts one of its main characters from Voltaire's *Candide*, *A Friend of the Earth* calls upon another text of the Western literary canon that thrives on irony: Molière's *Le Misanthrope*.[22] Yet, despite the satirical tone of Boyle's novel and its critique of the self-righteousness of radical activism as well as the precariousness of concepts such as Deep Ecology, an (unorthodox) environmentalist agenda is still extant in the text.[23]

Afraid of strong women, Tierwater is quick to judge and is no friend of political correctness. His long-time assistant Chuy, the reader learns, cannot remember his surname "since the crop-dusting accident that took his hair, his manhood and half his brain and left him as jittery as a cockroach on a griddle" (5). As in *The Tortilla Curtain*, the exposure of (im)migrant bodies to toxins becomes an important issue. Tierwater seems to rely on Chuy's suggestions though, and the latter, the text implies, is a man with a story to tell. But he never gets to tell it.

Mac's formerly majestic estate is now hemmed in by dilapidated condominiums. And when they start to slide, Mac's solidly built villa turns into an ark. The dangerous animals are put in the basement, the less ferocious ones and the mostly invisible cooks (immigrants from Pakistan), are put up in the middle. Above them there is ample room for Mac and his entourage as well as for Tierwater, Andrea, and April Wind, a former tree-hugger who gets to write Sierra's biography. Animals and humans alike live on the meat from Mac's gigantic meat locker. Events on the Southern Californian ark, however, refuse to repeat the biblical text. Peace is betrayed. When the end of the rain has finally come and the celebration is about to start, one of the lions escapes from the basement and tears up Mac, the servants, and the bodyguards. In the ensuing chaos Tierwater and Chuy release some of the exotic animals—the concept of local habitat no longer makes sense—and together with Andrea and a last remnant of Mac's menagerie Tierwater turns north.

---

22 Molière's play is actually mentioned: Tierwater takes his daughter to watch "*The Misanthrope* at a theater in Brentwood" (252)—the luxurious community bordering on the University of California campus.
23 Tierwater explains Deep Ecology as follows: "Deep Ecology [...] says that all elements of a given environment are equal and that morally speaking no one of them has the right to dominate. We don't preserve the environment for the benefit of man, for progress, but for its own sake, because the whole world is a living organism and we are but a humble part of it" (153).

Thoreau's cabin, the novel's ending suggests, is now located in Southern Oregon. If the landscape that was once experienced as a peaceful "embrace" (122) has turned into a wasteland, Oregon still carries hope. Along with the renewed commitment between Andrea and Tierwater, nature risks a new beginning. Trees start to grow and forest animals can be heard again. As in much of Boyle's fiction (strictly) heterosexual monogamy is asserted and becomes a paradigm of continuity and hope. Yet, in analogy to my reading of the final scene of *The Tortilla Curtain*, I want to claim that the ending of *A Friend of the Earth* provides a space for irony. Taking a stroll down the communally repaired street, Tierwater and Andrea meet a young girl with the looks and the voice of Sierra. She glances at the friendly animal next to the couple and asks whether that is "an Afghan." Tierwater's answer comes swiftly: "'That's right,' I say, 'that's right, she's a dog.' And then, for no reason I can think of, I can't help adding, 'And I'm a human being'" (275). Peace and order are restored to the world. The species are securely named. But perhaps the concept of the species has lost at least some of its relevance, since there is a problem to this reassuring statement: The perfectly domesticated dog named Petunia has simply forgotten that she was once a ferocious Patagonian fox.

Works Cited

Baudrillard, Jean. *America*. Trans. Chris Turner. New York, London: Verso, 1989.
Birnbacher, Dieter. "Wärmetod oder nuklearer Winter? Die zeitgenössische Apokalyptik in ethischer Perspektive." *Endzeitvorstellungen*. Ed. Barbara Haupt. Studia Humaniora 33. Düsseldorf: Droste, 2001. 359-383.
Boyle, T. Coraghessan. "After the Plague." *After the Plague*. New York: Viking, 2001. 281-303.
—. *Drop City*. New York: Viking, 2003.
—. *A Friend of the Earth*. London: Bloomsbury, 2000.
—. *The Tortilla Curtain*. London: Bloomsbury, 1995.
Davis, Mike. *City of Quartz: Excavating the Future in Los Angeles*. 1990. New York: Vintage, 1992.
—. *Ecology of Fear: Los Angeles and the Imagination of Disaster*. 1998. New York: Vintage, 1999.
—. *Magical Urbanism: Latinos Reinvent the U.S. City*. New York: Verso, 2000.
Emerson, Ralph Waldo. "Nature." 1836. *The Portable Emerson*. Ed. Carl Bode. New York: Penguin, 1981.

Freese, Peter. *From Apocalypse to Entropy and Beyond: The Second Law of Thermodynamics in Post-War American Fiction*. Arbeiten zur Amerikanistik 19. Essen: Die blaue Eule, 1997.

—. "T. Coraghessan Boyle's *The Tortilla Curtain*: A Case Study in the Genesis of Xenophobia." *English Literatures in International Contexts*. Ed. Heinz Antor and Klaus Stierstorfer. Heidelberg: Winter, 2000. 221-243.

—. "'Westward the Course of Empire Takes Its Way': The *translatio*-Concept in Popular American Writing and Painting." *Amerikastudien/American Studies* 41.2 (1996): 265-295.

Gysin, Fritz, ed. *Apocalypse*. Swiss Papers in Englisch Language and Literature 12. Tübingen: Narr, 2000.

Huntington, Samuel P. "The Clash of Civilizations?" *Foreign Affairs* 72.3 (1993): 22–49.

Molière, Jean Baptiste Poquelin. *Le Misanthrope*. 1666. Paris: Larousse, 1971.

Paul, Heike. "Old, New and 'Neo' Immigrant Fictions in American Literature: The Immigrant Presence in David Guterson's *Snow Falling on Cedars* and T.C. Boyle's *The Tortilla Curtain*." *Amerikastudien/American Studies* 46.2 (2001): 249-265.

Soja, Edward W. *Postmetropolis: Critical Studies of Cities and Regions*. Oxford: Blackwell 2000.

—. *Postmodern Geographies: The Reassertion of Space in Critical Social Theory*. London: Verso, 1989.

T.C. Boyle. 24 August 2001. http://www.tcboyle.com/friend2.html 1.

Thoreau, Henry David. "Walden." 1854. *Walden and Civil Disobedience*. New York: Penguin, 1986.

Voltaire. *Candide ou l'Optimisme*. 1759. Stuttgart: Reclam, 1987.

West, Nathaniel. *The Day of the Locust*. 1939. *Miss Lonelyhearts & The Day of the Locust*. New York: New Directions, 1975.

Performance / Film / Visual Arts

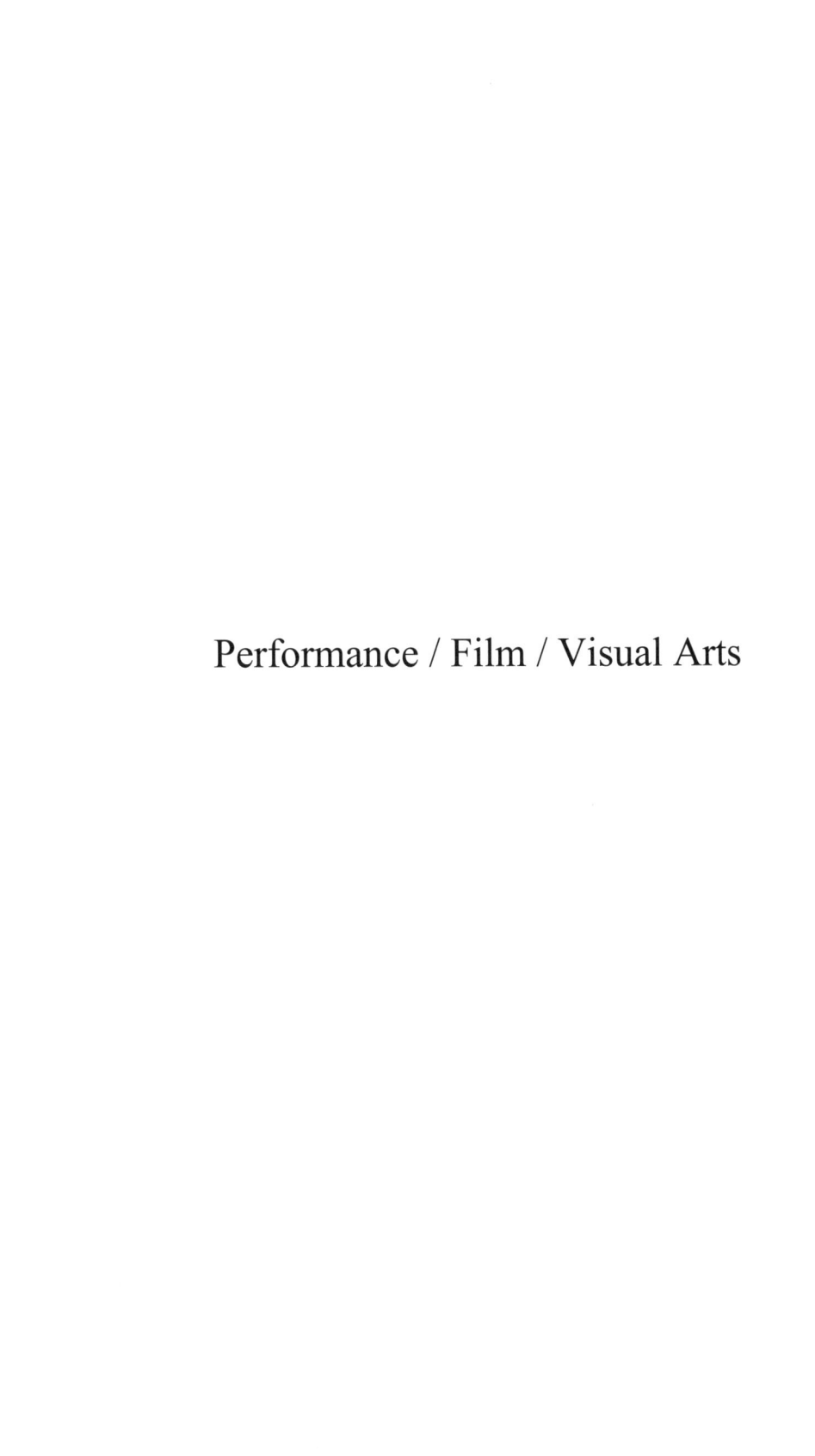

Theatrical Space and Mediatized Culture: John Jesurun's "Pieces in Spaces"

Kerstin Schmidt

> Even the most perfect reproduction of a work of art is lacking in one element: its presence in time and space, its unique existence at the place where it happens to be.
>
> Walter Benjamin

Analyzing the effects of technology and mechanical reproduction on works of art, Walter Benjamin noted the importance of a particular place and time for an art work, a distinct chrono-spatial environment in which original art unfolds. In a similar vein, traditional theater epitomizes a concept of art that is even contingent on "its presence in time and space." Major theories of drama and theater, from the Aristotelian unity of time, place, and action to Szondi's classical model of drama, have repeatedly pointed to this constitutive condition of theater. Small wonder then that the history of theater, and in particular its recent, postmodern history, is replete with experiments that question time and place as major constituents of theater and have turned this issue into a perennial topic.

The works by Puerto Rican American playwright John Jesurun are in striking contrast to this concept of theatrical presence in time and space. Jesurun's pieces, which he calls "pieces in spaces," explore the rapid mediatization and rampant technologization of contemporary society and feature a diverse array of techniques from television and video. A short description of two of his works should suffice at this point to give an idea of the sheer scope of the difference between traditional concepts of theatrical space and Jesurun's work. In his *Everything That Rises Must Converge* (1989/90), for example, a massive wall divides the quadrangular playing area. The audience is separated by this wall and sits on either side of the divided stage. Five monitors are placed above the wall on each side; they show the action on the respective "other" side of the stage. Each part of the audience thus sees the unmediated action on their respective side of the stage as well as the mediated action "of the other side" on the screens above the wall. Jesurun's plays hardly ever tell stories in the traditional sense of the word; rather, they dramatize a battle of perception between the fascination for the screen image and what appears to be real on stage. The presence of the actor, epitomizing the three-dimensional spatial experience of theater, competes with the video image, the two-dimensional "dead" representation on screen.

An even more radical experiment in problematizing theater space, Jesurun's *Blue Heat* physically separates the players from the audience.[1] What traditionally functions as the stage in theater remains conspicuously empty, as the action takes place in back rooms which the audience can only see by way of cameras and screens. Such a set-up for a play evokes fundamental questions on the art of theater: where does the play actually take place, what exactly is the theater play if it does not happen on stage in front of an audience, and in what ways does the mediatized set-up influence, if not determine, the contemporary theater experience?

The House Which Is None: Earlier Experiments with Stage Space

> To understand something is to understand its topography, to know how to chart it. And to know how to get lost.
>
> Susan Sontag

To provide a theoretical context for my reading of Jesurun's "pieces in spaces," I will first discuss earlier experiments with theatrical space in 20th century drama. Arthur Miller readily comes to mind when we think of reconceptions of the theater stage. Willy Loman's house, for example, is a 'house which is really none' in those scenes of *Death of a Salesman* that take up past experiences without further notice. Miller's extensive stage directions explain the curious setting: "*The entire setting is wholly or, in some places, partially transparent*" (130). The playwright is well aware of the far-reaching consequences that this

---

1 For a more detailed discussion of *Blue Heat*, see Lehmann 430.

particular setting entails for those involved in the theatrical production. For the actors, for instance, this means that

> Whenever the action is in the present the actors observe the imaginary wall-lines, entering the house only through its doors at the left. But in the scenes of the past these boundaries are broken, and characters enter or leave a room by stepping "through" a wall onto the forestage. (131)

When Miller questioned the mimetic stage in *Death of a Salesman*, he drew on a wide range of modern predecessors who equally interrogated the concept of time and space in traditional theater.

According to the German critic Peter Szondi, Strindberg was among the first modern playwrights to cast doubts on the idea of the stage as a stable, fixed space. If dialogue is constitutive for drama and creates that quintessential sphere in-between two people involved in a given dialogical section, the collapse of dialogue in Strindberg's expressionist drama certainly questions the stage as well. Rooted in autobiographical writing, Strindberg's so-called "subjective drama" could in many ways be seen as challenging the very possibility of drama because its focus on a single consciousness, the monagonist, radically disrupts the dialogic sphere constitutive of traditional drama. One could say that the play *To Damascus* (1898-1904) takes place within a single central consciousness, while all other characters on stage (the Lady, the Mother, the Stranger, etc.) remain but aspects of the monagonist's subjectivity. As a result, dramatic dialogue is reduced to the point where the Lady in *To Damascus* can, as Szondi notes, only tell the stranger what he already knows:

> Die Dame [zu ihrer Mutter]: Etwas ungewöhnliches ist er, und etwas langweilig ist es, daß ich nie etwas sagen kann, was er nicht schon gehört hätte. Das macht, daß wir sehr wenig sprechen..." (54)

If Strindberg actually believes, as Szondi (40) and Dahlström (99) argue, that one only knows one's own life, his epistemological skepticism spells out a disbelief in drama itself. Looking again at Strindberg's *To Damascus*, one immediately realizes that the concept of the so-called "Stationendrama" expresses the spatial orientation of Strindberg's plays. As the prototype of the expressionistic "Stationendrama," the trilogy *To Damascus* focuses on single episodes and sequences that are not necessarily related in any sequential or logical way. The stage eventually loses its traditional mimetic capacity and its power to sustain the theatrical illusion. The development of the monagonist in expressionist drama takes place in fractions of time and space and in unconnected sequences, and thus Strindberg dispenses with the idea of drama as an organic organization in the here and now. This strategy also serves to abolish the unity, even if only projected unity, of place and substitutes in its stead fragmented episodes of a character's life. In the author's note to Strindberg's *A Dream Play*, he explains:

> In this dream play, as in his former dream play, *To Damascus*, the Author has sought to reproduce the disconnected but apparently logical form of a dream. Anything can happen; everything is possible and probable. Time and space do not exist; on a slight groundwork of reality, imagination spins and weaves new patterns made up of memories, experiences, unfettered fancies, absurdities and improvisations. (3; trans. in Gilman 106-107)

Eugene O'Neill used the technique of the "Stationendrama" to develop his own version of expressionist theater in America. *The Emperor Jones* (1920), for instance, is essentially a monodrama, for only the first and the last scenes contain dialogue and build the realistic frame of the play. The middle part plays out Jones's psychological condition, his fears, hallucinations, visions, thoughts, etc. Since the principal part of the play is devoted to the exploration of a single consciousness, it could be argued that the play virtually takes place inside the monagonist's head. This curious location is taken up by Arthur Miller almost explicitly when he originally wanted to call his *Salesman* "Inside His Head." Even if Miller, compared to O'Neill, harks back to a more realistic vein of dramatic writing, he nevertheless questions the traditional stage concept, relocating the walls of Willy Loman's house in the imagination of both audience and actors.

Theatrical Space and Mediatized Culture: Theoretical Considerations[2]

> The present epoch will perhaps be above all the epoch of space. We are in the epoch of simultaneity: we are in the epoch of juxtaposition, the epoch of the near and far, of the side-by-side, of the dispersed. We are at a moment, I believe, when our experience of the world is less that of a long life developing through time than that of a network that connects points and intersects with its own skein.
>
> Michel Foucault

Many theater practitioners throughout the 20th century took issue with the intricacies of space in drama and theater; from expressionist plays to agit-prop theater, dramatists have been preoccupied with space, staging productions in lofts, cafés, and churches as well as simply on the next street corner. Even though economic expediencies often determined the choice of such locations, it was also informed by ideological considerations. Theater on location, in general, represents the attempt to reach out to the public, to lend a new air to the site where theatrical performance takes place, and to attribute new aspects to everyday spaces otherwise alien to the usage as stage—ideas mainly propagated by performance art and the Happening.[3] The locus of theater is thus reconceptualized and is turned into an important topic itself, a fact that also expresses the metadramatic thrust of postmodern drama. Such unorthodox theater locations expose a spatial turn that probably came to full swing in the many manifestations of postmodern theater.

The concept and role of space in postmodern drama and contemporary performance are in many ways contingent upon the shaping influence of postmodern mediatized culture. In addition to the pronounced metadramatic interest in the space of the theater stage, the

---

2   See also Schmidt, *The Theater of Transformation: Postmodernism in American Drama*, esp. ch. II.3.
3   The use of churches as theater spaces also indicates the interest in ritual and community and draws on the fact that theater has its origins in religious rituals.

diversified use of contemporary media has changed the concept of the postmodern stage considerably. As can be seen in plays by Don DeLillo, John Jesurun, Jean-Claude van Itallie, Megan Terry, Sam Shepard, Suzan-Lori Parks, and many more, a wide range of media technologies and devices from television, video, and the movies has transformed the theatrical space and its boundaries in order to represent and problematize a thoroughly mediatized culture in postmodern drama.

Talking about space always also involves a debate about time. In a seminal essay, Joseph Frank discusses the significance and function of space and time with regard to modernist literature. He focuses on modern poetry, Flaubert and Joyce, Proust and Djuna Barnes before analyzing the use of space in the visual arts, which he views as the model and forerunner of the use of the spatial paradigm in literature. Yet if Frank argues that "modern literature," by T. S. Eliot, Ezra Pound, Marcel Proust, and James Joyce specifically, "is moving in the direction of spatial form" (8), a number of other critics would claim that postmodern writing, too, embraces spatiality, and that space is even more pertinent to a postmodernist than to a modernist agenda. There is, however, a crucial difference between modernism and postmodernism with regard to space: in modern literature spatialization is to a large degree text-based, while postmodern dramatists have invented a host of new, mostly media-related, forms to express a spatial orientation in the postmodern theater of transformation. Spatial paradigms, in this context, endorse simultaneity and synchronicity, whereas time is associated with linear, progressive, and causal paradigms. William Spanos, therefore, discerns an effort among postmodern modes of writing to escape temporality and to attempt what he calls a "spatialization of time."[4] Referring to a variety of writers, critics, and artists including Barthes, McLuhan, Robbe-Grillet, Kaprow, Oldenburg, and Fiedler, he states:

> These modes of creativity and critical speculation attest to the variety of the postmodern scene, but this pluralism has also tended to hide the fact that, in tendency, they are all oriented beyond history or, rather, they all aspire to the spatialization of time. (166)

---

[4] At the same time, though, Spanos identifies this effort as an essentially modernist strategy, thus pointing out again that both movements cannot always be clearly differentiated and may overlap in certain contexts.

That space is increasingly conceived of as a governing principle of experimental theater in general and postmodern drama in particular is a claim backed up by many theater practitioners. In an interview, Liz LeCompte of the Wooster Group, for instance, pointed out that, in their postmodern theater projects, space is supposed to supersede time and that the organizational structural principle of their work is decidedly space, not time.[5]

A number of models and concepts in critical theory further stress the spatial orientation of postmodern writing. Gilles Deleuze and Félix Guattari's "rhizome" is as much an indication of postmodernism's spatial surface structure as is Katherine Hayles' notion of postmodern parataxis. Such models and theories foreground the surface structure of postmodern writing and identify its aim as that of overturning and transforming hierarchical relationships, replacing them with patterns of simultaneity.

Along with the theatrical space, the function of a scene in drama has also undergone changes in postmodern drama. The scene no longer presents a plot but is conceived of more as a landscape and a spatial image.[6] The predilection for spaces and images is actually an adoption of the visual arts to the theater. The theater of Robert Wilson, often labeled a "theater of images," readily comes to mind as a good case in point. His audio-landscapes—strongly reminiscent of cinematic practices—with the parallelism of images and speech patterns turn on the destruction of hierarchy. Flat characters or figures show hardly any interaction. All depends on the imaginative abilities of the spectator to compose a collage or montage of the theatrical landscape. It is only through associative processes that an interpretation of the stage presentations can be attempted. With regard to the concept of topic or theme in a given play, Wilson's mythic or pseudo-mythic

---

5   See Martins 33. LeCompte claims film and TV as main resources for her theater work. Whereas she is able to identify major influences of her work, namely Richard Foreman and The Living Theatre, she admits that an overall definition of contemporary theater has become quite difficult: "Wir wissen nicht, wie wir es nennen sollen. Ich denke, es ist Theater ..." (qtd. in Martins 34).

6   In drama this often leads to the substitution of ceremony for plot, as, for instance, in the requiem mass of the theater of Tadeusz Kantor. Kantor stresses the topics of memory, death, and the ritual incantation of the past. It is also Kantor who, like van Itallie and Craig, works with puppets larger than life-size and attributes to the puppets the function of the 'self in memory'.

Bilderbogen are demonstrably not interested in presenting a particular character's inner conflict or a dramatic interaction between characters, let alone socio-political problems of society at large. Similarly, postmodern theater in general presents landscapes and turns into what could be called an environmental theater. Borrowed from the visual arts, postmodern drama's emphasis on the 'environment' remains ephemeral and is mostly designed for physical experience. In many respects, this concept of theater marks a movement away from a form of drama that heavily relies on plot, action, character, and the transmission of a moral-didactic message. Here, by contrast, spatial and temporal aspects of drama and theater are highlighted at the expense of causally linked action or plot.[7] Scarcity of stage props, emphasis on the creation of an atmosphere, and stasis in the form of tableaux are among the prevalent characteristics of this new form of theater. The moment of speaking becomes important not so much as an idiosyncratic expression of character and story but as the sound of the word interacting with the space.

Postmodern drama furthermore aims at deconstructing time as a continuum and a linear progressive movement. Time is predominantly rendered as discontinuous and relative. The result is the production of new forms of presentation no longer based on progressive time concepts. The aesthetics of time in postmodern theater is grounded in an effort to present time itself, to exhibit time and trigger a metadramatic reflection on aspects of time. To this end, time is sometimes stretched and slowed down, as in filmic slow motion, and time frames are repeated to similar effects. Such repetitions also draw attention to detailed differences within the repetitions. Suzan-Lori Parks's plays, for instance, repeat certain gestures or phrases to the point of nausea until all meaning disappears. This metadramatic movement leads away from the perception of a train of action in which time and space serve as mere vehicles to the perception of time and space as such. This also entails a deconstruction of the self that is no longer certain of a coherent sense of time. Following the techniques of video-clip aesthetics, speed, acceleration, simultaneity, and collage are used to such an ex-

---

7   In a European context, the theater work of Klaus Michael Grüber may serve as an example of this environmental-spatial approach to theater. See here Hans-Thies Lehmann's extensive discussion of Grüber's theater in *Postdramatisches Theater* esp. 118-124.

tent that the temporal identification of realities is lost to an all-consuming sense of simultaneity. Postmodern drama may thus be said to stage the conflict between a given situation, a moment of life, and virtual, electronic surfaces in a fully mediatized environment.

Since we live in what Philip Auslander has called a "mediatized culture," the media are ingrained so irrevocably into everyday life that it no longer seems possible to tell apart lived from mediated experience.[8] By the same token, the postmodern stage has turned into a mediatized space. The significance and impact of media technologies on contemporary culture at large and on theater and drama in particular can hardly be overestimated. It has shaped contemporary dramatic writing and performance, especially with regard to the concepts of self and identity and other formal aspects of drama. Certainly, one may object that forms of communication have always left their mark on art and literature. But what has changed dramatically from the late 1960s and 1970s until today is the ubiquity and pervasiveness of new media technologies in their diverse expressions in life and literature. Therefore, the often proclaimed danger of overrating the significance of the media is probably not as great as the tendency to discern in the new only a variation of the old. Postmodern dramatists employ a variety of contemporary media—most prominently television, film, and video—in order to translate their idiosyncrasies into a language for the theater. This intertextual endeavor frequently challenges the borders between different art forms and dramatizes the relationship between a mediatized environment and the changing sense of subjectivity and self in postmodernity.

And yet, it is not so much the impact and influence that the media exert upon drama or society at large that is at stake here. Rather, the central issue is how the media change and constitute the frame of experience in postmodern culture. As Marshall McLuhan has so emphatically pointed out in his writings, the media are not merely vehicles for the mediation and transmission of given messages or ideas, but the media themselves have become a form of experience. In a double function, the media constitute the world that is experienced and act as the vehicles by which it is experienced (see also Roselt 112). They define the experience of reality in Western societies; they

---

8   Philip Auslander has contributed significantly to the discussion of "mediatized culture," notably in his monograph *Presence and Resistance*.

are a constant presence to which media critic Paul Virilio attributes such encompassing powers that he comes to the following conclusion:

> Seltsamerweise nehmen die Kommunikationsmittel in der bürgerlichen Gesellschaft göttliche Züge an: die Ubiquität (zu jeder Zeit allgegenwärtig sein), Augenblicklichkeit, Unmittelbarkeit, Allsichtbarkeit, Allgegenwärtigkeit. Jeder von uns ist in ein göttliches Wesen verwandelt.[9]

The ubiquity of public images generated by the media is indeed overwhelming. In his dystopian vision of media-dominated forms of the "real," Jean Baudrillard also testifies to the incursion of media imagery and communication into spaces which once were private and are now penetrated by the predatory gaze of the media: "Everything is exposed to the harsh and inexorable light of information and communication" ("Ecstasy of Communication" 130). The foundations of Baudrillardian media theory are outlined in his early essay "Requiem pour les media" (1972), in which he identifies the mono-directional nature of communication as the major characteristic of the new media: "il y est parlé, et fait en sorte qu'il ne puisse nulle part y être répondu" (209). As a result there is a growing social isolation of the spectator, who passively spends hours sitting in front of the TV set without being in the least forced to engage in meaningful exchanges. The power of the media resides exactly in this isolation, in not having to deal with one's environment, or in fully determining the condition of such communicative exchanges.

Arguably, the incursion of media images in our daily lives does not have to be greeted with such foreboding and can just as well be seen as a process of speeding up and intensification. The communication industry shapes consciousness and is able to ease out the real and replace it by its mediatized representation. Viewed with an eye on economical reasoning, the market offers new cultural expressions and attitudes in order to create new markets and outlets to sell products and commodities. It is hence no longer possible to separate image and reality, or media and society, as they are intricately intertwined and continually transformed. By referring constantly to other media im-

---

9 Virilio 270-271. On the effect of mediatization during the Gulf War, Virilio holds that CNN and its director Ted Turner set up a theater of real-time, of "life events" that led us to consider as truth that which was presented to us on television (270).

ages—and not to the real—in a self-referential move, the media create a network of interconnected images. Postmodern drama copies conspicuous strategies from contemporary television whose main thrust lies exactly in the creation of such a self-referential network of images. Concerning such tendencies, Umberto Eco extensively discusses television and establishes the contrasting categories of "paleo-TV" and "neo-TV":

> Its [neo-TV's] prime characteristic is that it talks less and less about the external world. Whereas paleo-television talked about the external world, or pretended to, neo-television talks about itself and about the contacts it established with its own public. ("A Guide" 19)

The recurrence and cross-referencing of fictions, images, and characters create an entirely new and vast field of popular knowledge, which shapes and transforms contemporary lives. Again, the simple fact that fictitious images invade our lives can rarely be considered a novelty, but it is their abundance and ubiquity, their fluctuation and evasiveness, that seem unprecedented today.

In this context, postmodern drama incorporates the brevity and speed of channel switching and other contemporary media mechanisms. Zapping on TV means switching back and forth between different representations and simulations, and TV evenings proliferate only fragments which are patterned after a randomly structured, multilayered collage. Hence, TV presentations no longer tell coherent stories, but rather evoke an endless flow of images through time (see Eco, "A Guide" 25). To describe the new television aesthetics, Raymond Williams uses the metaphor of "flow." It encompasses the fluid, illogical transmission of unrelated textual fragments, for example, from ads, TV programs, and diverse promotional material, and merges them into an all-consuming experience that we refer to as watching television. Previously static models of TV have thus been superseded by the model of flow, which is characterized by mobility and evanescence. This shift in TV aesthetics is crucial: "There has been a significant shift from the concept of sequence as *programming* to the concept of sequence as *flow*."[10] Flow, nevertheless, is somehow planned and thus deliberately unspecific. The idiom of "watching TV" or "lis-

---

10 Williams 83. For a discussion of Raymond Williams' concept of flow, see also Lynn Spigel's introduction to Williams's *Television: Technology and Cultural Form*.

tening to the radio" is indicative of this tendency: it denotes a habitual and rather vague activity. People refer to it as a general pastime and not as a specific interest and experience. Traditional cultural categories are smoothed out into a continuum of flow as artists and practitioners occupy and merge different positions. With regard to serialization as an important TV-form, Eco speaks of a "'concept of the infinity of the text'," a concept that also has its repercussions on the changed notion of dramatic textuality ("Innovation and Repetition" 29). By using media technology, the dramatic text turns into an unstable, ever-changing chameleon and textuality comes to be defined by its transformative abilities. The flow, the speeding up as well as the slowing down of theatrical action cut the ground from under the feet of plot. Plot has been replaced, and what has taken its place is the medium itself. In other words, form has superseded content and has assumed a role of prime importance: "Societies have always been shaped more by the nature of the media by which men communicate than by the content of the communication."[11] A society, however, thus shaped by a uniform media experience runs far-reaching political dangers. The homogenization of society at large and the reduction of plural to uniform viewpoints are ready consequences under such conditions. That contemporary society may develop into the dystopia of a lethargic society in which individuality is suppressed and in which the media have the power to narcotize individuals into a conformist Madison Avenue-stereotype of American society is a widespread concern in postmodern drama. Almost all of Jean-Claude van Itallie's postmodern plays, for example, express this dystopian vision.

---

11 In his classic *Understanding Media*, McLuhan describes the effect the media have on society: "In a culture like ours, long accustomed to splitting and dividing all things as a means of control, it is sometimes a bit of a shock to be reminded that, in operational and practical fact, the medium is the message." Marshall McLuhan and Quentin Fiore, *The Medium is the Massage* (New York: Bantam, 1967), 7-8. Raymond Williams strongly opposes McLuhan's famous dictum arguing that what matters is the way the medium is handled by people. This view, of course, coincides with his more positive view of the "masses," a term, by the way, which he refuses to use as denoting "mob." Williams, rather, argues for a democratization of "mass" media and hence for equal access. In *Television: Technology and Cultural Form*, he writes: "Thus whether the theory and practice can be changed will depend not on the fixed properties of the medium nor on the necessary character of its institutions, but on a continually renewable social action and struggle" (128).

The repercussions of a thoroughly mediatized culture on contemporary American theater are manifold and blatantly visible. Media culture and technology have provided dramatists with a variety of devices to stage postmodern concerns in their theater. Self-referentiality, for instance, is increasingly mediated by technological means, and the theater's bodily presence and materiality is contrasted with its medial representation when live actors, for example, are juxtaposed to their video images. Certain media present us with a meta-world where the link to the actual body is precisely its disembodiment in the virtual domain. Media technology at times also serves to make visible the invisible and to make heard the formerly unheard. Technology thus allows for further means to question the concept of representation and the concomitant focus on presence through its ability to create a 'virtual presence.'

Postmodern drama thus increasingly creates interfaces between human beings and the machine. The virtual realm often excludes the material body and is preoccupied with its mediatized immaterial appearance. Video art installations frequently proffer concepts of a mixed reality where the live action of the body is constitutive of the work of art but, at the same time, is present not in its materiality but in its screen image. In the same vein, a tape-recorded voice in the theater alters the concept of theatrical space because its origin can neither be determined nor localized. The virtual expansion of space not only offers new spaces, or a new concept of spatiality that requires different imaginative processes, it also marks a confrontation with a different sense of materiality. Ihab Hassan has drawn our attention to the fact that the culture of postmodernism largely "derives from the technological extension of consciousness," and thus has underlined postmodern drama's preoccupation with the mind and with the repercussions of technology on contemporary culture ("The Question" 124). With the intrusion of screens, video, TV, etc. into the theater, the actual body of the performer seems to disappear as a consequence of its reduction to a mere surface appearance. In this postmodern dramatic concept of space, the precise determination of the origin of voice, of thought, of authenticity becomes futile. Technologically-produced images and distortions turn the dramatic character into a constantly shifting and transforming ghost-like figure. Herbert Blau defined "ghosting" as an "idea of performance concerned, like Derridean theory, with appearance and disappearance and the following of a trace which is the origin of memory through which it appears" (*Take up the Bodies* xxvi). Such "ghost" figures are simulations, and can, according to Baudrillard's classification, be attributed to the third order of simulacra, namely that of the differential value of the sign. This is the order of the media as they form and control the code. In his 1981 essay, "The Precession of Simulacra," Baudrillard distinguishes four phases in the transformation of the image, culminating in the hyperreal as the stage in which the image is nothing but "its own pure simulacrum" and bears "no relation to any reality" (11).[12] According to Baudrillard's differentiation, the hyperreal does not include a concept of origin other than its reproduced simulation. The result, in more prosaic terms, is a paradigmatic ambiguity in which it is impossible to identify a real in the realm of the hyperreal. It is this very problem that has come to the fore in much of dramatic criticism, mostly in the form of the contested concept of reality and illusion in theater and the struggle to make believe that the stage —mimetically—represents the world.

Postmodern simulation, however, should not be confused with the familiar notion of mimesis, even though they have some common ground. As the German critic Dietmar Kamper argues, the two concepts differ decisively. He contends that simulation "verläuft in Automation. Sie ist wesentlich technisch organisiert und gehört dem sekundären Unbewußten an, das insgesamt Kultur heißt." Mimesis, in contrast, belongs to "Kunst, die das Ähnliche *als* Ähnliches setzt, die Fiktion *als* Fiktion betreibt und die Illusion *als* Illusion inszeniert." (Kamper 87). The goal of simulation, then, is the creation of a full identity of image and reality, whereas mimesis will always retain a recognizable difference between the two. Media and media technology, in this context, have added further means to achieve simulation. As soon as actual bodies are replaced by technologically produced images or substitutive machines, Kamper argues, mimesis will cease to exist and will completely be absorbed by simulation: "Insofern Körper durch Maschinen ersetzt sind, gibt es keine Mimesis mehr, ist Mimesis in Simulation aufgegangen" (86).

---

12   Baudrillard's position is by no means unassailable. His dystopic vision smacks at times of the metaphysics that he has rejected and leaves the reader trapped in a hyperreal realm over which we have no control. For a summary of critical commentary on Baudrillard, see Bertens, *The Idea of the Postmodern* 155-158.

The pertinent techniques adopted by the postmodern stage turn it into a hybrid which covers the fusion or blending of media as well as juxtapositions of their diverse manifestations.[13] The intertextual use of media in postmodern drama reflects patterns proposed and developed by the so-called intermedia art of the 1960s. Intermedia artists such as composer, fluxus-activist, film-maker, and theoretician Dick Higgins merged different forms of cultural expressions in their works and coined the term "intermedia" for the resulting hybrid entity. Higgins especially uses the Happening in order to demonstrate the concept of intermedia art:

> Thus the happening developed as an intermedium, an uncharted land that lies between collage, music and the theater. It is not governed by rules; each work determines its own medium and form according to its needs. The concept itself is better understood by what it is not, rather than by what it is. (22; see also Büscher 117-118)

Intermedia artists as well as postmodern dramatists are predominantly interested in the interface between body/human being and machine/medium. Consequently, they have discarded the notion that media and technology are alien, anti-human, anti-artistic forces and inhibit "true" art. Instead, they have reevaluated the possibilities which the different forms of media expressions offer for new artistic creation. For the theater, this means that the media's potential to transform the performing arts is duly recognized and put forth, concretely, in representations of the human body on stage as an object in the same manner as a chair or any other object. The strategy of doubling the body on stage as its movie image or using the body as a projection surface for the electronic image is one example of the mediated spatial simultaneity and the demonstration of the dispersed self in postmodern drama. The material body in this sense vanishes on the screen. Postmodern dramatists such as John Jesurun are increasingly concerned with the perception of technologically-induced movements in space and the expansion of space as a possible consequence of new technologies.

---

13   In his preface to *The Field of Drama*, Martin Esslin considers the rigid separation of stage drama from the cinematic media "absurd" and argues for a more inclusive concept of drama, film, and television (10).

To a considerable extent, film also has become an important tool for postmodern drama.[14] Filmic fragmentation and distancing is much more distinct compared to its theatrical counterpart. The actor's performance, for example, is more immediate in theater as compared to that in film. In drama, the actor performs directly in front of an audience, whereas in film there is no bodily encounter between actor and audience. They do not breathe the same air and do not share the same context of experience, which makes it impossible for the actor in film to react to the audience. In other words, film features a unilateral pattern of communication. In addition, the actor's performance itself is fragmented in film since it is split up in often disconnected shots. Filmic devices and tricks, such as stunts, montage, etc., may even further distance the actor from the end product to be seen on the screen. Most of all, the eye of the camera acts as an independent formative agent, apart from actors and audience. The camera eye presents and, what is more, controls the actor's performance. Special angles and close-ups, for instance, are movements undertaken by the camera and not by the actor. The camera thus acts as an additional contributor in the process of filmic communication, along with editing and cutting techniques which interfere in the making of a film and thus shape its signifying process.

---

14 If film served to transgress the traditional boundaries of theater, it was at the same time confronted with efforts to expand the boundaries of its own formal constraints. Experiments such as, for instance, the so-called 'expanded cinema' forayed into the modes and circumstances of perception. They tried to overcome the traditional context of watching movies and to create a different environment instead, as, for instance, in Stan Vanderbeek's "Movie-Drome"-experiments starting in the mid-1950s.

The Stage as Mediatized Environment: John Jesurun's "Pieces in Spaces"

> Tape my head and mike my brain, stick that needle in my vein.
>
> Thomas Pynchon

Since 1982 John Jesurun has written, directed, and designed more than twenty pieces for the theater including *Deep Sleep*, which won an Obie in 1986, *White Water* (1986), *Everything That Rises Must Converge* (1990) as well as over 50 episodes of the theater serial *Chang in a Void Moon*. The recipient of a number of awards and fellowships, Jesurun has sought to explore the role of video, television, and film for contemporary theatrical performance. The large-scale introduction of media in contemporary life has left such a decisive mark on theatrical performance that it has also reconfigured the concept of theatrical space. Jesurun, however, provocatively claims that "I wasn't interested in theatre or theatricality—just a space to make a presentation which could include all these things happening live in real time" ("Natural Force" 43). And he underlines the importance of spatial aspects for his work when he refers to his plays as "pieces in spaces" in an essay introducing the play *White Water* (76).

Jesurun, a sculptor by training, actively locates his theater at the intersections of different art forms: "My dimensional search went through painting, sculpture, film and video in rapid succession. Each of these disciplines dealt with time and space in a different way. My urge was to pull all these forms of perception together" ("Natural Force" 42). But even though he programmatically includes diverse forms of artistic expression in his work, film and filmic devices are probably easiest to notice in his plays. He explicitly emphasizes the role of film, but, at the same time, he supports a whole-sale paradigm shift when he denies the audience the role of a passive film spectator and, instead, assigns the additional role of a director to them: "The audience," he stipulates, "would be the camera and the film" ("Natural Force" 43). That film is a salient feature in Jesurun's work is also corroborated by the scattered academic responses that Jesurun's—often enigmatic—theater has triggered so far. One of the very few critiques consequently reads some of his pieces in the light of cinematic techniques only and, as a result, refers to Jesurun's work as "cinematic theater" (Fried 57-72).

But to see his work mainly as adapting filmic techniques, however, is to miss much of its impact and scope. More importantly, Jesurun creates a mediascape in his plays that goes beyond mere imitation or adaptation of filmic techniques. Rather, media are constitutive for his theater; they are not mere vehicles used to convey a message of sorts (cf. Lehmann esp. 416). Electronic media try to overcome physical limitations of time and space and radically call for a reconceptualization of the stage in theater. Jesurun's *Blue Heat* and *Everything That Rises Must Converge*, with their particular use of monitors and stage wall (as introduced above), trigger a radical opening of the interior space of theater, of the formerly closed space of the mimetic stage. Time and space as fixed concepts and concrete locations are surpassed when space is expanded infinitely and seemingly uncontrollably by using screen and video-recordings as well as a distinct stage architecture.

Jesurun expresses Pynchon's well-known quasi-nursery rhyme, that serves as an epigraph to this section of the paper, when he sees media as a large encompassing system: "the minute we turn on our set," he says, "we are connected to, influenced and disciplined by a large system" ("Relentless" n.p.). At the same time, he discloses his affinity to media theories in the vein of Harold Innis, Marshall McLuhan, Walter Ong, Jack Goody, Joshua Meyrowitz, Neil Postman, and others who view media as a totalizing, encompassing system not unlike the natural ecosystem on which it is based. It is indicative that spatial metaphors abound in this particular kind of media theory; Meyrowitz, for instance, theorizes media as environments (61), and McLuhan talks about "the unified field of organically interrelated structures that we call the present Age of Information" ("Role of New Media" 35). Neil Postman, also, explicitly analyzes structure and effects of media in terms of an environment; he compares media to a natural ecosystem, to an ecology, and concludes that a lot is to be gained if media are indeed studied in their spatial manifestation, as environments and complex message systems.[15] The main gain of dis-

---

15 See, e.g., Neil Postman and Charles Weingartner, *The Soft Revolution*; and Postman, *Teaching as Conserving Activity*.

cussing media in terms of environment and ecology, these theorists unanimously argue, is that one can analyze the complex and varied influences, cross-references, structures and interactions between technology and humans. Ursula K. Heise perceptively notes that the view of media as complex encompassing ecological systems does not necessarily reduce the significance of the human component, rather it "becomes a trope for thinking its active and creative connections with other elements" (159).

Calling the thus mediatized stage an environment asserts a spatial perception of experience. This spatial experience presupposes a certain arrangement, an architecture, of the stage: "It was an architecture of all the elements needed for a film. Script, actors, film technique (jump cuts, fragmentation of time, bird's eye views, etc.) became the structure of the pieces" (Jesurun, "Relentless" n.p.). A closer look at the setting for *White Water* will illustrate Jesurun's stage architecture. In addition to graphical representations of the set-up in the script, the stage directions specify:

> The playing space is rectangular, 18 feet by 36 feet. It is raked from floor level on one end to 3 feet in height at the other, and covered by industrial gray carpet.
>
> At each corner of the space is an upended television monitor (19") on a black boxlike pedestal 3,5 feet in height. Each of these monitors faces inward toward the playing area. From scene to scene talking heads appear on these monitors, as well as various images. The audience sits surrounding the playing space.
>
> Surrounding the audience are 16 additional upended monitors, each on a 15-foot pedestal. These monitors display numerous ambient images throughout the performance. The image on each of the 3 main floor monitors is duplicated so that a specific talking head can be seen from all sides. Images and heads shift from monitor to monitor as the piece progresses. (78)

This particular setting, meticulously described by the dramatist, brings to the fore the significance of a stage architecture that acts as a vital part in communicating the changed idea of the theatrical stage. In these "pieces in spaces," the monitors not only contribute television programs and prerecorded tapes to the action on stage, but they interact as dramatis personae in the theatrical performance. Jesurun's mediascapes probe the uncanny space where the human body interfaces with the technological and the non-living. The "vulnerability of live performance," as Jesurun has it, is mixed in an uneasy truce with the "seeming invulnerability of mechanized presentation."

Despite a certain degree of narrativity in *White Water*, a summary of its content is a challenging task. Fragments of a TV talk show alternate with pieces of conversation on the talk show and an interview with a character named Mack. Mack has seen an apparition, an obscure figure of a woman he can neither describe in detail nor claim with certainty that he has really seen the woman. Various characters involved in the production of the TV show doubt the apparition, constantly questioning Mack and pressing him for details he is unable to provide. Yet, the repetitive fragments of dialogue do not tell a story; they can rather be seen as competitive notions of a daydream or delirious ghost story, coming close to exaltation or hallucination. Curiously enough, Mack cannot specify the particulars of the woman's materiality; she remains uncannily disembodied and thus resembling in many ways the evanescent figures that we know from television:

> Mack: She doesn't really have a body like I told you. (85)

And when the producer of the show asks if Mack may have seen "*something from outer space*" or a coworker detects a "*form of energy*" (84), Mack unerringly defends the authenticity of the figure:

> Mack: It wasn't a vision she was there. (84)

The strangely immaterial body of the mysterious woman figure and the fascination it apparently exerts on all involved in the play bespeaks of a yearning for something spiritual or eternal that gradually takes possession of the other characters as well. And yet, there is always confusion as to what is actually seen, and, in the end, even Mack doubts his eyesight:

> Kirsten: Everything you've seen is true.
>
> Cortez: Everything I've seen is true.
>
> Mack: Except that it's not really true. I never saw it. That's all I have to say. Or I thought I saw it and the more I was asked the more I saw it but now I don't see anything. I never saw anything. (139)

The confusion does not stop at the obscure status of the woman figure but extends to the characters on stage and on screen as well. Kirsten in *White Water* recognizes that she herself is "only a simulacra, an ideology, a dialectic, the water table, poisoned water wells, a hippie dream" (138). Consequently, the question "How many people are in this room?" cannot be answered with certainty, and bets are cast from six down to one (141-142).

What was known as character has now been turned into ghost-like figures, embodied by the woman figure but also by the simultaneous encounter between actors on stage and on screen. When the traditional, illusionary stage propelled a certain intimacy, this intimacy is now perverted into an intimacy with a television network as in the TV talk show. Especially *White Water* makes it very clear that this intimacy is illusory as it presents all action and exchange under the terms and conditions of a TV talk show. The ghostly zone provides no possibility to escape but plays games with the notion of presence and absence. Seen this way, theater is, in many ways, at the "vanishing point," to allude to Herbert Blau's almost proverbial book title. In *White Water*, Cortez realizes that, in the end, all that remains is a paradoxical condition:

> Cortez: [...] The confusion was so clear in my mind [...]. (123)

The stage architecture, however, takes a leading role in the creation of the confusion on stage. When lines of a character are given in italic type, it means that this is prerecorded text spoken by the talking heads on the monitors. Additionally, these talking heads shift from monitor to monitor as the piece progresses. *White Water* links the yearning for spirituality explicitly to contemporary media, i.e. the television talk show, and to theater with its roots in religion and ritual. Interestingly enough, however, television and media technology are said to destroy spirituality while, at the same time, an awe-inspiring, sublime effect, a quasi-spiritual quality, is attributed to technology. In an interview, Jesurun affirms: "There is a fear that technology destroys spirituality but I actually see it as a symptom of spirituality and the search for it. It's the result of a very long line of irresistible human attempts to bring the inside to the outside, break free from physicality without having to pay the penalty of death" ("Natural Force" 45).

In addition, the use of spoken language, as a "most mysterious attraction" ("Natural Force" 43), contrasts with prerecorded "technological" language as actors on stage can communicate with their recorded, historical selves. This juxtaposition abolishes a progressive, measurable time concept as well as the concomitant concept of continuous space. "When live and mediated images communicate verbally," Jesurun envisages "a third reality [that] comes into place as a result" ("Natural Force" 45-46). The prerecorded voice whose origin cannot be localized with certainty on stage becomes exhibited in space, disseminated in a mediatized theatrical time-space.

Screens and video open up new spaces in theater, acting as doors or windows leading to new realms. In particular, Jesurun argues, the recorded images on screen open up "vast territories." He explains the process thus:

> A recorded image has been scrutinized and recorded by a camera as well as by a single human eye and then again by the audiences' eyes. The recorded human image also has the quality of scrutinizing the audience itself. It takes in the scene through seemingly dead eyes and through a face that appears to speak and think. These human images in particular open up vast territories for actors in the minute movements and vocal fluctuations. ("Relentless" n.p.).

Jesurun's *Blue Heat*, briefly discussed in the beginning, uses a different method to open up new spaces for the theater. Here, the audience is compelled to look at the spaces opened up by the monitors, simply because a wall has now taken the place of the traditional stage. The media are conspicuously, almost autistically, secluded in this play. Thus the focus is on the juxtaposition of the "dead" mediated world on screen with a presence and immediacy of the audience. This implies for the audience that its gaze oscillates between the video image and the empty stage, merely to check (in disbelief) that the live body, so characteristic for the theater experience, is conspicuously absent and only present as a mere representation on screen. This provocative set-up thematizes the transition from one environment to the next. Which one is chosen, for what reasons? Borders between real and virtual worlds and spaces and their interrelation are Jesurun's preeminent topics, thus it does not come as a surprise that the ambient monitors often show images from nature such as "wind-blown trees" (110) in *White Water* or "blue sky" (227) in *Deep Sleep*.

In *Deep Sleep*, both worlds are distinctly separated in the play's script. Each page consists of two columns, the left specifying the action on stage and the right column providing the simultaneous action on the screens. The contestation between both world is the main theme in *Deep Sleep*, and, in the end, it is no longer clear which world actually is which. While *Everything that rises must converge* (1989/90) has a wall on stage that rigidly, and visibly, divides the stage in two parts, inside and outside no longer seem to exist in *Deep Sleep*. Or, a formerly interior space has been opened up, expanded beyond any borderlines. Space becomes a virtual space, a mediascape that has occupied, possibly even annulled, the terrains of inside and outside. In Jesurun's work, these worlds are juxtaposed as environments, they collide, and sometimes they even try to communicate. If television, i.e. the screen, has become spatialized, it has virtually become "a place where we live" (McKibben 53).

The processes of competition and accommodation between the characters of the two worlds pose the question how an equilibrium may be achieved—and maintained—between the human and the recorded representation? In *Deep Sleep*, the competition leads to confusion, fear and uncertainty as well as mutual death threats. Whereas Manitas, for instance, claims that "We'll all be on the reel" (273) and Sparky asserts that "Nothing can convince me that I'm a projection" (272), Emily is determined to solve the problem: "I'm going to pull the plug and we'll see who goes where" (273).

Even when Smith in *Deep Sleep* warns that "You have to realize that you're chained into that machine" (268) and enlightens his fellow players "Those are the machines and you are coming out of the machines" (270-271), Jesurun's play does not voice the ubiquitous lament over the dehumanizing effect of contemporary media, it is not about "good" or "bad" media. If we talk about the contemporary stage as a mediatized environment, it does not simply mean that we have added "something" to the traditional stage, something that could also easily be withdrawn if no longer wanted. When Postman argues that "technological change [...] is ecological," he makes it very clear that this kind of change affects the whole landscape, instead of adding a new device. "After television," he writes, "the United States was not America plus television; television gave a new coloration to very political campaign, to every home, to every school, to every church, to every industry" (*Technopoly* 18). And Jesurun has expressed these circumstances in contemporary theater.

Drawing on the idea of a media ecology, the mediatized stage has been turned into an environment and characters have turned into nodes of information networks. An environment that has in many ways become so natural that it replaces the older, natural ecology and replaces both material and virtual habitats. In *Chang in a Void Moon (Episode Number 19)*, the following section of dialogue illustrates that technology has grown into more than an "extension of man":

SABARTES: Can you see the television anymore...?

ALMONDINE: No ... It's drifted away ... Gone. Our last contact with anything ... Gone. Have you ever held a telephone in your hand when it rings...? It's incredible really ... A chilling feeling all the way to your bones ... It happened to me once. I felt as if I had been electrocuted ...

(75)

Sections such as the following also cast doubt on the human capacities of characters, and the impression that they have acquired machine-like qualities is close at hand. In *Chang in a Void Moon*, Sabartes and Almondine are engaged in fast-paced calculations:

SABARTES: Almondine, help me calculate ... What is 36 divided by 78?

ALMONDINE: .4615384

SABARTES: Alright ... Now ... Add that to 467 and 879 and divide it by 7.367 ...

ALMONDINE: 182.7693

SABARTES. I see [...]

(75)

A recent newspaper article on the occasion of Jesurun's sojourn at the Berlin Volksbühne honors him as a virtual pioneer of video-theater and underlines the importance of speed for his theater (Wesemann 20). The fast-paced succession of dialogic bits and pieces and the rapidly shifting images and talking heads on the monitors could in many ways be read as a Virilian aesthetics of disappearance: by speeding up, images and dialogue sections can no longer be located in space, they virtually disappear and cannot be perceived. Jesurun identifies a thrill inherent in this process of speeding up when he says: "It's all about adrenalin" (Wesemann 20). The moving rollercoaster images on all screens in *White Water* visually underline this preoccupation with speed (118).

The adrenalin factor is constitutive of every performance because the prerecorded sections determine the play's pace. "Every performance," Jesurun sums up, "skirted the edge of chaos because the timing and speed of the language shared by live and recorded actors was so tightly knit. There was no way out after the piece began" ("Relentless" n.p.). The actors are thus engaged in an actual struggle as they try to "maintain a common ground with their own mediated images" ("Relentless" n.p.). Characters in the plays thus find themselves boxed in by technology, and the action on stage, too, is determined by a rigorous schedule.

In *Chang in a Void Moon*, the notion of speed is manifest in the process of the creation of the play itself. Imitating the structure of the popular TV serial, Jesurun writes a sequel each week, forcing the actors to learn the text in a couple of days and to rehearse the piece briefly before the performance a week later. In an interview, Jesurun establishes movement and mobility as driving forces in both his life and work: "Early on I got a sense of the world as a constantly moving, changing place where everything is happening simultaneously. [...] These ideas of motion and change can be found everywhere in my work from the structure to the content of the writing" ("Natural Force" 44).

These topics figure prominently in *Chang in a Void Moon*. In episode number 19, one of the players, Sabartes, is on a (slowly sinking) raft with Almondine, trying to teach her how to float. This raft directs our attention to Foucault's heterotopian space par excellence, the boat: "a floating piece of space, a place without a place, that exists by itself, that is closed in on itself and at the same time is given over to the infinity of the sea" (27).

*

Jesurun's theater can be seen as a new formalism that is mainly interested in a mechanical precision of dialogic sequences based on organizing principles of contemporary mediatized culture and devoid of expressions of human subjectivity.[16] It is a sort of technological functionalism that attempts to break free from physicality and that has fully discarded narrative and repudiated psychological, social, or even ideological concerns.

But what has then become of human agency? Are these players merely cogs in a huge socio-electronic machine? What is the relationship between the human body and the techno-body in this theatrical environment? Does the techno-body extend in space so as to finally

---

16   In this context, see also Michael Kirby's *A Formalist Theatre*.

consume the internal space of the human body? Again, what is the relationship between technology, media, and space? David Nye has reminded us that Americans have "used technologies to escape, to open new spaces, to create new landscapes" (184). He questions stories of supposedly autonomous technology and believes that "[h]uman beings, not machines, are the agents of change, as men and women introduce new systems of machines that alter their lifeworld" (180); however, Nye also realizes that we "quickly come to see these technologies [...] as 'natural'" (180). In the same vein, Bill McKibben notices that media and information ecology increasingly come to be seen "as a sort of substitute for the other, older, natural ecology (22) and indeed this triggers the crucial question how the application of ecological metaphors to such technologies transforms our understanding of natural environments" (Heise 164). After all, machines express culture, are not "'things-in-themselves'" and are thus not "inevitable" (Nye 180; 189).

The playwright considered in this paper should have a final word on the relationship between theater, space, and technology. Jesurun laments that whereas "[t]elevision, music and science have been much more innovative and experimental," theater "will have to be dragged kicking and screaming into the twenty-first century" ("Natural Force" 46). Consequently, Jesurun leaves the well-trodden terrain of theater and increasingly explores contemporary video art installations. Bill Viola's "The Sleepers" (1992), for instance, features seven barrels with water, each of which has a monitor at the bottom. These monitors show the faces of sleeping people. The viewers find themselves constantly looking for signs of life on these faces and are confused by the reflections and movement of the water in between their faces and the faces on the monitors. Just as the players in Jesurun's pieces, viewers may ponder on the faces on screen, wondering whether they are but dead representations, or if they themselves are simply bamboozled by the white water/noise of the media and media technology. Here, space is the location where both images and viewers meet; or, in Jesurun's terms, these works of art are also "pieces in spaces."

Works Cited

Auslander, Philip. *Presence and Resistance: Postmodernism and Cultural Politics in Contemporary American Performance*. Ann Arbor: U of Michigan P, 1992.

Baudrillard, Jean. "The Ecstasy of Communication." Trans. J. Johnson. *The Anti-Aesthetic*. Ed. Hal Foster. 1983. New York: The New P, 1998. 126-134.

—. "The Precession of Simulacra." *Simulations*. New York: Semiotext(e), 1983. 1-79.

—. "Requiem pour les media." *Pour une critique de l'économie politique du signe*. Paris: Gallimard, 1972. 200-228.

Bertens, Hans. *The Idea of the Postmodern*. New York: Routledge, 1995.

Blau, Herbert. *Take up the Bodies: Theater at the Vanishing Point*. Urbana: U of Illinois P, 1982.

Büscher, Barbara. "InterMedia—Material. Zur Verbindung von performativen Künsten und audio-visuellen Medien." *Grenzgänge: Das Theater und die anderen Künste*. Ed. Gabriele Brandstetter, Helga Finter, and Markus Weßendorf. Tübingen: Narr, 1998. 14-33.

Brown, Rebecca. "Blue Room, White Noise: John Jesurun's Intimate, Televised Theater." *The Stranger*. 21. August 2001. http://www.thestranger.com/2000-11-16/theater2.html

Caviola, Hugo. *In the Zone: Perception and Presentation of Space in German and American Postmodernism*. Basel: Birkhäuser, 1991.

Dahlström, Carl E. *Strindberg's Dramatic Expressionism*. Ann Arbor: U of Michigan P, 1930.

Deleuze, Gilles, and Félix Guattari. *Rhizome. Introduction.* Paris: Minuit, 1976.

Eco, Umberto. "A Guide to the Neo-television of the 1980s." *Framework* 25 (1984): 18-27.

—. "Innovation and Repetition: Between Modern and Post-Modern Aesthetics." *Reading Eco: An Anthology*. Ed. Rocco Capozzi. Bloomington: Indiana UP, 1997. 14-33.

Esslin, Martin. *The Field of Drama: How the Signs of Drama Create Meaning on Stage and Screen*. London: Methuen, 1987.

Foucault, Michel. "Of Other Spaces." *Diacritics* 16.1 (Spring 1986): 22-27.

Frank, Joseph. "Spatial Form in Modern Literature." *The Widening Gyre: Crisis and Mastery in Modern Literature*. New Brunswick: Rutgers UP, 1963. 3-62.

Fried, Ronald K. "The Cinematic Theatre of John Jesurun." *Drama Review* 29.1 (Spring 1985): 57-72.

Gilman, Richard. *The Making of Modern Drama*. 1974. New York: Da Capo, 1987.

Hassan, Ihab. "The Question of Postmodernism." *Bucknell Review* 25.2 (1980): 117-126.

Hayles, Katherine N. "Postmodern Parataxis: Embodied Texts, Weightless Information." *American Literary History* 2.3 (1990): 394-421.
Heise, Ursula K. "Unnatural Ecologies: The Metaphor of the Environment in Media Theory." *Configurations* 10 (2002): 149-168.
Higgins, Dick. "Intermedia" (1966). *Horizons: The Poetics and Theory of Intermedia*. Carbondale: Southern Illinois UP, 1984. 18-28.
Jesurun, John. "Breaking the Relentless Spool of Film Unrolling." *Felix*. 01. Oct. 2001. http://64.7.41.181/~felix/issue3/Jesurun.html
—. *Chang in a Void Moon (Episode Number 19)*. *Drama Review* 29.1 (Spring 1985): 73-83.
—. *Deep Sleep*. *Wordplays 5*. New York: PAJ, 1986. 223-304.
—. *Everything That Rises Must Converge*. Los Angeles, CA : Sun & Moon Press, 1997.
—. "A Natural Force: John Jesurun in Conversation with Caridad Svich." *Trans-Global Readings: Crossing Theatrical Boundaries*. Ed. Caridad Svich. Manchester: Manchester UP, 2003. 42-46.
—. "White Water." *On New Ground: Hispanic-American Plays*. Ed. M. E. Osborn. New York: Theatre Communications Group, 1987. 73-142.
Kamper, Dietmar. "Mimesis und Simulation. Von den Körpern zu den Maschinen." *Kunstforum* 114 (1991): 86-94.
Kirby, Michael. *A Formalist Theatre*. Philadelphia: U of Pennsylvania P, 1987.
Lehmann, Hans-Thies. *Postdramatisches Theater*. Frankfurt: Verlag der Autoren, 1999.
Martins, Kiki. "Avantgarde-Theater in New York: Kunst zwischen Chaos und Kommerz." *Theater heute* 10 (1984): 28-35.
McKibben, Bill. *The Age of Missing Information*. New York: Random House, 1992.
McLuhan, Marshall, and Quentin Fiore. *The Medium is the Massage*. New York: Bantam, 1967.
—. "The Role of New Media in Social Change." *Marshall McLuhan: The Man and His Message*. Ed. George Sanderson and Frank Macdonald. Golden, CO: Fulcrum, 1989. 34-40.
Meyrowitz, Joshua. "Images of Media: Hidden Ferment—and Harmony—in the Field." *Journal of Communication* 43.3 (1993): 55-66.
Miller, Arthur. *Death of a Salesman*. *Plays: One*. London: Methuen, 1988. 130-222.
Nye, David E. *Narratives and Spaces: Technology and the Construction of American Culture*. Exeter: U of Exeter P, 1997.
O'Neill, Eugene. *The Emperor Jones*. *Four Plays*. New York: Penguin/Signet, 1998. 109-153.
Postman, Neil, and Charles Weingartner. *The Soft Revolution*. New York: Delacorte, 1971.
—. *Teaching as a Conserving Activity*. New York: Delacorte, 1979.
—. *Technopoly: The Surrender of Culture to Technology*. New York: Vintage, 1993.

Roselt, Jens . "Vom Affekt zum Effekt—Schauspielkultur und Popkultur." *Transformationen*. Ed. Erika Fischer-Lichte, Doris Kolesch, and Christel Weiler. Berlin: Theater der Zeit, 1999. 111-120.

Schmidt, Kerstin. *The Theater of Transformation: Postmodernism in American Drama*. New York, Amsterdam: Rodopi, 2005.

Spanos, William V. "The Detective and the Boundary: Some Notes on the Postmodern Literary Imagination." *Boundary 2* 1.1 (1972): 147-168.

Strindberg, August. *Nach Damaskus. Dramen*. 3 vols. München: Hanser, 1984. 2: 5-232.

—. *Ein Traumspiel*. Stuttgart: Reclam, 1957.

Szondi, Peter. *Theorie des modernen Dramas (1880-1950)*. Frankfurt: Suhrkamp, 1963.

Virilio, Paul. "'Seinen Augen nicht mehr trauen.' Paul Virilio über Zeit, Beschleunigung und (Fernseh-)bilder." *Kunstforum* 114 (1991): 270-271.

Wesemann, Arnd. "Die Wölfe sind zurück: "Shatterhand", "Chang" und andere—der New Yorker Videotheater-Pioneer John Jesurun in der Berliner Volksbühne." *Süddeutsche Zeitung* 47 (26./27. Feb. 2005): 20.

Williams, Raymond. *Television: Technology and Cultural Form*. 1974. Hanover: Wesleyan UP, 1992.

Winthrop-Young, Geoffrey, and Michael Wutz. "Introduction: Media—Models, Memories, and Metaphors." *Configurations* 10.1 (Winter 2002): 1-10.

Dancing the Digital: American and European Visions of Digital Bodies in Digital Spaces[1]

Martina Leeker

Not without the Digital: Contemporary Concepts of Space

Contemporary concepts of space are not only contingent upon experiences in physical spaces, that is, spaces in which the body can act in a three-dimensional environment with perceivable resistance and obstacles. They also refer to digitally generated and controlled operations such as the Internet or virtual reality that are symbolic and not physical.[2] These operations are referred to as 'spaces' even though they do not correspond to the traditional sense of the word. They are graphical representations of concepts of physical spaces that are determined by digital operations having nothing to do with what is shown on the graphical user interfaces (GUI). Although these digital spaces are not 'real spaces,' we refer to them bodily and they have an impact on our psycho-physis. As a forum of experience, communication, and information, they are integrated in daily life and contemporary culture as a reality comparable to that of space and time.

When dealing with digital spaces, we are faced with mainly two problems: First, we need a representation in the digital space because we are unable to enter them physically. In order to enter digital spaces, users need interfaces, that is, devices allowing the user to control the digital circuits as, for instance, a keyboard or mouse. Additionally, user actions must be translated into digital operations which means that physical actions are transferred into data that can then be operated by the computer (touch-screens in train stations are a good case in

---

1   This essay is part of larger ongoing research project on digital performance art. Hence it formulates hypotheses and raises questions rather than presenting research results. I would like to thank Kerstin Schmidt and Klaus Benesch for their invitation to contribute to this collection.
2   Even if the physical space is covered with symbolic inscriptions, it can be experienced as resistance.

point). Or they are represented by an 'image' of the user in form of a digital structure (avatar), which can be governed by the user in so-called graphical chat rooms. The issue of representation raises crucial questions of identity in digital spaces and of the integration of experiences in physical and digital spaces. We need cultural techniques to integrate these different experiences and to adapt the digital as compatible to live-performances, as the digital is fundamentally different from analog human performances. The disturbing and questioning of a sense of identity and orientation in digital space also bears challenges and chances. In contrast to physical spaces, digital spaces are accessible for operations of a user, which can influence the symbolic structures so that space becomes in these technologies a fluid and contingent phenomena undermining concepts of stable space as well as that of a fixed viewpoint of the observer as we know it from the linear perspective.

Second, when dealing with the Internet, we operate in a somehow global space that allows us to connect with users from all over the world in real time beyond national frontiers.[3] The digital space is also global in the sense that users are represented as mere numbers and addresses that ignore every link to their physical and psychic reality and identity.[4] Based on this kind of translation of physical realities, the internet is often described as a global theater on a global digital stage, where users construct and perform virtual identities. Even if on the technological level the digital operations may be universal, because they seemingly do not touch on cultural inscriptions but only engage in the circulation of data, their graphical transformations are culturally

---

3   The concept of real time refers to technical time, i.e. the time of calculating digital operations. Real time is delayed in comparison to physical time, as we know from the delayed answers characteristic of telephone calls to overseas or videoconferences. The term real time describes the seemingly immediate, instantaneous reaction of the computer to a particular human performance. In the internet, real time is "extended time," as defined by Derrick de Kerckhove, because different time zones merge and the duration of communication is extended (we can, for instance, answer an email at once or with delay). See de Kerckhove, "Eine Mediengeschichte des Theaters" 518. Global access to the Internet is, of course, often limited by economical barriers as well as political censorship.
4   In *Identitäten im Netz*, Sherry Turkle examines the relationship between identity and the Internet. Turkle argues that any user can invent a new identity, i.e. physical appearance, sex, ethnic group, that has nothing to do with his of her "actual" identity.

determined metaphors, to be sure. In these we find icons, pattern and stereotypes of the human, which show a power play of integration and separation based on ethnicity, gender, and class. These observations become obvious in the avatars of chat rooms as well as in computer-games or in animation-programs.[5] Because the technological global is inundated by cultural differences, it is strongly determined by concurring culturally-based traditions, metaphors, concepts, and values.

In what follows I discuss two main problems. First, I will explore the ways in which physical performances are translated into digital ones and how digital bodies and digital spaces relate to the human and vice versa. I will investigate contemporary strategies of integrating digital bodies and adapting digital spaces into contemporary culture in order to assess the significance of the digital for contemporary culture. Second, the essay will present examples that illustrate processes of the inscription of cultural differences into the technological global. My aim is to analyze the quality and status of these differences in order to describe their cultural signification for an existence in and with digital spaces.

Motion Capture: Digital Dancers Become Global Players

Digital technology has been particularly influential in the contemporary performing arts scene. The performing arts have become a vital cultural forum to design and to experiment with present and future strategies and imaginations of human existence in digital spaces. Above all, contemporary dance has experimented with motion capture technology and has, since the 1990s, become a virtual cultural laboratory for the exploration of the intersections between dance and digital technology, focusing on the relationship between the physical body and digital spaces.[6]

Motion capture contributes significantly to an understanding the interfaces of the human and the digital. Motion capture is able to "read" and "write" physical actions of the body, that is, it translates them into distinct digital elements: to this end, sensors are attached to

---

5 The animation-software "Poser" would be a good example to illustrate this point: in this game, a human figure can be animated, and the figure is a white, well-done man or woman. See also "LifeForms."
6 For information about dance and technology, see the so-called dance-tech-list.

the articulations (e.g., knees or elbows) of a performer's body. Data produced by movements then is fed into a computer program in order to generate and/or direct a digitally-based graphical representation of the human body in the digital operation. Motion capture technology thus lets the human body enter digital spaces via the translation of physical movement into a sequence of digital data. Hence, motion capture addresses precisely the above-mentioned first problem, as it investigates the possibilities and problems of connecting the physical to digital operations. As systems tend to be wireless, it could be argued that the 'sensored' body itself becomes an interface with the digital. And in contrast to avatars, motion capture integrates data produced by the whole body to operate in digital processes and can thus be seen as an attempt to link the body directly with the digital. As a means of translation (avatars and other graphical representations), it deals with the transfers from analog to digital and their implications for notions of physicality. Motion capture puts forward three crucial questions: (1) How are physical bodies and spaces translated into digital ones? (2) What kind of relationship is created between the physical and digital body and space? (3) Which concepts of a digital space are generated and what is their cultural influence and signification?

I begin with the second problem: the inscription of cultural differences into the technical global motion capture technology and formats of their use can give hints to clarify the relation between globality and culturality in digital spaces. The reason is that motion capture technology itself is based on universal, digital operations, comparable to the Internet. Motion capture technology is interesting with regard to for the second complex because we can observe totally different forms of dealing with this technology in different dance companies. Different approaches use a universal technology to move from physical to digital space, namely, the Internet.

Yet there is a big difference in how American and European groups deal with motion capture. The question arises if the differences can be interpreted as inscriptions of the cultural in the universal technological. Do differences of physical and spatial representation and experience in the constitution of the global digital space exist? These differences may be a hint that global space is not transnational and transcultural, but constructed by cultural particularities. Moreover, what is the cultural signification of these concurring inscriptions for our life in digital spaces?

Motion capture technology in the field of performing art is especially interesting for an understanding of the interplay of technological standards and cultural and discursive inscriptions in the constitution of concepts of space in a digital culture. There is possibly even a third reason to analyze the use of motion capture in dance in Europe and the USA. Although there are fundamental differences in the use of motion capture, which arise from the cultural inscriptions into the universal technology of digital media, could it be that both approaches focus on similar intentions and effects? Does it suffice to connect the human to the digital—that it becomes a globality in the sense of 'the-best-for-all–humans—in order to legitimize cultural ownership in the digital space?

To understand more about the strategies of adapting the digital physically and about the power of cultural inscriptions into the technical global, we have to focus on the globalization of cultural ownership in the digital space, that is, we have to look at a concrete example. I have chosen two examples that should clarify the fundamental difference between European and American versions of a global digital space.

Time Lapses in Europe: Nik Haffner and Bernd Lintermann

Since 1999, the German artists Nik Haffner and Bernd Lintermann have experimented with motion capture in their project "Time Lapses" at the Zentrum für Kunst und Medientechnologie (ZKM) in Karlsruhe, Germany [ill. 039].[7] Haffner and Lintermann use Polhemus, a technology that determines the precise position of the body in space and its direction in space in a electromagnetic field by attaching sensors to the body.[8]

In their research, Haffner and Lintermann are mainly interested in the differences between movement in physical and in digital space, that is, they do not look for a direct representation of the body; they rather support the idea that the digital can detect and translate the physical in terms of one-to-one correspondences. Movements of the

---

7 For more information on "Time Lapses," see Nik Haffner and Bernd Lintermann at www.zkm.de.
8 For more information on the used wireless motion capture technology, see "Polhemus."

body in physical space are thereby transformed into abstract parameters like flow, direction, or the amount of movement in their digital representations. Digital calculations are used to interpret qualities of movement that cannot even be perceived without technical support.

In their work, the dancer moves in relation to her/his digitally-based representation on a projection screen; audiences simultaneously observe, in real time, the dancer's movements and her/his transformation on the monitor or projection screen. Aesthetically, Haffner and Lintermann focus on the processual aspects between dancer and technology; by refusing to present a finished work, they turn the creative process itself into a work of art. Haffner identifies four questions that guide their research: Are body, movement and dance perceived and defined differently in real space as opposed to digital space? Can the movement of a dancer disconnect from the physical body? How can the movement of the body be represented visually and what happens at the intersection, even confrontation, of real dance and digital dance?[9]

Haffner further describes two basic approaches: In the first work, a video-camera detects the dancer's movements, and the video-image of the dancer is projected onto a screen. Haffner is dancing with only one sensor activated on his body which shows as a distinct area in the video. This area can be manipulated by certain movements because, in the defined area, a computer program transforms parameters of space and time into, for example, the extension of time in graphical segments or the deformation of the video-image. This process sharply distinguishes the digitally produced part of the video-image from the unaltered, real video-image. Haffner appears to dance with his own mirror-image, transforming it by moving. During the experiment, the digitally-operated representation of the body gradually gains more independence: even when the dancer does not move, the video-image performs certain action, turns around, etc., and acquires a certain degree of agency by itself. In addition, Haffner dances often with his back to the audience thereby underlining the impression that it is a dance with a mirror (the public is looking over the shoulder of Haffner to the mirror video-image).

---

9   Haffner, "Time Lapses. Ein Motion Capture Projekt von Bernd Lintermann und Nik Haffner" 523–524.

Digital Bodies in Digital Spaces

The second project emphasizes the graphical representation of the dancer's movement as a delayed trace in the digitally-generated graphical representation. By capturing the movement, Haffner claims, an architectonic graver of the movement is created in physical space, thus visualizing the memory of movement in the digitally operated space. Dancer and computer-artist collaborate in this project and experiment with the program's inherent possibilities to extend, fragment, duplicate, and combine different layers of graphical representations of movement.

Haffner's and Lintermann's work thus focuses on aspects of connection and independence between movement in physical space and its representation as traces in digital space. Ultimately, their intention is to create a dance "in-between" physical dancer and digitally-generated traces, that is 'in-between' the gaps of physical movement and its real-time generated representations on screen. Seen this way, the dancer has to deal with two bodies and spaces via what could be called an "in-between body" in an "in-between space."

Spacing the Digital in the Far West: Merce Cunningham and Paul Kaiser/Shelley Eshkar

In 1999, the American computer artists Paul Kaiser and Shelley Eshkar created digital figures of dancers for *Biped*, a choreography by Merce Cunningham.[10] The figures were projected on stage during a given performance. They were created from data produced by a motion capture of choreographed sequences of movements performed by the dancers of the company in a motion capture studio during the performance. The digital representations of the body were always recognizable as outlines of a human *gestalt*, even if they transformed to mere moving sticks or circles. Floated in an undefined space, these figures lacked boundaries known from traditional concepts of physical space such as bottom or top [ill. 040]. Contrary to the work of Haffner and Lintermann, actors in *Biped* had no interactive access to these figures.

---

10 At that time, Kaiser and Eshkar worked under the name "riverbed." For works by Paul Kaiser, see www.kaiserworks.com. On Merce Cunningham, see www.merce.org.

In *Biped* the dancers moved behind a transparent tissue made of gauze. This partly concealed the action on stage, made it deliberately unclear. The dancers wear shining costumes reflecting the spotlights. The interplay of the transparent tissue, the shining costumes, and the lighting design question well-defined boundaries between the space and floor and instead create a space seemingly without borders. This space appears fragmented, created by chance out of an unlimited, somehow cosmic space, without bottom or top. The dancers almost miraculously appear and disappear on stage, emerging from nowhere because the limits of the stage could no longer be recognized. This lent the dancers an air of floating, without a physical connection to the floor, and beyond restrictions of gravity.

During the performance the motion capture figures were projected on tissues, fixed all over the stage. Thus the figures acquired a three-dimensional presence as they appeared both in the front as well as in the back of the stage. As vision is trained by linear perspective, these places in space signify rational proportions of depth and can be decoded as three-dimensional appearances. Paul Kaiser argued in an interview that, for him, the performance is successful precisely when the spectator are no longer able to tell apart the dancers from the motion captured figures, that is, if the spectator confounds both as equal inhabitants of one digital space.[11]

The Human Invasion of Digital Space: American vs. European Dreams

It seems as if motion capture technology is yet unable to solve the problem of entering digital spaces with the human body. Human agents can enter digital space such as the Internet, however, they are not physically present in these spaces. Motion capture technology mainly explores two approaches to the human invasion into digital space and offers probate strategies to investigate the doubling of the body in digitally-based telematic operations.

The work of Haffner and Lintermann is characterized by the attempt to interpret the digital and the relation between the human and

---

11 Interview with Kaiser in the film *Merce Cunningham. Une Vie de Dance* by Charles Atlas.

the digital as performative, with the underlying implication that the digital is defined as a self-regulated and self-organized performance. The basic relationship is that of exchange between dancer and digital representation, emphasizing the dynamic processes of the exchange and strengthening their performative quality. The performative quality is defined by temporality: the unrepeatable and non-fixable status of action as event. The performance itself thus becomes increasingly important, acting is conceived of as doing, that is, as a contingent event in space and time. What is more, the performance becomes the focal point in the digitally-supported graphical representation of the body. This performance is contingent on the visualization of human movement as traces, as something that disappears while appearing, that continually formalizes time without fixing it to a definitive shape. Also the relation between the digital and the human is shown as performative, that is, it is temporary, fluid, and contingent. The relation between the human and the digital becomes one of formalization and administration of time. Haffner and Lintermann convey the impression that a relationship between physical space and body and their digital representations is possible mainly because both follow the same law: that of performativity as a form of time-management.

Haffner claims to strive for the independence of the digital, that it may eventually create a performance of its own. Digital technology then acts as an autonomous mirror of the human performance. Technology can thus no longer be conceived as the medium of an imaginary self-representation (as in Lacan's mirror stage). On the contrary, it becomes its own imaginary, an imaginary technology.

Haffner and Lintermann create digital space as a kind of medium for a more thorough investigation of the human, based on the idea that the digital can show aspects unseen in non-technological environments. What is more, they make clear that the human and the digital are two separate worlds, with the digital acting as an autonomous mirror. The translation of the human into digitally-supported graphical representations also refers to a particular tradition of electronic formalization of human movement, namely, the experiments of Duchenne in the 19th century. When the emergent electro- and neurophysiology discovered electricity as an intrinsic part of both human being and electric appliances, facial muscles contracted by using alternating current; at the same time, the soul, formerly used as differentiating human being, animals, and machine, then came to be replaced by an uncontrollable unconscious of media and machines.[12] In contrast, the relation between the human and the formalized is modified in the digital era. They are no longer similar, but are seen as the outer points of reference of an "in-between-system" which defines the human as performative, as an continuing dynamics of change and temporality. The digital space as a kind of an exteriorized memory of movement is no longer a seismograph of human activities, but the relay of permanent change. The relation between physical body and space and their digital counterparts is one of exchange, of the constitution of an "in-between-system" of permanent translation and modification without any relation to ontological representations. In many ways, this expresses Derrida's concepts of "différance" and "iteration;"[13] the relationship between the body and its digital representation is as arbitrary as that between signifier and signified. The body leaves traces in digital space, but it lacks an origin because the recorded body vanishes precisely in the moment when its trace is discovered. Haffner's and Lintermann's performance thus become a continuous displacement of sense and referentiality. The digital becomes in a forum of memory, beyond the boundaries of three-dimensional materiality.

By referring the physical body and space to the digital, the digital, vice versa, also relates to the physical: without seeing the movements of the dancer, the origins of the graphical representations will remain unclear. It is, after all, physical movement that defines the graphical user interface (GUI). The digital operations are not marked as space, but as place which turns "dancing the digital" into an effort to make the physical a fluid, liquid, movable, changeable, contingent process instead of a fixed and resistible reality.

Cunningham's and Kaiser's/Eshkar's approach to digital space differs decisively from the above. Whereas Haffner and Lintermann refer to digital representations of the physical body as an autonomous mirror, Cunningham and Kaiser/Eshkar try to integrate the human body directly into the digital. When Haffner and Lintermann aim at the invasion of the digital by exploring a digitally-based language of human

---

12 See also Hans Christian von Herrmann, "Beseelte Statuen—zuckende Leichen. Medien der Verlebendigung vor und nach Guillaume Benjamin Duchenne" 66-98.
13 See Derrida, *Schrift und die Differenz* and *Grammatologie*. For a short introduction, see Münker/Roesler 36–49.

movement, Cunningham seems to spatialize two-dimensional graphical interfaces of digital operations as the Internet or virtual realities in which the human body is already integrated.

Haffner and Lintermann show the process of exchange. Cunningham and Kaiser/Eshkar avoid the exchange. The figures are prepared and projected as fixed images. The effects of technology are hidden in order to functionalize it as a means of expanding the limited physical space. Technology is proposed as an extension of the human body into a digital space. In this way technology proffers the imagination of a anti-terrestrial existence of the human, an angelic existence beyond the laws and limitations of gravity and, perhaps most crucially, death.

Quite similar to Haffner and Lintermann, Cunningham and Kaiser/Eshkar define the digital space as performative, in the sense that it is an event existing only in performance. The image of the digital space remains unclear, though, it can be limited or unlimited, human or digital, real or virtual, and, at the same time, being never only one or the other.

In many ways, Cunningham's and Kaiser's/Eshkar's work acquires a spiritual dimension, evoking the notion of immortality. This may be due to the representation of the digital in a three-dimensional space or to the complete transformation of the physical into the digital. The concept of digital space, in their work, seems to aspire to a dream of a life in harmony with the universe, integrated in flows of energy, information, and magnetic organization. Whereas the European dream, represented by Haffner and Lintermann, is one of performative exchange and iteration, the American version is characterized by performative illustration and illusion.

Performativity and Hybrid Identities in the Digital Era: Human Metaphors of the Digital since the 1990s

The emphasis on performativity since the mid-1990s differs considerably from the approach to the digital at the time of the introduction of the computer and its invention as mass-media in the 1980s. First, the concept of the separation of the physical from the digital, the material from the immaterial, and the real from the virtual that was characteristic of the anti-media as propagated by Jean Baudrillard,[14] is surpassed and has been replaced by an interrelationship which proves that mutual benefit and exchange is possible. There may not be an overlap of virtual realities, but a co-existence of different realities and experiences, as in Haffner's and Lintermann's work. Second, attempts to connect the body more or less directly to the digital, as, for instance, by devices such as data gloves and data helmets, are increasingly seen as a thing of the past. Today the physical and the virtual are conceived as two worlds that interrelate by translations, with the translation being always caught in a process of transformation (see Haffner/Lintermann). Cunningham seems to still work along the lines of immersion into the digital by connecting both spheres more or less directly. The contemporary approach, however, is predominantly marked by illusion. That is to say, Cunningham does not try to achieve the connection by technological means. He does not even look for a digital real-time operation in a given live-performance. He focuses, rather, on a mental training that will eventually lead towards a performative worldview—trained physically, so to speak, by the gauze-tissue which keeps the spectators' gaze from seeing and thinking clearly—as in cybernetic feedback-systems.

The question thus arises, where does this shift, or so-called "performative turn," come from?[15] Needless to say that this essay can only provisionally answer such a complex and contested question. The shift can also be understood in terms of an interruption of the electronic-cybernetic era (from the mid-1940s to the end of the 1980s) which is marked by the invention of the computer as a universal machine, based on a self-regulated feedback-system. In the mid-1940s binary computers were connected with cybernetic epistemology, according to which all areas of science follow the same patterns of information, feedback, and Boolean algebra.[16] This connection is based on the belief that neuronal interactions follow principles of logic and are thus

---

14 See, for instance, Baudrillard's concept of simulation and simulacra that defines the digital era as characterized by a loss of reality and physicality. See Baudrillard, *Agonie des Realen*.
15 For a detailed discussion of the "performative turn," see Erika Fischer-Lichte, *Ästhetik des Performativen* esp. 29, and Sybille Krämer, "Sprache—Stimme—Schrift: Sieben Gedanken über Performativität als Medialität" 323-346.
16 See Pias, "Elektronenhirn und verbotene Zone. Zur kybernetischen Ökonomie des Digitalen" esp. 296.

analogous and transferable to the "electronic brain" of a computer. Norbert Wiener's theories of feedback were influential to the development of this relationship between analog and digital operations. According to this theory, behavior is based on information theory processes, i.e. on differences and probabilities that can be measured discontinuously. What living beings and machines ultimately share is that they constantly produce their own signals and then feed them back into the system without any need for outside input. Eventually, Pias observes, a "hard" illusionary digitalization of analog processes succeeds despite severe doubts by Wiener, von Neumann, and a number of others.[17]

In the late 1980s, with the invention and cultural integration of graphical user interfaces (GUI), the metaphor of the human-machine feedback-system becomes more and more obsolete and is replaced by the metaphor of the performative digital. This new orientation is accompanied by a fundamental change in media theories and shed critical light on Marshall McLuhan's thesis of media as an extension and augmentation of the human.[18] McLuhan's approach to media seems contingent on an electronic worldview, but does no longer seem to capture the digital period. The electro-electronic world is analog and deals with calculable frequencies, waves, and amplitudes. The digital is, in contrast to the analog, symbolic and discrete, that is to say self-sufficient, without relation to yet other categories. By the end of the 1980s, the digital also seems to express the disappointment of dreams about man-machine-interaction or augmentation of human facilities by, for example, robots in projects of Artificial Intelligence. I would argue that the turn or shift in the performing arts as well as in other cultural fields to project the relation man-machine as performative is the strategy to deal with the non-human digital. It is based on the idea that the digital needs to be defined as performative which then enables its adoption to human performances, as can be seen in the above examples.

---

17 For more information on this debate, see Pias, *Cybernetics–Kybernetik*. For a critical critique, see Pias also, "Elektronenhirn" 295–310; and Hagen, *Die Camouflage der Kybernetik*.
18 "In the sense that these media are extension of ourselves—of man—then my interest in them is utterly humanistic. All theses technologies and the mechanisms they create are profoundly human," in Marshall McLuhan and Quentin Fiore, "Even Hercules Had to Clean Out the Augean Stables but Once" 294.

These examples demonstrate that there is no analog translation between digital and live performances. They rather engage metaphors of the digital and the body in digital spaces. Haffner and Lintermann are working on a graphic level, unaffected by digital operations. The only connecting point between the digital and the analog is time: the time to calculate—what becomes finally real time—and the time to move. Every operation in the computer needs time to produce the graphical image on the connected surfaces. Haffner and Lintermann cling to this approach even when they propose performativity as the center of digital space. Hence, the traces of Haffner's movements represent not so much insights in the translating processes between the digital and the human; they are rather a brilliant, perhaps intuitive visualization of a possibility to connect human and digital phenomena.

Cunningham adheres to the principles of illusion. He materializes a human dream or desire on stage: the angle-like existence, beyond age, gender, sex and pains, a floating existence. Additionally, he designs a physical impact of his performance: the illusion of putting oneself and situations at risk. The confrontation with Cunningham's *Bipeds* is risky precisely because it intrigues perception and traditional patterns of signification. We are confronted with hybrids in an environment that is also hybridized, never clear, always looking for frontiers. Cunningham thus spiritualizes the digital in a hybrid way: First, as an emergency exit out of a painful life into the digital by presenting the digital as a holy-gnostic universe and, second, as a new gauze-covered hybrid perspective on life, re-shaping the digital to develop a hybrid consciousness. In contrast to Haffner and Lintermann, there is no technical connection in Cunningham, but a mental or spiritual one.

Invading the Digital with Human Properties and Occupying the Digital with Old Dreams

To conclude, I would like to point out that the proposed differences between the European and the American approach to digital bodies and spaces are only first observations that would, ideally, inspire further research. In this sense, it should be fruitful to analyze, in a critical historical and cultural reconstruction and contextualization, the diverse traditions and discourses of body and space that feed into contemporary concepts of the digital. Both of the above discussed approaches can be analyzed as strategies of adaptation and of control over the non-human, digital space. It remains to be asked in which ways the intersection between traditional discourses and contemporary technologies facilitates the possibility to control the digital by invading it with human properties. Is there still an American dream of an unlimited space in digital spaces, which is, then, at the same time limited by the older tradition of presenting the digital as human? Is there still a European dream of geometric and calculated spaces in digital space that, although it exists beyond physical experience, offers the security of a non-contingent mathematical reconstruction beyond the unbearable changes of their performance?

As a second hypothesis I would suggest that both concepts of the performative digital represent strategies to occupy the digital and to make it one's own by cultural inscriptions. What does it then mean for the constitution of a digital existence to be confronted with two different concepts of digital bodies and spaces in a globally accessible environment? Further research should follow both directions and integrate them on a physio-technological level by exploring a system of time based on translations between the analog human and the digital as well as investigate the spiritual dimensions by hybridizing perception and mentality. If it were possible to show that both approaches are part of important cultural techniques and practices, then it could be researched in which ways they concur, or support each other. Could it not be possible that a definition of the human-digital relationship as a time-operation in fact needs a hybrid mentality? As the performative is contingent, pure change, it could be a functional strategy to use time calculation and manipulation as a way of formalizing vanishing existences. In what way could European and American attempts to occupy digital spaces concur? Will there be ownership of the Internet as the future ground for business and information/surveillance? Is there a chance that the angelic dream of life, as displayed by Cunningham's choreographies, could be stronger than calculations of formats and standards of times? The latter could possible occupy the digital as exterior memory of the human; but the first one could become a religious vision.

Works Cited

Baudrillard, Jean. *Agonie des Realen*. Berlin: Merve, 1978.
Derrida, Jacques. *Grammatologie*. Frankfurt: Suhrkamp, 1983.
—. *Die Schrift und die Differenz*. Frankfurt: Suhrkamp, 1976.
Fischer-Lichte, Erika. *Ästhetik des Performativen*. Frankfurt: Suhrkamp, 2004.
Haffner, Nik. "Time Lapses. Ein Motion Capture Projekt von Bernd Lintermann und Nik Haffner." *Tanz, Theorie, Text*. Ed. Gabriele Klein and Christa Zipprich. Hamburg: Lit-Verlag, 2002. 523–532.
Hagen, Wolfgang. "Die Camouflage der Kybernetik." 30.11.2004. www.w.hagen.de.
Herrmann, Hans-Christian von. "Beseelte Statuen—zuckende Leichen. Medien der Verlebendigung vor und nach Guillaume Benjamin Duchenne." *Körperinformationen*, Ed. Barbara Büscher, Hans Christian von Herrmann, and Susanne Holl. *Kaleidoskopien* 3 (2000): 66- 98.
"Interview with Paul Kaiser about *Biped*." *Merce Cunningham. Une Vie de Dance*, a film by Charles Atlas. La Sept, ARTE, INA, Thirteen/WNET New York, BBC, NPS, 2000.
Kerckhove, Derrick de. "Eine Mediengeschichte des Theaters." *Maschinen, Medien, Performances. Theater an der Schnittstelle zu digitalen Welten*. Ed. Martina Leeker. Berlin: Alexander Verlag, 2001. 501–525.
Krämer, Sybille. "Sprache—Stimme—Schrift: Sieben Gedanken über Performativität als Medialität." *Performanz. Zwischen Sprachwissenschaft und Kulturwissenschaft*. Ed. Uwe Wirth. Frankfurt: Suhrkamp, 2002. 323–346.
McLuhan, Marshall. *Die magischen Kanäle*. (Orig. *Understanding Media*) Düsseldorf/Wien: Verlag der Kunst, 1964.
McLuhan, Marshall, and Quentin Fiore. "Even Hercules Had to Clean Out the Augean Stables but Once." Ed. Gerald E. Stearn. *McLuhan: Hot and Cold—A Critical Symposium*. New York: The Dial Press, 1967. 266- 302.
Münker, Stefan, and Alexander Roesler. *Poststrukturalismus*. Stuttgart: Metzler, 2000. 36–49.
Pias, Claus. "Elektronenhirn und verbotene Zone. Zur kybernetischen Ökonomie des Digitalen." *Analog/Digital—Opposition oder Kontinuum. Zur Theorie und Geschichte einer Unterscheidung*. Ed. Jens Schröter, and Alexander Böhnke. Bielefeld: transcript, 2004. 295–310.
Pias, Claus, ed. *Cybernetics–Kybernetik. The Macy Conferences 1946–1953*. 2 vols. Zürich: Diaphanes, 2003.
Turkle, Sherry. *Identitäten im Netz. Identitäten in Zeiten des Internet*. Reinbek: Rowohlt, 1998.
Wiener, Norbert. *Cybernetics or Control and Communication in the Animal and the Machine*. Cambridge: MIT, 1948.

Webpages:
"Dance-tech-list." www.dance.ohio-state.edu/Dance_and_Technology/. 30. Nov. 2004.
"Dance-tech-list." www.art.net/~dtz. 30. Nov. 2004.
"LifeForms: Animation Software." www.CharacterMotion.com. 30. Nov. 2004.
"Merce Cunningham." www.merce.org. 30. Nov. 2004.
"Nik Haffner, Bernd Lintermann." Zentrum für Kunst und Medientechnologie. www.zkm.de. 30. Nov. 2004.
"Paul Kaiser." www.kaiserworks.com. 30. Nov. 2004.
"Polhemus: Wireless Motion Capture Technology." www.polhemus.com. 30. Mov. 2004.
"Poser: Animation Software." www.curiouslabs.com. 30. Nov. 2004.

Slow Spaces. Remarks on the Music of John Cage

Julia Kursell and Armin Schäfer

> "find ways of using instruments as though they were tools [...]. That's precisely what our tape-recorders, amplifiers, microphones, photo-electric cells, etc., are: things to be used which don't necessarily determine the nature of what is done."
>
> John Cage, *A Year from Monday* 123-124

John Cage liberated composition from its European tradition. He did so by introducing random operations, attributing a new function to silence, determining a composition's exact duration, and by allowing the performer a particular individuation. Thus, he redefined the relation between musical media—recordings, performances, and symbolic code. Music is neither a mere enacting of a notation, nor is the score simply an auxiliary device preceding the sounds. The same score can be played in so many ways that no recording may be considered the only valid presentation of a piece: "although people think they can use records as music they will have to understand that they have to use them as records" (Cage, qtd. in Kostelanetz 164).

The sound of Cage's music is never inert. The properties of a sound are never adopted by the following one. Accordingly, the sounds cannot be described by parameters, such as pitch, duration, articulation or loudness. The music is neither built along the rules of counterpoint and harmony, or even serialism, nor does it result from the composer's imposition of a form. Sounds follow sounds and line up to sequences, and it seems as if this could go on for any time, as if the piece could last twice or half as long, because the music lacks an organizing principle. There are no melodies or motifs and no coercive finalizing force; instead, there is only a stream of sounds resisting synthesis. The basic relation of the sounds in Cage's music is contiguity. The individual parts never constitute a whole. In these loosely coupled sound sequences, that may be interrupted at any moment or last any time, the only possible transition from sound to sound is effected by the listener's perception or association (cf. Erdmann). Yet the loose coupling should not be understood as arbitrariness, randomness, or chaos. There is a multiplicity—manifoldness instead of unity, juxtaposition instead of the blending of sounds, parts instead of wholes; this multiplicity results from an appositional increase, a growth that does not aim at organic unity. Sound is not added to sound, nor can the successor of a sound be predicted: Nothing indicates how to move from sound to sound, nothing can explain why a particular sound follows the other. But still, this music has astonishing effects because it sets free an anaesthetic perception of sound. This perception derives from a consciousness of time related to the experience of slow spaces.

*

Traditional music privileges the symbolic code: A "true" musical expert would not listen to music performed, but read the score. The audibility of a sound, as Thrasybulos Georgiades has pointed out, is no more characteristic of the specific musical phenomenon than its occurrence in space. And to read music, as Adorno puts it, means to listen to an inner theater of musical ideas, i.e. of tones. Listeners should be taught, he wrote, "to imagine music by the help of the inner ear as concretely and precisely as if it was bodily present sound" (103; our translation).[1] The symbolic code of music not only has the power to dominate the performance, recordings, and even the imagination, it also produces its own musical time. If a composition is written in the traditional symbolic code and is meant to be performed, it develops a performance-specific time, because its duration, tempo and temporal proportions may change. While Herbert von Karajan conducts Bee-

---

1 See also Karl Popper and John Eccles: "A musical composition has a very strange sort of existence. Certainly it at first exists encoded in the musician's head, but it will probably not even exist there as a totality, but, rather, as a sequence of efforts or attempts; and whether the composer does or does not retain a total score of the composition in his memory is in a sense not really essential to the question of the existence of the composition once it has been written down. But the written-down encoding is not identical with the composition—say, a symphony. For the symphony is something acoustic and the written-down encoding is obviously merely conventionally and arbitrarily related to the acoustic ideas which this written down encoding tries to incorporate and to bring into a more stable and lasting form" (449).

thoven's 9th symphony in d minor, op 125, in 74 minutes, it takes John Eliot Gardiner only 59 minutes. Although performances and recordings of the very same piece may differ greatly, there is a cohesion related to the type of the musical time of the piece.

As Boulez suggested it is possible to distinguish between two types of musical time: striated and smooth time. When music is organized by a constant pulse, it produces striated time, and when it is characterized by events and by soundplanes or blocks, it can be called smooth time. Striated time evolves from chronometrical time: it cuts marks or striae into time, as if the music were superimposed on empty time and laid out in an empty, yet dimensioned space. While the pulse of striated time divides temporal continuity into measurable, regular or irregular intervals, music characterized by soundplanes or blocks can be considered a mere succession of acoustic events with no distinguishable marks.

Striated time allows changing the structure of the music without abandoning its temporal cohesion: new elements can interfere, and the intervals between elements can change proportionally. In smooth time, however, no elements can be moved, as Boulez explains:

> Let's assume that a perfectly smooth surface and a regularly or irregularly—this does not matter—striated surface are disposed under a line of reference; when moved, the perfectly smooth surface will not allow us to grasp the speed or the direction of the movement, because the eye does not find any reference to which it can adhere; the movement of the striated surface, on the contrary, will appear immediately in its speed and in its direction. (100; our translation)

This distinction between striated time and smooth time was adopted by Gilles Deleuze and Félix Guattari: "the striated is that which intertwines fixed and variable elements, produces an order and succession of distinct forms, and organizes horizontal melodic lines and vertical harmonic planes. The smooth is the continuous variation, continuous development of form" (*A Thousand Plateaus* 478).

Striated time is based on one or a multitude of metric manifolds. The system's elements are countable and measurable; they can be compared and their properties determined; they may be combined into moveable units. Non-metric multiplicities, however, as they appear in smooth time, do not share a common measure, because smooth time can only be experienced as duration: "A time which is not pulsed confronts us, first of all, with a presence of heterochronic, non-coincident and qualitative durations" (Deleuze, "Pourquoi nous" n.p.). The metric multiplicity calls forth an elastic temporal cohesion that we shall call "the band." This band relates the performances of classical music. The symbolic code of the score produces an elastic band that connects the varieties of performances of one piece. The striated time of music guarantees the translatability of the different media of music, while smooth time threatens to tear up the band and thus the cohesion of these media. It does so, for instance, in the music of Morton Feldman (1926-1987), where symbolic code, performance, and recorded music drift apart, or in the music of Conlon Nancarrow (1912-1997), where the three media of music (recording, performance, score) fall into one. Feldman, like Nancarrow, composes pieces in which striated time is smoothed. In contrast to the multiple serialism of Boulez and Karlheinz Stockhausen, who tend to smooth tonal space by applying an ever finer matrix, defining parameters for the sounds and arranging their sequence according to a statistical distribution, Feldman and Nancarrow compose non-metric multiplicities, that is, their music may have definite pitches that follow the rules of counterpoint without co-ordination by a pulse.

Based on the experience that two musical instruments are never identical in tone and articulation, Feldman developed his so-called free durations (Claren 70-75). In his piano composition *Last Pieces* (1959) neither bars nor rhythm are written down. The notation specifies tempo and articulation, but the instructions accompanying the four pieces read "Durations are free" and, as for the fourth piece, even "Durations are free for each hand" (4). Additionally, the duration of sound is not prescribed, thereby lending a specific temporality to Feldman's music. In some of Feldmans compositions, as, for instance, in *Crippled Symmetry* (1983), a piece for flute/base flute, percussion, and piano/celesta, the temporal coordination of parts is weakened, if not given up. The three parts in *Crippled Symmetry* do not follow a shared pulse, but move independently from tone to tone. This is also why a recording of the piece requires a complete performance. As Feldman explains,

> Crippled Symmetry is conceived like a recording on tape or vinyl, which cannot be cut. That's why it cannot be spliced. [...] There is no splicing. It is written like a recording and like a performance, as well: it has to work out completely, otherwise ... If I recorded Crippled

Symmetry, we would have to play it through one or two times, at most, and then take the better version. ("Middleburg-Lecture" 11)

Classical music, by contrast, was recorded by cutting and splicing, thereby creating a patch work of "well-done" pieces. This was possible because the score coordinated the parts and prescribed a common pulse of striated time. The musical score of *Crippled Symmetry*, however, does not determine the temporal co-ordination of its parts, and therefore it does not allow a silent reading. Notation and performance are strictly separated by a difference of media. Since each part will be played in a different tempo, there are no identical performances. Furthermore, the performers interact with each other and occasionally change the tempo of their playing.

Feldman's music is not supported by striated time: there is no score that would prescribe when to set a mark; rather, the marks are produced in the performer's individual consciousness or, more precisely, in the spontaneous co-ordination of individual times. The performer's individual time is not coordinated by a presupposed pulse (as in a notation); rather, the individual times of the performers co-ordinate themselves.[2] A specific musical time in which the present can be experienced as stretched emerges from the feedback between the different individual times. The simultaneity of the playing does not reside in an exact coordination of the parts, rather, their coordination occurs in expanded simultaneity (cf. Schaffer 115-145). This musical time is both striated, since a pulse may be noticed in a single part, and smooth, because the next mark is often unpredictable. Feldman does not compose a single elastic band of time, but three bands, coordinated solely in a given performance. They are entangled in unpredictable ways and fixed in their specific extensions. Since the performer's feedback is crucial, a separate recording of the parts is impossible; without this feedback, the bands would lose their flexibility and fail to interconnect.

While Feldman stretches the band by interlacing the different time-bands, Conlon Nancarrow introduces a machine-readable band. In his cycle of compositions called *Studies for Player Piano* he fol-

---

2   Cage says in a conversation with Feldman: "[...] well, what it actually is that you're interested in is what superimposes what. What happens at the same time together with what happens before and what happens after" (*Radio Happenings* 13).

lowed an idea by Henry Cowell, who suggested using the player piano for the invention of complex rhythmical forms in his 1930 book *New Musical Resources*:

> Some of the rhythms developed through the present acoustical investigation could not be played by any living performer; but these highly engrossing rhythmical complexes could easily be cut on a player-piano roll. This would give a real reason for writing music especially for player-piano, such as music written for it at present does not seem to have, because almost any of it could be played instead by two good pianists at the keyboard. (Cowell 64-65)

Nancarrow does not compose for human beings. Number and sequence of notes is beyond the physical and cognitive capacities of the pianist: "Nancarrow's complete works could be heard in seven hours, but within half that time the listener would be as exhausted as though he had consumed Mahler's ten symphonies in a gulp" (Gann 3).[3] He himself produces the rolls for his piano: "When I punch," he explains the process, "I have what I call a punching score, which no one can read, [...] I need it for punching, and while doing so I correct the occasional mistake I made when printing, and only after that I write a score for people" (qtd. in Amirkhanian 39; our translation). This paper roll then runs at a constant speed in the player piano, which will play the punched notation invariably in the same mode. Also, the player piano eliminates subtle inconsistencies of tempo that characterize performances by a human pianist. No human performer has the cognitive capacity to perform the required frequency of touches—sometimes their number per second (!) exceeds a hundred. The deviation from temporal exactness typical of human performance and generally considered a sign of the player's individuality is thus effaced. The elastic band used by traditional interpretation is replaced by a machine-made time, organized by asynchronic layers. By the same token, rhythmic proportions such as 1 to square root of 2 or 60 to 61 are easily constructed on the paper role. This machine-made time does not depend on a coordination of pulse and does not require an individualized consciousness of time. In *Studies for Player Piano,* the multiplicities can neither be

---

3   Gann continues: "Within a three-minute study Nancarrow often fits a mass of notes that would have sufficed Liszt for a twenty-five minute sonata. Study No. 36, for example, is under five minutes, but its score is fifty-two pages black with ink" (3).

changed nor moved, and, although their elements can be counted on paper, the listener would not be able to detect rules of counterpoint or identify forms according to which these multiplicities are organized.

*

In classical music sounds obey a logic of representation, that is, a given letter designates a particular sound and vice versa.[4] Rather than understand music as an expression of metric multiplicity, Cage and Feldman use sounds that refuse to act as representatives or substitutes. Herein they followed Edgar Varèse: "[...] whatever sounds you hear, you know he really meant them. They're not substitutes for some other sounds. Most composers of his time wrote first for piano and then just colored it. But he didn't do that. He was using the sounds that he was using" (*Radio Happenings* 111). If sounds are no longer grounded in traditional counterpoint, harmony, or aesthetic forms, and no longer point to anything other than themselves, they have to be freed from the chains of aesthetic perception and alienated into non-resemblance.

Whereas in Varèse's music, sounds that cannot be described in terms of pitch, duration, articulation, and dynamics, are produced by orchestra and electronic instruments, Cage works with traditional notation and instruments that have to be released from the band of metrics, should they appear in smooth time. He composes for piano, an instrument that started its career as a substitute for other instruments. It was used as a tool in composition, where the simplification of the score was noted in an abridged "particell," and it was an instrument for reproduction, bringing the music otherwise played in concert hall or opera house into people's homes by means of a piano score (Wellmer 135).

From the very beginning, Cage had been unhappy with a music that recognizes only tones as its basis:

---

[4] Cage explains: "Before studying music, men are men and sounds are sounds. When studying music things aren't clear. After studying music men are men and sounds are sounds. That is to say: at the beginning one can hear a sound and tell immediately that it isn't a human being or something to look at. [...] While studying music things get a little confused. Sounds are no longer just sounds but are letters: A, B, C, D, E, F, G... If a sound is unfortunate enough not to have a letter or if it seems to be a complex, it is tossed out of the system" (*A Year* 96).

> Wherever we are, what we hear is mostly noise. When we ignore it, it disturbs us. When we listen to it, we find it fascinating. The sound of a truck at fifty miles per hour. Static between the stations. Rain. We want to capture and control these sounds, to use them not as sound effects but as musical instruments. ("Future" 5)

For the first time, he alienated the sound of the piano in his compositions for prepared piano in such a way that touches do not produce tones, but noise, and the piano thus reveals its nature as a percussive instrument. This noise escapes the frequency relations of tonality, and, simultaneously, questions the distinction between tone and noise, a distinction that has troubled psychology and acoustics since the nineteenth century.

"Sounds may be classed," writes John William Strutt, 3rd Baron Rayleigh, in his *Theory of Sound*,

> as musical and unmusical; the former for convenience may be called *notes* and the latter *noises*. The extreme cases will raise no dispute; every one recognizes the difference between the note of a pianoforte and the creaking of a shoe. But it is not so easy to draw the line of separation. In the first place few notes are free from all unmusical accompaniment. With organ pipes especially, the hissing of the wind as it escapes at the mouth may be heard beside the proper note of the pipe. And, secondly, many noises so far partake of a musical character as to have a definite pitch. [...] But, although noises are sometimes not entirely unmusical, and notes are usually not quite free from noise, there is no difficulty in recognizing which of the two is the simpler phenomenon. There is a certain smoothness and continuity about the musical note. Moreover by sounding together a variety of notes—for example, by striking simultaneously a number of consecutive keys on a pianoforte—we obtain an approximation to a noise; while no combination of noises could ever blend into a musical note. (4)

Even if the sound of a shoe and the sound of a piano were the same, the latter is, in contradistinction to the sound of the shoe, capable to be a representation of some other sound. Tonal sensations resulting from the perception of periodic and regular vibrations can only gradually be distinguished from noise sensations effected by the perception of a-periodic vibrations. Notably, even complicated periodic vibrations produce noise (see Stumpf 513). Thus the keys of the prepared piano separate the noise and sounds they produce from the order of striated space. They interrupt not only the connection of key and pitch, but sever the sounds from striated space-time as well.

Instead of manipulating the strings of a piano, in *Music of Changes* (1951), Cage uses a new device for alienating the sound of the piano and disengaging it from the function of being a representative: the succession of sounds and their properties now follow random decisions. To this purpose, he draws charts that contain the sounds and operations available for the particular composition. In some ways, these charts follow the principle of the prepared piano, i.e. they equal noise and tones, as Cage explains in "To Describe the Process of Composition Used in *Music of Changes* and *Imaginary Landscape No. 4*": "The sounds themselves are single, aggregates (cf. the accord sometimes obtained on a prepared piano when only one key is depressed), or complex situations (constellations) in time (cf. the Chinese characters made with several strokes)" (58). Similar to a Chinese character that consists of several syllables or different signs, the charts can contain sounds composed of a single tone, a tone complex or noise (Chao 448). In a letter to Pierre Boulez, Cage explains this new composition process by comparing it to a family structure: "each square of the chart [can] be taken as the (at that moment) visible member of a large family of sounds" ("18 December 1950" 78). Even though the sound charts—they are not "pitch charts"—specify rules as to the production of sound, they do not allow the description of a sound in terms of the traditional coordinates of a parameter system. The sounds are related to each other only by a family likeness, a resemblance that consists solely of the fact that everything heard is a sound. The succession and precise definition of the actual sounds by duration, sound shape, and speed is then guided by the chance operations of the *I-Ching*.

With *Music of Changes*, music enters the realm of thermodynamics. The relations between sound events cannot be defined according to the probability of their occurrence, because every element has the same chance of following a given sound (Luhmann 77-78). A retranslation of sound into traditional notation, which had guaranteed elasticity of the band in classical music, is impossible, because the choice of sounds is determined by complex rules beyond the intention of a composer. These rules treat sounds and silence in the same way; half of any sound chart, for instance, consists of empty squares, because not to strike a key produces something audible as well. The charts are changed considerably during the composition process: while some parts remain unchanged, others have to be emptied after being selected. This particular process renders impossible a reconstruction of the charts and the process of selection from its result. Commenting on this procedure, Feldman astutely observed that Cage had introduced the eraser in composition, not the ruler, as had been said about Marcel Duchamp (Schädler 194). This is also where the main difference to the multiple serialism of the 1950s can be located, even if the latter uses statistical distribution of sound. In the studios of the IRCAM, the Institut de Recherche et Coordination Acoustique/Musique founded by Pierre Boulez in 1977, any sound or noise is analyzed and re-synthesized according to given parameters and by the help of fast-fourier-transformation.

If the traditional symbolic notation of a musical score defines the relative duration of a piece and its parts, the notation of *Music of Changes* employs an entirely different system, exclusively developed for this piece: in contrast to traditional notation that produces striated time by noting parts and multiples of a base pulse, such as whole notes, half notes, quarter notes and so on, the notation of *Music of Changes* resembles a measuring tape. "The notation of durations is in space. 2 1/2 cm. = [quarternote]," Cage explains in his preliminary notes, "a sound begins at the point in time corresponding to the point in space of the stem of the note (not the note-head)" (*Music of Changes* n.p.).[5] In this notation, equal distances apparently refer to equal time intervals, but the speed in which this tape-like notation is to be read changes, thus resembling a tape recorder. The written time proportions rival the indications of velocity, which in turn determine a virtual sequence of tempos: "In the recent work the lengths exist only in space, the speed of travel through this space being unpredictable" (Cage, "To Describe" 57). While the unpredictability of sounds or marks arises from a reading process analogous to a machine, i.e. the tape recorder, *Music of Changes* has to be read by a human performer. If the tape separates the process of recording from the process of playing, both processes have merged in *Music of Changes*. The performance is not connected to the score by an elastic band, but it is an additional chance operator: "It will be found in many places that the notation is irrational; in such instances the performer is to employ his

---

5 According to Cage, the music should be printed in a way that the bars are given as units of ten centimeters. But his manuscript was not reproduced in full size, so the bars became smaller and the notes are in some places almost unreadable.

own discretion" (*Music of Changes* n.p.). Here, the notes do not indicate striae, but indefinite durations, even if the notation refers to some rhythmic structure, as Cage explains: "I keep, of course, the means of rhythmic structure feeling that that is the 'espace sonore' in which [each] of these sounds may exist and change" ("Letter to Pierre Boulez, 18 December 1950" 78).

In *Music of Changes*, the media of music shift from a time relation to a spatial relation. The charts contain, and this is important to Cage, graphic notations. "Composition becomes 'throwing sound into silence' and rhythm which in my Sonatas had been one of breathing becomes now one of a flow of sound and silence" ("Letter to Pierre Boulez, 18 December 1950" 78) The rhythmic structure of the sounds escapes metrical definition as the partition and distribution of written notation does not lead to audible regularity. The sounds, rather, have become unpredictable events, because there is no metrical multiplicity that could produce striated time and thus an elastic band.

If a composition determines pitch, duration, articulation and dynamics according to certain rules of composition, or, as in multiple serialism, probabilities of distribution, these rules or probabilities can be reconstructed from the sounds. *Music of Changes* has no rules of this kind, no predetermined distributions. Cage follows rules that deliberately thwart attempts at their own reconstruction, thus they have become 'inaudible,' that is, Cage tried to detach the sounds from aesthetic perception, as he explains in a letter to Boulez: "All this brings me closer to a 'chance' or if you like to an un-aesthetic choice"("Letter to Pierre Boulez, 18 December 1950" 78).

Similar to *Music of Changes*, *Winter Music*, also a composition for piano (1956/57), produces a flow of sound and silence. Its notation consists of twenty unbound sheets [ill. 041 and 042]. The staves are not drawn over the whole sheet, so it only partly resembles traditional notation. The preliminary notes explain: "The fragmentation of staves arose simply from an absence of events" (*Music of Changes* n.p.). In *Winter Music*, the music paper produced the notation as stains, spots, and irregularities of the paper become a random operator and are interpreted as note-heads. The sheets can be played in any order by one to twenty pianists. Although the duration of the piece is not determined, the performers have to agree upon the length of their performance. If they failed to do so, the performance might not even be recognized as a work of art at all. It is then the fixed total duration of the piece that enables the listener to recognize *Winter Music* because sounds are not fixed to specific moments and, in contrast to the performance of a traditional score producing an elastic band, in *Winter Music*, a sound occurs within a time tunnel.

"When we first played it," Cage later wrote, "the silences seemed very long and the sounds seemed really separated in space, not obstructing one other" ("How to Pass, Kick, Fall, and Run" 135). The low degree of determination is accompanied by a dispersing of sound events. Yet the isolation of sounds does not prevent a perception of differences and hence signification. The silence stimulates a peculiar activity: sounds are connected by listening, even if they are separated by large periods of silence, so that a melody will appear and the listener will produce a band by him- or herself. Christian Wolff had predicted that this would eventually happen: "No matter what we do it ends by being melodic" (qtd. in Cage, "How to" 135). In *Winter Music*, an effect of listening can be experienced which is described in phenomenology by the notions of "Retention" and "Protention":

> When a melody sounds, for example, the individual tone does not utterly disappear with the cessation of stimulus [...]. When the new tone is sounding, the preceding tone has not disappeared without leaving a trace. If it had, we would be quite incapable of noticing the relations among the successive tones; in each moment we would have a tone, or perhaps an empty pause in the interval between the sounding of two tones, but never the representation of a melody. (Husserl, *Phenomenology* 11)

In Cage's music, there is always more than "one tone in a moment," because there is always more than merely an abstract tone. At the same time, there is never anything more than the single moment and its sound. What has just resounded may be forgotten instantly, and what will sound afterwards is uncertain.

Cage wrote several pieces about stars—*Atlas Eclipticalis* (1961/62), *Etudes Australes* (1974/75), and *Etudes Boreales* (1978)—in which the randomness of sounds as well as the indeterminacy of their temporal distribution is related to a specific musical concept of space [ill. 043]. All these compositions are based on the same principle: Cage places transparent templates of an astronomical atlas on the pages and inscribes the position of stars chosen by *I Ching* on a paper sheet. These points are in turn written on music sheets, where they function as note-heads. By transferring the stars on the templates, Cage destroys every trace that explained their relation and function on the map of stars: the legend with the indication of size, the projection technique, the system of coordinates and so on. The astronomic map as well as the staves are symbolic codes, because they imply a certain knowledge which takes precedence over everything written in these particular codes, submitting the entire notation to the codes' rules. During the process of transference, the relations of sites between these points will be maintained, even if they finally become relations of sites among notes: "The Composition involved I-Ching operations together with the placing of transparent templates on the pages of an astronomical Atlas and inscribing the positions of stars" (Cage, "Directions" n.p.). But the points preserved on the templates are no longer symbols of stars, the points on the music-paper are not sounds, and the actually resounding tones do not refer back to the notation, let alone the astronomic map.

The astronomic map and the music-paper contain multiplicities by means of a metric system. The process of transferring the stars to music paper deprives the symbolic codes of their ability to metricize given multiplicities. Similar to the spots on the paper of *Winter Music* which had become note-heads and then produced relations of sites that did not imply tonal relations, the points on the transparent templates express only relations of sites. Hence, when they become metricized by the lines of the staves, they do not lose their relations of sites, rather, the latter are interpreted by an autonomous metric system that locates them in its own metrical, i.e. tonal space. Although the staves can grasp the non-metrical multiplicity of the relations of sites and transform them into musical notes, this process cannot be reversed. This expresses the difference between music as smooth time-space and traditional music, where sounds and symbolic codes are intertranslatable. And this is why these compositions do not emulate a music of spheres, which could, according to Norbert Wiener, be characterized by its independence of the actual resounding in time: "The music of spheres is a palindrome, and the book of astronomy reads the same backward as forward" (*Cybernetics: or Control and Communication in the Animal and the Machine* 31). Music that can be performed forwards and backwards is usually seen as most erudite, indicating the skills of a master composer. Cage's compositions are not so much characterized by erudition and scholarship but they display a high degree of precision and discipline: he strictly follows his own set of rules which replaces intention by decision and enables him to strictly differentiate between the media of music.

Every note in a traditional score is imperative and seems to say: Do that! Cage's notes, however, conceive alternative models of performance for musicians. In *Etudes Australes*, the hands of the pianist are disconnected. While traditional piano scores presuppose that the keyboard is split into a left and a right half, the notation of *Etudes Australes* gives instructions for the left and right hand to strike the whole keyboard. But if a key is not within the reach of the respective hand, it need not be played. *Etudes Australes* are a series of studies rather than etudes. They do not practice velocity, but they explore a slow space made up of non-metric multiplicities. Instead of making the anatomy of a pianist audible in the piece, every composition builds up its own sound space. *Etudes Australes* require certain keys to be struck and then fixed by small rubber pieces even before the piece starts. This procedure alters the sound of the piano. Because the strings of the fixed keys vibrate when other keys are struck, the overtones of their strings mix with the sounds of the keys that are actually struck.

This music triggers a somewhat paradoxical individuation: Its performance is no longer based on the pianist's *I-play*. A pianist like David Tudor, who premiered numerous compositions by John Cage, does not so much express his individuality by a particular way of playing. He plays something that exceeds his own self. But this 'something' is neither 'bigger' than the performer, nor is it meant to enhance the role of the performer. Here, the performance is not about an individualized interpretation of a composition; instead, the music provides an unpredictable and surprising experience of a musical space. Therefore, a piece like *Etudes Australes* strictly discriminates between the three musical media. There is only a pragmatic relation between them: the score has no imaginary sound in store which the performer then expresses. Instead, it becomes a prescript for the production of sounds; as Cage once remarked: "I do not hear the music I am writing, I write to hear the music which I haven't heard yet" ("Vorlesung" 22).

*

In the music of striated time and metric multiplicities, there is a canon of traditional forms that need not be developed from actual sounds. Traditional music, which used to be the métier of erudite musicians and whose material was tone, not sound, had a firm grip on this canon and could create learned forms out of tones, written in the respective symbolic code, as its material. But how can the durations of non-metric multiplicity be articulated in smooth time if they lack a common measure? Cage has created music beyond this savant form: His pieces are non-metric multiplicities, they develop a peculiar concept of space-time.

Any music not only produces its specific time, but also its specific space-time. From classical music theory on, the proportions of frequencies are conceived as a tonal space ordered by ratios of small integers. More than any other instrument, the piano visualizes this tonal space by the order of black and white keys, but it also requests fixed frequency relations. When the instrument is tuned, this leads to mathematical contradictions. "[T]hus a perfectly pure harmonious system of tones," Schopenhauer writes,

> is impossible not only physically, but even arithmetically. The numbers themselves, by which the tones can be expressed, have insoluble irrationalities. No scale can ever be computed within which every fifth would be related to the keynote as 2 to 3, every major third as 4 to 5, every minor third like 5 to 6 and so on. For if the tones are correctly related to the keynote, they no longer are so to one another, because, for example, the fifth would have to be the minor third to the third and so on. For the notes of the scale can be compared to actors, who have to play now one part, now another. Therefore a perfectly correct music cannot even be conceived, much less worked out; and for this reason all possible music deviates from perfect purity. It can merely conceal the discords essential to it by dividing these among all the notes, i.e., by temperament. (266)

When tuning a keyboard instrument, one has to negotiate a compromise between desired and possible intervals, between mathematically required and actually resounding pitches, if the piano is supposed to produce intervals which can build tonal scales from any possible key. Tonal scales can only be transposed willfully if all the intervals between neighboring keys are equidistant.

Since the Renaissance, such intervals have been calculated, and around 1800, with the rise of the piano, the well-tempered tuning system became the standard. The simplest interval with the proportion of one to two, i.e. the octave, is now divided into twelve equal intervals, in other words, semitones of 1 to $^{12}\sqrt{2}$. The Pythagorean concept of 'beautiful proportions' formed by small integers was consequently abolished, as well as the idea of music as a representation of the harmony of spheres, a harmony conceived according to the model of planetary orbits, imagining tones as surrounded by well-proportioned or pure intervals. The arrangement of black and white keys on the piano visualizes the tonal system and acts as an orientation of the moving and striking hands of the pianist, but it no longer refers to a privileged tonal center. Yet sounds are still considered as interrelated elements in a multi-dimensional time-space, represented by the keyboard as model. Even if acoustic phenomena are no longer described by tones but by parameters, the dominating parameters until the second half of the 20th century are based the model of the piano or, to be more precise, the 'pianoforte,' which discriminates pitch, duration, dynamics, and the mode of articulation.

But at the same time, the piano opposes the idea of a continuous tonal system. No matter how the piano is tuned, its keys indicate distinct pitches and prevent a continuous transition between sounds, because the sound production on a piano is actually that of a percussion instrument: once a key is struck, its sound cannot be modified, but quickly fades away. The piano became a model of musical space-time allowing a distinction of smooth and striated time because it produces a jointless contiguity of sounds, which, in turn, results from the connection of two principles: the principle of tonal equidistance and the principle of the discreteness of sounds.

In the nineteenth century, acoustics and the psychology of music discovered the psycho-physiological laws of tonal sensations. These laws describe the realm of tones as a continuously devisable space (see Stumpf 1:144; Révész 2). The dimension of pitch is characterized by internal and external infinity, external meaning the possibility of ever lower and higher pitches, and internal meaning the possibility of ever decreasing distances (Stumpf 1:144). In his *Entwurf einer neuen Ästhetik der Tonkunst*, Ferruccio Busoni postulates, typically for his times, the idea of an infinite number of discrete tone steps. The principle of discrete pitches embodied by keys bears the possibility of a continuous interpolation of tones. This smoothened tone space is no longer defined by marks or pulses, the occurring sounds can only be represented by statistics, or as a concentration of frequencies, but not as tonal proportions.

Cage's musical space-time no longer offers the transformation or reshaping of relations between musical elements. With reference to Michel Foucault's concept of "other spaces," we suggest calling the space-times or musical spaces of John Cage's compositions "slow spaces." Instead of a singular, which would indicate something common to all spaces, Foucault uses the plural and thus singles these "other spaces" out from a general idea of space. In fact, he opposes the idea of an empty space:

> we do not live in a kind of void, inside of which we could place individuals and things. We do not live inside a void that could be colored with diverse shades of light, we live inside a set of relations that delineates sites which are irreducible to one another and absolutely not superimposable on one another. (23)

Space is always actual space and can only be grasped in terms of the relations of sites between forms, things, persons, landscapes. These relations of sites are not necessarily rigid, as they are in a grid or matrix, rather, they can be dynamic and change in the course of time. Hence, a transformation of spaces is not effected by changing its elements, but by changing the relations between these elements. The appearance or disappearance of an element is not simply a supplement to the content or a reduction of it, but it reshapes all relations of this peculiar space (this is why some of Cage's compositions are defined by a predetermined total duration). Thus, the borders of spaces are defined by the range of their potential reshaping: changes of the relations of sites cause yet other changes of a second order whose scope, in turn, defines the extension of the space.

If space is defined by certain relations of sites, then space without order is slower because it takes more time to reshape its relations. Slow spaces are characterized by specific relations of sites. Zones of high density alternate with empty places showing no clear distributional order or functional cohesion. The lack of order impedes orientation or mere crossing of such a space. For neither condensation nor emptiness are sufficient criteria to determine a space's slowness. On the contrary, the homogeneity and the proportion of the relations of sites arranged in a grid or matrix facilitate tight packing, and emptying a space allows unimpeded, quick access to the remaining elements. A space is slow if its elements are not positioned in a definite, given structure and thus question the concept of position itself. Such spaces avoid the order assigned to each element to find for itself the best position within a given range of possibilities and thus to contribute to the functioning of a system.

John Cage and David Tudor once ordered two boxes of Indian spices:

> Two wooden boxes containing Oriental spices and foodstuffs arrived from India. One was for David Tudor, the other for me. Each of us found, on opening his box, that the contents were all mixed up. The lids of containers of spices had somehow come off. Plastic bags of dried beans and palm sugar had ripped open. The tin lids of cans of chili powder had come off. All of these things were mixed with each other and with the excelsior which had been put in the box to keep the containers in position. I put my box in a corner and simply tried to forget about it. David Tudor, on the other hand, set to work. Assembling bowls of various sizes, sieves of about eleven various-sized screens, a pair of tweezers, and a small knife, he began a process which lasted three days, at the end of which time each spice was separated from each other, each kind of bean from each other, and the palm sugar lumps had been scraped free of spice and excavations in them had removed embedded beans. He then called me up to say, 'Whenever you want to get at that box of spices you have, let me know. I'll help you. (*Silence* 193)

Works Cited

Adorno, Theodor W. "Zur Musikpädagogik." *Dissonanzen. Musik in der verwalteten Welt.* 2nd. enl. ed. Göttingen: Vandenhoeck & Ruprecht, 1958.

Amirkhanian, Charles. "Das Universum sollte wie Bach sein, aber es ist wie Mozart. Conlon Nancarrow und John Cage im Gespräch, 20.8.1980." *MusikTexte. Zeitschrift für Neue Musik* 31 (1989): 35-45.

Boulez, Pierre. *Penser la musique.* Genf: Gonthier, 1964.

Busoni, Ferruccio. *Entwurf einer neuen Ästhetik der Tonkunst.* Leipzig: Insel, 1916.

Cage, John. "To Describe the Process of Composition Used in *Music of Changes* and *Imaginary Landscape No. 4.*" *Silence.* 57-60.

—. "Directions for Conductor and Assistant." *Atlas Eclipticalis.* New York: Hennar P, 1961. n.p.

—. "The Future of Music: Credo." *Silence.* 3-6.

Slow Spaces

—. "How to Pass, Kick, Fall, and Run." *A Year from Monday. New Lectures and Writings.* Middletown, CT: Wesleyan UP, 1967. 133-141.
—. "Letter to Pierre Boulez, 18 December 1950." *The Boulez-Cage-Correspondence.* Ed. Jean-Jacques Nattiez. Cambridge: Cambridge UP, 1993. 77-79.
—. *Music of Changes.* New York, London, Frankfurt/M.: C.F. Peters, 1961. n.p.
—. *Silence.* Middletown, CT: Wesleyan UP, 1961.
—. "Vorlesung beim Commemorative Lecture Meeting." *du. Die Zeitschrift der Kultur* 5 (1991): 18-22.
—. *A Year from Monday.* Middletown, CT: Wesleyan UP, 1967.
—, and Morton Feldman. *Radio Happenings I–V.* Recorded at WBAI, New York City, July 1966-January 1967. Köln: Edition MusikTexte, 1993.
Chao, Yuen Ren. "Chemical Analogies in Chinese Grammatical Structure." *To Honor Roman Jakobson. Essays on the Occasion of His Seventieth Birthday, 11 October 1966.* Janua Linguarum, Studia Memoriae, Series Major; XXXI. The Hague: Mouton de Gruyter, 1967. 1:447-451.
Claren, Sebastian. *Neither. Die Musik Morton Feldmans.* Hofheim: Wolke, 2000.
Cowell, Henry. *New Musical Resources.* Rpt. New York: Something Else P, 1969.
Deleuze, Gilles. "Pourquoi nous, non musiciens?" Paper presented at *Le temps musical*. IRCAM. 1978. 28 July 2003. http://www.webdeleuze.com/html/TXT/-IRCAM78.html
Deleuze, Gilles, and Félix Guattari. *A Thousand Plateaus. Capitalism & Schizophrenia.* Transl. Brian Massumi. Minneapolis, MN: U of Minnesota P, 1987.
Erdmann, Martin. "Zusammenhang und Losigkeit. Zu Morton Feldmans Kompositionen zwischen 1950 und 1956." *Morton Feldman.* Ed. Heinz-Klaus Metzger and Rainer Riehn. Musik-Konzepte 48/49. München: edition text + kritik, 1986. 67-94.
Feldman, Morton. *Last Pieces.* New York, London, Frankfurt: Peters, 1963.
—. "Middleburg-Lecture." *Morton Feldman.* Ed. Heinz-Klaus Metzger and Rainer Riehn. Musik-Konzepte 48/49. München: edition text + kritik, 1986. 3-63.
Foucault, Michel. "Other Spaces." *Diacritics* 16 (Spring 1986): 22-27.
Gann, Kyle. *The Music of Conlon Nancarrow.* Cambridge: Cambridge UP, 1995.
Georgiades, Thrasybulos. *Nennen und Erklingen. Die Zeit als Logos.* Mit einem Geleitwort von Hans-Georg Gadamer. Göttingen: Vandenhoeck & Ruprecht, 1985.
Husserl, Edmund. *On the Phenomenology of the Consciousness of Internal Time (1893-1917).* Vol. IV of *Collected Works.* Trans. John Barnett Brough. Dordrecht, Boston, London: Kluwer Academic Publishers, 1991.
Kostelanetz, Richard. *John Cage.* Köln: DuMont, 1973.
Luhmann, Niklas. *Soziale Systeme. Grundriß einer allgemeinen Theorie.* Frankfurt/M.: Suhrkamp, 1984.
Popper, Karl R., and John C. Eccles. *The Self and its Brain.* Berlin: Springer, 1977.
Rayleigh Strutt, John William, 3rd Baron Rayleigh. *The Theory of Sound.* Vol I. 2nd rev. enl. ed. London: MacMillan, 1926.

Révész, Géza von. *Zur Grundlegung der Tonpsychologie*. Leipzig: Veit, 1913.

Schädler, Stefan. "Transformationen des Zeitbegriffs in John Cages *Music of Changes*." *John Cage II*. Ed. Heinz-Klaus Metzger and Rainer Riehn. München: edition text + kritik, 1990. 185-236.

Schaffer, Simon. "Astronomers Mark Time: Discipline and the Personal Equation." *Science in Context* 2.1 (1988): 115-145.

Schopenhauer, Arthur. *The World as Will and Representation*. Vol. 1. Indian Hills, CO: The Falcon's Wing P, 1958.

Stumpf, Carl. *Tonpsychologie*. Vol. 1. Leipzig: Hirzel, 1883.

Wellmer, Albrecht. "Das musikalische Kunstwerk." *Falsche Gegensätze. Zeitgenössische Positionen aus der philosophischen Ästhetik*. Ed. Andrea Kern and Ruth Sonderegger. Frankfurt/M.: stw, 2002. 133-175.

Wiener, Norbert. *Cybernetics: or Control and Communication in the Animal and the Machine*. 2nd ed. Cambridge, MA: MIT P, 1961.

African-American Contestations of Public and Ceremonial Space during the Civil War: Freedom Jubilees, 1861-1865

Geneviève Fabre

The conception African Americans developed of the public sphere is closely tied to the evolving idea of freedom in the eighteenth century, an idea kindled by the French and Haitian revolutions. Blacks persistently used every occasion for public appearances and they increasingly framed these performances on the idea of freedom. While my focus is on the Civil War years and on black participation in public ceremonial spaces in defense of the Union and, more specifically, in support of Emancipation, it is important to note that the tradition of black public ceremonies originated in the decades after the War of Independence, when freedom jubilees were organized in many northern cities. Public performance of slave songs must thus be seen in the broader context of the emergence of a new American civic culture that underwent tremendous changes when such displays became not only more popular but also more contested. They must be seen also in conjunction with African-American festivals observed throughout the formative years of the early national period.

Public Performances and Black Civic Culture in the Early Republic

From its birth, the New Republic was driven by the desire to set a calendar of public performances that would celebrate its independence, its constitution, its ideals and leaders. The invention of a new celebratory tradition, July Fourth, took place amidst heated debates over the uses of public space: questions were raised as to what occasion could serve best for a public performance, where, in what manner. Who would be the celebrants and their audiences, the organizers and sponsors? In a country where festivity could not to be taken for granted, or could give way to unwelcome disruption, it was important to establish an official calendar of public ceremonial life, with its rituals and appropriate spaces—a frame to herald a new era, cement the unity of the nation, start the narration of its beginnings, create a collective memory and history, and prepare for the future. If the principles underlying this policy were generally approved, the way it was put to practice was subject to many controversial debates. Thus July Fourth was viewed as exclusionary, undemocratic, and not representative of the country as a whole, and of the diversity of groups and classes that formed the new nation. Yet at the same time, ideally, these appearances in the public sphere could also hold great potentialities for all: in a truly republican state, they could provide a platform to express aspirations, faith and assent, but also dissent and grievances, propitious to foster a tradition of jeremiad.

The use of public space for marches and parades—originally the right of only few "representative" citizens—became an important claim on the part of groups that were eager to participate in the nation's ceremonial life. Those who felt excluded—Blacks, Irish, workers, women—often resented the silence and invisibility that was forced upon them. They increasingly claimed access to public spaces and defined the new civic culture on their own terms; if necessary, they were willing to create an alternative public sphere, with its distinctive rituals, icons and mottoes. When participation in official ceremonies, often staged near a capitol, on a hill, or along parks and main thoroughfares, was denied, they took to the streets, as a more plebeian site, or to their neighborhoods on the margins of the city.

The dispute over public appearances generated tensions and competition between various groups, a fact that inevitably influenced the performance itself. By the same token, celebratory contestation evolved as a response to the ever-changing social and political climate in early America. While the impact and efficiency of such events in bringing about change or in encouraging and supporting social protest and action may be arguable, the study of the uses of public space during the formative decades of the young nation can highlight overlooked aspects of American history or shed new light on allegedly familiar issues. Public displays functioned as a symbolic laboratory where power was asserted or challenged, where ideas and images were forged and, then, tested as well as contested. The social and political dynamic of these events cannot be overrated and it was certainly also perceived by official commentators who often tried to curb their subversive potential by describing these festivities as merely recreational and harmless events.

Even before the new nation had come into being, Northern Blacks had created a tradition of local public displays on the day of colonial elections, "Negro Election Day" or "Pinkster," events that had definite political overtones. In 1781, when the majority of African Americans was still enslaved and hopes entertained by free Blacks were often coupled with bitterness and disenchantment, the celebration of Independence Day was eagerly seized upon as an occasion to remind the nation of its republican ideals of social equality and justice and to question the ambiguity of the constitution and its silence over slavery. Obviously, the proclamation of Independence increased the legitimacy of African-American claims to freedom and full citizenship. Public performances provided African Americans, who had long been invisible and silenced, with visibility and a voice of their own; they also gradually placed both free blacks and slaves at the center of the nation's historical narrative and the collective memory of all Americans.[1]

It is important to note, however, that in their desire to join the new national civic culture, Blacks were moved by contradictory impulses: on the one hand, they were eager to participate in order to remind the nation of their presence and to voice claims to full integration; on the other, there was the necessity to define their own political agenda and to yield control over these public rituals. The appropriateness of black participation in the official Fourth-of-July celebration was much debated. Dispute in the black press over what strategy should be adopted eventually resulted in changes of the black festive calendar. African Americans began to focus on either the Fifth

---

[1] This essay is part of a larger study of African American Celebrative Culture, 1776-1877. The following essays have been published: "African American Commemorative Celebrations in the 19th Century," *History and Memory in African American Culture*, ed. G. Fabre and Robert O'Meally (New York: Oxford UP, 1994), 72-90; "Festive Moments in Antebellum African American Culture," *The Black Columbiad: Defining Moments in African American Culture*, ed. Maria Diedrich and Werner Sollors (Cambridge, MA: Harvard UP, 1994), 52-63; "Pinkster Festivals, 1776-1811," *Feasts and Celebrations in North American Ethnic Communities*, ed. Ramon Gutierrez and G. Fabre (Albuquerque: U of New Mexico P, 1995), 13-28; "Negro Election Celebrations as Political and Intellectual Resistance in New England," *Celebrating Ethnicity and Nation*, ed. Jürgen Heideking, G. Fabre, and Kai Dreibach (New York: Berghahn Books, 2001), 90-123.

of July or July 14th in order to emphasize protest and militancy. The Independence Day parades of the black population became increasingly elaborate, thus giving proof to the existence of a community that was well structured and could boast its own political institutions and cultural organizations. These organizations were marked by the contribution of many talents, orators, musicians and a careful and orderly orchestration of their diverse rituals. When the official celebrations fell into disgrace and were attacked for being too bawdy and uncontrolled, black Independence Day celebrations ironically became a model for the nation as a whole.

Yet the appearance of Blacks in public spaces also met with much hostility that often led to large-scale censuring and outbursts of violence. Although the serious political intent of these celebrations was officially denied, their potential for public display of black citizenship certainly also posed a threat to the dominant white power structure. Law and customs had always curtailed public assemblies and gatherings of African Americans; consequently, when the black public ceremonial calendar expanded during the antebellum period, it caused suspicion and immediately led to a more rigid system of control. And indeed, the fear that black Independence Day celebrations might foster plots of insurrection and rebellion was not altogether unfounded, since "The Fourth" was to become a symbolic landmark for black revolutionaries, such as Nat Turner who chose this date to start his famous rebellion.

The opposition they met on this contested terrain, the uses of public space, did not deter Blacks from holding on to the tradition. Their commemorative spirit remained strong; African Americans preferred to celebrate events and figures that were more meaningful to their own history and that figured large within a narrative of liberation and change. The conjunction of time and space is important here. After 1804, the celebration of the Haitian revolution replaced July Fourth, and after the Abolition of the slave trade in 1808, January First or July 14th were chosen as more significant dates. This new calendar initiated a number of public appearances centered on the issue of slavery and freedom and guided by an agenda of very precise goals: to demand emancipation, either gradual or, more often, immediate and total: to counter the ideological effects and political consequences of the pro-slavery crusade, to protest against the limited rights granted to free Blacks; and, finally, to lend a platform to the debate over colonization. Thus, after 1834, when slavery was abolished in the British West Indies, another significant shift in the black festive calendar occurred: from then on, August 1st became a major date for black public celebrations and the general abolition of slavery its key issue.

So far I have limited my remarks to the construction of an official African-American calendar and have emphasized how the uses of public space involved urgent social and political issues. What follows will focus more on the form and style of early black performances in order to show how Blacks celebrated and, at the same time, questioned Independence Day and how their celebratory acts blurred with vernacular traditions developed in semipublic spaces: in churches, meeting houses, lodges or cultural societies.

When the free black population grew as a result of manumission, state emancipation and migration, the African-American community became more structured and these places and institutions played a prominent role in public and ceremonial life. Three northern cities took the lead in the creation of a new black pageantry: Boston, Philadelphia and New York. Here Blacks had organized elaborate processions in the streets and established complex rituals of civic culture, including public debates, orations and speeches. These performances on the day of their political jubilee were demonstrations of the ability and willingness of African Americans to turn the national celebration of Independence into a movement for the abolition of slavery and a plea for black citizenship.

The new self-image these public displays tried to forge should not go unnoticed here. Black appropriation of public space during and after the antebellum period cannot be separated from the negative imaging of Blacks in official "white" parades, in minstrel shows that traveled widely through the country after the 1830s, and, more directly, in the Boston broadsides that ridiculed "the grand and splendid bobalition of slavery" (a term used to ridicule black pompousness and the inappropriate pronunciation of abolition) [ill. 044]. Black celebrations on July 5th or July 14th were largely considered inappropriate by working class whites and their symbolic claim to political participation was taken as a sign of arrogance and impudence. By using exaggerated black dialect to mock both participants and orators, Broadsides attempted to satirize African-American claims to full citizenship and advocated instead their exclusion from urban public space.

Yet these burlesque representations of African Americans, which were meant to marginalize Blacks in public life by way of physical and verbal abuse, can also be read as confirmation of the importance of black celebrations. Broadsides, their racist intentions notwithstanding, acknowledge through their explicit hostility to black performances the challenge freedom jubilees represented to the established order and they indicate that whites were quite aware of their political implications. If they ridiculed the alleged black imitation of white political culture and their ostentatious display, they also portrayed blacks as alert and committed to public life, as capable of contesting the official calendar and appropriating it to their own ends, and as inventive in the rituals they devise. Broadsides—the first appeared in 1816 as an invitation to July 14th—inadvertently advertised events that otherwise received very rare coverage in the press and thereby introduced them to a larger audience. Furthermore, broadsides were often followed by imagined replies to "Bobalition," in which African Americans appeared after the event to comment on whites' abuse of black celebrants. These counter-texts were equally sharp and satirical and they tried to capture the offensive spirit of the celebration. Broadsides, however, remained largely a Boston institution. In Philadelphia and New York, African Americans publicized their performances by coining their thoughts and aspirations in their own words and by reproducing and disseminating their speeches in print; thus they made yet another claim to the public sphere: namely, the realm of political literature and print culture.

Black celebrations created a civic and religious tradition that was to prevail through the antebellum years. Its stage was mostly northern cities, where churches and meeting houses of self-aid societies provided appropriate sites for celebrations of significant anniversaries. While audiences were often both white and black, its participants comprised northern slaves, freedmen, prominent black leaders, and abolitionists. Public gatherings were organized by either anti-slavery societies or political organizations such as the Negro Convention Movement. They became the public forum where strategies for emancipation and freedom were debated, where famous orators delivered speeches, where praise, prayer, and protest were voiced or resolutions drafted.

*

During the Civil War, African-American public displays assumed a new pace and, eventually, found a new, improvised scene: the South. Near the battlefields, in refugees and contraband camps or on abandoned plantations new actors began to emerge from among a population that had long been kept out official cycles of decision and public action. To the southern slave the war offered unexpected opportunities to appropriate the public sphere and to lift one's own voice, coin and celebrate one's own distinctive ideas of freedom and justice and impose them on public opinion. Four eventful years, from 1861-1865, signaled a decisive turning point in the history of black public life. This war, that for many commentators marks a major crisis in American history, simultaneously signified a revolutionary moment in the history of black emancipation, whose meaning for the millions of freedmen and slaves—who became involved in the conflict in diverse ways—, has not yet been fully understood.[2]

While references to major historical events of the War are necessary, I will try to avoid in the following a purely factual approach; I also do not claim to be exhaustive. Instead, I choose to analyze a few representative events, moments, and sites. What has long been neglected in the study of the Civil War from a black perspective is the new conception slaves and freedmen evolved by the variegated uses of public space. The story of the "Negro Civil War" was written mainly in terms of Negro contribution and participation in the war effort itself, with special emphasis on the North. In an attempt to assess the ways the slave population has influenced the course of the war and forced legislation to take action in favor of their own objectives, a new narrative now emerges among historians. In a time of deep trouble, African Americans reintroduced into public discourse ideas of inalien-

---

2   I am particularly indebted to major works on the Negro Civil War, and to a number of recent studies that offered a wealth of untapped sources and that emphasized the ex-slaves' point of view and action (see list of works cited). References in the text are to the page number and, if necessary, to the author or date of publication. I wish to thank Klaus Benesch for his careful reading of this piece and the Bogliasco Foundation for providing space and facilities to study these jubilees.

able rights, democracy, and equality, all promises that the Revolution of 1776 had failed to fulfill.

The Civil War, as I want to show, provided an opportunity for southern Blacks to make use of public space for action, reflection and resolutions. On this symbolic battlefield, slaves forged for themselves a conception of freedom and of the issues they should bring to the attention of the public. To examine this new space in more detail may also help us shed light on the important relation between the private and the public sphere, between pronouncements or political action and the underlying sentiments and emotions. From the outset, public encounters and gatherings of blacks, who were then converging toward the union army lines, generated a strong determination to act upon their own destiny. In this new public sphere African Americans exchanged information about the war, commented upon its course and, by way of public displays, allowed others to keep track of their progress in the struggle for freedom and emancipation. While they continued to use the "slave telegraph" or "grapevine," they turned these new public means of communication offered by the chaos of war into an informal platform on which they assessed advances and setbacks, evaluated the significance of war events, and discussed public opinion and the possibility of a radical change in their lives. They implemented, as far as their modest means would allow, a strategy of closely following the course of the war, government policy and the "due process of law"; they would then step in at the right moment and articulate openly their black agenda. This spontaneous and pragmatic use of public space required great mobility, an adjustment to the environment, sound judgment and an assessment of what the stakes were. Blacks showed their determination to become a force to be reckoned with in both spheres, in public decision making and actual military action.

Lincoln's election in 1860 and the victory of a party whose platform promised to usher in an era of freedom and equality opened up new avenues for public action. As Frederick Douglass pointed out in his August 1st speech that same year: "the slaveholders know that the day of their power is over when a Republican Party is elected" (Aptheker, *Civil War* 144). The ensuing secession encouraged both the slave population and free blacks to join in the demise of slavery. They were now able to contemplate their future in a nation that finally recognized the sovereignty of the people, the principle of equal rights and full citizenship and that had made a powerful pledge to change their social status and condition. Emancipation was at hand and would be accomplished in more radical ways than the Abolitionist Movement had foreseen. From then on the black population of the South would be instrumental in shifting the war effort towards a new goal: the destruction of the institution of slavery.

The anticipation of revolutionary changes and the dawn of a new era prompted Southern Blacks to take their fate into their own hands and to explore contested spaces that had long been denied to them. During the decisive years of the War, 1861-1863, spatial considerations became for them paramount, in particular, with regard to the distance from or closeness to military action.

New Spaces for Fugitives and Contrabands: The Military and the Battlefield

The year 1862 had propelled new actors onto the public scene: large numbers of blacks who offered their services to the Union army after the War Department had finally given legal approval of their enlistment. When martial law had been proclaimed in South Carolina, Florida, and Georgia earlier that year, it paved the way for the great jubilees that were to follow Lincoln's Preliminary and General Emancipation. From then on, the extent of black enlistment, as if in anticipation of Douglass's famous Call to Arms in March 1863, "Men of Color, To Arms," increased steadily.[3] And it entailed a crisis and, later, a revolution in the pictorial representation of African Americans [ill. 045].

In 1863, the campaign for enlistment intensified and spurred even more public debates. Conventions and mass meetings promoted black volunteers in the North (one was held at Poughkeepsie in November 1863). Manifestoes and speeches by famous speakers such as Highland M. Garnet or Lorenzo Thomas declared that the Negro was loyal and ready to bear arms and would make a first-rate soldier. In May 1863, when the War Department finally established the Bureau of Colored Troops, Blacks improvised a song titled "Do you think I will

---

3 In February, Douglass had become recruiting agent for the 54th Massachusetts Infantry which his own sons soon joined. His widely printed address immediately encouraged enlistment.

make a good soldier?" On July 18, 1863, the defeat at Fort Wagner, where black soldiers of the Mass. 54th Regiment had fought so valiantly, also boosted the spirit of colored troops; though the battle was utterly mismanaged, it renewed their faith in the struggle for freedom and their hope to win respect for their dauntless courage. Consequently, Blacks were even more eager to show their braveness and were determined to continue to fight.

At the same time, Black women began to enter the public sphere. In July 1863, contraband women such as Mary Carter in Virginia and Harriet Tubman, who had previously been active in the Underground Railroad, were given passes to go behind the lines. Tubman went to Hilton Head and Charleston, served in hospitals in the Sea Islands, embarked on scouting missions and encouraged the enslaved "to steal away." Susie King Taylor,[4] a free black woman from Savannah in Georgia, enrolled as a company laundress; she also acted as nurse and teacher in the Sea Islands. Sojourner Truth visited camps in the North, raised money, lectured and composed and sang in public a song to the John Brown tune entitled "The valiant soldier" (Quarles, *Lincoln* 225-229).

Between 1863 and 1865 the intensity of Freedom jubilees grew as the outcome of the war became clearer. Drilling and parades of black regiments were turned into public performances and were highlighted in many newspapers. They attracted crowds of on-lookers eager to see the "Sable arm" also called the "Grand Army of Liberation" (McPherson, *Negro's Civil War* 185-188). Parties were prepared in honor of soldiers before leaving. Flag presentation ceremonies were held (as in Union Square in March 1864), and, in 1864, July 4th was chosen to celebrate the conscription act issued that day. Although some of these festivals had been organized by civilians, yet many servicemen were invited. On the Fourth of July in Boston, a celebration was organized by the "ladies of the vicinity" with music and dancing, games and prizes, fireworks displayed from the railroad embankment overlooking the camp and a performance of the regimental band. Most of the songs were popular war tunes by white composers. Among the favorites were William Steffe's "John Brown's Body," honoring the martyr of the raid at Harper's Ferry in Virginia in 1859 or "The Battle Hymn of the Republic," written in 1862 by abolitionist and composer Julia

---

4   She is also the author of *Reminiscences of My Life in Camp* (Boston, 1902).

Ward Howe. The former was sung by the Fifty-fourth regiment of Massachusetts, one of the first black regiments to go south, as they marched down State Street in Boston on the way to Battery Wharf. The sight of black soldiers marching in military order, hailed by crowds and praised for their courage, became one of most compelling images in the new public ceremonials. It spelled out a victory over those who had objected that blacks would make poor soldiers and who feared that such parades would encourage arrogance and insurrection.[5] Yet the image of dignity that challenged contemporary prejudices and called for a revolution in representation could not entirely neutralize timeworn stereotypes. Ridiculing illustrations, broadsides, caricatures of enlistment or of training were still very widespread, even in northern newspapers [ill. 046 and ill. 047]. The figure of the black soldier was at the center of public attention: glorified by African Americans it was often vilified by whites, who held on to racist stereotypes.

Visual representations of this new black spirit are crucial for our understanding of African-American life during this important period because these images, at once more compelling than words or declarations, conveyed contradictory messages. The image of the valiant black soldier, that after 1862 had increasingly come to replace that of the fugitive and the black contraband, was actually not new: "Election day" and "muster day" parades of colonial times that were still vivid in the American collective memory endowed it with historical significance. Outstanding black military performance and courage in the decisive battles of 1863, as, for example, at Milliken's Bend or at Fort Wagner, silenced those who thought African Americans were poor fighters.[6] Sneers were now tempered by eulogies. The courage shown

---

5   When after the Enrollment Act of March 1863 the inequities of the conscription system were seriously questioned and riots broke out in New York in July, Irish immigrants who opposed the draft took the black New Yorkers as "the most visible and vulnerable symbols of the war" (Berlin et al., *Freedom's Soldiers: A Documentary History* 14). Black recruits also met violent white opposition within army ranks. Letters soldiers sent to their families, or pleas or petitions for equality and justice they addressed to the authorities, the War Department or the President's administration, give ample evidence of the enduring racial prejudices. These written documents and the print became another public space where to voice hopes and grievances (Berlin et al., *Freedom's Soldiers: A Documentary History* 83-175).
6   The valiant soldier image was even more controversial in the South where the Confederates refused to recognize armed African Americans as soldiers and con-

under fire won praise and respect for those who called themselves the "heroic" descendants of Africa and their feats were recorded not only in many detailed reports by officers and commanders, but also in popular music.

Celebrating Freedom in Songs and Tunes

African Americans responded to racial slurs and prejudice by improvising new variations on the "valiant soldier" song. It is perhaps in the words and tunes of marching songs heard on these black parades that the complex and, often, contradictory meaning of the war experience could be most readily found. Drawing on the tradition of spirituals, they blended the military and the religious and with parody and humor articulated the determination to carry on the fight for freedom. Public appearances and the songs that were sung on these occasions helped African Americans to sustain their spirit and to keep faith in their ability to act on their own behalf.

Antebellum slave songs, sung near burial grounds, at prayer meetings, in camps, or slave cabins—work songs, marching, rowing or hauling songs, dirges or Christmas chants, coffles or fugitives' songs—were now transformed into new wartime songs. They became Jubilee songs, Emancipation songs, performed at official ceremonies, in parades of regiments, in the streets and halls of big cities. Merging elements drawn from many traditions, these "new" spirituals, decidedly more secular as they reached the public sphere, never entirely lost their sacred character.

Many of the songs collected by Colonel Higginson, also known as "camp melodies," had been improvised as an immediate response to specific historical events and incidents. Taken together they constitute a long narrative of grievances, desire for and celebration of freedom composed of many tales and told by many distinct voices that belonged either to individuals or to a chorus.[7] Their sum total expressed a wide range of complex, contradictory feelings and emotions. Yet all

---

tinued to see them as insurrectionary slaves. If captured, black Union soldiers were not considered prisoners of war and were often subject to enslavement, corporeal punishment, or death.

[7] All songs quoted here stem from Higginson's collection (1870). References are to the roman numbers that he used for classification.

songs rang with anticipations and "imaginings" of freedom and articulated the hope for a new life and a new era. The question that an old slave, Uncle Silas, raised at a church service in Virginia: "Is us slaves gonna to be free in heaven?," a question never really answered by the minister, now met with a more radical response in songs such as "Done with driber's whips-cracking [and] massah's scoldin'" or "No more driver call for me," songs that deliberately expressed a reversal and negation of the slave system.

Freedmen songs or camp melodies were often patterned after the death songs that had long been a crucial part of the African-American musical tradition. Freedom jubilees revived that tradition and began to stage complex attitudes toward death as an appropriate means to deal with the dawn of freedom and the dramatic shift from slavery to self-controlled lives. Straddling two worlds, total dependency and incomplete emancipation, they used the shadowy realm between the living and the dead—the expression "the living dead" became emblematic for blacks during these uncertain years—to negotiate both the threat of death and total destruction that could result from warfare, and the prospect of triumphant new beginnings and rebirth in another (postbellum) life.

Death imagery, with coded references to the war events, thus became a vital ingredient of African-American freedom songs, yet the implicit hope of liberty endowed them with a different tempo and a new meaning. Encouraged by the expectations of freedom, slaves picked up and publicly performed the most daring themes and songs of their own musical tradition, an act of artistic creativity that during slavery would have incurred severe punishment. After 1861, however, African Americans had become increasingly dauntless and their songs, as Higginson notes in his diary, began to ring with self-confidence and the joy of impending freedom.[8]

Marching Songs, Songs of Fugitives

Many of the songs recorded by Higginson in the Sea Islands resumed another tradition, that of marching songs sung either by slaves who

---

8   "Leaves from an Officer's Journal," *Atlantic Monthly* 14 (Nov. 1864): 521-529. Repr. in *Army Life* 526-527.

were chained together and marched in coffles on dusty roads to the slave markets in Georgia or Mississippi or by those in the fields who were forced to sing under the whip of the driver. In addition to these work songs, they also recalled with a more ironic twist the chants sung by fugitives during their often strenuous wanderings at night, or the celebratory songs performed by slaves during processions to and from burial grounds and at clandestine, nightly meetings in their quarters.

It is not surprising that these old songs were revived by contrabands fleeing their rebel masters to find protection among Union lines. Death loomed large in these army camps, but so did hope; and the whole body of slave songs that had evolved around the representation of death during slavery was equally relevant to the shifting and unpredictable conditions during the war years. If the escape from slavery had been a deliberate act, so was the break with the past and the occupation of public celebratory space to welcome and speed up the liberation from bondage. By the same token, the symbolic invocation of death, on which many spirituals traditionally depended, now became the main metaphor to evoke the difficult and daring march toward freedom.

From the early 1860s onward, slave songs, increasingly based on an anticipation of deliverance and victory, were often replete with references to Union troops, to the black regiments that were formed both in the North and South ("One more valiant soldier" IV), and to the Confederate secessionists ("O, old Secesh, done come and gone / No man can hinder me," VI).[9] While their old masters were now often turned into "runaways" themselves, the former slaves, who had refused to follow them, instead joyfully welcomed the Yankees and slyly asked questions about their masters' future fate: "I wonder if my master be there (i.e., in heaven)" (VI). Small wonder that these songs which pointedly hinged on the ironic reversal between freedmen and their former masters were likely to be more exuberant and jubilant.

Songs such as "Jordan River, I'm bound to go / Bound to go, bound to go" (II) or "No man can Hinder me" (V) emphatically expressed a desire to leave and change one's life. Others evoked the inherent human drama of many thousands gone, the uncertainty of their

---

9 Other examples are "My army cross over" (V) or "O, Pharaoh's army drowned / We'll cross de mighty river / My army cross over; / We'll cross de danger water," in which the enemy's tumultuous defeat is hailed.

situation, or stressed the danger, the pain, and the willpower it took to look forward and not to falter in the belief in freedom ("I can't stay behind" III). Fear and fearlessness, patience and impatience, trust and doubt: these contradictory feelings were often expressed in a dialogue between verse and refrain. Gatherings were usually accompanied by extensive greetings and a roll call of parents, brothers and sisters whose names appeared in the songs as recitations. Separation from family of friends inevitably caused grief and mourning. The desire to "join the band" (XV) thus was often marred by the sorrow of leaving beloved ones behind. Leave taking or bidding farewell, which had been recurrent events in the lives of slaves, had to be endured with the same braveness and solemnity that was expressed in many death rituals. The overriding challenge was to sustain hope in the journey towards emancipation and a better world.

Every action towards freedom, either spontaneously or carefully planned and executed, was thus ritualized and made public by way of music: The communal gathering in an effort to organize support for the Union as in "Come along, come along, And let us go home" (xxviii), the summoning call to action in "O, is your bundle ready? [...] O, have you got your ticket?" (XXX), or the advice to spread the good news, "De angels brought de tidings down [...] As grief from out my soul shall fly" (XXXII). Occasionally, the incantation "let us go home" is directly answered by a qualifying, personal response such as "I want to go home" (VIII), "Dere's no" (VIII) or "No more" (XXV), which became a ritualistic way of bidding farewell to a life of toil and tribulations that was seen by many as an indelible part of the slave system: "Dere's no rain to wet you. Dere's no hard trials, Dere's no Whip-a-cracking [...] O push along, my brudder, / Where dere's no stormy weather, Dere's no tribulation, / many thousand go." In an amazingly direct, barely camouflaged manner the songs sung by contrabands and fugitives not only announced the impending escape from slavery but bore witness to the slaves' hope for a new, unified Nation in which all people, regardless of their race and skin color, would enjoy the rights to liberty and equality.

When slaves joined the camps of the Union army, the old images, words and tunes, while still relevant to express their feelings about this new experience, were marked by a different mood and a different emphasis. In many songs the image of the slave ship, on which African slaves had crossed the Atlantic, was replaced with that of the army. The gruesome memory of the Middle Passage slowly gave way to the more reassuring and stately image of "Dis de good ole ship o' Zion": "She's a-sailin' mighty steady / steady, steady [...] She'll neither reel nor totter, totter, totter / [...] King Jesus is de captain, captain, / And she's making for de Promise Land" (xxix). The "valiant soldier" became the new emblematic hero who was destined to fight and die, not so much to save the Union, but to save his black brothers and sisters. If the soldier was closer to the action and was confronting the enemy more directly, those who stayed behind on the plantation were equally determined to participate in the effort to overthrow the slave system that had maimed their lives for so long. These songs clearly had to respond to a swift and decisive succession of events: the cataclysmic change from "chattel" slavery to the life of freedmen and independent citizens, a situation that requested not only perseverance but also vigilance and inventiveness. One had to make sure that the prospects of emancipation and freedom actually materialized and would not become a "dream deferred."[10]

Above all else, however, these songs were devised to bring the "good tidings" and to prepare all slaves for their journey to freedom; both the singer and the many voices that were involved in the songs' basic call and response pattern mapped out the unwieldy landscape: "miry" roads to walk (VI), "mighty" rivers and waters to cross (in analogy to the biblical River Jordan or the Red Sea) or shores (Canaan's shore) to reach, cliffs and hills (Zion) to climb, valleys or wilderness to go through. These daunting acts were referred to as an ordeal but also as a "rite of passage," a triumphant way of overcoming death by seeking freedom and glory. Each song depicts a particular moment of this modern, reenacted "Pilgrim's Progress," with its varying prospects of failure or success, intimations of danger, trials and tribulations, before all obstacles are finally overcome. Although most images and metaphors are borrowed from the new military environment and the natural world, some of them evoke the great biblical battles, Old and New Testament figures and events; Pharaoh and Satan are the oppressors and traitors, Moses and Jesus the leaders and the "King" saviors. The meeting of Pharaoh's armies or Jacob's night-long wrestling with the angel are recurring, decisive moments (XIX). Biblical nouns and names expand religious history into the present,

---

10 As in Langston Hughes's famous long poem "Montage of a Dream Deferred."

thereby adding a mythic and sacred dimension to their current struggle for freedom. The slave who "got hard trials" on his way is symbolically joined by Moses, Jacob, Gabriel, and even Jesus, who travel with him to the promised land and elevate his journey to biblical importance: "Dere's a hill on my left, and he catch on my right / Dere ain't but one more river to cross" ("One more river" X). The singer knows how to distinguish allies from enemies, "And I run down the valley [...] Cappen Satan was dar [...] And I made him out a liar and I went my way" (XIII), he knows how to evaluate space and distances still to cover, how to call for help or give help to the brother on the wayside. Every move is carefully planned, and so is the time of day or night, the use of light and darkness. Soothing images of heaven, home and "the mansions above" alternate with apocalyptic scenes, often set in a valley or a lonesome place, and clad in verses that evoke familiar sounds and sights of raging warfare and impending death and rebirth.[11]

The coming day of deliverance "on that great getting' up morning" and the arrival in heaven or in the Heavenly City, the New Jerusalem, are heralded by trumpet sounds until the final songs break free: "We'll soon be free [...] When de Lord call us home [...] We'll walk de golden street [...] Where pleasure never dies. We'll fight for liberty / When de Lord will call us home"(XXXIV). Playing on forbidden, loaded words such as "pleasure," "free," "liberty," and "golden," slave songs conjure up a complex imagery that combines the awesome and the homely. The good tidings may take some by surprise, as in "O Sam and Peter were fishing in de sea, and dey drop de net and follow de Lord, / Don't you hear de trumpet sound? / Dere's a silver spade for to dig my grave / And a golden chain for to let me down" (XXVI). Yet gold and silver will surely be the reward for the "sacred" work slaves have to perform, a form of work that, as the changing of tools indicates, is replete with the prospects of free labor. As in the old spirituals, the slaves' grave on earth will be heaven, a place where they can

---

11 "De lightnin' and de flashin' / Jesus set poor sinners free / I can't stand de fire [...] / De green trees a-flamin' Jesus set poor sinners free, Way down in de valley, who will rise and go with me" (XII). The final battle often takes place "at the crossing": "We're a long time waggin' o'er de crossin' [...] Hear dat mournful thunder, Roll from door to door, Calling home God's children; See dat forked lightnin' / Flash from tree to tree" (XIX).

rest and rise again to a new life. The black celebratory repertoire of the early stages of the war thus tried to capture, in both narrative and dramatic form, the African American journey to freedom through ever-expanding and moveable space and feast, where dreams were both tangible and elusive and images of slavery mingled with the prospect of freedom and the beginning of a new era.

Slaves No More and Forever Free: African-American Freedom Jubilees

In September 1862, when the Preliminary Proclamation of Emancipation was issued, many questions were still unsolved. Obviously, the date set for the final edict would be decisive and highly symbolic. January 1st had for a long time been both dreaded and celebrated by slaves: dreaded because it was the end of a short period of rest at Christmas and the beginning of a new year of servitude and toil; celebrated because it marked the official date of the ending of the Atlantic slave trade in 1808. This long awaited event was seen by most as a major step toward the abolition of slavery. New Year festivities thus provided ample occasion for reflection and debate. By 1863, January 1st had became the "glorious" day and replaced August First, when Emancipation had been proclaimed in the British West Indies, as the most important date of the black celebratory calendar.

In Washington, D.C., where slaves had been freed by the first of the emancipation acts passed by Congress in April 11th, 1862, the Negro population, which counted many runaway slaves from the Border States, from Virginia, North Carolina and from many confederate states where the fugitive slave law was still in effect, the Proclamation was expected with great excitement. On the 31st, around noon, sixty Negroes from the contraband camp—men, women, children—assembled at the headquarters of Superintendent Nichols, ready to celebrate the second Emancipation edict, with songs and prayers, including an improvisation of the well-known spiritual "Go Down Moses" to which they added the line "Tell Jeff Davis to let my people go." Later that day, they assembled in a schoolhouse where the text of the Proclamation and the names of all counties, in which freedom had been declared, was read out aloud. This public performance was accompanied by shouts, prayers, and blessings to Lincoln. Everyone felt entitled to speak and testify, or offer a prayer. Reports repeatedly mention an individual gesture, an improvised step or a song, often by a woman, or the eagerness of male participants anxious to "shoulder the musket." At another location, the Israel Bethel Church, a more formal celebration was held, presided by the Reverend H. M. Turner, who read the Proclamation from a copy of *The Evening Star* where the text had been published. The fact that the document had appeared in a widely read journal seemed to bestow even more authenticity. While the reading itself had been a rather solemn event, it was immediately followed by outbursts of joy and happiness.

News of Emancipation spread at an amazing speed all over the South among slaves, who had either read or heard about it through soldiers, officers or through their masters. By the end of January most had been informed, whereupon some instantly declined work and claimed the privileges of free people. It mattered little that the Proclamation had been essentially a military measure and was criticized by radical abolitionists; enslaved African Americans chose to read it as a document that promised their freedom, and they knew that slavery could not continue after emancipation had been thus publicly proclaimed.

Juneteenth and Other Jubilees

However, one of the most striking Emancipation Jubilees, "Juneteenth," occurred in Texas, on June 19th, 1865, when General Granger issued an order emancipating 800,000 slaves, who had not been affected by the provisions of Lincoln's Proclamation.[12] The ensuing celebration, far away from the official ceremonials in the nation's capitol, offers yet another example of black jubilees organized "off-stage": jubilation burst out in prayer, song and dance, in storytelling and praise giving. These jubilees soon included popular and quite elaborate rituals: axes, carried by participants, symbolized the death of

---

12 In Texas, where the slave population had doubled by 1864, slave owners from other states "refugeed" their slaves away from where the battle was being waged. Slavery was widespread in antebellum Texas and the war had not led to abolition except in areas where the Union army did not invade. When Galveston was occupied in 1862-63, many slaveholders left and slaves were used to build massive fortifications. By listening to the news and passing them around, slaves were well aware that the Confederacy had lost and that they would soon be free. Official Emancipation, however, only came in 1864.

the masters; pine torches evoked the newly acquired freedom; new clothes were worn to express the break with the old slave life; the moonlight dance, in which a floating coffin was used to suggest the slave ship, dramatized the Middle Passage as a voyage towards death. These rituals, related to stories of escape and moonlight flight, honored the resistance of many slaves who had dared challenge enslavement. In contrast to the official jubilees these less formal celebrations improvised new public spaces and devised different styles of performance.

Colored Troops March into Southern Cities: Military Pageants

While initially most jubilees had focused on the Proclamation, public celebratory performances by African Americans soon turned again toward the battlefield. Since the edict contained a clause specifying that black volunteers for duty in garrisons or on war vessels would be accepted, it immediately increased the numbers of enlistment. In April 1863, the Bureau of Colored Troops was established. Already existing Negro units were gradually turned into full-sized regiments and the deployment of Northern black troops in the South, where they won frequent victories, had also spurred public celebrations.

By 1865, the marches of black regiments into southern cities had become symbolic moments. When they entered the capital of South Carolina, these former slaves returned as both conquerors and saviors of a nation in flames. They marched to the beat of the freedom drum, and, under a new banner, passed the old slave quarters and the auction block where many of them had been sold as chattel. After news of evacuation had reached the black population, crowds of slaves flocked into each surrendered city and greeted 'their' troops with the same rituals and festivities. On February 18 and 19, immediately after the white population had abandoned the city, the Twenty-first, Fifty-fourth and Fifty-fifth U.S. Colored Infantry arrived in Charleston and from there marched triumphantly to Mount Pleasant, where the black population had gathered to celebrate the "Black Yankees" and the fall of another rebel city in the heartland of Southern slavery. Two days later, as the regiments marched through the city, from the east side wharves to Charleston Neck, the streets were packed with slaves singing the old spirituals "Babylon is Falling" or "The Battle Cry of Freedom," by which they marked the solemnity of the moment.[13] One month after the evacuation, the black community of Charleston organized a march in honor of their recent emancipation. The "procession was led by horseback-riding marshals who wore red, white, and blue sashes." They were followed by a band, the Twenty-First Regiment of Colored Troops, a company of school boys, with the banner "We know no masters but ourselves," and the "Car of liberty" with girls being dressed in white. Then came the members of the Zion Bible Society, Preachers, Elders, and Sunday School Teachers of the several congregations of Charleston, all carrying a Bible and Hymn Book. Eighteen hundred school children participated, some carrying placards declaring "We know no caste or color." And finally, after the war "heroes" Sherman, Grant and Sheridan, followed tailors, "with their shears boldly displayed," firemen, carpenters, wheelwrights, blacksmiths, painters, barbers, masons, coach, carriage, wagon and dray drivers, and farmers, "some preceded by their band, all bearing some implement of their calling" (Powers 68-69).

*

The detailed documentation amply proves the importance of these processions many of which were designed to represent an urban or rural black population in its entirety. The diversity of trades, crafts, and professions clearly attests to the number of skills Blacks had been able to acquire as either freedmen or slaves. Yet their public presence on Southern streets delivered a quite complex, multi-leveled message: beyond the pride of achievement, there was also the will to show the coherence and structure of the community, its institutions, its members—in spite of the underlying conflicts between free Blacks and the recently freed slaves.[14] Processions, while often in keeping with established social hierarchy, also stressed solidarity and unity. What is

---

13   Colonel Charles Fox of the Massachusetts regiment distinctly recalled "the glory and the triumph of the hour [...]. It was one of these occasions," he wrote in a detailed report of the events, "[...] to be lived over in memory forever" (qtd. in Powers 68-72).
14   The city had a large black middle class of free Charlestonians, some of who had become slave owners, eager to establish a social distinction as free men of color.

more, in 1865, with the definitive demise of slavery and the beginning of Reconstruction, these public displays signaled the capacity of all Blacks to become responsible citizens and the legitimacy of their claim to full equality and social justice.

By thus endeavoring to dissipate prejudices and stereotypes, celebratory public performances could alleviate discrimination that had prevailed in both parts of the country. They also reminded "rebel" states, if not the nation at large, that all members of the community had contributed, through their toil and skills, to the prosperity of the South. And, finally, the parades provided a strong argument: the shift from slave to free labor could not be conditional and must be seen as an irreversible move towards full freedom and liberty. Above all, however, there was also the collective message to a President who was concerned about the increasing numbers of freed people; Lincoln and his administration repeatedly encouraged former slaves to contemplate emigration to the Caribbean or Africa.[15] By marching the streets and displaying the richness of their culture and their professional achievements, African Americans took a firm stand and publicly stated their determination to remain in the United States, a nation that,

---

15 This particular issue, emigration or then commonly called "colonization," had triggered heated debates both among black and white Americans. Ideologically, the colonization movement was based on the idea that racial differences would make full equality of the free black population impractical (an idea that originated during the late eighteenth century and had well persisted even after emancipation). Africa—where actual colonies had been founded in Liberia and Sierra Leone—, Haiti and, later, Canada, had been suggested as potential areas for the relocation of black Americans. As the number of free Blacks grew, so did the support for colonization. In 1816 the American Colonization society was created. Throughout the antebellum years, black leaders and abolitionists were divided over the issue, some like Martin Delany were strongly attracted to the idea but criticized the American Colonization Society for its inefficiency, others, like Douglass, were opposed to the idea as such. At the dawn of the Civil War, when full emancipation loomed large, the debate over colonization also gained new momentum. While Lincoln had become a strong advocate of colonization as a solution to the racial situation in America, for many emancipated slaves the prospect of staying in their native land seemed to offer greater opportunities than the rather uncertain future of relocation. And, besides, African Americans were convinced that they had earned "emancipation" as a reward for their loyalty to the Union and that, therefore, they had every right to capitalize on their newly won freedom. See R.J.M. Blackett, *Building an Antislavery Wall, Black Americans in the Atlantic Abolitionist Movement 1830-1860* (Ithaca, NY: Cornell UP, 1983), ch. 2, "Colonization's Nemesis" 47-78.

despite the stifling regime of slavery and lingering racism, had long since become their "native land."

The success of these black public appearances in conveying this complex message is, at least in part, due to the fact that they were closely patterned after the American tradition of pageantry and after the military parades of the early days of the Republic. Yet there were also significant differences: Blacks had long been excluded from such public events and were only now vehemently asserting their right to participate in the public sphere (many new Negro regiments were still not allowed to drill publicly). In contrast to earlier parades, the "processions" of 1865 included fewer military elements; they emphasized instead the presence of civilians, ready to take over the authority held by Union army officers.

Perhaps even more important, the event in Charleston was presented as a satire, a mock representation of the fallen order and a sly comment on the demise of slavery. After the trades and crafts had passed by, the crowd was suddenly confronted with an "auctioneer," mounted on a spring cart and accompanied by a slave driver with the auction bell and a number of Negroes, obviously on sale. Two colored women with their children were seated on the cart, while the rest of the Negroes followed, their hands tied with ropes. As the procession moved along, the auctioneer shouted vigorously: "How much am I offered for this good cook?" Next came a hearse, with the dead "body" of slavery, followed by the mourners all dressed in black. The hearse carried the inscriptions such as "Slavery is dead," "Who Owns Him? No One," or "Sumter Dug His Grave on the 13th of April, 1861" (qtd. in Powers 69-70). In another, equally symbolic episode, a slave broker leading a coffle of chained slaves into the railway station is forced by Union soldiers to take off the shackles and thus to free his property. This scene, that soon became part of the black collective memory, was also known as "the last coffle."

The Charleston Jubilee thus presented itself as a historical pageant, in which a travesty of a slave auction, a coffle march, and, eventually, the symbolic death of slavery itself were merged to dramatize the cultural and political landslide that had occurred between 1861 and 1865. In the Confederate capital, the streets were used as a stage for real events, war events that marked a decisive moment in the history of African Americans and of the Nation as a whole.

On April 3, the news of the Fall of Richmond was broken via telegraph to the War Office, finally sealing the defeat of the Confederacy. When Lincoln, without notice, arrived at a little-known landing place, he met a group of 40 Negro laborers who improvised a celebration that was instantly joined by hundreds of slaves [ill. 048]. The President was then led by a black soldier and six sailors to the General's headquarters at the White House of the Confederacy. Crowds of celebrants, dancing and shouting their blessings to the Great Liberator, "Massa Lincoln," who had declared them "forever free," followed in their wake; significantly, the term "liberator," originally ascribed to the Negro soldier, was immediately transferred to Lincoln himself. The fervor of the crowds, that clearly evoked the enthusiasm and craze of a slave revival, transformed an accidental encounter into a momentous political and historical event. While representatives of the black community had rarely been invited to official political ceremonies, on that very day ordinary African Americans were in direct, physical, and spiritual contact with the head of the nation. On this as well as on succeeding occasions (for example, in response to Lincoln's sudden death), Blacks came forward and organized spontaneous public manifestations of either exuberance or sorrow. Unplanned popular jubilees actually continued until after the war; all of them elaborated and, in a way, extended the Great Jubilee of January 1st—as if, by way of constant public celebration, African Americans desperately tried to sustain their faith in the promises associated with the Proclamation of Emancipation.

On April 14, 1865, a thanksgiving ceremony was held at Fort Sumter in Charleston harbor, on the very same site where the war had so dramatically begun and exactly four years after the federal surrender of the Fort. The Fall of Richmond and General Lee's surrender at Appomattox added symbolic meaning to the memorial, as did the hoisting of the old, star spangled banner. The Fourth anniversary of the surrender of Fort Sumter renewed recollections of slavery—in a celebration in Massachusetts, the famous abolitionist Frank Lloyd Garrison symbolically "mounted the steps of an original auction block from Charleston that was covered with Confederate flags captured by his son's regiment" (Quarles, *Lincoln* 336). Famous Northerners, such as Henry Beecher Stowe, who delivered one of the keynote speeches, foreign abolitionists, senators, judges, and a Supreme Court Justice attended the Charleston ceremony as official guests, thereby stressing the symbolic importance of the event and its role in the final victory. Most dignitaries came on a steamer provided by the government that brought them from New York to the Fort. They visited Hilton Head and from there embarked on boat trip to the neighboring, self-governed Negro settlement of Mitchville, named after General Mitchell who gave the order to build an African Baptist church at Port Royal (the visit was later to become an integral part of the official ceremony).[16]

To pay tribute to the important contributions of the Navy to the war effort, numerous vessels were also participating in the ceremony. Among them was the *Planter*, the former confederate steamer. Robert Smalls, its black pilot who was then in command of the ship, arrived with 2,500 recently emancipated slaves on board (Quarles, *Lincoln* 71-74; 91-93). For many Blacks, Smalls was the actual hero of the day; he was seen on deck with Major Martin R. Delany, who had been sent by Saxton to recruit additional black soldiers and, later, became commander of the 104th Regiment, and Robert Vesey, the son of Denmark Vesey (Powers 68-69). During the ceremony word arrived that Lee had surrendered to Grant.

By mere coincidence, a single geographical space had now become the symbolic focus of multiple strands in American and African-American history. The significance of the huge crowds, the prestigious celebrants and well-known public figures, the representatives of military and federal authority, the memories of defeat and victory and their concomitant icons and signs can hardly be overrated. Taken together they signaled the dawn of a new stage in the history of the nation. The Fort Sumter anniversary, on April 14, 1865, thus became the ultimate symbol of both change and renewal.

It should not go unnoted, however, that despite the large numbers of black participants there had also been limitations on their appearance in public space. While Smalls and Dickerson—a former slave and one of the orators at Fort Sumter—had been aboard the vessel that was chartered by the government, African-American dignities such Frederick Douglass or Harriet Tubman, who had played a prominent role in the "revolution," were absent. Likewise, when the funeral procession for Lincoln was organized in New York, the city council voted

---

16   See Charles Coffin," Four Years of Fighting," *The Atlantic Coast* (March 1868): 225-230; 245-47.

against black presence in the event. Although Blacks protested the decision and wrote a letter to the *New York Evening Post* (April 24, 1865) that forced the council to rescind, they still could only march at the rear of the cortege. Obvious discrimination notwithstanding, the outspoken commitment of the federal government to improve the legal situation of blacks and eventually to institute laws that would guarantee their equality spawned the jubilating spirit of this rather sad event.

*

In the celebrations that followed Lincoln's death, hundreds of African Americans mourned the President with a deep sense of loss. Lincoln, who at first had been reluctant to take action against slavery and hesitated to respond to the specific requests of African Americans, was nevertheless praised as hero and savior. In his Emancipation Proclamation he had uttered those magic words that declared slaves "then, thenceforth and forever free." Even though they could not yet vote, many Blacks acknowledged his historical role in the abolition of slavery. In Baltimore, former slaves presented him with a Bible whose cover design showed Lincoln in the cotton fields as he takes off the shackles from the wrists of a slave [ill. 049]. They had also celebrated the re-election of the President who stood forth to vindicate their rights (Franklin xxi). In the North, only a minority of black leaders, who had been opposed to his colonization project, his suppression of an earlier move towards emancipation initiated by his generals, and his injustice to colored troops, remained critical of Lincoln's Reconstruction policy. They feared that he would restore rebels to power and leave freedmen as little more than peons on the soil of their former masters. Yet by and large, the mood among black leaders of both North and South had been pro-Lincoln; especially after August 1864, when the Democratic Party presented an anti-emancipation peace platform, and, later, when the news of the Fall of Atlanta and the success of Sherman's army broke, radical black abolitionists had changed their minds about "Old Abe."

For many African Americans Lincoln had been the utmost embodiment of authority and power; what is more, he was seen to be at the center of the public sphere to which they so ardently aspired. Any occasion to come close to him was welcomed and many were bold enough to write letters or petitions. When the land issue was debated in the Sea Islands, a freedman sent the following request to a former teacher on his way to meet Lincoln in Philadelphia: "Tell Linkum dat we wants land. What dey want to carry from we all de witeness of de land, I tell you all stinctually and punctually, speak softly next time you meets massa Linkum and de Lord will keep you warm under he feathers" (qtd. in Franklin 299). Evidently, the Proclamations of September 1862 and January 1863 had turned Lincoln into the Great Emancipator-Liberator. Henceforth he would become a friend to be trusted or admonished, the ally to whom one could confide one's hopes or worries.

With eager anticipations of a brighter future, African Americans thus entered public sphere to symbolically put the old regime behind. Their performances were designed to construct a ceremonial space of their own and establish a calendar of feasts that would institutionalize a cultural memory primarily geared to black needs and experiences. Yet the public attention that the official black Emancipation celebrations garnered should not make us forget the rituals and private meetings that occurred backstage. Outside of white notice, Blacks had organized their own rituals of remembering and forgetting, of living and dying, and of oppression and rebellion. Both public and private events borrowed freely from a long festive tradition that addressed many aspects of slave life and, therefore, was apt to lend meaning and structure to the dawn of a new era.

"There's a meeting here to night," this line from a well-known song traditionally was an invitation to assemble for prayer, exhortation or supplication but also for deliberations or resolutions. The person who presided these meetings was often a former slave who now acted as pastor; the space, a deserted plantation, where a large parlor would be turned into a place for worship, or the open woods where slaves would "steal away" to stage their own celebrations of Union victory: processions, accompanied by songs and music, by circle dancing and shouts. Sometimes an impromptu celebration would be staged in a well-known historical site such as a former fort built by the Huguenots "long before the Mayflower cast anchor in Cape Cod Harbor" (Coffin 245-47), that later became Smith Plantation and, during the war, had been used as a drilling ground for the First South Carolina Regiment. The fall of this stronghold of slavery and its previous uses and metamorphoses clearly added to the symbolic meaning of this public site. It also revealed the importance and the symbolism of space in the African-American struggle for freedom and equality.

Conclusion

As slaves often said, slavery did not "die easy." In some areas constitutional amendments to abolish slavery had been rejected until 1865. Conversely, Blacks celebrated every single step towards complete abolition: they read out loud each new act or amendment, told tales of bravery—exceptional deeds of soldiers or laborers in the battlefield— or of other achievements such as successful escapes from slavery.

With the actual abolition of slavery, once the journey out of bondage was accomplished, both free blacks and former slaves began to reflect upon the full meaning of Emancipation and Freedom. Not surprisingly, they conceived a world without slavery more easily than their former masters could imagine. While publicly assessing the transformation from slavery to freedom, they staged the socio-economic implications of the change from slave to free labor, and were keenly aware of the importance of the new skills that their status as free people and their participation in public debate and decision making would necessitate. The war years not only offered a multiplicity of spaces and occasions to forge a strategy for these new commitments, they also helped African Americans to deal with the downside of emancipation, that is, the contempt of many white Southerners, oppressive authority and often violent outburst. Against this backdrop, the possibility to assemble and debate, to define and promote one's rights had become a priority. Within and beyond the much-contested spheres of the military and the political, African Americans managed to develop a critical understanding of democracy, to articulate their dissatisfaction with the gap between rhetorical declaration and practical action, and to acquire a greater versatility in the uses of public space. While making a clear distinction between the public and the private, Blacks constantly navigated the thin line between the two and claimed authority and legitimacy in both spheres. Thus access to public ceremonial spaces had been crucial for African Americans to act promptly upon threats or promises and to gauge critical situations; it also provided a platform to stretch the limits of knowledge, dream and desire and to imagine a better world: a world in which slaves and freedmen hoped to be finally acknowledged as acting, thinking, and speaking subjects.

Works Cited and Further Readings

Adams, Virginia Matzke, ed. *On the Altar of Freedom, a Black Soldier's Civil War Letters from the Front*. Amherst: U of Massachusetts P, 1991.
Allen, William Francis, Charles Pickard Ware, and Lucy McKim Garrison, eds. *Slave Songs of the United States*. New York: A. Simpson & Co., 1897.
Aptheker, Herbert. *The Negro in the Civil War*. New York: International Publishers, 1938.
—. "The Negro in the Union Jack." *Journal of Negro History* 23 (April 1947): 169-200.
Basler, Roy P., ed. *The Collected Works of Abraham Lincoln*. 9 vols. New Brunswick, NJ: Rutgers, 1955.
Berlin, Ira, ed. *Freedom: A Documentary History of Emancipation, 1861-1867*. 2 vols. New York: Cambridge UP, 1982-1990.
—, et al. *Slaves No More: Three Essays on the Emancipation and the Civil War*. Cambridge: Cambridge UP, 1992.
—, Barbara J. Fields, Steven F. Miller, Joseph P. Reidy, and Leslie S. Rowland, eds. *Free At Last. A Documentary History of Slavery, Freedom, and the Civil War*. New York: The New Press, 1992.
—, Joseph P. Reidy, and Leslie Rowland, eds. *Freedom's Soldiers: The Black Military Experience in the Civil War*. Cambridge, MA: Cambridge UP, 1998.
—, Marc Favreau, and Steven F. Miller, eds. *Remembering Slavery*. New York: The New Press, 1998.
Boatner III, Mark M. *The Civil War Dictionary*. New York: D. McKay Co., 1959.
Botume, Elisabeth. *First Days Amongst the Contrabands*. Boston: Lee & Shepard, 1893.
Brown, William Wells. *The Negro in the American Rebellion*. Boston: Lee & Shepard, 1867.
Coffin, Charles. "Four Years of Fighting." *The Atlantic Coast* (March 1868): 225-230; 245-47.
Colyer, Vincent. *Report of the Services Rendered by the Freed People to the United States Army in North Carolina*. New York: n.p., 1864.
The Confederate States of America Collection, 1861-1865. General Collection, Beinecke Rare Book and Manuscript Library, Yale University.
Cornish, Dudley Taylor. *The Sable Arm: Black Troops in the Union Army, 1861 1865*. 1956; Lawrence, KS: UP of Kansas, 1997.
Davis, Susan G. *Parades and Power. Street Theatre in Nineteenth-Century Philadelphia*. Berkeley: U of California P, 1986.

DuBois, W. E. B. *Black Reconstruction in America: An Essay toward a History of the Part Which Black Folk Played in the Attempt to Reconstruct Democracy in America, 1860-1880.* New York: Atheneum, 1935.

Eaton, John. *Grant, Lincoln, and the Freedmen.* New York: Cambridge UP, 1907.

Epstein, Dena J. *Sinful Tunes and Spirituals. Black Folk Music to the Civil War.* Urbana: U of Illinois P, 1977.

Era of the Civil War, 1820-1876. Carlisle Barracks, PA: U.S. Army Military History Institute, 1982.

Foner, Eric. *Nothing But Freedom. Emancipation and its Legacy.* Baton Rouge: Louisiana State UP, 1983.

—. *The Story of American Freedom.* New York: W.W. Norton & Company, 1998.

Forten, Charlotte. "Life on the Sea Islands." *Atlantic Monthly* 13 (May 1864): 587-594; (June 1864): 667-676.

Frank Leslie's Illustrated Weekly. New York, 1861-1864.

Franklin, John Hope. *The Emancipation Proclamation.* Garden City, NY: Doubleday, 1963.

French, A. M. *Slavery in South Carolina and Ex-Slaves.* New York: n.p., 1862.

Guthrie, James M. *Camp-Fires of the Afro-American.* Philadelphia: Afro-American Publishing, 1889.

Hallowell, Norwood P. *The Negro as a Soldier in the War of the Rebellion.* Boston: Little, Brown and Co., 1897.

Ham, Deborah Newman, ed. *The African Mosaic; a Library of Congress Resource Guide for the Study of Black History and Culture.* Washington, DC: Library of Congress, 1993.

Hepworth, George H. *The Whip, Hoe, and Sword.* Boston: Walker, Wise and Co., 1864.

Higginson, Thomas W. *Army Life in a Black Regiment.* Boston: Fields, Osgood & Co., 1870.

Holland, Rupert S., ed. *Letters and Diary of Laura M. Towne.* Cambridge, MA: Riverside P, 1912.

Horton, James O., and Lois E. Horton. *In Hope Of Liberty. Culture, Community and Protest Among Northern Free Blacks, 1700-1860.* New York: Oxford UP, 1997.

Image of War, 1861-1865. 6 vols. Garden City, NY: Doubleday, 1981-1984.

Jordan, Ervin L., Jr. *Black Confederates and Afro-Yankees in Civil War Virginia.* Charlottesville: UP of Virginia, 1995.

Keckley, Elisabeth. *Behind the Scenes: Or, Thirty Years a Slave, and Four Years in the White House.* New York: G. W. Carleton & Co., 1868.

The Liberator. Boston, 1861-1863.

Litwack, Leon F. *Been in the Storm So Long: The Aftermath of Slavery.* New York: Random House, 1979.

—. *North of Slavery.* Chicago: U of Chicago P, 1961.

Lockwood, Lewis C. *Mary S. Peake, the Colored Teacher at Fortress Monroe.* Boston: American Tract Society, 1862.
Lorini, Alessandra. *Rituals of Race. American Public Culture and the Search for Racial Democracy.* Charlottesville: UP of Virginia, 1999.
McPherson, Edward. *The Political History of the United States of America during the Great Rebellion.* 2nd ed. Washington: Philp & Solomons, 1865.
McPherson, James M. *Battle Cry for Freedom: The Civil War Era.* New York: Oxford UP, 1988.
—. *The Negro's Civil War: How American Negroes Felt and Acted during the War for the Union.* New York: Pantheon Books, 1965.
—. *The Struggle for Equality: Abolitionists and the Negro in the Civil War and Reconstruction.* Princeton, NJ: Princeton UP, 1964.
Miller, Francis Trevelyn. *The Photographic History of the Civil War.* 11 vols. New York: The Review of Reviews, 1911-1957.
Miller, Randall M., and John David Smith, eds. *Dictionary of Afro-American Slavery.* Updated with a new intr. and bibliogaphy. Westport: Praeger, 1997.
Nalty, Bernard C., and Morris J. MacGregor, eds. *Blacks in the Military: Essential Documents.* Wilmington, DE: Scholarly Resources, 1981.
Newman, Simon P. *Parades and the Politics of the Street. Festive Culture in the Early American Republic.* Philadelphia: U of Pennsylvania P, 1997.
Nordhoff, Charles. *The Freedmen of South Carolina.* New York: Charles T. Evans, 1863.
Pearson, Elisabeth Ware, ed. *Letters from Port Royal, Written at the Time of the Civil War.* New York: Arno Press and The New York Times, 1969.
Pictorial War Record: Battles of the Late Civil War. 2 vols. New York: Stearns & Co., 1881-1884.
Pinkerton, Allan. *Spy in the Rebellion.* New York: Carleton, 1883.
Powers, Bernard E. *Black Charlestonians A Social History,1822-1885.* Fayetteville: The U of Kansas P, 1994.
Quarles, Benjamin. *Black Abolitionists.* New York: Oxford UP, 1969.
—. *Lincoln and the Negro.* New York: Oxford UP, 1962.
—. *The Negro in the Civil War.* Boston, MA: Little, Brown, 1953.
Randall, J. G. *Civil War and Reconstruction.* Boston, MA: D. C. Heath and Company, 1937.
Ripley, C. Peter, ed. *Witness for Freedom. African American Voices on Race, Slavery, and Emancipation.* Chapel Hill, NC: U of North Carolina P, 1993.
Roark, James L. *Masters without Slaves: Southern Planters in the Civil War and Reconstruction.* New York: Norton, 1977.
Robinson, Armstead L. "Day of Jubilee: Civil War and the Demise of Slavery in the Mississippi Valley, 1861-1865." Ph.D. diss., University of Rochester, 1976.

Rose, Willie L. N. *Rehearsal for Reconstruction: The Port Royal Experiment.* New York: Oxford UP, 1964.

Silber, Irwin, ed. *Our War Songs, North & South.* Cleveland: S. Brainard's Sons, 1887.

—, ed. *Songs of the Civil War.* New York: Columbia UP, 1960.

Taylor, Susie King. *Reminiscences of My Life in Camp.* Boston: publ. by the author, 1902.

Times. New York, 1861-1863.

U.S. War Department. *The War of the Rebellion. A Compilation of the Official Records of the Union and Confederate Armies.* 128 vols. Washington, DC: Government Printing Office, 1901.

Wesley, Charles H., and Patricia Romero. *Negro Americans in the Civil War: From Slavery to Citizenship.* New York: Publishers Co, 1968.

Wiggins, William H., Jr. *O Freedom! Afro-American Emancipation Celebrations.* Knoxville: U of Tennessee P, 1987.

Wiley, Bell I. *Southern Negroes, 1861-1865.* New Haven, CT: Yale UP, 1938.

Williams, George W. *A History of the Negro Troops in the War of the Rebellion.* New York: Harper and Brothers, 1888.

Wilson, Henry. *History of Anti-Slavery Measures of the Thirty-Seventh and Thirty-Eighth United States Congress, 1861-1864.* Boston: Walker, Wise, 1864.

—. *The History of the Rise and Fall of the Slave Power in America.* 3 vols. Boston: Houghton Mifflin, 1872-1877.

Wood, Peter H., and Karen C. C. Dalton. *Winslow Homer's Images of Blacks: The Civil War and Reconstruction Years.* Austin, TX: U of Texas P, 1988.

The Ring and the Stage: African Americans in Parisian Public and Imaginary Space before World War I

Michel Fabre

In order to analyze the cultural implications inherent in the French popular and avant-garde stereotyped perceptions of Africans and African Americans it is helpful to focus on the ideological inscriptions and representations of black Americans in a natural and technological environment as they appeared in the French press and in Paris art circles at the outset of the twentieth century.

The French sense of nature in America, stereotyped, among others, in Chateaubriand's inspired evocations of Niagara Falls during the nineteenth century was linked both to utopian dreams and notions of immensity, abundance, and variety of fauna and flora. Later, this view of the New World was used as a foil for projecting mostly dystopian visions of American exceptionalism and for a critique of the urban and technological appropriation of natural spaces. Just like American attitudes towards space, French attitudes towards modern America varied greatly with time. Any attempt to analyze French images of black Americans, both in popular culture and in avant-garde circles in Paris at the outset of the twentieth century, reveals that places of public performance, like the stage and the ring, played an important role in this perception. They made the African American visible. During the nineteenth century, black Americans in Paris occasionally appeared on the stage in minstrels and variety shows, they gave concerts and sang in choirs, like the Fisk Jubilee Singers. Ragtime had been heard at the 1900 Exposition Universelle, but being performed by the John De Sousa orchestra, it was perceived as American rather than African American music. More visibly black was the "cakewalk," a dance launched by the Walker pickaninnies at the Nouveau Cirque in November 1902. Soon, leading music halls popularized a French version of that dance and cakewalk contests flourished.

Although black music and dance of the South of the United States were close to those in the Antilles, the French failed for some time to acknowledge the specificity of African-American culture. Cakewalkers were depicted humorously and mostly perceived as just another kind of Africans. When exhibited in fairs and zoos at the time of Béhanzin's war and the French conquest of Dahomey, these "Africans" were seen as primitive pagans, a race instinctively drawn to the pleasurable aspects of life and, even within the fervently religious context of New World camp meetings, engaging in highly sexualized music and dances.

One telling example of this geo-cultural misconception (be it deliberate or not) can be found in *Les Petits Cakewalk*, an illustrated book for children by Robert de la Nézière and Rodolphe Bringer, which was published in 1905. It tells the story of a couple of cakewalk dancers returning home after their success in Paris. Yet they do not sail to the US, as may be expected by the reader, but to the Congo where the gadgets they have acquired (mostly a movie projector, a gramophone, and a movie camera) enable them to establish a new royal dynasty. As it turns out, they are actually Africans. Here is how they describe the purpose of their journey:

> Now we rich, we want see Oubanghi. These two negro kids, no taller than a boot, were the famous creators of cake walk, the dance that went all around the world and brought to the Cirque Moderne more money in one year than it had earned in ten. (5)

French popular imagination obviously conflated the colonization of Africa with the settling of the American West. Both spaces were populated by threatening natives whose glaring primitivism had to be contained and, eventually, corrected by the ongoing influence of Western culture; as several contemporary cartoons show, the French conceived of America roughly the same way they conceived of Africa: as a wild, exotic place that would surely profit from the civilizing efforts of Europeans. For instance, in the Christmas 1902 issue of *L'Illustré national*, caricaturist G. Ri (for "j'ai ri," or "I laughed") clearly located in Africa his "Garden Party" where Blacks and whites wearing loincloths as well as minstrel show attire were used to satirize high society by having them dance cake walk to the sound of tom-tom drums.

It is worth noting here that the U.S. was then still heavily segregated. Blacks and whites either occupied different public spaces or they used the same space at different times. In France, however, there had been—at least *de jure*—no segregation, and the French government poignantly took pride in censoring America for its racial politics. By and large, the French public knew well that most of the black population in the South lived and worked on "plantations." Reports on both the "gospel of progress," as advocated by Booker T. Washington, and the horrors of lynching could be found in the French press.

Two decades later, in 1925, the history of Negro life in the U.S. would be more plainly apparent. Thus four major sets of the famous "Revue nègre" supposedly illustrated the history of black culture in Dixie, Harlem, and Africa. First, a steamer race on the Mississippi showed Josephine, an urchin in tatters, joking with stevedores and their girls in an idealized vision of the Old South. The second tableau, titled "New York Skyscrapers," featured Sidney Bechet as a street peddler playing "Tin Roof Blues," a reference to the great migration of Southern blacks. The third tableau, "Camp meeting in Louisiana," emphasized the mythmaking function of Negro religion and its sociocultural underpinnings. The last tableau, "A Charleston Cabaret," included a show in the show. Supposedly set in Africa, a "danse sauvage" featured Josephine Baker and Joe Alex in what soon became the main attraction in the "Revue nègre." But this was 1925, not 1905.

Yet for many Parisians the first encounter with African-American culture clearly was the boxing ring; in 1905, at a time when several black heavyweight boxers had gone to Paris to try their luck and escape the increasingly racist atmosphere back home, Sam McVea, "the Harlem coffee cooler," opened a boxing school there and, the following year, after his victory over Frank Haig, he immediately became a local legend. Later, in what was perhaps the most dramatic fight of the era, Sam McVea lost to Joe Jeannette on April 17, 1909. After four hours and fifteen minutes, McVea finally gave up during the 49th round. Overall McVea had been knocked down twenty-seven times, Jeannette nineteen times. The press later reported that, as a result of this record-breaking fight, McVea had been unable to rise from his bed for two weeks. There was no faking involved either. From then on, boxing fans in Paris expected every boxer to fight with the same kind of willpower and endurance displayed by these two record-setting champions.

By February 1910, there were no less than three training teams in the city, totaling about fifteen African-American boxers, all of them waiting for the arrival of Jack Johnson. They had been such a highly visible group in Paris that chronicler Henri Dispan noted with his usual touch of humor:

> I realize the emotions one can feel in the heart of Africa. I doubt that in any other portion of the globe one can find so many Negroes gathered at the same spot. There were enough of them on the ring tonight to fill the Belgian Congo, not counting the German Congo and the suburbs of mysterious Timbuctu. (*La Boxe et les Boxeurs* June 5, 1911; qtd. in Meunier 39)

Significantly, Dispan makes no distinction between Africans and African Americans in what he calls "a black invasion."

In fact, the boxers could be seen all over Paris: at Luna Park, their training ground; Les halles, where the actual fights took place; Fronton Bineau; the Nouveau Cirque; the Wonderland. Montmartre was their main recreation area, but they also frequented Montparnasse with its bars and flashy restaurants.

At that time there was a quartet of black boxers in Paris never to be equaled again—Jack Johnson, Sam McVea, Joe Jeannette, and "Battling" Jim Johnson. The French adored Jack Johnson, the gigantic Californian, "beautiful like an Apollo from the Congo," as painter Dunoyer de Segonzac wrote in his preface to the *Catalogue des oeuvres complètes de Dunoyer de Segonzac* (qtd. in Meunier 36).[1] Like Muhammad Ali in the 1960s, Johnson swaggeringly called himself "the greatest" and often behaved in a provocative manner. He was both a "bad nigger" and a "smart nigger." His initial visit to Paris in 1911 was mostly a publicity stunt: he rode in a huge 90 HP Thomas racing car to his three-room suite at the Grand Hotel, while his wife was chauffeured in a limousine by a Negro driver. Johnson managed to enter public space in Paris at the highest level—something he could never have done in the segregated U.S. where blacks were still widely discriminated against.

When Johnson returned to France two years later, his legendary fame had become even more pronounced: after his wife had committed suicide, he married a white employee at his Chicago Café, Lucille Cameron, and was arrested in October 1912 for violating the Mann Act by supposedly "kidnapping" a white woman. As a result, the

---

1   Géo Lefèvre also admiringly mentioned Johnson in *Le Plein Air* on April 7, 1911 (see Meunier 40-41).

French public saw him as a victim of American racism and, if somewhat self-righteously, offered their solidarity.

The other famous boxer, Jack Johnson, first participated in boxing performances staged at the Folies-Bergère and in catch-as-catch-can exhibitions at the Nouveau Cirque. On the eve of his December 1913 fight against Jim Johnson, he went to dance at the "Bal Bullier" with the cubist Sonia Delaunay, futurist Severini, and other Montparnasse painters in motley costumes. A few days later, in *La Boxe et les Boxeurs*, Henri Dispan depicted the American world champion as the incarnation of an "African" primitive,

> a kaffir king [...] endlessly masticating a piece of chewing gum, his rolling eyes so white and so ferocious that he seemed to be chewing the tough flesh of some insufficiently-cooked missionary. (qtd. in Meunier 92)

On June 27, 1914, Johnson had defeated the white American champion Bob Moran after twenty rounds without ceasing to smile. Colette Willy, not yet known as a great writer, reported on the fight in the newspaper *Le Matin*:

> Moran should have been in the right place after the first or second round, that is to say, far from this ring and, somewhat dazed, in the hands of expert soigneurs. And the other guy [Jack Johnson] would have left with his insolent smile, his beautiful Herculean stature already getting fat, his seven aides of all colors, his unguents and phials good for a sultan's wife. And we would have returned, some of us to supper, others home, instead of approving with our French longanimity the manifest chiqué and the gold and black smile, so deep, so hurtful and so contemptuous that we are forced to call it childish, in order to retain our dignity as white people. (qtd. in Meunier 46-47)

Her description of black pride as defiance of racism is a far cry from the image of the primitive African. Moreover, on January 20, 1914, when René Dalize (who, together with Guillaume Apollinaire, edited the review *Les Soirées de Paris*) covered the fight between Joe Jeannette and Sam Langford at Luna Park, he also noticed the *mondaine* ladies in the first rank, watching with blasé curiosity:

> [...] the two powerful and naked brutes, Joe supple like a cat, Sam like an orang-utang, meant nothing to those emaciated, sexless girls whose eyes shone only with fever; and yet, during the final rounds, the acrid smell of the flesh of the two laboring males had dispelled the scent of dainty perfumes. (qtd. in Meunier 49-50)

While *Art nègre* had been a tremendous inspiration for many, it also appeared too erudite for whoever wanted to enjoy life at the grassroots. Thus Parisian modernists would eventually embrace jazz music, as they had embraced African art and cakewalk. Both represented a capitulation of "civilization" to "savagery" and an alternative to Western tradition: those strange rhythms were taken to be simply a different expression and form of the grotesque shapes of African art. In a similar way, the black heavyweights' ballet-like sparring also seemed closely related to the primitive, pre-civilized energy lurking in all forms of black culture.[2]

It appears that during the pre-war years, black heavyweights, rather than black entertainers such as cakewalk dancers Freddy and Ruth Walker at the Nouveau Cirque in 1903, and Belle Davis's "pickaninnies" in 1906, changed the image of the American Negro in Paris, for the better. At that time, the perception of urban America was decidedly informed by new symbolical places abroad. While the Old Continent was perceived by many as a checkerboard of tamed nature and traditional habitats in a land shaped by its long history, the New World still appeared as the place of opportunity (even though the open spaces of native America and the Frontier had long been gone). More importantly, the U.S. was seen by modernist French artists and writers as a pioneer in creating a new urban space: in contrast with the stereotypical wilderness of the Hollywood western, there was the steel and stone world of Manhattan skyscrapers, suspension bridges and superhighways, an exciting world created by up-to-date technology. Accordingly, "Chicago" became a familiar French term for a brutal urban jungle. For the French modernists infatuated with horsepower, airplanes, and electricity, Jack Johnson, the black American fighter, represented, on the one hand, a sort of poetic initiation to the unlimited mechanical energy of New World space. He was splendid muscle machinery. While on the other, the African in him opened up the spaces of barbarism and primitivism, which catered to the French avant-garde's contempt for academic art and bourgeois conventions. The black boxer's main symbolic asset was therefore to represent both American modernism and African primitivism at one and the same time.

---

2   This is quite apparent in Guillaume Apollinaire's 1907 essay, "La Danse est un sport," as well as in the popular success of the so-called "Negro" dances.

Characteristically, in the August 1914 issue of *Les Soirées de Paris*, art critic Maurice Raynal published a story about a black boxer who had sold his shadow after being seized by fear during a shadow boxing session. Raynal concluded by humorously denouncing whites expectations:

> He was American, which was, in our opinion, a mistake, for we are inclined to think that the true Negro must be neither American, nor a student, nor even a boxer, as some have claimed, but African and anthropophagous. (qtd. in Meunier 85-86)

As a result, many French Modernists were among the first to hail black heavyweights and identify with them. Late nineteenth century artists and writers, who had traditionally depicted themselves as mountebanks, clowns, and prostitutes, now vicariously shared the tragic grandeur of black champions because they brought dignity to the theme of glory achieved through suffering. After the Negro circus performer and cakewalk dancer, and before the jazz musician, the black boxer embodied the theme of precarious fame. Adding to the modernists' enthusiasm for the New World, the black prizefighters combined the attraction of primitivism and, possibly, an attempt to go back to the people. The black champion blithely denounced, for a price, the vileness of sophisticated culture.

For painter Kees Van Dongen, the black American champion represented an intellectual license to be "ill-mannered." Van Dongen's most significant work along this line remains his 1919 full-size portrait of Johnson: the black giant is standing naked, holding a jewel-studded cane and a top hat, against a backdrop of palm fronds and exotic flowers. Johnson is characterized as a king: he represents the power of the black body. From within this artificial jungle setting, he looks at the white world and his solitude seems to hint at the mystery of his strength.

Black prizefighters won every fight so nonchalantly and so easily, it seemed, that they challenged established standards. Watching them in Paris, it was impossible not to question the aseptic order of white culture, which their primitive strength seemed to defy entirely. The presence of the black boxer in pre-World War I Paris made him an icon of rebellion and renewal for the avant-garde, even though the general public saw often only the African in him or wanted to do so. After the arrival of the cakewalk as an exotic dance, "American" but genuinely "African," Paris valued African-American heavyweights as the embodiment of New World raw energy. The image of the African American as entertainer was thus changed into that of a winner, a pugnacious and triumphant achiever. Johnson, McVea, Jeannette (who was called Joe "strategic" Jeannette) and other prizefighters had helped to modify the ubiquitous image of the cakewalker before France actually welcomed several hundred thousand black Americans in the U.S. Expeditionary Force. By then, African-American jazz would become the new space of freedom and expansion, the new icon of modernity and challenge to tradition in post-war Europe.

Works Cited

Meunier, Claude. *Ring Noir*. Paris: Plon, 1972.
Nézière, Robert de la, and Rodolphe Bringer. *Les Petits Cakewalk*. Paris: Felix Juven, 1905.
Segonzac, Dunoyer de. *Catalogue des oeuvres completes de Dunoyer de Segonzac*. Genève: Cailler, 1978.

Belizaire the Cajun and the Post-CODOFIL Renaissance of Cajun Cultural Capital and Space

Berndt Ostendorf

(dedicated to Franz Link, 1924-2001)

The two traumata of Cajun collective memory are displacement and diaspora. But these traumata are wrapped in a resilient culture of primitive hedonism: *Bon ton roulet*, as Clifton Chenier has circumscribed this remarkable immunity of Cajuns against adversity. Who are these people who would rather *fais do do* than fight? The origin of the New World Acadians lay in rural Normandie, Bretagne, Poitou and Guienne, whence they had migrated to what is today Nova Scotia. For two hundred years the Acadians were pushed around in Canada between the French and British, then between the Spanish and Americans in Louisiana where, to add insult to injury, their name was corrupted from "Acadiens" to "Cadiens" to "Cajuns." This odium of being a "backward" version of Western civilization settled heavily on the shoulders of these rural folk who, wherever they found themselves, ended up in a subaltern and despised social position, the butt of endless jokes. This persistent diasporic push factor stabilized a pattern of cultural behavior: A certain cussedness, a preference to avoid rather than confront problems, and a tendency to resort to backstage tricksterism.[1] As a consequence the Acadians and Cajuns remained a tightly knit, endogamic, ethnic group: "dedicated, stubborn, resilient, pettifogging, inventive, exasperating, peace loving," as a sympathetic historian calls them (Dormon 7). The social mortgage of a subaltern situation that seemed rather permanent was lifted dramatically after the 1960s and into the present time, when, to their own surprise, Ca-

---

1 The box office hit *The Big Easy* did much to popularize Cajun ethnicity; it also called attention to the fact that Cajun politics easily corrupts into mafiotic kinship networks that anthropologist Edward Banfield called "amoral familism" (e.g. 11).

juns and their culture became one of the hottest commodities on the American ethnic revival market. This revival embraced primarily their music and their cuisine with Paul Prudhomme cooking ahead of the rest; but even their architecture, their habitats, their backward cussedness and primitive hedonism suddenly were fashionable in a yuppified world. In that pastoral recovery of ethnic virtues that even some Cajuns did not know they had, their living spaces were radically revaluated and their diaspora turned into a privileged cultural realm. The film under review is an excellent vehicle to study this process of the gentrification of Cajun *Lebensraum*. The question remains: How can a lifestyle and a cultural space that for more than 200 years remained ignored, despised or repressed turn into an all-American red hot commodity and into cultural capital? Is this revival due to insurgent ethnic minority politics or is this a form of assimilation to the American multicultural marketplace?

The first dispersion, that the Cajuns refer to as the great *dérangement*, occurred when these rural French settlers were evicted between 1765 and 1785 from their "rural Acadia" in Nova Scotia by the British because they refused to swear allegiance to the crown, which in their view would have meant giving up their language and identity. After leaving Canada they were stranded in various places in France, the West Indies or along the coast of North America, from Massachusetts to Philadelphia, Maryland and Charleston. None of these places were to their liking, not even Catholic Maryland fit their bill, though in all these places some Cajun names persist. Finally they decided, more or less as a collective, that they could best reestablish their habitat in under-populated French Louisiana. By the time most of these wandering Acadians trickled in, the French colony Louisiana had been ceded to the Spanish. The Acadians negotiated long and hard with the Spanish governor; for they refused to be dispersed too far and wide, but insisted on adjoining holdings so that their community could remain spatially together. After a lot of fuss they settled mainly in two areas: 1) on the Acadian Coast and Bayou Lafourche, later after the second derangement they moved on to the Lafourche basin; 2) in the Attakapas and Opelousas Districts near Bayou Teche. The Spanish ruled lightly and left them pretty much alone, just what the Cajuns wanted. And they adjusted well to the new climate and became successful small farmers. Indeed the first Spanish Governor Antonio de Ulloa summarized the positive virtues of these newcomers when he confided in a letter in 1766 that the *Acadiens* were "a people who live as if they were a single family [...]; they give each other assistance [...] as if they were all brothers, thus making them more desirable as settlers than any other kind of people" (qtd. in Dormon 24). Surprisingly, the Cajuns kept separate from the older Francophone Creole population of Southern Louisiana, perhaps because the latter looked down upon them as crude and backward peasants, and by their standards they were right. Instead Cajuns chose to recreate their culture on the basis of a nostalgic memory of old Acadian-Canadian ways. Therefore Cajun life in Louisiana was already a reconstruction of a lost utopia. Because their culture remained tight, endogamic, centripetal and rigidly bounded, they, rather than acculturating to the surrounding groups, gladly absorbed and Cajunized smaller incoming groups, among them Creoles, Black slaves, Indians and even some Germans.[2] In a matter of one generation, by 1790, they had carved out a comfortable if not prosperous existence. Many of them thought that their odyssey had come to an end: Utopia was reconstructed and life was pleasant.

Two changes loomed large as a growing threat to their peace. The development of the sugar granulation process by Etienne Boré had given West Indian sugar makers a boost. Already during Spanish rule (1766-1803) there had been a steady growth of sugar cane production in Louisiana, which led to the expansion of cane fields. Louisiana, previously a complete economic failure, was fast becoming a money-making colony along the lines of the heavily capitalized sugar industry of the West Indies. Anglo-American investors and entrepreneurs and their black slaves began to trickle into Louisiana well before the Louisiana Purchase, hungry for real estate and new markets. When in 1803 Louisiana territory was sold by Napoleon to the young, purpose-

---

2   Shirley LeBoeuf writes about her Cajunness and her cultural conversion: "I didnt want to know, or be associated with my Cajun heritage. I avoided taking French in high school. I would quote the family line. 'Well, *my* LeBoeufs came straight from France, not Canada, so I'm not a Cajun,' conveniently forgetting about all the other Louisiana born descendants in my line. And also quoting, 'I'm German on my mother's side,' also conveniently forgetting about that my German great-great-grandfather Dinger settled in Morgan City and married a Cajun woman, and his descendants married Cajuns, too" (n.p.). The Germans had been recruited by John Law for the agricultural improvement of the colony. Law ascribed similar sterling virtues to the Germans that Ulloa did to the Cajuns. Hence the two groups bonded well.

ful American republic the Cajuns became a demographic and linguistic nuisance standing in the way of economic development and national unity. Not even their French cultural origin saved them from contempt; for it was corrupt and unsatisfactory, an estimate shared by the defrocked Austrian monk, Charles Sealsfield, who became an authority of Louisiana ways. He described them as uncouth, sexually challenged liabilities to progress and wellbeing.

The Louisiana Purchase (1803) accelerated this growing conflict over agricultural real estate: low intensity, subsistence economy of peasants vs. a high intensity, highly capitalized sugar and cotton production of entrepreneurially minded Americans.[3] "By 1820 the competition for the best of the agricultural lands—those best suited to plantation development—was becoming acute and the Louisiana/Acadian habitants were occupying substantial areas of this land, especially in the Mississippi River settlements and along the Bayou Teche and upper Lafourche," writes James Dormon (27). Hence a clash over space deepened between aggressive, heavily capitalized Anglos vs. soft, poor Cajuns on small ribbon farms. The latter farms were doubly desirable when fronting on the navigable waterways. Biotopic space as subsistence utopia vs. real estate for growth, industry and marketing. It is at this juncture when Ulloas positive ascription gradually turns into the negative Anglo-American stereotype, an ascription that Cajuns would henceforth have to live with. The stereotype became a function of real estate policy and national purpose.[4] Typically an Anglo-Saxon visitor, Sargent S. Prentiss, writes in 1829 about these Cajuns: "They are the poorest, most ignorant, set of beings you ever saw—without the least enterprise or industry. They raise only a little corn and a few sweet potatoes—merely sufficient to sup-

---

3   David Nye's typology of spatial legitimatizing places the Cajuns in the non-American camp (see Nye in this volume). The *New Yorker* comments on the dual thrust of American desire: In a cartoon two Puritans step of the Mayflower, one says to the other: "My initial motive in coming here is religious freedom, but eventually I plan to go into real estate."
4   Charles Sealsfield called part five of his series of novels *Exotische Kulturromane. Lebensbilder aus beiden Hemisphären* "Nathan der Squatter-Regulator" who has to deal with a group of pig-stealing Acadians. Needless to say, Sealsfield is firmly on the side of progress and improvement.

port life [...]."⁵ The contempt of the first sentence is paired with a sense of puzzlement in the second: "yet they seem perfectly content and happy, and have balls almost every day. I attended one and was invited to several others" (Dormon 25). It would take another century for that puzzlement to turn into celebration.

The principle of forced heirship, which was codified by Louisiana civil law, and the determination to keep the kinship group together led to the subdivision of family holdings into ever smaller units, which became easy fodder for real estate hungry Anglos. Many Cajuns sold out to *les Américains* and withdrew: a second expulsion and *dérangement*. The Cajuns had basically three options for their withdrawal: Either they moved further on into the prairie country of Southwest Louisiana where they became small subsistence farmers operating *vacheries*; or they moved to the non-arable swampland of Lafourche and Atchafalaya basins; if those two options did not work out, they moved to the uninhabited coastal marshland.⁶ Over time the Cajuns used all three options. Either they carried their rural culture to spaces where they were safe from *les Américains* or they withdrew to the Bayous, a virtually uncontrollable, fluid space, and became subsistence fisher-trappers using their pirogues for mobility. And others again set up the shrimp and crawfish industry on the Louisiana shoreline. But some stayed, made their peace with the dominant Americans and Americanized into genteel Acadians—often claiming "French-Creole" instead of their Cajun heritage.

The 1986 movie *Belizaire the Cajun* directed by Glen Pitre, which is set in 1859, focuses on this second displacement within antebellum Louisiana.⁷ The plot represents a morality play over real estate. Wealthy Anglo-Saxon regulators eager to develop and improve the land for large-scale cattle farming used vigilante methods and the rule

---

5   In January 1804, the first American governor of Louisiana, William C. C. Claiborne, wrote to James Madison with some exasperation that the francophone citizens of Louisiana were only interested in dance and leisure whereas the new American citizens were interested in industry and improvement (Kmen 3-4).

6   A film documentary by Robert Flaherty, *Louisiana Story* (1948, funded by Standard Oil), captures the confrontation between American progress in form of an oil rig and a heavily romanticized Cajun *locus amoenus* in the Bayous.

7   The date is a bit too late for the economic realignment he describes; another anachronism is the accordion used at the *fais do do* in the film. Accordions did not reach the Cajuns until the 1890s.

of law to rid the arable land of small time Cajun farmers with ribbon holdings. The Americans felt they had every right to roll out the rule of law since the beleaguered Cajun farmers reacted to the threat of displacement by employing guerilla tactics, that is, by becoming cattle rustlers. Thus the moral scenario contains formulas similar to those found in the Western: Put pressure on the Indians until they react with violence, then use the moral legitimacy to eliminate them. Indeed in this film we are given chase scenes of vigilante or posses going after thieves. The only difference is that posses in Cajun land have to slosh through swamps and bayous, which causes seasickness in the viewer and also looks a bit silly. At a crucial moment of general social derangement Belizaire, folk healer, trickster, Robin Hood, anarchist, cook and lover enters the stage. By motherwit, luck and sheer bravado, he manages to save his own endangered skin and through his successful negotiations with the powers that be opens two options for his group: peaceful association with the Anglo population on terms of mutual respect, but also the subsequent, large-scale retreat of the erstwhile Cajun farmers to the bayous.

The plot of the film unfolds as follows. Belizaire Breaux (played by Armand Assante of Sylvester Stallone fame, who despite his French name is not a Cajun but New York born) does not seem to have any regular job, but lives from hand to mouth as a folk medicine man and healer. Belizaire becomes embroiled in the struggle between Cajuns and wealthy vigilante groups who want to run them out of the state. Belizaire's life-long love, a Cajun woman named Alicia (Gail Youngs) lives in a common law marriage with one of the young Anglos, Matthew Perry (Will Patton), the son of the biggest landlord. Although this younger Perry is one of the vigilantes, he is enamored of Cajun ways and tries to steer a middle course between the two groups, always under suspicion of his extended Anglo family that he may be "going native." Yet Matthew is enough of an *American* alpha male to resent the continued ethnic bonding between Alicia and Belizaire. Younger Perry has to be doubly careful lest he lose the plantation to his brutal and unscrupulous brother-in-law, Willoughby (Steven McHattie), and he has to be wary of Belizaire, his rival for the undivided attention of his wife. Willoughby thoroughly disapproves of his brother in law for going slumming with the Cajuns, for his common law marriage with a Cajun, but mostly for his growing softness towards Cajun claims on the land. To get him out of the way of his inheritance he ambushes and shoots his brother-in-law. Suspicion falls on Belizaire's cousin Leger (Michael Schoeffling), a pathetic drunkard and cattle rustler, whom the dead Walter Perry had once given a cruel whipping. Therefore a revenge killing would make sense. Belizaire tries to save his cousin's neck by claiming that he, not Leger, shot Perry which, though nobody really believes it, is accepted by the authorities as a "compromise solution" in order to avoid further disruption. Meanwhile a vigilante group has captured and shot the cousin that Belizaire desperately tried to save. Belizaire makes the most of the new turn of events by making his confession contingent on major concessions of the Anglos and on having two of the vigilantes, who shot his cousin, hanged along with himself. The plot is resolved in a long gallows scene, where Belizaire framed by the two vigilantes is about to be hanged. The irony of the biblical quote is obvious. Before being hanged Belizaire distributes his folk pharmacy of healing potions and herbs to his people, an act of community bonding. He suggests that they ought to have a big gumbo in commemoration, a ribald quote of the Eucharist. He also gets the priest to lie about Matthew Perry and Alicia's union. The common law status of their union would have prevented Alicia from inheriting any of the Perry fortune; Alicia and her children by Perry would have been destitute. Belizaire twists the arm of the priest, who now claims that Alicia and Matthew Perry were married by him clandestinely—which makes Alicia a full heiress to the Perry fortune. Old man Perry and his daughter, Willoughby's estranged wife, tacitly accept Alicia and her children into the family by inviting them into the coach. Now Belizaire goes into high gear. With the help of a West Indian, killer-divining gris-gris doll he manages to terrorize Willoughby whose West Indian training had made him respectful of the power of root doctors. Willoughby's uncontrollable fear, which he exhibits in face of the gris-gris, outs him as guilty of the murder. Willoughby flees. Belizaire ends up a wealthy man, thanks to the deals he struck with the authorities, ready to marry Alicia, who will inherit half the plantation. A wholesale *Aufhebung* of all contradictions in a union of American and Cajun purposes.

    The film is both a product and mirror of the Cajun Revival: Let us return to the historical contexts, which allowed this film to emerge. During the Second World War Cajuns had their first cultural uplift. They found to their own surprise that knowing French was an advantage in and after the war. Cajuns understood and could talk to the Parisians, and were accepted by them as distant country relatives. This put Anglo-American soldiers in Paris at the mercy of the very Cajuns they had looked down upon for their peasant French. And their reception in France made Cajun soldiers heroes at home. They had discovered cultural capital in Frenchness. Motivated by the experience of Cajun veterans two politicians, Dudley LeBlanc and Roy Theriot, organized a bicentennial celebration of the Acadian exile in 1955. The cultural revival, this needs to be emphasized, was top-down, not bottom up. Not the working class, nor the ethnic power base, but elite Cajuns of South Louisiana, who determined that they must take action to preserve spoken French, were instrumental in effecting the turnabout. The revival effort by politicians was soon joined by the academic world. Professor Raymond Rodgers of Southwestern Louisiana University, not a Cajun but a Canadian by birth, and Congressman James P. Domengeaux of Lafayette joined forces. They established the State supported Council for the Development of French in Louisiana (CODOFIL). There were similar movements in other places of America such as the *Mouvement pour la Protection de la langue française in Nouvelle Angleterre* in New Hampshire. CODOFIL made French courses in public elementary and high schools mandatory. Yet, there was a serious problem. Since speaking French had been forbidden during the peak of the Americanization drive, there was no local tradition of teaching or learning French. No local teachers were available. So these had to be drawn from France, Belgium, and Quebec. And certainly, when the linguistic chips were down, CODOFIL had no intention of teaching Cajun French. Despite the moral uplift that the public attention via CODOFIL promised to Cajunhood, the real existing Cajuns were confronted with yet another derangement, this time linguistic. Their children were instructed, not in Cajun ways, but in high French in written and spoken form. Again the ordinary Cajuns felt classed down and deranged, for their dialect was identified as a broken tongue, now by the high French, who came in as teachers. In short, CODOFIL had little to do with the revitalization of Cajun ethnic identity, of ethnic folkways or of Cajun dialects.

But it had an unexpected, top down, spin-off effect. The revival helped create a talented tenth, an academic version of what used to be called genteel Acadians. The top down effort created a generation of educated, young Acadians who would go on to the best schools in the country. And due to the centripetal pull of Cajun ethnicity they all came home, a return to the folk pastoral. And in order to establish their own economic and ethnic *raison d'être* they began folk festivals, academic programs and public celebrations of Acadian ethnicity. In the new spirit of multicultural tolerance Cajuns came fully out of the regional closet. After 1968 there was an outreach to Quebec and a networking of francophone populations in North America. CODOFIL represented a strong internationalization of the effort by including people from Quebec, Belgium, France, and New Hampshire. Cajuns thus became part of a larger French family and now were on the public map. All of a sudden the previously negative ascription had become a positive value. New Yorkers began to dance to *fais do do music* and learned to blacken their fish (let alone their toast).[8] Cajun folklore became attractive and an object of study for outsiders. This revival had a latent pastoral-populist-leftist dimension as well: For the people called Cajun had survived all sorts of repression due to their stubborn resistance to class oppression. Just the thing for wine-and-cheese liberals. In 1974 Lafayette, which had become the center of Cajun revival activities, welcomed a huge festival called *Hommage à la Musique Acadienne* which attracted 12 500 visitors. This recreation of community affected a change from a focus on centripetal kinship to centrifugal marketing, from Cajun as private work culture to Cajun as public fun culture with music, cooking and dancing. Hollywood discovered the pastoral attractions of Cajunhood and *The Big Easy* became an international hit.

In this process the role of professional folklorists was not unimportant: Barry Jean Ancelet is typical of this new cohort as is the film director Glen Pitre. The former is director of the Folklore and Folklife Program of the Center for Louisiana Studies at the University of South Western Louisiana, and professor of French as well. Ancelet describes himself as an activist folklorist, that is, as a folklorist who does not only collect and archivize folk traditions, but nurture and "recreate dying" traditions. There was, in the sixties, a battle raging between the young action folklorists, represented by the Philadelphia group vs. antiquarian folklore, represented by Richard Dorson (see Ostendorf).

---

8   The Prudhomme recipe "Blackened fish" has nothing whatever to do with Cajun traditions. The *New Yorker* may be depended upon to comment on the zanier aspects of such revivals. A cartoon shows a toaster with two burned toasts sticking out, and the caption reads "Blackened toast."

Within the general cultural politics of revitalization the role of activist folklore gives an interesting twist to the Cajun revival. It turns political and social disadvantage into economic advantage, the Ur-American solution to all problems. Despite the empowerment of the group and the ultimate success of the revitalization movement, the new Cajun awareness does not seem to have any substantial political charge (Dormon 89). There is no Cajun nationalism within America, no cultural nationalism that has a political edge. Instead there is a strong commodification of Cajun ethnicity as a marketable capital gain (see Ancelet, "Cajun Ice").

This final, largely peaceful *Aufhebung* which the film charts also turns out to be the real historical fortunate fall, since as a consequence of the second derangement, Cajuns would find their spatial utopia, the Bayou, and their heraldic totems, shrimp and crawfish. The director Glen Pitre is a Cajun and a member of the post-CODOFIL cohort, the first generation to make Harvard where, in the citadel of knowledge and in the bowels of American power, I mean Widener Library, they could study books on Cajun folklore and ethnicity. Pitre received a degree in *Visual and Environmental Studies*, just the preparation to produce a film on a biotope. It is telling that Pitre's CV on his webpage identifies him first as a shrimp fisherman, then as a film-maker and only then as an academic, a populist presentation of self typical for many 1960s activists. This academically inspired cohort with a pastoralized sense of rural-ethnic self masterminded the revitalization of traditional Cajun culture from the top down. This occurred at the very moment, between 1950 and 1970, when Cajun culture, particularly Cajun French, had more or less gone under due to the massive modernization via oil and due to a relentless politics of Americanization (Huey Long) which lasted well into the fifties, an Americanization which left its trace in the habit of giving American first names to Cajun children: Barry Ancelet, Bruce Daigrepont, Clifton Chenier. The film was shot on the location of a reconstructed Acadian village and the drama unfolds, like the Western, as a power conflict over culture-in-space in a *paysage moralisé*; hence the plot is energized by a morally righteous spatial nostalgia which transforms the traumatic experience of repeated diasporic displacement into grounds for a celebration of cultural survival, and thus repeats the trajectory of Cajun historical eschatology: A resilient cultural identity which survived British, Spanish, and American power politics. The fictional trickster story is embedded in the very folk art that the Cajun renaissance had just helped to restore, thus the trickster myth is embedded in an overpoweringly real sense of Cajun thingness and Cajun place. The soundtrack is provided by Beausoleil's Michel Doucet with music played on authentic fiddles built from 1779 and 1793. Doucet is himself a key agent in the nostalgio-spatial, academic restoration of an Acadia that never existed in quite those purified, pastoral terms. The movie's celebration of particular Cajun motherwit is coupled with a dark view of American universalizing politics. This combination turns it into a Cajun version of the hip western and its nostalgio-spatial pastoralism of ethnic resiliency in an Americanocentric world. The overall aura of the film's closure is not revolution or rebellion but peace, made possible by this soteriological figure Belizaire who comes across as half wonder working, trickster Jesus, half as a non-violent, peace-giving Bayou Ghandi.

Did these activists know what they were doing? Of course they did. Barry Jean Ancelet, co-author with Glen Pitre of a book on Cajun culture, signifies on his own complex identity in the *Encyclopedia of Southern Culture*:

> Visitors to South Louisiana invariably bring their own cultural baggage. French Canadians, for instance, who seek in Cajuns a symbol of dogged linguistic survival in predominantly Anglo-Saxon North America, find virtually no Anglo-Franco confrontation and an absence of animosity in cultural politics. The French who seek vestiges of former colonials find instead French-speaking cowboys (and Indians) in pickup trucks. They are surprised that the Cajuns and Creoles love fried chicken and iced tea, forgetting this is the South; that they love hamburgers and Coke forgetting this is the United States; and they love cayenne and cold beer, forgetting this is the northern top of the West Indies. American visitors usually skim along the surface, too, looking in vain for traces of Longfellow's *Evangeline*. (422)

Yet, whatever the projections, reconstructions and commodifications, who would, at *fais do do* time, want to resist the inclusive pull of *bon ton roulet*? There are certain things worth fighting for, however tricksterish the strategies.

Works Cited

Ancelet, Barry Jean. " Cajuns and Creoles." *Encyclopedia of Southern Culture*. Ed. Charles Reagan Wilson and William Ferris. Chapel Hill: U of North Carolina P, 1989. 421-423.

—. "From Evangeline Hot Sauce to Cajun Ice: Signs of Ethnicity in South Louisiana." *Louisiana Folklore Miscellany* (1996). 15 March 2004 <www.louisianafolklife.org/LT/Articles_Essays/main_misc_hot_sauce.html>.

Banfield, Edward C. *The Moral Basis of a Backward Society*. Chicago: Free P, 1967.

Belizaire the Cajun. Dir. Glen Pitre. 1986.

Chenier, Clifton. *Bon Ton Roulet*. Arhoolie Records, 1967.

Dormon, James. *The People Called Cajun: An Introduction to an Ethnohistory*. Lafayette: U of Southwestern Louisiana P, 1983.

Kmen, Henry A. *Music in New Orleans. The Formative Years*. Baton Rouge: Louisiana State UP, 1966.

LeBoeuf, Shirley. "Some Stuff about Da Cajun Grrl." 15 March 2004 <http://members.tripod.com/Les_Abeilles/stuff.htm>.

Louisiana Story. Dir. Robert Flaherty. Lopert Films, 1948.

Ostendorf, Berndt. "Das amerikanische Folksong Revival: Ein Rückblick." *Jahrbuch für Volksliedforschung* 43 (1998): 93-99.

The Big Easy. Dir. Jim McBride. 1987.

Sealsfield, Charles. *Nathan, der Squatter-Regulator: oder der erste Amerikaner in Texas*. Nürnberg: Carl, 1948.

Wilson, Charles Reagan, and William Ferris, eds. *Encyclopedia of Southern Culture*. Chapel Hill: U of North Carolina P, 1989.

Brooklyn Bridge: Sign and Symbol in the Works of Hart Crane and Joseph Stella

Paul Neubauer

Brooklyn Bridge, seen here in one of its famous photographed presentations [ill. 050], has been and is the most recognizable and the most widely recognized landmarks of New York City—next to, of course, the Statue of Liberty.[1] Its status as a widely known image of modern city architecture rests only in part on its function—the breaching of a natural barrier, i.e. the bridging of the East River and thus convenient mass transportation as well as individual communication across one of the main water ways and transporting channels in the geophysical make-up of a city which itself has become a global cultural icon or rather an urban congregation of icons and images of modernity. Brooklyn Bridge is a major monument to the 19th century increase in man's capacity to overcome the natural limitations of his environment, and a document to the advance of the U.S. towards a technological civilization with an ever-growing socio-economical concentration in cityscapes. With its official opening in 1883, the everyday reality of the city has changed; because of its technical innovativeness as the world's first suspension bridge using cables spun from steel wire, Brooklyn Bridge was hailed as the eighth wonder of the world.[2] It

---

1   Even to this day, Brooklyn Bridge is one of the most often represented icons of the city of New York; it shared this status with the Flatiron building of 1902, then the Woolworth building of 1913, the Chrysler building of 1929, then the Empire State building of 1931, and later the WTC from 1966, which has now become Ground Zero. In 1964, the American government had proclaimed Brooklyn Bridge an official national monument. See, for example, www.endex.com/gf/buildings/bbridge/bbridge.html. The American Memory Collection of Pictures at the Library of Congress would be another excellent source for post-1930 pictorial representations of Brooklyn Bridge.
2   One newspaper listed it among the "seven fraudulent wonders of the New World" however, along with the Chambers Street Courthouse, the Northern Pacific Railroad, and the Washington pavements: "Conceived in iniquity and be-

connected the then independent cities of Brooklyn and New York (Manhattan) and could thus be seen as the last link of a continuous landlocked chain extending from the Atlantic to the Pacific.[3] The nation was united at last—and with a glance back at the painful divisions caused by the Civil War and Reconstruction, it appeared healed again in the eyes of the jubilant crowds.

In 1883, Brooklyn Bridge dominated the New York skyline; prints of the period show the supremacy of the building. But even thirty years later, the bridge evoked the prospect of the modern city of New York with its five boroughs, and a new generation of artists saw the challenge presented in this structure bringing ever increasing masses to and from Manhattan, transporting the goods into the city and the commuters to their flats in suburbia. Many artists had painted and photographed Brooklyn Bridge, but most—like Childe Hassam, John Twachtman, or Joseph Pennell—had outlined the bridge as a lofty presence resting above the cityscape. John Marin was the first to deviate from this mimetic representation of some part of the city dwarfed by the bridge; instead of that vista he chose to present its structure as a twirl of colors arranged in circles and wedges abstracted from a three-dimensional perspective, thus breaking up the architecture itself. Then Joseph Stella, another European artist in New York, seized upon this bridge as an up-to-date expression of "great forces at work."[4] His first full pictorial execution of the bridge was completed in the painting *Brooklyn Bridge* of 1917-18, a dissolution of the conventional cityscape both majestic and monstrous, a re-composition and displacement of the landmark architecture in two planes structured as well as distinguished by lines and colors;[5] both levels of this

---

gun in fraud," the paper exclaimed, "it has been continued in corruption" (cf. Trachtenberg 26-27).

3   Particularly so after the completion of the Union Pacific railroad line in 1869. "Now," wrote one observer, "with the completion of this bridge, the continent is entirely spanned, and one may visit, dry and shod and without the use of ferry boats, every city from the Atlantic to the Golden Gate" (cf. Trachtenberg 43).

4   Stella wrote: "Steel and electricity had created a new world. A new drama had surged from the unmerciful violations of darkness at night, by the violent blaze of electricity and a new polyphony was ringing all around with the scintillating, highly colored lights. The steel had leaped to hyperbolic altitudes and expanded to vast latitudes with the skyscrapers and with bridges made for the conjunction of worlds" (cf. Trachtenberg 87).

5   After his return from Europe in 1911, Stella moved to Brooklyn in 1916.

picture are connected in an upward movement of diagonal lines crossing at the top, where the topmost tower is bathed in light. But the direction of the lower half is leading us downward, under the bridge itself, so that the viewer's gaze is split into two vistas simultaneously: into a tunnel system going down under the construction, and beyond the towers themselves through the vertical lines leading our eyes upward.[6] Though Stella's later paintings of Brooklyn Bridge only quote this exacting tension between bridging und tunneling, the duality of the architecture, its functions and its contradictory appeal inform all five of his later pictures.

Presented here is the most popular of these, Stella's 1922 picture *The Bridge*, fifth and last panel of his polyptych *New York Interpreted* [ill. 051]. In this painting, the bridge appears more stable and consolidated than in the 1918 rendition, it appears far more insulated from the contagious frenzy of the city and has gained a solid independence of its own. The surface ambivalence of opposing principles in the earlier picture is reduced and seems almost overcome in a perspective of transcendence—the ambiguity of the split-level dichotomy, the dynamic of movements and the combination of perspectives is dissolved and is now grounded in a constructive choreography of power lines (cf. Saunders/Goldstein).[7]

The viewer is in the position of a pedestrian on the bridge's unique walkway, which is at the very center of the structure and popularly called "walkway to the stars," a centrality further emphasized by the quadripartite cable system establishing lines of vision which result in a clear upward movement of the viewer's glance. The painting concentrates on the arches and on one tower, featuring prominently the four main cables in their casing and including only a section of the city beyond. Manhattan as it is seen here, however, is not a real city— none of the buildings is recognizable and only one of skyscrapers now dominating its skyline had been erected at the time (what appears represented within the upper left arch is a fantasy city of some booming

---

6   The painting clearly resembles a stained-glass window juxtaposing depictions of heaven and hell in the tradition of medieval and Renaissance art.
7   Stella's 1922 painting *The Bridge* is often regarded as having introduced modern art to a large part of the American public; some critics considered it as America's most important futurist work, while others called it the most successful piece of American modernism.

modernist future). The point of view places the perspective in the middle of the bridge looking at the tower—actually both of them in line.

But the painter is playing tricks with the eye-level line, bending the lines of vision and thus allowing a simultaneous glance at the walkway and at the elevating arches with their Gothic points and at the understructure of the bridge underneath the promenade where I-beams, steel braces and supports can be perceived. Excluding the diagonal stays which support and stabilize the walkway, Stella painted multiple visual impressions of and from the bridge including the frantic traffic expressed in the dynamic colors of reds, blues, and greens at the corner angles and in the grid work below the eye level: in the lower half of the painting, these color arrangements combine the acoustic impressions with the visual in illustrating the constant roar of engines, the whining of tires in their steel gratings, the rattle of the carriages on the lower roadway.

The Bridge is basically a vertical painting: The three dominant lines of the towers meet and push the eye upward to the pointed Gothic archways. Underlining this vertical idea is the placement of the cables—the grand sweep of the three sets of cables is leading the line of vision ever upward—where the eyes find rest in the triangles of the two Gothic arches, in turn supported by the triangles formed by the three sets of cables. This 'triangulation' creates stability and symmetry in a combination of isosceles and right angle triangles. The symmetrical impression, however, is a designed illusion— the layout changes inside the arches that frame the viewer's very perspective: through the left arch the tall buildings of Manhattan can be seen in the distance, through the right the heavy structure of the bridge itself can be perceived together with its lower roadway. Thus the doubling archways create a double image or a doubled vision, one seemingly mirroring the other. This impression is supported through the repetition of the vertical buildings of the left archway in the vertical idea of the bridge in the right one. Stella's ultimately cubist strategy of creating pictorial simultaneity is going beyond the futurist application of lines of force; his are lines that curve, twist, dash and cut across those paintings to show dynamic energy, addressing the sights, sounds, smells, speed or *in toto* the mechanization of the modern civilization.

Stella's vertical city is pushing upward to unknown heights and unlimited goals. Once inside the structure of the bridge towards this city, however, the constant repetition of vertical lines feels more like the bars of a prison.[8] Thus he is capturing the contrasts of 1920s modernism: claustrophobia and crudeness, speed of mechanisms, majesty and grandeur of engineering achievements and the new modes of communication.[9] In Stella's commitment to an art of metaphor and symbol—his strategy of inclusiveness—the focal point of the painting, however, is generally ignored in critical commentary: it is opening up a vista transcending the structures and strictures confining the viewer. The perfectly round circle of brilliant azure just below the double curves of these Gothic gates points toward heaven and opens upon the vertical architectures of the modern cityscape. This blue circle established in a black square allows a glimpse of some beyond. Our vision, however, is barred by the middle pillar of the bridge, blocking any hope of a clearer view beyond our present predicament. Here the shifting forces of technology—both in the structure of the bridge itself and in the power lines it is supporting—achieve a focal point of balance, a counterweight in the symbol of unity, and a sign of hope with the color of truth. This central point of perspective, upon which the movement of lines, curves and colors can rest, solidifies the stabilizing choreography of the imagined structure: a simultaneity of multiple perspectives allows to view the underside as well as the different vistas of Brooklyn Bridge, to grasp its functions and its symbolic values, its sights and its sounds, its presence and its future in a structured kaleidoscope grounded in transcendence.

---

8 Although this city resembles a ship, it has the feel of a gigantic cathedral; but inside the cathedral is a hotbed of commotion. The effect is dizzying: life is whirling around at indescribable speeds and with ferocious energy.

9 The single precedent in the visual arts for Stella's synthetic ode to New York was *Manhatta*, the film collaboration of Charles Sheeler and Paul Strand that premiered in 1920. As if anticipating Stella's painting, the film opens with a ferryboat arriving in the port and closes with the sun setting on the Hudson River; and in between are views of Brooklyn Bridge, the harbor, railroad yards, skyscrapers, and buildings under construction. Punctuating these shots were quotes from Whitman's poems "A Broadway Pageant," "Crossing Brooklyn Ferry" and "Manahatta." The film achieved an epic drama that was at once contemporary and romantic. These are precisely the dualities that Stella combined in his composite panorama of the city, adding a blue circle to the blue flower of Romanticism.

Stella went on to do four more paintings of this bridge of all bridges: *American Landscape* (1929),[10] a simplified version of *The Bridge* in 1938,[11] *Brooklyn Bridge: Variations on an Old Theme* (1939)[12] and in 1941 at age 63 *The Old Bridge*, his last bridge painting, another panel markedly reducing the complexities of his second.[13]

This painting, rightfully considered his masterpiece, is an open act of secondary symbolism since Brooklyn Bridge had already been well established as a cultural icon of modern American civilization. Stella reinterprets the popular, abstracts from its public iconography and re-visualizes it as a private symbol of high ambivalence and ambiguity: with an above-below, upward-downward split running through the picture forcefully demonstrating the painterly representation and pictorial (self-)expression (both abstracted from the bridge's three-dimensional topography and subjectified from its cultural conventionality) the bridge turns into a modernist cathedral built on the daunting, yet also troubling, foundations of modern technology. Keeping the cool of the modern unbeliever together with his *angst* by presenting Gothic arches in cubist simultaneity, Stella is doubling our

---

10 It is a vertical landscape of buildings, factories, warehouses, and bridges. Solid buildings looking like a wall; grey and black with shafts of red, blue and green. The suspenders of the bridge are wider, more like the iron bars of a closed gate. As viewers, however, we are kept outside—we are not on the bridge, but beside it, off to one side. This picture is no longer an open door, it is a closed gate.

11 The lower structure is gone, and there is no second bridge in the right arch. The buildings are straighter and plainer. And the mysterious threatening darkness of the first bridges has been replaced by an insulating mistiness.

12 Here he repeated certain symbols and designs from the *New York Interpreted* panels. The skyscrapers are now more solid, rays of light project from the skyscrapers to the stars. Strips of bright yellow border the sides of the tower. The roadway is open. Blues and yellows replace the dark mystery of the subways and tunnels.

13 In his second and most famous picture, the heavy weight of the structure frames and even holds down all activity. As the bridge soars, it remains as solid as steel and stone (a private symbol for Stella the immigrant, the wanderer between countries and styles, a 20th century nomad). In the big paintings of the bridge, Stella chose 'abstract' art, perhaps because only in this style he was able to describe and make visual sense out of the towering city and the restless rush of modern urban life.

vision to present an intimation of transcendence in the very midst of the many activities that take place simultaneously in the picture.[14]

Joseph Stella's fashioning of an affirmative myth out of the crude realities of the technical world of the 1920s, his desire to resuscitate the contemporary, but decaying culture by arranging it around a mythical icon of old world art, is very close to Hart Crane's poetic design in *The Bridge* (even if the genres do shift). Crane's project does sound familiar in the context of aesthetic modernism.[15] unifying legends from American history with contemporary reality, re-animating the past in a contemporary culture with its railroads, subways, warplanes, and office buildings, and employing Brooklyn Bridge as an emblem of this unification, a passage between a trans-temporal ideal and the transitory sensations of history.[16]

*

In the winter of 1923, Crane had announced his plans for a long poem he intended to call *The Bridge*. It should be epic in scope, a mythical synthesis of America that would answer to "the complete renunciation symbolized in *The Waste Land*, published the year before" (Brunner 11; [ill. 052]). Taking Eliot's complex critique as his negative foil, Crane conceived of his poetic answer as projecting a myth of affirmation and he used the Brooklyn Bridge as a springboard against Eliot's London Bridge on which "each man fixed his eyes before his feet"

---

14 The machine was not to be ignored but absorbed into poetry, where its destructive forces would be countered through the creation of an alternative myth, a truly modernized romanticism.
15 As in Dorothy Landers Beall's verse-drama "The Bridge" (in *The Bridge and Other Poems* 1913) it also wants to 'bridge' the opposite impulses of love and power.
16 Stella's influence on Crane is still being questioned: His 1918 version was reproduced in the autumn 1922 issue of *The Little Review,* reproductions of *The Bridge* and *Skyscrapers* from *New York Interpreted* were printed in the February 1923 issue of *The Arts*. According to Crane, however, he first saw the paintings in late 1928 when Charmion von Wiegand showed him a copy of Stella's privately printed monograph *New York,* containing his essay on the Brooklyn Bridge and reproductions of *New York Interpreted*. Then Crane decided to use *The Bridge* as the frontispiece of the published version of his poem. For a variety of reasons, however, nothing came of his plan.

(Brunner 12) in a procession of the living dead. Crane moved physically closer to his poetic project—in 1923 he relocated to Brooklyn Heights, next to "the most beautiful Bridge in the world"—and in 1924 he lodged in 110 Columbia Heights, in the very house, and later even the very room occupied some fifty years earlier by Washington Roebling, son and heir of John Roebling, the visionary architect of Brooklyn Bridge. This room commanded the view of the bridge as it spanned the East River and had been used by the younger Roebling as his headquarters and command post after a crippling accident had retired him from the construction scene itself. During the next three years, Crane focused his imagination from the same vantage point upon that structure and its possible interpretations, transforming the concrete construction into a flight of fancy, turning the granite and steel into his emblem of eternity, making out of the passageway of thousands of commuters a passage between the Platonic ideal and the transitory moments of each day, a physical point of metaphysical import: a vision of harmony between realms of experience divided further and further.

Crane's epic poem recycles the myth of cyclical return, the antithesis to modern historical linearity. Its speaker evokes legends and legendary figures from American history beginning with Columbus, Cortez, and de Soto, and including the New England whalers, the frontiersmen, the 1849ers; and he is naming his models and precursors, calling upon Melville and Dickinson, Poe and Whitman. The action of the poem spans out over 15 sections in eight numbered chapters, and comprises one day—from dawn in "Harbor Dawn" to midnight in "Atlantis" [Fig. 1]. This single day and the single span of space between Brooklyn and Manhattan is broadened into both history and geography, stretching across the American continent—from Cape Hatteras on the Atlantic seashore, down the Mississippi to New Orleans, westward with the diggers to Colorado and finally to California. The reader is pushed back in time to Columbus on his voyage back to Spain, to the primeval world of the American Indians and one of their famous figures, Pocahontas. And he is brought back to modern times again—with the Wright brothers testing their flying machine, with three hoboes jumping trains to escape their economic woe, and with the speaker on a subway trip through the bowels of New York City scanning "the toothpaste and the dandruff ads" (Brunner 17). The relations between past and present, myth and modernity are far from arbitrary, though their correspondences are seldom spelled out and never arrested at a consistent and stable level of relevance or narration, presentation or stylistic framing. To give just one example: Pocahontas, the historic-mythical figure evoked by the section title, "II. Powhatan's Daughter," and in turn evoking Captain Smith's Virginia tall tales of near-death and miraculous escape, is equated with the very continent in "The Dance," three sections later; the perspective is that of an Indian poet/seer/ brave—and the next section is titled "Indiana." This increasing grandiosity in a mythology of Nature is sardonically deflated in "National Winter Garden," when the symbolic dance of the tribal braves is mirrored in a striptease performance, a pointed travesty of the Indian heritage as a form of modern entertainment, a reduction of mythical America to cheap sexual titillation, and a critique of the exclusively economic interest displayed in the popular 1920s New York vaudeville theater referred to in the section's title.

Grasping the reader's attention and playing upon his established association at the very opening of the epic, the first "Proem" is titled "To Brooklyn Bridge" [Fig. 2]. The setting is the familiar locale, New York Harbor and Lower Manhattan, and views of the Bay and the Statue of Liberty reinforce this sense of place. The point of view is mobile, shifting from an office in a skyscraper, down an elevator into the street, chancing into a dark movie house, and then returning to the sun-drenched walkway of the bridge. This bridge, or rather the view of the bridge, is changing also, until the perspective is directed upward from down under the structure, deep in its shadow. The shifting viewpoints and vistas circle around the immobile structure of Brooklyn Bridge, locating it as the link between the boroughs, but also isolating it, and gradually—through the concentration upon it—setting it apart from its surroundings, putting it into motion, activating, mobilizing it: "turn," "breathe," "lift," "sweep" are now the verbs associated with it. This realignment of the structure with the scenery around it can be seen in the play upon the geometry of the curve in the poem—from the flight of the gulls to the bend of the sails, the gradient is repeated several times in the movement around the architectural center of perspective and awareness—until the same curve is perceivable in the slide of the cables through the line of vision, in the bend of the lines from Brooklyn Tower to Manhattan Tower where the catenary's downward slope meets the upward convex of the roadway itself in the middle of the scene. Here the very architecture becomes sacerdotal.

Just as its planners and engineers had interpreted the bridge's structure as 'tensions at rest', Crane's bridge appears as a collection and a reflection of movements around, against and over it, taking them up, incorporating them and counter-pointing them in an image of movements arrested and abstracted. Collecting these visual attentions in their diverse zooms and zoomings, these reflections of motions against it, the structure itself is addressed as sign and symbol, signified and signifier. What is more, in stanzas seven and eight the bridge is partaking of divinity itself when its cables and suspenders, stays and truss work are turned into "harp and altar"—instrument and place of praise and prayer, jubilation and devotion, withdrawal from the material world in its very midst, and symbol of the greatness of human art in celebrating life.

In the last lines, the full potency of its meaning, its symbolic potential appears in the direct address of "curveship"—sign and signal of an epiphany, attaining to the deity itself which appears manifested in the design as well as in the associations which have been piled up upon it through the first ten stanzas: an imploration of the mythical manifestation of the divine.[17] This at least the bridge imports for the speaker of the poem who is also mask and figure of the poet: a promise of delivery, a structure of transcendence as well as imminence, a chance of retrieving the lost ideals of America, and a model for going after them—building bridges from the given and quotidian to attain the immanent, utopian, and transcendent.[18]

The bridge is no longer an object in the contemporary reality, not just Brooklyn Bridge, the image and icon used in aesthetic constructs, adopted and adapted in modern painting, not only a sign for and a

---

17 In the "Proem," Brooklyn Bridge metamorphoses into a feudal chieftain "Accolade thou dost bestow," a Roman Catholic rosary "Beading thy path," a "harp and altar" and so on. Likewise, in "Atlantis," the Bridge is divested of its status as empirical object and becomes a "Psalm of Cathay," the "whitest Flower" and a weaving machine for spinning yarns: "Pick biting way up towering looms [in weaving a *Pick* is being cast or thrown off the shuttle, a suitable image for the bridge's metaphorical *looms*]" (Simon 141).

18 Fittingly enough, the epigraph of the epic poem is taken from the Book of Job—it is Satan's reply to God's question where he might be coming from: "From going to and fro in the earth, and from walking up and down in it" (Simon 119). Here the connection of the many scenes on earth and their single metaphysical correspondence in the numinous is established through the dialogue of the opposing principles of Christian mythology—another moment of bridging.

symbol of America, it is a symbol for modern poetry itself, designating a process of sense building, connecting and bridging by leaps and bounds, jumps and curves and bends, alluding to the internal processes of composing and of reading the poem, and to the semi-conscious acts of construction and re-construction. The Roebling construction in the end signifies "Cathay," the land Columbus claimed to have found, and it is used as a designation of the speaker's search for himself, the meaning of his life, and of course, the meaning of his world, of America, of modernity and its constant negotiation with and renegotiation of the past, its heirlooms, monuments, memories, texts and subtexts, strata of submerging meanings and collected data, conscious, semi-conscious, unconscious. The reader's awareness of nexus, connection, negotiation and interrelation is thus both emphasized and is becoming unstable, shifting, toppling and reverted.

Crane's epic poem is trying to make the reader leap into a new consciousness as an answer to the troubles of modernity, the loss of sense and the blunting of sensibilities—at least this is Crane's intention: That the poem is also bewildering in its technical complexity; its authorial puns are part and parcel of its design, making it difficult to navigate its inter-connectedness of abstraction and subjectivity.

Conclusion

Both Joseph Stella and Hart Crane have employed the modern icon of New York's Brooklyn Bridge because of its monumental splendor and its well-established iconicity. The picture of its overwhelming architecture had been used to represent the technical advances of modern city building and the technological sublime associated with the new experiences of speed and noise of mass transportation, the collapse of distance and duration, and the new rhythm of the wheel around which the modern senses were reorganized in a new logic of time. Both Stella and Crane use the icon of the bridge, the access point to Manhattan with the supply lines for its businesses, as a focal image presenting cultural constructions of progress against a background of past achievements. And both artists utilize opposing principles of modernity and of modern art in the process and the mode of adapting this icon of New York City—the concept of abstraction and the mode of subjectification and individualization:

Stella is reconstructing the structural properties as well as the visual possibilities of the bridge in an attempt to capture the multitude of movements and the simultaneity of experiences of all people in one image; this image, abstracted from the physical conditions and the realistic limitations, provides a singular recombination of the cityscapes orchestrated here—focused in the perfect roundness of an azure circle in a black square which opens up a transcending vista in the midst of a mind-boggling concussion of movements and sights which are coming towards the viewer from many different directions all at once. This focalization corresponds to the structural grounding of the presented mobility and the low and long swing of the supporting tension upward, leading the gaze beyond the picture present. Here the interpretation of the modernity abstracted reaches back into the mythical justification of a central perspective—the foundation of the very act of seeing in a divine illumination. This transgression of modern self-reference allows for the painting's stark and startling focalization, its heavy structural swing against the plurality of details and perspectives, and the opening vision of a unifying principle for contemporary life in the very midst of the cacophonous bustle on the main thoroughfare in New York.

Crane, on the other hand, uses the very concept of bridging, connecting of naturally divided territories, as the forming and founding principle for his epic undertaking: the span that combines Manhattan to Brooklyn signals the modern interconnectedness of the American landmass and the American society, and combines this symbol of expansion and integration with the polarities of contemporary culture from aestheticism to commercialism and with the past and its so very different cultures and conceptualizations. Swinging is a recurrent image in "The Bridge"; the vacillation between opposites becomes the poetic attempt to assimilate multiple layers of linguistic meaning as well as referential difference and to reconcile them in an overarching harmony of movement as such. *The Bridge* as a visionary poem encapsulates a heroic quest, at once personal and epic, to find and enunciate "America."[19] The material bridge stands at the center of all the motion, it stands, finally, for the poem and for poetry itself. The fif-

---

19 When finally published in 1930 by the Black Sun Press in Paris, *The Bridge* contained three black-and-white photographs of Brooklyn Bridge by Walker Evans.

teen separate sections are arranged musically, with recurring, modulated themes rather than a narrative or an expository line. As in most modernist poems, the verse is open and varied, the syntax complicated and often ambiguous, the references too often dependent on the personal, consisting at times of inaccessible trains of thought. Crane wrote from the paradoxical, conflicting position of the outsider claiming to speak from and for the very center of America. At the same time, Crane's voice is charming the contradiction into a concert of sound, a pattern of relatedness, and a stance of awareness bordering on the sublime—the unifying vision of a transtemporal principle that bestows meaning and mission onto the arbitrariness of historical accident and aesthetic idiosyncrasy is sustained only by a modern prophet's vision and voice.

Both works of art are based on and set against the reality of the 1920s, the jazz age, flirtation and inflation, progress and prohibition, a time, which did not support many leaps of faith. It was also a period of frantic construction, of competition for the 'Tallest Building in the World'—a title won in 1930 by the Empire State Building. At the time the choice of the then forty year-old Brooklyn Bridge as poetic theme indicates in itself an interest in some historical grounding, some bridging between past and presence, some connection to the swiftly disappearing history of the USA.

The urge towards impersonality, abstraction, *and* subjectivity/individuality, that are at the core of all dichotomies of modern epistemology, results in principles of balancing in the art of both Stella and Crane: While Stella is establishing a ground swing of physical transgression, which is arrested and transformed in the focal push through the very center of the pictorial arrangements of his *Bridge*, Crane's ambiguities and contradictions in his poetic series is balanced by his principle of bridging, bringing disjunctive elements into a unity of unsystematic wholeness, with the elation of the speaking voice, its chiming leap of faith into a subjective cohesion of interpretation, blending obstacles and obfuscations in a sermon of self-transcending rhetoric.

Works Cited

Brunner, Edward. *Splendid Failure: Hart Crane and the Making of "The Bridge."* Urbana: U of Illinois P, 1985.
Haskell, Barbara. *Joseph Stella*. New York: Whitney Museum of Modern Art, 1994.
Saunders, Robert J., and Ernest Goldstein. *Joseph Stella: The Brooklyn Bridge—Let's Get Lost in a Painting*. Champaign, Il: Garrard Publishing Co., 1984.
Simon, Marc, ed. *The Complete Poems of Hart Crane*. London: Norton, 1993.
Trachtenberg, Alan. *Brooklyn Bridge: Fact and Symbol*. Chicago: Chicago UP, 1965.

Fig. 1

The whole poem is structured in these titled sections:

I. Ave Maria
II. Powhatan's Daughter
    The Harbor
    Dawn
    Van Winkle
    The River
    The Dance
    Indiana
III. Cutty Sark
IV. Cape Hatteras
V. Three Songs
    Southern Cross
    National Winter Garden
    Virginia
VI. Quaker Hill
VII. The Tunnel
VIII. Atlantis

Fig. 2

"Proem: To Brooklyn Bridge"

How many dawns, chill from his rippling rest
The seagull's wings shall dip and pivot him,
Shedding white rings of tumult, building high
Over the chained bay water Liberty—

Then, with inviolate curve, forsake our eyes
As apparitional as sails that cross

Brooklyn Bridge

Some page of figures to be filed away
—Till elevators drop us from our day ...

I think of cinemas, panoramic sleights
With multitudes bent toward some flashing scene
Never disclosed, but hastened to again,
Foretold to other eyes on the same screen;

And Thee, across the harbor, silver-paced
As though the sun took step of thee, yet left
Some motion ever unspent in thy stride,—
Implicitly thy freedom staying thee!

Out of some subway scuttle, cell or loft
A bedlamite speeds to thy parapets,
Tilting there momently, shrill shirt ballooning,
A jest falls from the speechless caravan.

Down Wall, from girder into street noon leaks,
A rip—tooth of the sky's acetylene;
All afternoon the cloud—flown derricks turn ...
Thy cables breathe the North Atlantic still.

And obscure as that heaven of the Jews,
Thy guerdon ... Accolade thou dost bestow
Of anonymity time cannot raise:
Vibrant reprieve and pardon thou dost show.

O harp and altar, of the fury fused,
(How could mere toil align thy choiring strings!)
Terrific threshold of the prophet's pledge,
Prayer of pariah, and the lover's cry,—

Again the traffic lights that skim thy swift
Unfractioned idiom, immaculate sigh of star,
Beading thy path—condense eternity:
And we have seen night lifted in thine arms.

Under thy shadow by the piers I waited;
Only in darkness is thy shadow clear.
The city's fiery parcels all undone,
Already snow submerges an iron year ...

O Sleepless as the river under thee,
Vaulting the sea, the prairies' dreaming sod,
Unto us lowliest sometime sweep, descend
And of the curveship lend a myth to God.

Contested Space: *Washington Crossing the Delaware* as a Site of American Cultural Memory

Karsten Fitz

> General Washington: "Our project is not to shed blood, but to protect our wives and children; to defend the land we have converted from a dark wilderness to a soil redolent with the fruits of industry. [...] Arouse, ye sons of freedom, and be free. Have your souls become smaller since with frost bitten feet we left our print in blood upon the shores of the Delaware, and bore in triumph a thousand Hessians in our victorious train?"
>
> (All shout.) "Onward, men!"
>
> Nathaniel Harrington Bannister, *Putnam, The Iron Son of '76* (1850)

The most often employed representations of national leaders and national history in the visual arts reveal much about the perception of particular historical events at a certain time and their impact on American cultural self-definitions. In their most persistent forms, visual images and the events they commemorate can turn into sites of national and cultural memory. Among the representations of George Washington, Emanuel Leutze's image of *Washington Crossing the Delaware* (1851, [ill. 053]) is one of the most vigorously enduring representations of American history: the 'father of the nation' leading his men out of a stormy darkness into a new dawn of freedom, surveying and appropriating a contested space—America. Leutze's painting is, as Barbara Groseclose points out, "one of the few works in American art history which deserves the label 'icon'" (*Art* 188). The spatial dimension of *Washington Crossing* oscillates between the geographical space (the Delaware River representing *the* American landscape), the historical/national space (the historical moment which allegedly determined the destiny of America), the local space and audience (the locations where these images were/are exhibited, i.e. the Capitol, museums, magazine covers, inexpensive lithographs, material items, etc.), and, most importantly, the 'ideological' space (evoking 'American' themes and concepts like Manifest Destiny, exceptionalism, nation-building, immigration, and the *rite de passage*-motif).

As Michael Kammen has pointed out in *A Season of Youth: The American Revolution and the Historical Imagination*, "[t]he narrative story of the American Revolution is reasonably well known, [...] yet the Revolution as a mythos, or part of our popular culture, is surprisingly blurry" (*Season* 9). This statement by and large still holds true more than twenty years after its publication. An investigation of how the American Revolution is represented in American works of visual art sheds some light on the function of the Revolution as 'mythos'. Focusing on the major visual representations of Washington's historical passage during the middle decades of the nineteenth century, this paper discusses variations on the theme of *Washington Crossing*—some of its reproductions or 'echoes'—as they inscribe American history in a mythologized form into an American national and cultural memory. Drawing from research within the fields of cultural studies, memory studies, cultural history, literary studies, and art history, I will explore the relationship between visual representations and cultural and historical memory (and forgetting) as well as between images and the historical and cultural construction (and self-interpretation) of a usable past.[1] Thus, this project concentrates on processes of remembering the American Revolution by means of visual representations in order to understand how individuals and groups connect to their collective national and historical experiences. The presupposition is that there exists something like a collective experience, a collective identity—either 'real' or constructed—which the French historian Pierre Nora has called "realms of memory" in his search for the roots of a French collective cultural memory.[2] I suggest that the ways in which land-

---

[1] Particularly the work by art historians Barbara Groseclose and Mark Thistlethwaite on George Washington and Emanuel Leutze, the studies by cultural historians Joyce Appleby and Michael Kammen on commemorating the American Revolution, and the research on cultural memory by Aleida Assmann are major influences for this project.

[2] For the concept of "lieux de memoire," cf., for instance, Pierre Nora, "Between Memory and History: Les Lieux de Memoire," *Representations* 26 (1989): 7-25. Identifying the spheres from which the French nation was collectively constructed, Nora considers the French Revolution as the crucial moment and genuine initiator of a French collective national memory. With regard to American culture a similar project still remains to be conducted.

scape functions in Leutze's version of Washington's historical passage, inscribing concepts like Manifest Destiny and American exceptionalism into an American cultural and historical memory, accounts for the enduringly powerful commemorative potential of this image.[3]

Images and Cultural Memory

In terms of theme, one reusable past for Americans to define their national identity and genealogy has always been the American Revolution and, in particular, the Revolution's personification: General George Washington. Portraits of Washington were first used to mediate between national identities and national ideologies, helping to establish a fertile ground on which ideas of community could be generated. As Barbara Mitnick has recently pointed out, in the early Republic "the United States was a nation in need of heroes, and Washington was in the right place at the right time and with the right credentials." This was important, Mitnick continues, because America

---

3   Of course, there is no *one* monolithic cultural memory (or cultural identity, for that matter) in a multicultural and dynamic society. However, by the mid-nineteenth century there was a strong tendency to construct a collective 'American' identity in the still relatively young American nation in which a consciousness of an American culture was just emerging, and the Revolution, the persona of George Washington, and Leutze's *Washington Crossing the Delaware* all served this larger purpose particularly well.
    There is also a second, very important layer to be studied in the reproductions of this image in prints for a mass audience, e.g. by the lithographic companies of Currier & Ives and Kellogg & Kellogg. Discussing the aspect of cultural memory with regard to Leutze's painting on a larger scale, one would also have to focus on the African-American patriot Prince Whipple, the figure pulling an oar at Washington's knee in Leutze's painting. A clear case of 'repressed' cultural memory, this historical figure is missing in the different versions reproduced by Currier & Ives and Kellogg and Kellogg in the second part of the nineteenth century (see, for example, the first version by Currier and Ives; [ill. 055]). And this is clearly no coincidence, since both versions of the historical crossing adopted by Currier and Ives—the one from Thomas Sully's *The Passage of the Delaware* and the one from Leutze's *Washington Crossing the Delaware*—erased the presence of the black patriot. These prints reflect the growing national tension connected with slavery, resulting in the omission of the black presence and thus in a repressed cultural memory. However, since this is too complex an issue to be discussed here, this will have to be addressed in a separate paper.

needed its own secular national icons "to replace the venerated saints of the Old World" in painted, carved, and printed images (55).

Among the representations of Washington, the image of Washington crossing the Delaware has been used in paintings, sculptures, cartoons, poems, plays, romances, films, and reenactments. The artistic commemorations of Washington during his historical passage over the Delaware River on Christmas Eve in 1776 provide us with important clues to how the Revolution and its most famous protagonist have been culturally re-appropriated over time. For good reasons, it is Emanuel Leutze's famous version of *Washington Crossing the Delaware*, which has become such a highly symbolic site of national and cultural memory and still serves as a model today.[4] It continues to serve as a site of American national and cultural memory in spite—or rather because of—the fact that the more prominent representations of the twentieth century represent parodies, satires or biting criticisms of the cliché produced in Leutze's image.[5]

---

4   There are two recent examples that take Leutze's version as a model: the 1999 New Jersey quarter, on which the image of *Washington Crossing the Delaware* has replaced the eagle on the back, thus creating the first circulating coin to feature Washington on both sides (this shows how powerful the image is to this day in a very serious context); the cover page of the German weekly news magazine *Der Spiegel* (No. 45) of November 6, 2000 (see http://www.spiegel.de/-spiegel/titelbilder), addressing the question "After Clinton: Where is America heading?" after the 2000 presidential elections ("Nach Clinton: Wohin steuert Amerika?"), exemplifies the transnational cultural knowledge and acceptance of Leutze's motif. Reenactments further foster the re-inscription of this image into an American popular cultural memory. The more famous examples of borrowing from Leutze are the Currier & Ives versions (initial version c. 1859, [ill. 055]), Grant Wood's *Daughter's of Revolution* (1932), Larry Rivers' *Washington Crossing the Delaware* (1953), Alex Katz's tableau *Washington Crossing the Delaware* (1961), Robert Colescott's *George Washington Carver Crossing the Delaware: Page From an American History Textbook* (1975), and Peter Saul's *George Washington Crossing the Delaware* (1975). There are also two versions painted by Roy Lichtenstein around 1951 (see Thistlethwaite, *Hero* 152n11).

5   Discussing Larry Rivers's abstract, expressionist version of 1953, which depicts an ill-defined Washington around whom vague spaces and indistinct forms are floating in a rather blurry composition consisting of thin washes of color, art historian Mark Thistlethwaite underscores that such parody and criticism of the Leutze painting nevertheless serves as a commentary on the commemorative power of the image in the twentieth century: "That [Rivers] chose to throw down the gauntlet by portraying a scene best known through Leutze's huge 1851 composition is both a mark of that nineteenth-century painting's celebrity and an in-

Memories—be they individual, historical or national recollections—can become what Aleida Assmann calls "imagines agentes" or "wirkmächtige Bilder" (221), which could be translated into "enduringly and creatively powerful images." These enduringly powerful images become unforgettable through their potential to leave a long-lasting impression and thus have a perpetually sustaining impetus on memory as opposed to other, less effective, images. Enduringly powerful images can thus be considered paradigmatic instruments of memory. By means of associated discourses within a given society particular images are selected, invested with meaning, and anchored in the repertoire of representations reflecting collective memory. What are the associated discourses which make this possible? How does the use of a particular composition in Leutze's painting contribute to make this image, produced in a German revolutionary context by a German-American liberal, fall on such fertile American ground nationally and culturally?

Interestingly, different versions of Washington's crossing were painted by important and influential American painters: two by Thomas Sully and Edward Hicks, respectively, before Leutze and one shortly after by George Caleb Bingham. In what follows, I will focus on how the representation of Washington's ordeal in Leutze's painting contributes to turn his version into the powerful image it has become, while the other versions did not make it as lastingly into the archive of American national and cultural memory. It is the composition of this painting, in particular, and the cultural and national narratives it implies, which serve as stabilizer, if not genuine initiator, of this representation's commemorative potential.

From 'Representation' to 'Site'

The American revolutionary effort was near extinction when George Washington led his ill-equipped army of 2500 hardly prepared volunteers against 1200 well-trained, well-equipped Hessian mercenary troops in a surprise dawn attack, allegedly turning the tide of the Revolution. In fact, if we look at what became of the United States in

---

dication of the low opinion modernists held of history painting, particularly if it involved George Washington" ("Hero" 145).

the decades after the Revolution, the following Battle at Trenton could easily be construed as one of the few battles that can be said to have changed the course of history not just of America but of the entire world.[6] Two future Presidents, James Madison and James Monroe, a future Chief Justice of the U.S. Supreme Court, John Marshall, and the famous rivals Aaron Burr and Alexander Hamilton accompanied Washington that night.

This historical event and the persona of George Washington fascinated Emanuel Leutze (1816-1868), who was born in Germany and came to Philadelphia at the age of nine. At the age of twenty-five, he went to Düsseldorf, Germany, to complete his training as an artist and later to teach at the Düsseldorf Academy of Arts. As a well-known painter he went back to America in 1859, where he died a few years later. Leutze started to paint the first version of *Washington Crossing* in 1849 in Düsseldorf, in a situation of political instability in Germany. The determination of the American revolutionaries and their courage to embrace new ideals is clearly expressed in his painting. The use of the metaphors of the boat and the crossing of the river were probably triggered by a poem by Ferdinand Freiligrath, "who marched with Leutze in the Festival of German Unity [August 6, 1848] and whose path was destined to cross the painter's often in the years of turmoil" (Groseclose, *Leutze* 36). In Freiligrath's poem "Vor der Fahrt," the Revolution is depicted as a ship searching for freedom on

---

[6] At least retrospectively, the event was constructed as being a turning point. John Frost, in his popular *Pictorial History of the United States* (first ed. 1844) describes the result of Washington's crossing of the Delaware as follows: "The enterprise was completely successful, in so far as it was under the immediate direction of the commander-in-chief, and it had a happy effect on the affairs of America. It was the first wave of returning the tide. It filled the British with astonishment; and the Hessians, whose name had before inspired the people with fear, ceased to be terrible. The prisoners were paraded through the streets of Philadelphia, to prove the reality of the victory [...]. The hopes of the Americans were revived, and their spirits elevated; they had a clear proof that their enemies were not invicible, and that union, courage, and perseverance would insure success" (220-221). The weight of the historical moment is similarly depicted by Joel Tyler Headley in *The Illustrated Life of Washington* (1859): Washington's "aspect and air were those of one who felt the crisis of his fate had come. He was about to put a large and almost impassable river across the only way of retreat, and the morning dawn would see his little army victorious, or annihilated, and his country lifted from the gloom that oppressed it, or plunged still deeper into the abyss of despair" (199).

its way to America. A direct reference points to Washington as one of the leaders of this ship called revolution.[7] It is very likely that Leutze, a "fourty-eighter" (the German revolutionaries supported the idea of a unified German nation and the establishment of a democratic legislative government) hoped to motivate his fellow Germans to rebel against the conservative governments, which had violently put down the uprising in Germany.[8] But it is more likely that he hoped to gain support for the German cause in America. After all, Washington's crossing of the Delaware River had been a symbolic moment in the American Revolutionary War.[9] At first sight, the Napoleonic gesture

---

7   Excerpt from Ferdinand Freiligrath's poem "Vor der Fahrt" from his collection *Ca Ira! Sechs Gedichte*, published in 1846 (qtd. and trans. in Groseclose, "Leutze" 36, 65n32; German version qtd.: Ferdinand Freiligrath, *Sämmtliche Werke* [New York: F. Gerhard, 1859] 6: 175-178).

Jenseits der grauen Wasserwüste / wie liegt die Zukunft winkend da! / Eine grüne lachende Küste, / ein geahndet Amerika! / ein geahndet Amerika! / Und ob auch hoch die Wasser springen, / ob auch Sandbank droht und Riff: / ein erprobt und verwegen Schiff / wird die Mut'gen hinüberbringen / . . .	Across the watery waste / The beckening future they saw / A green and smiling coast / A longed-for America! / A longed-for America! / And although the waters churn and toss / And sandbank and reef may threaten the trip / A hard-tested and daring ship / Will bring the brave across/ . . .
Ha, wie Kosciuszko dreist es führte! / Ha, wie Washington es gelenkt! / Lafayette's und Franklin's denkt, / und wer sonst seine Flammen schürte! . . .	Ha, how boldly Kosciuszko guided her! / Ha, how Washington did lead! / Lafayette and Franklin we remember / And whoever else these flames did feed! / . . .
Ihr fragt erstaunt: Wie mag es heißen? / Die Antwort ist mit festem Ton: / Wie in Österreich so in Preußen / heißt das Schiff: "Revolution!" / . . .	You ask astonished: "What's her name?" / To this question there's but one solution, / And in Austria and Prussia it's the same / The ship is called: "Revolution!" / . . .

Each stanza ends with the line "Stosst ab! Stosst ab! Kühn durch den Sturm! Sucht Land und findet Land" / "Shove off! Shove off! Boldly through the storm! Look for land and find land," clearly echoing the voices of plentitude, immigration, and Manifest Destiny.

8   For a more detailed analysis of the embeddedness of the painting within the German revolutionary context, see Groseclose, *Leutze* 34-47.

9   The interpretation of Washington's crossing and the following Battle at Trenton as turning point of the Revolutionary War was probably familiar to Leutze through George Bancroft's *History of the United States* (1834-74), of which he owned the first five volumes, and Jared Sparks's *Life of Washington* (1839), which he also possessed at the time of his death (cf. Groseclose, *Leutze* 65n31).

of Washington's left arm and hand seem to further support this reading within a German revolutionary context. However, this gesture which is characteristic for depictions of the French Emperor during the first half of the nineteenth century, and which is usually ascribed to Washington in Leutze's painting—and often used to support the point that this painting has to be interpreted more in a European than in an American context—is ambiguous. The first painting of George Washington prior to the outbreak of the Revolution was Charles Willson Peale's *George Washington in the Uniform of a Colonel in the Virginia Militia*, painted in 1772. It shows the later first President of the United States in the rank he held at the end of the French and Indian War (1754-1763). The painter, the artist-father of the Peale dynasty, for the first time depicts Washington with his right arm in his vest in a gesture usually considered as Napoleonic. Four years later, Peale painted another, less successful portrait of Washington, this time with his left arm in his vest. Thus it seems that Napoleon Bonaparte is much less the model for Leutze than Peale, which makes Leutze's painting more of an 'American' image than is usually acknowledged.[10] At any rate, neither this German context nor the assumed inspiration by earlier European depictions of the "storm-tossed boat tradition" (Thislethwaite, *Image* 89), do sufficiently explain the painting's success in America.[11]

---

10 Barbara Groseclose also stresses that as a painter Leutze thought of himself as an American first, since "[a]ll of his professional efforts were directed toward the establishment of an American career, and it was American fame he first sought. With the exception of portraiture, everything Leutze painted in these years was destined for American markets" (*Leutze* 25).

11 In art history, Théodore Géricault's *The Raft of the Medusa* (1819) is frequently discussed as one possible inspiration for Leutze's theme and composition. Eugène Delacroix's *Dante and Virgil in Hell* (1822) could have similarly inspired the German-American painter. Although Leutze's painting is, in contrast to Géricault's and Delacroix's, no disaster image, at least one figure in *Washington Crossing the Delaware*, the soldier at the rear of the boat (second from right) with his white, miserable face, recalls the suffering and sense of doom depicted in the two French paintings. It also establishes a connection to the suffering of Washington's army during the previous, devastating Jersey campaign of the year 1776 and relates to the motif of "bloody footprints in the snow," also used by the fictionalized General Washington in the epigraph to this essay and which is employed in virtually every pictorial history of the mid-nineteenth century. After all, a certain degree of suffering often seems to intensify the commemorative impact when it comes to visual depictions of the Revolution in American history

Only after learning about this first, original Leutze-version of *Washington Crossing*, which was soon badly damaged in a fire (but later repaired and exhibited, and eventually destroyed in Germany during WW II), did the American Art Union order a larger version of the image for exhibition in honor of the seventy-fifth anniversary of the American Revolution, to which Leutze gladly responded. In fact, still in 1851 the painting went on a tour in New York and 50,000 visitors paid to see it ("Black History").[12] Art historian Natalie Spassky says that almost immediately the painting gained a status nearly equivalent to a national monument (20).

It is fair to say that Leutze's depiction of the father of the nation leading his men—and, by implication, the American nation just about to emerge—into a glorious future instantly produced a site of cultural memory. In order to become part of the cultural memory, I argue, images of the American Revolution had to concurrently recount the past, make sense of the present, and project the nation's (real or imagined) self-understanding into the future. At the same time, these images had to invoke shared symbols.[13] Also, in order to be far-reaching and persistent within a multicultural and dynamic society, these images could not only be shared by some kind of elite or dominant group; rather,

---

    painting. See, for instance, Paul Revere's engraving of *The Boston Massacre* (1770), John Trumbull's *The Death of General Warren at the Battle of Bunker Hill* and *The Death of General Montgomery* (both 1786), John Vanderlyn's *The Death of Jane McCrea* (1804), and the various paintings of the painful winter camp at Valley Forge. The frequency at which particularly versions of these paintings were reproduced during the nineteenth century in pictorial histories, lithographs, historical prints, and drawings for pictorial magazines suggests that visual depictions of great historical moments of the American Revolution needed to include the element of suffering, if they were meant to be remembered.

12   Although until the 1970s, as Jochen Wierich points out, American art historians and critics in general produced negative responses with regard to Leutze's work, the American public could obviously easily relate to it ("Struggling through History").

13   In her introduction to *Acts of Memory*, Mieke Bal in a somewhat different study (focusing more on traumatic memory in psychoanalytic terms) describes "cultural memorization as an activity occurring in the present, in which the past is continuously modified and redescribed even as it continues to shape the future. Neither remnant, document, nor relics of the past, not floating in a present cut off from the past, cultural memory, for better or worse, links the past to the present and future" (vii). This definition could be similarly applied here.

they had to be ambiguous enough to strike responsive chords within the larger society.[14] Leutze's painting did all of that.

It was Thomas Sully (1783-1872), one of Philadelphia's leading portrait painters of the Romantic School, who first used the theme of Washington's crossing in 1819. His craving was to paint history by recreating authentic images of famous events. Sully's *The Passage of the Delaware* was painted for the Capitol building in North Carolina. In contrast to Leutze, Sully suggests a west-east movement. Washington, here on a horse, is looking back rather lost in thoughts than determined to lead America into a glorious future. Edward Hicks's *Washington Crossed Here* (c.1830), of which he produced six versions, is almost an exact copy of Sully's painting but seems to have been completely ignored.[15] As Mark Thistlethwaite remarks, Thomas Sully's *The Passage of the Delaware* of 1819 was regularly reproduced in the nineteenth century until this depiction of the historical event was replaced by reproductions of Emanuel Leutze's version of the subject after 1851.[16]

---

14 The phrase 'mystic chords of memory' originally stems from Abraham Lincoln's first inaugural Address, March 4, 1861: "The mystic chords of memory, stretching from every battlefield, and patriot grave, to every living heart and hearthstone, all over this broad land, will yet swell the chorus of the Union, when again touched, as surely they will be, by the better angels of our nature." Michael Kammen borrowed the phrase for the title of his book *The Mystic Chords of Memory: The Transformation of Tradition in American Culture*.

15 See Kammen, *Season* 82. The only traceable copy of Hicks's version can be found in Michael Kammen's *A Season of Youth* (here: fig. 5). Unfortunately, the size and quality of this copy does not allow further reproduction. Edward Hicks (1780-1849), a quaker preacher and folk painter, is probably best known for his painting *Peaceable Kingdom* (c. 1830).

16 Thistlethwaite, *Image* 8; 88. Indeed, as my own research on pictorial histories and historical print reveals, Sully's version is the most important one prior to Leutze's (and it remains a fairly important image even after 1851). The following pictorial histories and historical prints copied or at least borrowed Sully's version for their visual representation of Washington's passage: Robert Lincoln, *Lives of the Presidents* (Brattleboro, VT: Brattleboro Typographic Company, 1839); Samuel Goodrich's *The Life of George Washington. Illustrated by Tales, Sketches and Anecdotes* (Philadelphia: Desilver, Thomas & Co., 1837), and also Goodrich's *A Pictorial History of America; Embracing the Northern and Southern Portions of the New World* (Hartford: House & Brown, 1844; also 1848, 1849); William Croome, *The Young American's Picture Gallery* (Philadelphia: Blakiston, 1856); two Currier and Ives versions (one in 1876, engraved by John Cameron, and one undated); an undated nineteenth-century engraving by J. N.

George Caleb Bingham in his *Washington Crossing the Delaware* [ill. 054], which he began in 1856 and finished in 1871, also conveys a significantly different message. Although the theme was directly adopted from Leutze, Bingham (1811-1879), a genre painter and student of Leutze at the Düsseldorf Academy, used a completely different composition. Typical for Bingham, he staged the scene with a strongly pyramid-like formation in the center of the canvas. Poised and statuesque, Washington seems timeless—but motionless, too. There is no notion of movement and progression. Rather, the image exemplifies a standstill, symbolized by the mirror symmetry of the two poles and the relative tranquility of the water.[17] A direction is difficult to make out: the light is centered on General Washington, the east is fairly bright, and the west is very dark.

Up to this day it is the Leutze-image, sometimes referred to as guide painting, which is still considered an American treasure and treated as something of a documentary painting. This is, among other things, evidenced in the highly complicated selection process of choosing Leutze's version for the 1999 New Jersey quarter with the inscription "Crossroads of the Revolution."[18] Influenced by the

---

Gimbrede; a lithograph by Major and Knapp (c. 1870). Reproductions of Leutze's image are too numerous to be individually mentioned. As Gregory M. Pfitzer has recently pointed out, "Works such as *Washington Crossing the Delaware* were reproduced with such frequency in pictorial works such as the *History of the United States* that they came to seem synonymous in the popular mind with the events they described." And, Pfitzer adds, artists "contributed to the trivializing of its imagery by experimenting endlessly with the Leutze formula, even adapting its embarkation format for illustrations that had nothing to do with George Washington" (90).

17   Groseclose's analysis captures this notion of standstill well which, I would argue, explains to some extent why Bingham's version is largely forgotten: "the participant's wholly unbelievable expressions stifle the dramatic moment, just as the design, lacking both inspiration and a successful depiction of movement, brings the floatboat to a halt" ("Missouri Artist" 86). Michael E. Shapiro considers the painting as largely lacking movement and energy (cf. "River Paintings" 161).

18   As the United States Mint stresses on its homepage: "The selection process for the New Jersey quarter began November 17, 1997, when Assembly Joint Resolution Number 68 was passed to establish the New Jersey Commemorative Coin Design Commission. The 15 members of the Commission were selected for their backgrounds in history, art, and numismatics. The commission chose five design concepts for execution into drawings by the U.S. Mint's engravers. After consultation with the Citizens Commemorative Coin Advisory Committee, the Fine

Düsseldorf theater Leutze and others at the Düsseldorf Academy produced paintings similar to acted performances on stage, representing "living pictures" on canvas (cf. Norcross 38). As in portrait painting, theatricality and the staging of individuals—and of events—on canvas became important methods. Interestingly, in this context, Leutze had painted the picture in Düsseldorf, Germany, moulded the Delaware on the Rhine River, and used Americans visiting Düsseldorf as models. Besides Washington, only two of the figures have been identified. One is James Monroe, holding the "Betsy Ross" flag. To support the constructedness of this representation it is interesting to note that Leutze's design of this flag first came into existence some six months after the historical crossing; furthermore, Washington did not stand in the boat, the Durham boats (flat-bottomed iron-ore boats) used for the passage were much longer than the one depicted, and the event happened in the night and not at dawn. The other recognizable figure, pulling an oar at Washington's knee, is said to be the African-American patriot Prince Whipple. There seems to be no historical evidence, however, that Monroe or Whipple were in the same vessel as Washington.

One of the most striking elements that contribute to the success of Leutze's painting is its embeddedness in the philosophy of westward expansion, which is so deeply rooted in popular American self-definitions. The composition of Leutze's painting is the first of the various versions that emerged in the middle decades of the nineteenth century to strongly suggest such powerful ideological or mythic values. The east-west movement—the east symbolically represented by darkness, the west by light and the morning star—, which reverses the actual historical west-east movement from Pennsylvania to New Jersey, clearly suggests expansionism and Manifest Destiny, while Washington's stern pose in combination with effects of light and darkness evokes the concept of American exceptionalism.[19] In Leutze's

---

Arts Commission, and approval by the Secretary of the Treasury, three of these designs were returned to the New Jersey Governor, Christine Todd Whitman, for the final design selection. With her approval, the Commission chose the 'Washington Crossing the Delaware' design, creating the first circulating coin to feature George Washington on both the obverse and reverse sides" ("U.S. Mint").

19 After all, at that point in time America was just in the middle of a period of territorial expansion: the annexation of Texas, the proclamation of Manifest Destiny (both in 1845), and the War with Mexico, which caused a large increase of land

version, George Washington is not simply the commander-in-chief of the continental army: he is the *pater patriae*, the mythic father of an idealized nation, a fearless, statuesque, and invincible leader of unmatched determination and unprecedented moral virtues. All the values and virtues which had been projected onto the persona of Washington for eight decades in the visual arts, beginning with Charles Willson Peale's first portrait of him as leader of the Virginia militia in 1772, resurface in Leutze's painting. But the German-American painter adds a new dimension to it, the idea of a mission embedded in the contemporary context: Washington's glance is fixed and determined, his nose, arms, and knee almost form an arrow, pointing towards the west, towards the future. His mission is more than man-made, the image implies, it is guided by Providence, indicated by, once again, the light-effects in the painting as well as by the morning star (evoking the legend of the three Magi following the star at Christmas) guiding the American cause—and, by implication, representing hope for the rest of the world.[20] By comparison, Sully's, Hicks's and Bingham's paintings do not assume this mythic narrative quality. Neither do they suggest a west-east movement: it is either an east-west movement, as in Sully and Hicks, or standstill, as in Bingham.

The staging of the event in the way exerted by Leutze obviously appeals more enduringly to 'genuinely' American cultural and national values and self-constructions than the versions of the same event produced by other painters. The narratives Leutze's painting engenders seem to correspond with the American collective cultural imagination. This assumption is substantiated by the fact that Currier and Ives used this image (c. 1859; [ill. 055]) in at least two different versions (but the company also produced two versions which are roughly modeled

---

for the U. S. (1846-48), were still in everybody's mind and the Oregon Trail was just beginning to gather force.

20 The idea that Washington's undertaking was part of God's plan is also suggested in one of the mid-nineteenth-century plays, which includes Washington's crossing. In John Brougham's *The Miller of New Jersey; Or, The Prison-Hulk* (1858), the commander-in-chief says: "We must make a bold effort, and entrench ourselves on the opposite shore of the Delaware. At this season of the year, with the broken ice filling the channel, it will be almost as dangerous as the chances of battle, but with a firm reliance upon the assistance of Providence, we shall make the attempt" (24-25).

after Sully).[21] Although much cruder and less detailed than the original, their lithograph basically uses the same composition, background, and direction of the boat, thus also invoking a similar narrative. If Bryan F. Le Beau's recent assessment in *Currier & Ives: America Imagined* is correct—which is that no single person or institution has contributed more to the shaping of an American popular cultural memory in the nineteenth century than Currier and Ives—then the fact that the company used (and reused) this image is quite important. Quoting Harry T. Peters, the most prominent collector of Currier and Ives prints, Le Beau states that "Currier and Ives were businessmen and craftsmen [...] but primarily they [were] mirrors of the national taste, weather vanes of popular opinion, reflectors of American attitudes [...]" (qtd. in Le Beau 2). Currier and Ives had a feeling for what the larger public wanted and *Washington Crossing the Delaware* was an image, which promised to sell well.[22] This was obviously a quality not shared by the other visual versions of Washington's deed. In other words, those mystic chords of memory, to use Michael Kammen's phrase, were obviously not struck by any of the other paintings.

As indicated above, the Leutze-motif also became a prominent image in contemporary pictorial histories. In fact, the image was employed so enduringly as a 'carrier' of American cultural memory that it even heavily influenced the perception and visual reconstruction of Washington's life prior to the Revolution. In the colored wood engraving "Washington Descending the Ohio" used in Joel Tyler Headley's *The Illustrated Life of Washington* (175), Washington is depicted as a

---

21 Conningham lists five versions named *Washington Crossing the Delaware*, all classified as small (approximately 8.8" x 12.8"), and four are undated. It is safe to say, however, that the first two versions were produced before 1857 because they are published by Nathaniel Currier alone (James Ives became Currier's partner only in 1857); one of these versions is designed after Sully, the second is an altogether different version. The two undated versions after 1857 are modeled after Leutze, and one is listed as an engraving on stone by John Cameron. It is interesting that the version the company produced for the centennial in 1876 bears Leutze's title but pays homage to Sully's painting.

22 Concerning the issue of mass production of Currier and Ives prints, Le Beau asserts: "Rather than aspiring to have their work exhibited in the nation's fine-art museums and galleries, they sought to have them hung on the walls of America's homes, stores, barbershops, firehouses, barrooms, and barns. And in this they were widely successful." So successful, indeed, that at one point they created ninety-five percent of all lithographs in circulation in the United States (1).

land-surveyor in 1770 (which he actually was at one point).[23] Not coincidentally, I would argue, the future commander-in-chief assumes a similar pose as in Leutze's *Washington Crossing the Delaware*: the same determined look towards the west (in this case it is his hand which points to the future), a similar overall composition, and a suggested east-west movement (the east here, too, is depicted as much darker than the west). Instead of James Monroe holding the Betsy Ross flag, a Ohio River boatsman is depicted as casually leaning on the pole. Interestingly, the black patriot Prince Whipple, who is positioned at Washington's knee in Leutze's painting (and who is one of the men rowing the boat), gets replaced by another ethnic presence—a Native American in basically the same position, engaged in the same activity (although he is using a pole instead of an oar in order to move the boat). There is still a third man on the vessel, steering the Indian-style canoe, while the Indian is doing the actual physical work. The text to which the image belongs describes Washington as he initially "set out on horseback for the Ohio, to see the western lands for himself, in anticipation of having them surveyed and laid off in tracts for the army" (96). He commenced his journey "beyond the settlements of the whites" to "solitudes hitherto unvisited by the white man" (97). In addition, Washington is reconstructed as a pioneer and frontier's man—literally the spearhead of civilization. The symbolic function of the Indian clearly anticipates the symbolic function of the native presence in Leutze's famous later work *Westward the Course of Empire Takes its Way* (1861): he represents the native people in the west who are in the way of progress and civilization. And although Headley does not (directly) include an engraving of Washington as he crosses the Delaware, his textual depiction of this event—particularly the weather conditions and the marble-like pose of the commander—clearly echoes the one evoked in Leutze's:

> The night closed in dark and cold—the wind swept in gusts down the river, while the rapidly increasing ice threatened to prevent entirely the crossing of the troops in time for a night attack. A few boats reached the opposite shore, when a blinding snow storm set in, casting such a darkness on the river, that those which followed became lost,

---

23 Another such visual reconstruction of Washington's early life influenced by Leutze's painting is William Sidney Mount's *Washington and Gist Crossing the Allegheny* (1863). Here the movement of the boat and the light effects are arranged as in Leutze's image.

and drifted about in the gloom. [...] For nearly twelfe hours [Washington] watched on the banks of the Delaware, listening to the shouts and uproar of his scattered army, floundering in the gloom, and though an eternity seemed to intervene between the arrival of the boats, he showed no irritation, but stood like a column of marble amid the storm, his great heart almost bursting with anxiety, and yet not an indication of it in his voice and bearing. (199-200)

Although impossible to prove, Joel Tyler Headley had obviously studied Leutze's painting quite well.

Whether or not Leutze consciously applied the central theme of westward expansion and Manifest Destiny already in *Washington Crossing the Delaware* is impossible to say for certain. At any rate, he seems to have been heavily influenced by the ancient European paradigm of *translatio imperii*, which has always served as one of the philosophical foundations for westward expansion. This is underscored by Leutze's own words in the *Bulletin of the American Art-Union* in 1851, in which he recalled an epiphany that he experienced when visiting his native Swabian Alps in the early 1840s:

> [There] the romantic ruins of what were once free cities, with their grey walls and frowning towers, in which a few hardy, persevering burghers bade defiance to their *noble* oppressors, whose territories often extended to the walls and surrounded their towns, led me to think how glorious had been the course of freedom from those small isolated manifestations of the love of liberty to where it has unfolded all its splendor in the institutions of our own country. Nearly crushed and totally driven from the old world it could not be vanquished, and found a new world for its home.

Leutze was of course projecting his insight onto the United States, the country of which he was a citizen and to which he was to return after his Düsseldorf years, and he continued:

> This course represented itself in pictures to my mind, forming a long cycle, from the first dawning of free institutions in the middle ages, to the reformation and revolution in England, the causes of emigration, including the discovery and settlement of America, the early protestation against tyranny, to the Revolution and Declaration of Independence. (qtd. in Groseclose, *Leutze* 23-24)[24]

---

24 As Groseclose points out, the statement had already appeared (written in the third person) in Henry P. Tuckerman's *Artist-Life, or Sketches of American Painters* (New York: D. Appleton & Co.) in 1847 (*Leutze* 64n19).

Against this background it seems to be undeniable that Leutze was writing in the *translatio*-tradition, that is, with the assumption "that the idea of civilization's westward movement came into being as an analogy to the course of the sun from the East—*ex oriente lux*— towards the unknown territory beyond the Pillars of Hercules" (Freese 365), an interpretation projected upon America since the 'discovery' of the New World.[25] Ten years later, the immense influence of the *translatio*-paradigm and of the westward movement on Leutze could no longer be denied, as evidenced in his mural painting *Westward the Course of Empire Takes its Way* (1861) produced for the Capitol in Washington.

Despite the German context in which the painting was created and despite its historical inaccuracies—an excellent case in point with regard to the interrelation of myth and history—, *Washington Crossing* soon gained a mythic status. Unable to tell which loomed larger, Leutze's American experience or his European *translatio*-tradition, *Washington Crossing* was redefined and made usable within the American popular imagination. Besides the above-mentioned east-west movement there are at least three additional elements that helped pave the way of this image into the storehouse of American cultural memory the way it did: the landing-theme (immigration), the rite de passage-motif, and the aspect of nation-building.

The implied landing-topic probably also reflects Leutze's own immigration experience and that of Germans in general, whose number of immigrants soared after 1848.[26] "Before Leutze," as Thistlethwaite points out, "virtually no artist had shown Washington in a boat" ("Our Illustrious Washington" 11). As evidenced in Sully's,

---

25 For an excellent and detailed survey of the concept of *translatio imperii, religionis et studii*, see Freese.

26 As Jochen Wierich remarks: "In 1852, at the height of the immigration, 250,000 Germans entered the United States. In more than an abstract way, works such as *Washington Crossing the Delaware* spoke to the political aspirations of German immigrants who came to America in the aftermath of failed European revolutions, seeking a home where their liberal ideas could take root" ("Struggling through History"). But also Leutze's own immigration experience must have influenced the painter, particularly since his family did not merely emigrate from Germany for economic reasons: a poem dedicated to Emanuel's father Gottlieb upon his departure to the United States suggests that the Leutze family left Germany primarily to seek political liberty in America (cf. Groseclose, *Leutze* 14; thus also the subtitle to Groseclose's book, *Freedom is the Only King*).

Hicks's, and Bingham's paintings, Washington was usually represented on horseback in the first part of the nineteenth century. The landing-theme is even more apparent when viewed against the background of one of Leutze's earlier master pieces, *The Landing of the Norsemen* (1845). When he painted that picture, Leutze might have thought of the crossing of the Atlantic by the Norwegian Leif Erikson at the turn of the first millennium, who supposedly established a small settlement on the east coast of North America. Even if the romantic staging of this landing scene seems exaggeratedly melodramatic, it clearly reveals the range of feelings which accompany such an undertaking: a sad departure, anxiety about the future in a new and unknown place, and a cheerful hailing of the supposedly virgin space of freedom (cf. Bott 307). Of course, the paintings by Sully, Hicks, and Bingham also somehow suggest a landing. However, in these paintings the combination of west-east movement or even standstill (Bingham), the absent boat (Sully, Hicks), and the fact that any determined glance into a prospective future on the part of General Washington is missing do not support a landing-theme, which could, ideally, be connected to the topic of immigration. Nor do these images suggest the *translatio*-motif discussed above.

The rite de passage-motif is the most favorite and quintessential topic of American popular literature in the nineteenth century dealing with the American Revolution, and it serves as an important subtext here.[27] After all, earlier in his life Washington had led the Virginia militia for King George against the French, thus serving to secure English influence and control in the American colonies. Now—that is in the historical moment addressed in Leutze's painting—he is guiding the revolutionaries towards a decisive victory against the former 'parent' England. Thus, at least as is symbolically implied, there is a coming of age that is the separation from 'mother'/'father' England. In popular literature, inter-generational conflict and divided families often symbolize the divided empire: the leaving of home, patricide, con-

---

27 Defined by Arnold Van Gennep in *Les Rites de Passages* (1909) as ways in which adults incorporate adolescents into the community of mature men and women. Rites of passage are usually undertaken in conjunction with birth, adolescence, marriage, and death, as Alfred M. Tozzer describes in *Social Origins and Continuities*. For a detailed elaboration on rites of passages, cf. Turner, *The Ritual Process*.

frontations between parents and children, between brothers, among cousins. This specific rendering of the coming of age can be traced to the Puritan self-interpretation of the Atlantic crossing as a spiritual voyage towards a progression of souls into a state of grace (see Kammen, *Season* chpts. 5 and 6).

The aspect of nation-building is closely linked to the rite de passage-motif. As Joyce Appleby's recent study of autobiographical writing commemorating the Revolution demonstrates, the construction of the American Revolution in retrospect has always been shaped by two things: firstly, the writers' own remodeled experience since the event and, secondly, by how they imagined their country's self-definition and national creed for the future at the time of writing. Out of this rather complex tension of often conflicting conditions, "a new character ideal was created," as Appleby points out in *Inheriting the Revolution*: "the man who developed inner resources, acted independently, lived virtuously, and bent his behavior to his personal goals—not the American Adam, but the American *homo faber*, the builder" (11). What Appleby states with regard to autobiographical writing is also an important theme in *Washington Crossing*. Painted more than seventy years after the event, Washington here personifies the American ideal as builder of the new nation, particularly expressed through his pose, that is, being the spearhead. Also closely linked to the issue of nation-building is the allusion to the Columbiad, which was a very powerful image in nineteenth-century America because of its inference of going back to the beginning and the implication that something genuinely new was created when Columbus arrived in the New World. It is definitely no coincidence in this context that three earlier Columbus paintings by Leutze, *Columbus before the High Council of Salamanca*, *The Return of Columbus in Chains to Cadiz* (both painted in 1842), and *Columbus before the Queen* (1843) had already been great successes both in Europe and America (cf. Groseclose, *Leutze* 19-20). Here, the theme of nation-building and the *translatio imperii*-motif clearly go hand in hand.

Conclusion

As is most often the case when reading and interpreting 'texts', Emanuel Leutze's visual narrative *Washington Crossing the Delaware* reveals much more about the time in which it was produced than about the actual event. Beginning with its very production, the situating of Washington within this American landscape has immediately provided America with a national and cultural narrative (ostensibly) about the American Revolution. As I have tried to demonstrate, the conflicting narratives and interpretations of Leutze's painting were integrated and subsumed within a mid-nineteenth century cultural memory that was built on sufficiently clear images and messages with regard to an American past in order to construct an American cultural identity which could be shared by many. The conflicting potential of this image was only seriously tackled in the twentieth century. The success of Leutze's *Washington Crossing* in contrast to the other versions of this event is a particularly valid testimony to the belief that Americans had developed a sense of history, which they now emphatically claimed. As a writer enthusiastically put it in *The New York Review* in 1839, "we now have a glorious past, and it is time for us to value and venerate it" (qtd. in Thistlethwaite, *Image* 20). It needed a changed self-definition and national self-awareness to openly claim this glorious history. And this is, above anything else, what Leutze's painting most effectively does. In his study *The Image of George Washington*, Thistlethwaite describes this newly gained national self-awareness of the mid-nineteenth century: "No doubt existed in the minds of Americans concerning their history of uniqueness; America was conceived of as the New World, the New Eden, and the beginning of a new history. While this stress of 'newness' caused many Americans, particularly in the spirit of Manifest Destiny, to look forward rather than back, the assertive nationalism of the age" was employed as an increasingly important topic in the visual arts (20). To be sure, this process of assertive nationalism already began before the mid-nineteenth century. However, it was Emanuel Leutze who decisively helped to visually inscribe this process into the American cultural memory by reconstructing the American Revolution as the starting point of this new nation, positioning—or rather mythologizing—it within a contemporary context.

    It is the combination of national and cultural narratives and myths, which constitutes the crucial subtexts to the actual painting. The east-west movement, which signifies the various national and cultural concepts, is at the heart of the popular success of *Washington Crossing*: it directly or indirectly represents the *translatio imperii*-paradigm, expansionism and Manifest Destiny, landing-theme, *rite de passage*-motif, and nation-building. It is the combination of these various narratives that have turned *Washington Crossing* into a site of American cultural memory. Upon closer inspection, it is not so strange that a liberal German-American painter and patriot created a picture in Düsseldorf, which became appropriated by the American popular imagination. After all, Jewish immigrants established the Hollywood film industry at the beginning of the twentieth century and Roland Emmerich and Wolfgang Petersen, two German film directors who made their careers in Hollywood, currently produce highly patriotic American films (Emmerich made *Independence Day* in 1996 and *The Patriot* in 2000; Petersen directed *Air Force One* in 1997). I do not intend to equate mid-nineteenth century history painting with current Hollywood action movies. However, there seems to be a certain parallel. At least when it comes to visual representations, it appears that the 'author' is really and irrevocably dead: what counts is not so much *who* created the image but *what* the image generates within a given culture. As obvious as this insight into the power of cultural and national narratives appears to be in Leutze's particular case, a great deal of critical work remains to be done in order to uncover the culturally important narratives behind visual representations in American arts, particularly with regard to the cultural memory debate.

Works Cited

Appleby, Joyce. *Inheriting the Revolution: The First Generation of Americans.* Cambridge: Harvard UP, 2000.

Assmann, Aleida. *Erinnerungsräume: Formen und Wandlungen des kulturellen Gedächtnisses.* München: Beck, 1999.

Bal, Mieke, Jonathan Crewe, and Leo Spitzer. *Acts of Memory: Cultural Recall in the Present.* Hanover, NH: UP of New England, 1999.

Bannister, Nathaniel Harrington. *Putnam, The Iron Son of '76.* New York: S. French & Son, 1850.

Brougham, John. *The Miller of New Jersey; Or, The Prison-Hulk.* New York: S. French, 1858.

"Black History: Prince Whipple in American Painting." http://www.seacoastnh.com/-blackhistory/prince.html [Dec. 18, 2004].

Bott, Katharina and Gerhard, eds. *ViceVersa: Deutsche Maler in Amerika, Amerikanische Maler in Deutschland, 1813-1913.* München: Hirmer Verlag, 1996.

Conningham, Frederick A. *Currier & Ives. An Illustrated Check List*. 1949; 1970. New York: Crown Publishers, 1983.

Davidson, Abraham A. *The Story of American Painting*. New York: Abrams, 1979.

Freese, Peter. "'Westward the Course of Empire Takes Its Way': The *translatio*-Concept in Popular American Writing and Painting." *Amerikastudien/American Studies* 45.2 (1996): 365-395.

Frost, John. *The Pictorial History of the United States of America. From the Discovery by the Northmen in the Tenth Century to the Present Time. Embellished with three hundred and fifty engravings from original drawings, by W. Croome*. 4 vols. Philadelphia: Benjamin Walker, 1844.

Groseclose, Barbara S. *Nineteenth-Century American Art*. London: Oxford UP, 2000.

—. *Emanuel Leutze, 1816-1868: Freedom is the Only King*. Washington: Smithsonian Institution P, 1975.

—. "The 'Missouri Artist' as Historian." *George Caleb Bingham*. Ed. Michael Edward Shapiro et al. St. Louis, MO: The Saint Louis Art Museum, 1990. 53-91.

Headley, Joel Tyler. *The Illustrated Life of Washington. Giving an account of his early adventures and enterprises, his magnanimity and patriotism, his revolutionary career, his presidential life, and his final decease. With vivid pen-paintings of battles and incidents*. New York: G. & F. Bill, 1859.

Kammen, Michael. *Mystic Chords of Memory: The Transformation of Tradition in American Culture*. New York: Vintage, 1993.

—. *A Season of Youth: The American Revolution and the Historical Imagination*. Ithaca: Cornell UP, 1978.

Le Beau, Bryan F. *Currier & Ives: America Imagined*. Washington, DC: Smithsonian Institution P, 2001.

Meschutt, David. "Life Portraits of George Washington." *George Washington: American Symbol*. Gen. Ed. Barbara Mitnick. New York: Hudson Hills P, 1999. 25-35.

Mitchell, W. J. T. *Iconology: Image, Text, Ideology*. Chicago: U of Chicago P, 1986.

—. *Picture Theory: Essays on Verbal and Visual Representation*. Chicago: U of Chicago P, 1994.

Mitnick, Barbara, gen. ed. *George Washington: American Symbol*. New York: Hudson Hills P, 1999.

—. "Parallel Visions: The Literary and Visual Image of George Washington." *George Washington: American Symbol*. Gen. Ed. Barbara Mitnick. New York: Hudson Hills P, 1999. 55-69.

Nora, Pierre. "Between Memory and History: Les Lieux de Memoire." *Representations* 26 (1989): 7-25.

Norcross, Anne Rosseter. "Amerikanische 'Malerschulen' in Deutschland: Der Einfluß von Emanuel Leutze und Frank Duveneck." *ViceVersa: Deutsche Maler in Amerika, Amerikanische Maler in Deutschland, 1813-1913*. Ed. Katharina and Gerhard Bott. München: Hirmer Verlag, 1996. 37-43.

Peters, Harry T. *Currier and Ives: Printmakers to the American People*. 1929. New York: Doubleday, 1942.

Pfitzer, Gregory M. *Picturing the Past: Illustrated Histories and the American Imagination, 1840-1900*. Washington: Smithsonian Institution P, 2002.

"Review of the National Portrait Gallery of Distinguished Americans." *The New York Review* (April 7, 1839): 353.

Schwartz, Barry. "George Washington: A New Man for a New Century." *George Washington: American Symbol*. Gen. Ed. Barbara Mitnick. New York: Hudson Hills P, 1999. 123-139.

Shapiro, Michael Edward. "The River Paintings." *George Caleb Bingham*. Ed. Michael Edward Shapiro et al. St. Louis, MO: The Saint Louis Art Museum, 1990. 141-174.

—, et. al. *George Caleb Bigham*. St. Louis, MO: The Saint Louis Art Museum, 1990.

Spassky, Natalie. *American Paintings in the Metropolitan Museum of Art*. Vol. II: *A Catalogue of Works by Artists Born Between 1816 and 1845*. New York: Metropolitan Museum of Art, in Association with Princeton UP, 1985.

Stehle, Raymond L. "The Life and Works of Emanuel Leutze." Washington, 1972. Photographic reproduction of unpublished manuscript. Harvard University, Fine Arts Library, 1973.

Taylor, Joshua. *The Fine Arts in America*. Chicago: U of Chicago P, 1979.

Thistlethwaite, Mark. "Hero, Celebrity, and Cliché: The Modern and Postmodern Image of George Washington." *George Washington: American Symbol*. Gen. Ed. Barbara Mitnick. New York: Hudson Hills P, 1999. 141-152.

—. *The Image of George Washington: Studies in Mid-Nineteenth-Century American History Painting*. New York: Garland Publishing, 1979.

—. "'Our Illustrious Washington': The American Imaging of George Washington." http://www.mcconnellcenter.org/pdf.lectures/thistlewaite.pdf [Dec. 18, 2004].

Tozzer, Alfred M. *Social Origins and Social Continuities*. New York: MacMillan, 1925.

Turner, Victor W. 1969. *The Ritual Process: Structure and Anti-Structure*. Chicago: Aldine, 1995.

"The United States Mint: Mint Programs—New Jersey." http://www.usmint.gov/-mint_programs/50sqprogram/states/index.cfm?state=NJ [May 2, 2003].

Van Gennep, Arnold. *Übergangsriten. Les Rites de Passage*. Frankfurt/Main: Campus, 1999 (Trans. of *Les Rites de Passage*. 1909).

Wierich, Jochen. "Struggling through History: Emanuel Leutze, Hegel, and Empire." *American Art* 15.2 (2001): http://www.ewg.K12.ri.us/jhs/blackknights/NPR%-20Crossing%20Delaware%Story/wierich15n2.htm [Dec. 18, 2004].

Contributors

JOCHEN ACHILLES has been Full Professor and Chair of American Studies at Würzburg University since 1999. He taught at Mainz University for many years and was Visiting Professor at Georgia State University, Atlanta, Georgia, in the academic year 1992/93. His publications include *Drama als problematische Form* (1979) and *Sheridan Le Fanu und die schauerromantische Tradition* (1991). He co-edited *Irische Dramatiker der Gegenwart* (1996), *(Trans)Formations of Cultural Identity in the English-Speaking World* (1998), and *Global Challenges and Regional Responses in Contemporary Drama in English* (2003). Numerous book contributions and articles deal with American and Irish fiction and drama, the development of modernist aesthetics, and with individual authors such as Charles Brockden Brown, Washington Irving, Nathaniel Hawthorne, Edgar Allan Poe, Donald Barthelme, Eugene O'Neill, Alice Childress, Amiri Baraka, Adrienne Kennedy, James Baldwin, and August Wilson.

KLAUS BENESCH is Professor of English and American Studies at the University of Bayreuth (Germany). He was a 2004 Mellon Fellow at the Harry Ransom Humanities Research Center of the University of Texas (Austin) and has taught at the University of Massachusetts (Amherst) and Weber State University (Utah). Major publications include *African Diasporas in the Old and the New World* (co-edited with Geneviève Fabre/2004), *The Sea and the American Imagination* (editor/2004), *Romantic Cyborgs: Authorship and Technology in the American Renaissance* (2002), *Technology and American Culture* (editor/1996), and *The Threat of History: Geschichte und Erzählung im afro-amerikanischen Roman der Gegenwart* (1990).

HANJO BERRESSEM teaches American Literature and Culture at the University of Cologne. He has published books on Thomas Pynchon (*Pynchon's Poetics: Interfacing Theory and Text*, U of Illinois P, 1992) and on Witold Gombrowicz (*Lines of Desire: Reading Gombrowicz's Fiction with Lacan*, Northwestern UP, 1998). His articles are situated in the fields of poststructuralism, contemporary American fiction, media studies, and the interfaces of art and science.

ASTRID BÖGER is Assistant Professor of American Studies at Heinrich-Heine-Universität Düsseldorf, Germany, where she also received her M.A. (1994) and her doctorate degree (2000). In 2002/03 she conducted research as a Fulbright Scholar on her post-doctoral project on early American world's fairs. Her rescarch and teaching interests include 19th and 20th century

American literature and visual culture, with a particular emphasis on photography and film. She has published monographs on *Documenting Lives. James Agee's and Walker Evans's 'Let Us Now Praise Famous Men'* (Peter Lang, 1994) and on *People's Lives, Public Images. The New Deal Documentary Aesthetic* (Tübingen: Gunter Narr, 2001), which won the "drupa" prize of the German printing industry. She also co-edited the collection of essays *FrauenKulturStudien. Weiblichkeitsdiskurse in Literatur, Philosophie und Sprache* (with Herwig Friedl; Francke Verlag, 2001) and published critical essays on a wide range of subjects in American literature and film.

TRACEY JEAN BOISSEAU is Associate Professor of Women's and Cultural History at the University of Akron in Ohio. She has published articles on the history of the 1893 Chicago World's Fair in *Signs* and *Gender and History*. Her book, *White Queen: May French-Sheldon and the Imperial Origins of American Feminism* was published by Indiana University Press in 2004.

ROBERT W COLLIN is a Senior Research Scholar at the Center for Public Policy at Willamette University and an adjunct Professor of Law at the Willamette University College of Law. He is also serving as a faculty member in the University of Oregon Environmental Studies program. Collin holds advanced degrees in law, planning, and social work, and has written widely in all three areas, as well as collaborating extensively with Morris Collin in publications in the areas of sustainability and environmental justice. Together they helped to found the Conference Against Environmental Racism (CAER), the Governor's Environmental Justice Advisory Board, and a network of regional activists in the area of environmental justice in the Pacific Northwest. He researches the areas of multiple, synergistic, risks and their consequences for communities.

ROBIN MORRIS COLLIN is Professor of Law at Willamette University College of Law. She teaches Criminal Law, Remedies, Criminal Procedure and Sustainability and the Law. Among others, she practiced administrative law as a staff attorney in the Credit Practices Division of the Bureau of Consumer Protection at the Federal Trade Commission in Washington, D.C., and practiced criminal law as assistant county attorney in the Maricopa County Attorney's Office in Phoenix, Arizona. A graduate of Colorado College, Professor Morris Collin received her law degree from the Arizona State University College of Law. In 1993, she was the first professor to teach sustainability and the law at an American law school. Morris Collin is a member of the National Advisory Council for Environmental Policy and Technology, Standing Committee on Sectors (a federal advisory committee to the U.S. Environmental Protection Agency). She also serves on the board

Contributors

of her family's Red River Shipping Company, the first and only African American owned and operated vessel line.

FLORIAN DOMBOIS is Head of the Institute of Transdisciplinarity (Y) at the University of the Arts Berne (http://www.hkb.bfh.ch/y), Switzerland. He studied Geophysics and Philosophy in Berlin, Kiel, and Hawaii and received his M.A. in Theoretical Geophysics. His Ph.D. in Cultural Studies with Hartmut Böhme focused on the question "What is an earthquake?" His major areas of research are earthquakes, sound, art & science, and modes of depiction and he has conducted several projects on the relation between science and art for the Berlin Academy of Arts. A lecturer at universities and artschools in Berlin, Cologne, Delft, and Los Angeles, he was also a research scientist in charge of a project on earthquake data at the Fraunhofer Institute for Media Communication, St. Augustin, from 1999-2004, (http://www.-gmd.de/auditory-seismology).

GENEVIÈVE FABRE is professor emerita at the University Paris 7 where she is also the director of the Center of African American and Diasporas Studies. Co-author of books on *F.S. Fitzgerald* and *En marge: Les minorities aux États Unis* (1970), she is the author of *James Agee* (1977), *Le théâtre noir américain* (1982), translated as *Drumbeats, Mask and Metaphor: Contemporary Afro-American Theatre* (1983). She has edited various collections of essays on Hispanic literature and barrio culture in the USA, on ethnicity and identity, two volumes on feasts and celebrations among ethnic communities, on history and memory in African-American culture, and a book on Toni Morrison. More recently she has co-edited *Jean Toomer* (2000), *"Temples for Tomorrow": Looking Back at the Harlem Renaissance* (2001), *Celebrating Ethnicity and the Nation* (2001), *Écritures et représentations des diasporas* (2002), and, together with Klaus Benesch, *African Diasporas in the New and Old Worlds* (2004).

MICHEL FABRE is professor emeritus at the Université de la Sorbonne Nouvelle (Paris III) and president of the Cercle d'Etudes Africaines-Américaines. Recent books include *From Harlem to Paris: Black American Writers in France, 1840-1980* (University of Illinois Press 1991), *The French Critical Reception of African-American Literature, An Annotated Bibliography* (Greenwood Publishers 1993), and *The Several Lives of Chester Himes*, in collaboration with Edward Margolies (University Press of Mississippi, 1997).

WINFRIED FLUCK is professor and chair of American culture at the John F. Kennedy Institute for North American Studies of the Freie Universität Berlin. He has been a visiting scholar at Harvard University, UC Berkeley, Yale, Princeton, and UC Irvine. His work has focused on the changing functions of fiction, aesthetic theory, and on theories of American and cultural studies.

His books include *Ästhetische Theorie und literaturwissenschaftliche Methode: Eine Untersuchung ihres Zusammenhangs am Beispiel der amerikanischen Huck Finn-Kritik* (1975), *Populäre Kultur* (1979), *Theorien amerikanischer Literatur* (1987), *Inszenierte Wirklichkeit: Der amerikanische Realismus, 1865-1900* (1992), and *Das kulturelle Imaginäre* (1997). He is currently working on a history of American culture.

HELLMUT FRÖHLICH is a doctoral candidate at the Department of Urban Geography at the University of Bayreuth, Germany. He studied Geography and Urban Planning in Munich and Bayreuth and has dealt extensively with Southern California and the LA School of Urbanism in the context of his master's thesis. He also holds an M.A. in Urban Affairs and Public Policy from the University of Delaware. His research interests are in urbanism and urban geography, social geography and in the connections between cinematic representations and real-world images of cities.

BRIGITTE GEORGI-FINDLAY is Professor of North American Studies at the University of Technology, Dresden. Major areas of research include the cultural history of the American West (Native Americans, women, urban West), travel writing, and American photography. She is the author of *The Frontiers of Women's Writing: Women's Narratives and the Rhetoric of Westward Expansion* (Tucson: University of Arizona Press, 1996) and is currently working on a book-length study of the role of cultural diversity in the urban American West, 1860-1930.

MADELINE GINS and ARAKAWA: For the last forty years, artist-architects-poets Madeline Gins and Arakawa have created a visionary and widely admired body of work—museum installations, landscape and park commissions, experimental texts and films, residential and office designs, philosophical treatises and artistic manifestos—that challenge traditional notions about our built environments and the ways we inhabit them. Their transformations of physical space have consistently explored the poetics of architecture and the nature of contemporary life and thought. Since 1981, with the inception of their theory of *reversible destiny*—the belief that through radical forms of architecture mortality itself can be undone—they have dedicated themselves to rethinking the relationships between architectural environments and the body. In 1997 the Guggenheim Museum presented a retrospective of Arakawa and Gins's collaborative work, which received the College Art Association's highest award for that year (the Artist Award for Exhibition of the Year: Distinguished Body of Work, Presentation or Performance Award), and published a widely acclaimed catalogue of their work titled *Reversible Destiny: WeDestiny (We Have Decided Not to Die)*. Additionally, their work has been the subject of many critical studies by, among others, Jean-François Lyotard, Arthur Danto, Italo Calvino, George

Lakoff, and Hans-George Gadamer. Their more recent projects include "Nagi's Ryanji," a thirty-foot-diameter tube having both left-right and above-below symmetry, and "The Site of Reversible Destiny," a seven-acre park. Currently, two projects based on the design principles outlined in the present text are under way: construction has begun on Bioscleave House, a private dwelling commissioned by a family in East Hampton, New York, and schematic drawings have been completed and delivered for Reversible Destiny Eco-Housing Park—a reversible destiny community of several hundred units.

LOTHAR HÖNNIGHAUSEN is professor emeritus of English and North American Studies at the University of Bonn, Germany. He recently published *William Faulkner: Masks and Metaphors* (Jackson: UP of Mississippi, 1997) and edited/contributed to *William Faulkner: German Responses 1997*, *Amerikastudien/American Studies* (1997), *Regional Images and Regional Realities* (Tübingen: Stauffenburg, 2000), *Space, Place, Environment* (Tübingen: Stauffenburg, 2003), and *Concepts of Regionalism in the Global Age* (2 vols.; Madison: UP of Wisconsin, 2004).

KIRK ARDEN HOPPE is Associate Professor of African and World History at the University of Illinois at Chicago. His primary research interest is the environmental history of East Africa. His book, *Lords of the Fly: Sleeping Sickness Control in British East Africa, 1900-1960*, was published by Greenwood Press in 2003.

GERD HURM is Professor of American Literature and Culture and director of the Center for American Studies at the University of Trier, Germany. His publications include *Rewriting the Vernacular Mark Twain* (2003), *Fragmented Urban Images: The American City in Modern Fiction from Stephen Crane to Thomas Pynchon* (1991), and various edited volumes on American cultural identity and American political rhetoric: *The Fourth of July: Political Oratory and Literary Reactions, 1776-1876* (1992); *Important Speeches by American Presidents after 1945* (1994).

JULIA KURSELL is a researcher at the Max Planck Institute for the History of Science in Berlin. She is the author of *Schallkunst: Eine Literaturgeschichte der Musik in der frühen russischen Avantgarde* (Munich 2003).

MARTINA LEEKER is Assistant Professor for Theater and Media Studies at the University of Bayreuth, Germany. She studied theater, dance, and philosophy in Berlin and in Paris with Etienne Decroux and Jacques Lecoq. She has published on performance with electronic and digital technology and is the author of *Mime, Mimesis and Technology* (Munich: Fink, 1995). She is the editor of *Maschinen, Medien, Performances. Theater an der Schnittstelle zu digitalen Welten* (Berlin, Alexander Verlag, 2001; with cd-rom/dvd) and co-edited *Dance and Technology* (German/English, Berlin: Alexander Verlag, 2002). She is also a founding member of *transARTES, academy of performing art, media and culture*.

RUTH MAYER holds the chair of American Studies at the University of Hanover, Germany. She has written a dissertation on the interrelation of medicine, philosophy, and literature in nineteenth century American culture (*Selbsterkenntnis, Koerperfuehlen*, Fink, 1997), and published extensively on science studies and cultural studies as well as on the debates around cultural contact and transcultural communication. Her recent book publications are *Artificial Africas. Colonial Images in the Times of Globalization* (UP of New England, 2002) and *Virus! Zur Mutation einer Metapher* (co-edited with Brigitte Weingart, Transcript, 2004).

PAUL NEUBAUER studied at the Universities of Munich, Regensburg, Edmonton, and Vanderbilt. He received his Ph.D. in 1990 at the University of Regensburg, where he was Assistant Professor until 1998. He conducted research at Brown University, R.I., and at the Library of Congress in Washington, D.C. From 1998 until 2003 he taught at the American Studies Department of the University of Freiburg. His major publications include *Die Rezeption der US-amerikanischen Literatur der Postmoderne im deutschsprachigen Raum* (1991), *Die Rezeption der US-amerikanischen Erzählliteratur der Postmoderne in der deutschsprachigen Amerikanistik* (1994), and *Zwischen Tradition und Innovation: Das Sonett in der amerikanischen Dichtung des 20. Jahrhunderts* (2001).

DAVID E. NYE is Professor of American studies at Warwick University, and has been a visiting scholar at MIT, Harvard, Notre Dame, Leeds, Cambridge, and the Netherlands Institute for Advanced Study. He is the author of nine books on the relationship between technology and American culture, including *Electrifying America*, for which he won the Dexter Prize and the Abel Wolman Award.

BERNDT OSTENDORF is Professor of North American Cultural History at the Amerika-Institut, University of Munich, Germany. He has published *Black Literature in White America* (1982), *Die Vereinigten Staaten von Amerika* 2 Vol. (1992), *Die multi-kulturelle Gesellschaft: Modell Amerika?* (1995), and *Transnational America. The Fading of Borders in the Western Hemisphere* (2002). His major areas of interest include the cultural history of immigration; the politics of (ethnic) difference, multiculturalism, and public culture; creolization and circumatlantic diasporas; American popular culture and the culture industry; New Orleans and Louisiana. Among his recent articles are "Creolization and Creoles. The Concepts and their History;" "Subversive Reeducation? Jazz as a Liberating Force in Germany and Europe;" "The Politics of Ethnic Difference: Multicultural Theories and Practice in Comparative U.S.-German Perspectives;" "Why is American Popular Culture so Popular? A View from Europe;" and "Americanization and Anti-Americanism in the Age of Globalization."

ULFRIED REICHARDT is Professor of American Studies at the University of Mannheim, Germany. He studied at the University of Heidelberg, Cornell University, and the Free University of Berlin where he received his Ph.D. He was a visiting scholar at Columbia University, New York, and completed his Habilitation at the University of Hamburg. He taught American literature and culture at the John F. Kennedy-Institute of the Free University of Berlin, at the University of Hamburg, and the University of Cologne. His publications include *Postmodernity Seen from Inside: The Poetry of John Ashbery, A. R. Ammons, Denise Levertov, and Adrienne Rich* (1991) and *Alterity and History: The Representation of Slavery in the American Novel* (2001) (both in German); he edited special issues of *Amerikastudien/American Studies* on *Engendering Manhood* (with Sabine Sielke) and *Time and the African American Experience*. Major areas of research include the cultures of the African Diaspora, New York City, American Pragmatism, theories of "time," and the investigation of American cultural history with regard to modernization, individualization, and the "times" of the New World.

FLORIAN RÖTZER is editor of the online journal *Telepolis* (http://www.heise.de/tp/) and author/editor of numerous publications, such as *Französische Philosophen im Gespräch* (Munich 1985), *Kunst Machen. Gespräche und Essays* (with Sara Rogenhofer; Munich 1990), *Digitaler Schein* (Frankfurt 1991), *Philosophen-Gespräche zur Kunst* (Munich 1991), *Strategien des Scheins. Kunst—Computer—Medien* (with Peter Weibel; Munich 1991), *Cyberspace. Zum medialen Gesamtkunstwerk* (with Peter Weibel; Munich 1993), *Vom Chaos zur Endophysik* (Munich 1994), *Schöne neue Welten?* (Munich 1995), and *Die Telepolis. Urbanität im digitalen Zeitalter* (Mannheim 1995).

ARMIN SCHÄFER is professor of literature and media at the Bauhaus-University in Weimar, Germany. He is a member of the research group "Writing life. Media-technology and Life Sciences in 19th century" and has published *Biopolitik des Wissens. Hans Henny Jahnns literarisches Archiv des Menschen* (Würzburg 1996) as well as *Die Intensität der Form. Stefan Georges Lyrik* (Weimar 2003).

HEIKE SCHÄFER is Assistant Professor of American Studies at the University of Mannheim, Germany. She studied American and German literature at the University of Hamburg and the University of California, Davis. Her dissertation, *Mary Austin's Regionalism: Reflections on Gender, Genre, and Geography*, was published by the University of Virginia Press in 2004. Her major areas of research are ecocriticism, regionalism, digital culture, and the convergence of science, religion, and the arts in 19th- and 20th-century American literature and culture.

ELISABETH SCHÄFER-WÜNSCHE teaches American Studies at Rheinische Friedrich-Wilhelms-Universität Bonn, Germany. Her publications include the monograph *Wenn von Weißen die Rede ist: Zur afroamerikanischen Praxis des Benennens* (Tübingen: Francke, 2004), the co-edited volume on *The Civil Rights Movement Revisited: Critical Perspectives on the Struggle for Racial Equality in the United States* (Münster: LIT, 2001) as well as essays on American Literature, Popular Culture, and the politics of migration.

KERSTIN SCHMIDT is Assistant Professor of American Studies and Intercultural Anglophone Studies at the University of Bayreuth, Germany. She was a research fellow at the University of Toronto's McLuhan Program in Technology and at the University of British Columbia, Vancouver, on a scholarship from the International Council for Canadian Studies. She is also the recipient of a research fellowship from Indiana University/Bloomington in fall 2004. She has published on contemporary American drama, ethnic literatures, and the Harlem Renaissance. She is the author of *The Theater of Transformation: Postmodernism in American Drama* (Amsterdam: Rodopi, 2005) and co-edited the essay collection *America and the Sea* (Tübingen: Stauffenburg, 2004). She is also a founding member of the women's studies journal *Freiburger FrauenStudien*.

JOSEPH C. SCHÖPP is Professor of American Literature and Culture at the University of Hamburg. He is the author of *Allen Tate: Tradition als Bauprinzip dualistischen Dichtens* (Bonn 1975), *Ausbruch aus der Mimesis: Der amerikanische Roman im Zeichen der Postmoderne* (Munich 1990), and *Deciphering the Darkness of The Past: Essays zur amerikanischen Literatur*, ed. Bettina Friedl (Trier 1999). He has co-edited *Die Postmoderne—Ende der Avantgarde oder Neubeginn* (Eggingen 1989) and *Transatlantic Modernism* (Heidelberg 2001). His current research interest focuses on the American Transcendentalists.

SABINE SIELKE is Chair of North American Literature and Culture and Director of the North American Studies Program at the University of Bonn, Germany. Her publications include *Reading Rape: The Rhetoric of Rape in American Literature and Culture, 1790-1990* (2002), *Fashioning the Female Subject* (1997), the (co-)editions *18x15: amerikanische post:moderne* (2004), *Der 11. September 2001* (2002), *Making America* (2001), *Engendering Manhood* (1998), *Gender Matters* (1997), and *Theory in Practice* (1994) as well as essays on poetry and poetics, literary and cultural theory, African American culture, popular culture and twentieth-century art.

Illustrations

Berressem

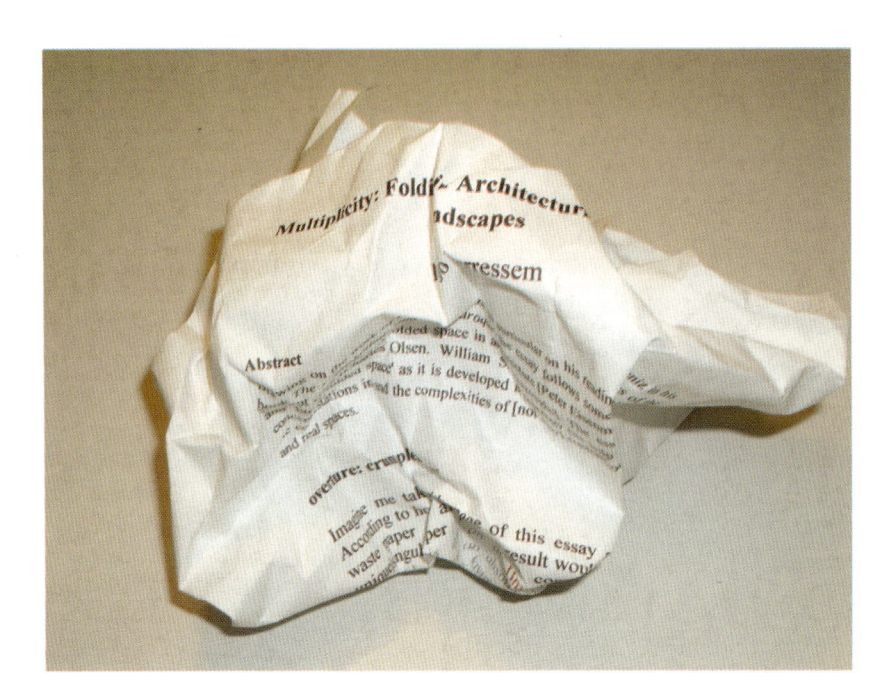

001

002

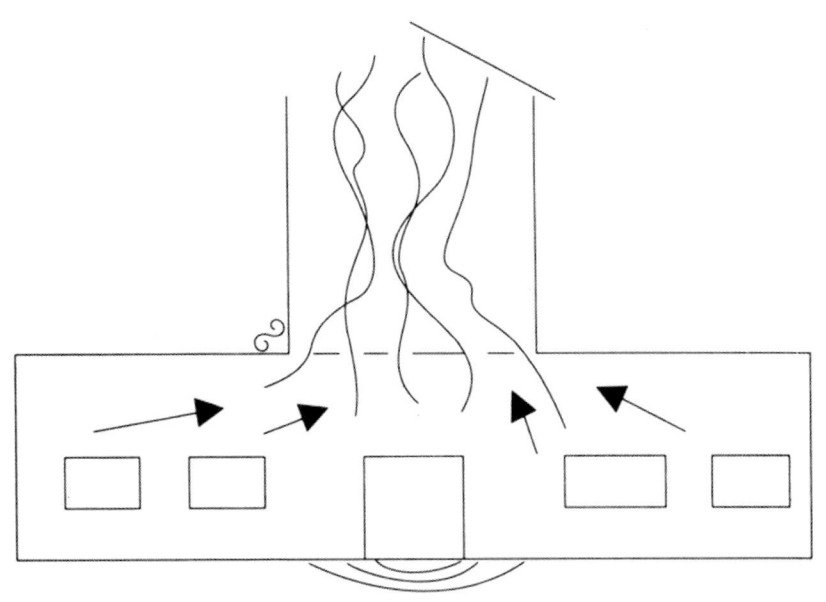

The Baroque House (an allegory)

004

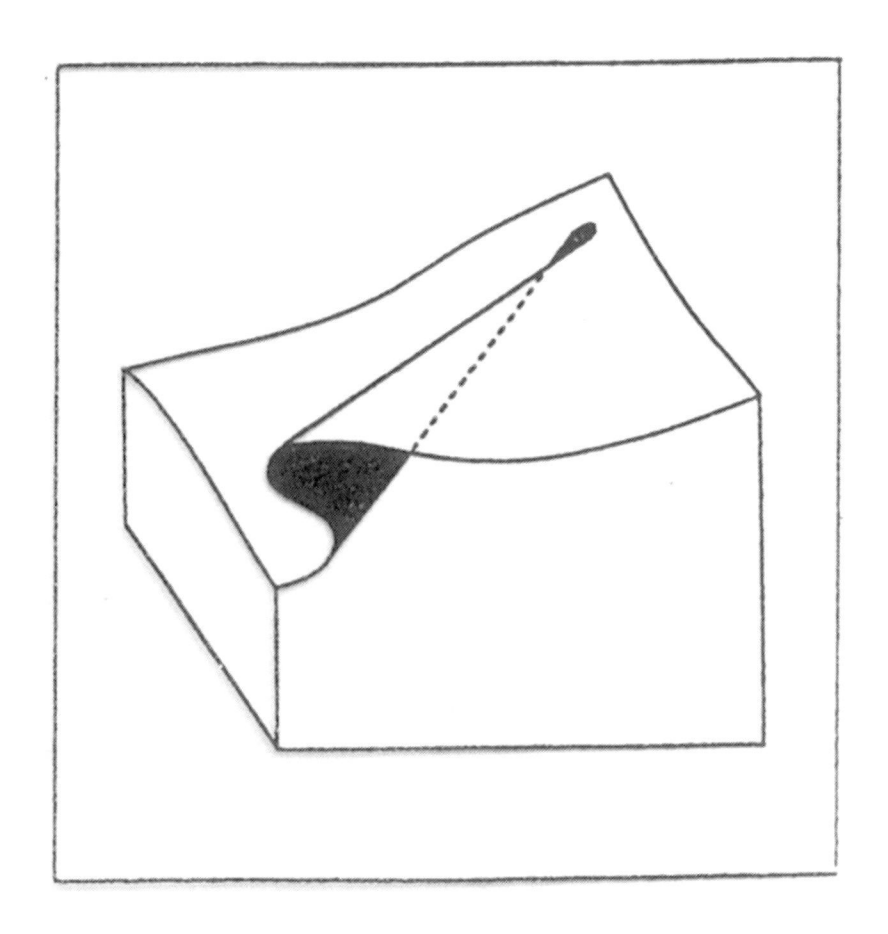

006

007

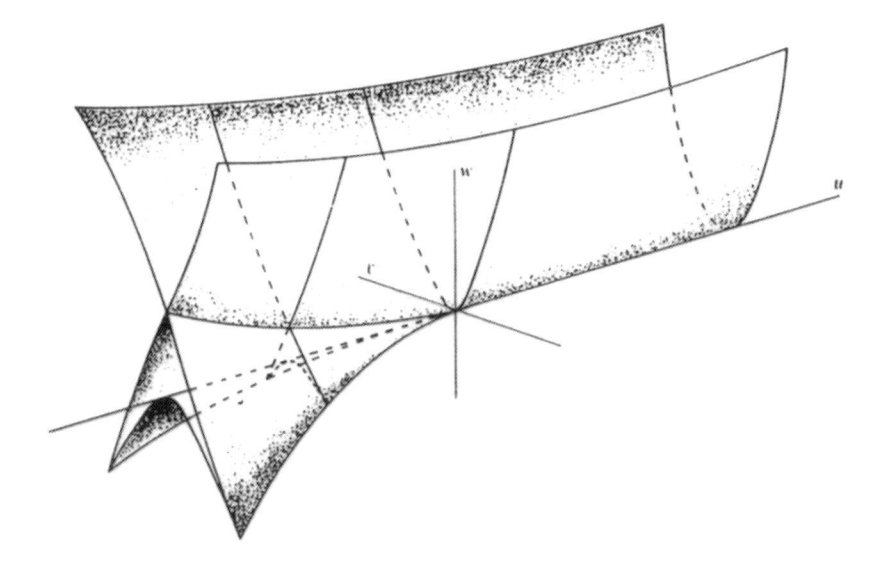

008

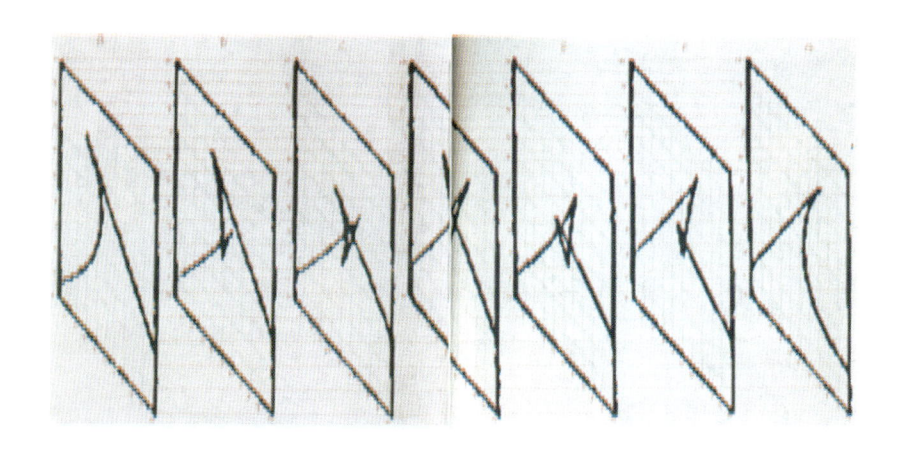

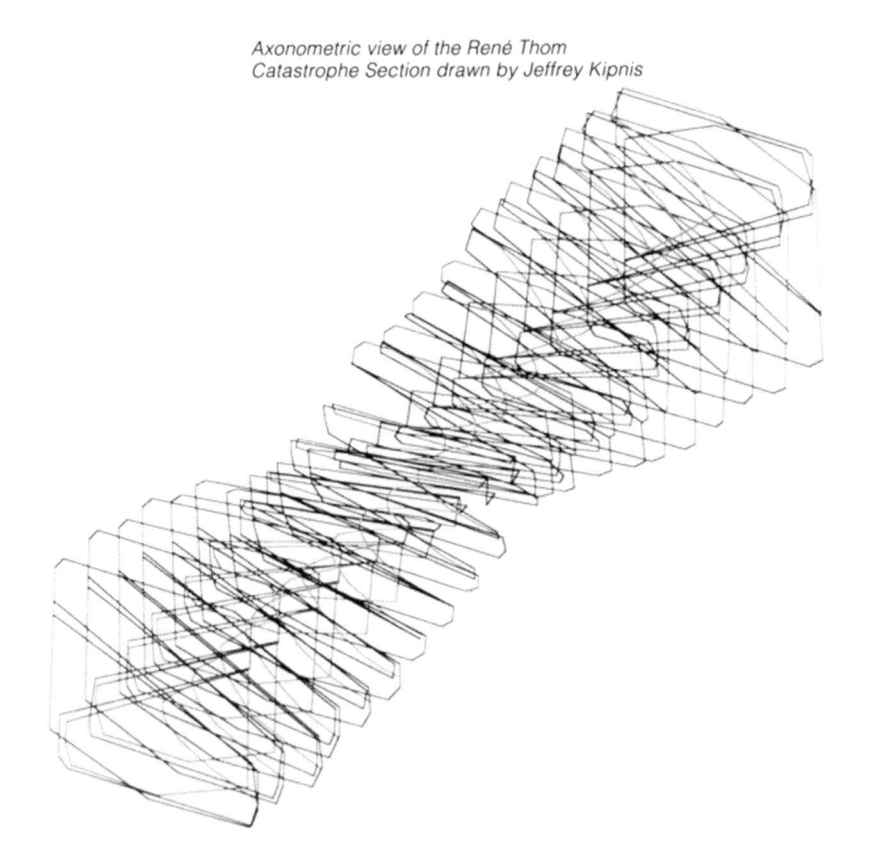

*Axonometric view of the René Thom
Catastrophe Section drawn by Jeffrey Kipnis*

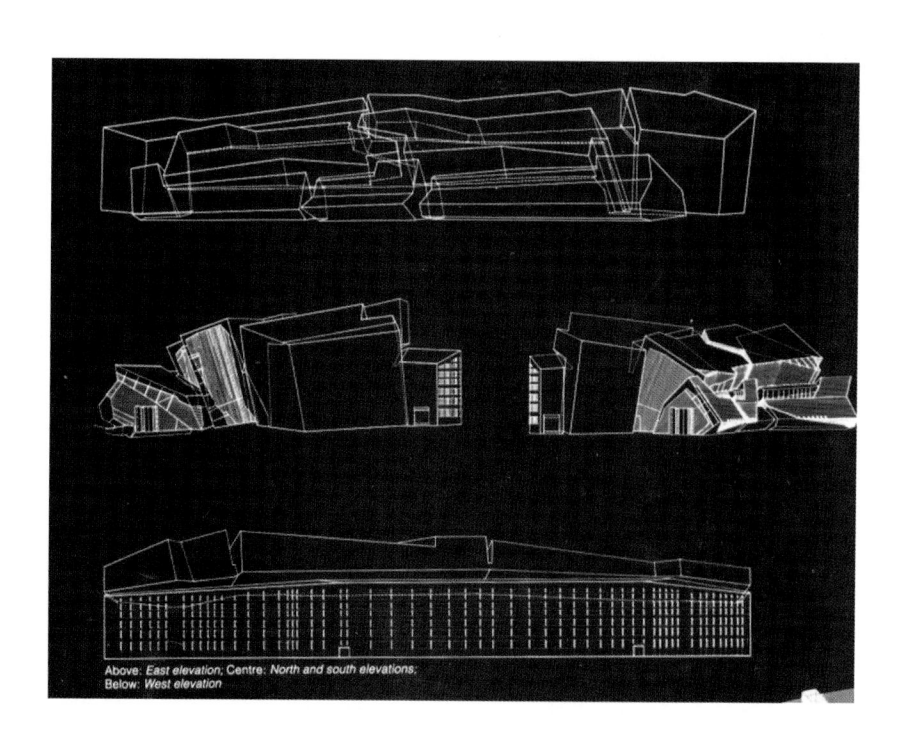

Above: *East elevation;* Centre: *North and south elevations;*
Below: *West elevation*

011

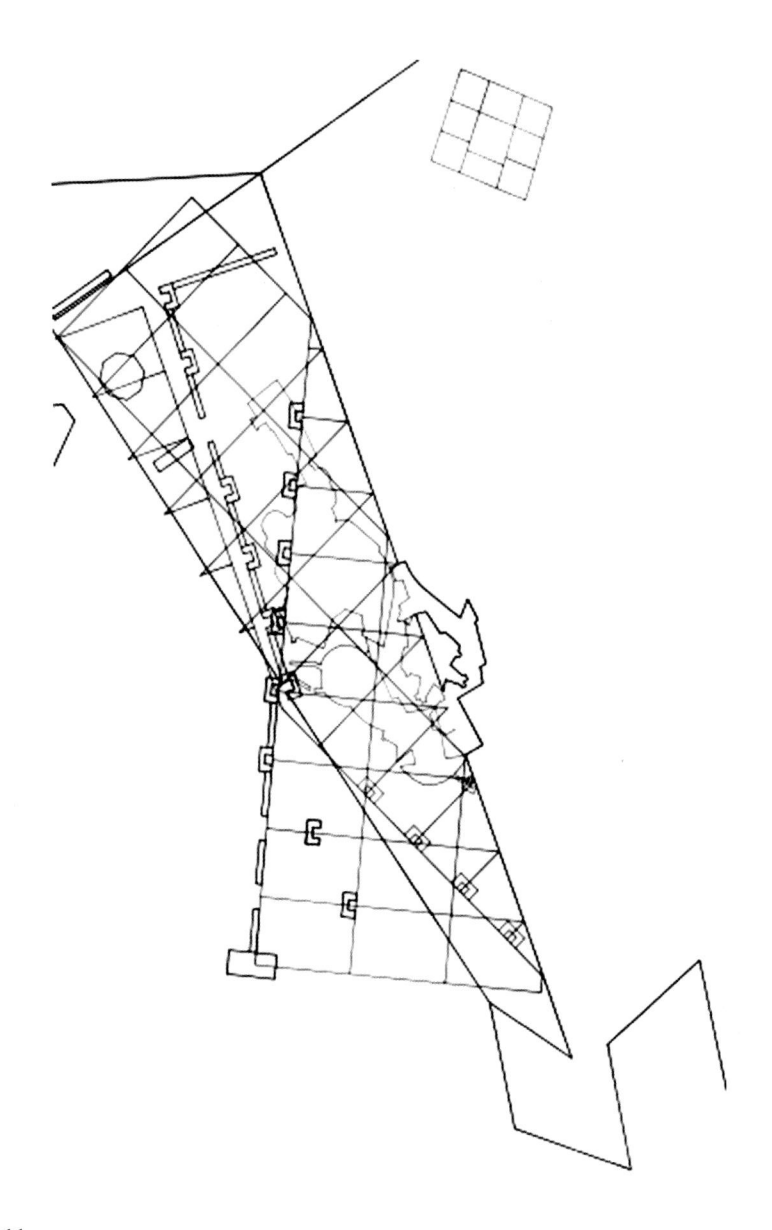

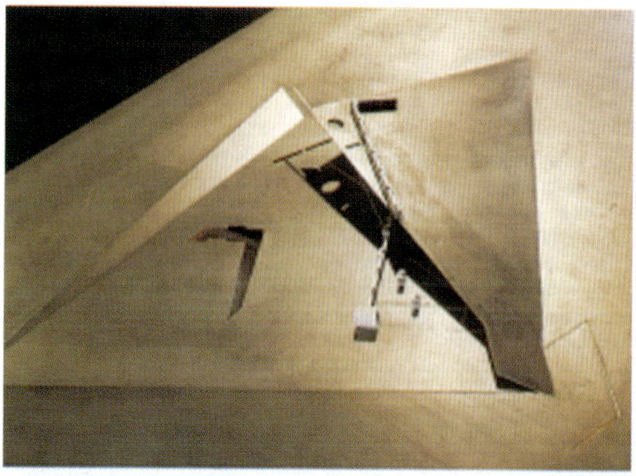

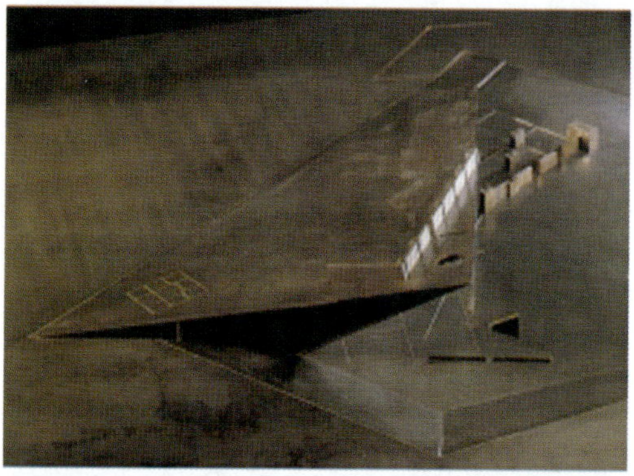

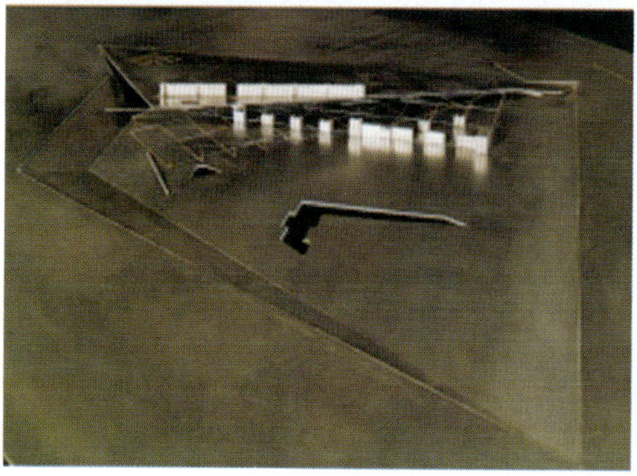

013

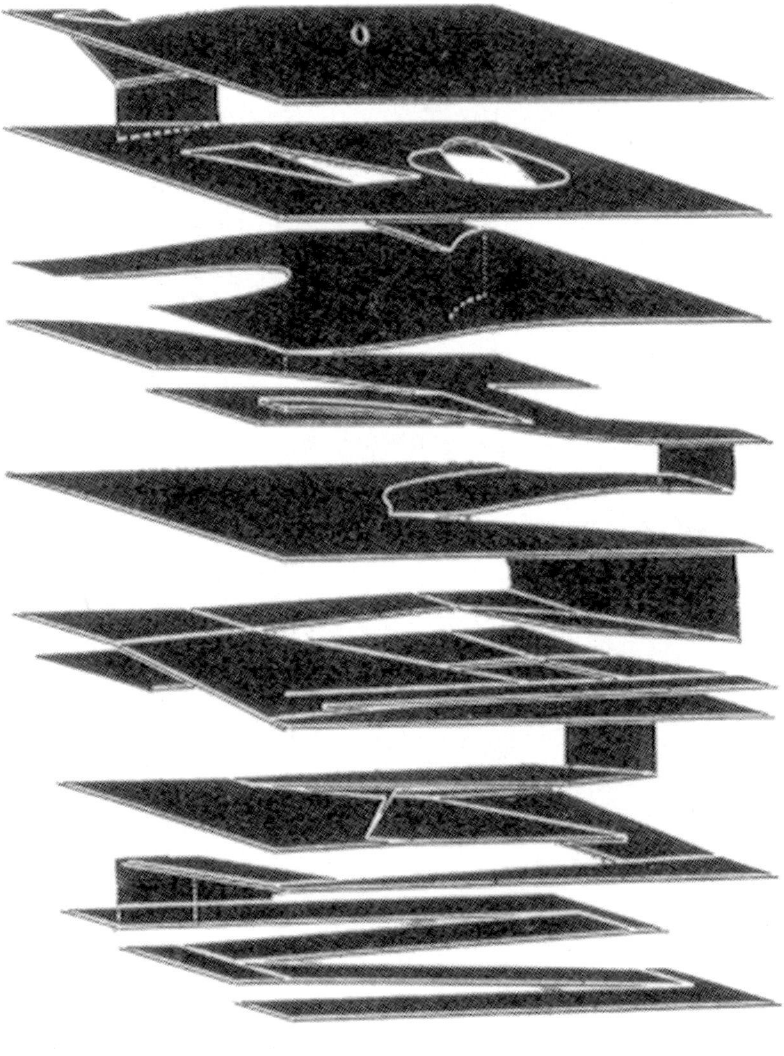

015

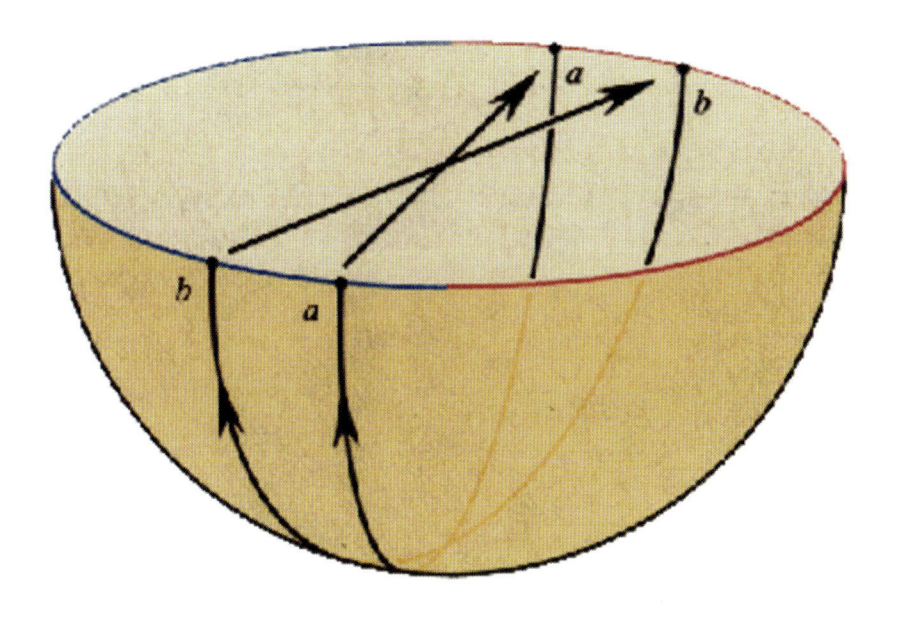

Fröhlich

	City of Los Angeles	Los Angeles County	Orange County	Riverside County	San Bernardino County	Ventura County	LA Region
Population 1990 (in 1,000)	3,485	8,863	2,411	1,170	1,418	669	14,531
Population 2000 (in 1,000)	3,695	9,519	2,846	1,545	1,709	753	16,372
Population Jan 01, 2003 (in 1,000)	3,864	9,980	2,979	1,706	1,833	791	17,289
Change 1990 – 2003 (in 1,000)	379	1,117	568	536	415	122	2,758
Change 1990 – 2003 (in %)	10.88	12.60	23.56	45.81	29.27	18.24	18.98

016   Recent population changes in Southern California (U.S. Census, California Dept. of Finance *E-1*)

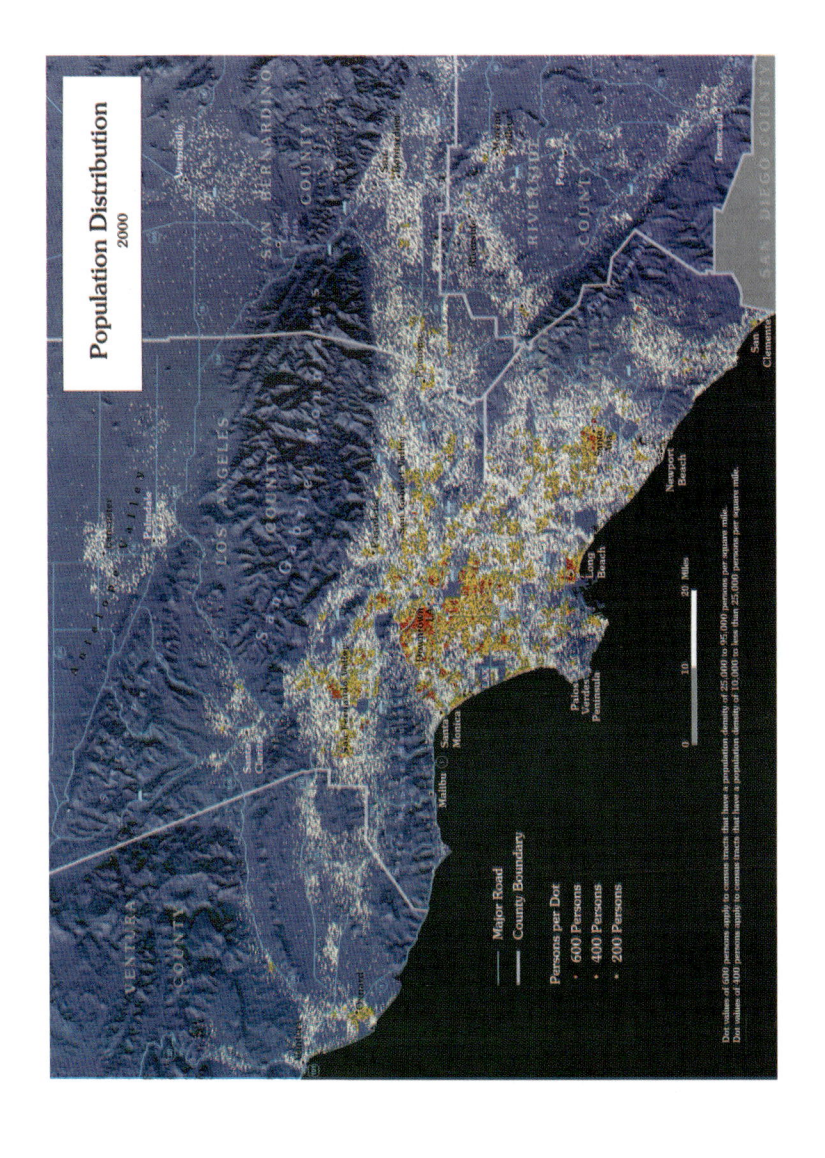

017   Population distribution in the LA region in 2000 (Allen/Turner 8)

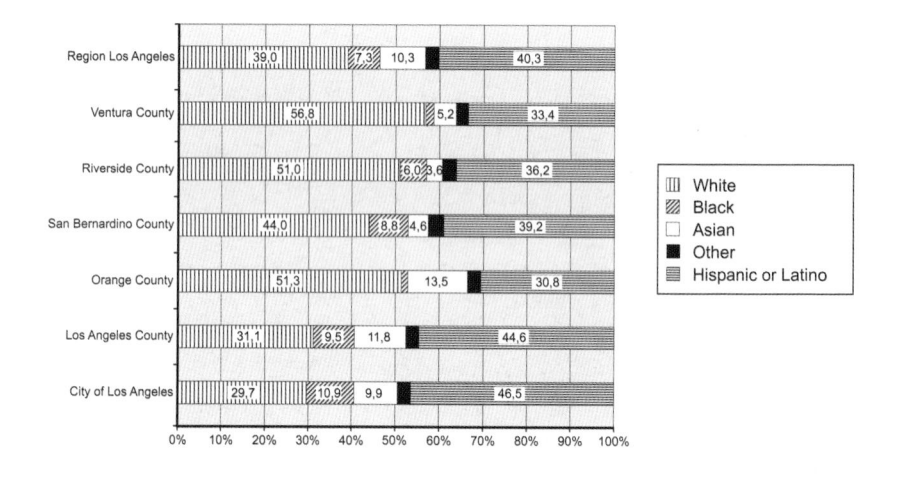

	White	Black	Asian	Other	Hispanic or Latino
Region Los Angeles	39,0	7,3	10,3		40,3
Ventura County	56,8		5,2		33,4
Riverside County	51,0	6,0	3,6		36,2
San Bernardino County	44,0	8,8	4,6		39,2
Orange County	51,3		13,5		30,8
Los Angeles County	31,1	9,5	11,8		44,6
City of Los Angeles	29,7	10,9	9,9		46,5

018   Ethnic groups in LA, 2000 (U.S. Census)

Rank	Language	LA region (total)	LA region (%)
1	Speak only English	7,771,538	52.51
2	Spanish or Spanish Creole	4,962,343	33.53
3	Chinese	356,223	2.41
4	Tagalog	269,439	1.82
5	Korean	232,897	1.57
6	Vietnamese	210,178	1.42
7	Armenian	147,291	1.00
8	Persian	95,205	0.64
9	Japanese	87,776	0.59
10	French (incl. Patois, Cajun)	58,970	0.40
11	German	52,185	0.35
12	Arabic	51,431	0.35

019   Languages in everyday use: more than 50.000 speakers, population over five years in the 2000 U.S. Census

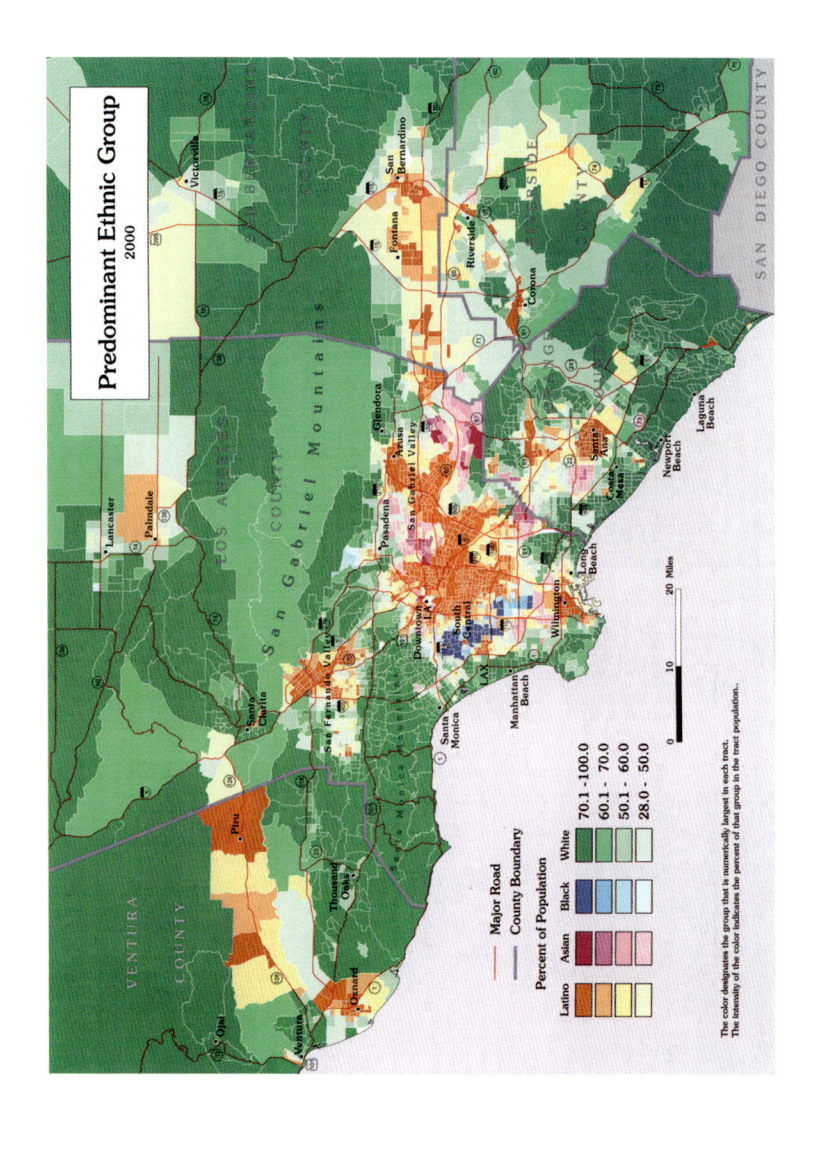

020   Leading ethnic group per Census Tract 2000 (Allen/Turner 47)

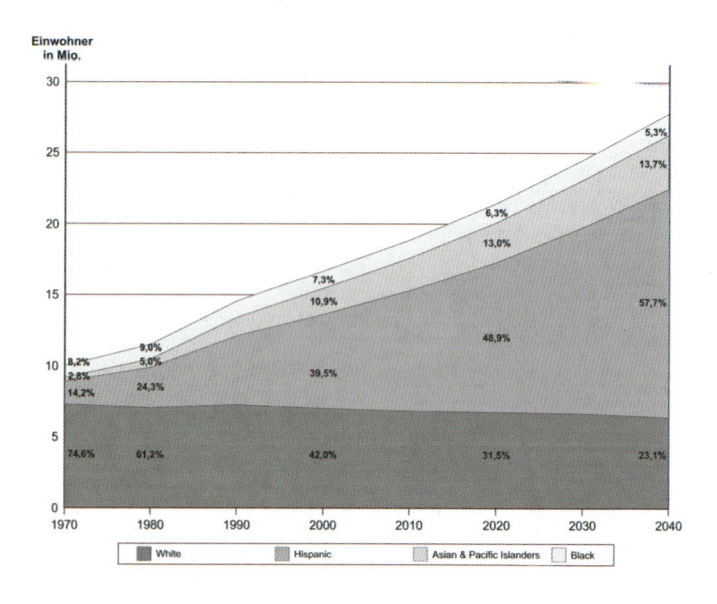

021   Population changes 1970 to 2040 (California Dept. of Finance, *Race/Ethnic Population*)

022   The New Plaza: privatized public space in Orange County (Doris Neukam 2000)

Gins and Arakawa

Site of Reversible Destiny, Elliptical Field, Yoro Park, Gifu Prefecture, Japan (1993-1995)

024　　Ubiquitous Site, Nagi's Ryoanji, Architectural Body; Nagi Museum
　　　　of Contemporary Art, Nagi, Japan (1992-1994)

REVERSIBLE DESTINY HOMES

DOUBLE HORIZONS
DOUBLE HORIZONS

IN EVERY VIEW, NOT ONE
BUT TWO (OR MORE!!) HORIZONS

MODEL NO. 17 UBIQUITOUS SITE HOUSE

In an extreme effort to oust death from the premises, the ubiquitous site, the site of a body-person inclusive of all that is within her perceptual ken, is reined in. As the body chews on the cud of its own expressivity, a monadology ensues. The architectural body is the ubiquitous site taken as an entity.

SPECIFICATIONS

Shape precludes entry, but entry can happen upon a resident's forceful insertion of herself into the pliant, half-structured muddle. Effort, having reentered infancy, flails about and cries out. Residents who open paths through chaotic amassings ferret out processes central to their own formation. The direct relation that bodily articulation bears to thinking becomes apparent and critically assessable.

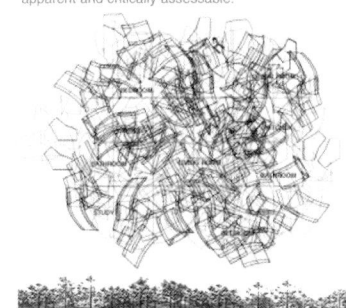

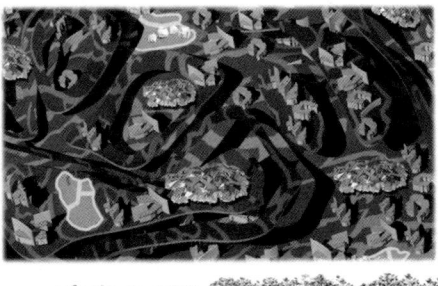

Put a reversible destiny home in your future and become a pioneer in eluding mortality.

Ubiquitous Site House, poster

REVERSIBLE DESTINY HOMES

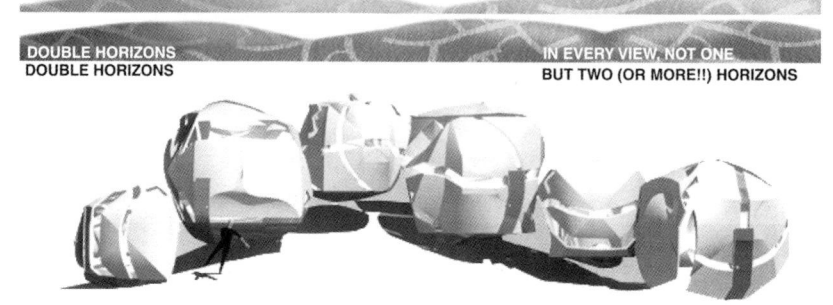

DOUBLE HORIZONS
DOUBLE HORIZONS

IN EVERY VIEW, NOT ONE
BUT TWO (OR MORE!!) HORIZONS

MODEL NO. 11   INFANCY HOUSE--LIGHT CHAOS

A resident of this dwelling launches an initial attack on mortality through ceasing to live a disposable existence. As the basic-generative unit rotates, the site of a person turns through itself. A continuity may be had in how landing sites disperse. Memory recycles through shape as rooms serve as mnemonic devices for each other.

SPECIFICATIONS

How architectural bodies form will be studied within these walls uninterruptedly. Residents hone in on that which animates them. Variously angled interiors, essentially identical, but no longer readily recognizable as such because they have been tumbled, cause those who move through them to form architectural bodies that contrast in revealing ways.

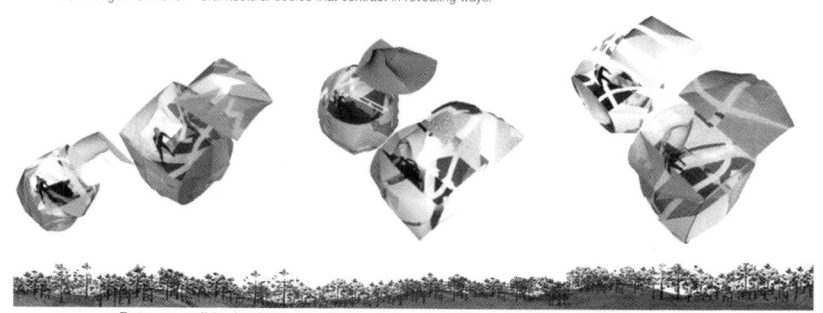

Put a reversible destiny home in your future and become a pioneer in eluding mortality.

026   Infancy House, poster

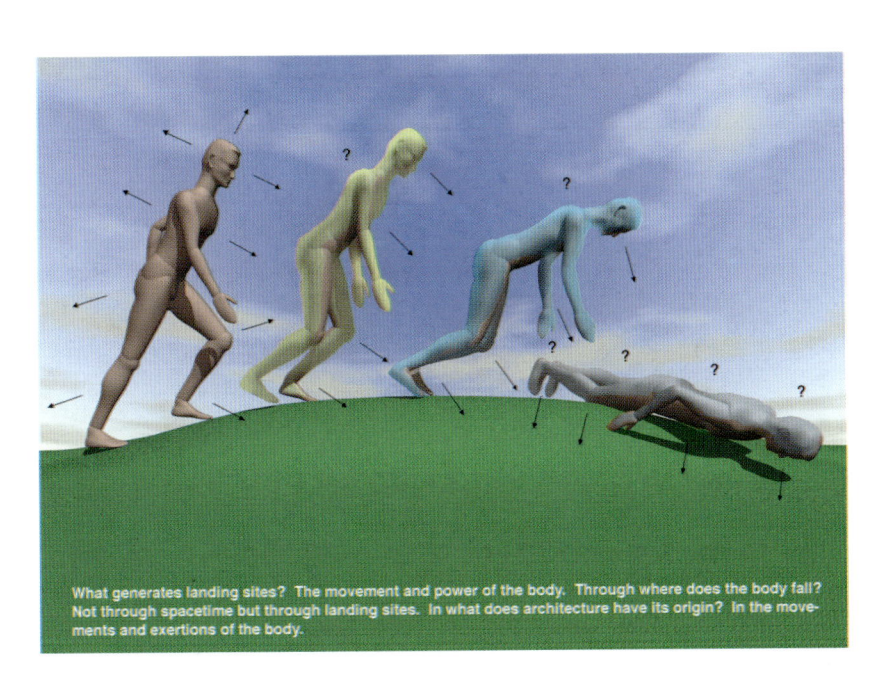

What generates landing sites? The movement and power of the body. Through where does the body fall? Not through spacetime but through landing sites. In what does architecture have its origin? In the movements and exertions of the body.

027   Landing Site Study I

Critical Holder

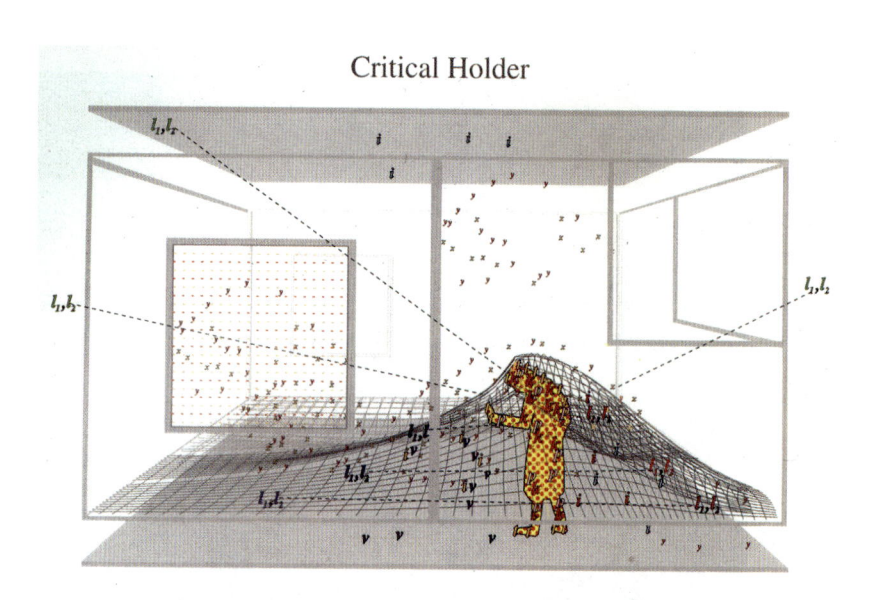

A tactile landing site marks any point of bodily contact.

A tactile-imaging landing site marks the envisioning of how anything might feel to the touch.

A micro-tactile landing site marks the minimum point of sentient contact. This might be said to be how that which cleaves feels to itself.

An atmospheric-kinaesthetic landing site marks ambient kinaesthesia, should such a thing be possible. Could the cleaving of the atmosphere get a feel of itself in action, in the process of forming, that would give rise to an ambient kinaesthesia.

Sets of micro-tactile landing sites and sets of atmospheric-kinaesthetic landing sites in various combinations could be what form all other perceptual landing sites. Tactile, kinaesthetic and proprioceptive landing sites might simply be accumulations of many smaller-scale tactile, or tactile-like, events with a kinaesthetic component. But what if imaging landing sites also owed their existence to these same micro-events? Were it then to be proven that the many other perceptual landing sites are, as we suspect, all to some degree a form of imaging landing site, then it could indeed be shown that all perceptual landing sites originate from micro-tactile and atmospheric-kinaesthetic landing sites in combination.

	zone of occurrent visual scanning formed by sets of imaging landing sites acting in conjunction with sets of visual landing sites	v	visual landing site	l_1, l_1, l_1, l_1, l_1	locator-perceptual landing site for establishing and maintaining distance (visual, kinaesthetic, aural, tactile, olfactory respectively)
		$\hat{v}, \hat{v}, \hat{v}, \hat{v}$	imaging landing site (blank, visual 1, visual 2, tactile respectively)		
	zone of occurrent imaging formed by active sets of imaging landing sites	p	proprioceptive landing site		
x	micro-tactile landing site	k	kinaesthetic landing site	l_2, l_2, l_2, l_2, l_2	locator-perceptual landing site for assessing of volume or distance (visual, kinaesthetic, aural, tactile, olfactory respectively)
y	atmospheric-kinaesthetic landing site	t	tactile landing site		

Landing Site / Architectural Body Study II

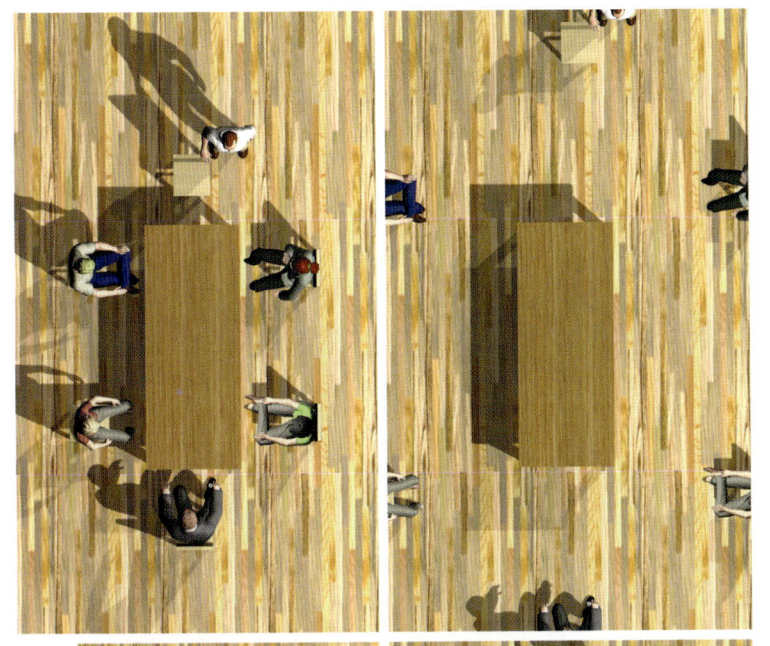

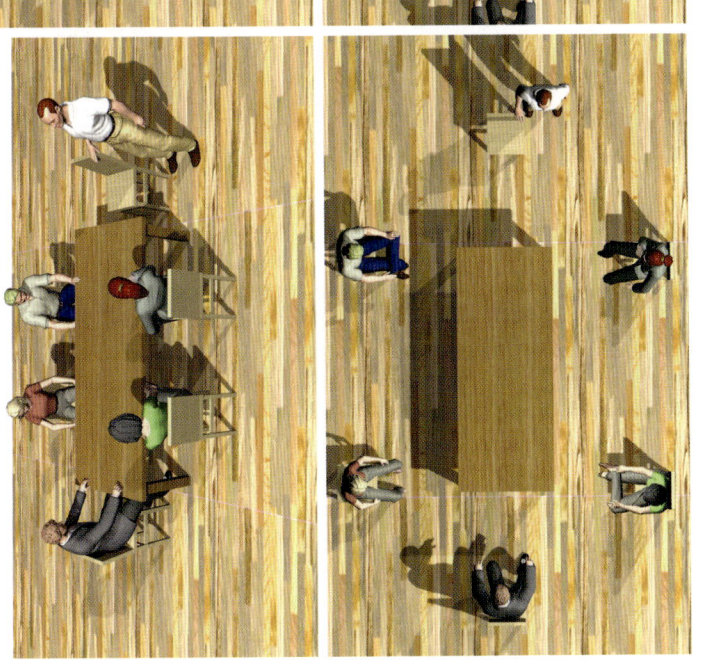

029 Landing Site / Architectural Body Study III

(Above Left) All that surrounds a person: ubiquitous site. The set of all landing sites of and for a person: ubiquitous site. A ubiquitous (landing) site: the sum of all landing sites. The sum of all landing sites equals a person or body plus world. *(Above Right)* The size of the ubiquitous site depends on the intensity of the perceiver's passion or concern. Simply by sensing herself to be where she is, a person defines a ubiquitous site within a locally circumscribed area. With the ubiquitous site outlined, the extent to which the view is determined by tactile and kinaesthetic sensations becomes more readily noticeable. *(Below Left)* Landing sites shift and the appearance of the world changes according to how the body moves. Reining in perceptual landing sites diminishes spacetime, making it all but vanish. *(Below Right)* One takes possession of a ubiquitous site within a locally circumscribed area in respect to a tentative plan by means of kinaesthetic outposts. Subject as Object. Subject? Object?

Ubiquitous Site House Study I

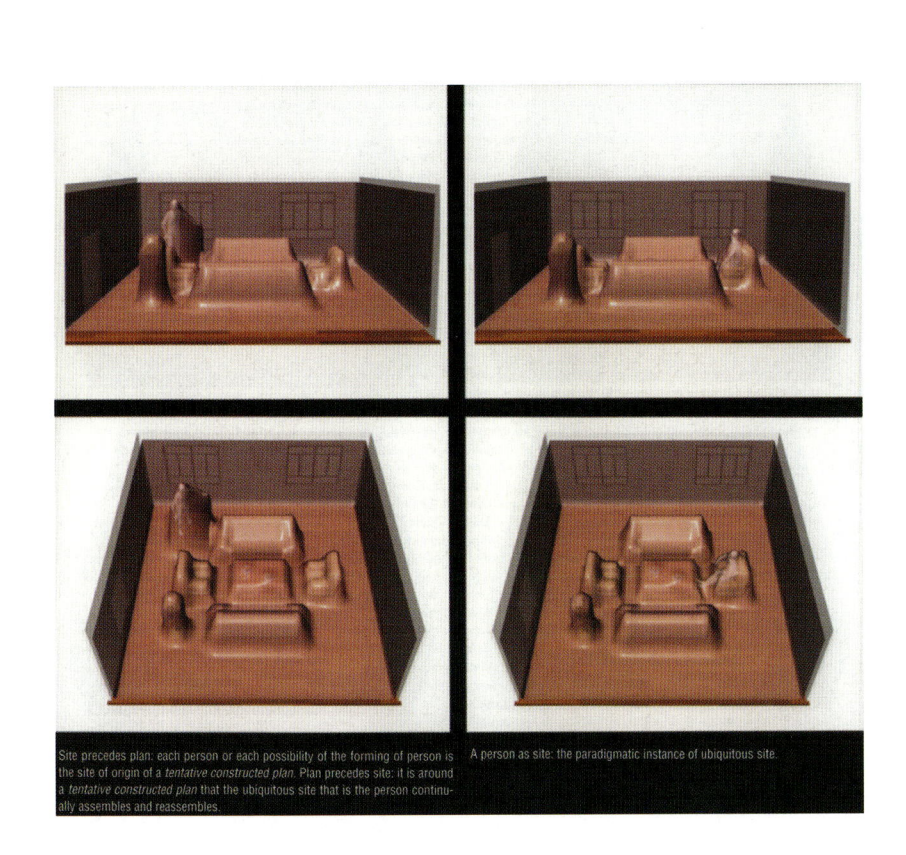

Site precedes plan: each person or each possibility of the forming of person is the site of origin of a *tentative constructed plan*. Plan precedes site: it is around a *tentative constructed plan* that the ubiquitous site that is the person continually assembles and reassembles.

A person as site: the paradigmatic instance of ubiquitous site.

031   Ubiquitous Site House Study II

032   Inside a Room Full of Trenches: Arakawa and Madeline Gins

033   Reversible Destiny Village / Museum of Living Bodies

Böger

034   Charles D. Arnold, Grand Basin and Court of Honor looking west from the Peristyle (Special Collections and Preservation Division, Chicago Public Library)

035   Unknown photographer, electric light display at night on the Grand Basin (Special Collections and Preservation Division, Chicago Public Library)

Chicago Public Library, Special Collections and Preservation Division

036   Charles D. Arnold, Edison's Electric Tower of the General Electric Company Exhibit (Special Collections and Preservation Division, Chicago Public Library)

037   Charles D. Arnold, a group of Dahomeyans (Special Collections and
        Preservation Division, Chicago Public Library)

Chicago Public Library, Special Collections and Preservation Division

038   Charles D. Arnold, scene in front of Arab-Bedouin encampment
       (Special Collections and Preservation Division, Chicago Public
       Library)

Leeker

039   *Time Lapses* (Nik Haffner); Photo: Bernd Lintermann

040   Paul Kaiser, Shelley Eshkar, still from motion captured animation ("forest sequence") for *Biped* (choreography by Merce Cunningham, 1999)

Kursell and Schäfer

041   John Cage, *Winter Music*, 1957 (Reprinted with permission of C. F. Peters Musikverlag, Frankfurt/M.)

WINTER MUSIC
FOR BOB RAUSCHENBERG AND JASPER JOHNS

THE 20 PAGES MAY BE USED IN WHOLE OR PART BY A PIANIST OR SHARED BY 2 TO 20 TO PROVIDE A PROGRAM OF AN AGREED UPON LENGTH. THE NOTATION, IN SPACE, 5 'SYSTEMS' LEFT TO RIGHT ON THE PAGE, MAY BE FREELY INTERPRETED AS TO TIME. AN AGGREGATE MUST BE PLAYED AS A SINGLE ICTUS. WHERE THIS IS IMPOSSIBLE, THE UNPLAYABLE NOTES SHALL BE TAKEN AS HARMONICS PREPARED IN ADVANCE. HARMONICS MAY ALSO BE PRODUCED WHERE THEY ARE NOT SO REQUIRED. RESONANCES, BOTH OF AGGREGATES AND INDIVIDUAL NOTES OF THEM, MAY BE FREE IN LENGTH. OVERLAPPINGS, INTERPENETRATIONS, ARE ALSO FREE. THE SINGLE STAFF IS PROVIDED WITH TWO CLEF SIGNS. WHERE THESE DIFFER, AMBIGUITY OBTAINS IN THE PROPORTION INDICATED BY THE 2 NUMBERS NOTATED ABOVE THE AGGREGATE, THE FIRST OF THESE APPLYING TO THE CLEF ABOVE THE STAFF. DYNAMICS ARE FREE. AN INKED-IN RECTANGLE ABOVE A PAIR OF NOTES INDICATES A CHROMATIC TONE-CLUSTER. THE FRAGMENTATION OF STAVES AROSE SIMPLY FROM AN ABSENCE OF EVENTS.

John Cage

STONY POINT, NEW YORK, JANUARY 1957

COPYRIGHT © 1960 BY HENMAR PRESS INC., 373 PARK AVE. SO., NEW YORK 16, N.Y.

042 John Cage, *Winter Music*, 1957 (Reprinted with permission of C. F. Peters Musikverlag, Frankfurt/M.)

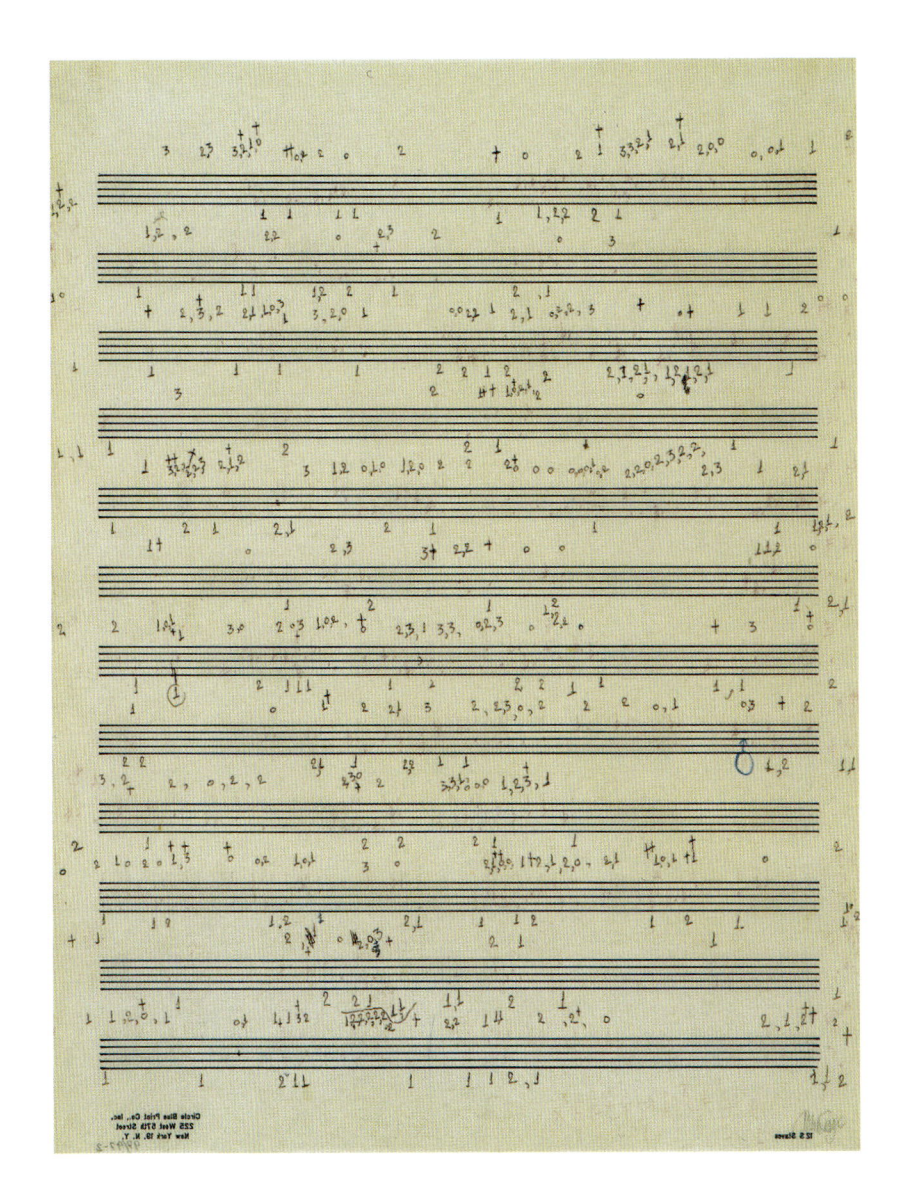

043   John Cage, *Etudes Australes for Piano Solo*, 1974/75 (Kunsthalle Bremen; reprinted with permission of C. F. Peters Musikverlag, Frankfurt/M.)

Fabre, Geneviève

044 *Grand and Splendid Bobalition of Slavery*, Boston 1822 (American Antiquarian Society)

045 *Hymn of the Freedman. Respectfully Dedicated to Mrs. Col. Chas. W. Fribley*. Published by the supervisory committee for recruiting colored regiments, 1210, Chestnut St. Phil. (P.S. Duval & Son. Lith. Phil.)

046   Unidentified artist, *Our Colored Militia. — A "Skid" Dressing for the Parade on the Fourth of July* in *Frank Leslie's Illustrated Newspaper,* 17 July 1875 (Library, University of Minnesota, Duluth)

047   Christian A. Fleetwood, sergeant major of the 5th Colored Troops, 3rd Division, 18th Army Corps, received the Congressional Medal of Honor on September 29, 1864, for action at Chaffin's Farm near Richmond (MSS. LC-USZ62-44731)

RECEIVING THE PRESIDENT.
Abraham Lincoln riding through Richmond, April 4th, 1865, after the evacuation of the city by the Confederates.

048   *Receiving the President, Abraham Lincoln riding through Richmond, April 4th, 1865, after the evacuation of the city of the Confederates* (New York Public Library)

FREEDOM TO THE SLAVES

Proclaimed January 1st 1863, by ABRAHAM LINCOLN, President of the United States. "Proclaim liberty throughout All the land unto All the inhabitants thereof" ___ LEV XXV 10

049   *Freedom to the Slaves*, Currier & Ives, ca. 1865 (Lilly Library, Indiana University)

Neubauer

Andreas Feininger / The Brooklyn Bridge New York 1948

050   Andreas Feininger, *The Brooklyn Bridge*, 1948

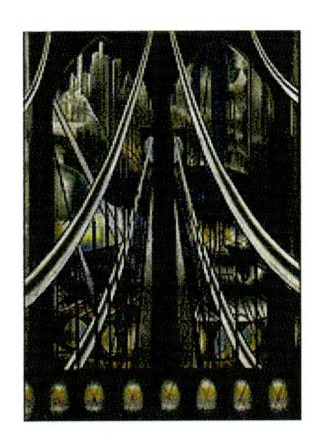

051   Joseph Stella, *The Bridge*, 1922

052   Richard Benson's photograph of Brooklyn Bridge, 1930, taken for
        Hart Crane's poem (cf. Saunders/Goldstein 10)

Fitz

Emanuel Gottlieb Leutze, *Washington Crossing the Delaware*, 1851

054   George Caleb Bingham, *Washington Crossing the Delaware*, 1856-1871

055 Currier & Ives, *Washington Crossing the Delaware*, 1859